Encountering
the New Testament

Encountering Biblical Studies
Walter A. Elwell, General Editor and New Testament Editor
Eugene H. Merrill, Old Testament Editor

Encountering the New Testament

A Historical and Theological Survey

Second Edition

Walter A. Elwell

and Robert W. Yarbrough

Baker Academic
Grand Rapids, Michigan

Book copyright © 1998, 2005 by Walter A. Elwell
and Robert W. Yarbrough
Design copyright © 1998 by Angus Hudson Ltd /
        Tim Dowley & Peter Wyart trading as
        Three's Company 1997
Published by Baker Academic
a division of Baker Publishing Group
P.O. Box 6287
Grand Rapids, MI 49516-6287 USA
www.bakeracademic.com
CD-ROM copyright © 1998, 2005 by Baker Book
House Company
ISBN 0-8010-3111-7

Designed by Peter Wyart, Three's Company, and
Dan Malda, Baker Book House Company

Worldwide coedition organized and produced by
Lion Hudson plc
Wilkinson House, Jordan Hill Road
Oxford, OX2 8DR, England
Tel: +44 (0) 1865 302750
Fax: +44 (0) 1865 302757
Email: coed@lionhudson.com
www.lionhudson.com

Printed in Singapore

Picture Acknowledgments

Illustrations
All maps by Jeremy Gower
James Macdonald: pp. 139, 322
Alan Parry: pp. 199, 216

Photographs
Ancient Art and Architecture: pp. 28, 210, 214, 218,
228, 265, 282, 300, 369, 377, 379
Jon Arnold: pp. 72, 100
Bible Scene Tours: pp. 240, 321
Billy Graham Evangelistic Organization: p. 389
British Museum: pp. 101, 197, 204
Tim Dowley: pp. 3, 21, 24, 39, 43, 51, 53, 55, 63, 71,
79, 81, 89, 91, 113, 121, 122, 123, 128, 129, 141, 143,
164, 186, 191, 192, 200, 213, 224, 238, 245, 252, 258,
267, 281, 283, 299, 309, 329, 337, 346, 349, 353, 367
Mary Evans Picture Library: pp. 157, 159, 170, 183, 275
Zed Radovan: pp. 31, 77, 78, 79, 162, 175, 198, 202,
291, 311, 364
National Tourist Office of Greece: p. 315
Clifford Shirley: p. 147
Jamie Simson: pp. 256, 289, 293, 295, 313, 329
Peter Wyart: pp. 26, 37, 38, 58, 60, 92, 98, 102, 107,
108, 111, 113, 118, 126, 131, 198, 201, 227, 229, 232,
243, 254, 261, 275, 277, 312, 345, 355, 363
Israel Government Tourist Office: pp. 47, 52
Illustrated London News: p. 154
SCM Press: p. 185
Italian State Tourist Office: p. 279

Library of Congress Cataloging-in-Publication Data

Elwell, Walter A.
    Encountering the New Testament : a historical and theological survey / Walter A. Elwell
and Robert W. Yarbrough—2nd ed.
        p.   cm.—(Encountering biblical studies)
    Includes bibliographical references and indexes.
    ISBN 10: 0-8010-2806-X
    ISBN 978-0-8010-2806-9
    1. Bible. N.T.—Introductions. I. Yarbrough, Robert W. II. Title. III. Series.
BS2330.3.E59 2005
225.6'1—dc22   2004054581

Contents in Brief

Contents

Preface

For this updated edition dozens of professors who use this book in the classroom made suggestions for improvements. We thank them for their thoughtful input and have accommodated many requests. Some suggestions, however, could not be incorporated because the recommendations for improvements were generally offsetting: Some wanted less exposure to critical matters, others more. Some wanted easier review questions, others wanted harder ones. Some complained of wordiness, others complained of brevity. Some wanted to see less theological emphasis and more Bible content, others called for the opposite. Pleasing some reviewers, then, would have meant frustrating others.

We have done our best to correct vague wording, update bibliography, rewrite outdated sections, and add material where the previous edition was culpably brief. We have not felt it wise to undertake a thoroughgoing revamping—to produce a different work as it were. Too many professors begged that we not tamper too much with a book that seems generally effective in classroom use. Students largely like it and seem well served by it.

The comments we have received are perhaps most striking in their diversity of theological vantage point: Baptist, charismatic, Roman Catholic, Reformed, Lutheran, Wesleyan, independent, Restoration, Salvation Army, and more. While most thoughtful reviewers proposed improvements, none found *Encountering the New Testament* inappropriate for use given their academic setting and associated community of faith. The book's broad appeal is also reflected in its translation into several languages, including Spanish, Dutch, German, and Chinese.

It seems the text succeeds at presenting the New Testament from an academic point of view yet also in a light compatible with an understanding of Christ and Scripture that predominates in confessional circles across many denominational lines on various continents. From the beginning this was our hope and goal.

We trust this revised edition will continue to contribute to Christian understanding, unity, service, and proclamation across a wide range of settings to the glory of Jesus Christ.

Walter A. Elwell
Robert W. Yarbrough

To the Professor

Surveying the New Testament in one relatively short book is, as someone has said in another connection, a bit like trying to whistle a Wagner opera. The authors wish to state in advance what this particular New Testament survey is, and is not, designed to accomplish.

Like all other surveys, this one is no substitute for earnest and repeated reading of the New Testament itself. It is at best an aid and encouragement to take up such reading.

The goal has not been to produce a running biblical exposition. In other words, this is not a commentary or a commentary survey—for that see D. A. Carson, *New Testament Commentary Survey*, 5th ed. (Grand Rapids: Baker, 2001). We have sought rather to provide enough theological and thematic discussion to do justice to most major New Testament themes, without necessarily generating this discussion out of verse-by-verse or even chapter-by-chapter explication.

The thematic treatment of the teachings of major figures like Jesus and Paul is summed up in chapters devoted to synthesizing their views. Chapters covering individual Gospels, or the Pauline letters, often omit or touch lightly on important themes, deferring their handling to the summary chapters.

Chapters on historical criticism, hermeneutics, and modern study of Jesus and the Gospels are placed after treatment of the Gospels and Jesus. This reflects a couple of convictions. One is that basic knowledge of the New Testament's content is necessary for intelligent consideration of critical and theoretical deliberation on how to construe that content. An analogy: Before delving very deeply into literary criticism of Shakespeare, we need to have read his works. Some who read this survey may have never read much of the New Testament.

Another conviction is that the New Testament's basic message is accessible to the general reader without knowledge of the sophisticated debates in technical New Testament studies since the Enlightenment. Historical criticism is important, and in due course we show why. But there are dangers in giving the impression that knowledge of secondary discussion is equal, or even superior, to acquaintance with the primary sources. We want to help readers survey the New Testament and not first of all debates about it.

Some may find this volume suitable for classroom use. Both of this book's authors have taught New Testament survey at various levels literally dozens of times. We have come to appreciate books that make our job easier. We trust that this will prove to be one of those books. In a number of ways we have sought to assist the busy teacher at the basic college (or advanced lay) level.

For instance, this book does not attempt to replace the teacher. We rather leave plenty of room for teachers to develop themes, doctrines, or issues as they see fit. We have provided much more foundation than finished superstructure. At the survey level, we believe, teachers should be given latitude to develop their own views. It is a pity to have to spend lots of class time correcting or disagreeing with a survey-level textbook that errs in being too specific, technical, and detailed.

The abundant illustrations, maps, charts, and other visual aids that we have included should likewise be useful for the teacher's task. Their inherent value alone merits the considerable space devoted to them. And they also break up the text, making it more readable. While skillful layout alone cannot guarantee that a book will be read, poor layout may guarantee that it won't. We have tried to improve on the drab and staid format of textbooks we have used (and lamented) in the past.

Still with the instructor in mind, with very slight modification we have followed the canonical order in our treatment.

Many teachers prefer this; those who don't are free to assign chapters in different orders. But we think that the preference of many teachers, combined with the weight of venerable church practice, points to the profound logic and good sense of starting with Matthew and continuing through to Revelation. In addition, that is the order in which most readers were first exposed to the New Testament corpus, and will continue to be exposed to it in their Bibles all their lives. In the absence of compelling good reasons to adopt some other order, we have followed established practice.

Further, we have written with the current young reader, or older nonspecialist, in mind. We hope the prose level reflects this. A glossary defines terms that may need explanation. Sidebars in some chapters point up the contemporary relevance of selected New Testament passages. While avoiding mere trend or novelty, we hope to have produced a treatment that will not scare readers away by too much jargon, or by an advanced level of prose more suited to a graduate or professional audience. On the other hand, we have resisted pressure to "dumb down" our treatment. The New Testament itself poses certain unavoidable intellectual and other challenges. It is fair, within reason, for a survey to follow suit.

In addition, study and review questions and carefully chosen books in the "Further Reading" section after each chapter can help generate classroom discussion, furnish homework or exam topics, and facilitate the efforts of students to do self-directed reading.

Outlines for each New Testament book are taken (with occasional slight modification) from *Baker Commentary on the Bible*, ed. Walter Elwell (Grand Rapids: Baker, 1989). Readers seeking verse-by-verse commentary not provided by this survey may be referred to this volume for further study.

Finally, professors will want to be aware of three items that supplement *Encountering the New Testament:*

1. Instructor's Manual with Test Bank. In addition to including numerous objective-type test items, this resource includes suggestions in using the textbook, chapter outlines, chapter objectives, chapter summaries, key terms, master transparencies, lecture outlines, media resources, and bibliography. Educational consultant Janet Merrill developed this tool along with the chapter outlines and objectives, Focus Boxes, review questions, and chapter summaries that appear in the text.
2. Student's Multimedia Interactive CD-ROM. Developed by biblical scholar Chris Miller and educational specialist Phil Bassett, this resource helps students become familiar with the material covered in *Encountering the New Testament* through interactive review questions and study aids, video clips and still photos of biblical lands, maps, and video clips of interviews with the authors.
3. *Readings from the First-Century World: Primary Sources for New Testament Study.* This collection of primary source readings related to the New Testament consists of material written in roughly the same era as the New Testament, including letters, legal documents, and treatises. The readings are arranged so as to correlate with the canonical order of the New Testament writings.

To the Student

Ethical and theological issues

Primary source material

Focus Box: key issues and relevant applications

Key terms, people, and places

Review questions

Study questions

Further Reading

Encountering the New Testament in a systematic way for the first time is an exciting experience. It can also be overwhelming because there is so much to learn. You need to learn not only the content of the New Testament but also a good deal about the Greco-Roman world of Jesus' and Paul's day.

The purpose of this textbook is to make that encounter a little less daunting. To accomplish this a number of learning aids have been incorporated into the text. We suggest you prepare for effective use of this textbook by reading the following introductory material, which explains what learning aids have been provided.

Sidebars

Material in yellow-colored boxes isolates contemporary matters of concern and shows how the New Testament speaks to these pressing ethical and theological issues. Material in blue boxes contains primary source quotes from various authors, whether ancient or modern, whose thoughts shed light on the New Testament material under discussion.

Focus Boxes

Each chapter has one Focus Box. These boxes add interest and relevance to the text by providing practical applications or devotional thoughts.

Chapter Outlines

At the beginning of each chapter is a brief outline of the chapter's contents. *Study Suggestion:* Before reading the chapter, take a few minutes to read the outline. Think of it as a road map, and remember that it is easier to reach your destination if you know where you are going.

Chapter Objectives

A brief list of objectives is placed at the outset of each chapter. These present the tasks you should be able to perform after reading the chapter. *Study Suggestion:* Read the objectives carefully before beginning to read the text. As you read the text, keep these objectives in mind and take notes to help you remember what you have read. After reading the chapter, return to the objectives and see if you can perform the tasks.

Summary

A list of statements summarizing the content of each chapter can be found at the end of each chapter. *Study Suggestion:* Use this summary list to conduct an immediate review of what you have just read.

Key Terms and Glossary

Key terms have been identified throughout the text by the use of boldface type. This will alert you to important words or phrases you may not be familiar with. A definition of these words will be found at the end of the book in an alphabetical glossary. *Study Suggestion:* When you encounter a key term in the text, stop and read the definition before continuing through the chapter.

Key People and Places

While studying the New Testament you will be introduced to many names and places. Those that are particularly significant have been set in SMALL CAPS. *Study Suggestion*: Pay careful attention to the people and places as you read the text. When studying for a test, skim the text and stop at each SMALL CAPPED term to see if you know its importance to the New Testament.

Review Questions

A short set of fill-in-the-blank questions follows each chapter. These can serve as a quick self-check after reading the chapter and/or a review for exams. Answers are provided at the end of the book. *Study Suggestion:* After reading each chapter and summary list, fill in the answers to the review questions as a way of checking your mastery of the content. Use them to review a group of chapters for examinations throughout the term.

Study Questions

A few discussion questions have been provided at the end of each chapter, and these can be used to review for examinations. *Study Suggestion:* Write suitable answers to the study questions in preparation for tests.

Further Reading

A short bibliography for supplementary reading is presented at each chapter's conclusion. *Study Suggestion:* Use the suggested reading list to explore areas of special interest.

Visual Aids

A host of illustrations in the form of photographs, maps, and charts have been included in this textbook. Each illustration has been carefully selected, and each is intended not only to make the text more aesthetically pleasing but also more easily mastered.

At the back of this text is a multimedia interactive program on compact disc. Designed to be pleasing to the eye and fun to use, this CD contains video clips of the authors and biblical lands, photos of the New Testament world, maps, interactive review questions, and visual organizers.

May your encounter with the New Testament be an exciting adventure!

Abbreviations

Old Testament

Genesis	Gn
Exodus	Ex
Leviticus	Lv
Numbers	Nm
Deuteronomy	Dt
Joshua	Jos
Judges	Jgs
Ruth	Ru
1 Samuel	1 Sm
2 Samuel	2 Sm
1 Kings	1 Kgs
2 Kings	2 Kgs
1 Chronicles	1 Chr
2 Chronicles	2 Chr
Ezra	Ezr
Nehemiah	Neh
Esther	Est
Job	Jb
Psalms	Ps(s)
Proverbs	Prv
Ecclesiastes	Eccl
Song of Songs	Sg (Song)
Isaiah	Is
Jeremiah	Jer
Lamentations	Lam
Ezekiel	Ez
Daniel	Dn
Hosea	Hos
Joel	Jl
Amos	Am
Obadiah	Ob
Jonah	Jon
Micah	Mi
Nahum	Na
Habakkuk	Hb
Zephaniah	Zep
Haggai	Hg
Zechariah	Zec
Malachi	Mal

Old Testament Apocrypha

Tobit	Tb
Judith	Jdt
Wisdom	Wis
Baruch	Bar
Sirach	Sir
1 Maccabees	1 Mc
2 Maccabees	2 Mc

New Testament

Matthew	Mt
Mark	Mk
Luke	Lk
John	Jn
Acts of the Apostles	Acts
Romans	Rom
1 Corinthians	1 Cor
2 Corinthians	2 Cor
Galatians	Gal
Ephesians	Eph
Philippians	Phil
Colossians	Col
1 Thessalonians	1 Thes
2 Thessalonians	2 Thes
1 Timothy	1 Tm
2 Timothy	2 Tm
Titus	Ti
Philemon	Phlm
Hebrews	Heb
James	Jas
1 Peter	1 Pt
2 Peter	2 Pt
1 John	1 Jn
2 John	2 Jn
3 John	3 Jn
Jude	Jude
Revelation	Rv

1 Why Study the New Testament?

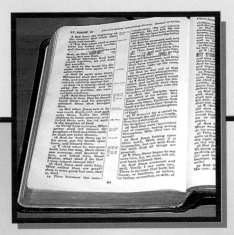

Outline

- **The Bible: A High Stakes Book**
- **Old and New Testaments**
- **Why Study the New Testament?**
  It Mediates God's Presence—
    and with It, Truth
  It Is of Ultimate Personal Significance
  It Is Foundational to Cultural Literacy
- **Why *These* Twenty-Seven Books?**
  Old Testament Precedent for a Canon
  The Divine Authorship of the
    New Testament: Inspiration
  Recognition of the Canon in the Church
- **The Integrity of the New
  Testament Text**
  Wealth of Evidence
  Brief Time Lapse
  Versions and Fathers
  So Many Translations!
- **Why *Study* the New Testament?**
  To Avoid the Tyranny of Preformed
    Personal Opinion
  To Avoid Misguided Reliance on the Holy
    Spirit
  To Enable Historical-Theological
    Interpretation

Objectives

**After reading this chapter,
you should be able to**

- Explain how the New Testament differs
  from the Old Testament
- Justify study of the New Testament
- List and classify the books
  of the New Testament
- Explain why the New Testament canon
  is regarded as reliable
- Give reasons for upholding the integrity
  of the New Testament text
- Discuss reasons for studying
  the New Testament

The Bible: A High Stakes Book

In the centuries since Christ's death and resurrection, Christians have sometimes died for refusing to hand over the Bible to hostile authorities.[1] Twentieth-century believers in the West took great risks to smuggle Bibles to eager readers behind the Iron Curtain, sometimes suffering dire consequences for doing so.

Even today Christians who cling to the Bible's words rather than the **Qur'an**'s are persecuted and killed in Muslim lands.[2] Millions of mainland Chinese Christians long fervently for a personal copy of the Bible; government printing and import restrictions limit the number available. No missionary traveling to Africa or Latin America can bring along enough Bibles to satisfy the demand that he or she will find there. Even in Western nations like Canada and the United States, where Bibles are not scarce, more of them are sold each year than any other single book published, including so-called best-sellers. New translations appear as steadily as the seasons.[3] *More copies of the Bible have been printed than any other single book in human history.*

Why such a fuss about a book? How is it that a volume you can hold in one hand has been instrumental in the rise and fall of nations, the life and death of civilizations, and—Christians believe—the salvation or damnation of multitudes of souls?

To answer such questions would fill the hours of a semester-long college-level course, entitled perhaps "The Christian **Scriptures** in World History." We cannot attempt to sketch that story here.[4] But we can say that it is one of the reasons why you are reading these words. The Bible, consisting of both Old and New Testaments, has shaped the world you live in. You may or may not have read much of it personally. You may or may not hear a sermon based on it in church each week. It doesn't matter. No one in today's world is free from the influence, whether direct or indirect, that the Christian Scriptures, both Old and New Testaments, have exerted.

Old and New Testaments

By Old Testament we mean the Scriptures that God gave, over the course of many centuries, to an ancient people with whom he chose to deal in a unique way (Dt 7:7). (In this book we will often refer to Bible passages. It would be wise to look them up as you are reading. A key to the abbreviations used, like "Dt" above, is found on p. 17.) These ancient people were known first as Hebrews or Israelites and later as Jews. People like Moses, David, and Isaiah were moved by God's Spirit to express divine truths in human words. The writings that resulted were eventually divided into three sections. The first was the **Torah** (the word means guidance, teaching, law). These were the five books of Moses. The second section was **the Prophets.** These consisted of longer works like Isaiah, along with some very short ones like Joel and Obadiah. The third section was called simply **the Writings** and consisted of historical writings, Psalms, Proverbs, and other works.

Together these books form what came to be called the Old Testament. They are God's ancient "testament" (solemn declaration) of his creation of the world and of humanity, their fall into sin, and God's saving work over many centuries to undo sin's disastrous consequences. These books point to a person who would save people from their sins and restore innocence and justice. They point to a savior. But the Old Testament ends with many eagerly longing for him. It looks ahead to a future fulfillment.

The New Testament tells of the fulfillment of what the Old Testament promises. It is the "testament" of God's saving work in more recent times. The savior, Jesus Christ, is born of the virgin Mary (Is 7:14) in Bethlehem (Mi 5:2). A prophet named John announces his coming (Is 40:3; Mt 3:3). Jesus preaches in Galilee as Isaiah predicted (Is 9:1–2). He attracts many followers and works miracles (Mt 12:15–21; see Is 42:1–14). His message remains a mystery to many (Mt 13:13–15), as the Old Testament had foretold (Is 6:9–10). Because his message and his very person were such an af-

Perennial best-sellers in the West, Bibles are often in short supply in other parts of the world.

front (Mt 15:3–9; see Is 29:13), steps were taken to silence him. Jesus could see it coming. He told his followers that even they would desert him, just as the Old Testament foresaw (Mt 26:31; see Zec 13:7). But he also predicted that he would be raised from the dead (Mt 26:32). Both his death and resurrection were foretold in Old Testament Scripture (Lk 24:45–46). So was the church and its ministry of preaching salvation through Jesus Christ (Lk 24:47).

The New Testament, then, announces the arrival of the Savior that the Old Testament awaits. Both Testaments also point to an eternal order beyond the world as we know it, a world of heavenly glory for those who seek God but of judgment for those whose lives remain centered on themselves. Old

Old Testament Apocrypha

Roman Catholics and some Eastern Orthodox churches recognize the writings listed below as Scripture. Protestants acknowledge their literary value and historical significance but do not view them as possessing spiritual authority.

Additions to Esther	Judith	Prayer of Manasseh
Baruch	Letter of Jeremiah	Psalm 151
Bel and the Dragon	1 Maccabees	Song of the Three Jews
Ecclesiasticus (Wisdom of Jesus Son of Sirach)	2 Maccabees	Susanna
	3 Maccabees	Tobit
1 Esdras	4 Maccabees	Wisdom of Solomon
2 Esdras	Prayer of Azariah	

and New Testament together are what we call the Bible. As we study the New Testament in this book, we will often refer to the Old Testament, for both stand together. But it is the New Testament that will be our main focus.

Some modern Bibles include a third section called the apocryphal/deuterocanonical books of the Old Testament. These were written after the last Old Testament prophet (Malachi, ca. 430 B.C.) and mainly between about 200 B.C. and A.D. 100. Some contain valuable historical and religious information.[5] But Protestants have historically maintained that these books lack the earmarks of divine authorship that distinguish the recognized Old and New Testament books. Jesus and the apostles did not quote them as Scripture. In citing the apocryphal books, we are recognizing their importance for our knowledge of the period without endorsing them as Holy Scripture.

Why Study the New Testament?

The New Testament has affected the whole world and also your life. That is one good reason to study it. This book will help you do that. But let us consider some other reasons why studying the New Testament is worthwhile.

It Mediates God's Presence—and with It, Truth

Assembled in solemn worship, Christians can often be heard singing hymns with lyrics like these:

> Our God is an awesome God.
> He reigns in heaven above
> With wisdom, power, and love.
> Our God is an awesome God.

Such words, when combined with the hymn's haunting tune, can make God's presence seem real. And why not? "He is not far from each one of us" (Acts 17:27). Hymns come to be cherished because through their message and emotional power they somehow convey God's presence.

The New Testament is loved for the same reason. God is present in it and through it. The Bible's words are God's words. By his own personal spiritual presence, God used various writers of long ago to observe events, record impressions, and convey truths. As a personal follower of Jesus wrote, "No prophecy of Scripture originates in personal explanation; for prophecy was not ever produced by human will; rather, men spoke from God, being moved by the Holy Spirit" (2 Pt 1:20–21, author's own translation). This means that the New Testament is worth studying because it is the Word of God. In a bewildering world of social change, political complexity, economic flux, and moral confusion, there is something firm to hold on to. There is light for the path ahead. There is meaning. There is even, to a far greater extent than mere mortals can grasp it, truth.

It Is of Ultimate Personal Significance

A second good reason for studying the New Testament follows from the first. While Scripture is of divine origin it is also of personal significance. It is important to you and me personally. The direction that our whole life takes depends on whether we embrace or ignore, or perhaps twist, the Word of God. And though we may be young now and not think much about dying, the New Testament has weighty things to say about the end of our lives, too: "It is appointed for mortals to die once, and after that the judgment" (Heb 9:27 NRSV). In life and in death, the New Testament has a status that no other book can rival.

The New Testament is important personally because it is the means God uses to heal searching souls. We all know what it is like to search. We experience times in our lives that seem unbearable. Our future is uncertain, our present unappealing. We are weighed down with vexing cares. We are crushed by questions. Who am I? Why am I alive? Does anyone really love me? What is the meaning of life? Why is there so much evil and suffering? What will happen to poor, polluted Planet Earth? What is the destiny of the human race? What is my own destiny? Why do I do things that I know are wrong? Is there any way to deal with my guilt feelings? Is there any way for my own life to be cleaned up so I can be part of building a better world?

These are searching questions. The New Testament invites them. Late one night a desperate prison guard about to commit

Is Everything Relative?

In his best-selling book *The Closing of the American Mind* Allan Bloom writes, "There is one thing a professor can be absolutely certain of: almost every student entering the university believes, or says he believes, that truth is relative." Today it is common to hear the word *relative* used when talk turns to ethics, morals, or religious matters.

Full knowledge of all truth belongs to God alone (Rom 11:33–34). But while there is much that mere mortals cannot discern, there is also much that God has revealed to them (Dt 29:29). If we accept the Bible as God's inspired and true Word, then there is at least one thing in this world that is not relative: Scripture.

Peter, like Paul (2 Tm 3:16) and other biblical writers, held a high view of Scripture. This does not mean that they thought they knew everything. But they were convinced that because God had spoken, they knew something. As Peter puts it, the Bible comes to us because God-appointed persons *"spoke from God as they were carried along by the Holy Spirit"* (2 Pt 1:21).

If God has spoken reliably and authoritatively—and Jesus Christ teaches that he has (Jn 10:35; 17:17)—then everything is not relative. There is a final standard. We can know some things for sure, because our God has told us.

It must be admitted that there is a measure of "relativity" in our perception of what the Bible says. But this doesn't mean that everything we read in it is cast in doubt. Throughout the centuries there has emerged a broad common core of conviction about the central teachings of Scripture. Only in recent generations have thinkers calling themselves Christian taught that we may doubt what the Bible says (see ch. 10) and still be considered Christians.

We should also remember that it is Almighty God we worship through his Son Jesus Christ, not the pages of a book. Yet God uses the Bible to make us *"wise for salvation through faith in Christ Jesus"* (2 Tm 3:15). Jesus asked skeptics, *"Since you do not believe what he [Moses] wrote, how are you going to believe what I say?"* (Jn 5:47).

Even in our relativistic age, disciples of Jesus Christ may build on the foundation of the words of their Master who said, *"Heaven and earth will pass away, but my words will never pass away"* (Mt 24:35).

---

suicide blurted out, "How can I be saved?" (Acts 16:30). He found the answer he was looking for. It was not a simplistic or pat answer—the New Testament is God's Word, not a 1–2–3 self-help pamphlet. But it is powerful. It reaches down to the depths of our hearts. It draws us out of our laziness, doubt, and misery—or perhaps our indifference and cocky self-confidence—and places us before One who hears, understands, convicts, and heals.

The New Testament is worth studying because it is what we may call a means of grace. To read it with the hungry curiosity of the needy sinner—not the haughty condescension of the smug skeptic—is to open yourself to rich depths of challenge, mercy, purity, and joy. It is to start down a path of profound and desirable personal transformation. It is to become part of the people of God, with all the privileges and responsibilities that entails. It is to be prepared properly for life to the fullest in this world—as well as in the age to come.

It Is Foundational to Cultural Literacy

The late University of Chicago professor Allan Bloom was not a Christian. But he spoke glowingly about the importance of the Bible in the lives of his grandparents:

My grandparents were ignorant people by our standards, and my grandfather held only lowly jobs. But their home was spiritually rich because all the things done in it . . . found their origin in the Bible's commandments, and their explanations in the Bible's stories and commentaries on them,

Dead Sea Scrolls

and had their imaginative counterparts in the deeds of the myriad of exemplary heroes.[6]

Bloom went on to say more about the importance of the Bible for informed and lively intellectual activity:

I mean . . . that a life based on the Book is closer to the truth, that it provides the material for deeper research in and access to the real nature of things. Without the great revelations, epics and philosophies as part of our natural vision, there is nothing left to see out there, and eventually little left inside. The Bible is not the only means to furnish a mind, but without a book of similar gravity, read with the gravity of the potential believer, it will remain unfurnished.[7]

We have already touched on the Bible's importance in what we might call spiritual matters. Bloom reminds us of its significance for the life of the mind. The New Testament (like the Old) has occupied the world's great thinkers ever since it appeared. Whoever wishes to engage in serious thought in the modern world is well advised to be conversant with its message and all the details it relates.

Studies show, however, that modern society is biblically illiterate. Even where lip service is paid to the Bible's importance, many have not read it through, and most possess little knowledge of even basic facts about it. If part of the decline in Western civilization in recent decades is due to failure to appropriate the cultural accomplishments of former generations, ignorance of the Bible is one of our chief sins. To build a better tomorrow, we need to lay a foundation of better understanding of the New Testament than we currently possess.

At issue here is cultural literacy. By this we mean acquaintance with at least the broad aspects of science, the humanities, and the fine arts. We also mean familiarity with the beliefs, social organization, and moral traits of a society. The shared knowledge of any society will influence what that society looks like. It can be argued that there was a time when our society was more influenced by such New Testament teachings as love for others (rather than violence), truth telling (rather than deceit and theft), sexual purity and veneration of marriage (rather than sexual laxity and easy divorce), and self-sacrificial living (rather than destruction of the unborn and neglect of children in the interest of adult self-gratification). True, there was no golden yesterday to which we should return. But many feel that how-

A society's heritage is expressed and passed on in various ways. The Bible and its teachings are important aspects of Western culture.

Ancient Devotion to Old Testament Scripture

Nearly two centuries prior to the rise of the church, Jewish communities showed the same zeal for Old Testament teaching and commands that Jesus and the early church did. These excerpts from the Old Testament Apocrypha dramatize that zeal. The hostile "king" is Antiochus IV Epiphanes, Syrian overlord of Jerusalem 175–163 B.C.

*. . . the king sent an Athenian senator [to Jerusalem] to compel the Jews to forsake the laws of their fathers and cease to live by the laws of God, and also to pollute the temple in Jerusalem and call it the temple of Olympian Zeus. . . . Harsh and utterly grievous was the onslaught of evil. For the temple was filled with debauchery and reveling by the Gentiles, who dallied with harlots and had intercourse with women within the sacred precincts.
. . . It happened also that seven [Jewish] brothers and their mother were arrested and were being compelled by the king, under torture with whips and cords, to partake of unlawful swine's flesh. One of them, acting as their spokesman, said, "What do you intend to ask and learn from us? For we are ready to die rather than transgress the laws of our fathers." The king fell into a rage, and gave orders that pans and caldrons be heated. These were heated immediately, and he commanded that the tongue of their spokesman be cut out and that they scalp him and cut off his hands and feet, while the rest of the brothers and the mother looked on. When he was utterly helpless, the king ordered them to take him to the fire, still breathing, and to fry him in a pan. The smoke from the pan spread widely, but the brothers and their mother encouraged one another to die nobly, saying, "The Lord God is watching over us and in truth has compassion on us, as Moses declared. . . ."*

—2 Maccabees 6:1–2a, 3–4a; 7:1–6a

ever lowly our cultural situation may have been before the cultural revolution of recent decades, it is even lower now. Renewed attention to the New Testament is sure to be an important part of a better tomorrow.

Certainly Christians who have come to know God through its pages and have had their own lives changed by its guidance will be eager to learn as much about it as they can. But everyone should share this eagerness given Scripture's widespread impact on past generations and centuries in cultures around the world. No culturally literate person can afford to disrespect the profound insights that the New Testament offers into the human condition. Far less should anyone be ignorant of the will of an all-knowing, sovereign, and personal God to change that condition from darkness into light.

"Regardless of what anyone may personally think or believe about him, Jesus of Nazareth has been the dominant figure in the history of Western culture for almost twenty centuries."[8] The premier source of information about this dominant figure is the New Testament.

Why *These* Twenty-Seven Books?

The New Testament consists of four books called Gospels, one book (Acts) that sketches the rise and spread of the early church, twenty-one letters, and one book of prophecy. What makes these twenty-seven documents so unique?

Old Testament Precedent for a Canon

By at least the time of Jesus (first century A.D.), the Old Testament consisted of the same writings that are familiar to us today. No one knows all the details or chronology of the process by which these writings gained recognition; the finer points are subjects of ongoing scholarly debate. But first-century sources like the New Testament, as well as extra–New Testament sources like the **Dead Sea Scrolls** and the Jewish writer JOSEPHUS (see next chapter), confirm that a unified and recognized body of writings existed. There was widespread agreement among Jewish authorities that in certain writings God had revealed his will to his people, and indeed to the whole world. This revelation was preserved in the documents that we have already mentioned: the Torah, the Prophets, and the Writings.

These writings became the standard for faith and life among people who loved and feared their God. They became a **canon**, an authoritative collection of documents. The Jewish people used this canon as the basis for their personal lives and their corporate existence. A Jewish writing called **2 Maccabees** tells of the torture of seven sons and the murder of their mother, resulting from their refusal to break the law of Moses during the tyrannical reign of ANTIOCHUS EPIPHANES (ca. 170 B.C.). At the heart of their refusal to betray their faith was their belief that in Moses' law God had made his eternal will known. Their brave trust in Scripture is emblematic of the high view of God's written revelation that the Jewish people shared, even if they did not all interpret that Scripture in the same way.[9]

Jesus, speaking as a Jew, said, "We worship what we do know, for salvation is from the Jews" (Jn 4:22). The community he founded, the church, recognized the Jewish Scriptures, the Old Testament, as the basis of its very existence. But just as Jesus himself fulfills the Old Testament, the community he founded gave rise to more than two dozen writings that stand alongside the Old Testament in importance and authority. These writings, written by close followers of Jesus, later came to be called the New Testament.

In other words, the Old Testament canon served as a precedent and analogy for the New Testament canon. It was to be expected that if God's people had found life and nurture through inspired writings pointing forward to the savior, they might also be given inspired writings to explain their savior to them and to the world after he had appeared. And that is exactly what happened. As New Testament scholar and translator Bruce M. Metzger writes, "the belief in a written rule of faith was primitive [i.e., existed from the very earliest days of the church] and apostolic."[10] We rightly treat the New Testament writings with particular care and reverence as a result.

The Divine Authorship of the New Testament: Inspiration

We devote careful attention to the twenty-seven-book collection called the New Testament for a second reason: They are inspired (God-breathed) writings.

Early in his ministry Jesus chose a dozen men, hand-picked pupils who would (except for one) carry on his legacy after he ascended into heaven. On the night Judas Iscariot betrayed him, he gave the remaining eleven several important pieces of information about their future roles. After his death and resurrection, Jesus' Spirit would come to them, sent by the Father, to give them insight. In Jesus' words:

> The Counselor, the Holy Spirit, whom the Father will send in my name, will teach you all things and will remind you of everything I have said to you (Jn 14:26).

> When the Counselor comes, whom I will send to you from the Father, the Spirit of truth who goes out from the Father, he will testify about me; but you must also testify, for you have been with me from the beginning (Jn 15:26–27).

> I have much more to say to you, more than you can now bear. But when he, the Spirit of truth, comes, he will guide you into all truth. He will not speak on his own; he will speak only what he hears, and he will tell you what is yet to come (Jn 16:12–14).

Christians grant Holy Scripture a place of high honor because of its divine origin.

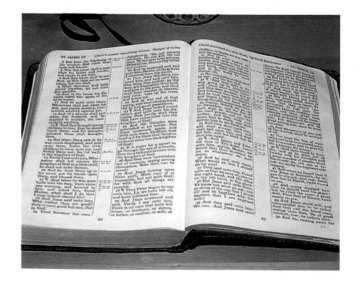

The Twenty-Seven Books of the New Testament

There must be no hesitation to state again the [books] of the New Testament; for they are these: Four Gospels: according to Matthew, according to Mark, according to Luke, and according to John. Further, after these, also [The] Acts of [the] Apostles, and the seven so-called Catholic Epistles of the Apostles, as follows: One of James, but two of Peter, then, three of John, and after these, one of Jude. In addition to these there are fourteen Epistles of the Apostle Paul put down in the following order: The first to the Romans, then two to the Corinthians, and after these, [the Epistles] to the Galatians, and then to the Ephesians; further, [the Epistles] to the Philippians and to the Colossians and two to the Thessalonians, and the [Epistle] to the Hebrews. And next two [letters] to Timothy, but one to Titus, and the last [being] the one to Philemon. Moreover, also the Apocalypse of John. . . .

—Athanasius (ca. A.D. 296–373)

gospel

inspiration

concursus

Good News about Jesus Christ—the **gospel**. We can surmise that it was Christ's intention that his story and commands be preserved in the witness, and eventually writings, of these closest followers. A direct result of Jesus' promise can be seen today in the writings we call the New Testament.[11]

Second, we should note that Jesus' words point to what theologians call **inspiration**. The Holy Spirit worked together with the minds and hearts of Jesus' followers to produce trustworthy understanding, recollections, and ultimately writings. The combination of divine and human elements is sometimes called **concursus,** the complementary interworking of God and the human writers in the composition of the Bible. As Gerhard Maier has written:

> Revelation, formed through the Holy Spirit, given written form by people, meets us as something unified and entire. . . . As Scripture took form, word of God and word of man became fundamentally intertwined: God wanted to speak in just this manner through human agency (2 Pt 1:21). Just as Jesus Christ is truly God and truly man, yet is not divisible into two persons, but remains thus the Son of God, so Scripture is simultaneously God's word and man's word, yet not divisible into two "words." It remains, finally and ultimately, God's word.[12]

All this points to a second major reason why we honor the New Testament writings, or the canon. It is inspired by God. In this sense Paul's statement applies to New and Old Testament alike: "All Scripture is God-breathed" (2 Tm 3:16).[13]

Recognition of the Canon in the Church

A third reason we recognize the importance of the New Testament writings lies in the preeminent role they gradually assumed in the ancient church. In the second through ninth centuries A.D. numerous writings arose that claimed to be written by Jesus' apostolic followers. Such works included so-called gospels, acts, epistles, and even books resembling Revelation in certain respects. There was much debate about these books. Christians who might be persecuted for hiding Christian Scriptures wanted to know which ones

Two things should be noted about Jesus' statements. The first is that after his departure, the Holy Spirit would teach the disciples and remind them of what Jesus had told them. On that basis, they would testify to Christ. The Spirit would assist them by guiding them "into all truth" and telling them "what is yet to come." These words establish a unique link between Jesus and a select group of his earliest followers. Through them he chose to disclose information about himself to subsequent generations. After his death the Holy Spirit would confirm among them the truth about who Jesus was and what he had accomplished. His followers were already grounded in Jesus' teachings and had witnessed his miraculous works. But by the Spirit, and in the light of Christ's resurrection and ascension, they were empowered to arrive at unique and authoritative accounts of the

manuscript

papyrus

uncials

Roman relief of a scribe.

they should be willing to die for. Pastors and theologians sought the most reliable possible documents for information about the faith they held dear. Over the span of about three centuries, the canon as we know it emerged. It comprised a standard by which all other writings were judged. The books in it possessed the marks of apostolic authorship (i.e., written by Jesus' hand-picked followers, the apostles, or their close aides). They bore evidence of their first-century origin. (Few noncanonical writings were written nearly so early. Only a few can even be dated to the second century and perhaps none with certainty to the first.) They also contained the apostolic message of the true gospel of Jesus Christ.

The twenty-seven New Testament writings are the ones that earned the recognition of early Christians as having been inspired by God and given to the church "for teaching, for reproof, for correction, and for training in righteousness" (2 Tm 3:16 NRSV). It is not naiveté, therefore, to honor this same canon today, but sober recognition of the Holy Spirit's work as well as humble acceptance of God's provision for knowledge of his will among Christians throughout all ages.[14]

Some years ago a scholar who rejected the distinctive place of the New Testament canon remarked that to accept it is to place yourself under the authority of second- to fourth-century bishops.[15] This comment is historically misleading. "Debates over the canon were so vigorous that no church council reached a decision about it before Trent in the sixteenth century."[16] The ancient church did not force the canon on unsuspecting members. "In the most basic sense neither individuals nor councils created the canon; instead they came to perceive and acknowledge the self-authenticating quality of these writings, which imposed themselves as canonical upon the church."[17] It can be reasonably argued that to reject the canon is to put yourself under the authority of the modern spirit of disbelief in Jesus Christ and his authority in the church through the Scriptures.

The Integrity of the New Testament Text

The printing press was not invented until the fifteenth century. Before that, writings had to be copied by hand. A hand-written copy is called a **manuscript**. All of the New Testament documents were passed down through the centuries in manuscript form. Our modern translations are made by scholars who consult these manuscripts and produce, say, English versions from them.

But as anyone who has tried to copy something (perhaps a newspaper quote or a recipe) by hand discovers, it is easy to make a mistake. If the New Testament writings were passed along for over a thousand years with one copy being made from another, can we be certain that our English translations reflect what Paul or Peter or Luke originally wrote in Greek?

Wealth of Evidence

Happily, the answer is a resounding yes. A major reason for this is the wealth of evidence available. *The New Testament is by far the best-attested writing of antiquity.* Over five thousand manuscripts containing at least a fragment of the New Testament have been catalogued. The earliest of these are written on **papyrus**, a paper made from reeds. Nearly three hundred others are called **uncials**; this means they record the New Testament in capital letters, usually on some kind of leather surface. The largest group consists of minuscules.

Greek Manuscripts of Part or All of the New Testament

Papyri Catalogued	115
Uncial Mss. Catalogued	270
Minuscule Mss. Catalogued	2,862
Lectionaries Catalogued	2,281
Total	5,528

(The statistics are derived from Kurt Aland, Barbara Aland, and M. Holmes.)

lectionaries

These display a kind of cursive writing that developed in BYZANTIUM around the ninth century. Finally, there are **lectionaries**, books used in church worship that include portions of Scripture. They, too, are important witnesses to the New Testament text as it was passed down through the centuries.

Brief Time Lapse

Another reason for confidence in our knowledge of what Matthew, Paul, and other writers originally wrote is the brief time span between the date when the documents were written and the date of the earliest copies we possess. It is not uncommon for a gap of a thousand years or more to separate an ancient work and the earliest known copy of it. Things are different in the case of the New Testament, where "several papyrus manuscripts . . . are extant which were copied within a century or so after the composition of the original documents."[18] A papyrus fragment of John's Gospel found in EGYPT is commonly dated to A.D. 125. This is barely one generation later than the A.D. 90s, when many scholars think the Gospel was first written. Textual evidence is consistent with the view that all four Gospels were written in the first century.

Versions and Fathers

Still another ground for optimism about our knowledge of the original text of the New Testament comes from the widespread distribution of it from a very early date. We refer here to what scholars call the ancient versions. As the gospel spread to non-Greek speaking lands, the New Testament was translated into languages such as Syriac, Latin, and Coptic. Over eight thousand manuscripts exist in Latin alone! These versions are generally less important for our knowledge of the ancient Greek text than the Greek manuscripts themselves are. But at some points they are quite significant. And overall they show that the New Testament was faithfully rendered as it passed from scribe to scribe and even language to language. Transmission was not perfect, but it was more than reliable enough for us to be in very little doubt about what the New Testament authors first wrote.

The writings of the early Church Fathers are still another important witness to the shape of the earliest Greek text. Dozens of church leaders like CLEMENT OF ROME (A.D. 95), JUSTIN MARTYR (A.D. 150), IRENAEUS (A.D. 170), and Origen (A.D. 250) quoted the New Testament in writings that are still extant.

We may conclude, then, that there are no grounds for doubting our knowledge of what the original manuscripts of the various New Testament writings contained. True, at individual points scholars debate precisely what the original said. Did Jesus send out seventy-two or seventy workers into the harvest (Lk 10:1)? There is confusion among various manuscripts here. Did the original copy of Matthew contain 12:47? Some ancient and important manuscripts omit it. And what about the woman accused of adultery (Jn 7:53–8:11)? Modern translations place it in brackets or mark it off from the rest of John's Gospel by other means. The original ending of Mark is also disputed as most modern Bibles indicate. All of this is a reminder that there are points of ongoing investigation into the precise wording of the original New Testament writings. (This scholarly pursuit is called textual criticism; books discussing its methods and findings are listed at the end of this chapter.)

But estimates of the degree of certainty in our knowledge of the New Testament text invariably run to near 100 percent. And experts agree that none of the points of discussion affect the gospel message or even any single Christian doctrine. While we may struggle with how to interpret the New Testament and find it challenging to apply what we interpret, we are free from serious doubts about the integrity of the text.

So Many Translations!

In recent decades English-language translations have multiplied rapidly. For centuries the King James Version (1611) dominated. But around 1950 the Revised Standard Version appeared, largely the product of mainline Protestant scholarship. Roman Catholics produced a pair of new translations: the Jerusalem Bible in 1966 and the New American Bible and in 1970. Evangelical scholars published the New American Standard version in 1960 and the New International Version in the 1978. The latter has become the most widely used translation for many, and an updated version (Today's New International Version or TNIV) is now available.

The Revised English Bible (1989) and the English Standard Version (2001), a revision of the Revised Standard Version, are recent examples of continuing efforts to make available the most accurate and readable renderings of Scripture possible. The Revised Standard Version had already appeared in an inclusive-language edition, the New Revised Standard Version (1989). In 2000 yet another team of scholars published a fresh translation of the New Testament, the Holman Christian Standard Bible. Also worth mentioning are paraphrases, renderings that are freer than translations in the strict sense but which still attempt to be faithful to the original languages of the ancient manuscripts. Examples include the New Living Translation (1996), itself a revision of the older Living Bible (1971), and the Contemporary English Version (1995).

The situation might appear chaotic, but these attempts mainly reflect the high value placed on the Bible's meaning and the importance of the clearest possible rendering of it into English. Translations vary depending on the target audiences and the commitments of the scholars who produce them. Study of different translations reveals that they differ mainly in emphasis, style, and nuance. Some are better for personal reading, others lend themselves to formal usage, such as public reading. They do not present radically differing pictures of God, Jesus, or Christian doctrine. They rather offer rich possibilities for serious students to delve into the finer and deeper aspects of the Bible's meaning for themselves. This brings us to the whole matter of formal *study* of the New Testament.

Why *Study* the New Testament?

We have already touched on good reasons for paying serious and extended attention to the New Testament and matters related to it. But is there really any need to *study* what it says? If it is inspired by God and its text is reasonably secure, then why is it necessary to expend energy pondering what it says; learning ancient names and dates; summarizing various New Testament teachings; exploring different writings and their contents? Why not just confess faith in it, learn a summary (like a catechism) of what it says, and go on to other things?

To Avoid the Tyranny of Preformed Personal Opinion

An obvious reason for *study* relates to what we have already said: The New Testament is an immensely important book, with much to offer the receptive reader. To reap the benefits of the whole, one must pay the price of mastering the various parts. But let us now go a step further.

The New Testament is a book with religious content, read by humans who are religious by nature. This can be a wonderful combination: The reader has a religious thirst; the New Testament satisfies it. What could be wrong with that?

The answer is, Plenty. We all stand in danger of seeing in the Bible, or anywhere else, only those things our prior experiences or convictions dispose us to see. And for some this is where *study* of the New Testament becomes nearly impossible. They already have their minds made up about their religious commitments—and therefore about the New Testament, too. They will perhaps read it for additional strengthening of what they already think. But they are not open to a depth and mode of *study* that might call into question their established outlook. While it is good (and

Archaeology is constantly adding to our knowledge of the world of the Bible.

rabbinic

inevitable) that we approach any book, including the Bible, with convictions, it is dangerous for those convictions to function as censors of the text's message to us.

A minister was once preaching from Acts 17:26: "From one ancestor he made all nations to inhabit the whole earth, and he allotted the times of their existence and the boundaries of the places where they would live" (NRSV). To the astonishment of some listeners, he angrily stressed the point that he resented seeing interracial dating and marriage between Caucasians and African Americans. "It makes my blood boil!" he declared. He explained that Acts 17:26 prohibited this—God "allotted . . . the boundaries of the places where they would live." To the minister this meant that blacks and whites ought to stay away from each other and remain on whatever side of the tracks they were born. But he could arrive at this conclusion only by ignoring the same verse's opening words: "From one ancestor he made all nations." Because Adam and Eve are, as the Bible teaches, everyone's first parents, we share a commonality that ought to rule out racist attitudes.

Apparently the minister had not *studied* the Bible sufficiently at this point but simply read into it the prejudices that he had before coming to this particular text. Unfortunately, this is what we all tend to do with Scripture, unless we gain wisdom and self-control in the way we handle it. "A fool finds no pleasure in understanding but delights in airing his own opinions" (Prv 18:2). Careful study can help us avoid misinterpretation and see what God really has to say rather than what we already think.

To Avoid Misguided Reliance on the Holy Spirit

A related danger, and enemy of *study*, is the notion that because the Holy Spirit influences our lives, he will somehow fill us with knowledge of the New Testament's truth without our having to work at mastering it ourselves. While we should not minimize our dependence on God's Spirit to understand Scripture aright, it is a mistake to substitute spiritual influence alone for the substantive means of grace that God has given in the form of Scripture. Without solid understanding of God's revelation of himself in Scripture, how can we be sure that the spiritual influence we sense is truly from God? The primary standard for making that determination must in the end be Scripture!

Martin Niemöller, heroic Christian leader and war prisoner in Nazi Germany, told of a young German minister who said that instead of study, he trusted the Spirit for his sermons. An older colleague commented: "As for me, the Holy Ghost never spoke to me in the pulpit. Yes, I remember, he did speak to me once. When I was going down the pulpit steps after a poor sort of sermon, the Holy Ghost spoke to me. He said only three words, and what he said was, 'Heinrich, you are lazy!'" In other words, "the Holy Spirit has much more important work to do than to substitute for human indolence."[19]

Based on the Gospels we can see that Jesus had learned, mastered, and was submissive to Scripture. Jesus' disciples were likewise serious students of Scripture—despite the benefit of personal instruction at Jesus' feet. Paul had extensive formal training in **rabbinic** interpretation and continued to develop his understanding of the Old Testament following conversion. Yes, all these people

Focus 1: The Old Testament Apocrypha

The Apocrypha contains approximately fourteen or fifteen documents that have not been recognized by the Protestant Church as part of the canon. These include books or parts of books that appeared in the two centuries before Christ and the first century after his birth. Whereas many of these documents provide insight into the religious, political, and social conditions during this period, they failed to meet the criteria for inspired Scripture that other biblical documents reflect.

The following story comes from a brief apocryphal text entitled "The History of the Destruction of Bel and the Dragon," which some took to be an addition to the Book of Daniel. The passage demonstrates how stories from the Apocrypha are blended with stories and ideas found in the Old Testament canon.

23 And in that same place there was a great dragon, which they of Babylon worshiped.
24 And the king said unto Daniel, Wilt thou also say that this is of brass? Lo, he liveth, he eateth and drinketh; thou canst not say that he is no living god; therefore worship him.
25 Then said Daniel unto the king, I will worship the Lord my God: for he is the living God.
26 But give me leave, O king, and I shall slay this dragon without sword or staff. The king said, I give thee leave.
27 Then Daniel took pitch, and fat, and hair, and did seethe them together, and made lumps thereof: this he put in the dragon's mouth, and so the dragon burst in sunder:
and Daniel said, Lo, these are the gods ye worship.
28 When they of Babylon heard that, they took great indignation, and conspired against the king, saying, the king is become a Jew, and he hath destroyed Bel, he hath slain the dragon, and put the priests to death.
29 So they came to the king, and said, Deliver us Daniel, or else we will destroy thee and thy house.
30 Now when the king saw that they pressed him sore, being constrained, he delivered Daniel unto them:
31 Who cast him into the lion's den: where he was six days.
32 And in the den there were seven lions, and they had given them every day two carcasses, and two sheep: which then were not given to them, to the intent they might devour Daniel.

trusted God and were empowered by the Holy Spirit. But the Spirit actualized the fruits of their prayer and *study*; he did not replace it. If study of Scripture was central to their lives, it probably should be to ours as well.

To Enable Historical-Theological Interpretation

A final reason for *study* of the New Testament is that it provides the historical dimension by which theological understanding and application must be informed.

God has seen fit to reveal himself, and to do his saving work, using historical means. The gospel is not the proclamation of an other-worldly, mystical experience. It is not an obscure insight or philosophical theory gained by skilled meditation or subtle reasoning. It is the message that through Christ God has acted in love and mercy in the affairs of the world over which he is Lord. It is the good word about God's moving and communicating himself across the gamut of human life in its broadest sense. It is God renewing human life, giving it heavenly quality and hope, in history—a word that here includes the whole spectrum of both the natural world and human civilization.

We have already established that Scripture is ultimately divine in character. It is God's Word. But it comes to us in earthly dress and through human agents. Understanding of the earthly and human components (history) is essential to realizing its theological meaning. These components include elements of geography, political and cultural history (Israelite, Egyptian, Assyrian, Babylonian, Persian, Greek, Roman, etc.), literature, and various languages. Informed interpretation of the New Testament may involve modern fields of study as varied as archaeology, social sciences, economics, linguistics, musicology, and many others.

All of this suggests that *study* of the New Testament is necessary for the kind of interpretation of it that is most basic and responsible in the long run. Admittedly, other kinds of interpretation are possible. A *devotional* interpretation may read the New Testament with little regard for historical considerations, seeking instead a word of encouragement or mystical guidance. A *literary* interpretation may examine how formal features like plot and structure help understand a book's message. A *political* interpretation may look for injustices that the Bible appears to sanction, or

Summary

1. The Bible has shaped the world in which we live, and no one is free from its influence.

2. The Old Testament tells of God's creation of the world, humankind's fall into sin, and God's saving work to undo sin's consequences. It is divided into three parts: Torah, Prophets, and the Writings.

3. The New Testament is the testament of God's saving work in more recent times and announces the Savior the Old Testament awaits.

4. Study of the New Testament is important because it mediates God's presence, is of ultimate personal significance, and is foundational to cultural literacy.

5. The twenty-seven books of the New Testament include four books called Gospels, one book that traces the rise of the early church (Acts), twenty-one Epistles or letters, and one book of prophecy.

6. The New Testament writings are inspired by God. The Holy Spirit worked together with the hearts and minds of the followers of Jesus to produce these trustworthy writings.

7. The New Testament canon is an authorized collection of writings that came together over a span of three centuries. It was given to the church for teaching, for reproof, for correction, and for training in righteousness (2 Tm 3:16).

8. New Testament manuscripts were first written on papyrus and later on leather. The manuscripts are of several types: papyri, uncials, minuscules, and lectionaries.

9. The New Testament text we have is secure because there is extensive evidence supporting it, the authors of the books wrote them within living memory of Jesus' life, and ancient versions of the text were widely distributed.

10. Christians should *study* the New Testament so that they will avoid misinterpretation based on preconceived ideas and misplaced reliance on the Holy Spirit, and so that they will have the appropriate historical foundation for understanding and applying its teachings.

Key Terms

canon
concursus
Dead Sea Scrolls
gospel
inspiration
lectionaries
manuscript
papyrus
the Prophets
Qur'an
rabbinic
Scriptures
2 Maccabees
Torah
uncials
the Writings

Key People/ Places

Antiochus Epiphanes
Byzantium
Clement of Rome
Egypt
Irenaeus
Josephus
Justin Martyr

place, but they are secondary to (because they are dependent on) the divine will and activity that created Scripture to begin with. Historical-theological interpretation—grasping the Bible's redemptive message to people *then* as a means of receiving and sharing its message *now*—is perhaps the most elementary and taxing, yet ultimately fruitful, way of approaching the New Testament that we can attempt. It involves learning and processing a good deal of information that may at first seem foreign and a little unnecessary. It takes work. It often requires (sometimes humbling) personal response, as increased understanding triggers conviction of personal need and awe at divine greatness. It will, in the sometimes daunting sense of the word, truly require *study*.

But the authors of this book, having gained a little more love for God and his Book through such *study* themselves, wish to help the reader along the path we have walked (and continue to walk). Generally the road ahead is engrossing and pleasant. But even if things get a little steep, dusty, and sweaty at points, we trust you will find it profitable as you make your way.

for insights about good government that it may contain.

But basic to all such interpretations is understanding of the Bible that most clearly approximates the purpose for which God inspired it. Devotional, literary, political, and other interests are valuable in their

Review Questions

1. In ancient times the three major sections of the Old Testament were Torah , Phrophets, and writings

2. The five books of Moses are called the Torah.

3. The word that means solemn declaration is Testement.

4. The books that provide useful historical and religious information but are not inspired are called Apo.calyptical/ deutromical

5. Apart from spiritual reasons, the Bible is also significant for Cultral literacy.

6. The four major kinds of writings in the New Testament are the Gospels, Acts, letters, and Phrophecy

7. The Jewish historian who confirmed a unified and recognized body of writing known as the Old Testament is Joshipus

8. An authoritative collection of documents is called a canon.

9. The working together of God and the human writers in the composition of the Bible is called concursul

10. The earliest manuscripts of the New Testament were written on papcysus

Study Questions

1. What does "testament" mean in the titles "Old Testament" and "New Testament"?

2. What is the relationship of the Old Testament to the New?

3. What is cultural literacy? What part does the New Testament play in acquiring it?

4. What is a canon? What are the ancient divisions of the Old Testament canon?

5. Give three reasons for special study of the New Testament canon.

6. What are the bases of our high level of certainty regarding the text of the New Testament?

7. What other subjects have you found it necessary to *study* in order to master? What differences are there, if any, between study of those subjects and study of the New Testament?

Further Reading

Bruce, F. F. *The New Testament Documents: Are They Reliable?* Leicester/Grand Rapids: InterVarsity/Eerdmans, 1988. Compact summation of evidence for holding a high regard for the integrity of the text and the validity of the canon.

———. *The Books and the Parchments*. Westwood, N.J.: Revell, 1963. A study of how the manuscripts of the New Testament came to us.

Carson, D. A. *The Inclusive Language Debate*. Grand Rapids/Leicester: Baker/InterVarsity, 1998. Shows the complexities involved in the seemingly straight-forward question of how to translate the Bible.

———. *The King James Version Debate: A Plea for Realism*. Grand Rapids: Baker, 1985. Explains why advances in knowledge of the original New Testament text require improved translations.

Evans, Craig A. *Noncanonical Writings and New Testament Interpretation*. Peabody, Mass.: Hendrickson, 1992. Comprehensive listing of extracanonical writings. Valuable bibliography.

Holmes, Michael W. "Textual Criticism." In *Interpreting the New Testament*. Ed. D. A. Black and D. S. Dockery. Nashville: Broadman & Holman, 2001, pp. 46–73. Summarizes the sources, tools, principles, and issues of the discipline.

Lewis, Jack P. *The English Bible from KJV to NIV*. 2nd ed. Grand Rapids: Baker, 1991. A survey and evaluation of many modern English translations of the Bible.

McDonald, Hugh D. *What the Bible Teaches about the Bible*. Wheaton, Ill.: Tyndale, 1979. An easy-to-follow discussion of the unique nature of the Bible as inspired by God.

McDonald, L. M., and James Sanders, eds. *The Canon Debate*. Peabody, Mass.: Hendrickson, 2002. Almost three dozen scholarly essays representing many points of view.

Metzger, Bruce M. *The Text of the New Testament: Its Transmission, Corruption, and Restoration*. 3rd ed. New York/Oxford: Oxford University Press, 1992. A standard work covering all important areas of New Testament textual criticism at considerable depth. Technical in places, but generally readable.

Wenham, John W. *Christ and the Bible*. 3rd ed. Grand Rapids: Baker, 1994. Probably the best brief compendium of why, given the authority of Jesus Christ, Christians are justified in holding a high view of the biblical text and canon.

Part
1

Encountering Jesus and the Gospels

2 The Middle East in the Days of Jesus

Outline

Objectives

After reading this chapter, you should be able to

- Describe the essential geographical features of Palestine
- Outline the major historical events occurring in Palestine from 539 B.C. to A.D. 70
- Explain how various factors unified Judaism
- Identify the differences asmong the major religious groups of this historical period
- Contrast the writings of the Old Testament, the Apocrypha, and the pseudepigrapha
- List the various rabbinic materials and what they teach

We live in an age of impersonal, consumer-driven communication. Billboards quietly drop seeds of discontent into the minds of passing motorists. The planet is bathed in radio waves directed at no one in particular. Newspapers barely slow down long enough to be read on their way to recycling bins and landfills, their sheer volume bespeaking a shotgun approach to communication. And now cyberspace is drilling yet another conduit into our homes and businesses through which an unprecedented flow of impersonal communication is made possible. Think of spam! All these forms of communication are designed to appeal to various sectors within the general marketplace, and in this sense they mimic the personal touch, but we all know how insulting it is to get a "personal" form letter in which our name is misspelled.

We as Christians are not unaffected by this. It is difficult to pick up the Holy Scriptures, especially when they are slickly packaged with the latest and greatest study aids, and somehow escape the feeling that this is not just another impersonal communiqué masquerading as personal communication. But nothing could be further from the truth. The biblical documents, while appealing to humans in general, are particular in nature. That is, they are rooted in history—real space and time. Indeed the redemptive flow of history cannot be divorced from the Scriptures that document it. God's Word speaks to the particular before it ever flows out into the general, which is just the opposite of much of the communication we encounter in a consumer-based society.

The New Testament especially is striking in its personal tone. Out of twenty-seven documents, twenty-four are personal letters[1] and the remaining three Gospels are personalized accounts of the life and work of Jesus Christ.

The apostle John begins his Gospel by telling us that the eternal Word of God, Jesus Christ, "became flesh and made his dwelling among us" (Jn 1:14); in his first Epistle John says that he and the other apostles saw him with their eyes and touched him with their hands (1 Jn 1:1–2). The Christian doctrine of the incarnation asserts that the Son of God became a human being and shared our human life

with us. This means, of course, that he had to appear at a certain time, in a certain place. To enter history meant that Christ became a particular person—Jesus of Nazareth; at a particular time—during the reigns of Augustus (27 B.C.–A.D. 14) and TIBERIUS CAESAR (A.D. 14–37); in a particular place—Palestine, on the MEDITERRANEAN SEA. When the apostle Paul spoke to the philosophers in Athens, he portrayed history as a prelude leading up to the coming of Christ, before whom we all must someday stand (Acts 17:22–31). This idea caused some of the early Church Fathers to speak of the history before Christ as a *praeparatio evangelium* (preparation for the gospel). Contemporary theologians speak of the "scandal of particularity"—the fact that Jesus is available for all, but was only to be found in one place. All of this is important for New Testament students because it speaks of the significance of the particular history of which Jesus was a part and of the place he filled in it.

It is for this reason that any study of the New Testament must begin with a look, however brief, at the circumstances that led up to and surrounded the major events that constituted the beginning of the Christian faith. Without that, it would be difficult to get a clear picture of Jesus, the apostles, or the early church.

The Land of Palestine

The land of Palestine has always been very important to the Jews and to the Middle East in general.[2] About one-third the size of Illinois, it is approximately 45 miles wide (east-west) and 145 miles long (north-south). The region as a whole divides into basically five longitudinal regions,[3] with several subregions of varying importance. The main regions, going from west to east, are the coastal plain, the Shephelah or foothills, the central mountain range, the wilderness and the Jordan Valley, and the eastern mountain range. The striking ruggedness of the territory produces marked changes of climate from place to place, so that snow might be found in one place while a few miles away are palm trees and sunshine. The map on p. 41 shows something of this contrast by

Gentiles

slicing into the land from west to east roughly through JERUSALEM. As you look at this, imagine yourself standing in the desert to the south of Jerusalem, looking north.

A look at the land as it lies north to south is also revealing, showing it to be almost impassable, except for the PLAIN OF ESDRAELON that cuts east to west between SAMARIA and GALILEE. In the picture on page 42 you are standing on the eastern side of the JORDAN RIVER looking west. Sea level is the straight line that cuts horizontally through the land.

In Jesus' day the land consisted of several administrative districts that were governed by the Romans. On the western side of the Jordan River there were three: Galilee, Samaria, and JUDEA. East of the Jordan to the north was a collection of smaller districts, ruled by Herod's son Philip. Another, called the DECAPOLIS, was a spread-out area containing ten cities that were given a rather large measure of self-government. South of this was PEREA, an area ruled along with Galilee by HEROD ANTIPAS. Let's take a brief look at these districts.

The district of Galilee to the north, where Jesus grew up, is of great physical diversity, an area about thirty-three miles wide and sixty miles long (north–south), bordered by PHOENICIA on the northwest, SYRIA on the north, the Jordan Valley with the SEA OF GALILEE on the east, and the Plain of Esdraelon on the south—Galilee, surrounded by the **Gentiles** (Mt 4:13–16).[4] The Sea of Galilee, which Jesus knew so well, is not really a sea at all but a medium-sized

lake about twelve miles long by eight miles wide. It supplied the region with an abundance of fish. On its northwestern edge was the marvelous PLAIN OF GENNESARET, which produced fruits and vegetables almost all year long, even in the dead of winter. This was possible because it was over six hundred feet below sea level and was not subject to the temperature extremes of higher altitudes.

Samaria stands between Galilee and Judea. Its northern boundary is the Plain of Esdraelon. On the west is the Mediterranean Sea and on the east is the Jordan River. To the south, it merges into Judea. The exact boundaries have always been somewhat fluid, so it is difficult to fix them precisely. Samaria was a mountainous area of rounded hills and fertile plains, where agriculture flourished along with fruits and grains of every sort. Large herds of sheep and goats also found pasture among its hills. It has stayed this way down to modern times. As William Thomson long ago observed, "one may be excused for becoming somewhat enthusiastic over this pretty vale of Nablus, sparkling with fountains and streams, verdant with olive groves and fig orchards, interspersed with walnut, apple, apricot, orange, quince, pomegranate, and other trees and shrubs."[5]

Judea is directly to the south of Samaria, and extends from the Mediterranean Sea on the west to the Jordan River and DEAD SEA on the east down to the desert on the south, including the old area of EDOM, or IDUMEA as it was called in New Testament times. Its major city was, of course,

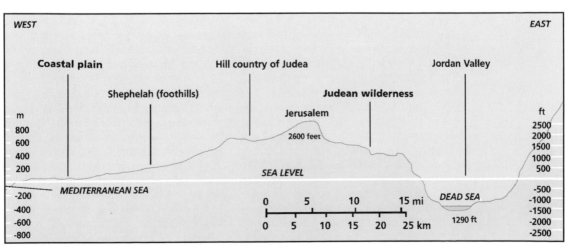

41

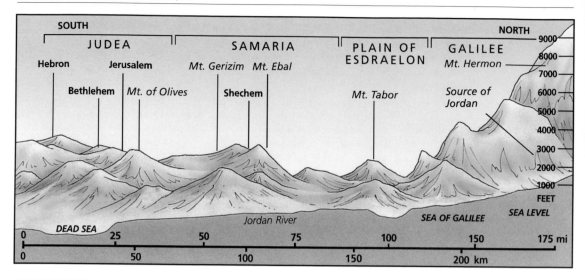

SOUTH   NORTH

JUDEA   SAMARIA   PLAIN OF   GALILEE
                                        ESDRAELON

Hebron   Jerusalem   Mt. Gerizim Mt. Ebal   Mt. Hermon

Bethlehem Mt. of Olives   Shechem   Mt. Tabor   Source of Jordan

DEAD SEA   Jordan River   SEA OF GALILEE   SEA LEVEL

9000, 8000, 7000, 6000, 5000, 4000, 3000, 2000, 1000, FEET

0   25   50   75   100   150   175 mi

0   50   100   150   200 km

Essenes

Jerusalem, but it also included many other ancient holy sites.

The physical features of Judea show the basic divisions of the land most clearly. The coastal plain and foothills were noted for their crops and pasturage. The west winds blowing off the sea provided enough moisture for everything to grow well, and throughout history these regions have been wonderfully productive. Up in the hills, olives and figs can grow, but the rough and stony land makes it difficult to farm. Flocks of sheep and goats abound. On the eastern side of the mountains lies the wilderness, a wild and barren area, utterly desolate, where little was to be found other than scorpions, jackals, and bandits. It was here that Jesus went to be tempted by the devil.

The eastern boundary of both Samaria and Judea is the Jordan River. In many ways it forms a region unto itself. It takes its rise in the mountains to the north, passes through the Sea of Galilee, and wanders through dense thickets for about sixty-five miles. It ends in the Dead Sea, so called because it is so salty from the evaporation of water that nothing can live there. JERICHO and its fertile plain are nearby, in stark contrast to the barrenness that surrounds it. The Dead Sea is the lowest natural place on earth (over 1,290 feet below sea level) and is surrounded by wilderness. A monastic group called the **Essenes** built a community here to get away from civilization and hid their precious library in its caves when the Romans attacked in A.D. 66. These documents were found in the mid-twentieth century and called the Dead Sea Scrolls.

The area to the northeast of the Sea of Galilee was ruled by HEROD PHILIP (4 B.C.–A.D. 34). It consisted of some smaller districts that included Batanaea, Trachonitis, Auranitis, Gaulanitis, and the territory surrounding Panias, a city Philip rebuilt and named CAESAREA PHILIPPI. The whole area was excellent for farming and herding. Jesus traveled infrequently in the area but did cross it on more than one occasion. Best remembered is his extraordinary self-revelation of divine sonship and his messianic mission of suffering and death at Caesarea Philippi (Mt 16:13–28). BETHSAIDA was also in Philip's territory, and it was here that Jesus performed some of his mighty works (Mt 11:21–22).

The Decapolis was an extended area, mostly on the eastern side of the Jordan River, which contained ten Greek cities and their surrounding areas. They were probably organized at the time POMPEY invaded Palestine (66–64 B.C.). The area was rich in farming and herding, being renowned in antiquity for its dairy products. Jesus made no extended trips through the area but did cross it on occasion (Mk 7:31). People from the Decapolis came to hear Jesus preach in Galilee (Mt 4:25). Jesus' memorable healing of an outcast demoniac took place in the Decapolis, on the eastern side of the Sea of Galilee. The pigs that rushed into the sea are evidence of the region's Gentile population (Mk 5:1–20).

Perea was a rather large area east of the

Jordan River and the Dead Sea that was ruled along with Galilee by Herod Antipas. JOSEPHUS, a first-century Jewish writer whom we will say more about at the end of this chapter, described it in this way:

> The greater part of it is desert, and rough, and not much disposed to the production of the milder kinds of fruits; yet a moist soil [in other parts] produces all kinds of fruits, and its plains are planted with trees of all sorts, while yet the olive tree, the vine, and the palm tree, are chiefly cultivated there. It is also sufficiently watered with torrents, which issue out of the mountains, and with springs that never fail to run, even when the torrents fail them, as they do in the dog days (Josephus, *War* 3.3.3).

There was a large Jewish population in Perea and many Jews from Galilee preferred to detour through it when traveling to Jerusalem rather than go through Samaria. John the Baptist preached and baptized in Perea (Jn 1:28; 10:40), and Jesus traveled extensively there in the six months prior to his death and resurrection. Jesus probably sent the seventy-two disciples into Perea to preach about the coming kingdom of God (Lk 10:1–17). MACHAERUS was a major fortress city of Perea. It was here that Antipas had his regional palace and that John the Baptist was imprisoned and, according to Josephus, was executed for denouncing Herod's illegal marriage (Josephus, *Ant.* 18.5.2. See also Mk 6:17–29).

Overall, Palestine is a small land, but it has been of immense value historically because of its strategic location as a land bridge between the mighty nations surrounding it. It has been fought over throughout history. But its significance is not just geographical. For Christians, it stands as the land promised to Abraham and the land of fulfillment for the Lord Jesus Christ. It was here that God chose to effect his great plan of salvation through the incarnation, death, and resurrection of his only Son.

The History of Palestine from the Return to the Destruction of Jerusalem

When CYRUS became the king of Persia in 559 B.C. his vast empire spread from Greece to India and from the Caucasus to Egypt. His enlightened policy allowed conquered peoples who had been sent into exile to return to their native lands and reestablish themselves as semi-autonomous units under his benevolent leadership. Numerous Jews living in exile

The Judean wilderness is a wild and barren area.

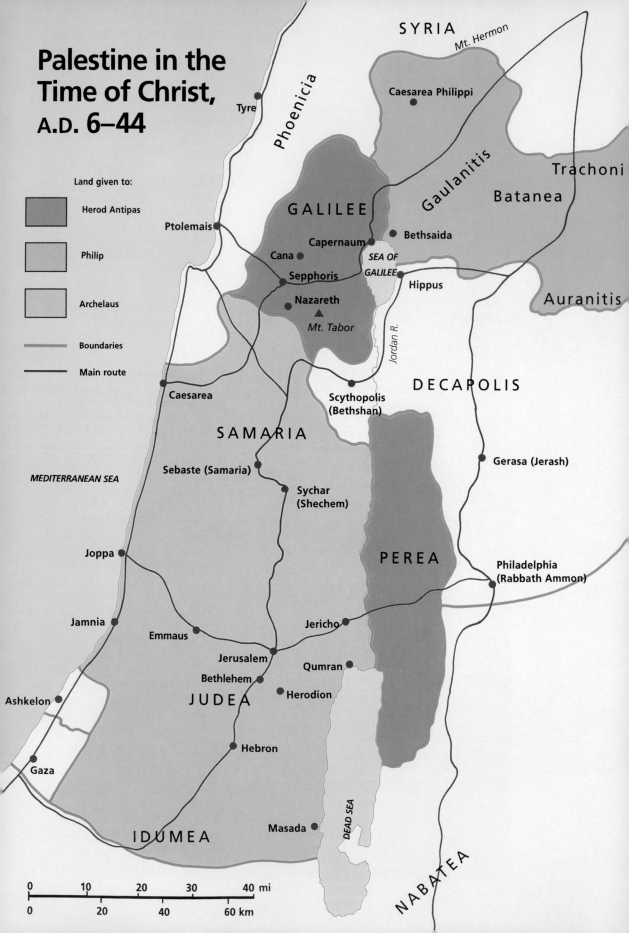

Palestine in the Time of Christ, A.D. 6–44

Land given to:

Herod Antipas

Philip

Archelaus

Boundaries

Main route

SYRIA

Mt. Hermon

Caesarea Philippi

Phoenicia

Tyre

GALILEE

Ptolemais

Cana

Capernaum

Bethsaida

SEA OF GALILEE

Sepphoris

Hippus

Nazareth

Mt. Tabor

Gaulanitis

Batanea

Trachoni

Auranitis

Jordan R.

DECAPOLIS

Caesarea

SAMARIA

Scythopolis (Bethshan)

Sebaste (Samaria)

Sychar (Shechem)

Gerasa (Jerash)

MEDITERRANEAN SEA

Joppa

PEREA

Philadelphia (Rabbath Ammon)

Jamnia

Emmaus

Jericho

Jerusalem

Bethlehem

Qumran

Ashkelon

Herodion

JUDEA

Gaza

Hebron

DEAD SEA

Masada

IDUMEA

NABATEA

| 0 | 10 | 20 | 30 | 40 mi |

| 0 | 20 | 40 | 60 km |

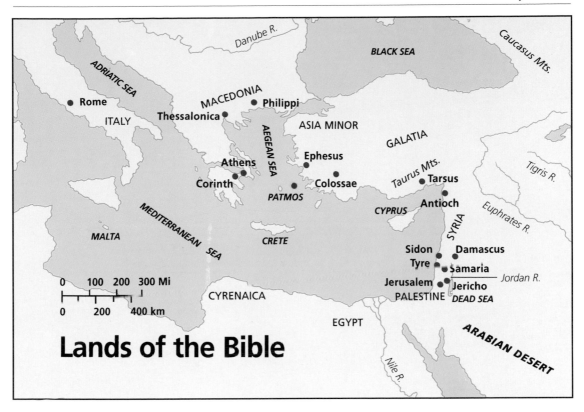

Lands of the Bible

Diadochi

in Babylon since the fall of Jerusalem in 587 B.C. were eager to return to their homeland. A series of emigrations brought many of them back to Palestine for a new start. This was the "time of restoration" as it is usually called in surveys of the Old Testament. Life was far from easy for these returnees, and as the decades went by it was hard not to become thoroughly discouraged. In time, however, the walls of Jerusalem were rebuilt, the temple was rededicated, homes were established, and an uneasy existence was begun. The Jews had come to realize that they were no longer in charge of their own destiny but were part of the larger world scene, subject to the changing fortunes of the huge nations around them.

During the fourth century B.C. Cyrus's Persian Empire began to crumble and European might was felt for the first time in Middle Eastern history. It came in the form of ALEXANDER THE GREAT. A century before, the Persians had attempted to extend their borders into Greece. They burned and pillaged Athens, seemingly invincible; a disastrous naval defeat at the Sea of Salamis in 480 B.C., however, forced their withdrawal back into Asia Minor. To avenge the desecration of the temple of Athena, Alexander pushed eastward to establish the rule of Greek civilization in what was formerly Persia's domain. He died in 323 B.C. and it was left to his military successors, called the **Diadochi**, to fight bitterly among themselves as they carved up his empire. Antigonus Cyclops seized the whole of Asia Minor, including Syria and Palestine; PTOLEMY took Egypt and North Africa; and SELEUCUS NICATOR took the enormous territory stretching from Mesopotamia eastward to India; others took smaller, insignificant portions. In 301 B.C., at the Battle of Ipsus, Antigonus was defeated and his territory was added, basically, to that of Seleucus, who founded the city of ANTIOCH in Syria in 300 B.C. and made it his capital. Meanwhile, Ptolemy had gained control of the Holy Land to the south of Syria. This set the stage for the bitter struggles over Palestine that raged until Roman military might made its presence felt there about a hundred years later.

In 198 B.C. ANTIOCHUS III THE GREAT, ruler of the Syrian (Seleucid) Empire, defeated his Ptolemaic rival at the Battle of

45

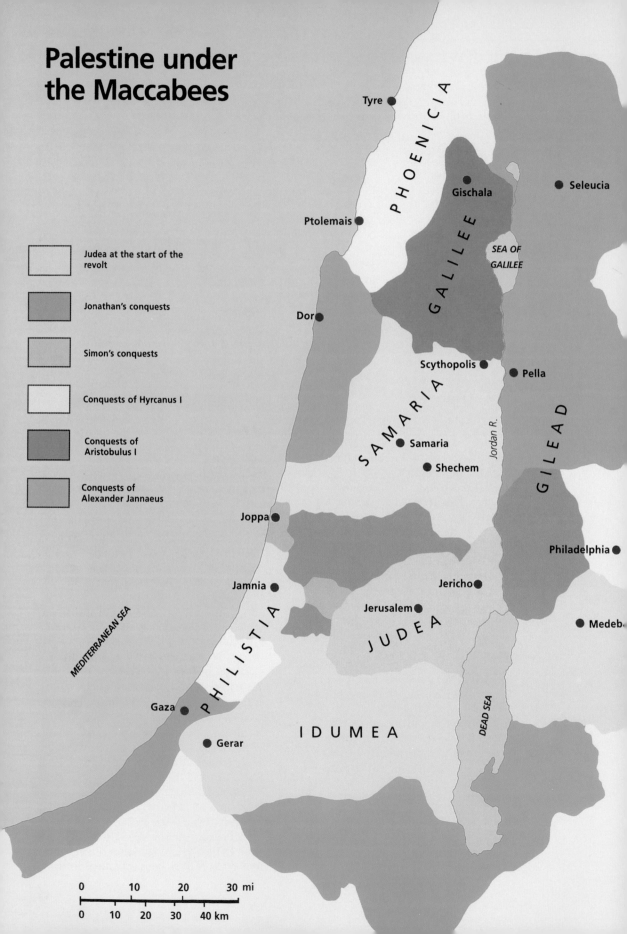

Palestine under the Maccabees

Legend:

- Judea at the start of the revolt
- Jonathan's conquests
- Simon's conquests
- Conquests of Hyrcanus I
- Conquests of Aristobulus I
- Conquests of Alexander Jannaeus

TYRE

PHOENICIA

Gischala

Seleucia

Ptolemais

GALILEE

SEA OF GALILEE

Dor

Scythopolis

Pella

SAMARIA

Samaria

Shechem

GILEAD

Jordan R.

Joppa

Philadelphia

Jamnia

Jericho

Jerusalem

Medeba

MEDITERRANEAN SEA

JUDEA

PHILISTIA

DEAD SEA

Gaza

IDUMEA

Gerar

0   10   20   30 mi

0   10   20   30   40 km

Hasidim

Hasmoneans

Feast of Dedication

Jewish children light the Hanukkah lamp for the festival that celebrates the rededication of the temple on Kislev 25, 164 B.C.

Panias and annexed Palestine to his territory. Later at Magnesia in Turkey, Antiochus was defeated by Scipio of Rome. The destiny of the region passed into Roman hands for the next five hundred years.

ANTIOCHUS IV, Epiphanes, was allowed by ROME to become the ruler of the Seleucid Empire in 175 B.C. He set about to hellenize (force Greek ways on) all of his territory. This included the worship of the Greek God Zeus (the Roman Jupiter). A series of outrages over two years, including murder, treachery, the ravaging of Jerusalem, and the establishment of a pagan citadel in Jerusalem called the ACRA, finally culminated in the establishment of an altar to Zeus in the temple. Swine's flesh was offered there in December 167 B.C. (1 Mc 1:54, 59; 2 Mc 6.2). Daniel had mentioned this sacrilege earlier in his prophecy (Dn 11:31; cf. Mt 24:15).

The Maccabean/Hasmonean Period (166–63 B.C.)

In the small town of MODEIN, about seventeen miles northwest of Jerusalem, an aged priest named MATTATHIAS resisted Antiochus's attempt to force pagan worship on all of Israel by killing the king's representative (1 Mc 2:19–26). He then fled into the hills with his five sons, John, SIMON, Judas, Eleazer, and JONATHAN. From there, with the help of the **Hasidim**, a group of pious warriors, they waged war against the Syrians. Leadership was exercised by this family, called the **Hasmoneans**, for the next 103 years until Pompey conquered Jerusalem in 63 B.C.

Mattathias died shortly after the revolt started. His son JUDAS (nicknamed "Maccabeus," probably meaning "the Hammer") assumed leadership of the revolt. After defeating the Syrians at EMMAUS (166/65 B.C.) and BETH-ZUR (165/64 B.C.), the temple mount was cleansed and rededicated on Kislev 25, 164 B.C., three years after it had been desecrated by Antiochus. The celebration lasted eight days and became known as the **Feast of Dedication** or of Lights (present-day Hanukkah) because the lamps in the temple were relit (see Jn 10:22). Judas won yet another decisive victory against a Syrian general, Nicanor, in 161 B.C., but was then killed in battle near Elasa that same year by the Syrian Bacchides.

Bacchides returned to Syria and an uneasy peace prevailed, despite sporadic civil unrest. Jonathan, Judas's brother, assumed leadership and extended his authority to numerous areas of Palestine. Jonathan was wise enough to reestablish relations with Rome, but in the end was foolish enough to trust a Syrian general named Trypho, who massacred a thousand of his unsuspecting troops and eventually Jonathan himself in 142 B.C. (1 Mc 12:46–48; 13:20–24).

Simon followed Jonathan as leader and from 142 B.C. until his death in 135/34 B.C. things were relatively calm. "He established peace in the land, and Israel rejoiced with great joy. Each man sat under his vine and fig tree, and there was none to make

them afraid. No one was left in the land to fight them, and the kings were crushed in those days. He strengthened all the humble of his people; he sought out the law, and did away with every lawless and wicked man" (1 Mc 14:11–14). The people were so grateful to Simon that they bestowed the high priesthood on him and his family in perpetuity. Thus was founded the Hasmonean dynasty of priesthood. Simon also renewed his alliance with Rome, which no doubt strengthened his position against Syrian attack.

Simon's son, JOHN HYRCANUS I, ruled over the land from 135/34 B.C. to 104 B.C. He secured his position by appealing to Rome for support, but he also hired a professional mercenary army rather than relying on a volunteer force of farmers and tradesmen. Because he was a good general and Syria's power was in decline, Hyrcanus was able, by a series of victories, to extend his territory through Samaria northward and Idumea southward until he ruled over a kingdom almost as large as that of David and Solomon. Hyrcanus had a falling out with the **Pharisees** (descendants of the Hasidim mentioned earlier). But his reign was generally remembered as a time of peace and prosperity. Josephus says, "He lived happily and administered the government in the best possible manner for thirty-one years. . . . He was esteemed by God worthy of three privileges—the government of his nation, the dignity of the high priesthood, and prophecy, for God was with him" (*Ant.* 13.10.7).

The disastrous reign of Hyrcanus's son, Aristobulus, lasted only one year (104–103 B.C.), and was followed by the turbulent twenty-seven years of ALEXANDER JANNAEUS, his brother. Alexander was constantly embroiled in war, turmoil, and internal political dissension. He was unprincipled and ruthless and is said to have had hundreds of captives crucified in the center of the city to entertain himself and his mistresses during a drunken party. The falling out that Alexander's father, Hyrcanus, had with the Pharisees became an outright break during Alexander's reign. They considered him totally unworthy to be the high priest because

of his evil ways. At one point Alexander had six thousand Jews massacred because they ridiculed him when he was officiating as the high priest (Josephus, *Ant.* 13.13.5).

When Alexander died in 76 B.C. his widow, Alexandra, became the queen. She was well liked by the people, but the Pharisees, at this time, basically dominated the country. After the death of Alexandra in 67 B.C. a war broke out between her two sons, HYRCANUS II and ARISTOBULUS II, with Aristobulus II managing to stay on top until 63 B.C., when the Roman general Pompey, who by this time had conquered virtually all the territory in Asia Minor up to Syria, arrived and conquered Jerusalem. In this way, the new power that was to control the area for centuries established its dominance and a new era had effectively begun.

The Domination of Rome (63 B.C.–A.D. 70)

After conquering Jerusalem, Pompey appointed Hyrcanus II as the high priest but without any royal title and sent Aristobulus II to Rome as a prisoner. Hyrcanus II's years of limited religious rule were filled with intrigues, political ups and downs, and ultimate humiliation. He was taken prisoner by the Parthians, mutilated by having his ears cut off to disqualify him for the priesthood, and replaced by Aristobulus II's ineffective son, ANTIGONUS II, in 40 B.C. Antigonus remained only a turbulent three years until the Romans confirmed Herod as the ruler in 37 B.C., after a series of military victories, even calling him king.

The Rule of Herod the Great (37–4 B.C.)
As we saw, when Pompey captured Jerusalem in 63 B.C., the fortunes of Palestine became tied up with those of Rome. During those uncertain years a new dynasty was arising in the person of ANTIPATER, an Idumean (from the ancient kingdom of Edom, just south of Judea), who was astute enough to support JULIUS CAESAR when he was in need of help in Alexandria, Egypt, in 48 B.C. For this, Antipater was rewarded by being made

Chronology of Herod the Great's Rule

B.C.

B.C.	
37	Herod conquers Jerusalem Executions
31	Earthquake in Palestine Herod defeats the Nabateans
30	Hyrcanus II executed Herod confirmed king by Octavian
29	Mariamme executed
ca. 29	Alexandra executed
ca. 25	Herod rebuilds Samaria and names it Sebaste Famine and pestilence
ca. 22	Herod starts to build Caesarea
19	Herod starts to build the temple
14	Herod's sons, Alexander and Aristobulus, fall out
12	Augustus settles quarrel between Herod's sons
10	Dedication of Caesarea Increasing discord in Herod's family
ca. 7	Alexander and Aristobulus executed at Sebaste Antipater all-powerful at Herod's court
5	Antipater tried for conspiracy Herod falls ill
4	Herod puts down popular uprising led by rabbis Judas and Matthias Herod's health deteriorates Antipater executed Herod names Archelaus king, and Antipas and Philip tetrarchs Herod dies five days after Antipater's execution

ethnarch

ethnarch (local governor or prince) of Palestine. In 47 B.C. Antipater appointed his son Phasael governor of Jerusalem and another son Herod as governor of Galilee. The assassination of Caesar on the Ides of March (March 15), 44 B.C., threw the Middle East into turmoil. Two factions were vying for power: Cassius and Brutus against Anthony and Octavian (later CAESAR AUGUSTUS). After Cassius and Brutus were disposed of, Anthony and Octavian fought for supremacy, with Octavian winning out. The Parthians had made Antigonus II the ruler of Palestine in 40 B.C., but in that same year the Roman

senate had made Herod the king of Judea. War followed and after a stubborn defense Jerusalem fell in 37 B.C. to the Romans; Herod was now the sole ruler of the territory. When Octavian became the supreme ruler (Caesar) of the Roman world after defeating Anthony in the Battle of Actium on September 2, 31 B.C., Herod switched his allegiance to Octavian; he was accepted by him as a loyal subject in 30 B.C. and confirmed as the king of Judea.

Herod had married MARIAMME, Hyrcanus II's granddaughter, to legitimate his claim to royalty, but he was also profoundly in love with her. His jealousy caused him to listen to court gossip started by his sister. Eventually he executed Mariamme and her mother, Alexandra. He had already had Aristobulus II and Hyrcanus II killed. After his ill-advised murder of Mariamme (she was innocent), Herod's none-too-stable mental condition deteriorated. His reign was filled with political intrigue, plots, murders, wars, and brutality until his death in April 4 B.C.

In spite of his many obvious shortcomings Herod accomplished some good for his territory. He could be quite generous when the occasion demanded it. He was often sensitive to the religious feelings of the Jews and was a master-builder of cities. He rebuilt the temple in Jerusalem, built a port city at Caesarea, beautified and refortified other important cities, and kept Rome satisfied, thus providing a stability Israel would not otherwise have known.

Herod died an agonizing death, perhaps from colon cancer, universally unmourned, "a man of great barbarity towards all equally and a slave to his passions" (Josephus, *Ant.* 17.8.1). It is ironic that during the reign of this brutal, inhumane ruler, the Prince of Peace was born.

The Rule of Herod's Descendants (4 B.C.–A.D. 66)

Immediately after the death of Herod riots broke out in Jerusalem that had to be put down by force. These riots continued while three of Herod's sons, ARCHELAUS, Philip, and Antipas, made their way to Rome to present their case before Caesar Augustus. Each wanted to be the sole ruler. After much scheming and intrigue, Augustus divided the land three ways. He gave

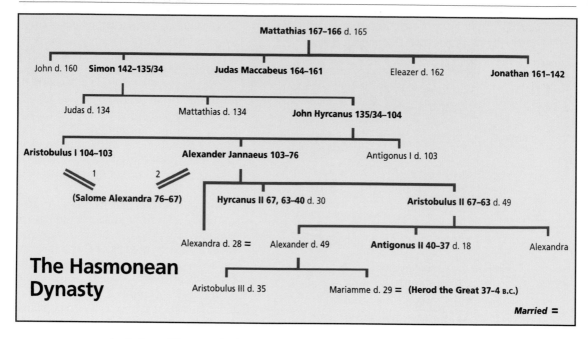

Mattathias 167–166 d. 165

John d. 160   **Simon 142–135/34**   **Judas Maccabeus 164–161**   Eleazer d. 162   **Jonathan 161–142**

Judas d. 134   Mattathias d. 134   **John Hyrcanus 135/34–104**

Aristobulus I 104–103   **Alexander Jannaeus 103–76**   Antigonus I d. 103

1   2

(Salome Alexandra 76–67)   **Hyrcanus II 67, 63–40** d. 30   **Aristobulus II 67–63** d. 49

Alexandra d. 28 =   Alexander d. 49   **Antigonus II 40–37** d. 18   Alexandra

The Hasmonean Dynasty

Aristobulus III d. 35   Mariamme d. 29 = **(Herod the Great 37–4 B.C.)**

Married =

Archelaus Idumea, Judea, and Samaria, and the title of ethnarch rather than king (Josephus, *Ant.* 17.13.5). Antipas was given Galilee and Perea and the title of tetrarch (local ruler). Philip received Batanaea, Trachonitis, and Auranitis, as well as other territories to the northeast and was also titled tetrarch. The riots that were occurring all over the country were brutally put down; Sepphoris in Galilee was destroyed, the temple in Jerusalem was burned and looted, and thousands were crucified by the Romans.

Archelaus (4 B.C.–A.D. 6)

The rule of Archelaus was "brutal and tyrannical" (*Ant.* 17.13.2) and was strongly resisted from the very beginning. His evil reputation forced Joseph and Mary to take Jesus back to Nazareth, rather than return to BETHLEHEM, which was in Archelaus's territory (Mt 2:22–23). He constantly interfered with priestly matters, caused great offense by his illegal marriage to a brother's widow, and harshly treated his subjects. When the Jews could stand it no longer they sent a delegation to Rome, bitterly complaining of Archelaus's misrule. He was summoned to Rome and in A.D. 6 was banished to Vienne in Gaul, where he died.

Archelaus's territory was placed under direct Roman rule that lasted from A.D. 6 to A.D. 41, when the nation was unified under

Agrippa I. There were six or seven Roman governors, mostly called procurators, during this time, but only the fifth one is of importance for New Testament studies: PONTIUS PILATE, who was in control from A.D. 26 to A.D. 36. As procurator he would have resided in Caesarea. Yet he visited Jerusalem for festivals and notable events. He was a harsh and insensitive ruler, with little consideration for his subjects. His excessive and brutal behavior caught up with him in the end. He was deposed and then exiled by Tiberius Caesar in A.D. 36.

Philip (4 B.C.–A.D. 34)

We know little about the reign of Philip except that he was universally praised. He limited personal ambition and kept extravagant building to a minimum. He rebuilt the ancient city of Panias north of the Sea of Galilee, renaming it Caesarea Philippi in honor of Caesar and himself. It was here that Peter made his great confession of Jesus' messiahship. Here too Jesus explained how he must go to Jerusalem to die and rise again (Mt 16:13–27). Bethsaida on the northeast coast of the Sea of Galilee was also rebuilt and renamed Julias in honor of Augustus Caesar's daughter. Philip died a natural death (unusual for Herod's family) in A.D. 34 after ruling for thirty-seven years. Josephus describes his reign in this fashion:

The volcano-like peak that was the citadel of Herod the Great's palace complex at Herodian, south of Jerusalem.

He had shown himself a person of moderation and quietness in the conduct of his life and government: he constantly lived in that country which was subject to him; he used to make his progress with a few chosen friends; his tribunal also, in which he sat in judgment, followed him in his progress; and when any one met him who wanted his assistance, he made no delay, but had his tribunal set down immediately, wheresoever he happened to be, and sat down upon it, and heard his complaint: he there ordered the guilty that were convicted to be punished, and absolved those that had been accused unjustly (*Ant.* 18.4.6).

Antipas (4 B.C.–A.D. 39)

Herod Antipas received the territories of Galilee and Perea, and hence was ruler of two areas where Jesus ministered extensively. He was a vain, arrogant ruler, who was also weak in times of moral crisis. He was married to the daughter of Aretas, the Nabatean king, but fell in love with HERODIAS, his niece, who was at that time the wife of his brother, Philip. He set plans in motion to marry her. Aretas was enraged and went to war with Antipas, decisively defeating him. It was Herodias who engineered the death of John the Baptist because he denounced the marriage as illegal (Mk 6:17–29). John had been imprisoned at Machaerus in Perea, east of the Dead Sea (*Ant.* 18.5.2). The Jews attributed Herod's defeat in battle to the judgment of God for

allowing John, whom they considered a prophet, to be executed.

It was this Herod to whom Jesus was sent by Pilate just before his crucifixion, while Herod was in Jerusalem for the Passover Feast (Lk 23:6–12). Herod seems to have had some spiritual sensitivity (Mt 14:9; Mk 6:20), but he was more interested in spectacular displays than in spiritual substance. The breach between Herod and Pilate, perhaps caused by Pilate's murder of some Galilean citizens (Lk 13:1), was, oddly, healed by their joint condemnation of Jesus (Lk 23:12).

Herodias proved to be Herod's undoing when she cajoled her husband into going to Rome and demanding of CALIGULA, the emperor, that he be made king rather than just ethnarch. For this he was banished to Spain, where he and Herodias died (*War* 2.9.6; *see also Ant.* 18.7.2).

Herod Agrippa I and II (A.D. 37–66)

AGRIPPA I was the son of Aristobulus and Bernice, and hence the grandson of HEROD THE GREAT and Mariamme. He had lived in Rome and was well known to Tiberius Caesar, his son Drusus, and Caligula. When Tiberius died in A.D. 37 and Caligula was made emperor, he bestowed the territories of Philip and Lysanias on Agrippa, after releasing him from prison. Agrippa was given the title of king (Acts 12:1). As we saw, Antipas and Herodias's jealousy

polytheistic syncretism

drove them to Rome in A.D. 39 to seek the same title, but it got them banished instead and so Galilee and Perea were also given to Agrippa (*Ant.* 18.7.2). In A.D. 41, after exceptional service to the new emperor CLAUDIUS, Agrippa was awarded Judea and Samaria, thus making his domain almost as large as that of his grandfather Herod the Great. Agrippa was very sensitive to Jewish feelings (*Ant.* 19.7.3), even to the point of executing James the son of Zebedee, one of Jesus' apostles, and putting Peter in prison (Acts 12:1–4). He died suddenly in A.D. 44, while attending a festival in Caesarea and accepting acclamation as a god (Acts 12:21–23; see *Ant.* 19.8.2).

In time, Agrippa's son, HEROD AGRIPPA II, was made nominal ruler of much of his father's old territory. It was not given to him immediately because he was not old enough to rule. He was more like his grandfather than his father and cared little for the feelings of the Jews (*Ant.* 20.7.11; 20.8.4). Paul appeared before Agrippa II while he was imprisoned in Caesarea (ca. A.D. 60), but Agrippa arrogantly dismissed the apostle's words (Acts 25:13–26:32). When the Jewish War broke out in A.D. 66, Agrippa sided with the Romans and after the destruction of Jerusalem retired to Rome where he died in A.D. 100.

The Jewish War and Destruction of Jerusalem (A.D. 66–70)

During the A.D. 44–66 period there was a succession of bad procurators over the territory of Judea and Samaria. This and other conditions would eventually lead to a disastrous revolt against Rome. These rulers were, in order, Fadus (44–46), Tiberius Julius Alexander (46–48), Ventidius Cumanus (48–52), Felix (52–60; see Acts 24:1–27), Festus (60–62; see Acts 25:1–22), Albinus (62–64), and GESSIUS FLORUS (64–66). Of these, the last two were exceedingly corrupt, greedy, and ruthless. The country by this time was in an uproar, heading toward the disaster that started in the spring of 66. There was enormous religious unrest, which the Romans never really understood because their **polytheistic syncretism** did not involve such unshakable convictions. The Jews, however, could not bend, convinced as they were that their law alone was from God and that rival religions amounted to blasphemy. In addition to the religious persecutions, there were economic problems, unfair taxes, bands of robbers roaming the country, excessive interest charged on loans, political assassinations, brutal treatment of innocent citizens, and government corruption. It was, in short, a nation ready to explode. In addition, the priesthood,

An aerial view of the mountaintop fortress of Masada in the Judean wilderness.

A carefully researched scale model of Herod's temple, which dominated the city of Jerusalem in Jesus' time.

which should have been leading the country spiritually, was as corrupt as everything else. The priests "used violence with the people, and were very ready to plunder those that were weaker than themselves. And from that time it principally came to pass that our city [Jerusalem] was greatly disordered, and that all things grew worse and worse among us" (*Ant.* 20.9.4).

The spark that ignited the fire began in Caesarea, where a synagogue was desecrated by some Greeks in the month of Iyyar (April–May 66). A riot broke out that spread to Jerusalem, where it was brutally put down by Gessius Florus; over 3,600 people were slaughtered. For the Jews the break seemed complete and the daily temple sacrifice in honor of the emperor was suspended, which meant the war had begun in earnest. Josephus puts it this way:

> And at this time it was that some of those that principally excited the people to go to war, made an assault upon a certain fortress called Masada. They took it by treachery, and slew the Romans that were there, and put others of their own party to keep it. At the same time Eleazar, the son of Ananias the high priest, a very bold youth, who was at that time governor of the temple, persuaded those that officiated in the divine service to receive no gift or sacrifice for any foreigner. And this was the true beginning of our war with the Romans: for they rejected the sacrifice of Caesar on this account: and when many of the high priests and principal men

besought them not to omit the sacrifice, which it was customary of them to offer for their princes, they would not be prevailed upon (*War* 2.17.2).

During the next three years the Romans systematically destroyed the country. The Jews occasionally met with some success against the battle-hardened Roman legions, but in the end were no match for them, in large part because they were fighting among themselves. By the summer of 69 all that remained to the Jews were Jerusalem, the Herodium, MASADA, and Machaerus. A civil war in Rome and the suicide of NERO in 69 caused VESPASIAN, the Roman general, to back off his conquest of Jerusalem, and in July 69 he was proclaimed emperor when he departed for Rome. But in the spring of 70 he sent his son TITUS to finish the destruction of Jerusalem, and with four legions of soldiers Titus accomplished the task. It took about four months for them to break through the walls one by one and ultimately subdue the city. It was completely leveled with the exception of a few towers and walls to show how mighty the city had once been and how invincible the Romans were. The siege of the city was horrible, almost beyond description, and the slaughter of people when it fell was excruciatingly brutal. Thousands were tortured, crucified, or sold into slavery, and the city was left in absolute ruin.

To complete the story, more ruin was to

follow. Masada fell in A.D. 73, thus ending the first Jewish revolt, and a second revolt occurred in A.D. 132–135, led by a messianic pretender named BAR KOCHBA, who promised a divine intervention that never came. The devastation of the city at that time was total and a law was passed that forbade any Jew from ever setting foot in it again.

Jesus' dreadful prophecy (Lk 21:20–24) had come to pass. The Jews did not know the time of their visitation. Most of them had rejected God's offer of salvation. Because of the hardness of their hearts, only a frightful judgment remained, and they were forced to drink the cup to the bitter dregs.

The significance of the fall of Jerusalem for the Christians and the Jews at that time can hardly be overestimated. From the Jewish point of view the break with the Christians was complete. Many of the Jewish Christians had fled Jerusalem because of Jesus' prophecy. Other Jews considered them traitors, with later rabbis even blaming the fall of the city on them. As for the Christians, they realized that they must now move out from Jerusalem; the center of Christianity would have to be elsewhere, in fact everywhere, just as Jesus had said to the woman in Samaria when he told her that God must be worshiped neither in Jerusalem nor in Samaria but in spirit and in truth (Jn 4:21–24). Paul also emphasized this in Athens when he pointed out that God does not dwell in temples made with human hands but is everywhere (Acts 17:24–28). The fall of Jerusalem also contributed to the Christians' developing a new theological vocabulary and worship styles designed to reach the Gentiles, who now became their primary mission. Out of this arose the New Testament canon that took its place alongside the Old Testament, thus creating the Bible we use today.

It is tragic that it had to end this way, but the apostle Paul surveys the situation with a note of hope. The rejection of the Jews was the reconciliation of the world. God has something yet in mind for Israel (Rom 11:25–29). In the great mystery of God's dealing with us, he has bound all over to disobedience so that he might have mercy on us all (Rom 11:32).

Jewish Religion in Jesus' Day

The brief look we have just taken at the complex history of the Jews leading up to the New Testament era should prepare us for the colorful diversity of Jewish religious thought as it existed in Jesus' day. There was no single, normative point of view but rather overlapping or even conflicting collections of ideas and practices that all together are called **Second Temple Judaism**. Josephus mentions four in particular as of importance, and there were more, some of which are themselves quite diverse. In spite of this, however, they did hold certain beliefs or at least attitudes in common that set them apart from other basic religious groups such as were found among the Romans and Greeks.

The Unifying Factors in Judaism

What must be emphasized at the outset is that Judaism was primarily a way of life rather than an accepted set of doctrines. It is not that theological ideas weren't important; it is just that no single interpretation was demanded with regard to them. There were frequently a number of ideas held within a group on a given point, but that did not force anyone outside the group. Deviation on a matter of life or lifestyle, however, such as eating, washing, or ritual purity, would bring about instant ostracism. A certain amount of doctrinal diversity could be accommodated, but not much variation in style of life. This was one reason Jesus was seen as a threat by the religious leaders—he took what they regarded as liberties in such matters.

The single most important idea that unified the Jews related to God and their own sense of uniqueness in the history of the world. They had been chosen by the one and only God to fulfill a singular destiny. He had established an eternal covenant with them. The experience of the exile (587 B.C.) had, of course, shocked them, but in the end they understood it as a punishment for their sins, especially their sin of putting other gods before the Lord (2 Mc 6:12–16). The exile had also forced them to see how small they really were when compared to the vast empires of the world, such as Babylon or Persia. They recovered from the initial shock with an even deeper sense of mystery—God chose them rather than any of the great nations of the world to be the bearers of truth. This called forth a profound sense of commitment to carry out their task. They had failed before, but nothing would shake them again. It was *God* who chose them, the *only* God. All the gods of the nations were idols and were to be despised. The uniqueness of the Jews was that they worshiped the one true God of the universe, who had revealed himself especially to them in choosing them to be his people. They would never again allow for the worship of idols, even if it cost them their lives.

Allied to this conviction regarding their historical uniqueness and their fierce monotheism was the idea that God had placed them in a particular place. God was the God of the whole universe and of all the nations, but he had placed the Jews in the land of Palestine, which was to be theirs forever. God had chosen Jerusalem to be the only place of true worship, and that city and the land of Israel must be protected and defended at all costs. What created a problem in Jesus' day, of course, was the fact that it was all under Roman occupation. How could this

be? When would God do something about it? The Jews agreed that God would do something and it would involve the land he had chosen, but they disagreed as to when and how this was going to be accomplished. Jesus looked beyond narrow nationalism to focus on the fact that God was seeking those whose worship was in the right spirit, not just in the right place (Jn 4:23–24). In fact, the days were coming when all these "right places" would be destroyed (Lk 21:5–6, 20–24; Jn 4:21). John the Baptist told the Jews that their ancient privileges would avail them nothing, if merely presumed upon. God could raise up children to Abraham from the rocks in the desert, if he so chose (Lk 3:7–8).

There was also messianic fervor at that time. There was widespread belief that God would send a Chosen One, a Messiah, who would defeat the Romans and usher in a time of universal peace, with the center of the world in Jerusalem. There were various opinions as to who the Messiah would be and precisely how he would accomplish the overthrow of the Romans. Some thought it would involve violence; others thought it would come in a more spiritual way. False leaders appeared in the midst of this confusion. Some even led peo-

This partially reconstructed synagogue at Capernaum on the Sea of Galilee probably dates from the fourth century A.D., but it is built over a first-century synagogue from Jesus' time.

diaspora

ple out into the wilderness to wait there for God's decisive intervention, only to be slaughtered by the Romans (see Acts 5:35–37; 21:37–38). But the hope persisted. God would send his Messiah to save his people.

The synagogue was also a unifying factor for the Jews, especially those Jews who did not live in Palestine—the scattered Jews, or **diaspora** as they are called. But even in Palestine there were numerous synagogues—at least one in every town, if some sources are to be believed. Jerusalem is said to have had 394 (Bab. *Kethub*, 105a) or 480 (Jer. *Megilla*, 73d), with a synagogue in the temple itself. The origins of the synagogue are lost in the mists of antiquity, but they apparently arose sometime during or after the Babylonian captivity. With so many Jews scattered over that part of the world the synagogue became the center of Jewish life. By Jesus' day it had four basic functions. It was primarily a school, where the children were taught the law and Jewish religious traditions. For some, such as the Jewish writer PHILO of Alexandria (20 B.C.–A.D. 45), this was the epitome of what it should be. It was also a place of worship, where there was recitation of creeds, reading of Scripture, a homily or exposition of Scripture, and prayers. The synagogue also functioned as a court where religious or civil questions were settled by the local council. Finally, the synagogue was a place of social interaction, where funerals and special meetings took place and even politics were discussed (see Josephus, *Life* 54). For the Christians in New Testament times, the synagogue served as the logical site to begin to preach the gospel ("to the Jew first, and also to the Greek") until the time when Christians were no longer allowed entrance to make known their message.

The law (Torah) and the traditions of the elders were also factors that bound most of the people together. Of central importance were those regulations that involved circumcision and Sabbath keeping. The Jews lived by the laws they believed God had given to them—not only the 613 commandments they found in the Pentateuch, but also the subsidiary regulations that surrounded them, which numbered in the thousands.

Finally, the temple, the priesthood, and the festivals also gave the Jews a sense of identity. The temple was a magnificent structure, and the Jews took great pride in it (Mk 13:1). Even the Romans respected Jewish commitment to the temple and its worship. At times they helped enforce the regulations prohibiting Gentiles from desecrating it and protecting the Jews who entered. To speak against the temple was to speak against God as far as the Jews were concerned. All of this helps explain why Jesus' cleansing of the temple so angered his countrymen. He said, "Destroy this temple [referring to himself], and I will raise it again in three days" (Jn 2:19). Jesus was claiming nothing less than that he would prove to be the true temple where the will of God was done; God's will was not confined to some physical structure, however magnificent, where vulgar commerce was taking place. Some scholars have suggested that it was Jesus' anti-temple attitude that ultimately led to his rejection by the Jews and his crucifixion.

Religious Groups

Pharisees

The best known of the religious groups in Jesus' day were the Pharisees.[6] Although they were a relatively small group (probably numbering about six thousand), they were extremely influential. Their point of view on many issues could be considered typical of a majority of Jews at that time. The name "Pharisee" probably derives from an Aramaic word meaning "separate"; hence, the Pharisees were "the separated ones." They came into being sometime before the New Testament era. According to Josephus they gained prominence during the reigns of John Hyrcanus I (135/4–104 B.C.) and Alexandra (76–67 B.C.).

By Jesus' time there were two different schools of Pharisaic thought—the followers of HILLEL and the followers of SHAMMAI. Hillel had revolutionized rabbinic thought with a new method of exegesis that allowed for a more liberalized interpretation of the law. GAMALIEL I (Hillel's son and teacher of the apostle Paul; Acts 22:3) was the leader of the Pharisees from A.D. 25 to 40. After the destruction of Jerusalem in A.D. 70, Johanan ben Zakkai undertook to reshape Pharisaism at JAMNIA in A.D. 90; the foundation for mainstream Judaism down to modern times was established.

Theologically, the Pharisees developed a set of views based on the Old Testament and their own oral traditions, both of which they considered equally authoritative. They "delivered to the people a great many observances by tradition which are not written in the law of Moses," says Josephus (*Ant.* 13.10.6). They believed in God (in almost a deistic fashion), angels and spirits, providence, prayer, the necessity for faith and good works, the last judgment, a coming Messiah, and the immortality of the soul. Much of what the Pharisees believed was also believed by the early Christians; Jesus could say of them, "You must obey them and do everything they tell you. But do not do what they do, for they do not practice what they preach" (Mt 23:3). Paul could say to the **Sanhedrin**, "My brothers, I am a Pharisee, the son of a Pharisee. I stand on trial because of my hope in the resurrection of the dead" (Acts 23:6). While not entirely denying the grace of God, many Pharisees tended toward legalism, so much so that Jesus accused them of nullifying the commandments of God by holding to human traditions (Mk 7:8). These traditions were gathered together at the beginning of the third century A.D. by RABBI JUDAH THE PATRIARCH in a book called the **Mishnah,** which, in turn, formed part of the **Talmud.** (These will be discussed shortly.)

The Pharisees were hostile toward Jesus because they felt he was lax with respect to their laws, was too accepting of sinful people, and was open to contact with Gentiles. He also made blasphemous claims about himself and his relation to God. For his part, Jesus opposed them because of their legalism, their hypocrisy, and their unwillingness to accept the kingdom of God as represented in himself.

Sadducees

The second major group of Jews in Jesus' day were the **Sadducees.**[7] Both their origin and precise nature are now difficult to determine because they faded into oblivion after the destruction of Jerusalem in A.D. 70 when the Pharisaic point of view became, in essence, Judaism. They came

into prominence during Maccabean times by supporting the Hasmonean political aims under John Hyrcanus I (135/4–104 B.C.), but under Alexandra (76–67 B.C.) and Herod the Great (37–4 B.C.), their power and numbers drastically declined. With the coming of the Roman procurators in A.D. 6, however, their fortunes rose and they played a significant role in the Sanhedrin and the priesthood until the Jewish revolt of A.D. 66–70 when the radical elements prevailed. After that the Sadducees disappeared from history.

Basically, the Sadducees were a priestly aristocracy that had made their way to power by way of their connection to high-priestly or aristocratic families. Theologically, they rejected almost everything the Pharisees (and most pious Jews) believed. They did not believe in angels or spirits, the resurrection, the last judgment, life after death, divine providence, or a coming Messiah. The Sadducees who sought to discredit Jesus did so by attacking his belief in the resurrection (Mt 22:23–32). Their opposition to Jesus lay basically in their desire to maintain their own privileged position, which Jesus threatened (Jn 11:48). They consequently made common cause with their political enemies, the Pharisees, in condemning Jesus to death (although the Pharisees wanted to be rid of Jesus for different reasons).

Essenes

The Essenes were another important group, numbering about four thousand in all.[8] We know about them from several sources, including Josephus, Philo, the Roman writer Pliny, the Church Father Hippolytus, and the Dead Sea Scrolls. We are unable to draw a completely consistent picture from these sources. Taken together, they indicate that the term "Essene," which perhaps means "the pious" in East Aramaic, describes a spectrum of views that fall under the same heading rather than a single close-knit movement.

The Essenes appear to have arisen sometime after the Maccabean revolt in 167–160 B.C., with a significant number settling between 150 and 140 B.C. east of Jerusalem near the Dead Sea. They deserted this location, probably after an earthquake,

Zealots

around 31 B.C., but some of them returned following the death of Herod the Great in 4 B.C. They were part of the revolt against Rome in A.D. 66–70 and fell along with the rest of the nation at that time. Some of their documents were hidden in caves near their community; they were discovered starting in 1947 and came to be called the "Dead Sea Scrolls." The ruins of the site they inhabited have been excavated since that time.

The Essenes at QUMRAN were a strict, highly disciplined community that lived together communally, that is, holding all their property in common. They observed rigid ascetic principles. They rejected anything that smacked of luxury and practiced celibacy, though Josephus does mention some Essenes who were married. They devoted their lives to the study of Scripture, the copying of their own documents, prayer, and frequent ritual washing. New members were allowed in only after an extended novitiate (two or three years; the sources differ on this) and a series of solemn vows.

Theologically, they were strict predestinarians, believing in the preexistence and immortality of the soul. They were anti-temple (perhaps because of their rejection of the Hasmonean control of the

high priesthood) and strongly legalistic in matters of ritual purity. They considered themselves the righteous remnant living in the last days and looked for a political Messiah or Messiahs and the end of the age.

Some theologians have tried to find a link between John the Baptist, and even Jesus, and the Essenes at Qumran. This is unlikely, especially in the case of Jesus. If there is a connection between John or Jesus and Qumran, it is certainly not a substantive one. There is no concrete evidence that either of them ever lived in or visited the community. In any case, the Essenes are never mentioned by name in the New Testament.

Zealots

Josephus refers to the **Zealots** as a fourth major group of Jewish opinion.[9] He speaks of JUDAS THE GALILEAN as its founder. But the roots of the movement probably go back to Maccabean times when those zealous for the law took matters into their own hands and sought by any means, including violence, to advance the cause of God. Josephus says of them:

> These men agree in all other things with the Pharisaic notions; but they have an inviolable attachment to liberty; and they say

Some of the caves in which the Dead Sea Scrolls were discovered in 1947.

apocalyptic

pseudepigrapha

that God is to be their only Ruler and Lord. They also do not value dying any kinds of death, nor indeed do they heed the deaths of their relations and friends, nor can any such fear make them call any man Lord (*Ant.* 18.1.6).

While acknowledging their high-mindedness, at least in theory, Josephus also points out that "all sorts of misfortunes also sprang from these men, and the nation was infected with their doctrine to an incredible degree; one violent war came upon us after another. [There were] seditions, murders, which sometimes fell on those of their own people and sometimes on their enemies, the taking and demolishing of cities, and at last, the very temple of God was burnt down by their enemy's fire" (*Ant.* 18.1.1). Although they considered themselves patriots, many of them were little different from what we call terrorists. One of Jesus' twelve apostles was a former Zealot (Lk 6:15).

The Apocalyptic Movement

This particular phenomenon was not a group of people as such, but a distinctive point of view that cut across many groups.[10] It produced a large and fascinating body of literature, some of which still exists today. The **apocalyptic** emphasis can be found in parts of the Old Testament, too, along with intertestamental literature, the New Testament, and early Christian writings.

The word "apocalyptic" comes from a Greek word meaning "to reveal." The information conveyed in such literature was thought to be a special revelation from God that unveiled the hidden secrets of the universe, especially the events surrounding the end of the age. Apocalyptic writings often took the form of some extravagant vision, highly symbolic in nature, which mapped out events to come. The one who received the vision was often puzzled, and needed an angelic interpreter to explain it. The writer frequently wrote in the name of some ancient saint, such as Enoch or Elijah. For this reason the material is sometimes called **pseudepigrapha**, meaning "wrongly titled." The book of 4 Ezra is an excellent example of apocalyptic literature:

It came to pass as I lay on the grass that my heart was again troubled as before. And I lifted up my eyes and saw a woman upon the right and lo! she was mourning and weeping and her clothes were rent and there were ashes upon her head. And I said, "Why are you weeping?" She said to me, "I was barren for 30 years but God looked upon my affliction and gave me a son, but when he was grown up and entered his wedding chamber, he fell down and died. Now I am grief-stricken and wish to die." I said, "No, woman, do not do so; be consoled by Jerusalem's sorrows." And it came to pass, while I was speaking to her, her countenance shone exceedingly and her aspect became bright as lightning, and my heart was terrified. Then, lo! an angel came to me as I lay on the ground as dead and said, "The matter is as follows: the woman thou saw is Zion and the son is the city David built after 3000 years of barrenness. The fall of Jerusalem is the death of the son in his wedding chamber, but her glory is yet to come" (9:26–10:57, selected portions).

The main theological characteristics of apocalyptic thought are as follows:

- Stress on the sovereignty and transcendence of God.
- Description of the cosmic struggle of good and evil, God and Satan, angels and demons.
- Dominance of a mood of strain and tension, with pessimism concerning the present.
- Expectation of the ultimate triumph of God, seen as imminent, future, and wholly supernatural.
- Deemphasis on human wisdom and strength in the declining world situation—this age is passing away. The age to come will arrive by divine intervention and according to the divine plan. Nothing can stop it.

There is obviously much in apocalyptic thought that rings true scripturally. One hears echoes of the Old Testament books of Daniel, Ezekiel, Zechariah, and Isaiah and of Jesus' words in Matthew 24, to say nothing of the book of Revelation, the "Apocalypse," itself. Such literature may have given the oppressed Jewish people of Jesus' day hope for the future. It undoubtedly provided a backdrop for what Jesus and the early Christians had to say.

tephillin

mezuzah

A Jewish father and son at Jerusalem's Western Wall wear tephillin, or phylacteries: small cubic boxes of black leather containing biblical texts.

Peter drew this practical point from his own apocalyptic outlook: "The heavens will disappear with a roar; the elements will be destroyed by fire, and the earth and everything in it will be laid bare. Since everything will be destroyed in this way, what kind of people ought you to be? You ought to live holy and godly lives as you look forward to the day of God and speed its coming" (2 Pt 3:10–12).

Other Groups in Palestine

In addition to the groups already mentioned there were other groups, or at least emphases, which form a background for understanding the rise of Christianity.

The Herodians are mentioned three times in the Gospels (Mt 22:16; Mk 3:6; 12:13).[11] They probably represent more of a political party than a religious group, but the two were not easily separated at that time. Josephus mentions a party of Herod the Great (*Ant.* 14.15.10; *War* 1.16.6), and if these groups are the same, their origin goes back to that time. In this case the Herodians who joined forces with the Pharisees in seeking to do away with Jesus would be those who remained loyal to the Herodian dynasty in the person of Herod's son, Antipas. Some have sought to identify the Herodians with the Sadducees, but this is by no means certain. They could not have been a very large group.

Philo's *On the Contemplative Life* speaks of a group called the Therapeutae, contemplative mystics who were prominent in Egypt but apparently widely dispersed. They are probably to be identified with the Essenes in some loose way and represent the mystical tradition that was also to be found in varying degrees within Judaism.

The influence of Greek thought on Palestinian Judaism has also been established to a degree not previously realized. Although no single party or group representing it explicitly was dominant in Jesus' day, it was quite pervasive. It was probably to be found at all levels of society but was most in evidence among the educated and in the more urban areas. Some scholars argue that Greek influence was so widespread that Jesus even taught in Greek as well as in Aramaic.[12]

The *Am ha-Aretz* (people of the land), or common people, were the largest group numerically but the least significant in terms of political influence. They formed that vast majority of people who affiliated with no specific group but simply tried to live their lives each day in the will of God to the best of their ability. Their views were closest to that of the Pharisees, but they were despised by the latter as rabble that knew nothing of the law (Jn 7:49). Later rabbinic literature describes them as those who do not tithe regularly, do not read the *Shema* (Dt 6:4–9; 11:13–21; Nm 15:37–41) morning and evening, do not wear **tephillin** (a small leather box containing Scripture), have no **mezuzah** (a portion of Scripture in a case) on their door posts, fail to teach their children the law, and do not associate with the scholars of the law.[13] To Jesus, these were the lost sheep of the house of Israel (Mt 10:6), sheep without a shepherd on whom he had compassion (Mk 6:34). They were the common people who listened to him with

Samaritans

monotheistic

Apocrypha

delight (Mk 12:37), as opposed to the religious leadership who were angry about his teachings and sought to kill him. They were, in the end, the focus of his ministry. From their ranks came most of his apostles and disciples, the primary witnesses to the truth of the gospel.

The Samaritans

Finally, it is necessary to look at the **Samaritans** as part of the background for understanding the New Testament. Samaria was roughly the region occupied by the Old Testament kingdom of Israel. It had been destroyed by the ASSYRIANS in 722 B.C. but was later resettled by the king of Assyria with pagan peoples to replace the Israelites. "Each national group made its own gods in the several towns where they settled, and set them up in the shrines the people of Samaria had made at the high places. . . . They worshiped the LORD, but they also served their own gods in accordance with the customs of the nations from which they had been brought" (2 Kgs 17:29, 33).

Samaria was a mixed population both racially and religiously. During Ezra's time its inhabitants were forbidden to help build the temple in Jerusalem (Ez 4:3–4), causing them to set up their own temple on MOUNT GERIZIM; they never forgave the Jews for the insult. Bad feelings persisted over the years and about 128 B.C. John Hyrcanus invaded Samaria, devastated the land, and destroyed their temple (Josephus, *Ant.* 13.9.1). After the removal of Archelaus in A.D. 6, the Samaritans sneaked into the temple in Jerusalem and defiled it by scattering corpses around (Josephus, *Ant.* 18.2.2). Later, the Samaritans killed a number of Jewish pilgrims at GINAE, which started a civil war that ended only by Roman intervention in A.D. 51 (Josephus, *Ant.* 20.6.1–3). The hatred that each group felt for the other was longstanding and deep, and in Jesus' day the Jews had no dealings with the Samaritans (Jn 4:9).

Religiously, the Samaritans considered themselves to be Jews but worshiped in their own distinctive way. They were **monotheistic,** kept the festivals, were committed to the law, practiced circumcision, and looked for a coming Messiah. They did not acknowledge the Jerusalem temple, however, but worshiped on Mount Gerizim (Jn 4:20), using only their own version of the Pentateuch as their Bible. It is said that they did not believe in the resurrection of the dead (*Bab. Sanh.* 50b). Most of what we know about the Samaritans comes from a later period of time, so many details of their faith are obscure to us.

It is remarkable that Jesus was so open to the Samaritans, traveling through their territory and even discussing theology with a Samaritan woman, revealing the profound truth to her that God seeks those who worship in the right spirit, not in the right place (Jn 4:1–42). He later speaks the parable of the "good Samaritan" (Lk 10:25–37)—to many Jews, there was no such thing—and at his ascension says the gospel must go out from Jerusalem to Judea, to Samaria, and then to the ends of the earth (Acts 1:8).[14]

The Literature of the Jews

The Old Testament

First and foremost of the literature that forms a background for understanding the New Testament are the Scriptures of the Old Testament.[15] The Old and the New Testaments comprise one Bible today, but in Jesus' day only the Old Testament existed. He (and the New Testament writers) used the formula "it is written" (which means "this comes directly from God") only of the Old Testament Scriptures. Jesus never quoted any other sources, whether rabbis, Greek writers, **Apocrypha**, or other well-known sources of his day. For him, the Old Testament Scriptures alone were the Word of God. Until heaven and earth disappeared not the smallest part of it could be disregarded—all of it must be fulfilled (Mt 5:18). The reverence that Jews felt for the Scriptures went back at least to Ezra's day (Neh 8–10). A thousand years before that, Moses called for God's people to love God by loving his commands (Dt 6:4–6). Allegiance to the law was so important that the rabbis would later say, "Whoever says that the Torah (Law) is not from heaven, he has no share in the world to come" (*mSanh* 10:1). By Jesus' time the three sections that comprise the Old Testament had been acknowledged as Scripture (Lk 24:44;

Septuagint

Vulgate

The Hebrew Bible: Its Divisions and Contents

Torah (Law)
Genesis
Exodus
Leviticus
Numbers
Deueronomy

Nevi'im (Prophets)
Joshua
Judges
Samuel
Kings
Isaiah
Jeremiah
Ezekiel
Minor Prophets

Kethubim (Writings)
Psalms
Job
Proverbs
Ruth
Canticles
Ecclesiastes
Lamentations
Esther
Daniel
Ezra–Nehemiah
Chronicles

see also the prologue to Ecclesiasticus). That it was written in Hebrew (with a small portion in Aramaic) created some problems for the Jews outside Palestine, as well as for some in Palestine who could no longer read Hebrew. A translation was made into Greek, called the **Septuagint** (abbreviated LXX). This was done more than a century before Jesus and probably over a period of time, judging from the various versions of it that exist. The early Christians quote from it as often as they quote from the Hebrew Old Testament.

The Old Testament Apocrypha
The Apocrypha is a group of fourteen books, existing in Greek, which appeared roughly between 200 B.C. and A.D. 100. They are listed on page 21. They deal mainly with the religious ideas and history of the Jews.[16] They are never quoted

in the New Testament and were excluded by the Jews of Judea from their canon of Scripture. Because some of these books were included in part of the Septuagint, there were second- and third-century Christians who made use of them along with the Old Testament. But there was never any discussion at that time as to whether they were part of the Bible, nor any agreement as to which of them should be used. When Jerome translated the Bible into Latin around A.D. 400 (the **Vulgate**, as it is called), he made a distinction between those books that were canonical (i.e., Scripture) and those that were not. The Apocrypha, he concluded, were not. They continued to be used by medieval Christians to varying extents until the Reformation, when the Protestants rejected them as Scripture. The Roman Catholic Council of Trent, at Session IV in 1546, accepted them as Scripture along with the Old Testament and the New Testament. The Thirty-Nine Articles (1562) of the Church of England stated: "The church doth read [them] for example of life and instruction of manners; but yet it doth not apply them to establish any doctrine." In 1566 Sixtus of Sienna coined the word "deuterocanonical" to designate these books. Today Protestants pay respect to the apocryphal books as valuable sources of information about Jewish life and thought, but not as Scripture, while Roman Catholics and others revere them as part of their Bible.

The Old Testament Pseudepigrapha
These books are a large and diverse collection of writings that arose between approximately 200 B.C. and A.D. 200. They are falsely ascribed to some well-known ancient person, such as Enoch, Solomon, or Ezra. Hence the designation "falsely titled" or pseudepigrapha.[17] There were a great many of them, most of which have been lost, but we retain portions or at least knowledge of over fifty. Fourth Ezra, itself one of these pseudepigrapha dating from around A.D. 120, notes the existence of seventy such books at that time (4 Ezr 14:45–46). To organize and classify this material is difficult because much of it has gone through complicated stages of editing, in some instances turning the books from Jewish into more or less Christian writings.

tractates

J. H. Charlesworth's literary classification is perhaps the most satisfactory. He finds five major groupings: apocalyptic literature and related works; testaments; expansions of the Old Testament and legends; wisdom and philosophical literature; prayers, psalms, and odes. There are also fragmentary remains that include poetry, oracle, drama, history, and romance. The reason why this material was written under an assumed name from antiquity was presumably to assure its acceptance in a day when the prophetic voice was muted or even absent. The subjects dealt with are varied but often concern fundamental theological issues such as God and the world; humanity, sin, and judgment; the kingdom of God and the future; heaven and hell. For this reason they provide an invaluable look at Jewish thought at that time as well as, in some later instances, what some Christians were thinking. Yet the pseudepigraphical books were never considered Scripture by anyone, Jew or Christian.

The Dead Sea Scrolls

The term "Dead Sea Scrolls" is used to describe those literary works that were discovered beginning in 1947 at about eleven locations near the Dead Sea community of Qumran.[18] Tens of thousands of fragments were found; from Cave 4 alone the remains of nearly five hundred different volumes were discovered. From 1953 to 1956 a complex of buildings was excavated near the caves that is most certainly the community from which the scrolls came. The scrolls were probably copied or written between 250 B.C. and A.D. 68, when the community was destroyed by the Romans. The scrolls, which represented the library of over eight hundred volumes belonging to the community, were hidden in the caves to save them from destruction.

As we saw earlier, the Jews who lived here were probably Essenes, who believed they were living in the last days.

The scrolls naturally reflect the interests of the community. There are biblical texts representing every book in the Old Testament except Esther. There is apocryphal and pseudepigraphical material of the sort mentioned above; devotional material such as psalms, prayers, blessings, and hymns; Bible commentaries and paraphrases (targums); and numerous documents designed to govern community life, the Manual of Discipline being the best known. Taken all together these eight hundred volumes show how rich and varied the literature and theology of the Jews were during the time of Jesus.

Rabbinic Writings

This material developed over a period of some six hundred years, receiving final form in two large collections known as the Jerusalem Talmud (compiled at the end of the fourth or early fifth century A.D.) and the Babylonian Talmud (compiled at the end of the fifth century A.D.).[19] These large, complicated works (the Babylonian Talmud runs to some six thousand pages) represent Pharisaic teaching gathered together over the centuries. The core of the Talmud is the Mishnah,[20] a collection of rabbinic sayings that was written down by Rabbi Judah the Patriarch at the beginning of the third century A.D. It consists of six major sections, divided into sixty-three **tractates** dealing mainly with legal matters related to temple ritual, civil and criminal law, marriage, the Sabbath, and the like. A good bit of this comes from Jesus' day and before, but it is often hard to date the material precisely because it has been edited at a later date. To the Mishnah were added later sayings, comments, and expansions, collectively called the Gemara, and together they became the Talmud.

All this material is very helpful in understanding the content of the New Testament, although care must be exercised in using it.[21] In some ways it is helpful in

Part of the excavated Essene community buildings at Qumran. The Dead Sea can be seen in the distance.

targums

showing us what the New Testament is *not*, namely, a vast collection of minute and often contradictory rules. The emphasis found in Jesus and Paul is on the grace of God, who forgives sins and does not impose a weight of requirement that simply cannot be borne. It was rules such as those found in the later Mishnah that Jesus said were heavy burdens (Mt 23:4) in contrast to the "burden" that he offered, which was light or easy to bear (Mt 11:28–30). But it must also be remembered that Jesus said the law contained matters of great consequence—justice, mercy, and faithfulness—and these must be done (Mt 23:3, 23). Jesus taught much the same things as the rabbis, because like them he was building on God's revelation in the Old Testament. Unfortunately, many of the rabbis had so buried that revelation beneath a mountain of rules that the truth could no longer be found. It was that fact that Jesus was objecting to.

Other Writings

By the time of Jesus and Paul, Hebrew was no longer the major language of the Jews. As we saw, this necessitated an Old Testament in Greek (the Septuagint) for the Jews outside Palestine. It also created the need for Aramaic Scriptures in Palestine, because that was now the major spoken language there. These translations of the Bible into Aramaic were called **targums**. They arose in the synagogues and schools to train ordinary Jews in matters of religious ritual and moral life. Tradition puts the origin of this material back in Ezra's day (fifth century B.C.), but even if it is not that old, it arose before the time of Christ and became an important part of Jewish life. Targums for all of the Old Testament, except for Daniel, Ezra, and Nehemiah, still exist. The targums do more than just give a translation of the Old Testament material. They also include paraphrases, discussions of

Key Terms

apocalyptic
Apocrypha
Diadochi
diaspora
Essenes
ethnarch
Feast of Dedication
Gentiles
Hasidim
Hasmoneans
mezuzah
Midrash
Mishnah
monotheistic
Pharisees
polytheistic syncretism
praeparatio
  evangelium
pseudepigrapha
Sadducees
Samaritans
Sanhedrin

Second Temple Judaism
Septuagint
Talmud
targums
tephillin
tractates
Vulgate
Zealots

Key People/ Places

Alexander Jannaeus
Alexander the Great
Antigonus II
Antioch (Syrian)
Antiochus III the Great
Antiochus IV (Epiphanes)
Antipater
Archelaus
Aristobulus II
Bar Kochba
Beth-Zur
Bethlehem
Bethsaida
Caesar Augustus
Caesarea Philippi
Caligula

Claudius
Cyrus
Dead Sea
Decapolis
Edom
Emmaus
Galilee
Gamaliel I
Gessius Florus
Ginae
Herod Agrippa I
Herod Agrippa II
Herod Antipas
Herodias
Herod Philip
Herod the Great
Hillel
Hyrcanus II
Idumea
Jamnia
Jericho
Jerusalem
John Hyrcanus I
Jonathan
Jordan River
Josephus
Judas "Maccabeus"
Judas the Galilean
Judea
Julius Caesar

Machaerus
Mariamme
Masada
Mattathias
Mediterranean Sea
Modein
Mount Gerizim
Nero
Perea
Philo
Phoenicia
Plain of Esdraelon
Plain of Gennesaret
Pompey
Pontius Pilate
Ptolemy
Qumran
Rabbi Judah
Rome
Samaria
Sea of Galilee
Seleucus Nicator
Shammai
Simon
Syria
Tiberius Caesar
Titus
Vespasian

Focus 2: Tradition!

If you have seen the movie *Fiddler on the Roof* you should have some insight into the meaning of "tradition" in the Jewish religion as it was emphasized by Tevye. Since the earliest times Judaism has been primarily a way of life. This doesn't mean that theological ideas aren't important, but deviations there can be tolerated more than they can be tolerated in lifestyle.

The lifestyle of tradition can dictate matters of eating and washing as well as the celebration of numerous festivals. There are many laws and traditions in Judaism. Some examples from the Mishnah are:

Laws pertaining to agriculture
• various benedictions for the consumption of fruit
• common prayers after meals
• which corner of the field should be left for the poor
• illicit mixture of seeds
• how the firstfruits are to be brought to Jerusalem

Festival days
• Sabbath
• Passover
• Day of Atonement
• Feast of Booths
• New Year's Feast
• Purim
• Feast of Weeks

Laws pertaining to women
• marriage contracts
• sisters-in-law
• how to cancel a wife's vows
• certificates of divorce
• how to acquire a wife

Midrash

words, grammatical points, and explanations of various passages. The targums give us insight into Jewish thinking at that time, but it must be remembered that because they arose over a long period of time (over five hundred years) it is often difficult to date them exactly. They were used quite widely, and fragmentary targums on Job and Leviticus were found even at Qumran.[22]

Another large body of material, called **Midrash**, also seeks to explain the Old Testament Scriptures. This material consists of commentaries, homilies, explanatory notes, exegetical comments, and exhortations. It is all to be dated later than the New Testament, indeed, after the compilation of the Mishnah in the early third century A.D., and some of it comes from the early Middle Ages. However, it is possible to trace some of the ideas and material back into New Testament times. If used cautiously this material can be of genuine benefit to students of the New Testament.[23]

The Tosefta (meaning "supplement") is still another large collection of material that arose more or less at the same time as the Mishnah. It is arranged in orders and tractates that parallel the Mishnah and almost all the areas covered. This material was not deemed as authoritative as the Mishnah at that time, so it was excluded

from it, but for the modern student the ideas found there are very helpful in understanding the Judaism of the first and second centuries A.D.

Finally, we mention two well-known Jewish writers, Philo (ca. 20 B.C.–A.D. 50)[24] and Josephus (ca. 37–100).[25]

Philo was an Alexandrian (Egypt) philosopher and theologian whose goal was to reconcile Greek and Hebrew thought. He wrote extensively, and most of his writings still exist today. He developed the allegorical method of interpreting the Old Testament. This method allowed him to find underlying Greek ideas in the Hebrew Scriptures. Later Christian thinkers such as Clement of Alexandra and Origen made extensive use of Philo's allegorical method, but it is not clear whether any New Testament books were influenced by his thought. Some see traces of it in the Logos (Word) idea in John 1:1–14 and the Book of Hebrews, but this is by no means universally acknowledged. That aside, Philo gives us some rare insight into Jewish mystical thought during the time of Jesus and Paul.

Josephus was a Jewish military commander who lived through the difficult days leading up to the destruction of Jerusalem in A.D. 70. He survived by surrendering to the Romans early in the rebellion. In return for his cooperation with Roman invaders, he was later given an apartment in Rome where he wrote several famous works. His *History of the Jewish War*, published in A.D. 77–78, is our primary source of information about those awful days as well as the events that led up to them. Josephus mentions James, John the Baptist, and even Jesus, saying he was "a wise man, if it be lawful to call him a man, for he was a doer of wonderful works—a teacher of such men as receive the truth with pleasure" (*Ant.* 18.3.3).

Conclusion

So what do all these complex ideas, this vast literature, and this complex history add up to? Three things stand out.

First and foremost is how God's overarching plan is being accomplished in the world. History is not just the meaningless interplay of purely this-worldly forces—human greed and violence, natural events like earthquakes, economic factors, political upheavals. Rather, woven through it

Summary

1. The personal tone of the New Testament is seen in the fact that its twenty-seven books are made up of twenty-four personal letters and three personalized accounts of the life and work of Christ.

2. Viewed north to south, Palestine consists of five regions: the coastal plain, the foothills, a central mountain range, the wilderness and the Jordan Valley, and the eastern mountain range.

3. Palestine had several administrative districts in Jesus' day: Galilee, Samaria, Judea, Philip's territory, the Decapolis, and Perea.

4. Herod's descendants who ruled Palestine from 4 B.C. to A.D. 66 were: Archelaus, Philip, Antipas, Herod Agrippa I, and Herod Agrippa II.

5. Jerusalem was destroyed systematically by the Romans from A.D. 66 to 70.

6. Jesus was seen as a threat by the Jews because he made controversial claims about himself and took liberties with Jewish customs.

7. The most significant unifying factors for the Jews were their relationship to God and their sense of uniqueness in world history.

8. Other factors that unified the Jews were: (a) the idea that God had placed them in Palestine forever; (b) the messianic fervor of the time; (c) the synagogue; (d) the Torah and tradition, which included Sabbath keeping and circumcision; (e) the temple; (f) the priesthood; and (g) the festivals.

9. The best known religious group in Jesus' day was the Pharisees, who had two major schools of thought: the followers of Hillel and the followers of Shammai.

10. Other groups of this period included the Sadducees, the Essenes, the Zealots, the Samaritans, the Herodians, and the *Am ha-Aretz*.

11. The Apocrypha includes over a dozen noncanonical books written between 200 B.C. and A.D. 100.

12. Rabbinic materials were developed over a period of six hundred years and were put in the form of the Talmud, of which the Mishnah is the core.

Review Questions

1. The land of Palestine divides into _____ main regions.

2. The district where Jesus lived as a boy is called _____.

3. The Middle East first was influenced by Europe during the military campaigns of _____.

4. Before the crucifixion, Pilate sent Jesus to the ruler of Galilee named _____.

5. In A.D. 70 Vespasian sent his son _____ to destroy Jerusalem.

6. Initially Judaism was primarily a _____ rather than a set of doctrines.

7. Religion was so important to the early Jews that every town had a _____.

8. The _____ were the most well known religious group in Jesus' time.

9. The Dead Sea Scrolls were produced by a religious group called the __ ___, who lived at Qumran.

10. The body of literature that is most important for understanding the New Testament is the_____.

Study Questions

1. What were the main theological beliefs of the Pharisees?

2. What factors unified Judaism in Jesus' day?

3. What is the Apocrypha?

4. Why did the Jewish War of A.D. 66–70 take place?

5. Why was the destruction of Jerusalem in A.D. 70 significant for Christianity?

6. What are the major geographical regions of Palestine?

7. Who were the Hasmoneans and why were they important?

8. What were the strengths and weaknesses of Herod the Great?

9. How was the land of Palestine divided after Herod the Great, and what was the rule of his sons like?

10. What are the distinctive features of "apocalyptic"?

all is a higher purpose, often discernible (at least in retrospect) to those who know God. They are able to see God at work, accomplishing his own purposes. Paul saw all of history this way (Acts 17:24–28), and the Book of Revelation shows in dramatic fashion how the real spiritual world stands behind the events of this less real material world where "history" is taking place.

Second and equally important is the observation that human beings are not left out of the picture. Human choices are being made, and the consequences for good or ill are always being felt. We could almost wish that God did step in more directly sometimes, but most often, he does not. He allows us our choices. We are responsible for them and their consequences. And sometimes the courage of a single person or family, such as the Maccabees, can change the whole course of history.

Third, the Christians of the New Testament era saw all of past history as pointing to the coming of Christ as its fulfillment. The prophecies of the Old Testament, the unifying of the world under Rome, a universal language that related peoples together, a time of relative calm that allowed travel and exchange of ideas, the restless spiritual hunger of people for something more—all of this together converged at the coming of Christ and his offer of the gospel. The coming of Christ brought the end of all the earlier ages and the beginning of a new era of salvation. The time of preparation was now over and the time of fulfillment had come.

Further Reading

Barnett, Paul. *Jesus and the Rise of Early Christianity*. Downers Grove: InterVarsity, 1999. A historian reviews the sources and developments leading to the existence of early Christianity. Perceptive and reverent in its approach and findings.

Bruce, F. F. *New Testament History*. Garden City, N.Y.: Doubleday, 1972. Readable treatment of the Second Temple period.

Davies, William D., and Louis Finkelstein, eds. *The Cambridge History of Judaism,* vol. 2, *The Hellenistic Age*. Cambridge: Cambridge University Press, 1989. A standard history of Judaism during the time of Jesus and the early church.

García-Martínez, Florentino. *The Dead Sea Scrolls Translated*. 2nd ed. Grand Rapids: Eerdmans, 1996. The definitive translation of the Dead Sea Scrolls in English.

Helyer, Larry R. *Exploring Jewish Literature of the Second Temple Period*. Downers Grove: InterVarsity, 2002. A valuable guide to the beliefs and extant writings of Jewish groups leading up to the time of Jesus. Shows connections between New Testament developments and Second Temple Judaism.

Magness, Jodi. *The Archaeology of Qumran and the Dead Sea Scrolls*. Grand Rapids: Eerdmans, 2002. Updates and furthers research into the identity of the Essenes and offers the best interpretation of archaeological remains in the Qumran area.

McRay, John. *Archaeology and the New Testament*. Grand Rapids: Baker, 1991. An authoritative and comprehensive treatment of how archaeology relates to the New Testament.

Montefiore, C. G., and H. Loewe. *A Rabbinic Anthology*. New York: Schocken, 1974 [1938]. A selection of readings from the rabbis, topically arranged, taken from the Talmud. Helpful explanatory material is included.

Nickelsburg, George W. E. *Jewish Literature between the Bible and the Mishnah: A Historical and Literary Introduction*. Philadelphia: Fortress, 1981. An introduction to ancient Jewish literature.

Pritchard, J. B. *The Harper Atlas of the Bible*. San Francisco: Harper, 1987. One of the best geographical guides to biblical places and times.

Richardson, Peter. *Herod*. Columbia: University of South Carolina Press, 1996. The definitive work on Herod the Great and his times.

Sanders, E. P. *Judaism: Practice and Belief 63 BCE– 66 CE*. Philadelphia: Trinity Press International, 1992. Standard introduction to the life and thought of the Jewish people from the coming of the Romans to the Jewish War.

Schürer, Emil. *The History of the Jewish People in the Age of Jesus Christ*. Rev. and ed. Geza Vermes, Fergus Millar, and Matthew Black. 3 vols. Edinburgh: T & T Clark, 1973–87. The standard scholarly compendium of information about the period. Covers the history, literature, and institutions of Judaism in this era.

Scott, J. Julius. *Jewish Backgrounds of the New Testament*. Grand Rapids: Baker, 1995. A thorough study of the Jewish backgrounds of the New Testament. Good for those with no background in this area.

Vander Kam, James C. *The Dead Sea Scrolls Today*. Grand Rapids: Eerdmans, 1994. A comprehensive introduction.

Witherington, Ben, III. *New Testament History: A Narrative Account*. Grand Rapids/Carlisle: Baker/Paternoster, 2001. Unfolds the story of Jesus' life and early church development in a lively and memorable way.

3 The Gospel and the Four Gospels

Outline

- **The Content of the Message**
- **The Growing Body of Material**
- **The Distinctive Gospel Form**
- **Why the Gospels Were Written**
- **The Trustworthiness of the Gospels**

Objectives

After reading this chapter, you should be able to

- Explain how the kerygma embodies the gospel message
- Identify material used to describe the Gospels
- Give an example of a biographical sermon
- Discuss the reasons why the Gospels were written
- List reasons why the Gospels are regarded as trustworthy

kerygma

One early summer day a ten-year-old boy noticed a large turtle in a dry midwestern creek bed. He had heard about "snappers" and wondered if this could be one. He dangled a dry sycamore twig in front of its jaws to find out. Snap! Yes, it was a snapper. He very nearly lost a finger. If he had known beforehand what he was dealing with, he would have saved himself a scare.

People sometimes approach the New Testament's first four books, called Gospels, with a similar idle, childish curiosity. They have heard the word "gospel" and may even have learned a verse from it (like Jn 3:16). But they really don't know what they are dealing with. They have little idea of what Gospels are, what message they contain, how and why they were written, and whether they merit full trust.

The Gospel writings (which are wonderful) are mostly unlike a snapping turtle with its lunging bite (which is not). But they share this: Both are worthy of careful respect. To deal with them as they deserve we need something more than vague familiarity. In this chapter we consider information about the New Testament's first four documents that will make our encounter with them informed and mature rather than childish and haphazard.

The Content of the Message

The message that Jesus is the Lord who died and rose again for our salvation is the heart of the gospel but not the whole of it. An analysis of the preached message, the **kerygma**, as New Testament theologians call it, reveals that certain other facts and doctrines are also included.[1] Peter's sermon to Cornelius (Acts 10:34–43) is a good example. The gospel message outlined there (see box below) includes the lordship of Jesus; the ministry of John the Baptist; the life of Jesus in Galilee; Jesus' power, miracles, healings, and exorcisms; the death of Jesus by crucifixion and his resurrection; his appearances to the believers in full bodily form after his death; the command to preach forgiveness of sins through faith in Christ; and the assertion that the Old Testament prophecies pointed to all these things. Other sermons in Acts (2:14–36; 3:17–26; 4:8–12; 5:29–32; 7:2–53; 13:16–41) add elements to this summary, but this embodies the essence of the gospel as preached: God's offer of salvation; the life, death, and resurrection of Jesus; and the call to faith in light of coming judgment.

Peter's Sermon in Acts 10:34–43

[34]Then Peter began to speak: "I now realize how true it is that God does not show favoritism [35]but accepts those from every nation who fear him and do what is right. [36]You know the message God sent to the people of Israel, announcing the good news of peace through Jesus Christ, who is Lord of all. [37]You know what has happened throughout the province of Judea, beginning in Galilee after the baptism that John preached— [38]how God anointed Jesus of Nazareth with the Holy Spirit and power, and how he went around doing good and healing all who were under the power of the devil, because God was with him.

[39]We are witnesses of everything he did in the country of the Jews and in Jerusalem. They killed him by hanging him on a tree, [40]but God raised him from the dead on the third day and caused him to be seen. [41]He was not seen by all the people, but by witnesses whom God had already chosen— by us who ate and drank with him after he rose from the dead. [42]He commanded us to preach to the people and to testify that he is the one whom God appointed as judge of the living and the dead. [43]All the prophets testify about him that everyone who believes in him receives forgiveness of sins through his name" (TNIV).

Remains of the Roman aqueduct, Caesarea. Cornelius, a centurion of the garrison at Caesarea, was the first Gentile converted to Christianity by Peter.

The Apostles and the Gospel

We lay it down first of all that the Evangelical instrument has Apostles as authors, upon whom this duty of promulgating the Gospel was laid by the Lord himself. And if [it be true that] there are also Apostolic men [among them], yet they are not alone but with Apostles and after Apostles, since the preaching of disciples could be suspected to be done because of a desire for glory, if the authority of the masters did not assist it, nay rather, [the authority] of Christ, which made the Apostles masters. So then, of Apostles, John and Matthew instill us with faith; of Apostolic men, Luke and Mark renew it, beginning with the same principles [of faith] so far as it pertains to one God, the creator, and his Christ, born of a virgin, the fulfillment of the Law and the Prophets.

—Tertullian (ca. A.D. 155–222)

The Growing Body of Material

When Peter preached his sermon to Cornelius he could say, "You know what has happened throughout Judea, beginning in Galilee" (Acts 10:37), and "we are witnesses of everything he did in the country of the Jews and in Jerusalem" (v. 39). But what of those who had *not* seen those things or heard Jesus preach? They needed to know them as well because it was part of the gospel they were to believe. No doubt at first it was all done by simply recounting it; the people who heard remembered it. But as time went on and the Good News spread beyond the borders of Palestine to Cyprus, Syria, and Asia Minor, something more needed to be done. Christians began to put together collections of material relating to Jesus.

It is possible, but not certain, that one of the first things done was to gather a collection of prophecies from the Old Testament that related both to Jesus' life and to themselves as the heirs of Jesus' ministry. This collection could be used to show the Jews that Jesus was not an innovator but part of God's plan, promised of old. It would also provide the Gentiles who knew nothing at all about Israel with some background for their understanding of Jesus, Israel's Messiah. In all, there are about eighty such prophecies recorded in the New Testament. They cover everything from Jesus' preexistence to his birth, life, death, resurrection, and the outpouring of the Holy Spirit. Other collections could certainly have been the things that Jesus did and said, and these would have been especially treasured. In time they could have taken a more specific shape as "Jesus and his story," as more of the facts of Jesus' life were woven into it. There had been several such attempts at this by the time Luke wrote because he begins his Gospel by telling Theophilus that "Many have undertaken to draw up an account of the things that have been fulfilled among us" (Lk 1:1). Luke was not implying that all these accounts were wrong as the reason for his writing; in fact, they went back to those who were eyewitnesses and servants of the Word from the very beginning. But Luke had some special material that he had gathered, some of it from Mary, Jesus' mother, and he wanted to include that in his Gospel. He also wanted to write an "orderly account" (Lk 1:3) for

Theophilus so that he could see the reason why Christians can be certain of what they believe.

The Distinctive Gospel Form

The earliest description we have of the Gospels as books comes from JUSTIN MARTYR in A.D. 155, when he calls them "memoirs" (1 *Apol.* 66). His readers would have understood this to mean that the Gospels were essentially biographical accounts of Jesus similar to the *Memorabilia* that XENOPHON had written about Socrates. It was in this way that the Gospels were understood from Justin's day until the beginning of the twentieth century. This was true whether the reader was approaching them from a very conservative or a very liberal perspective. But with the rise of form criticism in the 1920s (see ch. 11 below) came loss of faith in the Gospels as biography. Form criticism saw the Gospels as arising out of jumbled oral tradition to assume a new shape that had never existed before. This view, in turn, fell out of vogue[2] and has given rise to the present situation in which although there is no complete consensus, biography is again

suggested as the best way to describe the Gospel genre. In the ancient world biography covers such a large group of writings that the New Testament Gospels fit quite comfortably there, at least better there than anywhere else.[3]

But the Gospels are not just biographies, following some mechanical idea of what a biography ought to be, whether ancient or modern. A simple reading of them discloses that they differ even from one another. Each writer has a special point, or series of points, he is trying to make.[4] Perhaps the best way to describe them would be to call them expanded biographical sermons.[5] They tell the story of Jesus' life and teaching so they are biographical, but they also contain the elements found in early Christian sermons. Their primary purpose is to present the gospel message and call people to faith. It is for this reason that many things that could have been said were left out. Often Jesus' activity is summarized by simply saying he healed them all or he traveled through all their towns and villages teaching and preaching (Mk 1:38, 39; Lk 4:40). John puts it this way: "Jesus did many other miraculous signs in the presence of his disciples, which are not recorded in this book. But these are writ-

Part of the Egnatian Way (or Via Egnatia), near Philippi, a vital Roman imperial road. The early Christian evangelists were able to utilize the impressive Roman infrastructure to spread their faith.

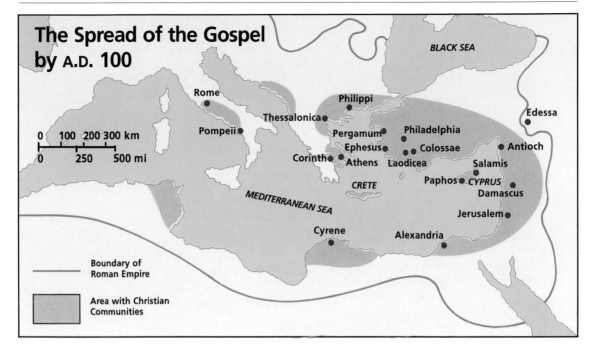

The Spread of the Gospel by A.D. 100

BLACK SEA

Rome
Philippi
Edessa
Thessalonica
Pergamum Philadelphia
Pompeii Ephesus Colossae Antioch
Corinth Athens Laodicea
Salamis
CRETE Paphos CYPRUS
Damascus
MEDITERRANEAN SEA
Jerusalem
Cyrene Alexandria

0 100 200 300 km
0 250 500 mi

—— Boundary of Roman Empire

▢ Area with Christian Communities

ten that you may believe that Jesus is the Christ, the Son of God, and that by believing you may have life in his name" (Jn 20:30–31). He later adds, "Jesus did many other things as well. If every one of them were written down, I suppose that even the whole world would not have room for the books that would be written" (Jn 21:25).

Why the Gospels Were Written

The Gospels are in essence the combining of the gospel message with other important material as it relates to Jesus' life and teaching. They are called "Gospels" because they embody the gospel—the story

Focus 3: A Call to Courage

There are many reasons why early Christian leaders compiled the Gospels. But one reason may be largely overlooked: to instill courage in Christians. The fate of their leader had been death, and their own lives may have been in peril because of their obedience to him.

Fight or Flight by Geoffrey Regan (New York: Avon, 1996) is the title of a fascinating study of bravery in wartime situations. Regan underscores that courage does not mean

the absence of fear. Not to be afraid in the face of war's carnage would be insanity. Courage is not insanity but the intellectual and emotional toughness that enables soldiers to stand their ground, not desert it. Regan reports (p. 257) that in World War II many American soldiers lacked toughness, with as many as twenty thousand deserters huddling in Paris alone.

The early church needed toughness to survive. The

information found in the Gospels would not, by itself, produce courage. But without such information it is unlikley that the first Chrisitans could have steeled themselves for the reproach they often attracted. The Gospels served, not merely to inform, but to galvanize early believers. For modern readers who dare to take up Christ's cross, they serve a similar function today.

Summary

1. The essence of the gospel as preached includes God's offer of salvation; the life, death, and resurrection of Jesus; and the call to faith in light of the coming judgment.

2. The material for the Gospels was first preserved by eyewitnesses.

3. The earliest Christians collected information about Jesus, which included Old Testament prophecies about the Messiah and things that Jesus did and said.

4. An early description of the Gospels comes from the writings of Justin Martyr in A.D. 155.

5. The primary purpose of the Gospels is to call people to faith.

6. The Gospels can best be described as biography.

7. Written Gospels were needed because it was impossible to disseminate the message quickly, widely, and reliably via the spoken word alone.

8. The Gospels are trustworthy because they were written when those who knew Jesus were still alive, they are directly linked to the apostles, and God guided the authors.

Key People

Justin Martyr
Xenophon

Key Terms

gospel
kerygma

of who Jesus was and what he did. But why did they arise at this particular time? Why wasn't it good enough just to pass the word along orally from one generation to the next or from one place to another?

One of the main reasons written Gospels were needed was the speed and extent of the spread of the gospel message. This made it simply impossible for the church to spread the word by oral means alone. Within forty years—and by this time at least three of the four Gospels had been written—the Word of God had spread across the vast Roman Empire, and many thousands had believed. It was impossible for the apostles or accredited teachers to travel across that whole area to all the remote corners where believers

could be found and there speak the word personally. The *written* story of Jesus could go and be read to groups and by individuals. They could be read repeatedly, studied, and memorized, so that who Christ was could become a part of who they were.

Another reason for writing the Gospels was that as time went on the apostles aged and passed from the scene. We do not have abundant concrete facts to go on here, but by A.D. 70 most had perished for their faith. There was a sense of urgency that the material be recorded before those who knew it best were gone.

Another reason could have been that the early believers were looking to the future. They sincerely believed that Christ was going to return soon, but who knew when that would be? If it were almost immediately, there would be no need to write anything down. But who was to say how long it would actually be? As the years went by, it only made sense to record what was known of Jesus so that it could be remembered right up to the end, whether it came very soon or much later than expected.

It was also possible that inauthentic or perhaps distorted accounts were begin-

Review Questions

1. The message that Jesus died and rose again for our salvation is the _____ of the gospel but not the _____ of it.
2. The core content of the preached word is called the _____.
3. The New Testament records _____ (number) Old Testament prophecies.
4. One of the reasons that Luke wrote his Gospel was so there would be an account that was _____.

5. The earliest description of the Gospels refers to them as _____.
6. The Gospels can best be described as what form of literature? _____
7. By the time three of the Gospels were written, the Word of God had spread across the _____.
8. Of the four Gospels, how many were directly linked to the apostles? _____

Study Questions

1. What elements of the life of Jesus were included in the preached gospel message of the early church?
2. What is the "Gospel form"?

3. Cite five reasons why the Gospels were written.
4. Why may the Gospels be trusted?

ning to make their appearance. We're not sure of this, but if they were, this would be yet another reason to record the truth while it could still be verified.

But perhaps the main reason for writing the Gospels down was the need for factual material to use in the instruction of new converts. It wasn't long before virtually everyone who was converted to the new faith came without any knowledge of who Christ was. They needed to be instructed in the basic facts of Christ's life. They needed to know of Old Testament history and prophecies, Jesus' birth, his preaching, his miracles, his healings, his teachings, his triumph over demons, something of his travels, and the facts relating to his trial, death, and resurrection. These new believers were becoming "Christians," those who followed Christ. It was mandatory that they be taught who Christ was, so they could become disciples just as those who had followed him in Galilee.

The Trustworthiness of the Gospels

For these reasons, and possibly others, the four Gospels came to be written. Many people today emphasize the human element of production to such a degree that the Gospels appear to be little more than pious fiction. But three things must be remembered about this process.

First, it took place while those who had known Jesus were still alive and the information could be traced back to them, because either they said it or they wrote it down. Second, according to the best evidence available from the early years of the church, three of the four Gospels are directly linked to the apostles; the fourth, Luke, by his own testimony (Lk 1:1–4), was dependent on eyewitnesses and those who had known Jesus from the beginning. Matthew and John were themselves apostles, and

Mark depended on the recollections of the apostle Peter. This means that all four Gospels derive from Jesus' life itself.

Third, it must never be forgotten that God had a hand in all this. It is part of the Christian faith that God is active in human affairs and has made his will known to his people. Jesus and the apostles accepted the Old Testament as the inspired word(s) of God, and the early church attributed to Jesus that same sort of inspiration. What he said was just as true as the Old Testament because he *was* the Word of God, just as the Old Testament was the words of God. It was only a matter of time before they realized that what was written about Jesus by the apostles and their close associates was also true. In time the writings of Paul (as an apostle) were also recognized as Scripture and made equal to the Old Testament and the accounts of Jesus' life and words (2 Pt 3:15–16). The Gospel accounts of Jesus' life are believed to be true by Christians not just because they can be judged as inherently probable by historians, but because the guiding hand of God stands behind them, assuring their trustworthiness. The holy people of old "spoke from God as they were carried along by the Holy Spirit" (2 Pt 1:21; 2 Tm 3:16), and so did the dedicated followers of Jesus who wrote the New Testament.

Further Reading

Aune, David E. *The New Testament in Its Literary Environment.* Philadelphia: Westminster, 1987, pp. 17–76. Fine introduction to the whole subject of the Gospel genre and the Gospels as ancient biography.

Bauckham, Richard, ed. *The Gospels for All Christians: Rethinking the Gospel Audiences.* Grand Rapids: Eerdmans, 1998. Significant proposals for reading the Gospels in a fresh and more justifiable way than many scholars have in recent generations.

Blomberg, Craig L. *The Historical Reliability of John's Gospel.* Downers Grove: InterVarsity, 2001. Demonstrates the historical plausibility of John's authorship of the Fourth Gospel. Shows the reasonableness of regarding this Gospel's claims as factually true.

———. *The Historical Reliability of the Gospels.* Downers Grove: InterVarsity, 1987. An excellent treatment of the questions that surround the truthfulness of the Gospels, showing that they indeed may be trusted.

Burridge, Richard A. *What Are the Gospels? A Comparison with Graeco-Roman Biography.* Cambridge: Cambridge University Press, 1992. Demonstrates that the Gospels are a form of ancient biography.

Capes, David B. "*Imitatio Christi* and the Gospel Genre." *Bulletin for Biblical Research* 12, no. 1 (2003): 1–19. Fascinating brief study of how the Gospels served to help early believers follow Jesus. In other words, they served as practical guides for discipleship. (*Imitatio Christi* means "the imitation of Christ.")

Dodd, C. H. *The Apostolic Preaching and Its Developments.* 2nd ed. New York: Harper & Bros., 1951. Standard text that discusses the early Christian preaching and how it stood behind the Gospels as they developed.

Guelich, Robert. "*The Gospel Genre.*" In *The Gospel and the Gospels,* ed. Peter Stuhlmacher. Grand Rapids: Eerdmans, 1991, pp. 173–208. A good survey of the concept of Gospel form, especially as it relates to the Gospel of Mark.

Hurtado, Larry W. "*Gospel (Genre).*" In *Dictionary of Jesus and the Gospels,* ed. Joel B. Green, Scot McKnight, and I. Howard Marshall. Leicester/Downers Grove: InterVarsity, 1992, pp. 276–82. An up-to-date and easy-to-understand summary of the discussion.

Millard, Alan. *Reading and Writing in the Time of Jesus.* Sheffield: Sheffield Academic Press, 2000. Challenges the view that the Gospels were transmitted orally to such an extent that the reliability of their written forms cannot be trusted.

Moule, C. F. D. *The Birth of the New Testament.* New York: Harper & Row, 1962. Looks at the early church and its role in giving rise to the New Testament.

Talbert, Charles H. *What Is a Gospel? The Genre of the Canonical Gospels.* Macon, Ga.: Mercer University Press, 1985 [1977]. A standard introduction to the subject of Gospel as form.

4 The Gospel of Matthew
The Messiah Has Come!

Outline

- **Author**
- **Date**
- **Place of Writing**
- **Outline**
- **Purpose and Characteristics**
- **Jesus the Fulfillment of God's Intention**
- **Jesus the Savior of Israel and the World**
- **Jesus the Supreme Authority**
- **Jesus the Teacher, Preacher, and Healer**
- **The Followers of Jesus and the Church**
- **Critical Issues**
- **Conclusion**

Objectives

After reading this chapter, you should be able to

- List the pros and cons regarding the authorship of Matthew
- Discuss the dating of Matthew
- Outline the content of Matthew
- Use Scripture references to support the idea that God was involved in the events related to Jesus' life
- Enumerate the areas over which Jesus had supreme authority
- Illustrate with Scripture that Jesus was a teacher
- Describe the ways Jesus was both a preacher and a healer

Coin of Caesar Augustus. Matthew was a tax gatherer—an unpopular position as taxes were paid to the Roman authorities.

Most of us are skilled at letting words go in one ear and out the other. That skill may be fine for some, but not for a court stenographer. Somehow this person must learn to funnel those words into her or his fingertips. It seems almost impossible. How can a person sit over that little keypad machine and capture every single word of testimony that the judge allows? In some ways it's the human equivalent of a tape recorder.

Matthew, the author of the first Gospel, was not a human tape recorder. His task was much more complicated than that of a court stenographer. That is not to say his account is inaccurate. Rather, it is to say that accuracy was only the first step. As a personal disciple of Jesus Matthew emphasizes certain aspects of his Master's ministry that he is uniquely equipped to see. Matthew arranges his data to demonstrate that Jesus indeed fulfilled God's intention to provide Israel, and even the whole world, with a savior. Not only this, but Christ is everywhere shown to be in charge, yet never at the expense of his compassion and concern for instructing and redeeming his followers. Matthew was no

court stenographer. He has delivered to the church something far more, and greater, than a mere transcription of the life and words of Christ.

Author

The only person ever suggested as the author of the first Gospel until recent times was the apostle Matthew. Among the Church Fathers, IRENAEUS, ORIGEN, and EUSEBIUS, quoting earlier sources, all attest to this. There was some discussion by these early writers as to the precise nature of what Matthew wrote and what language he used (Aramaic, Hebrew, or Greek), but they never disputed that it was Matthew who wrote it. The title, "According to Matthew," is found in one major Greek manuscript, but it is not absolutely certain whether this was attached to the original document. Recent studies by Martin Hengel suggest rather convincingly that the Gospel titles including each author's name were used from the very beginning.[1] The titles as we know them, or superscriptions, are in any case no later than A.D. 125. Matthew's name was likely attached to the first Gospel since very early times.

Since the rise of critical studies (see chs. 10–12 below), however, Matthew's authorship of the Gospel has been denied by a great many New Testament scholars. Among the reasons for this are: Matthew nowhere claims to be the author, so the book is technically anonymous; because it reflects a later period in the church's history, it *could not* have been written by Matthew; it makes use of a Gospel written by a nonapostle (Mark), and it is unlikely that an apostle would have done this; it doesn't have the "feel" that an eyewitness account should possess. No one else is named as the possible author, but suggestions include a converted rabbi, a Christian Jew, a provincial schoolmaster, a Hellenistic Christian, or even a "school" of people or a church. From one point of view, the message of the Gospel isn't changed if Matthew were not the author. Yet all alternate selections are purely speculative. Those who were closest and knew best named the apostle Matthew as the author. There is no com-

pelling reason their testimony should be rejected.[2]

Date

For those who reject Matthew as author, dating the Gospel is largely a matter of how developed the redactional (editorial) process is considered to be and how advanced the theological ideas are. Because Matthew is considered to be dependent on Mark, and Mark is viewed as being written somewhere between A.D. 65 and 70, Matthew is put somewhere between A.D. 80 and 100. Paul Minear puts it as late as 110.[3] Others date Matthew much earlier, sometimes as early as the 50s. John Wenham[4] and John A. T. Robinson[5] have both attempted a comprehensive restructuring of thought, arguing for early dates for all the New Testament books. Wenham puts the date of Matthew at A.D. 40.[6] There is no compelling reason why this could not be correct but it need not be that early. That it was written before the fall of Jerusalem in A.D. 70 is most certainly correct.

Place of Writing

Two general localities qualify as the potential place of origin (or destination; they could be the same thing if Matthew was written for local believers). SYRIA, or Antioch of Syria in particular, is one, and Palestine is the other. The majority of scholars favor one of these two places. The former is suggested because of supposed affinities with some later works such as IGNATIUS's letters and the *Didache*, both identified with SYRIAN ANTIOCH. Antioch's status as a center of early Christianity causes others to favor it as the point of origin of such a central church document.[7] The latter, Palestine, is proposed because of the Jewish flavor of the Gospel as a whole, and because it seems to have been written with Jews in mind. Caesarea, Phoenicia, and Alexandria have also been suggested, but not many support these hypotheses. All things being considered, Antioch seems the most likely candidate, though Palestine can hardly be ruled out.

Outline

The outline of a book has to take into consideration authorship, date, place of writing, and the purpose for which the book was written. Because there are so many diverse theories on these topics one is not surprised to find many different suggested outlines. The one offered here is based on the premise that Matthew is the author and that one of his primary purposes was to present a life of Jesus—not necessarily a biography in the strict sense of the word, but Jesus' life as he remembered it. For that reason the basic facts of Jesus' life form the substance of the outline, which proceeds along geographical lines, with emphasis on Jesus as teacher and preacher.

I. **The Birth and Preparation of Jesus** (1:1–4:16)
   A. The Birth and Childhood of Jesus (1:1–2:23)
   B. Preparation for Ministry (3:1–4:16)

II. **Jesus' Public Ministry in Galilee** (4:17–16:20)

magi

A. Jesus Begins His Public
Ministry (4:17–25)
B. Jesus' Teaching on Discipleship
(5:1–7:29)
C. Jesus' Authority Manifested
(8:1–9:34)
D. The Disciples' Ministry
(9:35–11:1)
E. Jesus' Ministry Receives
Diverse Responses (11:2–12:50)
F. Jesus' Parables of the Kingdom
(13:1–53)
G. Jesus' Teaching and Parables
Receive Diverse Responses
(13:54–16:20)

III. **Jesus' Private Ministry in Galilee**
(16:21–18:35)
A. Teaching on Jesus' Mission
(16:21–17:27)
B. Teaching about Relationships
among Jesus' Followers (18:1–35)

IV. **Jesus' Ministry in Judea**
(19:1–25:46)
A. Teaching on the Way to
Jerusalem (19:1–20:34)
B. Arrival in Jerusalem (21:1–22)
C. Confrontations in Jerusalem
(21:23–23:39)
D. Jesus' Teaching about the
Future (24:1–25:46)

V. **Jesus' Passion and Resurrection**
(26:1–28:20)
A. Preparation for the Passion
(26:1–46)
B. Jesus' Arrest and Trial
(26:47–27:26)
C. Jesus' Crucifixion (27:27–56)
D. Jesus' Burial and Resurrection
(27:57–28:20)

Purpose
and Characteristics

Matthew nowhere formally states his
purpose, unlike Luke and John, so it is
left to the reader to determine what he or
she thinks the basic purposes are. The
only way that can be done is by a careful
reading of the material and noting what
characteristics stand out. Some of these
are obvious and are agreed on by most
commentators; others are not, especially
if they are based on some highly special-
ized theory regarding the structure of
Matthew. Some of the more technical theories understand the Gospel to be a Christian lectionary (readings for the church
year), a midrash (expanded commentary), a manual of instruction for the
church, or perhaps a modified Greco-
Roman biography. There is merit in some
of these ideas, but they are all in the realm
of conjecture. Too rigid a use of them
could detract from what Matthew was
really trying to say. Fundamentally,
Matthew wrote his Gospel to preserve
what he knew about Jesus' life and words.
That was his basic purpose, as it was the
underlying purpose of each of the Gospel
writers. He wanted to make sure that the
truth about Jesus would never be lost. In
order to accomplish this he focused on
certain specific things that to him were
the essence of what that meant.

Jesus the Fulfillment
of God's Intention

Matthew emphasizes that the coming of
Jesus cannot be understood as just another
event in history. It is the *supreme* event in
history, planned and prophesied by God
centuries before it ever occurred. Virtually
every circumstance that surrounded the
birth, life, teaching, death, and resurrection of Jesus is seen as the fulfillment of
prophecy (e.g., 1:22; 2:15, 17, 23; 4:14–16;
8:17; 12:17; 13:35; 21:4; 26:53–54; 27:9). Jesus
came to fulfill the destiny mapped out for
him in advance by God.

Not only was Jesus' life prophetically
set out in advance; when the time of
Jesus' arrival came, God was actively involved in the unfolding events that constituted Jesus' life. There was constant
involvement on the part of God to ensure that all went according to plan. It
began with the divine birth of Jesus of
the virgin Mary (1:18). Then God spoke
through his angel to Joseph in a dream
(1:20); he warned the **magi** not to return
to Herod (2:12); he sent the holy family
to EGYPT to escape Herod's wrath (2:13)
and then to GALILEE (2:22); at Jesus' baptism, God assured him of his divine sonship with a voice from heaven (3:17); the

God spoke through his angel to Joseph in a dream and sent the holy family to Egypt to escape Herod's wrath.

Holy Spirit led Jesus into the wilderness to be tested by the devil (4:1) and then to be ministered to by angels when it was over (4:11); Peter's confession of Jesus' divine sonship is called by Jesus a direct revelation of God (16:17) and, at Jesus' transfiguration, God's voice again affirms Jesus as Son (17:5); supernatural events take place at Jesus' death (27:51–53) and Jesus is raised from the dead by God (28:2–7). Not only was God with Jesus in all these remarkable ways, but Jesus was, indeed, God with us as well (1:22–23).

Jesus the Savior of Israel and the World

Jesus came as the fulfillment of Israel's prophetic Scripture but also as the fulfillment of Israel itself, of all its hopes and dreams. Matthew introduces Jesus to his readers as "Jesus Christ the son of David, the son of Abraham" (1:1). Just as Abraham began the nation that made up God's people, so Jesus brings it to completion. Just as David ruled the nation, so Jesus will rule on his throne over all of Israel (2:6; 19:28). For Matthew, the God of Israel is the true God, and when Jesus worked his wonders, the people burst forth in praise (15:31). Jesus' mission is to Israel (10:6; 15:24), and he is to save his people from their sins (1:21), minister to them as God's Chosen Servant (12:15–21), fulfill the whole of their law (5:17), and be for Israel what they had never seen before (9:33). For Matthew, the title "Messiah" (or "Christ") sums it up (1:17; 26:63–64). Jesus is the one who was to come; there would be no other. He is the final Word of God to his people.

Matthew also emphasizes the fact that Jesus came to minister to Gentiles as well, and that the Gentiles have a central place in God's kingdom. So Gentiles (the magi) are the first to acknowledge Jesus in Matthew's Gospel (2:1–12). When Herod threatens the life of Jesus, Jesus and his family escape to Gentile territory (Egypt; 2:13–15). A Gentile centurion is extolled for faith such as did not exist in Israel (8:10). Many (Gentiles) will come from east and west to sit down with the (Hebrew) patriarchs of old (8:11–12). The extraordinary faith of the (Gentile) Canaanite woman is rewarded with the healing of her daughter (15:21–28). The parable of the tenants and the landowner points clearly to a renewed people who will bring forth fruit, while the original tenants (symbolizing stubborn Israel) are re-

Apostolic Teaching in Matthew and the Other Gospels

Now Matthew published also a book of the Gospel among the Hebrews in their own dialect, while Peter and Paul were preaching the Gospel in Rome and founding the Church. After their departure, Mark, the disciple and interpreter of Peter, he too handed down to us in writing the things preached by Peter. Luke also, the follower of Paul, put down in a book the Gospel preached by that one. Afterwards John, the disciple of the Lord who also leaned upon his breast, he too published a Gospel while residing in Ephesus [in] Asia.

And all these have handed down to us [the doctrine that there is] one God, maker of heaven and earth, proclaimed by the Law and the Prophets, and one Christ, the Son of God. If a person does not assent to these [doctrines], he surely rejects the followers of the Lord; he rejects even Christ the Lord himself; he rejects indeed also the Father and is self-condemned, resisting and fighting against his [own] salvation—which thing all the heretics do.

—Irenaeus (ca. A.D. 125/140–200)

jected (21:33–45). Matthew ends his Gospel with Jesus' command to his disciples to go into all the nations—the word can also be translated "Gentiles"—baptizing in the name of the Father, Son, and Holy Spirit (28:18–20). A major theme of Matthew is the engrafting of the Gentiles into the one people of God.

Jesus the Supreme Authority

Throughout the entire Gospel of Matthew constant emphasis is placed on the inherent supreme power and authority of Jesus (28:18). Nothing can stand in his way, and his actions or words bring instant compliance from anything that comes in contact with him.

His authority was supreme:
- over people (4:20, 22)
- over paralysis and suffering (8:6, 13)
- over illness and disease (9:22; 14:35, 36)
- over blindness (9:30)
- over leprosy (8:3)
- over the wind and the water (8:23–27)
- over the temple (12:3–6)
- over sin (9:2)

- over demons (8:31–32; 15:28)
- over nature (21:18–19)
- over history (26:64)
- over the individual destinies of all human beings (7:21–23; 11:27; 13:40–43)
- over his own destiny (16:21; 20:17–19; 26:45–46)
- over his mission on earth (10:1)
- over space, time, and the future (18:19–20; 28:20)

The natural reaction of people to the divine authority of Jesus, both before and after his resurrection, was to fall down and worship him (8:1; 14:33; 28:9, 17). Yet for all this, Matthew also stresses the compassion that Jesus felt when confronted with human need (9:36; 14:14; 15:32; 20:34). Jesus' authority was not that of despotic power, but of divine love; it was used to alleviate human suffering, not to impose an arbitrary or impersonal will.

Matthew also makes use of titles or comments that were either used by Jesus or of him that stress his supreme authority. He is the Lord of the Sabbath (12:1–8); the coming Son of Man who is ruler and judge (24:29–31); the ultimate revealer of God (11:27); the Son of God (3:17; 14:33; 16:16; 17:5); the giver of rest to the weary of the world (11:28–30); and a man of wisdom and miraculous power (13:54).

Jesus the Teacher, Preacher, and Healer

For Matthew, Jesus is *the* Teacher, called so by himself (10:24–25; 23:10) and by others (8:19; 19:16; 22:16, 24, 36; 26:18). His whole public ministry was directed toward instructing the people. He took advantage of every opportunity to lead them into a deeper understanding of God. He taught in the farms and villages of Galilee (9:35; 11:1); in JUDEA and across the Jordan (19:1–3; cf. Mk 10:1); on the road to Jerusalem (20:17–19); on the MOUNT OF OLIVES (24:3–25:46); in the temple courts (21:23); in synagogues (4:23; 13:54) and houses (13:36–52); in grainfields (12:1–8); in hill country (5:1–2); from a boat (13:1–3); on weekdays and the Sabbath (26:55). Jesus was filled with compassion for the ill-taught people and saw them as sheep without a shepherd, harassed and helpless, as a plenteous harvest without enough workers (9:36–38). The crowd was constantly astonished and amazed at his teaching (7:28; 13:54; 22:33); the religious leaders were indignant (26:1–4) because he taught with unsurpassed authority (7:28–29). Matthew ends his Gospel with Jesus commanding his disciples to go to all the nations and teach them to obey everything he commanded (28:19–20). Jesus' ministry of teaching is never to end.

As a preacher, Jesus had the prophetic ministry of expounding the Word of God, calling the people to repentance, warning of the coming judgment of God on sin, announcing the arrival of the kingdom of God (4:17), and proclaiming the end of the age with his glorious second coming (24–25).

As a healer, Jesus delivered the people from physical and spiritual bondage by restoring them to health and expelling demons. There are several summaries of Jesus' healing activities that speak of this extensive power over pain, suffering, disease, sickness, epilepsy, paralysis, demon possession, lameness, blindness, muteness, and crippled limbs (4:23–25; 9:35; 14:34–36; 15:29–31; 21:14). There are also numerous examples of individual healing that illustrate the above categories and show Jesus' deep concern for the people he healed. At one point, when the task had gotten too large for one person, Jesus sent out his disciples, filled with his own authority, "to drive out evil spirits and to heal every disease and sickness" (10:1). Matthew sees all this as fulfilling prophecy in Isaiah (8:16–17; Is 53:4) and elsewhere.

The Followers of Jesus and the Church

Matthew is the only Gospel that mentions the church by name. At CAESAREA PHILIPPI, after Peter's great confession of Jesus as the Messiah, Jesus says that he will build his church on the rock-solid fact of his messiahship and that the gates of Hades will not overcome it. He also gives to Peter, representing all the disciples, symbolic keys of authority over the kingdom of heaven to confirm entrance to it or restriction from it (16:17–19), an authority specifically conferred on all the apostles both here and in 18:18. Later Jesus gives instructions for the settling of disputes within the church, including the use of expulsion if the offender refuses to regard the admonitions of the community (18:15–17).

Matthew also records lengthy sections of Jesus' instructions to his followers. Some commentators have suggested that Matthew saw Jesus as a new Moses giving a new "law" to his people, because the instructions can be grouped in five large sections all ending with the same stylized formula "when Jesus finished saying these things" (7:28; 11:1; 13:53; 19:1; 26:1). The five sections may be likened to a new "pentateuch" (5–7; 10; 13; 18; 24–25). Whether that is true or not, Matthew certainly presented Jesus as the founder of the church, understood as the true Israel (16:18). His words are to guide all God's people as they live their lives in the kingdom of God.

Critical Issues

In addition to questions about author, date, and place of writing (see the beginning of this chapter), scholars debate whether this Gospel is written from a Jewish or a Gentile Christian point of view—and even whether this distinction as long understood is still meaningful today. Data support various possibilities. There is ongoing discussion of how Matthew may (or may not) have made use of written sources like Mark (or a version of Mark) or the Sayings Source Q (on this see ch. 11 below).

Recent research continues to scrutinize the theological intention of Matthew's author. How do the Gospel's individual sections relate to its overarching message(s)? Here attention has focused on such matters as the ethics of the Sermon on the Mount, the conflict between Jesus and the rulers of Israel (when Matthew is subjected to literary-critical analysis), and the role of Old Testament elements in Matthean understanding.

Conclusion

Matthew was writing to show his audience that Jesus was the fulfillment of God's promises to Israel, coming as Israel's Messiah and Redeemer. And because the original promise to Abraham included the promise that Abraham's descendants (Israel) would be a blessing to the nations, or Gentiles, Matthew also pointed out that Jesus came to be the Savior of the world, as well as the Savior of Israel. As the fulfillment of God's ultimate intention for all who trust him, Jesus is depicted as the sole supreme authority,

---

Key Term

magi

Key People/ Places

Antioch (Syrian)
Caesarea Philippi
Egypt
Eusebius
Galilee
Ignatius
Irenaeus
Judea
Mount of Olives
Origen
Syria

Focus 4: Dealing with Temptation— A Hermeneutics Lesson

Jesus was mightily tempted, Matthew records (4:1–11). How did he keep from sinning? He seems to have relied on the truth of Old Testament Scriptures that he had memorized. He also had a strong sense of his personal identity as a servant of God, not Satan.

The famous Egyptian Chrstian teacher Origen (A.D. 85–254) once took a different approach. Because of Jesus' teaching (found only in Matthew's Gospel, 19:12) that some become eunuchs for the sake of the kingdom of heaven, he underwent castration. He felt this would make him less susceptible to charges of sexual involvement with the women who flocked to hear his brilliant teaching.

It is hard not to stand in awe of Origen's commitment and courage. But was his act true to the spirit of Jesus' statement? Neither Jesus nor any known early Christian took this drastic step. In general they affirmed the lawful expression of sexuality within the covenant of marriage. They did not present sexual temptation as an evil to be avoided, if necessary, at the cost of personal mutilation.

While we should not sit in personal judgment of Origen's extreme measure, we may decide for Jesus' more positive approach. Clinging resolutely to the heavenly Father, his Word, and his purpose for his people is the main line of defense when temptation pays its unwelcome visits.

teacher, preacher, and healer. The Old Testament Scriptures prophesied it; Jesus fulfilled it. But Matthew lived after Jesus' saving death and resurrection in the time of the church, so he pointed out that this, too, was part of God's intention. Jesus had said that his church would be established and hell itself could not overthrow it. We live now in the time of that church with Jesus' personal presence supporting us, awaiting the end of the age when God will bring to a close what he began with Abraham long ago.

Review Questions

1. _____, _____, and _____ all identified Matthew as the author of the Gospel bearing his name.
2. The date for Matthew has been placed at A.D. 40 by New Testament scholar _____.
3. The three locations suggested as the place where Matthew was written are _____, _____, and _____.
4. Matthew's purpose in writing his Gospel was to preserve the truth about the _____ and _____ of Jesus.
5. Every event in the life of Christ was a fulfillment of Old Testament _____.
6. Matthew introduces Jesus to his readers as the Son of _____ and the Son of _____, two Old Testament figures.
7. In regard to sin, demons, and nature, Jesus was the _____.
8. When Jesus was at the city of _____, he announced that he would build his church.

Study Questions

1. What was Matthew's basic purpose in writing his Gospel?
2. In what ways did Jesus fulfill God's intention?
3. How does Matthew emphasize that Jesus is Savior of both Jews and Gentiles?
4. In what ways was Jesus the supreme authority?
5. How does Matthew depict Jesus as the Teacher?

Summary

1. Matthew arranged his Gospel to emphasize how Jesus provided Israel and the world with a savior.

2. Until recent times Matthew was the only author suggested for the Gospel bearing his name.

3. The traditional dating for Matthew places it some time prior to A.D. 70.

4. Although the Jewish flavor to the Gospel of Matthew suggests that it might have been written in Palestine, most scholars favor Antioch of Syria.

5. Matthew's basic purpose in writing his Gospel was to preserve what he knew about Jesus' life and words.

6. Matthew demonstrates that Jesus' coming was the supreme event of history and that every circumstance of his birth, life, teaching, death, and resurrection was a fulfillment of prophecy.

7. Matthew emphasizes that Jesus is the final Word of God to his people.

8. Matthew focuses on the inherent power and supreme authority of Jesus.

9. Matthew highlights the fact that Jesus was primarily a teacher but was also a healer and preacher.

10. Matthew is the only Gospel that mentions the church by name.

Further Reading

Carson, D. A. *The Sermon on the Mount.* Grand Rapids: Baker, 1978. A sound, challenging, and uplifting exposition of Jesus' teachings in one of the most renowned passages of the whole Bible.

France, R. T. *Matthew: Evangelist and Teacher.* Grand Rapids: Zondervan, 1989. A good overall introduction to the Gospel of Matthew covering most of the significant areas of discussion today.

Goodspeed, Edgar J. *Matthew, Apostle and Evangelist: A Study of the Authorship of the First Gospel.* Philadelphia: Winston, 1959. An interesting study of Matthew the apostle; helpful in understanding who he was and why he wrote the Gospel.

Hagner, Donald A. *Matthew.* 2 vols. Dallas: Word, 1993, 1995. A comprehensive evangelical commentary on Matthew.

Keener, Craig S. *A Commentary on the Gospel of Matthew.* Grand Rapids: Eerdmans, 1999. A lengthy but user-friendly discussion. Strong on historical and cultural background.

Luz, Ulrich. *The Theology of the Gospel of Matthew.* Cambridge: Cambridge University Press, 1995. Tries to distill from Matthew a complete theological outlook and agenda. For the advanced student.

Mounce, Robert H. *Matthew.* San Francisco: Harper & Row, 1985. A good entry-level commentary on Matthew.

Senior, Donald. *The Gospel of Matthew.* Nashville: Abingdon, 1997. An introduction to the interpretations, themes, and content of Matthew.

———. *What Are They Saying about Matthew?* Rev. ed. New York: Paulist, 1995. Useful classification and discussion of Matthean scholarship.

Stanton, Graham N. *A Gospel for a New People: Studies in Matthew.* Edinburgh: T & T Clark, 1992. A fine treatment of the ideas found in Matthew's Gospel.

———, ed. *The Interpretation of Matthew.* 2nd ed. Edinburgh: T & T Clark, 1995. A current survey of issues related to Matthew's Gospel.

5 The Gospel of Mark
Son of God, Servant of All

Outline

- **Author**
- **Date**
- **Place of Writing**
- **Outline**
- **Purpose and Characteristics**
- **The Supernatural Nature of Jesus**
  The Unfolding Mystery of Jesus' Divine Sonship
  The People's Confirming Reactions
- **The Death and Resurrection of Jesus**
- **The Ministry of Jesus as Servant**
- **Be Silent!**
- **Critical Issues**
- **Conclusion**

Objectives

After reading this chapter, you should be able to

- Present the position of the early church on the authorship of Mark
- Identify where Mark was written and explain why this location is thought to be the place of writing
- Outline the content of Mark
- Outline the missionary activities highlighted in this Gospel
- Give examples of how Jesus' divine sonship is illustrated in Mark
- Identify the chief ministries of Jesus as recorded in Mark
- List the three sets of circumstances in which Jesus commanded silence and the reasons for each

presbyter

Novels are a well known literary form, but they can be time-consuming to plow through. A popular alternative is the short story. Brief stories can leave us with much of the effect of a larger book without making such heavy demands on us as readers. Because they can be read more quickly, moving rapidly to their conclusion, short stories have a better chance of holding an audience spellbound from beginning to end. In a long novel there is the danger of getting lost, or just losing interest.

If we were to think for a moment of Matthew (28 chapters) and Luke (24 chapters) as short historical novels of Jesus' life, Mark (a scant 16 chapters) could be called a long short story. The most concise, vivid, and in some ways exciting of the Gospels, it has been rather neglected throughout the history of the church. This was due in part to the view, universal until the nineteenth century, that Matthew was written first, then Luke, and finally Mark. In other words, it was supposed that Mark simply condensed or sometimes enlarged on what had already been written. An attitude seems to have arisen like this: Why read Mark when you can have the whole of Matthew or Luke instead?

But with the rise of modern biblical scholarship, Mark has become the favorite Gospel and one of the two main sources of Gospel tradition (Mark and Q) postulated by critical theory. So the importance of Mark has received due recognition. In some ways, this is a positive development, for Mark is a very readable and valuable source for the life of Jesus.

Author

The only name ever attached to the second Gospel is that of Mark. There is an unbroken testimony that includes PAPIAS, IRENAEUS, the Muratorian Canon, CLEMENT OF ALEXANDRIA, TERTULLIAN, ORIGEN, JEROME, and EUSEBIUS the church historian, who supplies a good bit of the evidence. All of this is to be dated before A.D. 325. One well-known reference is of particular importance. It is the statement of Papias, who was bishop of HIERAPOLIS in PHRYGIA during the opening years of the second century. He is quoted by Eusebius as saying:

> And the presbyter [John the apostle; see below] used to say this, "Mark became Peter's interpreter and wrote accurately all that he remembered, not indeed in order of the things said or done by the Lord. For he had not heard the Lord, nor had he followed him, but later on, as I said, followed Peter, who used to give teaching as necessity demanded but not making, as it were, an arrangement of the Lord's oracles, so that Mark did nothing wrong in writing down single points as he remembered them. For to one thing he gave attention, to leave out nothing of what he had heard and to make no false statements in them."[1]

There are six things to observe about this statement by Papias:

1. He is quoting an earlier source, "the **presbyter**," who is best identified as the apostle John. If this is so, Papias's statement has the highest possible authority.
2. Mark is named as the author of the Gospel.
3. Mark relied on the apostle Peter for his information because he was not personally an eyewitness.
4. Mark wrote what he remembered comprehensively, leaving nothing out and making no false statements.
5. Mark's writing was episodic—"writing down single points."
6. Mark was not striving for "order" but for accuracy.

We can sum up the position of the early church very simply: Mark recorded Peter's recollections and was striving for accuracy but not a tightly connected, strictly chronological narrative.

The question then arises as to who this Mark is. Here, again, only one suggestion was ever made by the early believers, and that was John Mark, one who worked so closely with Peter as to be called his "son" (1 Pt 5:13). He was a cousin of Barnabas (Col 4:10), a traveler with Paul and Barnabas (Acts 13:5), and the son of a wealthy family in JERUSALEM (Acts 12:12–14). Although he disappointed Paul by going back to Jerusalem during the first missionary journey (Acts 13:13), he later proved his worth so well that Paul said to Timothy, "Get Mark and bring him with you, because he is helpful to me in my ministry" (2 Tm 4:11).

form criticism

Recent scholarship has tended to deny that Mark is the author of the second Gospel. However, no new evidence has been found nor has any other name been suggested. A reason for the change in many cases is the theoretical requirement of **form criticism**, which requires that stories float rather freely through communities for a while, being reshaped numerous times so that in the end the final story is the product of numerous anonymous hands. This theory cannot really allow an eyewitness or a single hand to be the source of most, if not all, of the material found in a Gospel. So on dogmatic, not historical or factual grounds, Mark is denied as author of the second Gospel.[2] Recent research affirms the likelihood that eyewitness recollection is a better explanation for the Gospel accounts, including Mark, than anonymous community formation.[3]

The external evidence points to Rome as the most likely site of the composition of the Gospel of Mark.

Date

There are two apparently conflicting testimonies coming from the early days of the church. Both are preserved in Euse-

bius's *Historia Ecclesiastica* (H.E.), or church history, in which Irenaeus says, "After the departure of [Peter and Paul] Mark . . . handed down to us in writing the things preached by Peter" (H.E. V.8.2–4). But Eusebius also records Clement of Alexandria's statement that Mark wrote while Peter was still alive (H.E. VI,14.6–7). These statements conflict only if the word "departure" means death, which it might. In all probability, however, it means only "departure," and Mark wrote while Peter was still alive, which would date it before the early 60s.[4] W. C. Allen dates it around 50[5] and J. A. T. Robinson has argued that a first draft was written around 45.[6] John Wenham also favors 45, but says any date between 44 and the early 50s is possible.[7] Somewhere in this time range (i.e., the 40s–60s) accords well with the evidence we have.

Those who have dated the book later, such as B. W. Bacon[8] or S. G. F. Brandon,[9] usually do so by finding allusions to later events in the Gospel, such as the fall of Jerusalem in A.D. 70. On examination these allusions are invariably found to be questionable.

Place of Writing

The external evidence points to Rome as the most likely site of composition. Internal evidence points in the same direction. Mark clearly has a Gentile audience in mind. Hence he explains the Aramaic expressions he uses (3:17; 5:41; 7:11, 34; 14:36; 15:34). He also uses expressions reflecting the Latin language, or "Latinisms" (e.g., 12:42; 15:16). A Galilean origin for Mark has been suggested by some, but the evidence does not seem to warrant this. The "Jewishness" of Mark reflects the writer and his source (Peter) rather than the place of origin.

Outline

Numerous outlines have been suggested for the Gospel of Mark. This one sees Mark as focusing primarily on the kerygmatic activity of Jesus. He is "producing a short, pithy, but intense manual for missionary work as well as for teaching and Christian instruction that calls for absolute commitment to Christ and to preaching his gospel, no matter what the cost may be in suffering."[10] Mark dramatically highlights the major episodes of Jesus' life that prove him to be the Son of God, the great servant-preacher who is ushering in God's saving reign, the kingdom of God.

  I. **Thematic Prologue: The Gospel of Jesus Christ, Son of God** (1:1–15)
  A. The Beginning of the Gospel (1:1)
  B. John the Baptist's Preaching in the Wilderness (1:2–8)
  C. Jesus' Baptism (1:9–11)
  D. Jesus' Temptation in the Wilderness (1:12–13)
  E. The Beginning of Jesus' Proclamation (1:14–15)

  II. **Jesus Invades Wilderness and City with Good News** (1:16–8:26)
  A. Jesus' Inaugural Ministry in Galilee (1:16–3:6)
  B. Jesus' Itinerant Ministry in Galilee (3:7–6:29)
  C. Jesus' Withdrawal to the Wilderness beyond Galilee (6:30–7:23)
  D. The Gentile Mission (7:24–8:10)
  E. Questions Concerning Signs and Seeing (8:11–26)

  III. **Jesus Invades the Hostile City of Jerusalem** (8:27–15:47)
  A. The Journey to Jerusalem (8:27–10:52)
  B. Jesus Confronts Jerusalem (11:1–13:37)
  C. Jerusalem Opposes Jesus (14:1–15:47)

  IV. **Unfinished Epilogue (16:1–8)**

Purpose and Characteristics

As is true with all of the Gospels, the central theme of Mark is the story of Jesus of Nazareth. Mark is concerned to record a description of who Jesus was and the impact he had on those who came in contact with him. Mark realized Jesus' identity—he was the Son of God—and he wanted to make this point as the story of Jesus unfolded. The supernatural nature of Jesus is the central theme of the Gospel of Mark, so we will begin with that and then look at other themes as well.

The Supernatural Nature of Jesus

Mark begins his Gospel (1:1) with his own confession and closes it with the confession of the Roman centurion (15:39). Jesus is no ordinary human being; he is the Son of God. Let's look at this confession as it unfolds in the Gospel and then observe how the reactions of those around Jesus corroborate it.

The Unfolding Mystery of Jesus' Divine Sonship

Mark begins his Gospel with a quote from the prophets: "Prepare the way for *the Lord*" (Is 40:3). The Lord is coming, and he will bring the Holy Spirit with him (1:8). All the preliminaries of Jesus' birth and early years are skipped over, moving quickly to Jesus' baptism by John, where

Fishing vessels on the Sea of Galilee. Many incidents in the Gospel of Mark refer to the important fishing industry.

God himself tells us who Jesus is: "You are my Son, whom I love" (1:11). The supernatural forces of evil, the demons, know instantly who Jesus is: the one who will destroy them, because he is the Holy One of God (1:24). In Capernaum Jesus magisterially says to the paralytic, "Your sins are forgiven" (2:5), and then reads the hearts of his critics and discloses their thoughts to them (2:8–10). Later the Pharisees complain to Jesus about his actions on the Sabbath only to be told in return that "the Son of Man is Lord even of the Sabbath" (2:28). Wherever Jesus went the evil spirits would cry out, "You are the Son of God" (3:11), but Jesus would silence them.

In the stormy crisis on the sea Jesus rebukes the pounding wind and waves. "Who is this? Even the wind and waves obey him," is all the disciples can say. In the Gentile region of the Gerasenes Jesus is pronounced the "Son of the Most High God" (5:7). On his return to Jewish territory, a mere touch draws power from Jesus that instantly heals a woman (5:27–30). Jesus raises Jairus's daughter (5:40–42), feeds five thousand with five loaves and two fish (6:39–44), and walks on the water at night (6:47–50). The crowd later confesses, "He has done everything well" (7:37), but Peter's confession is more specific—"You are the Christ" (8:29). That confession is followed by the extraordinary

disclosure by Jesus at the transfiguration of his own inherent divinity. God again says, "This is my Son, whom I love" (9:2–7). During the last week of Jesus' life, when asked about the source of his authority, Jesus affirms it is from heaven (11:27–33). In a confrontation with the jealous religious leaders Jesus asserts that he is the King's Son and the prophesied Rock of Scripture (12:1–12).

In yet another confrontation, Jesus stuns his opponents by arguing that David's Lord is David's Son, the Messiah (12:35–37)—and Jesus claims to be that Messiah. At his trial, when asked point-blank, "Are you the Christ, the Son of the Blessed One?" Jesus answers, "I am, and you will see the Son of Man sitting at the right hand of the Mighty One and coming on the clouds of heaven" (14:62). When Pilate asks, "Are you the king of the Jews?" Jesus replies, "Yes, it is as you say" (15:2). Then finally at the crucifixion, the story ends where it began, with the centurion confessing, "Surely this man was the Son of God" (15:39).

The People's Confirming Reactions

The divine reality of Jesus is expressed by everyone he came in contact with—with the notable exception of the religious leaders. John the Baptist shrinks back as not worthy to stoop down and untie Jesus'

Niches for Greco-Roman statues carved into the rock at Banyas, site of the city of Caesarea Philippi, where Peter made his confession of Christ (Mk 8:29).

sandals (1:7). After defeating Satan in the wilderness, Jesus is unharmed by the wild animals and attended to by the angels (1:13). The call of Jesus brings instant response from Peter, James, John, and Levi (1:16–20; 2:14). The people are amazed at an exorcism as Jesus speaks with supreme authority (1:27). Later, when a paralytic is healed, it "amazed everyone and they praised God, saying, 'We have never seen anything like this'" (2:12). Jesus' power over the storm terrified the disciples (4:41), and the raising of Jairus's daughter completely astonished everyone (5:42), as did the healing of the deaf and dumb man (7:37). On occasion after occasion, the only response is that of utter amazement (6:2, 51; 9:15; 10:24, 26; 11:18; 12:17). When Jesus was transfigured, his clothes became an unearthly dazzling white, and he talked to the long-dead Moses and Elijah. His disciples were so frightened they could not speak coherently (9:5–6). On his way to Jerusalem Jesus' disciples were strangely disconcerted by his presence, as the crowd hung back in fear (10:32); the intentions of Jesus were profoundly incomprehensible to them. Jesus' words delighted the crowd (12:37) just as it silenced his critics, so that not even the experts dared to ask him any more questions (12:34).

Everyone and everything recognize that Jesus is divine—John the Baptist, the demons, disease, the wind and the waves, the disciples, even God himself—except the religious leaders. It is a supreme irony that those who should have been the first to see the supernatural nature of Jesus were unwilling to acknowledge it. The power they acknowledged, but they attributed it to the devil (3:22). Mark attributes their spiritual blindness to the mysterious purpose of God foretold by prophets centuries earlier (4:11–12; 7:6–7).

The Death and Resurrection of Jesus

In addition to the divine sonship of Jesus, Mark also emphasizes his death and resurrection. In this regard Mark focuses on the ministry of Jesus' actions and not just his words. The very structure of the Gospel shows this. Mark spends ten chapters on the whole of Jesus' life (some thirty years) and six chapters on just the last week of his life. Mark is a Gospel of action. Jesus is at work bringing in the kingdom of God, ultimately through his death and resurrection. After a hint at this in 2:20, it becomes plainly visible when Jesus announces in very specific terms at CAESAREA PHILIPPI what awaits him in Jerusalem (8:31, 32). Jesus repeats this at least three times (9:9–12, 30–31; 10:32–34), and adds an explanation: "The Son of Man did not come to be served but to serve, and to give his life as a ransom for many" (10:45). At the

Focus 5: A Foreign Exchange Office or a Temple?

Jesus was infuriated when he arrived in Jerusalem and went to the temple only to find a bustling commercial center in the Court of the Gentiles, the outer court Gentiles were allowed to enter. Caiaphas had authorized a market there where ritually pure items could be sold for temple sacrifices. This was unnecessary because there were certified markets elsewhere in the city.

In addition, all male Jews over the age of twenty were required to pay an annual half-shekel temple tax. Three currencies circulated in Palestine: Roman (imperial money), Greek (provincial money), and Tyrian (local money). Since the Roman and Greek coins featured human portraits that were considered idolatrous by the Jews, these coins could not be used for the temple tax and had to be exchanged for Tyrian coins. In effect, then, Caiaphas had made the temple a bank. To make matters worse, fraud and extortion were present in these transactions, despite the fact that the moneychangers were allowed to charge a small surcharge.

This Court of the Gentiles also was made a thoroughfare from one part of the city to the other since people loaded with merchandise took shortcuts through it.

Jesus' actions included overturning the moneychangers' tables and the dove-sellers' benches; he also stopped people from using the Court as a thoroughfare.

To think about
What can contemporary houses of worship learn from this? What theological deductions can be drawn from the fact that Jesus felt competent to challenge the authority of the temple?

Last Supper, Jesus is deeply aware of his divine destiny on earth as he speaks of his broken body and blood—"The Son of Man will go," he says, "just as it is written about him" (14:21). The last words of the angelic being to the trembling women is, "He has risen! He is not here! . . . He is going ahead of you into Galilee. There you will see him just as he told you" (16:6–7). Jesus' death was no accident; it was the plan of God. Mark wants to emphasize that by the way he puts his Gospel together.

The Ministry of Jesus as Servant

The Son of Man chose to be a servant (10:45). Mark highlights two aspects of Jesus' ministry of service. First, he portrays him as a teacher/preacher. There is nothing equivalent to the Sermon on the Mount (Mt 5–7) or Jesus' final discourses (Jn 14–17) in Mark, but it is clear from what Mark says that Jesus is the proclaimer— he has come to teach what people need to know about God (1:14–15, 21–27, 38; 2:2;

3:13–14; 4:1; 6:2, 6, 34; 8:31, etc.). Jesus was called "Teacher" by his own followers (4:38; 9:38; 13:1), those in the crowd (5:35; 9:17), and even his enemies (12:13–14).

Second, Jesus is depicted as a worker of miracles with power over disease and demons. He was filled with compassion when he saw the suffering of those around him. He spent long hours healing them of their diseases. Mark gives numerous examples of this but is often content to summarize a large block of time spent in healing or expelling demons in this fashion: "That evening after sunset the people brought to Jesus all the sick and demon-possessed . . . and Jesus healed many who had various diseases. He also drove out many demons" (1:32–34; see also 3:10–11; 6:54–56). When the task becomes too large, Jesus gives his apostles authority over disease and demons and then sends them out. They, too, drove out many demons and healed the sick (6:12–13) as they preached. Jesus' miraculous ability even extends to the created elements themselves. This terrifies the disciples (6:35–41). After the resurrection, when they finally understand who Jesus is, the terror gives way to joyful celebration.

Key Terms

form criticism
presbyter

Key People/ Places

Caesarea Philippi
Clement of Alexandria
Eusebius
Hierapolis in Phrygia
Irenaeus
Jerome
Jerusalem
Origen
Papias

Be Silent!

One of the distinctive things about Mark's Gospel is the heavy emphasis he places on Jesus' commanding those who had been healed, or told some profound truth, not to disclose it but to remain silent. This emphasis, sometimes called "the messianic secret," has fascinated and puzzled modern interpreters of Mark. Some have even made it the crux of their understanding of Mark and the key to understanding his Gospel.[11] A careful reading of Mark reveals that in three sets of circumstances Jesus gave the command to silence. In each case it was for a different reason.

First, in exorcisms, demons are commanded to silence because Jesus did not want the evil spirits to shout out testimony to the truth, even if what they said was true. Jesus did not want to be associated with them in any fashion whatsoever (1:32–34; 3:11–12). After he had healed the demon-possessed man, however, Jesus gave him instructions to return home and tell everyone what the Lord had done for him (5:19).

Second, in some instances, but not all, people who were healed of disease were commanded to be silent. In this case the command was to relieve the pressure of the crowds on Jesus' total ministry. So many people sought Jesus out after a healing that he was often forced to spend excessive amounts of time in just that aspect of his ministry. At times he scarcely had time to pray. So when moving into different areas he sought to devote himself to preaching and teaching before the great and needy crowds found out that they could receive physical healing. Hence Jesus commands the ones who are healed to silence (1:44; 5:43; 7:36). Mark observes that often the people talked anyway and that, "as a result, Jesus could no longer enter a town openly but stayed outside in lonely places. Yet the people still came to him from everywhere" (1:45).

In the third instance, Jesus tells his disci-

Review Questions

1. The Gospel of Mark contains _____ chapters.

2. Extrabiblical sources written before A.D._____ attest to the Gospel of Mark.

3. In writing his Gospel, Mark did not attempt to have a connected _____.

4. Mark obtained the information about Jesus in his Gospel from the apostle _____.

5. The Gospel of Mark was written for an audience of _____.

6. Mark highlights parts of Jesus' life that prove him to be the _____.

7. The central theme of the Gospel of Mark is the _____ nature of Jesus.

8. The Gospel of Mark begins and ends with a _____.

9. The only group that rejected Jesus' divine nature was the _____.

10. The supreme acts of establishing God's kingdom were Jesus' _____ and _____.

ples to remain silent about his messiahship because they simply did not understand it and in fact would not until after the resurrection (8:29–30; 9:9–10, 31–32). It would have been unwise for them to go forth proclaiming something of which they had such poor and partial understanding. Only after Jesus' instructions to them and prayers for them (see Jn 14–17) would they publicly preach Jesus' kingship, armed with the knowledge of his resurrection and the power of the Spirit whom God would send.

Critical Issues

In addition to questions about author, date, and place of writing (see the beginning of this chapter), scholars have examined the narrative structure of Mark in fresh ways using the tools of literary criticism. Mark's depiction of Jesus' approach to discipleship has received careful attention, and future expectation (eschatology) proves to be vital to Jesus' concept of training his followers. There has also been focus on Mark's understanding of faith, which combines acceptance of Christian confession with intensely personal commitment and trust.

Recent interest in these and other topics indicates that a decades-long preoccupation with "the messianic secret in Mark" (see p. 94) is dissipating. It can no longer be regarded as the sole or even central element of Markan intention. What is clear is that Mark sets forth a narrative that in-

Study Questions

1. Who was Mark?

2. When was the Gospel of Mark most likely written?

3. Describe how Jesus' divine sonship is developed in Mark.

4. How do the "people" confirm that Jesus is the Son of God?

5. In what ways was Jesus a servant?

6. Why did Jesus command people to silence about his identity?

Summary

1. The author of the Gospel of Mark was John Mark, who worked with Peter and recorded his recollections of the life and work of Jesus.

2. The Gospel of Mark was most likely written in Rome with a Gentile audience in mind.

3. The Gospel of Mark has as its central theme the story of Jesus.

4. Mark focuses on the mystery of Jesus' divine sonship, beginning with his baptism.

5. In the Gospel of Mark, the divine reality of Jesus was apparent to everyone and everything except certain religious leaders.

6. Mark emphasizes the ministry of Jesus rather than his teachings.

7. Jesus commanded many whom he had helped or told something significant to be silent about it.

vites readers to a suffering discipleship based on Jesus' walk from baptism to the cross.

Conclusion

Mark's Gospel is a vivid portrayal of how Jesus Christ, the Son of God, accomplished the establishment of the kingdom of God. He came embodying it in all of the wonderful things he did and taught.

It was there for everyone to see. What kept it hidden from people's eyes was the hardness of their hearts. The supreme act of establishing God's kingdom was Jesus' death and resurrection. It was there that the ultimate enemies of humanity—sin and death—were conquered forever. Mark's Gospel invites readers to share the fruits of that victory by faith in the risen Son of God.

Further Reading

Recent years have seen a spate of commentaries on Mark, including studies by D. H. Juel (1990), M. D. Hooker (1991), J. Brooks (1991), P. Perkins (1995), J. Painter (1997), B. M. F. van Iersal (1998), and Joel Marcus (1999; chs. 1–8 only). The following works may also be noted:

Donahue, John R., and Daniel J. Harrington. *The Gospel of Mark.* Collegeville, Minn.: Liturgical, 2002. A readable study making use of up-to-date methods.

Edwards, James R. *The Gospel according to Mark.* Grand Rapids: Eerdmans, 2002. Informed by scholarly discussion but written at an accessible level.

France, R. T. *The Gospel of Mark.* Grand Rapids: Eerdmans, 2002. A scholarly analysis of the Greek text with attention to cultural and historical context.

Gundry, Robert H. *Mark: A Commentary on His Apology for the Cross.* Grand Rapids: Eerdmans, 1993. A definitive commentary on Mark by a contemporary evangelical scholar.

Hengel, Martin. *Studies in the Gospel of Mark.* London: SCM, 1985. Studies in various aspects of Mark's Gospel by an eminent German New Testament scholar. Rather technical in places.

Martin, Ralph P. *Mark: Evangelist and Theologian.* Grand Rapids: Zondervan, 1973. A good introduction to the study of Mark, dealing with the basic issues.

Morgan, G. Campbell. *The Gospel according to Mark.* Westwood, N.J.: Revell, 1927. An older but reliable and spiritually concerned commentary.

Nineham, Dennis E. *The Gospel of Mark.* Harmondsworth, U.K.: Penguin, 1963. A modern-style commentary, making full use of form criticism.

Schweizer, Eduard. *The Good News according to Mark.* Atlanta: John Knox, 1976. An easy-to-follow commentary by a well-known German scholar.

Stein, Robert H. Review of *The Gospel of Mark,* by John R. Donahue and Daniel J. Harrington; *The Gospel according to Mark,* by James R. Edwards; and *The Gospel of Mark,* by R. T. France. *Journal of the Evangelical Theological Society* 46, no. 2 (June 2003): 342–48. Illuminating discussion of the fruits of recent Markan scholarship.

Stonehouse, Ned B. *The Witness of Matthew and Mark to Christ.* London: Tyndale, 1944. An excellent study of Mark (and Matthew) as it relates to Jesus, especially his authority.

Telford, W. R. *The Theology of the Gospel of Mark.* Cambridge: Cambridge University Press, 1999. Attempts to locate Mark's theology in several historical contexts: the Markan community and its Greco-Roman world; the first-century church; the history of interpretation; and the contemporary setting. Reflects both strengths and weaknesses of current approaches.

Witherington, Ben, III. *The Gospel of Mark: A Socio-Rhetorical Commentary.* Grand Rapids: Eerdmans, 2001. Skillfully combines attention to historical, literary, social, and theological concerns.

6 The Gospel of Luke
A Savior for All People

Outline

- Author
- Date
- Place of Writing
- Outline
- Purpose and Characteristics
- God's Universal Work
- Jesus as Savior of the World
- Events of Jesus' Early Life
- The Place of Women in Jesus' Ministry
- The Ministry of the Holy Spirit
- Critical Issues
- Conclusion

Objectives

After reading this chapter, you should be able to

- Identify Luke's activities as a character in his own Gospel
- Outline the content of Luke
- Demonstrate the universal nature of God's dealing with the world
- List events from the early life of Jesus as presented in this Gospel
- Explain how Jesus included women in his ministry

"Seeing is believing." It's a common saying, and we are sometimes tempted to think that our modern scientific age is the most demanding ever when it comes to asking for evidence to back up beliefs. So it might surprise us to find out that the ancient world was just as demanding. Every reasonable person wanted to know what was really being asked of them when a new teaching appeared. Luke, the author of the Gospel that bears his name, spent a great deal of time and effort digging up just such evidence to present to Theophilus, the Roman official who wanted to know what Christianity was all about. The opening lines of his Gospel reveal this plainly:

Many have undertaken to draw up an account of the things that have been fulfilled among us, just as they were handed down to us by those who from the first were eyewitnesses and servants of the word. Therefore, since I myself have carefully investigated everything from the beginning, it seemed good also to me to write an orderly account for you, most excellent Theophilus, so that you may know the certainty of the things you have been taught (Lk 1:1–4).

Rather than being upset with Theophilus for wanting to know the facts, Luke did the research work necessary to assure him of the certainty, the reliability, of the things he had been taught. And not only did he do this for the life of Jesus, but he continued his work in a second volume dealing with the early church that we know as the Book of Acts (cf. Acts 1:1–2).

A look at Luke 1:1–4 shows that Luke's procedure included the following elements:

- Gathering information
- Checking evidence
- Verifying the sources—in this case, eyewitnesses and accredited servants of the Word
- Critical evaluation
- Orderly arrangement of the material

Luke could have gone into more detail, but this was enough to describe the approach he used to put together an account of Christian origins.

Author

All of the early evidence, including Irenaeus, Clement of Alexandria, Tertullian, Origen, Eusebius, and Jerome, states that Luke, the traveling-companion of the apostle Paul, was the author of this two-volume work (Luke–Acts). Even the early opponent of the church, Marcion, affirmed this, as the anti-Marcionite prologue to Luke shows. Those who reject this uniform testimony do so on what they perceive to be internal, not external evidence. They see indications of lateness in Luke's Gospel itself, arguing that it reflects a time after which Luke had died, during which conflicts rage, both theological and historical, between Acts and the letters of Paul. If Luke had really been Paul's companion, these would not have occurred. Although some of the material in Luke–Acts lends limited support to these arguments, they are far from conclusive and certainly not strong enough to outweigh

Marble tombstone of a Greek physician examining a child with a swollen belly. Luke was trained as a physician.

Luke and His Two Books

Luke, in regard to race being of those of Antioch, but by profession a physician, since he had been very much with Paul and had no mean association with the rest of the Apostles, left us examples of the therapy of souls, which he acquired from them, in two inspired books: the Gospel which he testifies that he also wrote according to what those handed down to him who were eyewitnesses from the beginning and ministers of the word, all of whom he also says he had followed even from the beginning; and the Acts of the Apostles which he composed from what he had learned, not by hearing but with [his] eyes. But men say that Paul was accustomed to refer to his Gospel whenever, writing as it were about some Gospel of his own, he said, *"according to my Gospel."*

—Eusebius (ca. A.D. 265–339)

the clear testimony of three centuries of ancient church teaching.[1]

Who then was Luke? The only reliable information comes from the New Testament itself. Luke was a well educated Gentile, a doctor and close friend of Paul (Col 4:14), one who traveled with Paul extensively and was with him near the end of his life, when Paul was apparently otherwise alone (2 Tm 4:11). The sections from the Book of Acts where Luke becomes part of his own narrative can be easily identified, because Luke switches from "they" to "we," including himself in the group (16:10–17; 20:5–21:18; 27:1–28:16). Chapters 14–16 below discuss this in more detail.

Luke is mentioned in two of the four Prison Epistles, which were probably written from ROME (Col 4:14; Phlm 24). We know nothing of Luke's whereabouts during the three or so years between Paul's first and second imprisonments in Rome, but he is with Paul at the end, just before his death (2 Tm 4:11). The fact that the Book of Acts ends with Paul's first imprisonment suggests to some scholars that Luke intended to write a third volume covering the period between that and Paul's death. Although possible, there is no concrete evidence for this.

Date

In order to fix the date when Luke was written, it is also necessary to fix the date of Acts, because they were written as a joint project, and Luke was written before Acts (Acts 1:1). It is not likely that Acts was written any later than A.D. 62 or 63, because nothing in Acts reflects a later period of time. The book ends with Paul's first stay in prison, with no date set for his trial and Rome still at peace, which would place the book before NERO's persecutions in late A.D. 64. If they had taken place Luke would most certainly have mentioned it. Because the Gospel of Luke was written earlier, it must have been completed somewhere in the late 50s or early 60s.

Those who place it later, some putting it even into the second century, do so on speculative rather than concrete grounds. One argument is that Jesus' predictions of the fall of JERUSALEM (Lk 19:43, 44; 21:20–24) are so specific that they must have been written after that event in A.D. 70. This argument assumes that Jesus could not have made such a specific projection. If Jesus could have accurately predicted the future, this argument disappears. Another argument is that Luke made use of Mark and was written roughly at the same time as Matthew. This would mean that a later Mark would require an even later Luke. But there is no reason why Mark should be dated later. Nor has it been conclusively proven that Luke used Mark in the first place. Finally, it is argued that the theology of Luke is late, reflecting a so-called early catholicism,[2] and that it would have taken time for the church to have evolved through its Jewish and Gentile phases to reach that developed compromise. But here again, why must one make this assumption? It is a highly questionable construct and can be accepted only if the historicity of Acts is completely set aside. If one does not feel compelled to do so, there is no reason to date Luke any later than the early 60s.[3]

Place of Writing

No agreement exists among scholars as to the most likely place that Luke wrote his Gospel. GREECE, CAESAREA, ALEXANDRIA, and Rome have all been suggested. The anti-Marcionite prologue suggests the Gospel was written somewhere in ACHAIA. These are all conjectures and in the end it is of little consequence where Luke wrote his Gospel. It is relatively clear, however, that wherever he wrote it, it was intended for Christians who had a pagan background. If he envisioned Jewish readers, he seems to have assumed that they would not be residents of Palestine.

Outline

There is a general consensus among scholars that Luke had a theological purpose in writing his Gospel that is reflected in the way he put his material together. The structure is as follows: prologue (1:1–4), Jesus' early years (1:5–2:52), Jesus in Galilee (3:1–9:50), Jesus en route to Jerusalem (9:51–19:27), and Jesus in Jerusalem (19:28–24:53). This structure puts emphasis on the work of Jesus as he proclaims salvation, calls to discipleship, and fulfills his destiny in Jerusalem.

I. **Prologue: A Reliable Account of Salvation History** (1:1–4)

II. **Preparation for Jesus' Ministry** (1:5–4:13)
   A. Two Births Predicted (1:5–56)
   B. Two Sons Born (1:57–2:52)
   C. The Baptist's Ministry: Preparation for the Lord (3:1–20)
   D. Jesus: Endowed by the Spirit for Ministry (3:21–4:13)

III. **Jesus Proclaims Salvation in Galilee by the Power of the Spirit** (4:14–9:50)
   A. Proclamation of Good News in Galilee (4:14–5:16)
   B. Conflict with the Pharisees (5:17–6:11)
   C. Good News for the Poor (6:12–8:3)
   D. Revelation and Obedience (8:4–21)
   E. The Revelation of Jesus' Identity (8:22–9:50)

IV. **Galilee to Jerusalem: Discipleship** (9:51–19:27)

Roman crypt at Philippi, Greece, tentatively identified as the prison from which Paul and Silas were freed after an earthquake.

Caesar Augustus
(31 B.C.–A.D.14)

Purpose and Characteristics

As we have already seen, Luke tells us his fundamental purpose in writing his Gospel. He wants Theophilus to know that faith in Jesus rests on historical facts that stand up under the most severe scrutiny, founded as they are on firsthand testimony. As Luke develops the life of Jesus to substantiate this, he makes use of numerous details and themes. Below we recount five areas of particular Lucan interest.[4]

God's Universal Work

The first distinctive characteristic of Luke is its emphasis on the universal or comprehensive nature of God's dealings with the world. Matthew traces Jesus' ancestry back to David and Abraham (Mt 1:1), the great founders of the Jewish nation. Luke traces Jesus' ancestry back to the very beginning of the human race, Adam himself, the direct creation of God (3:38).

Luke places Jesus' birth during CAESAR AUGUSTUS's reign, when QUIRINIUS was governor of SYRIA (2:1–2). The beginning of Jesus' public ministry is specifically located by seven verifiable facts: the reign of TIBERIUS CAESAR, the fifteenth year of that reign, HEROD's tetrarchy of GALILEE, PHILIP's rule of ITUREA and TRACHONITIS, LYSANIAS's tetrarchy of ABILENE, the high priesthood of Annas and Caiaphas, and the preaching of John the Baptist in the wilderness. Jesus is a part of concrete human history. Jesus' coming was for all to see and everyone was addressed by his message, even the Gentiles.

This was evident from the very first, when the angels announced that peace was for all on whom God's favor rests (2:14). Shortly thereafter Simeon speaks of Jesus as "a light for revelation to the Gentiles" (2:32). It is Luke alone who records Jesus' references to the Old Testament Gentiles who experienced the grace of God—the widow of Zarephath and Naaman the Syrian (4:25–27; see 1 Kgs 17:8–24 and 2 Kgs 5:1–14). The Queen of

The huge Basilica of the Annunciation, Nazareth, stands over the traditional site of the angel Gabriel's visit to Mary to foretell the birth of Jesus.

the South and the men of Nineveh, all Gentiles, will put Israel to shame because of their spiritual discernment (11:31–32). The hated Samaritan, not one of the Jews, is good according to Jesus' estimation in the parable given to define neighborliness (10:25–37). None of this excludes the importance of Israel (1:30–33), but it does broaden the idea of Israel's blessedness by presenting it as the means to God's mercy reaching all nations, not just Abraham's descendants.

Jesus as Savior of the World

Luke also focuses on Jesus as the Savior of the world. From the announcement of the angels (2:11) to his last appearances on earth (24:46–47) Jesus is seen as the only one who can provide forgiveness of sin and a new life (see also Acts 4:12). When Jesus began his ministry he opened the scroll of Isaiah in his home synagogue in NAZARETH and read, "The Spirit of the Lord is on me . . . to preach good news to the poor . . . to proclaim the year of the Lord's favor" (4:16–19). This was the

theme of Jesus' ministry. He was to preach the Good News and the favor of God that would be realized through his death and resurrection. Jesus went to Jerusalem for that specific purpose, after predicting on several occasions that he must die and rise again (9:22, 44; 13:32–33; 18:31–33). It is the death and resurrection of Jesus that will provide salvation for all the world.

Events of Jesus' Early Life

Luke also has a special interest in the events of Jesus' early life and of Mary, Jesus' mother. It is conceivable that Luke derived this information directly from Mary herself. He would have been in a position to do so when he was in Palestine with Paul. He could quite possibly have found Mary and talked to her about those things. It is only Luke who records the events surrounding the announcement of John the Baptist's birth and the fact that Elizabeth, John's mother, is Mary's kinswoman (1:36). Only Luke records the annunciation to Mary (1:26–38), her visit to Elizabeth (1:39–45), the Magnificat of Mary

(1:46–55), the birth and childhood of John (1:57–80), the birth of Jesus, the coming of the shepherds and the announcement of the angels (2:8–20), the circumcision of Jesus (2:21), the presentation of Jesus in the temple (2:22–24), the praise of Simeon and Anna in the temple (2:25–38), comments regarding the childhood of Jesus (2:40, 51–52), and the trip to Jerusalem when Jesus was twelve years old (2:41–50). These facts are reasonably explained by the theory that Luke had contact with Mary as he compiled the information that became his Gospel.

The Place of Women in Jesus' Ministry

A fourth emphasis in the Gospel of Luke is the place of women in Jesus' ministry.[5] Jesus is exceptional for his day in the way he treated women. He accorded them a dignity and respect that was virtually unknown among the rabbis of Palestine. All of the Gospels record how Jesus welcomed the presence of women among his followers, but Luke especially emphasizes this. He records the praise of Anna at Jesus' presentation in the temple (2:36–38) and the raising of the widow's son at Nain

(7:11–17). The Pharisee's haughty disdain of Jesus and his treatment of a sinful woman is contrasted with the penitence and love exhibited by the woman herself (7:36–50). Women played an active role in Jesus' ministry. Luke puts it this way:

> After this, Jesus traveled about from one town and village to another, proclaiming the good news of the kingdom of God. The Twelve were with him, and also some women who had been cured of evil spirits and diseases: Mary (called Magdalene) from whom seven demons had come out; Joanna the wife of Cuza, the manager of Herod's household; Susanna; and many others. These women were helping to support them out of their own means (8:1–3).

Jesus praises Mary for her desire to know spiritual things and allows her to "sit at his feet" as a learner, just like any other disciple (10:38–42). He heals a crippled woman of her infirmity (13:10–17). Only Luke and Mark record the episode of the widow who put her minute treasure into the temple collection box, which in God's eyes was vastly superior to the more extravagant offerings of the Pharisee (21:1–4; see also Mk 12:41–44). Jesus also casts women in his parables in a favorable light (13:20–21; 15:8–10; 18:1–8).

Focus 6: Jesus Chose Women

One of the realities that stands out in the minds of women as they study the life of Christ is that Jesus himself set an example with regard to their treatment and role. At many points, Christ included women not only as objects of his ministry but also as co-laborers in that ministry. The Gospel of Luke is replete with such examples.

Consider Joanna. In Luke 8:3 we learn that Joanna had been a recipient of Jesus'

healing power. She had an illness that had controlled her life; after she was healed, she decided to follow Jesus and serve him.

Joanna was a wealthy woman. Her husband, Cuza, was Herod Antipas's steward—a position of power and status. He was undoubtedly able to provide her with many luxuries. Since the women who served Jesus had a difficult life, Joanna would have had to give up

many of these material benefits. She did this gladly and gave her time, energy, and worldly goods to support Jesus' work.

Joanna was with the women at the cross and was one of the first to witness the empty tomb. Because of her faithfulness and her willingness to sacrifice her own comfortable life for his work, Joanna's ministry of service was greatly valued by Jesus.

Summary

1. Luke's procedure in writing his Gospel included: gathering information, checking the evidence, verifying the sources, evaluating critically, and arranging the material in an orderly manner.

2. All of the early evidence indicates that Luke was the author of the Gospel bearing his name.

3. The dating of Luke must be closely related to the dating of Acts.

4. Luke organized his Gospel for a theological purpose and arranged the story accordingly, starting with a prologue and then discussing Jesus' early years, his years in Galilee, his trip to Jerusalem, and his time in Jerusalem.

5. Luke emphasizes the comprehensive nature of God's dealings with the world from the beginning of the human race to the resurrection of Jesus.

6. Jesus is seen as the Savior of the world in Luke.

7. Luke gives special emphasis to Jesus' early life.

8. Luke demonstrates how Jesus treated women differently than the rabbis did.

9. The Holy Spirit plays a central role in the Gospel of Luke and continues to be emphasized in Acts.

The Ministry of the Holy Spirit

Finally, Luke shows a special interest in the work of the Holy Spirit. It is the Holy Spirit who overshadows Mary at the conception of Jesus (1:35). John the Baptist is to be filled with the Holy Spirit (1:15), as was his mother Elizabeth (1:41) and his father Zechariah (1:67). Simeon, in the temple, was guided by the Spirit as he recognized the infant Jesus as the Messiah of God (2:25–27). Jesus was to be the supreme mediator of the Holy Spirit to the world (3:16) and was endowed by the Holy Spirit in a special way at his baptism (3:22). From then on Jesus' life was characterized by the power and the presence of the Holy Spirit at work in him.

- Jesus left the scene of the baptism filled with the Holy Spirit (4:1).
- The Spirit led him into the wilderness (4:1).
- Jesus returned to Galilee in the power of the Spirit (4:14).
- Jesus began his ministry as the fulfillment of Isaiah's prophecy about the Spirit of the Lord who would anoint God's special Servant (4:18; see Is 61:1–2).
- Jesus lived his life "full of joy through the Holy Spirit" (10:21).
- Jesus promised the Holy Spirit as God's supreme gift, who will supply our deepest needs (11:13; 12:12).
- Jesus warns of the dire consequences of blaspheming the Holy Spirit (12:10).

The Book of Acts, also written by Luke, continues this emphasis on the Holy Spirit, showing how the Spirit guided the lives of the believers and empowered them for service (1:2, 5, 8, 16; 2:4, 17, 18, 33, 38, etc.).

Critical Issues

In addition to questions about author, date, and details of composition (see the beginning of this chapter), scholars have noted that Luke is dominated by theological ideas like salvation history, the Twelve and their apostleship, the Holy Spirit, and the proclamation of the kingdom. Studies suggest that Luke stresses Jesus' identity and function as a prophet and as the Son of Man (the term occurs twenty-five times in Luke) and the Son of God from start to finish (see 1:35; 22:70). The same source-critical interest found in Matthean studies is present in Lukan scholarship (see ch. 11 below). In comparison to the other Gospels, Luke underscores the centrality of prayer in the life of Jesus, a force and example which made a great impact on the early church.

Luke's affirmations, many scholars stress, are firmly based on the historical research and eyewitness testimony to which his Gospel's prologue refers.

Conclusion

Luke's Gospel focuses on history as the place where God's salvation was effected and on Jesus as God's savior. From Adam on, there is one human race and one flow of time, with all nations, Jews and Gentiles, and all people, men and women, seen as universally loved by God and prospective recipients of salvation. This does not mean that everyone and everything are identical in all respects, but it does point to a higher redeemed unity in which certain differences no longer separate. In order for this extraordinary salvation to be experienced here and now, God sent his Holy Spirit, without whom it would never have been accomplished.

Key People/Places

	Jerome
	Jerusalem
	Lysanias
Abilene	Marcion
Achaia	Nazareth
Alexandria	Nero
Caesar Augustus	Origen
Caesarea	Philip
Clement of Alexandria	Quirinius
Eusebius	Rome
Galilee	Syria
Greece	Tertullian
Herod	Theophilus
Irenaeus	Tiberius Caesar
Iturea	Trachonitis

Review Questions

1. Luke wrote an orderly account of Christ especially for _____.

2. The opponent of the church who affirmed Luke's authorship of this Gospel was _____.

3. In order to identify the date of Luke, it is essential to fix the date of _____.

4. Luke wrote to show that faith in Jesus rests on _____ _____.

5. Luke makes Jesus an essential figure in human _____.

6. It is possible that Luke may have obtained information about the early life of Jesus from _____.

7. _____ and _____ were two elderly figures who recognized the special status of the infant Jesus.

Study Questions

1. How does Luke describe his writing of his Gospel?

2. Who was Luke?

3. When was the Gospel of Luke written?

4. How does Luke emphasize the universal nature of Jesus' work?

5. What special place did women play in Jesus' ministry?

6. How is the Holy Spirit emphasized in Luke's Gospel?

Further Reading

Bock, Darrell L. *Luke.* 2 vols. Grand Rapids: Baker, 1994, 1996. A definitive evangelical commentary on the Gospel of Luke with practical as well as exegetical sections.

Bovon, François. *Luke the Theologian: Thirty-three Years of Research (1950–1983).* Pittsburgh: Pickwick, 1987. A survey of earlier studies on Luke's theology.

Caird, George B. *The Gospel of St. Luke.* Harmondsworth, U.K.: Penguin, 1963. A helpful, mildly liberal commentary dealing with contemporary issues.

Ellis, E. Earle. *The Gospel of Luke.* London: Thomas Nelson, 1966. A commentary on the Revised Standard Version text by an eminent evangelical scholar.

Evans, Craig A. *Luke.* Peabody, Mass.: Hendrickson, 1990. An easy-to-read treatment of the New International Version text by a contemporary evangelical.

Fitzmyer, Joseph A. *The Gospel according to Luke.* 2 vols. New York: Doubleday, 1981, 1985. A standard work by an eminent Roman Catholic scholar.

Gooding, David. *According to Luke: A New Exposition of the Third Gospel.* Leicester/Grand Rapids: InterVarsity/Eerdmans, 1987. A close and insightful reading stressing content and literary flow.

Green, Joel B. *The Theology of the Gospel of Luke.* Cambridge: Cambridge University Press, 1995. Stresses the narrative structure and flow along with Luke's major theological interests and intentions.

Green, Joel B., and Michael C. McKeever. *Luke-Acts and New Testament Historiography.* Grand Rapids: Baker, 1994. Lists over five hundred books and articles dealing with Luke and Acts. Each listing includes a brief but informative annotation.

Manson, William. *The Gospel of Luke.* London: Hodder & Stoughton, 1948. An older style commentary, but useful, containing much spiritual insight.

Marshall, I. Howard. *Luke: Historian and Theologian.* Rev. ed. Downers Grove: InterVarsity, 1988. While some scholars stress Luke's historical aims and others his theological agenda, Marshall argues that Luke's theology centers on "salvation," and that this salvation rests on the historical events that Luke's Gospel describes.

Nolland, John. *Luke.* 2 vols. Dallas: Word, 1989–93. Technical study dealing with the Greek text.

Stonehouse, Ned B. *The Witness of Luke to Christ.* London: Tyndale, 1951. A devout look at Luke as it relates to the person of Christ.

Taylor, G. A. *St. Luke's Life of Jesus.* New York: Macmillan, 1955. An introductory study of Luke's Gospel. Easy to follow for beginners.

Wilcock, Michael. *The Savior of the World: The Message of Luke's Gospel.* Downers Grove: InterVarsity, 1979. Well-written and easy to follow. A good place to begin the study of Luke.

7 The Gospel of John
Eternal Life through His Name

Outline

- **Author**
- **Date and Place of Writing**
- **Outline**
- **Purpose and Characteristics**
- **In the Beginning Was the Word**
  Jesus' Divine Qualities and Essence
  Jesus as Unique Divine Messenger
  Jesus' Fulfillment of Israel's and
    All Humanity's Hopes and Needs
- **The Word Became Flesh**
- **The Principle of Faith**
- **Other Themes in John**
- **Critical Issues**
- **Conclusion**

Objectives

**After reading this chapter,
you should be able to**

- Contrast John with the other Gospels
- Present the evidence for John's author-
  ship of this Gospel
- Demonstrate John's emphasis on the
  divine glory of Christ
- Illustrate how the challenge to Jesus'
  humanity was met in the Gospel of
  John
- List the beliefs a follower of Christ
  should have
- Identify the individuals John notes as
  having held these beliefs

Synoptic

A young married student once told how he met his wife for the first time in an attic. Later he changed his story: He claimed to have met her at a Bible study. Still later he seemed to change the story yet again: He reported that he and his wife first met on a couch. But in the end, all three facts were true. The Bible study was held in an attic apartment, and the man and his future wife sat next to each other on a couch. Sometimes an incident can be described in such different ways that the accounts at first sound contradictory. But upon closer examination the different perspectives complement rather than contradict each other.

This insight is useful as we continue our look at the four Gospels, this time focusing on John. The first three Gospels are called the **Synoptic** Gospels (meaning when placed in parallel columns they reveal striking similarities). They look at Jesus' life from the same perspective in certain respects. They share similar stories, chronologies, teachings, and emphases. The Gospel of John stands apart from them, if for no other reason than that at least 90 percent of it lacks direct verbal parallel in the three Synoptics. John also implies a somewhat different chronology (postulating a three-year ministry, whereas there is an apparent one-year ministry in the Synoptics). John also stresses different aspects of Jesus' teachings (Jesus' close relationship to the Father and his descent from heaven; 3:13; 5:18; 10:30; 17:5; but see Mt 11:27), and emphasizes Jesus' ministry in and around Jerusalem in a manner not found in the Synoptics. For these reasons some scholars have questioned whether John even knew of the Synoptics.

In none of this does John's Gospel contradict the Synoptics, however; rather it supplements them, giving us a richer picture than if we relied on the Synoptics alone. It must be remembered that none of the Gospels intends to give us an exhaustive picture of Jesus' life, but rather a selection that drives home the point(s) that the writer had in mind. Other secular writers of antiquity wrote this way, too. Plutarch tells us that when he wrote, he chose what was needed to make his point. Regarding those historic figures who were his subjects he says, "we . . . select from their actions all that is noblest and worthiest to know."[1] John selects, as well (as do the Synoptics), and makes the comment that if everything Jesus did were written down the world could not contain the books that would be written (20:30; 21:25).

Fishing on the Sea of Galilee. The view that John, the fisherman son of Zebedee, wrote the Fourth Gospel was held uniformly by the early Church Fathers.

internal
criticism

Christology

Author

The view that John, the son of Zebedee, one of the original twelve apostles, wrote the Fourth Gospel, was held uniformly by the early Church Fathers and for this reason became the traditional view held by the Christian church until modern times.[2] Today, however, "the traditional view that the Fourth Gospel is the work of John the son of Zebedee . . . has few supporters among critical scholars."[3] The influential modern commentary by R. Bultmann did not even discuss the subject. It simply assumed that John could not have written it. Let's look briefly at what the early church thought and the differing situation today.

The Gospel of John was known and used authoritatively from the very earliest times. This can be seen in the early papyri, IGNATIUS OF ANTIOCH (ca. 110–115), JUSTIN MARTYR (ca. 150), TATIAN, and ATHENAGORAS. Explicit references to John's authorship of the Fourth Gospel are found in THEOPHILUS OF ANTIOCH (ca. 180) and IRENAEUS (ca. 180). Irenaeus says, "John, the Disciple of the Lord, who also had leaned upon His breast [see Jn 13:13], did himself publish a Gospel during his residence at EPHESUS in Asia."[4] What is especially significant about Irenaeus's testimony is that he derived much of what he says from POLYCARP (who died in 156 when he was eighty-six years old), who was a follower of John the apostle himself and other of the apostles.[5] In reminiscing on his childhood, Irenaeus said:

> I remember the events of those days more clearly than those which have happened recently, for what we learn as children grows up with the soul and becomes united to it, so I can speak even of the place in which the blessed Polycarp sat and disputed, how he came in and went out, the character of his life, the appearance of his body, the discourse which he made to the people, how he reported his converse with John and with the others who had seen the Lord, how he remembered their words, and what were the things concerning the Lord which he had heard from them, including his miracles and his teaching, and how Polycarp had received them from the eyewitnesses of the word of life, and reported all things in agreement with the Scriptures.[6]

B. F. Westcott summarized the situation in this way: "The chain of evidence in support of the authenticity of the Gospel is, indeed, complete and continuous . . . not one historical doubt is raised from any quarter."[7]

At the present time this historical testimony is entirely discounted. The situation is described by Robert Kysar:

> The observer of current Fourth Gospel criticism is able to trace certain broad movements and tendencies. The Fourth Gospel took its origin within a "Christian school" which was related to a marginal and non-normative form of Judaism. It preserved a distinctive tradition all its own (in either oral or written form) which was at the same time related in some way to the synoptic tradition. Out of that tradition the community developed a unique theological perspective amid a struggle with the synagogue. The Johannine community was marked among other characteristics by a special concern with a Logos Christology and with a figure of the past to whom they looked as their founder. In this enigmatic document we have, it appears, a pristine example of community and Gospel.[8]

The basis for this change of attitude from the traditional view to the modern rejection of John as author of the Fourth Gospel is not historical evidence or any newly found material that casts doubt on the traditional view. In fact new evidence found (papyri, the Dead Sea Scrolls) tends to show the untenability of the more extreme modern views. As L. T. Johnson has recently noted, it is not unthinking traditionalism to link the Gospel with apostolic times.[9] The arguments used against Johannine authorship are based on **internal criticism** (e.g., the **Christology** is too developed, the Gospel is too theological and mystical, the words of Jesus are not on the same order as those in the Synoptics, the material reflects a church situation outside PALESTINE). Robert Grant argues in this fashion: "Was the author a disciple of Jesus? If the synoptics are taken as the norm for the life of Jesus . . . we may wonder how a disciple could have written as John does. . . . We conclude that the author was probably not the son of Zebedee, but a Jerusalem disciple of Jesus who wrote his gospel around the time of the Roman-Jewish War of 66–70."[10] Grant may wonder why the Synoptics and John seem so different to him, but others may wonder why that "Jerusalem disciple of Jesus" could not have been the son of Zebedee himself. That's what the early church thought. At any rate, there seems to be no necessary reason to reject the uniform testimony of the early church in favor of speculative theories on which there is no agreement, even among the critics themselves.

Date and Place of Writing

The traditional view put the writing of John's Gospel in Ephesus in the A.D. 90s. Some nineteenth-century critics put it about one hundred years later (ca. A.D. 180) on dogmatic grounds, but that has been gradually whittled down to the original date offered by the early church. As Werner Kümmel says, "The assumption that John was written probably in the last decade of the first century is today almost universally accepted."[11] Indeed, there are some who would push John farther back, to A.D. 70 or earlier.[12] Ephesus still remains the most likely place of writing, because John was located there late in life. The intimate knowledge of Palestine that the Gospel displays is due to the author's personal experience of the events described.

Outline

I. **The Prologue** (1:1–18)

II. **The Book of Signs** (1:19–12:50)
  A. The Testimony of John the Baptist (1:19–51)
  B. Jesus and the Institutions of Judaism (2:1–4:54)
  C. Jesus and the Festivals of Judaism (5:1–10:42)
  D. Foreshadowing of Death and Resurrection (11:1–12:50)

III. **The Book of Glory** (13:1–20:31)
  A. The Passover Meal (13:1–30)
  B. The Farewell Discourse (13:31–17:26)
  C. The Passion (18:1–19:42)
  D. The Resurrection (20:1–29)
  E. Conclusion (20:30–31)

IV. **Epilogue** (21:1–25)
  A. The Miracle of One Hundred Fifty-Three Fish (21:1–14)
  B. Jesus and Peter (21:15–23)
  C. Appendix (21:24–25)

Purpose and Characteristics

As is true with all the Gospels, John's goal is to paint a portrait of Jesus by drawing from what he and others witnessed (see 1 Jn 1:1–4) and shaping these recollections to convey an appropriate message. In the case of John (as in Lk 1:1–4), we have the author's own words to guide us. John is writing in order that readers might believe that Jesus is the Christ, the Son of God, and by believing have life in his name (20:31). There is a lot more to John's Gospel than this, however. In accomplishing his purposes John emphasizes a number of truths about Jesus' person and work.

In the Beginning Was the Word

The first, and most distinctive, feature of John is his emphasis on the divine glory of Christ—he is nothing less than God himself, incarnate in human flesh. This extraordinary claim pervades the entire Gospel and unfolds in literally dozens of ways. These can be placed in three major groupings: first, Jesus' divine qualities and essence; second, Jesus as unique divine messenger; third, Jesus' fulfillment of Israel's (and the Old Testament's) hopes and images, the One who is the answer to humanity's deepest needs. There is some overlap among these categories. They all ultimately coalesce in the one person Jesus Christ. But looking at them this way can help focus our attention on how John is trying to present Jesus, the One and Only Son of God, to us.

Jesus' Divine Qualities and Essence

There are a dozen or more groups of designations that emphasize Jesus' essential

The magnificent theater and marbled Arcadian Way, Ephesus. Ephesus is the most likely place of writing for John's Gospel because John was located there late in life.

deity. The arrangement below moves from the abstract to the concrete. Jesus is or embodies life (1:4; 5:21; 6:57; 11:25; 14:6), light (1:4, 5, 9; 3:19; 8:12), truth (1:14; 14:6; 18:37), glory (1:14; 2:11; 11:4; 12:41; 17:5, 24), and grace (1:14, 17) because he is the Word of God (1:1). All of these ideas have deep Old Testament roots and are divine qualities. But Jesus is more than just the embodiment of what might be called transcendent divine attributes; he is, more concretely, the *personal* expression of God as the Son (1:34, 49; 3:16–18; 3:36; 5:25, 26; 10:36; 17:1; 19:7), or the one and only Son (1:14, 18), of God himself. There might be lesser beings who qualify as God's fam-

ily; in fact, even sinful humans may become God's children by faith in Christ (1:12). But only Christ is God's eternal Son. In John's Gospel Jesus is referred to as the Son of God, but even more explicitly than this, as God the Son. Jesus is referred to as Lord (13:14; 20:28; 21:7) and God (1:1; 5:18; 10:30, 33, 37–39; 14:11; 20:28), nothing less than the One who existed before Abraham and revealed himself to Moses as the great "I AM" (8:57–58).

There is both profound unity and yet also diversity within the Divine Being. In time, this gave rise to the Christian doctrine of the **Trinity**, by which this profound truth was expressed. This unity and di-

God's Unutterable Word

But when God determined to do the things which He had purposed, He brought forth this unutterable Word, the first-born of all creation: He himself was not emptied of the Word but bringing forth [the] Word He always had consort with His Word. Hence the Holy Scriptures and all the inspired [writers] teach us [as] one of these, John says: "In the beginning was the Word, and [the] Word was with God"; showing that at the first God was alone

and the Word was in Him. Then he says: "And the Word was God; all things were made by Him, and without Him not a thing was made." Therefore, the Word, being God and proceeding by nature from God, whenever the Father of the universe determines, He sends Him to a certain place; coming He is both heard and seen; being sent by Him, He is also found in [that] place.

—Theophilus (ca. A.D. 170–180)

The "I Am" Statements of Jesus in John

I am the Bread of Life (6:35–48).

I am the Living Bread (6:51).

I am the Light of the World (8:12).

I am from above; I am not of this world (8:23).

I am the Gate for the Sheep (10:7).

I am the Good Shepherd (10:11).

I am the Resurrection and the Life (11:25).

I am the Way, the Truth, and the Life (14:6).

I am the True Vine (15:1).

Gnosticism

versity, seen as intimate personal relationship, is epitomized in John 1:18: "No one has ever seen God, but God the One and Only, who is at the Father's side, has made him known."

Jesus as Unique Divine Messenger

Jesus is presented by John as the one who finds his eternal source in God (3:31; 8:23), coming down to earth from him (3:34; 5:24; 6:38; 8:16, 18, 42; 15:21; 17:18). As such, he is the one who qualifies as a teacher come from God (3:2; 13:13–14), the true bread from heaven (6:32–33, 50, 58), the one who possesses all power (13:3), the one through whom the Holy Spirit speaks (14:26; 15:26), the one who conquers the world (16:33), the judge who raises all up at the last day (5:22, 27–30; 6:39, 54; 11:25), and the one who when his earthly mission is finished returns to his true home in heaven with God above (16:28).

Jesus' Fulfillment of Israel's and All Humanity's Hopes and Needs

The Old Testament as a prophetic book points beyond itself to the time of its fulfillment. Israel was also prophetic in this sense; it, too, looked to a fulfillment of what it was historically, as representative of humanity at large. It is with this in mind that John points to Jesus as the Messiah (1:41; 4:25–26; 7:41; 10:24–25; 11:27), the King of Israel (1:49; 18:37;

19:19), the Lamb of God (1:29, 35), the Son of Man (1:51; 3:13–14; 6:27, 53, 61; 13:31), the Prophet par excellence (4:44; 6:14; 7:40; 9:17), and the one to whom the Old Testament pointed (1:45; 5:39, 45–47; 8:56; 12:41; 19:36–37). He fulfills the mighty work of God begun in ancient times, promised and mediated through God's people. As the fulfillment of all of these promises Jesus is also the fulfiller of the larger world's dreams. He is, in fact, the Savior of the world (4:42), the one who gives eternal life (6:68; 10:28), who sets people free from sin (8:36), who is the light of the world (8:12; 9:5; 12:46) and the light of life (8:12). He becomes the gate of the sheep (10:7, 9), the good shepherd (10:14), the true vine (15:1, 5), the bread of life (6:35), the only way (14:6), and the resurrection unto life itself (11:25).

The Word Became Flesh

It is surprising to some people that it was the humanity of Jesus that was first called into question rather than his deity. This trend is already evident in a first-century document like 1 John. By the middle of the second century comparable views had developed into a strange and complex system called **Gnosticism**. But in his Gospel John says that "the Word became flesh and made his dwelling among us" (1:14), emphasizing that "he was in the world" (1:10). Throughout the Gospel of John there is an emphasis on Jesus' human nature. Jesus comes from NAZARETH (1:45), travels with his mother and brothers (2:12), asks for a drink of water in SAMARIA (4:7), crosses the Sea of Galilee in a boat (6:1), spits on the ground to make mud for a blind man's eyes (9:6), weeps over Lazarus's death (11:35), washes his disciples' feet (13:5), dies and is buried (19:30, 42), and even after the resurrection bears nail marks in his hands (20:20, 27). Jesus' incarnation (becoming human) was not a mere appearance on earth but a real entering into human life and flesh. The theological importance of this for John is that only one who was truly human could be the true redeemer of the human race. To

John points to Jesus as the Lamb of God.

- Jesus himself (3:18; 4:39; 10:42; 12:42, etc.)
- Jesus as the Son of Man (9:35–38)
- Jesus' miracles (10:38)
- Jesus as the Messiah (11:27; 20:31)
- what Jesus says (8:45–46; 14:11)
- the fact that Jesus is in the Father and the Father is in Jesus (14:10; 7:21)

While today "faith" is sometimes understood as undefined religious experience, for John it means a personal trust in Christ informed by certain facts and truths. John also wants to point out how many different people or groups of people actually believed in this way, so he mentions

- John the Baptist (1:34)
- Jesus' disciples (6:69; 16:27, 31; 17:8)
- a woman in Samaria (4:28–29)
- a group of Samaritans (4:39, 41–42)
- a royal official and his household (4:53)
- a large group in Jerusalem (7:31)
- many of the Jewish leaders (12:42)
- groups of Jews (8:31; 12:11)

It is interesting to note that the Judean religious leaders were afraid that *everyone* would believe in him (11:47–48), and that the whole world had gone after him (12:19). Looking into the future, a special blessedness is pronounced on those who will not see Jesus as his early followers did and yet will still believe in him (20:29). Jesus prays specifically for them (17:20)—and thereby for readers of John's Gospel today.

rob Jesus of his humanity—or even to diminish it in some way—would imperil his status, which he claimed for himself, as Savior and Lord.

The Principle of Faith

The principle of faith is fundamental in the Gospel of John. Faith is a dynamic activity: "believe" occurs in various verbal forms about 100 times in this Gospel while the noun "faith" is absent. Those who believe have everlasting life (3:16) and will never die (11:26); they are the children of God (1:12). Those who do not believe are condemned (3:18) and will not see life, but will experience the wrath of God (3:36). Sometimes John uses the simple term "believe" as the expression to define what God desires (4:53; 9:38), and Jesus' followers are called "believers" (4:41). But more often John defines what Christ calls people to believe in. It is an impressive list. John's readers are to believe in

- God (14:1)
- God as the one who sent Jesus (12:44)
- what the Old Testament says (2:22; 5:46–47)
- Jesus as the one sent by God (6:29)
- Jesus' name (2:23)

Other Themes in John

The Gospel of John has many other themes that flow out of the basic idea of Jesus as the divine-human Savior who was sent by God to call forth faith.[13] Some of these themes are

- The nature of eternal life
- The future resurrection of the dead
- The work of the Holy Spirit
- The special place of Jesus' miraculous signs
- The personal relation of Jesus to the believer

Focus 7: Holding Fast the Faith

On a cold November Sunday in 1994, a small group of elderly women, their heads covered with brightly colored scarves, huddled together outside a tiny church in Balabanovo, Russia. Transformed from a small house into a church, this House of Prayer was the first church building these women had known since the Bolshevik Revolution in 1917 and the subsequent repression of religion.

It was nearly thirty minutes before the service was scheduled to begin, but in spite of the bitter cold these eager women were awaiting the arrival of their pastor to unlock the door. As visitors from America approached them, a small, wizened woman began to smile. She was eager to welcome her American brothers and sisters, yet she was unable to speak English. Instead, a seemingly unending stream of Russian poured from her smiling mouth. The interpreter told the Americans that she was quoting Psalms—the Word of God she had hidden in her heart throughout the many years of trials and persecution. As she spoke, tears began to flow gently down her wrinkled cheeks as she pointed a trembling hand at the church and said, "I have waited seventy years for this!" This woman manifested a faith that had sustained her all those years. At last she was able to worship God with freedom.

The following year, this saint went to be with her Lord at the age of one hundred. She is a modern-day example of the principle of faith so fundamental to the Gospel of John.

Key Terms

Christology
Gnosticism
internal criticism
Synoptic
Trinity

Key People/ Places

Athenagoras
Ephesus
Ignatius of Antioch
Irenaeus
Justin Martyr
Nazareth
Palestine
Polycarp
Samaria
Tatian
Theophilus of Antioch

- The love of God
- The conflict of the believer with the world
- Fundamental theological principles such as light, glory, truth, and revelation

It isn't possible to develop all these themes here, but the Gospel is replete with profound truth and rewards a careful reading with rich dividends. One could spend a lifetime and not exhaust the content of the Gospel.

Critical Issues

In addition to questions about author, date, and details of composition (see the beginning of this chapter), scholars debate such issues as the background against which John should be read: Hellenistic, Jewish, or some combination of the two. Also of interest is the meaning of so much conflict in John's Gospel: Jesus' conflict with followers of John the Baptist as well as with various segments of the mainstream Jewish leaders. Even his own followers are shaky allies at times (6:64–66). John's literary integrity—was it a document shaped and reworked over time—and possible sources have provoked extensive discussion. Did he know the Synoptic Gospels, and if so, how did he use them? The evidence receives varying assessments. At present many conclude that John's testimony taps into early tradition that is parallel to what informed the Synoptics. If so, John is an independent and authoritative voice not a spiritual restatement of older Gospel documents.

Traditional scholarship focusing on history and theology in John's Gospel has given way in many quarters to rhetorical criticism. Here current theories of communication are applied to John, and the

Review Questions

1. The Gospel of John covers a period of _____ years in the life of Christ.

2. The most likely place for John to have written his Gospel is _____.

3. All the references that emphasize that Jesus is the embodiment of transcendent divine attributes have roots in the _____.

4. The fact that there is unity and diversity within the Divine Being eventually produced the Christian doctrine of the _____.

5. John's writing shows that Jesus fulfills the hopes of _____ and _____ _____.

6. The first thing that was questioned about Christ was his _____.

7. Fundamental to the Gospel of John is the principle of _____.

Study Questions

1. How is the Gospel of John different from the Synoptics?

2. Why are Irenaeus's reflections of his childhood important for understanding John?

3. How does John emphasize Jesus' divine essence?

4. How did Jesus fulfill Israel's hopes?

5. How is Jesus' humanity emphasized in John?

6. What is the importance of "faith" in John's Gospel?

---

text's message is determined by each reader who interacts with it. In this outlook creative analysis reflecting personal interest dominates. One might ask how pleased the author or the main character of John's Gospel would be with this approach and its outcomes.

Conclusion

John's Gospel is a rich document that offers salvation in an impressive array of fashions. Indeed, its fundamental purpose is to be "Gospel," that is, the Good News that we may be saved by faith in Jesus Christ. It accomplishes this by presenting Jesus as the unique divine-human person, the one who came down from God to become one with us, so that by faith in him we might be made new and return to God with him. This saving purpose of God was displayed through Jesus' life, and human redemption was accomplished through Jesus' death and resurrection. John goes on to emphasize that ultimate future redemption—bodily resurrection, a dwelling-place in the immediate presence of God, and eternal life—awaits those who respond in faith. John invites us not to look merely at what God is doing in someone else's life, but what is happening in our own: "What is that to you? You must follow me" (Jn 21:22).

Summary

1. The Gospel of John differs from Matthew, Mark, and Luke because 90 percent of it has no direct parallel with these three: It postulates a ministry of three years rather than one, it focuses on different parts of Jesus' teachings, and it emphasizes Jesus' ministry in a different manner.

2. John, the son of Zebedee, wrote the Gospel of John in the A.D. 90s in Ephesus.

3. The fact that Jesus is God incarnate in human flesh is found in passages that (a) emphasize his divine qualities; (b) focus on Jesus as God's unique divine representative; and (c) show Jesus as the fulfillment of Israel's and all humanity's hopes.

4. John emphasizes Jesus' human nature in many incidents, including (a) traveling with his mother and brothers; (b) asking for a drink of water in Samaria; (c) crossing the Sea of Galilee in a boat; (d) spitting on the ground to make mud for the blind man's eyes; (e) weeping over Lazarus's death; (f) washing his disciples' feet; and (g) dying and being buried.

5. John represents the principle of faith in his Gospel and makes clear that only those who believe in Christ will receive the gift of eternal life.

6. John notes many people who believed in Christ, starting with John the Baptist.

7. The Gospel of John has many themes but all flow out of the basic truth that Jesus is a divine and human savior who was sent by God for us to believe in and follow.

Further Reading

Beasley-Murray, G. R. *Gospel of Life: Theology in the Fourth Gospel.* Peabody, Mass.: Hendrickson, 1991. A helpful study of theological themes in the Gospel of John.

Blomberg, Craig L. *The Historical Reliability of John's Gospel.* Downers Grove: InterVarsity, 2002. Challenges the view that John is unreliable as a historical source. Since John's theology is rooted in a reported history, this book does much to uphold the Gospel's claims about Christ and his teaching.

Burge, Gary M. *Interpreting the Gospel of John.* Grand Rapids: Baker, 1992. A guide on how to understand John's Gospel.

Carson, D. A. *The Gospel according to John.* Leicester/Grand Rapids: InterVarsity/Eerdmans, 1991. An excellent, full-length commentary by a contemporary evangelical scholar.

Köstenberger, Andreas J. *John.* Grand Rapids: Baker, 2004. A recent scholarly study of the Greek text.

Ridderbos, Herman. *The Gospel of John: A Theological Commentary.* Grand Rapids: Eerdmans, 1997. A long and complex book, but it brings out the depth and texture of the Fourth Gospel's astounding claims.

Tenney, Merrill C. *John: The Gospel of Belief.* Grand Rapids: Eerdmans, 1948. A somewhat older style commentary by an eminent evangelical scholar.

Yarbrough, Robert W. *John.* Chicago: Moody, 1991. An easy-to-read, basic commentary on John.

8 Man from Galilee
The Life of Jesus Christ

Outline

- **The Gospels and the Life of Jesus**
- **Outline of Jesus' Life**
- **Jesus' Birth and Youth (6 B.C.–A.D. 26)**
- **The Beginning of Jesus' Public Ministry (A.D. 26–27)**
- **The Galilean Ministry (A.D. 27–29)**
- **Jesus' Travels outside Galilee (A.D. 29)**
- **The Perean and Judean Ministry (A.D. 29–30)**
- **Jesus' Last Days on Earth and Crucifixion (April A.D. 30)**
- **The Resurrection and Ascension of Jesus (April–June A.D. 30)**
- **The True Meaning of Jesus of Nazareth**

Objectives

After reading this chapter, you should be able to

- Write an account of Jesus' life using content from the Gospels
- Enumerate the highlights of Jesus' birth, childhood, and youth
- Trace the locations of Jesus' ministry
- Outline the final days of Jesus on earth, including the crucifixion
- Discuss the true meaning of Jesus

A census sent Mary and Joseph to Bethlehem, where Jesus was born.

The Gospels and the Life of Jesus

The New Testament Gospels are our primary source of information about Jesus. Other ancient historians such as Josephus, Suetonius, and Tacitus, as well as the Jewish Talmud, also mention Jesus and the early Christians, but, as valuable as they are, they add little to what we find in the New Testament.[1]

The world at that time had little concern about events that were taking place in a remote region like Palestine and among a conquered people like the Jews. Two thousand years of history have straightened out this indifference, however, and today it is the Roman rulers who are largely forgotten while Jesus stands out as the most extraordinary person who ever lived. Indeed, more has been written about Jesus Christ than about anyone else in history.

The Gospel writers were well aware of Jesus' significance from the very beginning. Matthew begins his Gospel by tracing the ancestry of Jesus, "who is called Christ" (Mt 1:16), back to the mighty king of Israel, David, and to the founder of that nation, Abraham (Mt 1:1). As we saw, this was in keeping with Matthew's conviction that Jesus was the founder of a new era for the people of God. He would bring the old era to completion. Luke, looking beyond the more narrow limits of Israel to the whole of world history, traces Jesus back to the very first human being, Adam, who was a direct creation of God (Lk 3:23–38). It is John who catches the ultimate significance of Jesus by tracing him back beyond recorded time to the very depths of God himself, from whom he came as the Word of God, the bearer of life and light for all humankind (Jn 1:1–5).

Although the Gospels do not provide us with enough material to construct a complete biography of Jesus in the modern sense,[2] we do have enough to draw together a life of Jesus sufficient to satisfy our need to know who he really was.[3] Various outlines have been suggested, but for our purposes, we will arrange Jesus' life under seven headings.

Suppose you want to gain an overview of the life of Martin Luther (1483–1546). As a result, you decide to read his writings. Imagine your shock at discovering that these writings, in English translation, fill nearly sixty volumes! After reading them, you would still have to do the work of piecing together the general understanding that you were looking for in the first place.

Gaining a general understanding of the life of Jesus Christ is not quite such a daunting task. For one thing, the main sources for our knowledge of his life are concise enough to fit nicely into just one book, not dozens of volumes. For another, the major focus of his life was the brief period when he ministered publicly, died on the cross, and then repeatedly appeared alive. This does not mean that figuring out all the details of Jesus' life is easy or even possible. But it does mean that we can arrive at a basic overall understanding without years of immersion in ponderous volumes crammed with footnotes and fine print.

Below we move toward gaining an overall grasp of the major sources, periods, and activities of the life of Jesus Christ. We will also attempt to summarize the meaning of his life, the most important human life ever lived, for us today.

Jesus the Wise Man

Josephus finished his book *Antiquities* in the A.D. mid-90s. In it he describes Jesus from his point of view. Some scholars doubt that he called Jesus "the Christ," but this is the text as we have it today.

Now, there was about this time, Jesus, a wise man, if it be lawful to call him a man, for he was a doer of wonderful works—a teacher of such men as receive the truth with pleasure. He drew over to him both many of the Jews, and many of the Gentiles. He was [the] Christ; and when Pilate, at the suggestion of the principal men amongst us, had condemned him to the cross, those that loved him at the first did not forsake him, for he appeared to them alive again the third day, as the divine prophets had foretold these and ten thousand other wonderful things concerning him; and the tribe of Christians, so named from him, are not extinct at this day.

—Josephus, *Antiquities* 18.3.3

Nisan

Passover

Outline of Jesus' Life

1. Jesus' Birth and Youth (6 B.C.–A.D. 26)
2. The Beginning of Jesus' Public Ministry (A.D. 26–27)
3. The Galilean Ministry (A.D. 27–29)
4. Jesus' Travels outside Galilee (A.D. 29)
5. The Perean and Judean Ministry (A.D. 29–30)
6. Jesus' Last Week and Crucifixion (April, A.D. 30)
7. The Resurrection and Ascension of Jesus (April–June, A.D. 30)

You will notice that this chronology puts the birth of Jesus at 6 B.C. and his death in A.D. 30, with a public ministry of about three and a half years.[4] The reasons for this are as follows. First, in A.D. 30 **Nisan** 14 of the Jewish calendar, the day on which Jesus died, fell on a Friday, satisfying the account of John. (The Synoptics followed another calendar.) Second, at the **Passover** when Jesus began his public ministry, the temple had been under construction for forty-six years (Jn 2:20). That temple was begun by Herod in 19 B.C., putting this in A.D. 27, and Jesus' baptism sometime before that, probably in A.D. 26. Third, Luke 3:21–23 says Jesus was about thirty years old when he was baptized and began his ministry. Putting this in A.D. 26 would take us back to 4 B.C. Since Herod died in March or April 4 B.C., Jesus' birth had to be be-fore that. How long before depends on how far one wants to stretch Luke's "about thirty years old." Putting Jesus' birth in 6 B.C. stretches it the least. Finally, there are three Passovers (2:13; 6:4; 12:1) and one unnamed feast (5:1) mentioned in the Gospel of John. Assuming that the unnamed feast was a Passover, that gives the time needed for a three and a half year ministry.

There have been other chronological schemes suggested for Jesus' life that put his birth earlier (up to 7 B.C.), make his ministry shorter (two and a half years or less), or put his death later (up to A.D. 33). Some of these have genuine merit, but the chronology suggested above answers the most questions and has the fewest diffi-culties, so it is followed here as the one most likely to be historically accurate.[5]

Jesus' Birth and Youth (6 B.C.–A.D. 26)

The story of Jesus' birth is one of the best known in all the world. Near the end of HEROD THE GREAT'S reign (37–4 B.C.) the angel Gabriel appeared to Zechariah the priest announcing the birth of John the Baptist (Lk 1:5–20). He later announced to a virgin named Mary that she, too, would bear a son, who would be the Son of the Most High and whose kingdom would never end (Lk 1:26–38). A census proclaimed by CAESAR

AUGUSTUS sent Mary and her husband Joseph from NAZARETH to BETHLEHEM, where Jesus was born. Shepherds, not kings, were the first to be told of the Savior's birth, as they were watching their flocks that night in a nearby field. A vast company of angelic beings appeared to announce Christ's coming in a blaze of glory and light. The initial terror of the shepherds became joy and praise as they heard the words, "Glory to God in the highest heaven, and on earth peace to those on whom his favor rests" (Lk 2:14 TNIV). Their reports amazed all those who heard them.

After the ancient rites of circumcision and presentation in the temple had taken place, the family returned to Bethlehem. While there, some magi, probably astrologers from MESOPOTAMIA, guided by a miraculous star and apparently their own study of the Old Testament, arrived to offer worship and gifts to Jesus.[6] They had inquired of Herod in JERUSALEM as to where the Messiah was to be born, and, being warned by God in a dream not to go back to Herod, returned home by a different route (Mt 2:1–12). Herod's response was to have all the male children two years and younger in Bethlehem killed, hoping to eliminate any possible rival. Mary and Joseph had taken Jesus to EGYPT according to instructions God gave Joseph in a dream, so Jesus escaped Herod's wrath.

After Herod's death in 4 B.C. Joseph and Mary were guided by God to take the child from Egypt back to the land of Israel—no doubt, in their minds, to live in Bethlehem again. But divine guidance led them to Nazareth, both to take them away from Herod's son and successor, ARCHELAUS (who ruled over Judea), and to fulfill prophecy as to where the Messiah would live (Mt 2:19–23; Lk 2:39).

Only one episode of Jesus' young life is recorded in the Gospels. He was twelve years old and went to Jerusalem with his family where he astounded the teachers of the law with his knowledge and wisdom. Jesus' worried parents could not fully comprehend what he meant when he said, "Didn't you know I had to be in my Father's house?" (Lk 2:41–50). In other respects Jesus grew up as any normal child would, obeying his parents and developing physically and maturing spiritually, intellectually, and socially (Lk 2:52).

This is an altogether extraordinary story. Just about every aspect of it has been subjected to intense and often negative scrutiny. None of it, however, is inherently improbable given the nature of the Gospel writers' fundamental theology. They believed that God existed and was able to act according to his own will in the world that he had made. The events described are recounted with restraint and dignity, entirely lacking any of the wild exaggerations commonly found in other ancient stories. That it should offend a secular modern outlook is certainly no surprise, but that is hardly evidence against it. Fashions change, if slowly, and with increased knowledge of ultimate things, belief in the miraculous intervention of God in our affairs might become easier again for the world at large. But whether easy to believe or not, the fact remains: The Gospels present us with the astounding claim that God himself broke into history by way of the virgin Mary's son, surrounded by both divine glory and human opposition.

The Beginning of Jesus' Public Ministry (A.D. 26–27)

All four Gospels associate Jesus with the ministry of John the Baptist, who burst on the scene in the wilderness east of Jerusalem to call people to repentance in the face of imminent divine judgment.[7] John was a striking figure reminiscent of Elijah (see 1 Kgs 17–2 Kgs 2:14), wearing camel-hair and leather clothes and living in ascetic austerity. His message was as startling as he was. Like Old Testament prophets before him he preached that the end of the age, the coming of the Messiah, and the final judgment were at hand. Traditional religious behavior and observance alone could not replace authentic obedience and love for God. John was anti-temple, anti-nationalism, and anti-establishment. Ancestral privilege alone was meaningless. What God required was repentance, confession of sin, baptism, and ethical behavior to prove one's sincerity, no matter how inconvenient that might be.

Jesus went to the Jordan River to be baptized by John in order to "fulfill all righteousness."

John recognized himself as a transitional figure who was a forerunner to the Messiah. The Messiah would gather the righteous together and would "burn up the chaff with unquenchable fire" (Lk 3:17). John saw his baptism as transitional as well. He baptized with water, but the Messiah would baptize with the Holy Spirit and fire. John gathered a group of disciples around him. In time, however, many switched their allegiance to Jesus at John's urging. He was a fearless preacher of righteousness and publicly rebuked HEROD ANTIPAS for illegally marrying Herodias, his brother's wife, as well as for other immoral behavior. For this, John was arrested, thrown into prison at MACHAERUS, and later executed by beheading as a result of Herod's drunken oath (Mk 6:14–29).

In A.D. 26 Jesus went from GALILEE to a place called BETHANY, on the eastern side of the Jordan River, to be baptized by John in order to "fulfill all righteousness" (Mt 3:15; Jn 1:19–28). With these profound words and symbolic acts Jesus was identifying with our lost human race by becoming one with our sin and offering himself to God on our behalf. He later referred to his coming death as a baptism yet to be endured (Mk 10:38; Lk 12:49–50). He began his ministry with a confession of sins that were not his own and ended his ministry with a death for sins that were not his own. John at first refused to baptize Jesus, but relented when Jesus insisted. In a profound experience of divine affirmation Jesus heard the words, "You are my Son, whom I love; with you I am well pleased," and the Holy Spirit descended on him like a dove (Mk 1:10–11).

After his baptism Jesus was led by the Holy Spirit into the wilderness, there to be put to the test by the devil. Jesus endured forty days of fasting and temptations. Three are of special significance. Jesus was tempted by Satan to turn stones into bread to relieve his hunger, to cast himself down from the heights of the temple to prove that God would preserve him, and to seek control of the kingdoms of the world by compromising his commitment through worship of him, the Tempter. Jesus knew the inner meaning of these temptations. They were designed to divert him from accomplishing God's will in God's way by substituting an alien plan. In each case Jesus found guidance and strength from the Scriptures. Satan was forced to withdraw when confronted by God's Word. Jesus would later teach his disciples to pray, "Lead us not into temptation" (Mt 6:13), having endured the worst that Satan had to offer.

Jesus returned to Galilee after the arrest of John the Baptist by way of SAMARIA,

The monastery on the Mount of Temptation. After his baptism, Jesus was led into the wilderness to be put to the test by the devil.

ration for the extensive ministry that was to follow.

The Galilean Ministry (A.D. 27–29)

It is not possible even to mention all the events that took place during the year and a half that constituted Jesus' Galilean ministry.[8] More than seventy are recorded in the Gospels. It is possible, however, to summarize what happened and to give some representative examples.

When Jesus arrived in Galilee after the Baptist's imprisonment, he immediately began to proclaim that the time of fulfillment had arrived. With the coming of the kingdom of God, the people must repent and believe the Good News (Mk 1:14–15). He began teaching in the synagogues of Galilee and, when he reached his hometown of Nazareth, he made a startling announcement. Reading from the Book of Isaiah where the coming of the Messiah is prophesied (61:1–2), Jesus stopped at the statement "to proclaim the year of the Lord's favor." After handing the scroll back to the attendant, he said, "Today, this scripture is fulfilled in your hearing" (Lk 4:16–21). Jesus was presenting himself as the fulfillment of Old Testament prophecy, the Messiah who was to come and the Savior of the world.

Jesus' preaching got a mixed reception. Many spread his fame throughout Galilee, praising him (Lk 4:14, 15), while others were furious because he seemed to be opening up the kingdom to sinners, tax collectors, and Gentiles (Lk 4:24–30).

Back in Capernaum, Jesus began gathering disciples (Lk 5:1–11), some of whom were later made special envoys called apostles. Jesus' days were filled with activity as he traveled about preaching the Good News, calling people to repentance, healing the sick, teaching, and casting out demons. Matthew summarizes it this way:

Jesus went throughout Galilee, teaching in their synagogues, preaching the good news of the kingdom, and healing every disease and sickness among the people [and driving out demons, Mk 1:39]. News about him

where he stopped at SYCHAR to talk to a woman about spiritual worship (Jn 4:23, 24). He ultimately settled in CAPERNAUM, making it the center of his Galilean ministry.

The period of time between Jesus' baptism and John's arrest by Herod was an important one for Jesus. During this time, which lasted about a year, he worked out his basic understanding of a spiritual ministry, which was based on faith in God and included ministering to the needs of people by doing good to them and healing them. The message that Jesus developed included announcing the arrival of the kingdom of God. He issued a call to repentance and faith in himself as Messiah. He gathered disciples around him but in this early period of his ministry had not yet made any formal calls to apostleship, nor had he sent anyone out on preaching missions. It was, in fact, a time of prepa-

spread all over Syria, and people brought to him all who were ill with various diseases, those suffering severe pain, the demon-possessed, those having seizures, and the paralyzed, and he healed them. Large crowds from Galilee, the Decapolis, Jerusalem, Judea and the region across the Jordan followed him (4:23–25).

The Gospel writers make no attempt to record every healing that Jesus performed. They rather recount examples of the various kinds of diseases or other maladies that Jesus healed: lameness (Jn 5:2–47); paralysis (Lk 5:17–26); leprosy (Mk 1:40–45); fever (Mk 1:29–31); deformity (Mk 3:1–6); muteness (Mt 12:22–30); hemorrhage (Mk 5:25–34); blindness (Mt 9:27–31); and many more.

In addition to Jesus' power over disease, he was also in control of his surroundings and capable of performing astounding miracles, such as raising the dead (Lk 7:11–17), commanding a storm to cease (Mk 4:36–41), walking on water (Mt 14:23–33), and feeding over five thousand people with a few loaves of bread and fewer fish (Lk 9:10–17).

Another outstanding feature of Jesus' ministry was his triumph over the evil forces of Satan and the demons. Whenever the demons saw Jesus they cried out in terror, knowing their destruction had come. Many examples are given in the Gospels, but perhaps the most outstanding took place across the lake at Gergesa (Mk 5:1–20).

Jesus apparently made regular circuits preaching and teaching. On occasion he delivered lengthy discourses like the Sermon on the Mount (Mt 5–7). He seems to have had the goal of reaching all of Galilee with the Good News of the kingdom of God, and at one point sent out his twelve apostles on a preaching mission to cover territory he might not reach (Mt 10:1–42). When he was not going out to the people with the power of God, the people found a way to come to him. Sometimes this hectic pace forced Jesus to withdraw so that he could commune alone with his heavenly Father (Mk 1:35–38). Jesus recognized that there were times when his overworked followers needed rest, too (Mk 6:30–32). Even at these times, however, Jesus' compassion was stirred, and he found ways, sometimes miraculously, to meet their needs (Mk 6:34–44).

One would think that all of Jesus' kind and generous acts would get him nothing but praise—and many people did praise him—but not everyone was happy with what was going on. It comes as something of a surprise to read of how hostile the religious leaders were toward Jesus. They never seemed to tire of criticizing him, attempting to trip him up in some state-

Why Jewish Leaders Opposed Jesus

1. Their jealousy—He was accepted readily by common people.
2. His authority—He taught with authority that superseded theirs.
3. Perceived recklessness—He made messianic claims which Roman rulers might interpret as treasonous.
4. His liberal attitudes—He simplified the law and rejected established customs.
5. His social practices—He associated with the wrong people.
6. His lack of rabbinic education—He was not educated under a recognized teacher.
7. Their embarrassment—He publicly contradicted them.
8. His power—He did miraculous work they couldn't.
9. Their political fears—He was neutral regarding Roman rule.
10. His call for repentance—He denied their righteousness.
11. His knowledge—He won debates by referring to Scripture.
12. His popularity—Large numbers of people traveled to hear him.

eral important things. First, he set an example for them by embodying what he taught. In this way, they could see what they would have to do. Second, he established organization by gathering disciples and appointing twelve as apostles over them. By selecting twelve, he was drawing a parallel between the work of God in the Old Testament (the twelve tribes of Israel were chosen by God) and his own work in the New Testament. Third, Jesus sent his apostles on a preaching mission so they could get the experience they would need when the time came for them to do it alone. Fourth, he sent them out endowed with his own power and authority. Nothing would be able to resist them as long as they relied on the strength that he would provide. Finally, he went to great lengths to teach them the things they would need to know for their future ministry.

It was difficult for them to take it all in. At times, they woefully misunderstood what Jesus was saying and doing. But after his death and resurrection, they remembered and went on to establish the church that has endured until this day.

This phase of the Galilean ministry ended after the Passover of A.D. 29 when Jesus became embroiled in two major conflicts—one with the fickle crowd that wanted to make him a king because he had fed them in the wilderness, and the other with the religious leaders over some questions of ritual law. This latter conflict heated up to such a degree that the Jewish authorities in Judea began devising ways to take Jesus' life (Jn 7:1).

ment, arguing with him, falsely accusing him, trying to stir the crowd up against him, and, in general, trying to discredit his ministry. There were, no doubt, many reasons for this animosity, ranging all the way from simple jealousy at his popularity to a sense of threat because of his extraordinary power. Jesus knew that doing what was right did not always bring praise and predicted persecution for his followers as they sought to live in the kingdom of God (Mt 5:10–12).

During all this time, Jesus was training his followers for what was to come.[9] There would come a time when he was no longer with them. They would have to carry on without his physical presence. In order to accomplish this, Jesus did sev-

Jesus' Travels outside Galilee (A.D. 29)

Jesus now left Galilee and traveled in a northwesterly direction toward TYRE, an ancient Phoenician city about forty miles from Capernaum, trying to keep his whereabouts a secret. However, a Greek woman found Jesus, and her extraordinary faith moved him to heal her daughter of demon possession. Jesus continued his journey through that area, going back to DECAPOLIS, near the Lake of Galilee. His presence could not be concealed for long. Matthew summarizes the situation this way: "Great crowds came to him, bringing the lame, the blind, the crippled, the mute and many others, and laid them at his feet; and he healed them. The people were amazed when they saw the mute speaking, the crippled made well, the lame walking and the blind seeing. And they praised the God of Israel" (15:30–31).

After feeding a crowd of four thousand in a manner similar to the miraculous feeding of the five thousand, Jesus and his disciples departed northward for the pagan city of CAESAREA PHILIPPI, center of the ancient worship of the god Pan. It was here that Jesus clarified for his disciples

exactly who he was and what his mission on earth was to be. He began by asking them who people thought he was. Peter, speaking for the group, said, "You are the Christ, the Son of the living God" (Mt 16:16). Jesus then explained what he, the Messiah, the Son of God, must do, in words that startled them all: "The Son of Man must suffer many things and be rejected by the elders, chief priests and teachers of the law, and . . . must be killed and after three days rise again" (Mk 8:31). This so contradicted their ideas of messiahship that Peter actually began to rebuke Jesus. Peter was, in turn, rebuked by Jesus

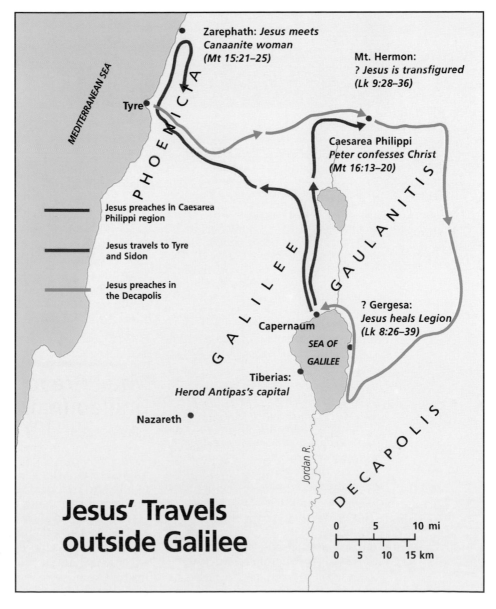

Zarephath: *Jesus meets Canaanite woman* (Mt 15:21–25)

Mt. Hermon: *? Jesus is transfigured* (Lk 9:28–36)

MEDITERRANEAN SEA

Tyre

PHOENICIA

Caesarea Philippi *Peter confesses Christ* (Mt 16:13–20)

—— Jesus preaches in Caesarea Philippi region

—— Jesus travels to Tyre and Sidon

—— Jesus preaches in the Decapolis

GALILEE

GAULANITIS

? Gergesa: *Jesus heals Legion* (Lk 8:26–39)

Capernaum

SEA OF GALILEE

Tiberias: *Herod Antipas's capital*

Nazareth

Jordan R.

DECAPOLIS

Jesus' Travels outside Galilee

0   5   10 mi

0 5 10 15 km

Jesus took his closest disciples up a high mountain (probably Mount Hermon), and there he was transformed in their presence.

for playing Satan's role; Jesus told the disciples what discipleship should mean to them:

> If anyone would come after me, he must deny himself and take up his cross and follow me. For whoever wants to save his life will lose it, but whoever loses his life for me and for the gospel will save it. What good is it for a man to gain the whole world, yet forfeit his soul? Or what can a man give in exchange for his soul? If anyone is ashamed of me and my words in this adulterous and sinful generation, the Son of Man will be ashamed of him when he comes in his Father's glory with the holy angels (Mk 8:34–38).

A few days after that profound revelation, Jesus took his closest disciples up to a high mountain (probably Mount Hermon) and there, while he was praying, he was transformed in their very presence. The inner divine glory of Jesus flashed forth with the brightness of lightning, and he was seen speaking of his coming departure from this earth with two great saints of old, Moses and Elijah. It was all brought to an end when, for a second time, God himself spoke from a cloud saying, "This is my Son, whom I have chosen; listen to him" (Lk 9:35).

While traveling again southward through Galilee toward Capernaum, Jesus continued to teach his disciples about his coming death and resurrection in Jerusalem (Mk 9:30–31), but it was too much for them to digest. An argument arose as to which of Jesus' followers was to be the greatest. In the house back in Capernaum, Jesus admonished them to become like little children and to give up their claims to greatness so that they could be genuinely great in the kingdom of God. Jesus continued to teach them about humility, forgiveness, and service.

The Perean and Judean Ministry (A.D. 29–30)

In the fall of A.D. 29, Jesus knew that the time had arrived for him to go to Jerusalem to fulfill the purpose of his life, which was to die and rise again for the sins of the world. He started out through Samaria but was refused hospitality at the border. He took the longer route, crossing the Jordan River and then traveling south through PEREA. On the way, Jesus stressed with a new urgency the cost of discipleship to his

Feast of
Tabernacles

followers. It could include the loss of comfort, forgoing natural human affections, and costly endurance.

When Jesus arrived in Jerusalem for the **Feast of Tabernacles** in October of A.D. 29, he healed a man who had been born blind. Rather than causing the rulers to rejoice, the healing led to a series of disputes because it had not happened under their auspices. However, the man's commonsense reply of "I was blind but now I see!" (Jn 9:25) was impossible for them to oppose.

Jesus then traveled into Perea and at one point sent out seventy-two of his followers in groups of two (Lk 10:1–24), just as he had sent out the twelve apostles earlier, to preach the gospel and cast out demons. In this way, many more people could be reached and many more trained in the remaining months of his life on earth than if he had tried to do it all by himself.

Jesus returned to Jerusalem in December for the Feast of Dedication. He presented

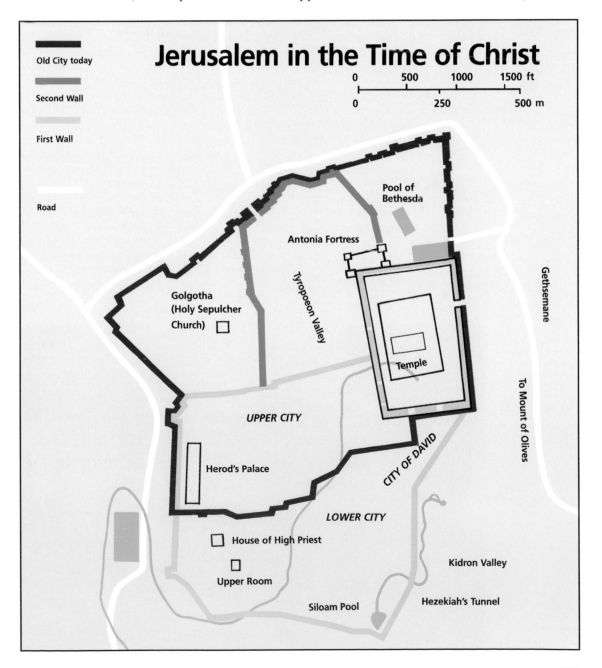

Jerusalem in the Time of Christ

Old City today

Second Wall

First Wall

Road

Pool of Bethesda

Antonia Fortress

Golgotha (Holy Sepulcher Church)

Tyropoeon Valley

Gethsemane

Temple

UPPER CITY

To Mount of Olives

Herod's Palace

CITY OF DAVID

LOWER CITY

House of High Priest

Upper Room

Kidron Valley

Hezekiah's Tunnel

Siloam Pool

himself as the good shepherd and, in defense of that, appealed to the good works he had been doing. After that, he retreated again to Bethany beyond the Jordan where John had baptized before (Jn 10:40). After teaching the people there, Jesus traveled throughout Judea extensively during the winter of A.D. 29–30. Luke alone describes this period of time in extended fashion (Lk 11:1–18:17). While on this preaching mission, Jesus traveled from village to village (Lk 13:22) with large crowds following him (Lk 11:29; 12:1; 14:25), teaching in the synagogues (Lk 13:10), eating with prominent Pharisees (Lk 11:37; 14:1), and welcoming tax collectors, sinners, and even little children (Lk 15:1; 18:15).

Jesus' message at this time covered the cost of discipleship (Lk 9:57–62; 14:25–33), the importance of salvation (Lk 14:15–24; 15:1–32), the joy of life in the kingdom of God (Lk 12:22–34), the nature of prayer (Lk 11:1–13; 18:1–8), humility (Lk 14:1–14; 18:9–14), the evils of hypocrisy (Lk 11:39–52; 12:1–3), the future coming of the kingdom (Lk 12:54–59; 17:20–37), and much more.

Jesus continued his healing ministry during this time. In many ways, it resembled the days of Galilee when large crowds gathered and were healed (Mt 19:2). He restored sight to the blind (Mt 20:29–34; Jn 9:1–41), cured lepers (Lk 17:11–19), healed a man with dropsy (Lk 14:1–4), and restored a crippled woman's health (Lk 13:10–17). The fierce opposition of the Pharisees only increased when Jesus refused to abide by many of their ceremonial practices (Lk 11:37, 38, 53; 13:14; 14:1, 6; 15:1–2). Jesus knew what was in store for him in Jerusalem (Lk 12:49–50; 13:32–35) but moved steadily in that direction as Passover drew closer.

Among the most memorable events of this time was Jesus' raising of Lazarus from the dead (Jn 11:1–44). Lazarus was the brother of Mary and Martha. All three were close friends of Jesus. They lived in Bethany just east of Jerusalem beyond the Mount of Olives. Jesus was away when Lazarus died, intentionally not returning for four days so that the miracle would be seen for the astounding thing that it was. Jesus used the occasion to teach his disciples that he was the source of all resurrection and life, as well as to express his true humanity by weeping at Lazarus's graveside. News of this remarkable event spread quickly to Jerusalem, where the Jewish rulers intensified their plot to take Jesus' life (Jn 11:53). They reasoned that if he kept doing such extraordinary things, everyone would believe in him and the Romans might interpret Jesus' growing popularity as open revolt (Jn 11:47–48).

A Franciscan church marks the supposed site of Jesus' raising of Lazarus at Bethany.

After Jesus' last Passover meal, he led his disciples to the Garden of Gethsemane, east of Jerusalem.

After this, Jesus left Bethany and retired northward to Ephraim, on the edge of the wilderness (Jn 11:54). He then made a circuit through Samaria to the border of Galilee, east to Perea, south to JERICHO, and back to Bethany, where he was greeted by Mary in a lavish display of devotion during a banquet given in his honor (Jn 12:1–8).

Jesus' Last Days on Earth and Crucifixion (April A.D. 30)

On the Sunday before Passover in April A.D. 30, Jesus presented himself to the city of Jerusalem as the Promised One of God, the Messiah, by riding into Jerusalem in triumph to the acclaim of the crowd. He was hailed as the Son of David, the One who comes in the name of the Lord, the fulfillment of prophecy (Mt 21:1–11). Upon entering the city, Jesus again denounced the money changers' activity of turning God's house of prayer into a common marketplace (Mk 11:15–18).

The next few days were spent in con-flicts with the authorities who were trying to trap him in his words in order to discredit him in the eyes of the crowd. He also continued to prepare his followers for what was to come (Mk 11:27–12:40).

Events moved quickly. On Thursday plans were made for Jesus' last Passover meal with his disciples (Mk 14:12–16). Judas, who was also at this meal, had already made arrangements with the Jewish leaders to betray Jesus to them. At the meal, Jesus established what was to become "the Lord's Supper," perhaps the most important celebration of the church. Jesus drew upon the prophecies of Jeremiah (31:31–34) concerning the new covenant that God would make with his people and solemnly pointed out that the time had arrived. His blood about to be shed was the blood of the covenant, symbolized by the wine, and his body about to be broken was symbolized by the bread (Mt 26:26–29). During the course of the meal, Judas, the betrayer, departed and Peter's coming failures were predicted. Jesus also used this occasion to instruct his disciples in matters relating to himself and what was to come in some of the most memorable passages of the Bible (Jn 14–17). He concluded with a prayer of intercession for them, after which they departed for the Garden of Gethsemane.

129

Jesus' Seven Last Statements from the Cross

1. *"Father, Forgive them, for they do not know what they are doing."* (Lk 23:34)

2. (To Mary) *"Woman, here is your son"*; (to John) *"Here is your mother."* (Jn 19:26–27)

3. (To the criminal on the cross) *"I tell you the truth, today you will be with me in Paradise."* (Lk 23:43)

4. *"I am thirsty."* (Jn 19:28)

5. *"My God, my God, why have you forsaken me?"* (Mt 27:46; see Ps 22:1)

6. *"It is finished."* (Jn 19:30)

7. *"Father, into your hands I commit my spirit."* (Lk 23:46)

Opposite: Detail from *Ecce Homo*, by Richard Westall. The painting, presented by King George IV, hangs in All Souls Church, Langham Place, London.

It was late in the evening when Jesus entered the garden, a park-like area. While his disciples kept nodding asleep, he agonized in prayer over his coming death. In his humanity, he cried out for release from the coming ordeal, knowing that it was not just death that awaited him, but a desolate death in which God's wrath would be poured out on him. But in his commitment to the will of God for the salvation of the lost, he concluded these prayers with a thrice-repeated "Your will be done" (Mt 26:36–45).

At that point Judas arrived with the temple police and pointed Jesus out to them by greeting him with a kiss (Mk 14:43–46).

Jesus was taken to a complex building known as the high priest's house where he was interrogated by Annas, the former high priest and father-in-law of Caiaphas, the current high priest.[10] Annas was able to ascertain nothing, so he sent Jesus to Caiaphas. Much false testimony was offered, but it was not until asked by the high priest, "I charge you under oath by the living God: Tell us if you are the Christ, the Son of God?" that Jesus broke his silence. He said, "Yes, it is as you say . . . and in the future you will see the Son of Man sitting at the right hand of the Mighty One and coming on the clouds of heaven" (Mt 26:64). Jesus was declared worthy of death for uttering such blasphemy. By the time daybreak approached, the whole Sanhedrin had gathered together and Jesus again acknowledged that he was the Son of God. While all this was going on, Peter, who had made his way into the courtyard, denied at least three times that he ever knew Jesus, and, catching Jesus' eye, fled from the scene weeping bitterly (Mt 26:69–75).

Early on Friday morning, Jesus was taken to the palace of Pilate, who was told that Jesus was a dangerous criminal who subverted the nation, opposed paying taxes to Caesar, and claimed to be a king (Lk 23:1–2). In a private interview with Jesus, Pilate could find no basis for a charge against him. When Pilate told this to the assembled Jews, they raised a stir and insisted that he was causing riots all the way from Galilee to Jerusalem (Lk 23:5, 14). Hearing the word "Galilee," Pilate sent Jesus to Herod Antipas, who ruled in Galilee and was in town for the festival. Herod, wanting to stay out of the affair, sent Jesus back to Pilate, who again insisted that he found no basis for the charges against him.

Pilate made an effort to have Jesus freed by offering to release a prisoner, but when given the choice between Jesus and the prisoner, a murderer named Barabbas, the Jews chose Barabbas for release instead (Lk 23:18–19). Pilate then had Jesus brutally flogged, perhaps hoping to evoke pity on the part of the crowd, but they kept shouting, "Crucify him!" When the Jewish leaders insisted that Jesus should die because he claimed to be the Son of God, Pilate became afraid, perhaps thinking it could be true. So Pilate redoubled his efforts to get Jesus released (Jn 19:8–12). When the Jews threatened to expose Pilate as being no friend of Caesar if Jesus were released, he relented, washed his hands of the whole affair, and delivered Jesus over to be crucified (Mt 27:24; Jn 19:12–16).

Jesus was taken to the execution grounds called Golgotha, where he was nailed to a cross. Two convicted criminals were crucified along with him. A sign was put above Jesus' head that read, "Jesus of Nazareth, the king of the Jews," and Jesus' clothing was divided among the soldiers. It was 9:00

in the morning when he was crucified. His first words from the cross were a prayer of forgiveness for his torturers (Lk 23:34). Jesus suffered the agonies of dying for six hours. At noon, a mysterious darkness shrouded the earth until Jesus died with a dramatic suddenness at 3:00 P.M., after crying out in quick succession, "My God, My God, why have you forsaken me? It is finished," and "Father, into your hands I commit my spirit." At that point an earthquake shook the earth, split rocks in half, and tore the curtain in the temple that separated the holiest place from the rest of the building in two from top to bottom (Mt 27:51). And so Jesus died, offering his life in payment for our sins, just as he said he must do.

Because the Sabbath was approaching (the next Jewish day began at 6:00 P.M.) the legs of the two criminals were broken to hasten their death. Jesus' side was pierced with a spear to ensure that he was dead. Joseph of Arimathea requested the body from Pilate and he, together with Nicodemus, prepared the body of Jesus for bur-

ial and laid it in an unused tomb in a nearby garden (Jn 19:31–42). A Roman seal was then placed on the tomb and guards were posted to protect it (Mt 27:62–66).

The Resurrection and Ascension of Jesus (April–June A.D. 30)

Early Sunday morning, the women who followed Jesus went to the tomb to anoint his body, but were surprised to find the tomb empty and to be told by a shining angel, "Don't be alarmed. You are looking for Jesus the Nazarene, who was crucified. He has risen! He is not here. See the place where they laid him" (Mk 16:6). They ran to tell the apostles. Quickly Peter and John verified that the tomb was indeed empty.

That first Easter Sunday, Jesus made several appearances to his followers, beginning with Mary Magdalene (Jn 20:10–18) and the other women (Mt 28:8–10). Far-

Focus 8: The Life of a Liberator

You've probably never heard of Agnes Gonxha Bojaxhiu (1910–97), the daughter of an Albanian grocer—but in fact you have, if you've heard of Mother Teresa. The service of this Roman Catholic nun to lepers, the blind, and others in Calcutta, India, made her name legendary in her own lifetime. Her identity is known, finally, by the life she lived.

You may also think you have never heard of Joshua ben Joseph. But you have, because that is one rendering of the Semitic name of Jesus. Like Mother Teresa, his life is famous because of what he accomplished.

The list of his accomplishments is enormous. African theologian Malcolm McVeigh points to several major outcomes of Jesus' life. One is liberation from sin. (The Hebrew word Joshua, *Iesous* or Jesus in Greek, means "the LORD is salvation"; see Mt 1:21.) Another is liberation from enslaving social conditions. A third is liberation from evil forces thought to lie behind life's setbacks and tragedies, like sickness and death.

"Liberation theology" has been too critical of earlier forms of Christian expression and too uncritical of totali-

tarian socialism. But it has been useful in calling attention to Jesus' role as liberator.

Jesus' life is the story of a man who came to set people free from whatever stands between them and unfettered worship of God. Mother Teresa helped lessen suffering for some in one city of India for a few decades. By his life, her master Jesus established a kingdom that liberates lives and transforms circumstances both now and forever.

Key People/ Places

Key Terms

Feast of Tabernacles
Nisan
Passover

Archelaus
Bethany
Bethlehem
Caesar Augustus
Caesarea Philippi
Capernaum
Decapolis
Egypt
Emmaus
Galilee
Herod Antipas
Herod the Great
Jericho
Jerusalem
Machaerus
Mesopotamia
Nazareth
Perea
Samaria
Sychar
Tyre

ther away on the road to EMMAUS, west of Jerusalem, two of Jesus' followers were despondently returning home when Jesus made himself known to them, expounding the Scriptures and explaining the reason why he had to die (Lk 24:13–32). They hastily returned to Jerusalem to tell the assembled apostles that they had seen the risen Lord and to confirm that he had also appeared to Peter (Lk 24:33–35). Jesus then appeared to the same group, minus Thomas who was away at the time, and pronounced peace on them (Lk 24:36–43). Thomas would not believe until Jesus appeared to the group a second time a week later (Jn 20:26–31).

During the next few weeks Jesus continued to make appearances, both in Galilee and in Jerusalem, to small groups and large (Mt 28:16–20; Jn 21:1–24; Acts 1:3–8; 1 Cor 15:6–7).[11]

When the time came for Jesus to be received back into heaven, he pronounced a benediction on the disciples and disappeared heavenward out of their sight, with a promise to return (Lk 24:50–53; Acts 1:9–11).

Review Questions

1. Besides the New Testament, ancient sources that mention Jesus include _____, _____, _____ and the _____.

2. Jesus lived from 6 B.C. to A.D._____.

3. After the death of Herod the Great, Jesus' parents took him back to _____, where he grew up.

4. The only event of Jesus' childhood that is recorded occurred when he was _____ years old.

5. Jesus was baptized by John the Baptist on the east side of the Jordan River at _____.

6. Jesus' triumph over evil was seen with the destruction of _____.

7. Jesus knew that doing what is right did not always bring _____, and he predicted _____ for his followers.

8. Jesus disclosed to his disciples his true identity and the nature of his mission at the city of _____.

9. Jesus returned for the Feast of Tabernacles, the Feast of Dedication, and Passover to the city of _____.

10. Charges were brought against Jesus to Pilate and Herod by the _____.

The True Meaning of Jesus of Nazareth

This is the story of Jesus as it is remembered in the four Gospels in the New Testament. From it, Christian believers have taken strength for the past two thousand years. No one pretends to understand it fully, but certain things do stand out as of supreme importance if we are to comprehend it at all. The first is the uniqueness of Jesus. He is not just another religious leader, equal to or even better than Mohammad, Buddha, or Moses. He is in a class by himself. The early believers could find no better way to describe him than to call him "King of kings and Lord of lords," indeed, God himself. Though unalterably monotheistic, they felt justified in doing this because Jesus had made such claims himself and the only Jesus they remembered was the Jesus who taught them with absolute authority, as never a mere man spoke.

Second, the story of Jesus is supernatural from beginning to end. Any attempt to remove this element from the accounts destroys them entirely. The story abounds with references to God, angels, demons, Satan, miraculous events, divine healings, the Holy Spirit, and the eternal dimension breaking into time. The very fabric of all four Gospels consists of the many singular occurrences in Jesus' life, such as the virgin birth, his transfiguration, his resurrection from the dead, and his ascension to heaven. These are not ancient myths, but historical realities, the foundation on which the Christian faith is built. Take these away and there is no Christian faith left. Without them it is also impossible to account for the undeniable effects of Jesus in history at that time and since.

Third, there is the challenge to us to believe and the command of Jesus to follow him. This is not easy for us today, any more than it was for the original followers of Jesus. They came to realize the truth of who Jesus was and what he said only as they responded in a positive way. To those who had, more was given. A negative response brought only more doubt and darkness. But either way, the call to follow and the challenge to believe remain. If we step out in faith we will become new people in the same way that those who knew Jesus while he was on earth were transformed when they yielded their

Study Questions

1. Look up the references related to the chronology of Jesus' life and work out for yourself what you think it should be.

2. Reconstruct for yourself the events that preceded and surrounded the birth and early years of Jesus.

3. Discuss the ministry of John the Baptist as Jesus' forerunner.

4. How did Jesus prepare his followers to continue on after he was gone?

5. What are the major elements of Jesus' ministry in the north (Galilee and travels outside Galilee)?

6. Discuss Jesus' Perean and Judean ministry.

7. Recount in detail the events of Jesus' last thirty-six hours on earth.

8. Work out a sequence of events from Jesus' burial to his ascension.

9. Write a brief essay on the miraculous elements of Jesus' life (miracles, healings, expulsion of demons).

10. What do you think is Jesus' true significance?

hearts to him. There is no other way to find out who he really is.

Fourth, the story of Jesus tells us that death is not the end of anything, but for Christ's followers the beginning of a glorious new existence. Just as Jesus broke the power of the grave, so will death's power over us be broken as we believe in him. He challenged Martha with this question, "I am the resurrection and the life. He who believes in me will live, even though he dies; and whoever lives and believes in me will never die. Do you believe this?" (Jn 11:25–26). These are extraordinary words, but that is the promise. Because Jesus lives, those who trust him will live forever with him.

Finally, all the above is true because the final point is true—that Jesus is alive and promises to be with us now and to the end of the age. What more could anyone ask? The same Jesus who walked on Galilee's shores, healed the sick of their diseases, forgave sinners of their transgressions, and performed extraordinary miracles of power is the Jesus who is with us today.

Summary

1. The New Testament Gospels provide the primary source of information about Jesus.

2. The story of Jesus' birth is presented in the Gospels, but only one incident about his childhood is recorded.

3. Jesus is linked with the ministry of John the Baptist in all of the Gospels.

4. Jesus' ministry in Galilee lasted a year and a half, and more than seventy events from it are recorded in the Gospels.

5. Jesus trained his followers for the future by setting an example for them, by gathering disciples with twelve apostles to lead them, by sending them on preaching missions to gain experience, by sending them out with his own power, and by teaching them things they needed to know.

6. Jesus presented himself as the Messiah to the city of Jerusalem on the Sunday before Passover in April A.D. 30.

7. Jesus was sent to Pilate, Herod Antipas, and back to Pilate before he was taken to Golgotha to be crucified.

8. After the resurrection on the first Easter, Jesus appeared to Mary Magdalene, the other women, two followers on the road to Emmaus, Peter, and the apostles who were assembled in Jerusalem.

9. The story of Jesus is uniquely supernatural; it challenges us to believe and commands us to follow him, and it teaches us that death is not the end but rather the beginning of a new existence.

Further Reading

Blomberg, Craig L. *Jesus and the Gospels.* Nashville: Broadman & Holman, 1997. An excellent textbook for advanced study of Jesus and his teachings.

Bock, Darrell L. *Studying the Historical Jesus.* Grand Rapids/Leicester: Baker/Apollos, 2002. A clear and well-informed assessment of sources and methods used in critical study of Jesus and the Gospels.

Bockmuehl, Markus. *This Jesus: Martyr, Lord, Messiah.* Edinburgh: T & T Clark, 1994. A helpful book that answers the question, "which Jesus?" with the answer, "Lord and Messiah."

Bornkamm, Günther. *Jesus of Nazareth.* New York: Harper & Row, 1970. The definitive life of Jesus written by a neo-orthodox proponent of the "New Quest."

Bruce, F. F. *Jesus and Christian Origins outside the New Testament.* Grand Rapids: Eerdmans, 1974. A careful study of what can be known of Jesus outside what the New Testament says. Establishes the full historicity of Jesus.

————. *Jesus: Lord and Savior.* Downers Grove: InterVarsity, 1986. A very helpful and easy-to-read book on the life of Jesus and an interpretation of who he is.

Drane, John W. *Jesus and the Four Gospels.* San Francisco: Harper & Row, 1979. A fine survey of Jesus' life, suitable for beginners.

Green, Joel B., Scot McKnight, I. Howard Marshall, eds. *Dictionary of Jesus and the Gospels.* Downers Grove: InterVarsity, 1992. The standard evangelical dictionary that deals with all aspects of Jesus' life and times.

Green, Michael. *The Empty Cross of Jesus.* Downers Grove: InterVarsity, 1984. A careful study of the death and resurrection of Jesus.

Marshall, I. Howard. *The Origins of New Testament Christology.* 2nd ed. Downers Grove: InterVarsity, 1990. An excellent treatment of who Jesus really was by a well-known evangelical scholar.

Meyer, B. F. *The Aims of Jesus.* London: SCM, 1979. A difficult but excellent book on who Jesus was and what he wanted to accomplish.

Morgan, G. Campbell. *The Crises of the Christ.* Grand Rapids: Kregel, 1989. An evangelical treatment of Jesus' life, looking at seven major crises in which his uniqueness shone forth.

Prat, Ferdinand. *Jesus Christ: His Life, His Teachings and His Work.* Milwaukee: Bruce, 1963. A full-length life of Jesus from a conservative Roman Catholic perspective.

Scroggie, William Graham. *A Guide to the Gospels.* Old Tappan, N.J.: Revell, 1948. Still one of the best introductions to the Gospels and the life of Jesus.

Shepard, John W. *The Christ of the Gospels.* Grand Rapids: Eerdmans, 1956. A full-length life of Jesus.

Stewart, James S. *The Life and Teaching of Jesus.* Nashville: Abingdon, 1978. An excellent, readable life of Jesus, suitable for beginning students.

Theissen, Gerd, and Dagmar Winter. *The Quest for the Plausible Jesus.* Louisville/London: Westminster John Knox, 2002. A technical study arguing for a more realistic approach to validating facts of Jesus' life than scholars have often tended to use. Deals particularly with the "criterion of dissimilarity," urging its replacement with a "criterion of historical plausibility."

Twelftree, G. H. *Jesus the Exorcist.* Peabody, Mass.: Hendrickson, 1993. An analysis of one important aspect of Jesus' ministry, defending its authenticity.

Wells, David F. *The Person of Christ.* Westchester, Ill.: Crossway, 1984. A biblical and historical study of the incarnation from an evangelical perspective.

Wenham, John W. *Easter Enigma: Are the Resurrection Accounts in Conflict?* 2nd ed. Grand Rapids: Baker, 1992. A brilliant treatment of a difficult subject, showing that the accounts do not conflict.

9 Lord, Teach Us
The Teaching Ministry of Jesus Christ

Outline

- **How to Understand Jesus**
- **Jesus the Preacher**
  Jesus' Use of Language
  The Form of Jesus' Message
  Jesus and His Message
- **The Teaching of Jesus**
  God, the Kingdom of God, and Jesus'
    Relation to the Kingdom
  The Uniqueness of Jesus
    Jesus' Special Relation to God
    Jesus' Special Relation to Other
      Human Beings
    Jesus' Sense of Mission
- **Human Life, Human Sinfulness,
  and God**
- **The End of the Age, the Second
  Coming, and the Life to Come**

Objectives

**After reading this chapter,
you should be able to**

- Discuss how Jesus was able to
  communicate his message effectively
- Identify the reasons for Jesus' effective
  preaching style
- List the four major theological areas that
  Jesus touched upon in his teaching
- Explain Jesus' relationship to the
  kingdom of God
- Note the way Jesus was unique among
  men
- Describe the human characteristics that
  Jesus understood and the way he
  treated them
- Use Scripture references to describe
  the second coming

A man decided to build a custom house. He hired a local architect to draw up the plans and within a few weeks obtained blueprints containing all the information needed to begin construction. Being very cautious, he decided to construct a scale model of the house from the blueprints using foam-board, just to ensure there were no problems.

A good friend openly questioned the need for this, since it seemed obvious from the blueprints that everything was in order. But the man ignored his friend's opinion. A couple of weeks later he called him over to take a look at his finished product. He had discovered a problem after all! An exposed ceiling beam crossed right in front of a clerestory window, which would have been an ugly feature of the completed living room. Even though the design error was documented in the two-dimensional architectural drawings it was very difficult to see. Only by constructing a three-dimensional model did the error become apparent.

We can experience this same difficulty when studying the teachings of Christ from a contemporary perspective. Even though most necessary information is contained in the Scriptures, our vantage point—or lack of one—makes some things in Christ's teaching difficult to see. A careful look at the factors relating to Jesus' situation will go a long way toward clearing up any possible misunderstandings.

How to Understand Jesus

For a clear grasp of Jesus' teaching, four points must be kept in mind. First, Jesus came primarily as a preacher-teacher who was delivering his message in spoken fashion to his hearers. He was not a researcher and writer who sat down and wrote out systematic treatises on theology. In fact, we have no books written by Jesus, as we do from Plato, Aristotle, and Philo. This means that what we do have of Jesus' teachings are taken from live situations where the needs of the audience, the moods and circumstances of the moment, and Jesus' own specific intentions supplied the shape that his message took. Because these factors were always changing, sometimes even during the course of the same conversation, Jesus was constantly shifting his focus to communicate most effectively. It is up to us as readers of the Gospels to think ourselves out of our day and back to these situations so that we can enter into what Jesus was really trying to say to his audience.

Second, Jesus generally shared fundamental assumptions with his audience. They had a common understanding of the theological principles Jesus wanted to get across. There was broadly similar understanding on such points as the existence of God, angels, providence, sin, revelation, salvation, and miracles. This is not to say that everyone believed precisely the same thing. But the basic concepts were agreed on. Jesus was not speaking to a group of Hindus or Buddhists, in which case his ideas would have been so unfamiliar that each point would need to be defined and explained in detail. Both Jesus and most of his hearers were familiar with and at least theoretically committed to the Old Testament. It was from that common basis that Jesus spoke. Jesus' task was generally not so much to impart completely new information as to remind them of what they knew and to correct the many misunderstandings that had arisen over time.

Third, one of Jesus' most formidable challenges was how to convey his (in some ways basically familiar) message. At numerous points the people knew *too* much and had become complacent. They didn't need to be taught every last bit of what Jesus had to say because they knew it already. The problem was it had little or no effect on their lives. So Jesus had to devise ways to wake the people up to the truth once more. Jesus sought to find ways to penetrate this wall of casual familiarity and complacency in such a way that they could see the truth again in a personal and living way. For some this would mean a revitalization of their lives; others would get things straight for the very first time. In many ways Jesus was confronted with the same problem that preachers today face on a Sunday morning—how to tell people something they have some acquaintance with, but in such a way that they will see it afresh and be changed by it.

kingdom

Fourth, Jesus' task was not confined simply to communicating ideas. He had a far more important goal in mind. He was attempting to challenge his hearers to make a decision to enter the **kingdom** and establish a personal relationship with God himself. As a result, Jesus' words were designed to confront and convince his hearers. He was not concerned to receive mass affirmation of what a wonderful speaker he was. He rather wanted hearers to see the greatness of God, the seriousness of their situation, and the new life that was being offered to them, if they would repent and believe the Good News. Jesus came to offer them life, not just good ideas.

In sum, Jesus had the task of figuring out how to build on what the people already knew, but in such a way that they would be challenged to go beyond it and apply it to themselves, adding to it his own new insights and understanding. How he did it marks him as one of the greatest communicators ever known.[1]

Jesus the Preacher

Jesus' Use of Language

"The traditional site of Jesus' Sermon on the Mount on the north shore of Galilee."

Jesus was a master of creative use of language. He knew how to take everyday

words and use them in such a way that it took his hearers by surprise. His vocabulary in most settings was that of his audience, the common people, and he avoided the technical, theological jargon of rabbis. He understood even technical rabbinic issues quite well, however, and when he needed to he could make his point forcibly on their terms (see, for example, the dispute about "corban," Mk 7:1–13). Usually, however, Jesus stayed away from obscure conflicts and spoke directly to the broad cross-sections of people in words they could grasp.

To get his message across, Jesus would sometimes bury his meaning somewhere below the surface in order to force listeners to think about what he said. An example of this is Luke 9:60, where Jesus said, "Let the dead bury the dead." In some instances, Jesus went on to explain what he meant, but in most cases he let the words he had spoken do the work.[2]

Sometimes, Jesus would use highly graphic language to make a point. A well-known example of this is when he said, "Why do you look at the speck of sawdust in your brother's eye and pay no attention to the plank in your own eye?" (Mt 7:3–5).

Other times Jesus used paradoxical or seemingly self-contradictory language to force his hearers to think or to make a decision, as when he said, "Whoever wants to save his life will lose it, but whoever loses his life for me will find it" (Mt 16:25) or "Many who are first will be last, and the last first" (Mk 10:31).

Jesus could also use the language of calculated overstatement to arrest attention or even to shock his hearers. An example of this is in Mark 9:42–48, where Jesus speaks of cutting off a hand or a foot or plucking out an eye to enter the kingdom of heaven.

In all of this, Jesus was exercising an extraordinary creativity by taking the common language of his day and making it do things it had rarely if ever done before.

The Form of Jesus' Message

The form that Jesus used to communicate his message was much like that of any rabbi of his day. He knew that if he had chosen a totally foreign way of presenting his message the people would have been

parable

allegorical

proverbial

Son of Man

unable to grasp it. So he gave it a style or pattern that they were familiar with. His favorite teaching device was the **parable**, of which there are dozens recorded in our Gospels.[3] This device can also be found in the Old Testament as well as in the writings of the rabbis. By definition a parable can range from a short, compact saying to a complete, almost **allegorical** story. Its purpose was to reveal just enough truth to raise intense curiosity, promising more if listeners went along, but also concealing enough of the truth that the complacent could walk away uninspired. In some ways the parable was a concrete example of one of Jesus' sayings, "Whoever has will be given more; whosoever does not have, even what he thinks he has will be taken from him" (Lk 8:18). In some cases Jesus explained the meaning of the parable to his followers (Mt 13:18–23, 36–43), but not always (Mt 13:44, 45).

Jesus was fond of using illustrations, down-to-earth examples from everyday life. To name just a few, he refers to animals, birds, houses, work, fields, farmers, women, children, money, landowners, trees, vines, food, meals, clothes, taxes, music, slavery, education, the weather, doctors, and illnesses. By using illustrations from daily life Jesus identified with the people and made his point accessible to virtually all of them.

Occasionally, Jesus used objects as lessons, as when he put a child in front of them (Lk 9:46–48) or pointed to the image of Tiberius on a coin (Mt 22:18–21). Sometimes Jesus would command people to do things as a lesson to them (Lk 5:4, 14), or he would do something as a lesson, as when he washed the feet of his disciples (Jn 13:2–17).

Jesus on occasion used **proverbial** sayings that were current among the people (Lk 5:31). But most frequently he would quote from the Old Testament when he wanted to make a point. The Old Testament was the Word of God, and its authority was not open to dispute.

In all of this we see Jesus' creativity being expressed in ways that were familiar to the people. But he took the familiar and transformed it by both what and how he communicated.

Jesus and His Message

The most striking feature of Jesus' teaching is the way he related himself to it. The rabbis of Jesus' day were in the habit of quoting one another or well-known rabbinic teachers from the past. In not one instance did Jesus do this. He spoke either on the basis of Scripture or on his own inherent authority, prefacing his words with "*I* say unto you," or "Truly, truly, *I* say unto you." He was aware that what he said carried divine attestation, and the fact that he spoke the words was enough to give them finality and power. The uniqueness of his words was a reflection of his own uniqueness, and the people knew it. Never a man spoke as he had spoken (Mt 7:28–29; Jn 7:46).

Basically, by his words Jesus was offering *himself* to the people, not just what he said, true as those words in fact were. So he could say, "If anyone is ashamed *of me and my words* in this adulterous and sinful generation, the **Son of Man** will be ashamed of him when he comes into his Father's glory with the holy angels" (Mk 8:38). Jesus' words were not offered as general moral axioms or eternal truths open to the unaided insight of human thought, but as part of the gospel message that required faith, obedience, and acceptance of the kingdom that he offered. Ultimately, in order to understand the things that Jesus said we must heed Jesus' call to repent of our sins, trust in his death for our salvation, and place our lives at his command. Does he deserve this kind of commitment? This is the question that was thrust on the hearers of Jesus' day and that confronts us as well.

The Teaching of Jesus[4]

In light of the preceding section we should not expect a systematic presentation of theology by Jesus, nor do we get it. However, the basic points of theology are all touched on in the course of his preaching. These can be summarized as follows.

• God, the kingdom of God, and Jesus' relation to the kingdom

Jesus was fond of using down-to-earth illustrations from everyday life.

- The uniqueness of Jesus—his special relation to God, his special relation to other human beings, and his sense of mission
- Human life, human sinfulness, and God
- The end of the age, the second coming, and the life to come

Below we take up each of these themes in turn.

God, the Kingdom of God, and Jesus' Relation to the Kingdom[5]

The first thing to note about Jesus' teaching on the kingdom of God is that it is *God's* kingdom, not man's. Consequently, in order to understand what Jesus said about the kingdom, we need to understand what Jesus said about God. For Jesus, the fact that God existed was taken for granted. He apparently never asked if people believed in God, nor did he set out to prove that God existed. We do not validate God's existence by human thought; God validates human existence by being creator, sustainer, and redeemer. Jesus' thinking was from the top down, not from the bottom up. God is primary; we are secondary. If heaven and earth should pass away, God would still remain in his unchanging eternal glory. Jesus also assumed that God was present with us as we live our lives on earth. He is not far off and unconcerned, but near us as helper and sustainer. The personality of God is

also taken for granted. As a person, God is able to understand our needs, comprehend our thoughts, hear our prayers, accept our praise, deliver us from evil, provide our wants, guide our lives, and forgive our sins. In the depth of his person, God is supremely Father, a heavenly Father, and is everything a father should be in compassion and concern for his children here on earth.

Throughout Jesus' teachings, he constantly refers to who God is and what he is like. Jesus tells us that God is a Spirit (Jn 4:24) who is good (Mt 19:17), glorious (Jn 11:40), true (Jn 17:3), loving (Lk 11:42), holy (Jn 17:11), righteous (Mt 6:33), perfect (Mt 5:48), all-powerful (Mk 10:27), all-knowing (Lk 12:6–7; 16:15), wise (Lk 11:49), and sovereign (Mt 11:25). What God does, according to Jesus, is equally impressive. God created the world (Mk 13:19) and the human race (Mk 10:6), cares for the inanimate and animate order (Mt 6:30; Lk 12:24, 28), is involved in human affairs (Mt 19:6; Jn 4:10), works according to a plan (Lk 4:19), and is establishing his kingdom (Lk 17:20–21).

This is just some of what Jesus says about God. In actuality, there is a great deal more, as well as a great deal that Jesus did not need to say, because he was building on a common understanding of what the Old Testament taught.

It is this God who is establishing his kingdom here on earth. The idea that God

141

has a kingdom and exercises his sovereignty over it is taught throughout the Old Testament. Jesus could build on that fact. As Jesus speaks of it, it is a heavenly kingdom that will be established by God and not by human effort. Nor is it to be confused with ideas of earthly geography. It is not so much a "kingdom" (a territory ruled by a sovereign) but a kingship (the exercise of that sovereignty). "Kingdom" denotes nothing less than the exercise of divine rule in human affairs. Its extent is unlimited. In some respects, this kingly rule of God is virtually equivalent to the providence of God because God accomplishes his will throughout the whole created order. In a narrow sense, however, the kingdom of God is to be understood as the realm where God's *saving* will is being done, and hence is identified with salvation.

Jesus came offering this kingdom to those who were willing to accept it. He says a number of things about entering into the kingdom but they boil down to this. In order to enter the kingdom we must become changed individuals. We cannot stay the same, either in essence or in action, and expect to be part of God's community of redeemed people. Jesus describes entering the kingdom in the following ways: We are to repent and believe the Good News (Mk 1:14–15); we are to be converted and become as little children (Mt 18:3–4); we are to be born again (Jn 3:3, 5); we are to exert strenuous effort, breaking free from our past (Mt 11:12); we are to acknowledge Jesus as Lord in sincerity and not in pretense (Mt 7:21–23); we are to make whatever sacrifice is necessary (Mt 18:8–9); and we are to be made inwardly righteous by a divine act, not by relying on our outward behavior (Mt 5:20). Putting all this together, Jesus says God is establishing his saving kingdom and has invited us to become a part of it by allowing God to do his saving work in us. In this way, we will be miraculously transformed into individuals who qualify for entrance into the kingdom and who delight in our inmost being to do the will of God.

This new life is to be experienced as a change within our hearts and as a different way of relating to those around us. The change within produces new individuals, in whom faith, humility, meekness, righteousness, purity, dependence on God, peace, and love reign (Mt 5:3–9; 22:37). We are those who no longer harbor lust in our hearts, let alone commit adultery (Mt 5:27–28). We do not hate, let

Was Jesus a Revolutionary?

It is common today to read about murder and violence in the name of God. This also existed in the time of Jesus, and some contemporary scholars suggest that Jesus was also a revolutionary. They believe that Jesus had a social/political agenda that included the overthrow of the Roman government, using armed violence if necessary. He was crucified before his political "kingdom of God" could be established.

This view totally misunderstands Jesus and, ironically, is not radical enough. Jesus did not want to change society politically; he wanted to change people. The only way society will change is when the people are changed and put their new principles of life into action. When people's hearts are renewed in the true kingdom of God, all barriers are broken down and Pharisees, tax collectors, Gentiles, and sinners may all become spiritually one.

Jesus was a revolutionary—a spiritual revolutionary offering people a whole new life, for both time and eternity. He was crucified as a king, and King he was, but as he told Pilate, *"My kingdom is not of this world"* (Jn 18:36). It was of an entirely different order and someday all the world will acknowledge that he is *"King of kings and Lord of lords"* (Rv 19:16).

Jesus describes entering the kingdom in the following way: We are to be converted and become as little children (Mt 18:3–4).

alone murder our foe (Mt 5:21–24). We are changed in the way we relate to those around us: We now love our enemies and pray for those who persecute us (Mt 5:43–45). We forgive others their sins (Mt 6:12, 14 15); we refrain from censorious judgment (Mt 7:1); we do the will of our Father who is in heaven (Mt 7:21, 24–27); we feed the hungry, give a drink to the thirsty, give shelter to the homeless, clothe the needy, minister to the sick, and visit the desperate (Mt 25:31–46). We strive to be as perfect both inwardly and outwardly as our Father in heaven is perfect (Mt 5:48).

Jesus tells us that this kingdom is present with us now as we experience God's saving grace, and is also coming someday as a glorious fulfillment of God's promise to us. So we seek first the kingdom of God and his righteousness in order to experience the work of God in our lives now (Mt 6:33). But we also pray, "Your kingdom come" (Mt 6:10), longing for the day when the knowledge of the Lord will cover the earth like the waters cover the sea (see Hab 2:14).

Jesus was convinced that in his own person and work the kingdom of God had arrived. He is uniquely its proclaimer and its embodiment. He told Pilate that his kingdom is not of this world. He told his followers that because he is overthrowing Satan by casting out demons, the king-

dom of God has arrived (Mt 12:28), and he rejoiced to see Satan fall from his place in heaven (Lk 10:18). Later, Jesus' followers would refer to the kingdom of God as the kingdom of Christ, because Christ was the essence of the kingdom and their entrance into it. Because Jesus brought in the kingdom, and the kingdom was the realm of salvation, it was appropriate to preach Jesus as the Savior. In his death and resurrection Jesus was the saving act of God. While on earth he offered the salvation of God by inviting people into God's kingdom. So whether he was on earth preaching the Good News of the kingdom or risen again offering himself in the preaching of the gospel, Jesus is uniquely the essence of God's salvation and kingdom.

The Uniqueness of Jesus[6]

Jesus was unlike any other person who ever lived. It is true that he was fully human. A simple reading of the Gospels shows that very clearly. He grew tired and slept (Lk 8:23), was hungry and thirsty (Mt 21:18; Jn 19:28), felt compassion and love (Mk 8:2; 10:21), and was sometimes angry and exasperated (Mk 3:5; 8:12). At times he needed solitude or companionship (Mt 27:38; Lk 4:42), and sometimes he was moved to tears (Jn 11:35). Luke describes Jesus' growing up as normal human growth that included his intellectual, physical, spiritual, and social life (Lk 2:52). Everything that human beings legitimately are Jesus was. That is not *all* Jesus was, of course, but it is important that this be emphasized. When the church, centuries later, was called on to define the nature of Jesus, they included the expression in the **Nicene Creed**, "He became flesh . . . and was made man." Any theory that rejected the full humanity of Jesus was rightly branded as heresy.

But the Jesus who is presented to us in the Gospels is more than just a human being. He is unique in the strict sense of the word, one of a kind. This uniqueness was evident in three ways: in Jesus' relation to God, in his relation to the rest of the human race, and in his special sense of mission while here on earth.

Jesus' Special Relation to God

Jesus bore a relationship to God that can only be described as equality. This is the way in which the early church later expressed it (Phil 2:5–11), and believers felt no embarrassment in calling Jesus both Lord (Rom 10:9; 1 Cor 12:3; Phil 2:11) and God (Jn 1:1; Rom 9:5; Ti 2:13). Anything that could be said about God, they also said about Jesus.

Both God and Christ are glorious (Rom 5:2; 1 Pt 4:13); the Spirit is from God and Christ (Rom 8:9; Phil 1:19); divine power is from God and Christ, and Christ is the power of God (1 Cor 1:24; 2 Cor 6:7; 12:9); grace comes from God and Christ (Gal 1:6; Col 1:2); peace comes from God and Christ (Eph 2:14; Phil 1:2); God and Christ forgive our sins (Col 1:13; 2:13); God and Christ love us (Rom 5:8; Gal 2:20); God and Christ sanctify us (Acts 20:32; 1 Cor 1:2). We are to live by the will of God and Christ (Eph 1:11; 5:17); we are to obey God and Christ (Acts 5:29; 2 Cor 10:5); we are to glory in God and Christ (Rom 15:17; Phil 2:11); we are to live in the presence of God and Christ (Acts 10:33; 2 Tm 4:1); and we will ultimately appear before the judgment seat of God and Christ (Rom 14:10–12; 2 Cor 5:10).

Many other things are said exactly like this because Jesus presented himself while he was on earth as uniquely one with God. The early believers were not simply making all this up out of their own heads or imaginative experience. They had the remembrance of Jesus himself to base it on

and were only reflecting what they remembered of him.

They recalled that at no time did Jesus ever put himself in the same category as other human beings. He was aware of his own sin*less*ness and of his followers' sin*ful*ness. He never spoke of a common relation to God, including himself and them together. He always spoke of "my Father" and "your Father"; God was not Father to him and his followers in the same way. In one place Jesus' confession reaches the point of saying that no one on earth even knows the Father, except he himself, and that no one knows him except the Father (Mt 11:27). So profound and complete is the relationship that Jesus can say, "I and the Father are one" (Jn 10:30) and "Before Abraham was born, I am" (Jn 8:58), using the words of God spoken at the burning bush to Moses (Ex 3:14).

Jesus assumed the authority of God and forgave people their sins (Mk 2:1–12; Lk 7:44–50). He accepted worship, something that is due to God alone (Mt 14:33; 28:17). Everyone knew that the Scriptures were God's Word, yet Jesus claimed to speak with final authority over them and claimed that they were written about him (Lk 4:20–21; Jn 5:46) and that he came to fulfill them (Mt 5:17). The truth of Scripture endures forever because it is the Word of God, but so do the words of Jesus. Indeed, heaven and earth will pass away, but his words will never pass away (Mt 24:35).

The early believers later recalled the close relationship that existed between the Word of God and Jesus and could find no better way to describe him than as *the* Word of God (Jn 1:1–14; Rv 19:13). They were also able to find virtually the whole of his life predicted in prophecy and referred no fewer than eighty passages of Scripture prophetically to him. One of the most notable is Isaiah 9:6–7, where the promise is made that a child will be born, a son given, who will be the "Mighty God, Everlasting Father." The unfathomable mystery of the Son who is the Everlasting Father is the unfathomable mystery of Jesus Christ.

Jesus' Special Relation to Other Human Beings

Because of the relationship that Jesus had with the Father, he also bore a special relationship to the rest of the human race.

second coming

inter-
testamental

The Gospel of John remembers this best in the "I am" sayings of Jesus (Jn 6:35; 8:12; 10:7, 11; 11:25; 14:6; 15:1).[7] In these he presents himself as the absolute answer to all human need.

Jesus believed that our ultimate destiny depends on our relationship to him and his evaluation of us. Merely calling him Lord is not enough; we must sincerely mean it and follow that confession by a life lived in submission to the will of his Father (Mt 7:21–23). On the great day of Jesus' **second coming** those who have been ashamed of him and of his work, having refused to take up the cross and follow him, will be denied by Jesus and forfeit their souls (Mk 8:34–38).

Nothing can hinder the relationship of Jesus to his own; where two or three are gathered together in his name, he promises to be present with them (Mt 18–20). He will remain with them throughout all time until the end of the age (Mt 28:20). Neither space nor time can place a limit on him.

Jesus' Sense of Mission

From the earliest days of Jesus' life he was aware that God had a special mission for him. When he was only twelve years old he became so engrossed in the calling of God that he could not leave the temple. When asked by his parents about his absence, he replied that he simply had to be in his father's house (Lk 2:49). When Jesus began his ministry some years later, he told John it was proper that he be baptized to fulfill his mission (Mt 3:15). Shortly after that Jesus expelled unscrupulous entrepreneurs from his "Father's house" (Jn 2:16).

Throughout his life he was aware of a special sense of timing and conveyed this to his followers. He knew when his hour had come and when it had not (Jn 2:4; 7:30; 8:20; 12:23, 27; 13:1; 17:1). In all of this Jesus was guided by a supreme desire to do his Father's will (Mt 26:42; Jn 5:30; 6:38). Jesus epitomized it this way: "My food is to do the will of him who sent me and to finish his work" (Jn 4:34). At the time of Jesus' crucifixion, Pilate mistakenly thought that he had the power of life and death over Jesus but was told, "You would have no power over me if it were not given you from above" (Jn 19:11). No one had authority over Jesus except his heavenly Father, and Jesus knew this to the very end.

Jesus sensed that Scripture had long before predicted the course his life would take. He was aware throughout his entire life that prophecy was being fulfilled by what he was doing. He had read the Book of Isaiah carefully and knew well of the Servant who was prophesied to come (Is 42:1–4; 49:1–7; 52:13–53:12). Of the many things that it was said the Servant would do, it stood out in Jesus' mind that he would be pierced for our transgressions and crushed for our iniquities (Is 53:5), that the Lord would lay on him the iniquity of us all (Is 53:6), and that he would be cut off from the land of the living (Is 53:8–9). Jesus took special pains to point out to his disciples that his mission was to suffer and die for the sins of the world (Mt 16:21; 20:17–19, 28; 26:27–29).

There are several titles that are either used by Jesus of himself or are accepted by him in the Gospels that reflect in one way or another what his mission in life was, such as Teacher (Mt 8:19; 19:16; 26:18; Mk 4:38), Rabbi (Mk 9:5; Jn 1:49; 3:2; 6:25), and Son of David (Mt 15:22; 20:30–31; 21:9, 15).

The favorite self-designation of Jesus, however, is the title "Son of Man." It is a term found both in the Old Testament (Ez 2:1–3; 3:1, 3, 4, 17; Dn 7:13–14) and in **intertestamental** literature. It probably had messianic overtones in Jesus' day. It was sufficiently ambiguous that Jesus could use it to affirm his messiahship while at the same time putting his own meaning into it. He needed to do this because the current expectation of the Jews was for a Messiah who would crush the Roman oppressors, whereas he came to be the Servant-Savior of the world, who only at his second coming would rule the earth in glory. There were at least three things that Jesus wanted to emphasize when he used the term: his authority (Mt 12:8; Mk 2:10; Lk 5:24), his coming death and resurrection (Mk 8:31–32; 9:12, 31; 10:33–34), and his second coming in glory (Mt 16:27; 24:26–31; 26:64; Mk 8:38). It is possible that Jesus was also underscoring his humanity and his prophetic ministry.

The Ethics of Jesus Summarized

We have written enough to you, brothers, about the things which pertain to our religion and are particularly helpful for a virtuous life, at least for those who wish to guide their steps in holiness and righteousness. For we have touched upon every subject—faith, repentance, genuine love, self-control, sobriety, and patience—and have reminded you that you must reverently please almighty God in righteousness and truth and steadfastness, living in harmony without bearing malice, in love and peace with constant gentleness, just as our fathers, of whom we spoke earlier, pleased him, by being humble toward the Father and God and Creator and toward all men. And we have reminded you of these things all the more gladly, since we knew quite well that we were writing to men who are faithful and distinguished and have diligently studied the oracles of the teaching of God.

—1 Clement 62:1–3 (ca. A.D. 95)

Human Life, Human Sinfulness, and God

As we have already seen, one of Jesus' chief concerns was to make God real again in the lives of his people. As against the prevailing views of his day that emphasized judgment, duty, legal requirements, and strict observance of the law, Jesus wanted to stress the closeness, love, and concern of God. In order to do this he almost invariably refers to God as "heavenly Father." It is striking that when speaking of God's work on earth Jesus' favorite expression is "the kingdom of God," but nowhere does Jesus call God a king or judge. Jesus knew very well that God was both king and judge, but that was not the point he wanted to emphasize. The kingdom of God is ruled by a heavenly Father, not by a despotic judge or cruel king. Jesus says that our heavenly Father knows our needs, cares infinitely for us, and even has the very hairs on our heads numbered (Mt 10:30). The beautiful picture of the father waiting for the return of his lost son epitomizes what Jesus had to say of God (Lk 15:11–24). It is the fact that God cares for us that gives human life its ultimate meaning.

Jesus was well aware of the complexity of human life. We are created beings (Mk 10:6) of great value to God (Mt 6:25–26; 10:30; 12:12). We have the ability to appreciate beauty (Mt 6:28–29). Our inner nature includes heart, mind, soul, strength, spirit, and will in one complex whole (Mt 22:37; Mk 8:35–36; 12:30). We are social and moral beings (Mt 12:33–37), bursting with emotions (Mt 5:4, 12). Although subject to the limitations of the flesh, we are destined to live forever (Lk 16:19–31; Jn 6:38–40).

Jesus is also aware of human sinfulness and our inability to do what God requires of us (Mt 7:11). Human beings are, simply put, sinners (Lk 5:32). Yet our sins can be forgiven (Mt 9:2, 5; 12:31). Those who were considered to be the worst of sinners felt comfortable in Jesus' presence (Mk 2:15). He became known as the "friend of tax collectors and sinners" (Mt 11:19). Jesus never used people's sinfulness as a club to beat them with or to demoralize them. If they were caught in sin, they were forgiven and told to sin no more (Jn 7:53–8:11). He does, however, single out for severe condemnation those who are self-righteous and unwilling to acknowledge their sinfulness (Mt 23:13–32; Lk 18:9–14). He also has strong words for those who reject the work of God as offered in himself (Mt 11:21–24; 12:39–42).

To find the true meaning of life, people must come to Jesus, there to find rest for their souls as they become his followers or disciples (Mt 11:28–30). Although a person may have to make many sacrifices to become a follower of Jesus (Lk 14:25–35), the yoke of Jesus' discipleship is bearable, and in the end God rewards his own with eternal life. The disciple of Jesus knows that human life as God intends it does not consist of amassing wealth (Mt 6:19–21; Lk 12:15–21), having an estab-

We are created beings (Mk 10:6) of great value to God (Mt 6:25–26; 10:30; 12:12). We have the ability to appreciate beauty (Mt 6:28–29).

lished position of privilege (Mt 21:43), being outwardly religious (Mt 6:16), getting all our heart ever desired (gaining the whole world), or reaching our full potential as we project it (saving our life) (Mk 8:35–37). Rather, life consists of denying ourselves for Christ's sake (Lk 9:23–25), living in the kingdom of God (Mt 6:33), and fulfilling Jesus' two great commands that comprehend the full meaning of existence—love of God (Mk 12:30) and love of neighbor (Mk 12:31).

If we truly love God, we will do all that he wants of us, and if we truly love our neighbor, we will be all that he or she needs us to be. Jesus epitomized this principle in the story of the banquet, where kindness is shown to those who cannot repay (Lk 14:12–14). When asked to define who the neighbor is whom we are to love, Jesus responded with the parable of the good Samaritan, which taught, in essence, that a neighbor is anyone who is in need (Lk 10:29–37).

The true disciple is the one who follows in the footsteps of his Master. To that one Jesus promises life in abundance, the only life really worth living (Jn 10:10).

The End of the Age, the Second Coming, and the Life to Come[8]

Although the Sadducees of Jesus' day rejected the idea that there was any afterlife, Jesus affirmed that life did not end with the grave. History as we know it will not continue on forever. Just as there was a beginning at the initial creation, so there will be a consummation at the end of the age.

Jesus had a great deal to say about what would happen in the future. As he looked beyond his own time he saw the destruction of Jerusalem coming in the very near future (Lk 21:5–6, 20–24)—it happened in A.D. 70—but he also saw how the world itself would someday end. In Jesus' mind the end of the age would be ushered in with his second coming (Mt 13:39–40, 49; 24:3). Before that happened, however, a number of things needed to take place. Jesus carefully instructed his followers so

Events That Will Precede Jesus' Second Coming

- Apostasy (Mt 24:10)
- The rise of Antichrist (Mt 24:5, 23, 26)
- Betrayal (Mk 13:12; Lk 21:16)
- Earthquakes (Mt 13:7; Mk 13:8)
- False Christs (Mt 24:24; Mk 13:6, 21–23)
- False prophets (Mt 24:11, 24; Mk 13:21–23)
- False signs and miracles (Mt 24:24; Mk 13:22)
- Famines (Mt 24:7)
- Increase of evil (Mt 24:12)
- International strife (Mt 24:7)
- Persecution of believers (Mt 24:9; Mk 13:9–13)
- Pestilence (Lk 21:11)
- Unparalleled distress (Mk 13:17–19)
- Wars and rumors of wars (Mt 24:6; Mk 13:7)
- Worldwide proclamation of the gospel (Mt 24:14; Mk 13:10)

that they would not be misled concerning it.

No one knows exactly when it will take place, so speculation on that point is useless (Mt 24:36, 42; 25:13). Only God knows when the second coming of Christ will be (Mt 24:36). Human beings are sure to be mistaken as to when Christ will return. It will be unexpected (Mt 24:44; Lk 12:35–40), sudden (Mk 13:33–36), like a thief in the night (Mt 24:42–44).

The event itself will be powerful (Mt 24:30), glorious (Mt 16:27), personal (Mk 8:38), and visible (Mk 13:26). When Jesus returns to earth he will be accompanied by angels (Mk 8:38), descend from the clouds (Mt 24:30) in the midst of immense cosmic and earthly distress (Mt 24:29; Lk 21:25–26), and gather together the saints of all time to himself (Mt 24:31; Mk 13:27; see also 1 Cor 15:50–54; 1 Thes 4:13–17).

Jesus also speaks of the coming resurrection of the human race, both generally (Mk 12:26–27; Lk 20:37–38) and specifically (of the righteous and the unrighteous; Jn 5:21, 25, 28–29; 6:39–40; 11:21–25). Jesus spoke of the end of the age and the consequent last judgments in some well-known parables, such as the net cast into the sea (Mt 13:47–50), the sheep and the goats (Mt 25:31–46), and the wheat and the weeds (Mt 13:24–30).

The redeemed will be gathered together in heaven (Mt 6:19–21; Lk 10:20), which is the ultimate kingdom of God (Mt 25:34; Lk 22:29–30). They will possess eternal life (Jn 3:15–16; 10:28–29) in their Father's house (Jn 14:1–4), feasting with the saints of old (Mt 8:10–11) and fellowshiping with Jesus Christ himself (Jn 12:26; 17:24). It is a place of ultimate joy, blessing, and reward (Mt 5:12; 25:34; Mk 10:21; Lk 18:22).

The lost will be cast into outer darkness (Mt 8:10–12; 22:13) where there is anguish (Mt 25:29–30) and destruction (Mt 7:13). It is the place of the devil and his angels (Mt 25:41). It is a place of evil (Mt 13:38–42) and unbelief (Lk 8:11–12; Jn 3:18, 36), likened to a fiery furnace (Mt 13:42). It is ultimate condemnation (Mt 10:28; Jn 5:29).

In the light of all that is to come, Jesus challenged his hearers (and us!) to make a decision. We cannot serve two masters; we cannot walk down two roads; we cannot be both good and bad trees at the same time; we cannot love God and material goods. We must decide whether to build our house on sand, only to see it come crashing into ruin in the end, or to build on the solid foundation of Jesus Christ and have our lives endure throughout all of eternity in the glory and the blessedness of God (Mt 7:24–27; 13:43; 25:34).

Key Terms

allegorical	parable
intertestamental	proverbial
kingdom	second coming of Jesus
Nicene Creed	Son of Man

Focus 9: The Teachings of Christ in the Nicene Creed

The early church highly valued the teachings of Jesus, which formed the basis of Christian doctrine. Church leaders recognized that it was vitally important for Christians to know what they believed and why they believed it, especially in the face of false teachers and heretical sects that were spreading perverted versions of Christ's teachings. And, given the exponential growth of the church, it was also important for new converts to be instructed quickly and carefully in Christian doctrine.

For these reasons, church leaders decided to incorporate the teachings of Jesus into creeds, or short summaries of Christian belief (the word "creed" literally means "I believe"). There was good biblical precedent for this, as several brief credal passages are found throughout the New Testament, including this one in 1 Timothy 3:16, which focuses on the life and nature of Jesus—"*Beyond all question, the mystery of godliness is great: He appeared in a body, was vindicated by the Spirit, was seen by angels, was preached among the nations, was believed on in the world, was taken up in glory.*"

Prominent in the creeds are the teachings of Christ regarding the kingdom of God, God the Creator, his relationship with God his Father, the resurrection of the dead, his judgment of humanity, and life after death. These teachings are all found in the Nicene Creed, which was named after the Council of Nicea in A.D. 325 when church leaders endorsed biblical teaching concerning the divine-human nature of Jesus. Note how much of the creed—perhaps 50 percent or more—directly mirrors Jesus' own teachings as recorded in the Gospels.

I believe in one God the Father Almighty, Maker of heaven and earth, And of all things visible and invisible.

And in one Lord Jesus Christ, the only-begotten son of God, Begotten of his Father before all worlds, God of God, Light of Light, Very God of very God, Begotten, not made, Being of one substance with the Father, By whom all things were made: Who for us men, and for our salvation came down from heaven, And was incarnate by the Holy Ghost of the Virgin Mary, And was made man, And was crucified also for us under Pontius Pilate. He suffered and was buried, And the third day he rose again according to the Scriptures, And ascended into heaven, And sitteth on the right hand of the Father. And he shall come again with glory to judge both the quick and the dead: Whose kingdom shall have no end.

And I believe in the Holy Ghost, The Lord and giver of life, Who proceedeth from the Father and the Son, Who with the Father and the Son together is worshipped and glorified, Who spake by the Prophets. And I believe one holy catholic and apostolic Church. I acknowledge one Baptism for the remission of sins. And I look for the Resurrection of the dead, And the life of the world to come. Amen.

Summary

1. Jesus came primarily as a preacher-teacher who communicated his message so that people would be able to build their own knowledge base on his teachings and would also be challenged to apply the teachings to their lives.

2. Jesus communicated his message in a form similar to the rabbis of his day and used parables, illustrations, object lessons, contemporary proverbial sayings, and quotes from the Old Testament.

3. Jesus taught extensively about the kingdom of God and his own relationship to it as its proclaimer, embodiment, and fulfiller.

4. Jesus is unique because he has a special relationship to God and to the human race and a special sense of mission here on earth.

5. Jesus believed and taught that our ultimate destiny depends on our relationship to God through him and on his evaluation of us.

6. Jesus realized his special mission early in life, at least by the age of twelve.

7. Jesus used and/or accepted the titles of Teacher, Rabbi, Son of David, and Son of Man.

8. Jesus' chief objective was to make God real in the lives of his people by stressing the love and concern of God instead of legal requirements.

9. Jesus made clear that a true disciple is one who follows in his footsteps.

10. Jesus emphasized that life does not end at death; the world will end someday at his second coming, which will be powerful, unexpected, glorious, personal, and visible.

Review Questions

1. Jesus came not as a researcher or writer but as a _____ and _____.

2. Jesus was able to teach and get his points across because everyone understood the _____.

3. Jesus was one of the world's greatest _____.

4. The favorite teaching device of Jesus was the _____.

5. Jesus taught that the kingdom of God belonged to _____, not to us.

6. In order to enter the kingdom of God, people must first _____.

7. _____ designates the exercise of divine rule in human affairs.

8. Jesus had a special relationship to God in that he was _____ to God.

9. Jesus was aware throughout his life that he was fulfilling prophecy from the Book of _____.

10. Jesus' favorite self-designation was _____.

Study Questions

1. What are some of the things that help us understand Jesus as a communicator?

2. What are some of the ways Jesus used language when he preached?

3. What was Jesus' favorite teaching device? Look up how Jesus used this form to communicate his message.

4. How and why did Jesus relate himself so directly to his message?

5. Discuss Jesus' teaching on the kingdom and how he related himself to it.

6. In what ways was Jesus unique?

7. What did Jesus teach about human life and sinfulness?

8. According to Jesus, what will the end of the age be like?

Further Reading

Anderson, Norman. *The Teaching of Jesus.* London: Hodder & Stoughton, 1983. An easy-to-read introduction to Jesus' teachings.

Bruce, F. F. *The Hard Sayings of Jesus.* Downers Grove: InterVarsity, 1983. A look at those hard-to-understand sayings of Jesus, with helpful solutions on how to handle them.

Gempf, Conrad. *Jesus Asked: What He Wanted to Know.* Grand Rapids: Zondervan, 2003. A fresh and stimulating analysis of Jesus' teaching from the standpoint of the questions he posed to listeners.

Hess, Richard S., and M. Daniel Carroll R., eds. *Israel's Messiah in the Bible and the Dead Sea Scrolls.* Grand Rapids: Baker, 2003. Essays that shed light on messianic expectations and realities in biblical times and since.

Morris, Leon. *New Testament Theology.* Grand Rapids: Zondervan, 1986, parts II, III, pp. 91–297. An easy-to-follow theology of the whole New Testament. Parts II and III deal with the Synoptic Gospels and the Johannine Writings. This is an excellent introduction to what Jesus said as recorded in the Gospels. Written from an evangelical perspective.

Smith, Gordon T. *The Voice of Jesus: Discernment, Prayer, and the Witness of the Spirit.* Downers Grove: InterVarsity, 2003. Help for the task of understanding Jesus' leadership amidst the complexities of contemporary life.

Stassen, Glen H., and David P. Gushee. *Kingdom Ethics: Following Jesus in Contemporary Context.* Downers Grove: InterVarsity, 2003. Reflections on how to live the daily Christian life based especially on the Sermon on the Mount.

Stein, Robert H. *Difficult Passages in the New Testament.* Grand Rapids: Baker, 1990. The first part deals with the Gospels.

———. *The Method and Message of Jesus' Teachings.* Philadelphia: Westminster, 1978. A very helpful introduction to how Jesus taught and what he said.

Stott, John R. W. *The Message of the Sermon on the Mount.* Downers Grove: InterVarsity, 1978.

Wenham, David. *The Parables of Jesus.* Downers Grove: InterVarsity, 1989. A very fine study of Jesus' parables.

Zuck, Roy B. *Teaching as Jesus Taught.* Grand Rapids: Baker, 1995. A good introduction to the way Jesus taught and how we should understand it.

10 Modern Approaches to the New Testament

Historical Criticism and Hermeneutics

Outline

- **Two Ways of Reading the New Testament**
- **The Necessity of Criticism**
- **Roots of Historical Criticism**
- **Contribution and Limitations of Historical Criticism**
- **The Promise of Hermeneutics**
  Conditions
  Methods
  Aims
- **Invitation to Further Hermeneutical Study**

Objectives

After reading this chapter, you should be able to

- Trace the highlights in the development of higher criticism
- Give examples of the challenges parts of the New Testament present to the reader
- State the non-Christian assumption about the Bible made by some critics
- Name and define the methods of historical criticism
- Identify scholars who belong to the historical-critical and historical-theological traditions
- Explain the field of hermeneutics
- Discuss the aims for interpreting the New Testament

hermeneutical

Two Ways of Reading the New Testament

During World War II a learned pastor and teacher named Martin Albertz (1882–1956) was imprisoned by Nazi authorities for his church activity. After the war he began work on a book somewhat like the one you are reading—a survey of the New Testament. Eventually his study swelled to four volumes. He dedicated the third one to a pair of his students.

The first, Erich Klapproth, was a gifted young minister listed as missing in action on the Russian front in 1943. The other was a valiant pastoral assistant, a young woman named Ilse Fredrichsdorff. She ministered so selflessly that she starved to death outside Berlin alongside the people she served in November 1945, well after the war's end. What sustained both young believers through these devastating years was their unshakable faith in Christ and their certainty that the gospel was true.

Albertz's New Testament introduction was one of the first theological books to come off the presses in East Germany after the war. A few years later a New Testament scholar named Werner Kümmel reviewed it. Students should be discouraged from reading Albertz's books, he wrote, because they assume we know a great deal about the rise and proper understanding of the apostolic testimony[1]

The reviewer's complaint raised an important question still pertinent now. Have modern findings made it impossible to speak confidently about the origin and meaning of the gospel message? Should an introduction to the New Testament focus on modern theories about the New Testament and perhaps argue for the ones currently in vogue? (They change steadily.) Must a "modern" reading of the New Testament focus on current doubts about the biblical message?[2]

Surely it is appropriate for a New Testament survey to see in the biblical books the sure message of redemption from sin through Jesus Christ that Christians have long found there and deal primarily with what the New Testament says "on the surface" as we pick it up and read it.[3] Certainly we must bear in mind all relevant important **hermeneutical** considerations and background factors, but in the light of the Bible's excellent historical credentials, it ought to be treated as a trusted friend rather than a potential enemy.

Not everyone approaches the Bible in this way. Different readers make different assumptions that influence how they understand the New Testament and there-

In times of war, the foundations of religious belief are tested. The truth of the Bible has given strength and comfort to many.

Areas of Controversy in New Testament Study

Some have raised questions about the New Testament's historical reliability. Scholar I. Howard Marshall lists the following areas of controversy. He is one of many who believes that satisfactory answers exist in each of these areas.

1. Discrepancies between parallel narratives
2. Comparison with nonbiblical material
3. Historical improbabilities
4. Supernatural occurrences
5. Creation and modification of material in the early church
6. Literary genre
7. Insufficient evidence

historical criticism

fore how they commend it to others. Previous chapters of this book have made clear that we think the New Testament is quite reliable indeed. We think that it makes good sense to read the New Testament against the backdrop of such ancient Christian doctrines as the inspiration of Scripture, the divinity of Jesus Christ, the sovereignty of a personal God in the world who does miracles like raise his crucified Son to life, and a coming day of judgment.[4]

But many New Testament interpreters would disagree. In recent generations, and still today, various writers claiming scholarly support have argued things like: The New Testament writings are no different or better than dozens of other writings we possess. Jesus never founded the church (more likely Paul did) and never claimed to be divine. He never rose from the dead. Or even more extreme: He was probably a member of the QUMRAN sect who married twice and had three children. His mother was not a virgin but was raped; Jesus was the illegitimate result. And so the theories go.

Now part of handling the New Testament properly is understanding modern approaches to it. Below we survey what is distinctive about some of these modern approaches. We will briefly sketch the development, value, and risks of what has come to be called **historical criticism**. In this chapter we will deal with historical criticism generally. (Chapters 11 and 12 treat it more specifically as it pertains to

the study of Jesus and the first three Gospels.) Then, after general treatment of historical criticism, we will go on to explore how the New Testament is best read given the contemporary setting. That is, we discuss the meaning and value of a field of study called hermeneutics.

The Necessity of Criticism

In chapter 1 we spoke of the need for *study* of the New Testament. It was written in ancient times in another language. It reflects customs that differ from our own. Its message may well be foreign to the understanding we bring to it. For many reasons we need to proceed with diligence, thoroughness, and rigor if we wish to glean from the New Testament the message its authors sought to convey. Otherwise we risk imposing our views on it instead of discerning its claims on us.

So, there is a legitimate sense in which a "critical" reading of the New Testament can only be welcomed. Some years ago George E. Ladd defined criticism as "making intelligent judgments about historical, literary, textual, and philological questions which one must face in dealing with the Bible, in the light of all the available evidence, when one recognizes that the Word of God has come to men through the words of men in given historical situations."[5]

More recently I. Howard Marshall has called attention to a number of challenges that various parts of the New Testament pose to the careful reader (see box above).[6] These challenges require careful, reasoned investigation for their solution.

Marshall goes on to point out that whether we like it or not, "the Bible needs interpretation," and this involves a type of criticism. While the seeking soul may find the basic message of the New Testament in a single phrase or verse like John 3:16, maturing believers are wise to proceed to a more advanced understanding of the New Testament based on extensive study, careful analysis, and logical explanation in view of the full range of relevant evidence.

This insight is not new to Marshall, of course. Even in antiquity scholars wrestled with Scripture's meaning in a comparable, though not identical, way. Augustine and John Chrysostom in the fourth and fifth centuries, Calvin and Luther in the Reformation, Bengel and Wesley in the eighteenth century, all worked hard to interpret the New Testament in a reasoned and intellectually responsible fashion. For that reason their comments often still repay study as we seek all the relevant evidence that we can.

But just what is the relevant evidence? For scholars like Marshall and Ladd, as well as the figures just cited from earlier in church history, the uniqueness of Jesus Christ, the Bible's status as the Word of God, and the real presence of God in human affairs are highly relevant to how the New Testament ought to be read. But it is precisely at this point that much recent study disagrees. This brings us to another kind of "criticism"—not just rigorous analysis, but analysis based on certain convictions quite different from those shared by Ladd, Marshall, and their classical Christian predecessors.

Roots of Historical Criticism

There came a time in seventeenth- and eighteenth-century European history called the Enlightenment when "fundamental Christian beliefs" became "problematic." The Bible began to be interpreted in the light of different, non-Christian assumptions.[7] These assumptions included the following:

- The church has misread the Bible. Intelligent, independent readers need to free themselves from church doctrine and interpret the Bible in the light of human reason alone.
- Jesus Christ was not the divine Son of God. He was a superior ethical guide and spiritual example. He taught about God's moral law, but not salvation through his death for our sins and his resurrection. These ideas were inventions of the early church.
- Miracles in the New Testament, including Jesus' resurrection, can no longer be the basis for Christian belief, since modern reason doubts that they happened as the Bible reports.

- The Bible calls for ridicule, not reverence, since much of it is offensive to the modern mind. In advancing this view writers like Voltaire, Tom Paine, and Thomas Woolston sowed seeds that helped destroy the Bible's privileged place in Western society by encouraging skepticism toward it.
- The only legitimate way to interpret the Bible is the "historical" way. This is not "historical" in the sense held by Ladd and Marshall. It is rather "historical" in the sense of the non-Christian assumptions just listed. A "historical" reading in this vein assumes that cardinal Christian doctrines are rationally unacceptable, that Jesus was no more than a mere mortal, that miracles should be rejected or at least radically reinterpreted—and that no other interpretation of the Bible but this one deserves personal acceptance and public recognition.

And so it happened that by the nineteenth century, many scholars in Europe and particularly in Germany were arguing for an understanding of the New Testament that flatly contradicted Christian belief of all previous centuries. "Historical criticism" in the Enlightenment sense had been born. And "it laid the foundations on which modern biblical studies still rest."[8]

The rise of historical criticism is a vast subject. In reality there is not just a single type.[9] From the beginning it existed in numerous forms. Scholars around the world work constantly to understand its developments and effects. It is a fascinating field of study. Names like Galileo, Descartes, Locke, Semler, Lessing, Kant, Baur, Strauss, and many others come into view. A grasp of their distinctive ideas often goes far toward explaining not only their times but ours too.[10]

For in one form or another historical criticism is still very much with us. Books about the New Testament that insist on a "historical" reading of the New Testament often mean "historical-critical" and assert that the Bible is to be treated like any other book. The New Testament's central claims—as many Christians over many centuries have understood them—are cast into doubt. Then new or at least different meanings are proposed. A well-publicized example of this was a book called *The Five Gospels*, written in 1993.[11] It appealed to many Enlightenment figures in supporting its views and placed the reader before a stark either/or: ignorant belief in a human-divine savior as proclaimed in an authoritative Bible; or a reinterpretation of the canonical Gospels using later Gnostic documents to arrive at an egalitarian, anti-establishment Jesus who proclaimed witty though obscure philosophical wisdom.

Because the influence of historical criticism is widespread, we do well to pay attention to it, understand what it might have to teach us, and be aware of why we do not accept its doctrines if we find them unsatisfactory.

Contribution and Limitations of Historical Criticism

Historical criticism is sometimes denounced out of fear of the harm it can cause—and this is not without good reason. "This apprehension cannot be dismissed as merely reactionary. Some influential scholars of the modern period, identified as 'historians of early Christianity,' proposed radical revisions of traditional views of Christian beginnings."[12]

Voltaire (1694–1778) was one of many European intellectuals who cast doubt on the Bible's trustworthiness during the Enlightenment period.

For example, early Christianity has come to be treated as a free-for-all social movement of competing sects. The ancient apostolic church that upheld a central core of biblical teaching is portrayed by many as mythical. In fact, "modern accounts portray the mainstream church as suspect and devious, and the canonical gospels as weapons wielded by the powerful."[13]

These radical views have created many unnecessary sidetracks in scholarly thought. As Marshall points out, careful scholarship has often solved "problems" that careless criticism wrongly supposed it had found.[14] So caution toward historical criticism and skepticism toward its excesses are reasonable, though care must be exercised that disavowals be moderate in tone and fair to all parties concerned. Such an approach is apt to be more effective than shrill charges and complaints.[15]

It is only fair to grant historical criticism—or, as some would say, the historical-critical method—the credit it deserves. In broadest terms it has fostered many exciting discoveries over the past two centuries. During that time numerous ancient manuscripts have come to light. In the twentieth century this included the Dead Sea Scrolls and other important ancient works. Our knowledge of ancient languages and cultures has grown markedly. Scholars are able to defend the public from apparent forgeries like the ossuary (storage box for a dead person's bones) "discovered" in Israel in 2002. Reported to contain the remains of James, the half-brother of Jesus, closer examination seems to indicate that it was a hoax all along. New fields of study like semantics have refined the way we define biblical words. The life and milieu of Jesus are understood more clearly as new evidence comes to light and new methods are applied. The New Testament is seen in more graphic detail through application of methods like source, form, redaction, and literary analysis.

Scholars pay more attention to Jesus' Jewishness and its significance than they sometimes did in former times. Through historical criticism the nature and implications of various philosophical systems have been dramatized, as the New Testament has been interpreted in the light of philosophers like Kant, Hegel, Heidegger, Gadamer, Ricoeur, and Derrida, or philo-

157

Neo-Kantianism

phenomenology

existentialism

sophical movements like **Neo-Kantianism**, **phenomenology**, **existentialism**, and postmodernism. The serious Bible student will find that historical-critical scholarship has produced startling numbers of monographs, reference works, and commentaries. Many of these are invaluable even if their theological outlook is less than ideal.[16]

It should also be noted that many who use historical-critical methods in some form do not share Enlightenment convictions about Jesus Christ, miracles, and church doctrine. Historical criticism has pioneered methods that can prove useful when grounded in a worldview that leaves room for the truth of cardinal Christian doctrines. Any number of important critical studies today are written by Christian scholars who make use of historical-critical methods to varying degrees.

But caution is advised here. A prominent body of opinion insists that to use historical-critical methods without historical-critical convictions about the historical process is fudging. James Barr asserts that "History means only what we mean by our use of the word 'history.' . . . We do not apply the term 'history' to a form of investigation which resorts to divine agency as a mode of explanation."[17]

Is it possible to rule out the real influence of "divine agency" and still do justice to the New Testament? Can we really reject the incarnation, the virgin birth, and Jesus' divinity, resurrection, and ascension—all involving "divine agency"—and still give an adequate account of what the New Testament writers wrote and why? Many would rightly answer in the negative. Some even reject historical criticism entirely as a result. This is the strategy of a former historical critic who now renounces her earlier work and calls for radical reform in biblical scholarship.[18]

Yet others find use of a modified historical-critical approach fruitful. "One of the great challenges currently facing evangelical biblical scholarship is precisely that of modifying the historical-critical method so that it becomes productive and constructive."[19] It is not inappropriate to give historical criticism, as used by those who employ it in a responsible way, the credit it deserves for the refinement it can bring to the interpretation process.

In spite of the potential good of historical criticism, it still has its major difficulties. "To speak of the crisis of the historical-critical method today is practically a truism."[20] Many are convinced that in its classic forms it has seen its best days and call for major overhaul.[21] Maier lists thirteen criticisms lodged by critics themselves.[22] E. Heller offers insight from another quarter. As a literary critic he speaks of the "trust" and "heroism" of the postmedieval West's quest for "objectivity."[23] Its trust is "the conviction that the argument of critical inquiry will lead to something that is not only of use, but of true value." Its heroism is "the readiness not to flinch if it does not." But Heller goes on to diagnose a deadly fallacy, which consists in

> [t]he assumption that values, banned from the method of inquiry, will yet make their way into the answer; that means, indifferent to values, can yield an end justified not merely by its "correctness" or its usefulness, but by its intrinsic value. . . . [This is fallacious, for] things lose their value for man if he is set on withholding it from them.[24]

Applying Heller's broad insight to our own subject, there is certainly a trust and heroism underlying historical-critical

---

Criticisms of Historical Criticism

Gerhard Maier cites over a dozen problems with historical criticism voiced by critics themselves. They include:

- destabilization of faith
- inability to provide any suitable basis for faith
- belief that its method is the only method
- unlimited plurality of hypotheses
- capitulation to the spirit of the age
- enthronement of reason as sole source of authority
- elimination of the supernatural
- elevation of theologian over the Bible

—From Gerhard Maier, *Biblical Hermeneutics*, trans. Robert W. Yarbrough (Wheaton, Ill.: Crossway, 1994), 256–60.

Conditions

If we learn anything from the procedure of the Tübingen School it is this: that *Biblical exegesis and interpretation without conscious or unconscious dogmatic presuppositions is impossible.* The interpretation of the Bible and Biblical history demands an open, unconcealed, and honest statement of the fundamental historical principles by which it is to be interpreted. The validity of all Biblical exegesis and interpretation rests upon its readiness to set forth clearly and unflinchingly the dogmatic presuppositions on which it is based.

—Horton Harris, *The Tübingen School,* 262

Philosophers like Immanuel Kant (1724–1804) have had great influence on how the Bible is understood in the modern world.

labor. But a fallacy is also often at work. For what the procedure too frequently bans at the outset—a divine-human sin sacrifice; the resurrected Lord; the very gospel of redemption itself as classically understood—is unlikely to make it back into the results at some later stage.

Historical criticism has not produced the results so generously promised over the past two hundred years, as everyone, even its supporters, admit. But that does not mean progress cannot be made. There is yet

another way to approach the New Testament writings. We spoke of it in chapter 1 as the historical-theological approach. In chapters 2 through 9 we explained the Gospels and Jesus along these historical-theological lines. We now turn to a field of study that will assist us in thinking more deeply and clearly about the nature of a historical-theological outlook: hermeneutics.

The Promise of Hermeneutics

The word "hermeneutics" refers to the theory and practice of interpretation. We may break hermeneutics down into three basic aspects. When we approach the biblical text, we must ask: What are the necessary *conditions* for apprehending and entering into fruitful dialogue with its message? What *methods* are most appropriate for analyzing the data? What are the *aims* that shape our observation and the application of our findings?

These are some of the basic questions that hermeneutics highlights. If we do not take these into consideration, wrong interpretations can be the result. The price for such error can be high if the interpreter is trying to base life decisions on his or her interpretation, as readers of the New Testament often do. Let us now take a brief look at the three major factors that affect us when we interpret Scripture so that we can work on making our interpretations sound rather than random or even erroneous.

Conditions

Interpreting the New Testament works best under certain conditions. Some of these relate to the interpreter personally. Is he or she willing to receive the message that the text contains? If not, it is unlikely to emerge. Is the interpreter sufficiently equipped emotionally and intellectually? A six-year-old may be able to read but lacks the emotional maturity to probe the depths of Paul's praise of married love in Ephesians 5. Without a great deal of background knowledge it is difficult to make much sense of the Book of Revelation. Is the interpreter regenerate? That is, does he or she live in dependence on Christ so that Christ's Spirit lends aid to his or her interpretive efforts? "Herme-

Genres in the Bible

Different types of literary forms, called *genres*, can call for different ways of interpretation.

Typical genres found in the Bible include:

- narrative
- epistle
- law
- poetry
- prophecy
- wisdom

genre

neutics when utilized to interpret Scripture is a spiritual act, depending upon the leading of the Holy Spirit."[25] These are only a few of the conditions that affect the hermeneutical process at the personal level. Others include personal qualities like courage, character, and credibility.[26]

Other conditions involve assumptions about the data being interpreted. The New Testament is best seen as ultimately divine revelation and not merely a collection of human ideas. The "historical" explanation, although very important, must not be allowed to crowd out other kinds or levels of meaning. Maier speaks of the importance of what he calls dynamic and ethical understanding, too; and he makes "historical understanding" only one of five types of "cognitive understanding."[27] The other four are doctrinal, typological, allegorical, and prophetic.

Perhaps the major condition affecting interpretation is the interpreter's stance toward the authority of Scripture. But another important issue is Scripture's unity. While some claim to find disagreements and contradictions, a high view of Scripture's inspiration and authority justifies seeing various parts in the light of a unified whole. Here the principle of progressive revelation becomes important. This principle teaches that God's revelation of himself in Scripture grows in fullness and clarity as the centuries of his dealings with humanity progress. Many times parts of the Bible that were written earlier become clearer in light of what was written later. Another important area where assumptions make a big difference concerns the **genre** (literary form) of the writing being interpreted. When we open our Bibles we need to be aware of the kind of literature we are reading. Is it history? Poetry? Both? Neither? Different ways of reading apply,

depending on whether we are dealing with a parable, a narrative, a sermon, or a proverb.[28] The right decision here can be crucial to sound interpretation.

To sum up, interpreting the New Testament involves numerous *conditions* that will shape the way that interpretation proceeds from the outset. Being clear about the conditions that influence what we see and how we understand it, and working to make these conditions more suitable, is an important first step—and at the same time a lifelong process—toward a historical-theological approach.

Methods

A graduate theology student was once asked to talk to a college-age church group on the subject of hermeneutics. After the presentation he asked if there were questions. A Welsh art student named Vyvyan offered this response: "I think this hermeneutics business is quite mistaken. Here is my method. I seek the shade of a willow on the banks of a river. I let the wind blow the pages of my Bible. And when it stops, I look down and read. That is God's word for me."

This method did not serve Vyvyan very well. He drifted away from the church, fell into immorality, and eventually took his own life. In the long run most readers wisely seek more reliable methods of handling Scripture. It was a strength of historical criticism that it worked hard to formulate proper methods. But that strength became a weakness when the methods were dominated by assumptions inappropriate to the data being interpreted. As we refine the *conditions* under which we engage in interpretation, we should at the same time be on the lookout for *methods* that are sound and fruitful.

At a basic level we might think of methods like consulting a biblical concordance, or the cross-references in our Bible, when we seek more information about a verse or the meaning of a biblical word. Or we might keep a Bible handbook at our side as we read the New Testament, consulting the handbook to give us information we lack. Looking up a verse in different translations can be illuminating. Certainly we should be aware of the need for prayer, not as a substitute for intellectual under-

Tips on Meaningful Bible Reading

Helpful hints for reading the New Testament with profit:

1. Read it like any other book—the Bible is more than a regular book, but it is not less.
2. Read it with personal interest.
3. Interpret narratives in the light of doctrinal passages.
4. Interpret unclear passages by clearer passages.
5. Determine word meanings with the help of a good Bible dictionary.
6. Give careful attention to genre.
7. Make use of the realities of prayer and the Holy Spirit's guidance.

textual criticism

source criticism

form criticism

redaction criticism

literary criticism

canonical criticism

sociological criticism

discourse analysis

structuralism

standing but as a means of opening our whole selves to the living God who is able through Scripture to make us "wise for salvation" (2 Tm 3:15). The Holy Spirit's role in sound interpretation, while difficult to quantify, is real and important.

In an immensely helpful and readable book R. C. Sproul offers a number of "practical rules" that amount to a method for approaching any biblical text.[29] At a more advanced level, scholars and serious students make use of a number of critical methods and measures designed to arrive at the proper interpretation: **textual criticism**, **source criticism**, **form criticism**, **redaction criticism**, **literary criticism**, **canonical criticism**, **sociological criticism**, background studies, **discourse analysis**, and **structuralism**.[30] These modes of analysis are normally just one step in a larger process of arriving at the right or best understanding of a text.

Like conditions, methods affect interpretation in decisive ways. Inappropriate methods, or methods used ineptly, may make proper understanding difficult. An important part of growing in knowledge of *what* Scripture says is growing in wisdom regarding the *method* we use to interpret it. Wrong methods are obviously dangerous, but having no thought-out method at all may be little better. Most Bible readers find that their reading grows more rewarding as their method matures.

For example, readers who read whole biblical books in consecutive fashion on a daily basis are apt to arrive at sounder understanding than those who use a "lucky dip" method—on days when they think to read the Bible at all.

Aims

A third vital hermeneutical consideration is our *aims* in interpreting the New Testament. Reading can become stale or even heretical if aims are not sound. A number of aims may be suitable, depending on why we are approaching Scripture. We may wish to grow spiritually. Our aim may be to read as a springboard for devotional worship. Or we may have a class assignment on some portion of the New Testament. Now the aim has shifted from a purely devotional one. Or we may be teaching a lesson or giving a sermon. Once more the aim is different. None of these aims is any better than the other. They are also not mutually exclusive. But each is hermeneutically significant because it may cause us to see different dimensions of the text. Being aware of our aim, or aims, can help us avoid faulty interpretation and instead enjoy the fruit of sound understanding and application.

Unsound aims are not difficult to imagine. Reading the New Testament to find verses that will prove a parent or roommate wrong can easily lead to forcing the wrong meaning on the text because we so dearly wish to prove we are right. Meditating on a verse that promises forgiveness of sins (like 1 Jn 1:9) when at the same time we are engaging in an immoral relationship will inevitably result in twisting or ignoring Scripture's overall message (which does not extend free pardon to conscious and willful rebellion; see 1 Jn 2:4). Interpreting the New Testament with no thought of responding to it personally can hinder understanding. Interpretation that is so me-centered that the New Testament's real subject matter—Jesus Christ—becomes a mere accessory to the "blessing" I think I need, or the prayer I want answered, can obviously result in skewed results. Interpretation whose aim is to disprove or discredit historic Christian faith will likewise arrive at unsatisfactory findings.[31]

Maier speaks of the need for "communicative interpretation." Our aim ought to

> Apply yourself wholly to the text.
> Apply the text wholly to yourself.
>
> —Johann Albrecht Bengel (1687–1752)

doxological

exegesis

Historical criticism has shed light on many exciting discoveries, such as the Dead Sea Scrolls. This is the "Temple Scroll."

be to apply the New Testament to our lives.[32] In J. A. Bengel's words: "Apply yourself wholly to the text. Apply the text wholly to yourself." But, Maier continues, our aim ought to go further then self-application if this merely means moral or practical guidance. It should have a *doxological* aim—that is, it should lead to the worship of God, to personal communion with him. And it should include a *missiological* aim—the intention of passing on to others some of what Scripture has disclosed to us.

Osborne speaks similarly. Hermeneutics is important because of its highest aim: "to allow the God-inspired meaning of the Word to speak today." Osborne states that the ultimate aim of hermeneutics is "not systematic theology but the sermon."[33] This does not mean that the text's original mean-ing (**exegesis**) or personal application is unimportant. But it recognizes that the New Testament was written in and for a community (the church) whose lives centered on living out and spreading the gospel. Only if this is our aim, too, can we hope to arrive at something approaching the full range and depth of the New Testament's meaning. In this sense we see once more that the interpreter's *aim* is crucial in shaping the interpretation at which he or she arrives.

Invitation to Further Hermeneutical Study

"Only a carefully defined hermeneutic can keep one wedded to the text."[34] Interpreting the New Testament calls for care in arriving at the text's meaning and applying it properly.

In this chapter we have spoken of the pros and cons of historical criticism. We concluded that there are good reasons for declining to go along with historical criticism's excesses. At the beginning of the

chapter we noted a point of disagreement between two scholars, Albertz and Kümmel, and a question they raised: May a New Testament survey legitimately center on the New Testament's message, or should it focus on critical problems and uncertainties? While agreeing that a certain type of criticism can be fruitful, on the whole we sided with Albertz. We have also surveyed the importance of hermeneutics, especially in terms of the conditions, methods, and aims that influence how we understand and apply the Bible's message.

We have spoken of the need for a sound hermeneutic in order to support the idea of a historical-theological approach to the New Testament. Such an approach recognizes that the New Testament intends to relate the story of Jesus Christ as ancient Scripture foreshadowed it (the Old Testament), as various witnesses depicted this story (the Gospels), as the story spread (Acts), as the story was applied in various settings (the Epistles), and as the story will one day climax in world judgment and redemption (Revelation). The New Testament is not "history" in terms of purely natural cau-

sation. This was the historical-critical error. Nor is it "theology" in the sense of spiritual or doctrinal teaching apart from its original setting and meaning. This would be the mistake of some who interpret it solely for devotional or church application. It is both history and theology simultaneously. The hermeneutic used to interpret it is crucial to correct understanding and application.

In this chapter, then, we have sought to lay a foundation for productive reflection on formulating an appropriate hermeneutic—a lifelong process that every responsible reader of the New Testament is well advised to begin. Subsequent chapters of this book, like earlier ones, are designed to give assistance in raising issues and, where possible, proposing solutions that will enlarge the hermeneutical foundation that readers may already possess.

It is difficult to overestimate the complexity and magnitude of the discussion that hermeneutical questions have generated in recent decades. And the debate continues to surge forward. Recently evangelicals have excelled in shrewd interaction in this debate and constructive for-

F. C. Baur (1792–1860) and Historical-Critical Hermeneutics

F. C. Baur was a professor in Tübingen, Germany, whose views have greatly influenced the way many scholars and churches in the West read the Bible. Baur's was a historical-critical hermeneutic rather than a historical-theological one. Baur's biographer Horton Harris comments on Baur's scholarly agenda, achievement, and error. Taking "full account of its dogmatic premises" (see below) is precisely what a historical-theological hermeneutic seeks to do.

What Baur desired was a total view of history and in particular of the history of the Christian church. In this desire he was right. Any view of early church history must be a total view based on clear historical facts into which the unclear pieces of history are fitted. The tragedy was that Baur chose the wrong historical total view and then spent the rest of his lifetime distorting the evidence in order to maintain it. The problem that still confronts the investigation of the historical sources of Christianity is to set forth a historical total view that takes full account of its dogmatic premises.

—Horton Harris, The Tübingen School, 262

Focus 10: It's a Miracle! (Or Is It?)

The ministry of Jesus was characterized, among other things, by many miracles. He turned water into wine at the wedding feast in Cana; he raised Lazarus from the dead; he cured blindness, lameness, and a host of other ailments. And his time on earth culminated with the miracles of his own resurrection and ascension to his Father in heaven.

From its beginning, the church accepted the historicity of these miracles. But in the eighteenth century, doubt crept in as the Enlightenment notion of skepticism toward everything that couldn't be "scientifically" proven gained a foothold among scholars. The philosopher John Locke had this to say: "Whatever God hath revealed is certainly true; no doubt can be made of it. This is the proper object of faith: but whether it be a divine revelation or no, reason must judge." In other words, it is up to us to determine whether the Bible is truly God's Word to us.

The so-called argument from miracles was one way of deciding whether a revelation had a divine source. If we accept that only God can empower people to perform miracles and that God only confers this power on his true representatives, then a person who performs a miracle thereby gives us evidence that any revelation he delivers is from God. This argument was widely accepted as late as 1705, when Samuel Clarke declared that "the Christian Revelation is positively and directly proved, to be actually and immediately sent to us from God, by the many infallible *Signs and Miracles*, which the Author of it worked publicly as the Evidence of his Divine Commission."

However, in a matter of only twenty years this argument came under severe attack. One of its chief opponents was Thomas Woolston. In his *Discourses on the Miracles of our Saviour* (1727–29) he analyzed fourteen of Jesus' miracles, as well as the miracle of the resurrection. His conclusion was "that the literal History of many of the Miracles of *Jesus*, as recorded by the *Evangelists*, does imply Absurdities, Improbabilities, and Incredibilities; consequently they, either in whole or in part, were never wrought."

Woolston died in prison in 1733, where he had been detained on charges of criminal blasphemy. But his skepticism did not die. It was to be the seed from which other Enlightenment critics would doubt and ultimately reject not only miracles, but any part of the Bible that would not withstand the dogmas of historical criticism.

Earthenware pots commemorate Jesus' turning water into wine at one of the churches in Cana, Galilee.

Key Terms

canonical criticism
discourse analysis
doxological
exegesis
existentialism
form criticism
genre
hermeneutical
historical criticism
literary criticism
Neo-Kantianism
phenomenology
redaction criticism
sociological criticism
source criticism
structuralism
textual criticism

Key Place

Qumran

mulation of hermeneutical strategies. At a time when historical criticism in many circles has collapsed, at least as a basis for theology,[35] a wealth of studies have emerged that point ahead to ways of analyzing the New Testament rigorously without employing a method that constitutes an attack on its fundamental claims. Hermeneutical reflection is one of the most exciting and promising aspects of evangelical biblical scholarship as the twenty-first century gets under way.

Summary

1. Interpreting the New Testament is essential and should be done within a framework that recognizes the uniqueness of Jesus, accepts the Bible as the Word of God, and acknowledges the real presence of God in human affairs.

2. The Enlightenment critics who interpreted the New Testament typically held the following assumptions: (a) the church has misread the Bible; (b) Jesus was not the divine Son of God; (c) miracles in the New Testament may not have been real and cannot be the basis for Christian belief; (d) the Bible should be ridiculed because it is offensive to the modern mind; and (e) the only legitimate way to interpret the Bible is to use the historical-critical method.

3. Philosophical movements like Neo-Kantianism, phenomenology, and existentialism have influenced modern critical methods.

4. Hermeneutics is the theory and practice of interpretation.

5. In interpreting the biblical text, it is important to consider which conditions are necessary to enter into the text, which methods are appropriate for analyzing it, and which aims shape our observation and application of our findings.

6. Some methods of historical criticism include: textual criticism, source criticism, form criticism, redaction criticism, literary criticism, canonical criticism, sociological criticism, and structuralism.

7. The purpose of interpretation of the New Testament should be to apply it to our lives, to lead us to worship God in the context of the church, and to equip us to share this knowledge with others.

8. The New Testament is both history and theology simultaneously.

9. A sound hermeneutic recognizes that the New Testament relates the story of Christ as the Old Testament foretold, that various witnesses depicted this story, that in Acts the story was spread, that the story was applied in various settings in the Epistles, and that it will culminate one day in cosmic judgment as prophesied in Revelation.

Review Questions

1. Part of handling the New Testament properly is understanding _____ _____ to it.

2. Scholars like Augustine, Calvin, Luther, Bengel, and Wesley struggled to interpret the Bible in a _____ and intellectually _____ fashion.

3. Voltaire, Paine, and Woolston helped destroy respect for the Bible's truth in Western society by encouraging excessive _____.

4. The theory and practice of interpretation is called _____.

5. An essential assumption for interpreting New Testament data is that the New Testament must be seen as divine _____.

6. The major condition affecting interpretation is the interpreter's position on the _____ of Scripture.

7. In addition to the various methods to be used in interpretation, it is important to recognize the need for _____.

8. The aims for interpretation should be personal, doxological, and _____.

9. Recovering the text's original meaning is called _____.

10. For every believer, developing an appropriate hermeneutic should be a _____ process.

Study Questions

1. What issue did Kümmel's review of Albertz's New Testament introduction raise?

2. Why does the Bible need interpretation?

3. Cite some contributions of historical criticism.

4. How does a historical-theological approach differ from a historical-critical one?

5. What is the meaning of the word "hermeneutics"?

6. Give five characteristics of a sound hermeneutic for interpreting Scripture.

Further Reading

Bray, Gerald. *Biblical Interpretation: Past and Present.* Downers Grove: InterVarsity, 1996. An excellent history and survey of how the Bible has been interpreted through the centuries.

Doriani, Daniel M. *Getting the Message: A Plan for Interpreting and Applying the Bible.* Phillipsburg, N.J.: Presbyterian & Reformed, 1996. Ground level discussion of how to approach the Bible fruitfully. Full of practical insights yet academically well informed.

Elwell, Walter A., and J. D. Weaver, eds. *Bible Interpreters of the Twentieth Century.* Grand Rapids: Baker, 1999. Examines the life and work of some three dozen Christian scholars. Shows the human side of biblical interpretation and teaches sound hermeneutics by example.

Fee, Gordon. *New Testament Exegesis: A Handbook for Students and Pastors.* 3rd ed. Louisville: Westminster John Knox, 2002. A step-by-step guide for interpreting a biblical text with a view to preparing a research paper or sermon. Shows the advantage of a methodical approach to interpreting Scripture.

Fee, Gordon, and Douglas Stuart. *How to Read the Bible for All It's Worth.* Rev. ed. Grand Rapids: Zondervan, 1993. A much-used practical handbook covering both Testaments.

Hayes, John H., ed. *Dictionary of Biblical Interpretation.* 2 vols. Nashville: Abingdon, 1999. An advanced reference work covering many of the topics mentioned in this chapter.

Kaiser, Walter C., Jr., and Moisés Silva. *An Introduction to Biblical Hermeneutics: The Search for Meaning.* Grand Rapids: Zondervan, 1994. Wrestles with the issue of the Bible's relevance in a world where the possibility of textual meaning is disputed. Both practical and theoretical in scope.

Maier, Gerhard. *Biblical Hermeneutics.* Trans. Robert W. Yarbrough. Wheaton, Ill.: Crossway, 1994. A leading German evangelical scholar analyzes the conditions under which interpretation and application of Scripture take place. Valuable chapters on criticism and need for method.

McKim, Donald K., ed. *Historical Handbook of Major Biblical Interpreters.* Downers Grove/Leicester: InterVarsity, 1998. This invaluable reference volume summarizes how various periods and scholars have pursued the hermeneutical task.

O'Collins, Gerald, and Daniel Kendall. *The Bible for Theology: Ten Principles for the Theological Use of Scripture.* New York/Mahwah, N.J.: Paulist, 1997. Roman Catholic attempt to arrive at normative principles for theological use of the Bible.

Oden, Thomas C. *The Rebirth of Orthodoxy.* San Francisco: HarperSanFranciso, 2003. Discusses the recent return to classic Christianity in circles that had abandoned it. Shows the importance of appropriate theological convictions and personal commitment to God in order to understand the word of God.

Osborne, Grant R. *The Hermeneutical Spiral: A Comprehensive Introduction to Biblical Interpretation.* Downers Grove: InterVarsity, 1991. As the subtitle indicates, no aspect of the hermeneutical debate escapes mention. Valuable because of its scope and consistency.

Soulen, Richard N., and R. Kendall Soulen. *Handbook of Biblical Criticism.* 3rd ed. Louisville: Westminster John Knox, 2001. Valuable reference guide covering a wide range of concerns central to hermeneutics. These include methods, technical terms, abbreviations, and major names in the field.

Sproul, R. C. *Knowing Scripture.* Downers Grove: InterVarsity, 1977. Valuable basic study guide.

Thiselton, Anthony C. *New Horizons in Hermeneutics: The Theory and Practice of Transforming Biblical Reading.* Grand Rapids: Zondervan, 1992. Comprehensive survey and analysis. Brings the world of academic hermeneutical discussion into dialogue with the concerns of practical biblical interpretation.

Vanhoozer, Kevin. *Is There a Meaning in This Text?* Grand Rapids: Zondervan, 1998. Advanced discussion of postmodern trends and how they impact hermeneutical theory and practice. Defends the concept of authorial intent.

11 The Modern Study of the Gospels

Outline

- The Rise of Source Criticism
- The Rise of Form Criticism
- The Rise of Redaction Criticism
- The Current Situation

Objectives

After reading this chapter, you should be able to

- Outline some major approaches to the study of the New Testament
- Identify major scholars who are associated with each approach
- Define and contrast the methods of source, form, and redaction criticism
- Discuss current methods of approaching the study of the Gospels
- Formulate a Christian response to methods that are needlessly skeptical

Augustine believed that Matthew was the first Gospel written and that the apostle by that name wrote it.

John Calvin, *(far right),* like Augustine, wrote about the problematic passages in the Gospels.

R. M. Ogilvie has written that "the determining ideas of a civilization have always been the prerogative of the few."[1] By this he means that the way society views the world is heavily influenced by key ideas held by esteemed thinkers and leaders of each generation. Ogilvie shows how the ruling classes of England from the seventeenth to the early twentieth centuries drew on certain ancient writers to enliven their minds and thus to shape the thinking of their whole nation. The ideas of an intellectual elite, informed by such classical writers as Ovid, Horace, Plato, and Homer, shaped the vision of the larger society.

A similar story can be traced in how the Gospels have been read and understood over the past two and a half centuries. Prior to that time, as we shall see below, the view prevailed that the four Gospels were inspired by God and therefore true and binding for all persons. But with the rise of what has come to be called "modern" thought in the seventeenth century, the Bible began to be viewed from a different viewpoint.[2] This new viewpoint dramatically altered how the Gospels were read. The effects of this new viewpoint persist to the present time.

The modern study of the Gospels is to be dated from the Enlightenment in the eighteenth century.[3] Until that time the Gospels were studied, and many books and commentaries were written on them. All four Gospels were considered of equal value both historically and theologically, having been produced by human authors through divine inspiration. The view that prevailed regarding their interrelationship was generally that of AUGUSTINE (354–430). He believed that Matthew was the first Gospel written and that the apostle by that name wrote it. John Mark had the apostles Peter and Matthew as his sources, abbreviating the latter. Luke and John were then written independently, or perhaps with some knowledge, of Matthew and Mark. For over a thousand years this view, or one similar to it, held sway.

Everyone knew very well that differences existed among the four Gospels and that some of these differences were significant. The opponents of Christianity also knew this. CELSUS, for one, as early as the second century, used this as one of his arguments against the faith. There were many responses to such challenges as his. ORIGEN responded directly to Celsus. He also produced a massive work called the *Hexapla,* which was a carefully researched comparative version of the Old Testament Scriptures designed to show their trustworthiness. Augustine later composed a work entitled *The Harmony*

Augustine on the Gospels

> However the evangelists may each have reported some matters which are not recorded by the others, it would be hard to prove that any question involving real discrepancy arises out of these.
>
> —Augustine, *Harmony of the Evangelists*, Book IV, X.II

Marcan Hypothesis

Q

Synoptic Problem

of the Gospels, in which he painstakingly went through a lengthy catalog of problematic passages in the Gospels with a view to explaining them. John Calvin, during the time of the Reformation, wrote a book similar to Augustine's, as did others after him. So the Gospels were not uncritically swallowed during all those centuries. Believers were well aware of the difficulties that existed in the Gospel narratives. But their faith in the power of God to override any tendency toward human error kept them from believing that the Gospels contradicted one another in fundamental ways.

The Rise of Source Criticism

In the same year that the United States declared its independence (1776) a German scholar named J. J. Griesbach wrote a *Synopsis of the Gospels of Matthew, Mark and Luke*. In it he arranged the first three Gospels in parallel columns for ease of study. The Gospel of John was only incidentally included. Thus arose a new term ("Synoptic Gospel") and a new approach to Gospel study (comparing the first three Gospels against one another, while leaving John out as being too different to warrant comparison). This did not, at first, discredit the Gospel of John. Yet by the time the twentieth century arrived John was considered by the critics to be too theological to be of any real historical value. Griesbach, by constructing his synopsis, was not attempting to advance any radi-

cally new theory of Gospel authorship. In fact, he accepted Augustine's view that Mark abbreviated Matthew, adding the modification that Mark also made use of the Gospel of Luke.

In the next thirty years, many new ideas arose, but one in particular became the reigning theory of Gospel relationships. The idea was that Mark was the first of the written Gospels and that both Matthew and Luke used Mark as their primary source. Thus arose the "**Marcan Hypothesis**," or the "Priority of Mark" as it is sometimes called. There were numerous variations of this and in 1863 H. J. Holtzmann added another source that was ultimately dubbed simply "**Q**." This source comprised the 230 or so verses that Matthew and Luke have in common that are not found in Mark. So the Marcan Hypothesis took shape as a two-source hypothesis, the sources being Mark and Q. Swirling around all this was a virtual explosion of theories dealing with such questions as the content of Q, whether the canonical Mark was the original Mark (some theories suggested as many as four different Marks that preceded it), which of the many revisions of Mark Matthew and Luke used, whether Matthew and Luke used the same Mark, and so on. All the problems that involved how the first three Gospels related to one another were collectively called "the **Synoptic Problem**" by scholars.

With the coming of the twentieth century came almost microscopic studies of the Gospels in such well-known works as Sir John Hawkins' *Horae Synopticae* (1898) and the *Oxford Studies in the Synoptic Problem* (1911). This approach to the Gospels reached its logical conclusion in 1924, when B. H. Streeter wrote his monumental *The Four Gospels: A Study in Origins*. He proposed a four-document hypothesis, the documents being Mark, Q, L (material peculiar to Luke), and M (material peculiar to Matthew). From these four sources our three canonical Gospels were constructed. Streeter's was not the last word, of course. Many others attempted to refine the process of Gospel origins, moving away from singular written sources, whether two or four, to multiple sources for the Gospels. A typical example of this is F. C. Grant.[4]

Formgeschichte

pericopae

Sitz im Leben

The Rise of Form Criticism

Streeter had not yet written *The Four Gospels* when its days were already numbered. A new approach had appeared—*Formgeschichte* (form history), or form criticism, as it came to be known.[5] Those who developed the form-critical approach to the Gospels were interested in more than just the final written stage of the Gospel tradition (i.e., the Gospel itself). They were also keen to go beyond the question of literary sources. They were primarily concerned about the stages through which the earlier material passed in its oral phase before it reached that final written stage. To trace that development, it was necessary to begin with the written Gospel material, but then, for purposes of analysis, to break it into isolated, independent units (called **pericopae**) and to identify the form that the tradition took. Then, these independent pericopae were to be located within their original life setting, or *Sitz im Leben*, as it was called. For the vast majority of the Gospel pericopae, the *Sitz im Leben* was the life of the early church, not the life of Jesus.

The fundamental postulate that underlay this theory was that the Gospels were not analogous to classical literary works. They were more akin to ancient folk literature, and the Gospel writers were just recording the short pithy stories or sayings that circulated orally among the early Christians. So, the Gospel writers were not really writers at all, but compilers of traditions that had been adapted to their own communities.

The first major written work that suggested using this methodology was Martin Dibelius's *Die Formgeschichte des Evangeliums* (1919), which was revised in 1934 and made available in English as *From Tradition to Gospel*. Dibelius argued that the preaching of the early church was the matrix out of which the traditions arose. He found such "forms" of tradition as sermon, paradigm (a brief account of an event), tale, legend, and exhortation. This was followed by RUDOLF BULTMANN's *The History of the Synoptic Tradition* (1921; ET 1963). Bultmann's was a more thoroughgoing work than Dibelius's, adding many refinements of form; it was also more radical. In the hands of Bultmann, there was little left of the Gospel material that went back to Jesus. A considerable portion could

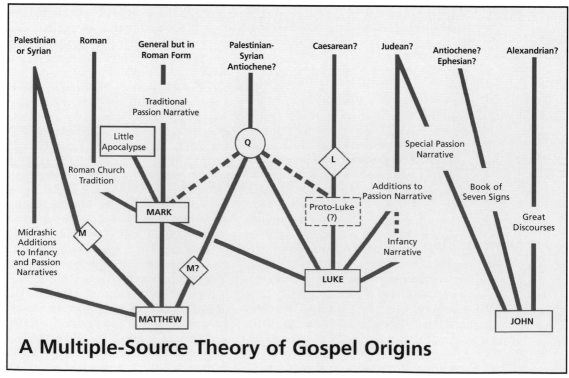

A Multiple-Source Theory of Gospel Origins

Are the Form Critics Right?

If the Form Critics are right, the disciples must have been translated to heaven immediately after the Resurrection.

—Vincent Taylor, *The Formation of the Gospel Tradition*

munities as we know them from the letters of the New Testament. Often we are virtually forced to read these needs into the synoptic text. The term '**community construction**' which is used so readily today, usually without further explanation, can seldom elucidate actual historical circumstances; more frequently, it tends to obscure them."[7] Many other criticisms were also leveled at form criticism and by the 1950s a new method had arisen to take it one step farther—and in some instances to challenge or even replace it.

community construction

be traced to the myth-making instincts of the early believers.

Critics of the new methodology such as Erich Fascher and Martin Albertz condemned the "brazen skepticism" of Bultmann, but the method soon established itself as part of New Testament studies. Form criticism was toned down by more moderate scholars such as Vincent Taylor in *The Formation of the Gospel Tradition* (1933). Although acknowledging the limited value of form criticism, he disagreed with its radical formulations and even argued that many of the Gospel sayings go back to the original eyewitnesses.[6]

In the hands of the form critics the focus shifted from the written Gospels (they were end-products of an earlier process) and from Jesus on earth (Gospel recollections of him are uncertain) to the community that kept Jesus' memory alive by adapting and inventing material related to him that later became the written Gospels. Since there were many such communities, there were many such collections of stories and in the end a conflicting set of "memories" about Jesus. So the search for these early churches began. Obviously, if we want to know what the creative memories were we would have to know something about their originators.

But here the fundamental problem arose. We know almost nothing about them, and what we do know comes from the Gospels themselves. The Gospels claim to tell us about Jesus, not the early church. In addition, when we do know something about the churches, the picture is very different than the one imagined by the form critics. As Hengel says, "It is in fact amazing how few signs the synoptic gospels show of the 'needs' of the com-

The Rise of Redaction Criticism

Aside from the fact that Jesus virtually disappeared in the hands of the form critics, the Gospels did too. But they wouldn't go away so easily (nor would Jesus, for that matter); after all, they *were* in the Bible. Critics had to account for their coming into existence in the first place. These Gospels had obvious unity and a sense of purpose as literary productions. This being the case, *someone* had to have produced them. Abstractions such as "communities" don't write books. So the focus shifted to the redactors (compilers, writers) of the Gospels in a scholarly movement known as *Redaktionsgeschichte* or redaction criticism.[8]

Although anticipated by earlier writers, redaction criticism began with the writings of some of Bultmann's students. Günther Bornkamm's work on Matthew set the pace,[9] followed by Hans Conzelmann's *Theology of St. Luke* (1954; ET 1960) and Willi Marxsen's *Mark the Evangelist* (1956; ET 1969). What these writers were doing, in effect, was adding another consciously acknowledged life situation (*Sitz im Leben*) to the developmental process of the Gospels. The first *Sitz im Leben* could be Jesus' life; the second, the oral period of the early church; the third, the Evangelist and his circumstances. But, as Marxsen said, "Redaction history is not merely the continuation of form history"; it is something else again.[10] Norman Perrin summarizes what that something else is in four points.[11] First, form criticism saw the Evan-

narrative
criticism

gelists as compilers of tradition; redaction criticism sees them as authors in their own right. Second, form criticism was concerned with small units of tradition and how they came to be; redaction criticism is concerned with large units, up to the whole Gospels themselves. Third, form criticism, with its concern for small units, never did justice to the intent of the Evangelists; redaction criticism is concerned with the theological intent of the writers. Fourth, form criticism is concerned with only one *Sitz im Leben* (the early church); redaction criticism is concerned with all three *Sitze im Leben* of the Gospel material.

But redaction criticism did not go on to establish itself as the overarching method that could solve all of the basic problems of Gospel research. Quite the contrary, by 1991, R. H. Stein could write, "Today redaction criticism has fallen on hard times. In part this is to be expected, since the fever pitch of redaction-critical studies could not maintain itself. Like other movements in biblical research, this one would also peak and then recede. This was only natural, and the excess of some redaction-critical studies, the lack of clear methodology (especially in regard to Marcan studies), and the narrow focus of redaction criticism aided in its receding from the dominating position in New Testament scholarship."[12]

The reason for this was that during the past forty years the inherent limitations of the redaction-critical method, as well as the other critical methods, were gradually recognized and other approaches began to make their voices heard.

The Current Situation

It is not possible at the present moment to speak of any dominating theory on which all scholars would agree when approaching the study of the Gospels. Indeed, that was probably never the case, although some points of view stood out above the others, as we have seen. But some current trends can be observed.

For one thing, although the complex edifice of German-dominated form-critical and redaction-critical studies is less dominant, there are those who hold that whatever the limitations in those methods we can't get along without them. Some continue to place faith in these methods, hoping that an answer will be found there.[13]

Others have looked at alternate ways of approaching the Gospels. One such approach was called structuralism,[14] part of a large group of related approaches, collectively called literary criticism.[15] Structuralism arose around the turn of the century with linguist Ferdinand de Saussure and folklorist Vladimir Propp. It wasn't until the 1970s that their insights were applied seriously to biblical narratives, notably by Roland Barthes. The essence of structuralism is that there underlies all expression and narrative a structure in our minds, a "deep structure," which determines courses that our thoughts and expressions take. When we understand that deep structure, we can understand the "real" meaning of any narrative or story. Variations of this approach abound, and adaptations were made to it by yet others, such as A. J. Greimas and Claude Lévi-Strauss. By the time it was applied to the Gospel stories, it had become such a complicated and esoteric enterprise that it found little widespread support. It seemed to promise much, but in the end produced few agreed-on results. It is generally conceded that there is considerable value in giving serious consideration to the formal structures of narrative as story, but few are willing to buy into the idea that the mind has a single structure, still less that structuralist theorists have discovered it.

Another literary approach to the Gospels is called **narrative criticism**.[16] It is not really a new way of looking at Scripture; in fact, it has been around for about a century. It was eclipsed by some of the newer, more fashionable movements earlier in this century but is now being revived. As presently practiced, it tries to incorporate modern insights in the study of both ancient and modern literature into more technical New Testament studies, giving full weight to the Bible as literary production in all its manifold complexity, not just as fragmented bits of folk tradition. The focus is on literary techniques, plot, structure, ordering of events, dramatic tension, intended impact on the reader, and other such literary elements. There is compara-

reader–response theories

rhetorical criticism

deconstructionism

tively less emphasis on the specific theological ideas present, grammar and lexicographical matters, and historical reference. In some cases, **reader–response theories** are being integrated into the analysis. These shift the focus even away from "what happened back then" to "what is happening now to me as I read the text."[17] A related, though significantly different, approach is **rhetorical criticism**.[18] It seeks to be more dynamic than a narrow literary approach to the text and looks at the quality or techniques of discourse by which the writer seeks to impact the reader. When the focus on the reader is pushed to the extreme it becomes known as **deconstructionism**, a view in which the text loses all objective meaning and becomes whatever the reader takes it to mean. New Testament scholars have generally resisted sweeping application of this approach.

Another collection of approaches to the New Testament falls under the heading of "social scientific criticism of the New Testament."[19] As is the case with the literary approaches, these views are not really new either. The importance of such things as historical background, social context, and economic matters were being explored as early as the 1920s. One such example was F. C.

Grant's *An Economic Background to the New Testament* (1927). By the 1940s the expression "criticism by social environment" had arisen.[20] What distinguishes these earlier attempts to bring social-historical factors to bear on New Testament studies from the present approaches is that whereas formerly the New Testament was seen as *illuminated* by sociology, now sociology is seen as *explaining* the New Testament. The New Testament is being forced into the mold of categories predetermined by the sociological analysts. Most scholars are proceeding with caution. Social scientific methodologies, even in sociology, are of recent vintage, and have not worked themselves out to any consensus as yet, so how they will apply to the New Testament is a matter of debate. To the extent that an assumed social determinism underlies these methodologies, wise interpreters will apply them with critical caution.

Most scholars agree on the importance of understanding the Gospels in the context of their decidedly Jewish setting and this marks real progress over some older approaches. Jesus' Jewishness has rightly become a focal point of study.[21] This can be overstated so that Jesus becomes little more than just one other Jewish thinker of his

Excavating a Roman period capital in Jerusalem. Since the 1920s, historical background, social context, and economic matters have been explored in approaching the New Testament.

A Reader–Response Hermeneutic

The New Testament with one voice describes the twelve apostles of Jesus Christ as being men. Matthew, for example, lists the twelve whom Jesus sent out to preach and perform mighty signs and wonders, and without exception they are males (Mt 10:1–20). The same twelve (with the exception of Judas) became the foundation stones of the early Christian church, as recorded in Eph 2:20—"built on the foundation of the apostles and prophets, with Christ Jesus himself as the chief cornerstone."

Some radical readings of these texts adopt what is sometimes called a reader-response hermeneutic, which asserts that the meaning of a text does not lie in its words but in its relevance to contemporary sociological or cultural circumstances. Since the first-century world was dominated by a male chauvinistic point of view, these critics argue, the choice of male apostles was to be expected. In our enlightened and liberated age, however, gender roles no longer matter, so women are free to hold any office or ministry open to men.

Were Jesus to have lived today, some say, he would have chosen women to be apostles.

The question of women's ordination is complex. But we can see from this example that the choice of hermeneutic is significant for our application of biblical teachings to the church today. Whereas a feminist reader–response theory would simply assume that women should be free to hold all church offices, other readings of the text would place greater stress on the author (Matthew) or the subject (Jesus) rather than the current reader.

time.[22] But in general, study of the Gospels has benefited greatly from more careful attention to the Old Testament and the Jewish substructure of Jesus' life and teaching.[23]

The Synoptic Problem is another issue that will not go away. Throughout the entire twentieth century the Marcan Hypothesis reigned supreme. Most New Testament scholars begin with the assumption that in one way or another Mark was the first written Gospel and a primary source of both Matthew and Luke, who also used another source called Q. Although dominant, this view has not gone unchallenged. Dom John Chapman's rejection of Mark's priority in *Matthew, Mark, and Luke* appeared in 1937. B. C. Butler continued with *The Originality of St. Matthew* (1951) and in 1964 W. R. Farmer began arguing for an updated version of the Griesbach Hypothesis.[24] This trend was continued by H. H. Stoldt[25] and again, Farmer.[26] E. Linnemann asks even more fundamental questions in *Is There a Synoptic Problem? Rethinking the Literary Dependence of the First Three Gospels* (1992). Some are beginning to argue for the virtual independence of the three Synoptics.[27]

Of course, defenders of Marcan priority continue and still dominate the field. However, among scholars there is still very little agreement on how to proceed. Symptomatic of this is the result of twelve years of study by the Synoptic Seminar of the Society for New Testament Studies. When it disbanded in 1982, their report was that they did not agree on a single thing. All of this has led some to argue that the Synoptic Problem might be ultimately insoluble.

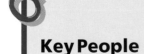

Key People

Augustine
Bultmann
Celsus
Origen

Key Terms

community construction
deconstructionism
Formgeschichte
Marcan Hypothesis
narrative criticism
pericopae
Q
reader–response theory
rhetorical criticism
Sitz im Leben
Synoptic Problem

Q has also come in for renewed analysis recently. As one of the foundational documents of the two-source theory it had been more or less taken for granted. Some had attempted to dispense with it,[28] but unsuccessfully, because the reigning theory required that something like it exist. Currently, its nature, theology, structure, and content are being vigorously explored.[29]

There are also a number of minor currents that could be observed, but this gives an idea of where we are today. There are a great many ideas competing for dominance, but little agreement on anything among the critical scholars. The root cause of this could well be the scholarly critics' unwillingness to allow God any significant part in the production of the Gospels and their commitment to treat the New Testament as "just another book."

David Alan Black speaks for many in questioning the wisdom of "modern" and "postmodern" approaches[30] that refuse "to admit the existence of a supernatural order and the intervention of a personal God in the world through special revelation, miracles, and prophecies."[31] The current confusion is a reminder of the need for continued refinement of methods, study of primary sources, and dialogue among parties holding various views. It is a reminder too of the need for courage in upholding long-standing and intellectually defensible Christian convictions regarding the saving message of the Gospels despite the loss of appetite for Jesus' lordship among most of the West's intellectual elite.

Summary

1. Prior to the seventeenth century, the Gospels were widely believed to be inspired by God and therefore true and binding for all persons.

2. New impetus to Synoptic study was given by Griesbach's work on the Gospels published in 1776.

3. In form criticism, the material in the Gospels was broken down into isolated, independent units called pericopae for further study.

4. Form critics held that the writers of the Gospels were not writers at all but compilers of tradition.

5. The focus of the form critics was on the community that kept the memory of Jesus alive.

6. Redaction criticism focuses on the writers in their own right.

7. There is currently no one method of Gospels interpretation on which all scholars agree.

8. Newer methods of criticism include structuralism, which is part of literary criticism. It maintains that there is a structure within our minds that determines the direction of our thoughts, and that it is necessary to understand that deep structure in order to understand a story.

9. Some newer methods of criticism are narrative criticism, reader–response theory, rhetorical criticism, and deconstructionism.

Review Questions

1. Until the Enlightenment, the general approach to the Gospels was based on the view of _____.

2. The German scholar whose work began the new approach to the Gospels was _____.

3. The emphasis on the priority of Mark is called the _____.

4. The set of problems that involve the relationship of the first three Gospels is known as the _____.

5. Those who were most concerned about how the material of the Gospels passed through oral to written stages developed the method known as _____ criticism.

6. Form critics focused on the _____ that kept Jesus' memory alive.

7. Central to redaction criticism are the redactors, who are the _____ and _____.

8. A newer theory that focuses on what happens to the reader as he or she reads is called _____ theory.

9. Recently there has been a renewed interest in the analysis of _____, the verses that Matthew and Luke, but not Mark, have in common.

Study Questions

1. What is the "Synoptic Problem," and how did it arise?

2. What is form criticism? What can be said for and against it?

3. Why did redaction criticism arise and what does it teach?

4. Discuss some of the current trends of Gospel study.

5. How should evangelicals relate to critical biblical studies?

6. What is your opinion of modern biblical studies? Does it help or hinder understanding the New Testament?

Further Reading

Bailey, James L., and L. D. Vander Brock. *Literary Forms in the New Testament*. Louisville: Westminster/John Knox, 1992. An introduction to the various literary types that exist in the New Testament from a critical point of view.

Bultmann, Rudolf. *History of the Synoptic Tradition*. San Francisco: Harper & Row, 1976. The standard form-critical study of the Synoptic Gospels from a radical perspective.

Dungan, David Laird. *A History of the Synoptic Problem*. New York: Doubleday, 1999. Proposes that traditional approaches that either simply harmonize or criticize are misguided. Implies that the "problem" is really an issue of recognizing God, or Christ, more than solving "a scientific riddle" (394).

Farmer, William R. *The Synoptic Problem: A Critical Analysis*. Macon, Ga.: Mercer University Press, 1964. Excellent history of the problem. Argues that Mark was not the first Gospel and Q did not exist.

Gerhardsson, Birger. *The Reliability of the Gospel Tradition*. Peabody, Mass.: Hendrickson, 2001. A Swedish scholar's important defense of the Gospel's accuracy based on what we know about the transmission of oral teaching in other Jewish circles of Jesus' day.

Hall, David R. *The Gospel Framework: Fiction or Fact?* Carlisle: Paternoster, 1997. An important analysis of early form criticism, especially the work of K. L. Schmidt, whose work on the Synoptic Gospels continues to wield influence. Hall shows that Schmidt's work was to a large extent flawed.

Harrisville, R. A., and W. Sundberg. *The Bible in Modern Culture*. 2nd ed. Grand Rapids: Eerdmans, 2002. A survey of contemporary historical-critical methodology with strong words of caution.

Kümmel, Werner G. *The New Testament: The History of the Investigation of Its Problems*. Nashville: Abingdon, 1972. A useful survey of New Testament studies emphasizing the German contribution to the subject.

Longman, Tremper, III. *Literary Approaches to Biblical Interpretation*. Grand Rapids: Zondervan, 1987. A nicely written and easy-to-follow introduction to the whole question of the Bible as literature. Both Old Testament and New Testament examples are given.

Malina, Bruce J., and Richard L. Rohrbaugh. *Social Science Commentary on the Synoptic Gospels*. 2nd ed. Minneapolis: Fortress, 2002. Investigation that reflects the strengths and weaknesses of social-scientific assumptions and methods.

McKnight, Scot. *Interpreting the Synoptic Gospels*. Grand Rapids: Baker, 1988. An easy-to-follow introduction to synoptic studies. Most modern methods are evaluated.

Neill, Stephen, and Tom Wright. *The Interpretation of the New Testament: 1861–1986*. Oxford: Oxford University Press, 1988. A standard history of New Testament interpretation.

Patzia, Arthur G. *The Making of the New Testament*. Downers Grove: InterVarsity, 1995. Assesses methods in Gospels research and describes how the Gospels may have been composed and collected.

Reicke, Bo. *The Roots of the Synoptic Gospels*. Philadelphia: Fortress, 1986. A rather technical study of the Synoptic Problem that contains a brief history of the discussion and an attempt to work out a constructive mention that goes beyond mere literary relationships.

Stein, Robert H. *The Synoptic Problem: An Introduction*. Grand Rapids: Baker, 1987. Examines modern methods of analyzing the Gospels favorably. Argues that Mark was the first Gospel and Q did exist.

Taylor, R. O. P. *The Groundwork of the Gospels*. Oxford: Blackwell, 1946. An original and courageous work that challenges many of the skeptical beliefs accepted in Gospels scholarship. Far ahead of its time in arguing that Hellenism influenced first-century Judaism, that Jesus spoke Greek, and that when the Gospels came to be written, various circumstances served to assure the accuracy of their contents.

Taylor, Vincent. *The Formation of the Gospel Tradition*. London: Macmillan, 1933. A moderate statement of the form-critical theory.

Wenham, John W. *Redating Matthew, Mark and Luke*. London: Hodder & Stoughton, 1991. A complex, scholarly work that argues for very early dates of the Gospels, dating Matthew about 40 and Mark about 45.

12 The Modern Search for Jesus

Outline

- **The Search for the Real Jesus**
  A Brief History of the Search
  The Current Situation
- **The Search for the Real Words of Jesus**
  A Brief Look at the Search
  The Criteria Used to Find Jesus' Real Words
  A Positive Approach to the Problem

Objectives

After reading this chapter, you should be able to

- Construct a brief outline of the three phases of the search scholars have made for the "real" Jesus
- Identify the scholars who have played major roles in this debate
- Evaluate the current status of this search
- Discuss the search for the real words of Jesus
- List the criteria used to find what Jesus really said
- Suggest a suitable approach for evangelical scholars interested in this debate

A Cambridge University professor begins a recent book with a profound question: "At the end of the 20th century, is it possible to affirm a view of Jesus of Nazareth that relates with integrity both to historical scholarship and to orthodox Christian faith?"[1] For over two hundred years now in Europe and North America, debate has raged over what we know for sure about Jesus. Most of us do not need to become experts in this debate. But all of us can benefit from learning how it arose, how it continues to affect our world's approach to the Bible, and how we can adopt a more responsible outlook in our own understanding of the four Gospels.

The Search for the Real Jesus

A Brief History of the Search[2]

It would have sounded strange to Christians before the eighteenth century to be told that they needed to "find" Jesus in the Gospels. Jesus was not lost, so why would they have to search for him? The Gospels were divinely inspired books that contained no errors, so all one had to do was to gather the material together and arrange it in some comprehensive way.

Jesus, the Center of History

Regardless of what anyone may personally think or believe about him, Jesus of Nazareth has been the dominant figure in the history of Western culture for almost twenty centuries. If it were possible, with some sort of supermagnet, to pull up out of that history every scrap of metal bearing at least a trace of his name, how much would be left? It is from his birth that most of the human race dates its calendars, it is by his name that millions curse and in his name that millions pray.

—Jaroslav Pelikan

Thoughtful believers were aware that some of the accounts differed and that in some places, like the trial and resurrection accounts, it was very difficult to work everything out precisely. But that did not invalidate the story. It simply meant that the events in question were being looked at from different angles and were emphasizing different things. The resulting picture was the true story of Jesus of Nazareth, guaranteed by God who had protected the Gospel writers from saying anything that was untrue. In fact, the writers themselves, in one way or another, had direct contact with the events they were describing. Matthew and John were disciples of Jesus; Mark was recording the remembrances of Peter; and Luke had interviewed many people who had been eyewitnesses and servants of Christ from the beginning (Lk 1:1–4).

With the coming of the Enlightenment in the late eighteenth century, however, all that changed. A rationalistic spirit swept over scholars in the European universities, including many Bible and theology professors.

It did not happen all at once, or to the same degree everywhere, but the general attitude was that the old way of looking at the Gospels would not work anymore. The newer attitude went something like this. The Gospels were not considered to be the story of Jesus, but only stories about Jesus, written by people who had not known him and perhaps a hundred years after Jesus died. During that time many myths, legends, and heavily edited accounts had arisen and become part of the tradition. Hence, the real Jesus was buried in a mass of questionable material and had to be rediscovered. In addition to this, the idea that God had divinely inspired the Gospels was also being abandoned. There was no guarantee that anything found there was necessarily true. If it could be "proven" to be true on rational "scientific" grounds, then it could be accepted, but only then. Any other attitude would be naive and uncritical. The Bible was, after all, just another book and needed to be read that way. The fact that it talked about religious things did not warrant giving it special treatment.

How would one decide what was "historical" and what was not? For most scholars the answer seemed obvious enough.

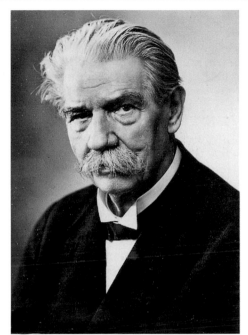

Albert Schweitzer surveyed more than two hundred books on the life of Christ in *The Quest of the Historical Jesus.*

Far right: D. F. Strauss's *The Life of Jesus Critically Examined* caused enormous controversy.

Anything that sounded supernatural had to be ruled out or reinterpreted. "History" was declared to be a closed system that ruled out any divine intervention. Anything miraculous like a virgin birth, a resurrection, divine healings, casting out of demons, or predictive prophecy had to be either removed or explained in some "historically" acceptable way.

Thus began the search for Jesus, a Jesus of "history" as Enlightenment thinkers defined it, who could fit selected basic human categories. The reason he appeared to be more than just human in the Gospels is that the early believers created someone to believe in—a Christ—because their faith needed it. They are not necessarily to be blamed for doing this because they did not know any better, being uneducated, superstitious peasants. However, it was thought, in the modern age we know better and can correct their misunderstandings. Using the newer tools of scientific Bible study we can write a life of Jesus as he really was, not as someone wished he had been.[3]

By the time the twentieth century arrived, numerous attempts had been made to reconstruct the life of Jesus along these lines, some of them standing out as centers of enormous controversy, such as D. F. Strauss's *The Life of Jesus Critically Examined* (1835) and E. Renan's *Life of Jesus*

(1863). In 1906 Albert Schweitzer surveyed over two hundred such lives of Jesus in *The Quest of the Historical Jesus,* and convincingly showed that none of them had found the real Jesus. In fact, those historians had found in Jesus only a reflection of their own preconceived ideas. They had taken Jesus out of his own time by transporting him into our times and had modernized him beyond recognition.

Schweitzer's book as well as other more technical and critical studies on the Gospels had a profound effect on the search for Jesus. Because the Gospels could be trusted so little, the search was, in time, abandoned, and a theological encounter with the Christ of faith was offered as the only viable approach to the reality of Jesus. In 1926 Rudolf Bultmann attempted to pull together what could be known about Jesus in *Jesus and the Word,* but the results were meager in the extreme. When he finally wrote his *Theology of the New Testament* (2 vols., 1951, 1955), only thirty pages were allotted to Jesus, and Bultmann pronounced him only the "presupposition" of New Testament theology. He was convinced that almost nothing could be known about the Jesus who had lived on earth two thousand years ago, nor did it really matter. The only thing that mattered was *that* Jesus was, not *what* Jesus was or taught. In support

demythologiz-
ing

of the rationale for this, Bultmann explained his new program for understanding him in a paper first delivered in the early 1940s, "New Testament and Mythology."[4] He called it **demythologizing**. He said that we must take the early Christian "myths" of incarnation, deity, death for sins, and resurrection and translate them into acceptable twentieth-century categories, so that modern people could believe them. These myths have no literal truth, but can become true for us as we incorporate them into a new self-understanding. Here Bultmann drew on the philosophy of a former colleague at Marburg, Germany, Martin Heidegger.

It was not long before Bultmann's view came under attack by other theologians and even by his own students. In 1953 the "post-Bultmannian" era began with an essay entitled, "The Question of the Historical Jesus" delivered at Marburg by Ernst Käsemann, one of Bultmann's followers. In it Käsemann accused Bultmann of espousing a modern Gnosticism, an intellectual system of faith devoid of any historical basis and in danger of losing Jesus entirely. Käsemann and other ex-Bultmannians then set out on a new quest of the historical Jesus. Günther Bornkamm published the first book on the subject, *Jesus of Nazareth*, in 1956. This was followed by an attempt to explain the principles involved in such a program by James M. Robinson in *A New Quest of the Historical Jesus* (1959). Nothing much came of this new quest for Jesus because it was too closely associated with radical form-critical views and the existentialist approach of Bultmann, so that today it is virtually nonexistent. Efforts to modify it by using a new hermeneutic based on a supposed "later Heidegger" also came to naught.

The Current Situation

The quest for the "real" Jesus has up until recently gone through basically two phases. The first phase began with the Enlightenment in the late 1700s, and is generally called the "old quest" of the historical Jesus. This was followed by the rejection of that quest beginning around World War I (1914–18) and lasting through the 1950s. This, in turn, was replaced by the "new quest" of the historical Jesus, undertaken mainly by Bultmann's disenchanted students in an attempt to find Jesus again. This phase did not outlast those theologians, and as they retired or passed away the new quest gradually disappeared. This phase lasted about twenty years or so, taking us into the 1980s.

The failure to produce anything of substance as far as our knowledge of Jesus Christ was concerned caused a new wave of thought to arise. After all, Jesus is the essence of Christianity, so if we want to be Christians, we must know who Jesus is. This new wave is sometimes called the "third quest," but it is difficult to find anything that really binds it together into some unified movement. In fact, its very disunity is its most prominent feature. There is no agreement on what is to be done, how to go about doing it, or what results from the attempt to find Jesus. Because of this we have a bewildering variety of reconstructed Jesuses. We are currently offered Jesus defined as a political change agent,[5] a street-corner Greek preacher,[6] a zealot,[7] a magician,[8] a moralistic prophet,[9] a confused Galilean peasant,[10] a Marxist-atheist,[11] or an outright fraud.[12] Included in this new collection of Jesuses are also some serious attempts to see him in a more favorable light.[13]

John Reumann has tried to pull the whole of these efforts (he tracks them back to 1900) into twenty different categories that he lists as "Types of Lives—Some Key Examples," but he actually just scratches the surface of the diversity in scholarly opinions over this era.[14] If he had included more than just "some key examples" it is hard to say how many categories he would have found. He concludes that "within certain parameters of what is possible or likely, no final historical answer can be given on Jesus."[15] Crucial here is the word "historical." If we are looking for an answer that makes Jesus merely a part of our historical processes, then, indeed, no final answer can be given.

So where does this leave us? In all probability, right where we began. The attempt to find a "real" Jesus by using basically secular methods will result only in an unconvincing portrait of a Jesus who looks very much like the assumption of the one who painted the picture.

Adolf von Harnack's book *What Is Christianity?* summarized the case for the nondivine Jesus.

Jesus Seminar

The Search for the Real Words of Jesus

A Brief Look at the Search

As one might expect, the search for the real words of Jesus has traveled along the same road as the search for the real life of Jesus. If, in the end, there is a fundamental skepticism about the value of the Gospels as sources for the life of Jesus, then the same would hold true regarding his words. They can no longer be trusted either.

In broad terms the attempt to recover Jesus' words can be described like this. During the nineteenth century, when the Gospels were being gradually discredited as historically reliable and as the supernatural elements of Jesus' life were being turned into myths or legends, the focus shifted from what Jesus did to what Jesus said. It was hoped that here the real Jesus could be found, a human Jesus who taught his disciples how to love God and serve their neighbors. This was epitomized by Adolf von Harnack in his *What Is Christianity?* (1900), a book that summarized the significance of Jesus in his teaching on the fatherhood of God, the brotherhood of all human beings, and the infinite value of the human

soul. But with the abandonment of the liberal old quest of the historical Jesus, this view of Jesus also collapsed, to be followed by a period of skepticism about whether we could know anything about the real Jesus—his life or his teachings. With the coming of the "new quest" in the 1950s came a renewed attempt to find Jesus, either through his intentions or his words, with the heaviest focus being on his words. This in turn gave rise to renewed attempts to find what Jesus *really* said.

It is here that the problems arose. The question now became how to sift the material, so that the later additions and changes made by the church communities, the redactors, the oral transmitters of the tradition, and the final "author" of the finished Gospel could be set aside, leaving us the "real" words of Jesus. In the past thirty years, no fewer than twenty-five criteria have been suggested to accomplish this. It has not gone particularly well. As M. J. Borg says, "For the most part, this century's scholarship has been more skeptical [than last century's] about being able to recover the teaching of Jesus, and reluctant to ascribe much theological significance to historical reconstructions of Jesus' message."[16] John Riches says simply that "we do not have hard and fast tests to enable us to establish what Jesus said."[17] With that statement almost all of those who use these methods to reconstruct Jesus' message would agree. There are so many combinations of criteria that can be used and so many interpreters using them that no two reconstructions are ever alike. The best one can hope for is a collection of sayings about which there is a general consensus that Jesus might have said that.

Sometimes the results are not even that encouraging. Over a decade ago a group of some seventy scholars banded together in a group called the **Jesus Seminar** whose intention was to answer the question: What did Jesus really say? After working six years on the project, they published their results in *The Five Gospels: The Search for the Authentic Words of Jesus* (1993). They came to the conclusion that "Eighty-two percent of the words ascribed to Jesus in the gospels were not actually spoken by him."[18] They also concluded that not a single saying in the Gospel of John can be trusted and, to cite but one example from the Synoptics, in the Lord's Prayer we may be certain only that the words "Our Father" go back to Jesus.

The Criteria Used to Find Jesus' Real Words

How is it that scholars can come to such conclusions as these? The answer lies in the skeptical attitude they bring to the Gospels and the methods they use to establish what Jesus really said. It isn't necessary to list all twenty-five criteria sometimes used to find Jesus' authentic words, but some examples can be given. Among the most commonly used are these:

- *Multiple Source Attestation:* A saying found in more than one place in the Gospels may be judged to be authentic.
- *Palestinian Environment:* A saying that presupposes first-century Palestine for its background may be judged as authentic.
- *Aramaic Language:* A saying that contains words that in Greek are awkward, but in Aramaic make better sense, is likely to be authentic.
- *Dissimilarity:* A saying that differs from what first-century Judaism and/or the

early church believed is likely to be authentic.
- *Embarrassment:* A saying that was embarrassing to the church would hardly have been made up by them, so it must go back to Jesus.
- *Consensus of Scholars:* A saying is judged to be authentic when most New Testament scholars agree it goes back to Jesus.
- *Multiple Forms of Statement:* A saying is more likely authentic when it is found in more than one form in the Gospels.

By the use of these and numerous other criteria, New Testament scholars hope to be able to find what Jesus really said. But the results will always be tentative, because the methodology employed builds so heavily on limited human knowledge and judgment. Thankfully, not everyone who uses these methods comes up with a negative assessment of what Jesus said. Yet that is probably not because of the methods used but because these scholars are of a more reasonable bent to begin with.[19]

A Positive Approach to the Problem

Not everyone has followed the lead of this critical scholarship.[20] Many have looked at the fundamental principles that underlie this essentially negative approach to the Gospels and refused to accept them. After all, if some people believe that God did not inspire a trustworthy Bible and that Jesus could not be God incarnate, others opt to reject that point of view. They are sympathetic to the long-held view that the Gospels were written within a context of faith and can only be understood in that way. This is not a stance of blind credulity. It is only to observe that all of us approach a subject from a point of view, as everyone, even Bultmann, acknowledges.[21] As we saw in Chapter 10, we can either approach the Gospels open to what they have to say about the divine events being spoken of or we decide in advance that such things cannot be true and should be explained in some other way. The past two hundred years have shown the failure of trying to make sense of the Gospels by attempting to remove the supernatural dimension.

The Basilica of the Beatitudes, on the traditional Mount of the Beatitudes, where the Gospels present Jesus teaching the Lord's Prayer.

In the light of that history, it is not unreasonable to suggest that we re-adopt the traditional view that the Gospels can be trusted because they are inspired by God. The story of Jesus as it is depicted in the Gospels should be analyzed on the assumption that the material is reliable and can be trusted—innocent until proven guilty, as it were. As C. H. Dodd says, "It is surely significant that when historians of the ancient world treat the Gospels, they are quite unaffected by the sophistications of *Redaktionsgeschichte*, and handle the documents as if they were what they professed to be."[22] The resulting picture of

Jesus has at least this to say for it, that it is not an imaginary modern reconstruction of what someone thought took place. It is the story of Jesus as presented in the Gospels as understood by those who were closest to the event, almost two thousand years closer than we are. It is also the picture of Jesus that has been preserved in the church from the beginning, and has sustained it during times of persecution and stress. The Jesus of history and the Christ of faith are in fact the same person, just as the Gospels say, and the One who lived on earth is the One who lives today and meets us in the pages of the New Tes-

Focus 12: Jesus Studies: The Handmaiden of Islam?

While many scholars who study Jesus are faithful Christians, others (like the so-called Jesus Seminar) have received national publicity by denying the Gospels' claims that Jesus was the Son of God who was born of a virgin, died for people's sins, and rose from the dead. Like Jesus Seminar member

Robert Funk (*Honest to Jesus* [San Francisco: HarperCollins, 1996], 306), they argue that we should "give Jesus a demotion" by understanding him as a religious visionary, a sort of prophet perhaps, but not as the one-of-a-kind Savior presented in the New Testament.

Islam, the religion of

perhaps one-fifth of the world's population, would applaud this judgment. It is ironic that "Christian" scholars in the West provide fuel for the scaled-down Jesus presented in the holy book of the Islamic faith, the Qur'an.

New Testament Testimony	Qur'anic Teaching (Surah = chapter)
Jesus an uncreated being (Jn 8:58; Col 1:16–17)	Jesus created from dust like Adam (Surah 3:59)
Jesus a unique divine figure (Jn 1:14)	Jesus simply a messenger like many others (Surah 5:75)
Jesus given all authority on earth and in heaven (Mt 28:18)	Allah alone possess all power—he could "annihilate the Messiah" if he wished (Surah 5:17)
Jesus affirmed by God the Father as his eternal Son (Mk 1:11; cf. Ps 2:7)	Jesus' divine sonship is "a lie" (Surah 18:4–5)
Jesus brings salvation through faith in him (Jn 3:16)	Salvation is through good works and faith in Muhammad's message in the Qur'an (Surah 47:1–3)
Jesus died on the cross and will return in glory for all believers (Acts 1:11; 2:23)	Jesus was not crucified—the Gospels are false at this point—and on judgment day he will be a witness against Christians (Surah 4:157–59)

tament as we read them.[23] It is only on this assumption that the Gospels can make any real sense.

This should not be misunderstood, however. To approach the Gospels in this fashion in no way denies that either Jesus or the Gospels are part of human history. The Christian doctrine of the incarnation and a proper formulation of the doctrine of biblical inspiration assert the very opposite. Jesus was God incarnate in human flesh, and the Scripture is God's Word incarnate in human words. As such, they are open to both human observation and scrutiny. The apostle John even makes a point of saying this, when he asserts, "That which was from the beginning, which we have heard, which we have seen with our eyes, which we have looked at and our hands have touched . . . we proclaim to you" (1 Jn 1:1–3). When historical research is properly pursued without presuppositions that rule out God's involvement, it is to be welcomed, even encouraged by the church. Such investigation helps put us in touch with a very important element of the Christian faith, namely, the historicity of Jesus of Nazareth as the tangible embodiment of the eternal Son of God.

There is a lot to learn from the historical research that has accompanied the study of the Bible, even that of the past two hundred years. But one should only copy the good that is there and avoid the mistakes and pitfalls that have nearly brought current academic New Testament studies to a standstill and in the process virtually lost Jesus and his words for more than one generation.

Summary

1. Skepticism fostered in scholars since the Enlightenment dictates that anything that seems supernatural be ruled out or reinterpreted.

2. Schweitzer pointed out that most nineteenth-century scholars seeking to find the historical Jesus removed Jesus from his place in history and placed him in their own historical period.

3. Bultmann developed a method called demythologizing to reinterpret the early Christian myths such as the incarnation and deity of Christ.

4. The quest for the historical Jesus has had three phases: the Old Quest, the New Quest, and the Third Quest.

5. A group of seventy scholars called the Jesus Seminar worked over six years to validate the words of Jesus and concluded that 82 percent of the words ascribed to Jesus were not actually spoken by him.

6. There are over twenty-five criteria used to find authentic words of Jesus.

7. When historical research is conducted without presuppositions that rule out God's involvement, it can bring greater understanding of the Bible.

Review Questions

1. A rationalistic attitude began with scholars in universities and seminaries in _____.

2. After the Enlightenment, the Gospels were not considered to be the story of Jesus but only stories _____ Jesus.

3. In order for Jesus to be historical, critical scholars believe they have to rule out the _____.

4. Jesus was said to be "the presupposition of New Testament theology" by _____.

5. Reinterpretation of deity and incarnation is called _____.

6. The current attempt to reconstruct a historical portrait of Jesus is called the _____.

7. The Jesus Seminar concluded that out of all the words attributed to Jesus, _____ percent were not spoken by him.

8. The criterion of _____ requires that the sayings of Jesus be found in more than one place in the Gospels.

Study Questions

1. Recount briefly the modern search for Jesus.

2. What was Rudolf Bultmann's contribution to this search?

3. Why did the "post-Bultmannians" reject Bultmann's views?

4. What are some of the current emphases in the search for Jesus?

5. What is your evaluation of the search for Jesus?

6. Recount briefly the search for Jesus' real words.

7. What are some of the criteria used to establish Jesus' real words?

8. Is there a way to integrate faith and research together in analyzing Jesus as historical figure? Explain.

Key Terms

demythologizing
Jesus Seminar

Further Reading

Anderson, Charles C. *Critical Quests of Jesus.* Grand Rapids: Eerdmans, 1969. A fine survey of life of Jesus studies from the Enlightenment to the New Quest.

———. *The Historical Jesus: A Continuing Quest.* Grand Rapids: Eerdmans, 1972. A carefully written book on the question of how to find the historical Jesus, from an evangelical point of view.

Bonhoeffer, Dietrich. *The Cost of Discipleship.* Rev. ed. New York: Collier, 1963. A classic treatise on following Jesus. May help explain the myriad of theories about who Jesus is: To affirm Christ's identity as the New Testament presents it demands costly repentance and a life of obedient faith.

Burridge, Richard A. *Four Gospels, One Jesus?* Grand Rapids: Eerdmans, 1994. A survey of the Gospels' picture of Jesus that is scholarly, spiritual, and easy to understand.

Dawes, Gregory W., ed. *The Historical Jesus Quest: Landmarks in the Search for the Jesus of History.* Louisville: Westminster John Knox, 1999. Excerpts from the work of major players in the history of Jesus research, including Spinoza, Reimarus, Strauss, Ritschl, Troeltsch, Wrede, J. Weiss, Schweitzer, Kähler, Bultmann, and Barth.

Farmer, William R., ed. *Crisis in Christology.* Dallas: Truth, 1995. Important essays calling for adjustment in modern approaches to studying Jesus.

Funk, R. W., Roy W. Hoover, and the Jesus Seminar. *The Five Gospels.* New York: Macmillan, 1993. Radical book that argues that 82 percent of the sayings of Jesus in the Gospels do not necessarily go back to him.

Jenkins, Philip. *Hidden Gospels: How the Search for Jesus Lost Its Way.* New York/Oxford: Oxford University Press, 2001. A historian analyzes contemporary study of Jesus, the Gospels, and early church origins. Debunks claims that "secret" texts like the Gospel of Thomas and the Gospel of Mary undermine the historical value of the New Testament.

Johnson, Luke Timothy. *The Real Jesus.* San Francisco: HarperCollins, 1996. A critical account of current radical theorizing about Jesus, in particular the Jesus Seminar, pointing out its many weaknesses. It refocuses the debate back onto the fundamental issues.

Pelikan, Jaroslav. *Jesus through the Centuries.* New York: Harper & Row, 1985. An excellent survey of how Jesus has been viewed throughout the history of the church.

Sanders, E. P. *Jesus and Judaism.* Philadelphia: Fortress, 1985. A modern scholar's attempt to find Jesus as part of Judaism using historical-critical methods.

Schweitzer, Albert. *The Quest of the Historical Jesus.* New York: Macmillan, 1961. The standard work that ended the old quest of the historical Jesus in 1906.

Stanton, Graham N. *The Gospels and Jesus.* Oxford: Oxford University Press, 1989. A study of Jesus from a moderate, contemporary perspective.

Strobel, Lee. *The Case for Christ: A Journalist's Personal Investigation of the Evidence for Jesus.* Grand Rapids: Zondervan, 1998. A former atheist interviews various scholars to uncover reasons why people view Jesus the way they do.

Stuhlmacher, Peter. *Jesus of Nazareth, Christ of Faith.* Peabody, Mass.: Hendrickson, 1988. Argues forcefully that Jesus is the Christ and that critical studies can be properly used.

Theissen, Gerd, and Dagmar Winter. *The Quest for the Plausible Jesus.* Louisville: Westminster John Knox 2002. Deals particularly with the "criterion of dissimilarity," urging its replacement with a "criterion of historical plausibility."

Turner, H. E. W. *Jesus: Master and Lord.* London: Mobray, 1953. An excellent treatment of Jesus' life by an eminent English scholar.

Wilkins, M. J., and J. P. Moreland. *Jesus under Fire.* Grand Rapids: Zondervan, 1995. Excellent collection of essays showing that the Jesus Seminar's negative conclusions are based on shaky foundations.

Witherington, Ben, III. *The Jesus Quest.* Downers Grove: InterVarsity, 1995. A careful look at the most recent themes about Jesus known as the Third Quest. An excellent introduction to the current situation from an evangelical point of view.

Wright, N. T. *Who Was Jesus?* Grand Rapids: Eerdmans, 1992. A critical look at some modern reconstructions of Jesus, arguing that the traditional view is right after all. Easy to read.

———. *Jesus and the Victory of God.* Minneapolis: Fortress, 1996. A brilliant treatment of Jesus' life—technical but well-written.

Part

2

Encountering Acts and the Earliest Church

13 The World and Identity of the Earliest Church

Outline

Objectives

After reading this chapter, you should be able to

- Assess the role of the Roman emperor
- List and characterize the key emperors of the New Testament era
- Evaluate the reigns of the emperors of the New Testament era
- Discuss the effects of the emperors on the early church
- Define Hellenization
- Identify the philosophies that the early church encountered
- Explain the beliefs of early Christians

Introduction

Previous chapters have dealt extensively with Jesus, the Gospels, and the historical setting of first-century Judaism. As we prepare to study Acts and the New Testament letters beginning in the next chapter, we need to pause and consider the larger world of the first-century Roman Empire. What was life like? Who were the reigning authorities? How was government set up and conducted? How did people view themselves? What were their hopes and fears? What were the popular religions and outlooks?

Such questions are important because they help explain why those who heard the gospel responded the way they did. Some welcomed it. Others were indifferent or skeptical. Still others were hostile. Why such different reactions? What effect did becoming a Christian have on a person, or a whole family, when it occurred? We cannot answer all such questions, but we can sketch enough details of first-century life to shed light on how the New Testament message was received and why.

Knowing some things about the first-century Roman world is no substitute for knowledge of the New Testament itself. But it is useful at many points for interpreting the New Testament rightly. The New Testament, Christians believe, was written by divine inspiration. Yet the people and events that gave rise to it are people and events of another era and, in some ways, of a different world. This chapter will enable the modern Bible reader to see the New Testament and the people it describes more clearly in its original setting in order to apply it more responsibly in today's world.

The Reality of Empire

As chapter 2 has already indicated, Rome was the dominant military and political power of the first century A.D. All inhabitants of the Roman world were naturally affected by its rule. Generally Rome pursued a relatively benevolent approach to government, allowing as much local control of the areas it ruled as possible. Native persons and structures were often used to maintain order and see to the collection of taxes. Roman legions, legendary for their battlefield ef-

ATLANTIC OCEAN

LUGD.

AQUITANIA

TARRACONENSIS

NARB.

LUSITANIA

CO

BAETICA

MAURETANIA

| 0 | 100 | 200 | 300 mi |
| 0 | | 250 | 500 km |

fectiveness, stood by to ensure compliance with imperial policies, supplementing local police forces where necessary.

The history of Rome is long and complex, but its first-century shape was dominated by the office of emperor. As Rome grew in size and influence during the second and first centuries B.C., various parties and persons vied for power. The successful military general and brilliant administrator JULIUS CAESAR seemed on the verge of uniting the Roman republic under his personal leadership in the 40s B.C.[1] But he was assassinated, and more than a decade of political and military confusion followed. Emerging as victor from the swirl of plots and battles was OCTA-

VIAN, known in the New Testament as CAESAR AUGUSTUS (see Lk 2:1). He ruled 27 B.C.–A.D. 14 and was thus emperor at the time of Jesus' birth.[2]

The Roman Empire thus came together as a stable, homogeneous unit under imperial control, as if by design, roughly at the start of the New Testament era. In the two centuries prior to Christ's coming, Roman influence had slowly but steadily expanded both on the south European mainland and in coastal regions of the Mediterranean. MACEDONIA, where Paul would plant his first church on European soil, came under Roman sway in 168 B.C.; ACHAIA, where CORINTH was located, in 146 B.C.; and the province of Asia, whose

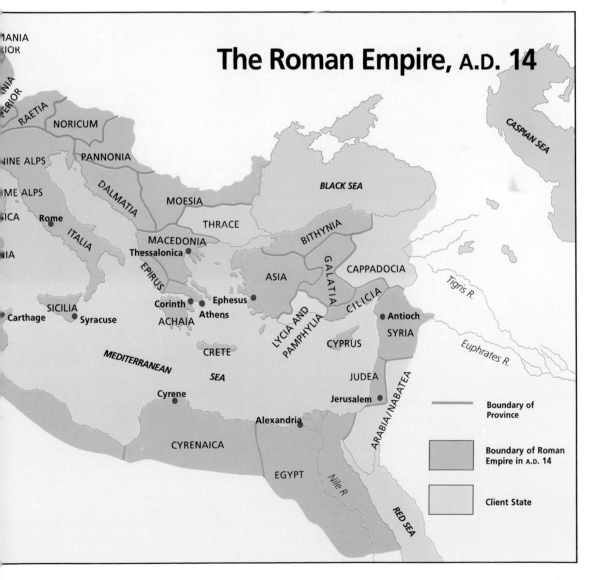

The Roman Empire, A.D. 14

Boundary of Province

Boundary of Roman Empire in A.D. 14

Client State

195

The Roman Emperors of the First Century

Years	Names	Events	References
30 B.C.–A.D. 14	Augustus	Birth of Christ	Lk 2:1
A.D. 14–37	Tiberius	Ministry and death of Christ	Lk 3:1
A.D. 37–41	Caligula		
A.D. 41–54	Claudius	Famine	Acts 11:28
		Expulsion of Jews from Rome	Acts 18:2
A.D. 54–68	Nero	Trial of Paul	Acts 25:10–12
		Persecution at Rome	Acts 27:24
			2 Tm 4:16,17; Rv 13:1–10(?)
A.D. 68	Galba		
A.D. 69	Otho		
A.D. 69	Vitellius		
A.D. 69–79	Vespasian	Destruction of Jerusalem	
A.D. 79–81	Titus		
A.D. 81–96	Domitian	Persecution (?)	Rv 6:9; 7:14; 12:11; 20:4(?)
A.D. 96–98	Nerva		
A.D. 98–117	Trajan		

capital was EPHESUS, in 133 B.C. Conquests by the Roman general Pompey resulted in the creation of the province of Syria in 66 B.C. This province included the lands of GALILEE and JUDEA where Gospel events took place. Its capital was Antioch, the place where Christ's followers were first called Christians (Acts 11:26).

Following Octavian's death a succession of less illustrious emperors followed, some of whom are mentioned in the New Testament. His successor TIBERIUS ruled A.D. 14–37 and is mentioned in Luke 3:1. Whenever the Gospels refer to the Roman emperor, as when Jesus speaks of rendering to Caesar what is Caesar's, Tiberius was the figure then in power. Next was GAIUS (A.D. 37–41), also known as CALIGULA. He is not mentioned in the New Testament and plays little direct role in early church developments. Slightly more important is CLAUDIUS, Caligula's uncle, who reigned A.D. 41–54. He showed some administrative skill. It was his decree that evicted Jews from Rome (Acts 18:2). He met his end, it seems, at the hand of his niece (and wife) AGRIPPINA. A few years after their marriage, she fed him poison mushrooms. This enabled her son by another marriage to assume the throne. Because he was only thirteen at the time, Agrippina was effectively in command. Her son's name: NERO.

Nero's rule (A.D. 54–68) seems to have been reasonably stable at first, perhaps because it was largely in the hands of others. As he grew in age and power, he made a name for himself by murdering his mother and many others. He kicked one of his wives to death and committed many other atrocities that scandalized even the pagan world. Ancient reports are therefore quite believable that he set Rome ablaze to divert attention from the empire's decline under his disastrously corrupt oversight and then blamed a minority sect—the Christians—for the damage. Widespread persecutions followed, Nero torturing many Christians in public and setting some on fire while they were still alive.

The last emperor of possible direct importance to the New Testament is DOMITIAN (A.D. 81–96). More interested in government than Nero was, he was scarcely less cruel. He is said to have used "Lord

pax romana

and God" as his regular title in both writing and conversation. Some scholars think that persecutions mentioned in the Book of Revelation reflect conditions existing during Domitian's reign.

This brief description of prominent Roman emperors during the New Testament period serves two purposes. One is to spark interest in reading more about them. For example, few books are more fascinating and informative for the student of the first century than SUETONIUS's *The Twelve Caesars*.[3] It may not be accurate in every detail (though scholars give it generally high marks for reliability), but it makes aspects of the first-century Roman world come alive in unforgettable ways. The New Testament world is not an island, and any knowledge of persons and events of that time is valuable for better grasp of New Testament documents. Another memorable study is Paul Maier's *Pontius Pilate*,[4] a novel rich in the historical light it sheds on Roman power and its effect in provincial areas like Judea.

A second reason why knowledge of Roman imperial rule in the first century is important is the definition it gives to the celebrated *pax romana* (Latin for "Roman peace") of the New Testament era. Histo-

rians have long observed that conditions in the first century were just right for the spread of Christianity. There was relative peace, a common language (Greek), some level of social order enabling safe travel, and an increasing network of roads and sea routes.

But it was far from an ideal world. Leadership was often corrupt. While approaching its economic and military zenith, the empire was beginning a downward political and moral spiral. The Roman world in which Paul and other apostles preached was a world in which a very large empire could protect, but could also threaten, the individual person and new movements like early Christianity. In other words, Roman rule was a mixed blessing, because its power for good was ultimately matched by its capacity to suppress and harass. The social order in which the church was first formed was often far from friendly to the gospel message and its bearers.

Hellenistic Civilization

As a culture the Roman Empire was dominated by Greek, or Hellenistic, features. Think of how the United States owes many of its cultural distinctives to Great Britain: language, legal code, history, literature, and in many cases religion. In some ways the situation was similar in the Roman world of New Testament times. While Rome excelled in organizational and military achievements, Greece had set a high standard of literary and intellectual accomplishment. Greek ways were widely spread in the wake of ALEXANDER THE GREAT, and Rome gradually took over many of the lands he conquered. Thus it happened that the Roman world is also aptly called the Greco-Roman world. Territorially it belonged to Rome; culturally it was dominated by various Hellenistic features.

Take language. The native Roman language was Latin. Yet the language of culture and commerce was Greek. From Spain, or even Britain, in the west to Syria in the east, a traveler was well advised to brush up on Greek. It was spoken by at least the ruling and trading classes nearly everywhere, while Latin was not. This linguistic uniformity was not just convenient

Whenever the Gospels refer to the Roman emperor, as when Jesus speaks of rendering to Caesar what is Caesar's, Tiberius (A.D. 14–37) was the figure in power.

Pentecost

Hellenization

Nero (reigned
A.D. 54–68)
committed
atrocities that
scandalized even
the pagan world.

from a trader's or tourist's point of view; it was also important for the missionary expansion of the early church. Christian preachers could count on ready hearers if they proclaimed their message in Greek whether in JERUSALEM, Alexandria, or Rome itself. This was undoubtedly an important factor in the rapid spread of the Christian gospel after **Pentecost**.

Hellenization also shaped social consciousness. Its notion of human society involved founding and cultivating cities. Ideally, this would mean access by many to the services and relationships that masses of people in close proximity can provide. Practically, however, it often meant ghetto existence, loss of personal hope as the individual was swallowed up in the masses. The gospel found a ready audience under such conditions where large numbers of people living under bleak conditions were ready to hear a message of renewal, hope, justice, and joy.

 # Domitian's Cruelty

Ancient Christian sources suggest that the Roman emperor Domitian was a vicious enemy of Christianity. Secular sources agree that Domitian was exceedingly cruel, quite apart from persecuting the church. Roman historian Suetonius (paragraph 11 of his *The Twelve Caesars*) writes:

Domitian was not merely cruel, but hot-headed and cunning into the bargain. He summoned a Palace steward to his bedroom, invited him to share his couch, made him feel perfectly secure and happy, condescended to share a dinner with him—yet had already given orders for his crucifixion on the following day! He was more than usually gracious to the ex-Consul Arrecinius Clemens, a favourite agent, just before his death-sentence, and invited him out for a drive. As they happened to pass the man who had informed on Arrecinius, Domitian asked: "Shall we listen to that utter scoundrel tomorrow?" And he impudently prefaced all his most savage sentences with the same little speech about mercy; indeed, this preamble soon became a recognized sign that something dreadful was on the way. Having brought a group of men before the Senate on a treason charge, he announced that this must be a test of his popularity with the House; and thus easily got them condemned to an "old-style execution." [Suetonius explains elsewhere what this means of death involves: "the executioners stripped their victim naked, thrust his head into a wooden fork, and then flogged him to death with sticks."]

A Roman centurion *(foreground)* and legionary soldier. In the first century the Roman Empire was approaching its economic and military zenith.

religious syncretism

Hellenization also brought with it an air of **religious syncretism**. As Roman power gradually brought together dozens of smaller kingdoms, each with its own local gods and goddesses and rituals, the idea gained favor that all deities and religions ultimately amounted to the same thing. There was one overarching spiritual reality, though innumerable ways of expressing it. Local religious traditions by no means always died out. But they tended to lose their traditional exclusive status. This was good for the gospel in that new religious claims might receive a ready audience. But it was bad in that the God of Christianity could not simply be thrown in alongside other gods and goddesses of polytheistic belief. When pagans realized this, they sometimes responded with hostility to gospel proclamation (Acts 19:28). Nor were early Christians content to let the emperor worship of the late first century claim the devotion that they were

willing to give only to Jesus Christ.

In several ways, then, Hellenization set the tone for the outlook of people who heard the gospel as it first spread. A brief look at Greco-Roman religions and philosophies will give a still clearer picture of popular convictions that affected first-century hearers of the gospel.

Religions and Philosophies

By New Testament times popular belief in ancient Greek and Roman religious mythology seems to have declined, though it had not disappeared. In one instance Christian missionaries were hailed as Zeus and Hermes (Acts 14:12). But other beliefs were more prevalent.

Chief among these was belief in the occult (the reality and activity of supernat-

Stoicism

Cynicism

ural powers). Masses of people from all social classes feared and tried to placate the spirit-world that they felt controlled their lives. Governmental decisions were commonly made with the aid of priests interpreting the entrails of slaughtered animals for guidance. Some cities were famous for their oracles—men or women thought to have the power of foretelling events or divulging personal mysteries. Astrology was widespread, as were various magic practices. Among both Gentiles and Jews there was often a strong sense of the presence and power of unseen spiritual beings and forces.

Modern Westerners should not be too quick to write off all such beliefs as ancient superstition. Much of it was bogus, to be sure. But the Bible itself speaks of an unseen world of spiritual beings and conflicts (Eph 6:12). Jesus cast out many unclean spirits and had personal encounters with the prince of the demons. Acts 16:16 speaks of a hapless slave-girl who made money for her owners by fortune-telling; by Christ's power Paul liberated her from her bondage. The proof of her liberation is the beating Paul took for his action.

Overall the New Testament religious

Isis and Horus. Isis, originally an Egyptian goddess, came to be worshiped under many names. Temples to her were scattered among cities of the Roman world.

world was diverse and confused. In chapter 2 we saw the fragmented nature of first-century Judaism itself, even in the local setting of Judea and Galilee. The situation was still more fragmented in the larger Greco-Roman world. Life posed tough questions, and people were casting about for answers offered by various religious means.

Philosophy was a prevalent option, too. In the first century it was much more religion-like than it claims to be today. It was not an academic discipline so much as a formal way of discussing and posing solutions to life's ultimate questions. Unlike both Judaism and Christianity, which insisted that valid human knowledge must first make room for the revelation of Scripture that God has given, ancient philosophies (like nearly all modern philosophies) made their starting point human rationality, experience, will, or some combination of these. No single philosophy commanded universal acceptance, though we can speak of several dominant tendencies. These often intertwined in their practical outworking; philosophies of the age were as syncretistic as religions were.

Stoicism stressed fate. The world is beyond our control as individuals. The individual must therefore create his or her own stability by forsaking excesses of both pleasure and sorrow. The Stoic person is unmoved by emotion, reflecting in personal life the conviction that the world is running a preordained course in which all things are already determined. There is no good or evil as such, only an inscrutable, all-powerful, and impersonal cosmic logic that causes all things to have their being. Stoicism called for strict ethical conduct, and if moral codes alone could change the human heart, it might have revolutionized its age. But it fell far short of, and stood in marked contrast to, the Christian doctrine of a personal God. This God cares and loves and answers prayer; he is a God whose sovereignty and control over all things by no means rules out the real choices that all persons face, and which they are free to make.

Other philosophical currents included **Cynicism**. The Cynics gloried in radical personal freedom of act and speech. They were the radical activists of antiquity. Cynics ridiculed those who conformed to accepted social standards, which they reviled. In the

Sculpture of a Sophist philosopher from Ephesus.

cupy our attention in the chapters that follow as we trace the spread of Christian claims to areas and persons that did not always welcome what they heard. For now, let us attempt to give a preliminary summary sketch of early Christian life and the main beliefs on which it was based.

The Early Christians: New People in Christ

So who were the early Christians? Two months had not yet passed since Jesus' death and resurrection when Christ's Spirit moved afresh among his core followers in Jerusalem. It was during the festival of Pentecost. Suddenly this small band of disciples were transformed people, speaking the Good News of God to fellow Jewish pilgrims from around the ancient world in their own native languages. Three thousand were converted to Christ on that day alone.

The coming of the Holy Spirit on the day of Pentecost was a watershed event. True, in some ways the disciples were no different than before. They still shared the same memories of being with Jesus during his life, witnessing his shocking death, marveling at his resurrection and ascension, and patiently awaiting his promise to return to make them powerful transmitters of a saving message for the whole world (Acts 1:8). Moreover, as the years went by other aspects of their lives were normal: They still had jobs, families, houses, and lives to live. This was less true, of course, for the many who pursued callings into missionary service, or who suffered persecution for their faith.

But in another sense they would never be the same again. They had become new people in Christ.

The spread of the gospel got an early boost through the thousands of worshipers converted at Pentecost. When they returned to their homes and synagogues in faraway Parthia or Rome or Spain, they brought word of Jesus the Messiah with them.

But the core group of Jesus' earliest followers, enlarging steadily as they continued to preach and care for each other, at first stayed close to Jerusalem. In time some chose to move elsewhere, often due to persecution. They took their message and way

Skepticism

same way that Cynics held ethics up to ridicule, Skeptics derided knowledge. **Skepticism** held that knowledge grew out of experience alone, that all experience is unique to the individual, and that therefore no truth exists that is binding on all persons.

Christianity differed from both. Against the Cynic impulse, it held to a way of life taught by Scripture and modeled by Christ and others (see, e.g., Heb 12) that was truly virtuous. Freedom is not irresponsible and unchecked self-expression; it is, through Christ, receiving a new heart that finds its joy in walking the path that a loving God prescribes and enables. Against the Skeptics, Christians could insist that truth is rooted in God's creation, existence, and self-disclosure, not in human experience alone. And God has become human in Jesus Christ, putting to flight the notion that humankind has no access to a transcendent word of truth. In Christ God's word was made flesh (Jn 1:14).

Other philosophies and religions marked the first-century landscape,[5] but the ones mentioned suffice to give a sample of the disparate marketplace of ideas popular at the time. The New Testament message did not echo in a vacuum, nor did it encounter naive persons who had never entertained religious or philosophical options. It rather collided, sometimes violently, with firmly established ideas and movements.

Details of these confrontations will oc-

What Early Christians Believed in Common with the Jews

The Bible of the early church was the Old Testament. Old Testament scholar Christoph Barth lists nine key statements (below) about God that are basic to Old Testament theology. All are restated by New Testament writers. The last three statements are not Barth's but are certainties shared by Old and New Testament writers.

1. God created heaven and earth
2. God chose the patriarchs of Israel
3. God delivered Israel out of Egypt
4. God led his people through the wilderness
5. God revealed himself at Sinai
6. God granted Israel the land of Canaan
7. God raised up kings in Israel
8. God chose Jerusalem
9. God sent his prophets
10. God delights in communion with each and all of his people
11. God calls his people to a life of holiness
12. God is faithful to his covenant—his promise to save a people for his eternal praise

—From Christoph Barth, *God with Us: A Theological Introduction to the Old Testament*, ed. Geoffrey W. Bromiley (Grand Rapids: Eerdmans, 1991).

even language differences, with some speaking Aramaic or Hebrew and others speaking Greek (see Acts 6:1).

It was a time of reevaluation as they attempted to retain their ties with the past, yet also sharpen their focus on what made them a new community. Eventually, in the A.D. 40s, conflicts arose over Jewish customs like the practice of circumcision. Ministry by Philip, Peter, and especially Paul in Gentile areas raised related issues of whether Christians from non-Jewish backgrounds must always follow traditional Jewish practices. Eventually church leaders convened a summit to settle the matter. The **Jerusalem Council** took place about A.D. 49 and is summarized in Acts 15. It will be discussed more fully in a later chapter.

What emerged from these years of tension, decision, and growth was the conviction that the Christians were ultimately not a subset of any of the established sects of Judaism. In certain respects it was time for a parting of the ways. But Christians did not feel that *they* were leaving God's work in past centuries behind or veering off in some novel, unheard-of direction. On the contrary, they believed that God had foretold the Christian movement in ancient prophecies and more recently in the preaching of John the Baptist and Jesus himself. Jewish Christians felt that it was the non-Christian Jews who were abandoning their own ancient heritage by rejecting God's promised deliverer, Jesus of Nazareth, risen and exalted to God's right hand. They knew from Scripture that the inclusion of the Gentiles among God's covenant people had long been prophesied. So they felt they were fulfilling, not defying, the message of the Old Testament by the steps they took to adjust Jewish customs to the realities of non-Jewish communities. They held firmly the

Jerusalem Council

of life with them, seeking to combine their former Jewish customs with what seemed appropriate to their new life in Christ. But it became increasingly difficult to hold the two together. Tensions developed. Early Christians in predominantly Jewish Palestine continued to worship in the Jerusalem temple and in synagogues. But they also began to meet in private homes for prayer, worship, and study of Scripture and the apostles' teaching. There were cultural and

Synagogues were found throughout the Roman world. Missionaries preaching the Jewish Messiah Jesus often made them their first stop. This stone lintel from Corinth is inscribed "Synagogue of the Hebrews."

The Apostles' Creed

I believe in God the Father Almighty,
   Maker of heaven and earth.

I believe in Jesus Christ, his only Son, our Lord,
   who was conceived by the Holy Spirit,
   and born of the virgin Mary.
He suffered under Pontius Pilate,
was crucified, died, and was buried;
he descended into hell.
The third day he rose again from the dead.
He ascended into heaven
and is seated at the right hand of God the
   Father Almighty.
From there he will come to judge the living and
   the dead.

I believe in the Holy Spirit,
   the holy catholic church,
   the communion of saints,
   the forgiveness of sins,
   the resurrection of the body,
   and the life everlasting. Amen

Although not written by the apostles, the Apostles' Creed is a concise summary of their teachings. It originated as a baptismal confession, probably in the second century, and developed into its present form by the sixth or seventh century.

17:26), but Christians joined other children of Abraham (Gal 3), true believers in the living God from earlier times, to form an extended spiritual family chosen by God to worship him and to mediate salvation to the world. Their message was called "the gospel," or the Good News. It centered around Jesus Christ—who he was and what he had done—and they were witnesses of this. By definition, witnesses bear testimony to something or someone else, not to themselves. So it was with the early Christians. They preached not themselves, but Jesus Christ as Lord. They described themselves, or were described, in many other ways—as followers of the way, servants of Christ, the remnant of Israel, the true Israel, the church, witnesses, Christians—all of which pointed in one way or another to how they were living out their new life in Christ.

What Early Christians Believed

Because the early Christians used the Old Testament as their Bible, there was fundamental agreement with a great deal of what the Jews around them believed. All agreed that there was only one God, the Creator of the world, who was holy, loving, just, and true. All agreed that God revealed himself in the Scripture, thus making himself and his will known to his people. All believed in the necessity of prayer, worship, and moral living in the presence of God. Christians and many Jews alike believed in life after death, a bodily resurrection, the coming end of the age, the last judgment, and eternal consequences in the form of heaven or hell. In a speech to the Jewish high court in Jerusalem, the apostle Paul could even say, "I am a Pharisee, the son of a Pharisee. I stand on trial because of my hope of the resurrection of the dead" (Acts 23:6).

The Uniqueness of Jesus

But Christians and Jews did not agree on everything. Their differences centered especially around who Jesus was and what he had done. Christians made the startling assertion that in Jesus, God himself had taken human form. Yet they did not think that this meant there was more than one God. Rather, God was more than one, without compromising his oneness. The Father was God, but so was the Son and the Holy Spirit. We are dealing here, of

essentials of Old Testament doctrine Jesus himself had observed, endorsed, and elaborated in his own teaching.

All this took place in an increasingly complex, even hostile environment, as we have already seen. The social and political situation in Palestine was worsening as the Jewish revolt against Rome of the A.D. 60s drew near. Gentile reaches of the Roman Empire were already witnessing occasional persecution of Christians. The early Christians had a great deal to explain to themselves and to others during those years. What they said centered around who they were and what they believed.

How Early Christians Saw Themselves

The early Christians saw themselves as the people of God and inheritors of the Old Testament promises. God was at work among all peoples, certainly (Acts

203

A chariot race at the Circus Maximus, Rome; from a clay lamp.

believed this very thing, asserting that he and the Father were one (Jn 10:30). His opponents likewise thought he was making claims to be equal with God (Jn 5:18).

The Decisive Fact of Jesus' Death and Resurrection

The early Christians also held distinctive beliefs about what Jesus had done. Everyone agreed that Jesus died. But for the Christians it did not end there. They also believed that it was the Lord who had died—however impossible that statement might sound—and that he was raised again from the dead, in resurrection life. They also said that the death of the Lord Jesus was for the sins of the world, so that God's people might be saved through him. And because he was the *Lord* Jesus Christ he was (and remains) the only Savior of the world. Salvation can be found nowhere else than through faith in his name (Acts 4:12).

course, with what later came to be called the doctrine of the Trinity. The Son existed eternally in the very form of God (Phil 2:6) and in him dwelt all the fullness of the Godhead bodily (Col 2:9). This conception of God as threefold diversity (Father, Son, and Holy Spirit) in unity (one God, not three) was a distinctive of Christianity and is found in early Christian writings all the way back to the very beginning. In fact, Jesus himself said things that indicate he

These distinctive facts about who Jesus was and what he had done constitute the heart of the gospel as the early Christians believed and preached it. As the apostle Paul put it in summary form, "If you confess with your mouth, 'Jesus is Lord,' and believe in your heart that God raised him from the dead, you will be saved" (Rom 10:9).

Focus 13: Belief and Behavior

Early Christian belief—what difference does it make? The fact is that beliefs can play a large role in how people live out their daily lives.

This truth is understood in an important study of German resistance to Adolf Hitler, *Plotting Hitler's Death,* by Joachim Fest (New York: Metropolitan Books, 1996). Repeatedly Fest shows that religious or spiritual beliefs were the basis for opposition to Hitler and the police state he established.

Sometimes these beliefs meant a desire to save

Germany from Hitler's draconian policies. Sometimes they meant a sense of outrage about the imprisonment and execution of Jews. Often they involved a sense of personal obligation before God—not to try to stop Hitler would one day result in personal judgment.

In January 1944 Prussian field marshal Count Helmuth James von Moltke (1907–45) was arrested for involvement in an anti-Hitler plot. At his trial his Nazi "judge" exclaimed, "Christianity and National Socialism [the Nazis] have one thing in common, Count von

Moltke, and only one: we both demand the whole person." In part because von Moltke believed that his whole person belonged to God, not Hitler, he was executed.

Early Christians placed full trust in Jesus' kingdom message. It changed their lives, and working together they eventually changed the life of an entire civilization. Belief can, it is true, be abstract and meaningless. But when directed to Christ (and combined with the love that Christ gives) there is perhaps no stronger force on earth.

Key Terms

Cynicism
Hellenization
Jerusalem
  Council
pax romana
Pentecost
religious
  syncretism
Skepticism
Stoicism

Key People/ Places

Achaia
Agrippina
Alexander the
  Great
Antioch
Caligula
Claudius
Corinth
Domitian
Ephesus
Gaius
Galilee
Jerusalem
Judea

Julius Caesar
Macedonia
Nero
Octavian
(Caesar
Augustus)
Pompey
Rome
Suetonius
Syria
Tiberius

Conclusion

In a complex and daunting world ruled by the Roman Empire, shaped by Hellenism, buzzing with religious activity, and echoing with competing philosophical claims, early Christians lived out a reality that would outlive them. Christians today know that same reality; their own faith grows out of the powerful message about Christ and his followers that Scripture enshrines (Rom 10:17). Acts and the New Testament letters give glimpses, and sometimes full views, of how Christians of old were faithful to God in their times, and thus transformed their world. In following chapters we trace out details of how this came to pass, aware that we in our own world stand in desperate need of that same gospel light and life.

Summary

1. The dominant military and political power of the first century was centered in Rome.

2. The early church suffered at the hands of several of the Roman emperors, but especially Nero and Domitian.

3. The first century produced conditions that made the spread of Christianity possible: There was relative peace, Greek was the common language, social order made travel safe, and roads and sea routes were increasing.

4. The Roman Empire was dominated by Hellenistic features that affected the growth of Christianity: the use of Greek as a common language, the development of cities, and religious syncretism.

5. Religion in the world of the Roman Empire was characterized by belief in the occult and in astrology.

6. The early church had to deal with the influence of a variety of philosophies, especially Stoicism, Cynicism, and Skepticism.

7. The disciples were transformed at Pentecost.

8. The majority of early Christians remained in Jerusalem and worshiped there.

9. Early Christians viewed themselves as the people of God and inheritors of Old Testament promises.

10. Early Christians held a variety of distinctive beliefs, but the critical common beliefs were Jesus' divine uniqueness and his saving death and resurrection.

Review Questions

1. The dominant military and political power of the first century world was the _____.

2. The Roman general Pompey conquered the province of Syria, where Christ's followers were first called Christians in the capital city of _____.

3. Early Christians suffered great persecution under the reigns of the emperors _____ and _____.

4. While Latin was the native language of Romans, the language of culture and commerce was _____.

5. Social consciousness in the first century was shaped by a process called _____.

6. The most influential religious belief in Rome was belief in the _____.

7. There was also great influence from _____, which was much more religion-like than its modern counterpart.

8. The philosophy of Stoicism stressed _____.

9. The disciples were never the same after _____.

10. Early Christians believed in the _____ of Christ and his _____ with God, a belief that quickly expressed itself as the doctrine of the Trinity.

Study Questions

1. List five questions that knowledge of the first-century Roman world can help answer.

2. Who are the Roman emperors mentioned by name in the New Testament?

3. What is meant by the term *pax romana*?

4. List some ways that Roman civilization was influenced by Hellenism.

5. What was Stoicism? How did it differ from Christianity?

6. Why did tensions arise between the early Christians, nearly all of whom were Jewish, and other Jews?

7. In what ways were the Old Testament Scriptures foundational to the faith of early Christians?

8. What were the main distinguishing features of early Christian belief? In what ways was Jesus Christ central?

Further Reading

Bell, Albert A., Jr. *Exploring the New Testament World.* Nashville: Thomas Nelson, 1998. Examines most aspects of first century Mediterranean culture, majoring on Greco-Roman aspects like religion, philosophy, societal structure, morality, personal relations, and Roman law. Some information on Jewish backgrounds. Contains valuable lists of books and articles for further study of every topic covered.

Bowder, Diana, ed. *Who Was Who in the Roman World.* Ithaca, N.Y.: Cornell University Press, 1980. Useful reference tool for identifying major figures, their contributions, and their writings.

Evans, Craig A., and Stanley E. Porter, eds. *Dictionary of New Testament Background.* Downers Grove: InterVarsity, 2000. Articles on most aspects of the New Testament world. Covers both Jewish and Greco-Roman subjects. Valuable bibliography included with most articles.

Ferguson, Everett. *Backgrounds of Early Christianity.* 3rd ed. Grand Rapids: Eerdmans, 2003. Concise discussion, rich in bibliography, on the whole range of political, sociocultural, religious, and philosophical topics and evidences relating to the New Testament.

Finegan, Jack. *Myth and Mystery: An Introduction to the Pagan Religions of the Biblical World.* Grand Rapids: Baker, 1989. An easy-to-follow introduction to the complex religions, cults, and ideas in which Christianity arose. It shows the sharp contrast between what pagans believed and what Christians taught.

Frazee, Charles A. *Two Thousand Years Ago: The World at the Time of Jesus.* Grand Rapids: Eerdmans, 2002. Gives a global perspective on the New Testament era by looking at each of the world's major regions and their religions during Jesus' era.

Grant, Michael. *The Twelve Caesars.* New York: Barnes & Noble, 1996. An excellent study of the twelve Caesars of New Testament times by an eminent contemporary historian.

Grant, Robert M. *Augustus to Constantine.* New York: Barnes & Noble, 1996. A survey of the history of Rome during the early Christian era.

Excellent on the flow of events as it affected the believer.

Guthrie, Donald. *New Testament Theology.* Downers Grove: InterVarsity, 1981. Extensive description, topically arranged, of early Christian beliefs.

Johnson, Luke Timothy. *The Writings of the New Testament: An Interpretation.* Rev. ed. Minneapolis: Fortress, 1999. Pages 1–153 offer a perceptive though advanced synopsis of background issues, critical theories, and scholarly bibliography.

Kee, Howard Clark, et al. *Christianity: A Social and Cultural History.* New York: Macmillan, 1991. Pages 1–143 treat the rise of the early Christian movement and identity. Stress is placed on cultural and social forces faced by Jesus and his followers. Early Christian history is traced into subsequent centuries down to about A.D. 300.

Keener, Craig S. *The IVP Bible Background Commentary: New Testament.* Downers Grove: InterVarsity, 1994. Covers the whole New Testament verse by verse and notes background data that may shed light on a passage's meaning. Focuses mainly on Jewish sources, but Greco-Roman writers and beliefs are frequently highlighted.

Maier, Paul. *Pontius Pilate.* Wheaton, Ill.: Tyndale, 1976. A professional historian uses the form of a novel to give an unforgettable and factually sound portrait of life both in Rome and in the provinces.

Newsome, James D. *Greeks, Romans, Jews: Currents of Culture and Belief in the New Testament World.* Philadelphia: Trinity, 1992. Readable though often technical discussion of ancient sources and historical developments. Valuable in exploring the nature of Hellenism and its influence on Judaism. Assessment of religions and philosophies of the period.

Suetonius. *The Twelve Caesars.* Trans. Robert Graves. New York: Penguin, 1989. One of the most informative, and entertaining, ancient sources for our knowledge of the early imperial period.

14 Acts 1–7
The Earliest Days of the Church

Objectives

After reading this chapter, you should be able to

- Identify the author and purpose of the Book of Acts
- Explain why the Book of Acts is important
- Suggest practical guidelines for studying Acts
- Outline the content of Acts 1–12
- Identify Jesus' legacy as found in Acts 1
- Discuss the first Christian Pentecost
- Illustrate three major themes in Acts 3–7
- Identify the two major divisions in Acts

In Plato's *Republic*, Socrates tells his listeners that "the most important part of every task is the beginning of it." History makes clear that in the wake of Jesus' brief public ministry a world-changing movement arose. To understand that movement, we must study its beginnings. There is no more illuminating guide to Christian beginnings than the Book of Acts.

Each of the four Gospels relates that in about A.D. 30 Jesus of Nazareth died on the cross and rose from the dead. After his resurrection, Jesus instructed his disciples to live out and spread the message that he had delivered to them. The next book in the New Testament after the four Gospels, the Acts of the Apostles, tells the story of the earliest church's birth and growth. Before we consider that story, several introductory matters demand our attention.

> Acts was written by Luke, a doctor who sometimes worked alongside Paul (Col 4:14).

Acts: Volume 2 of Luke

Author and Purpose

The opening words of Acts declare, "In my former book. . . ." This clearly refers to an earlier work. Scholars agree that this work is the third Gospel, Luke. Ancient tradition as well as similar literary features of the two documents establish their common authorship. If Luke, the physician and co-worker of Paul (Col 4:14), wrote the Gospel that bears his name, then he also wrote Acts.

The opening verses of Luke's Gospel (1:1–4) are worth recalling as one comes to Acts. Luke informs the reader of three things. First, reliable traditions about Jesus and the early Christian movement have been handed down by eyewitnesses. Second, Luke has made careful investigation of these experiences and reports. Third, he dedicates his work to the reader's knowledge of and growth in the Christian faith. These three statements apply not only to Luke but to Acts as well. They help account for the plausibility, careful reporting, and theological sensitivity of the book.

Date

When did Luke write Acts? The answer depends on the date one assigns to the third Gospel. It was probably written no later than the early 60s, when Paul was under house arrest in Rome awaiting trial. This is the time, at any rate, when Acts concludes (see Acts 28:30). The most likely reason why it ends here is that at the very time he writes, Luke comes to the end of the history he can recount.

No one knows just when Luke began to write Acts. Presumably it was after he finished his Gospel. One should not overlook the possibility that Luke completed his Gospel considerably earlier: ancient interpreters held that the gospel referred to by Paul ("my gospel"; see Rom 2:16; 16:25; 2 Tm 2:8; cf. 2 Cor 8:18) was none other than the Gospel of Luke.[1] Perhaps Luke compiled his Gospel before and during his early years of association with Paul, then composed Acts as a sequel. Key portions of Acts imply that the writer was part

The Muratorian Canon on Luke–Acts

An ancient document (named after its discoverer L. A. Muratori) probably dating from the late second century preserves the following information about the New Testament books written by Luke:

The third book of the Gospel is that according to Luke. Luke, the physician, when, after the Ascension of Christ, Paul had taken him to himself as traveling companion, wrote in his own name what he had been told, although he had not seen the Lord himself in the flesh. He set down the events as far as he could ascertain them, and began his story with the birth of John. . . . Moreover the Acts of all the Apostles are included in one book. Luke addressed them to the most excellent Theophilus, because the several events took place when he was present; and he makes this plain by the omission of the passion of Peter and of the journey of Paul when he left Rome for Spain.

—From Henry Bettenson, ed., *Documents of the Christian Church* (New York/London: Oxford University Press, 1947), 40f.

of the narrative he relates. Scholars call these portions the "we sections" (16:10–17; 20:5–21:28; 27:1–28:16).

Title

Some maintain that the title "Acts of the Apostles" is not entirely apt. Only one of the original twelve, Peter, receives extensive attention. Otherwise the book is primarily concerned with Paul's ministry. Some have suggested that titles like "Acts of the Holy Spirit" or "The Growth of the Gospel through the Church" (see 6:7; 9:31; 12:24; 16:5; 19:20) might serve better.

Themes in Acts

Luke wrote with historical interest, but his topics were of theological importance. They include:

World Mission
The Providence of God
The Power of the Spirit
Restored Israel
Inclusive Gospel
The Gospel's Triumph

—Adapted from John B. Polhill, "Interpreting the Book of Acts," in *Interpreting the New Testament*, ed. D. A. Black and D. S. Dockery (Nashville: Broadman & Holman, 2001).

On the other hand, "apostles" in the broad sense refers simply to early Christians who were specially authorized and empowered by the Spirit of Jesus Christ. Numerous persons in Acts fit that description. In addition, the accomplishments of Peter and Paul may be seen as representative of the work of other apostles in other places of which Luke had less ready firsthand knowledge. Acts may be likened to a survey of the American presidency entitled "The Work of Presidents" that centers on, say, Washington and Lincoln, with brief reference to less significant presidents.

In any case it is not easy to come up with a better title than the one the document bears in the ancient manuscripts.

Characteristics and Importance

Acts is distinguished on two counts: its historical value and its theological insight.[2]

Historically, Acts mentions over thirty countries, more than fifty towns or cities, numerous islands, and nearly one hundred persons, about sixty of whom are not mentioned elsewhere in the New Testament. The author of Acts demonstrates impressive knowledge of geography, local politics and customs, seafaring, and the first-century Mediterranean world generally, as studies by scholars like F. F. Bruce, C. Hemer, M. Hengel, and W. Ramsay show.

Theologically, Luke does not set out to

write a systematic account of early church teaching. Yet in powerful fashion he narrates the development, discussion, and at times dissension surrounding the spread of early preaching about Jesus Christ. Particularly in Acts' speeches and sermons, which account for some one-fifth of the book, the body of early apostolic teaching emerges. Whether in a Petrine sermon (Acts 2), Stephen's defense (Acts 7), or a Pauline address before a skeptical pagan audience (Acts 17), the word of Jesus Christ goes forth clearly and effectively.

Taken together with Luke's Gospel, Acts makes up over one-fourth of the entire New Testament. Its position—between the Gospels, which tell of Jesus Christ's coming, and the Epistles, which explain Christ's significance in concrete local church situations—indicates its theological importance. Acts explains how the kerygma, the earliest proclamation about the dead and risen Jesus, made its way into the ancient Roman world and thus acquired universal significance. This in turn assures its importance as a witness to early church practice and doctrine, or theology, for all ages since.

Literary Features and Structure

Acts is notable for its high literary quality. Its prose possesses elegance and polish without succumbing to rhetorical excess. Like Luke, Acts employs a wide-ranging vocabulary: It uses over four hundred words not found elsewhere in the New Testament, with an additional sixty of its words appearing elsewhere only in Luke's Gospel (which uses over 250 words not found elsewhere in the New Testament). By comparison, Matthew has just over, Mark just fewer than, a hundred such words.

While no single description of Acts' literary structure has gained universal acceptance, many agree that the book divides naturally into two large sections. Taking note of Jesus' programmatic words in 1:8 ("you will be my witnesses in Jerusalem, and in all Judea and Samaria, and to the ends of the earth"), they suggest that chapters 1–12 recount the gospel's spread in and around Jerusalem, Judea, and Samaria. Chapters 13–28 relate the early church's witness to Christ as it radiated out into "the ends of the earth" during the early church's beginning decades.

How to Interpret Acts

Like the Gospels, Acts contains a large amount of narrative. That is, it narrates historical events. Unlike the Gospels, much of what it narrates does not directly relate to Jesus' own deeds and teaching. It tells how Jesus' followers, and many other persons as well, were part of, and sometimes opposed to, the gospel's spread. The alert reader will ask the question: How much of Acts merely *describes* what once took place, and how much *prescribes* what *should* take place in other times and settings?[3]

An answer to this question must result from study and reflection on each individual passage in the light of all of Scripture and other relevant factors. Must speaking in tongues accompany every manifestation of the Holy Spirit (Acts 2)? Probably not. Should Christians worship each day at the Jewish temple, as Peter and John did (Acts 3:1)? Again, surely not. Both of these passages are, then, primarily descriptive, though they may also contain important prescriptive insights (the Holy Spirit is powerful and opens hearts to the meaning of the gospel; worship should be a daily event for Christians).

Other passages, however, seem both descriptive and prescriptive in nature. Is Jesus Christ the only Savior, as Acts 4:12 claims, or can one stand before God in the final judgment by one's own merit, or by the merit of some other religion? Did the Holy Spirit truly inspire David as he penned various psalms (Acts 4:25), or was that just an ancient belief or figure of speech? In these and many other cases, it is likely that Acts not only *describes* but also *prescribes* what those who follow Christ ought to affirm as true. Its description relates to other biblical events or statements, whether in the Old Testament, Gospels, or Epistles, in such a way that it seems to be furnishing trustworthy doctrinal affirmation (or teaching), not simply reliable historical information.

The point is that care is warranted in reading Acts due to the type, or genre, of literature it is. Acts furnishes, generally speaking, **historical narrative**, and it understandably relates events that persons in later times should not expect to see repeated (e.g., Jesus' ascension in Acts 1). Yet much of what it describes has at least indirect analogies with Christian experience in all times and places. The careful reader will exercise due caution in light of the special interpretive challenge that Acts presents.

Outline of Acts 1–7

Much of the world Luke writes about believed in the existence of many deities. Christians proclaimed only one.

Initial Witness to Christ in and around Jerusalem (1:1–2:47)

Jesus' Legacy (1:1–11)

Acts takes up where Luke's Gospel ends: focused on Jesus Christ. Luke 24:51 relates that several weeks after his resurrection Jesus ascended into heaven. Acts opens with an additional disclosure of what Jesus said and did prior to his physical departure from the earthly scene.

First of all, he left his own personal presence. Curious as it sounds, New Testament writers are agreed that although Jesus plainly and publicly died, his physical departure did not mean he was no longer a factor in earthly affairs. His real, though nonphysical, presence remained, as he had promised it would (see Lk 24:49; Jn 14:16). Thus Acts 1:2 speaks of Jesus "giving instructions through the Holy Spirit." The Holy Spirit is the Spirit of the risen Jesus. Acts, along with the Gospel of Luke, makes extensive mention of the Holy Spirit, so much so that scholars speak of the Spirit being a pervasive Lucan theme.

Second, Jesus left standing orders. He instructed his disciples, who were expecting him to establish some kind of earthly reign (1:6), not to waste energy speculating on the Father's timetable, which he would bring about in due course. Instead, they should ready themselves for a transforming divine visitation in the immediate future (1:8). After Jesus left, his Spirit would furnish fresh impetus for them to carry out the mandate he entrusted to them. That mandate involved testifying to who they knew Jesus Christ to be: the Lord of all creation, redeemer of all who trust in his death for their deliverance, and stern judge of all who reject his call to repent and pledge their life's loyalty to him.

With no drama or fanfare, 1:9–11 soberly recounts Jesus' ascension. While it is not easy to understand or describe the technical details of what the onlookers saw, the validity of their experience is no less trustworthy than their testimony to Jesus' physical reappearance following his un-

Luke's account of Jesus' ascension into heaven has inspired many artists. This depiction is from an eleventh-century Latin sacramentary.

observance and is still celebrated by Jews today. Pentecost Sunday is likewise a day of celebration in the Christian calendar. The Spirit's intensive presence on this particular occasion (2:2–4) serves to symbolize the completion of God's redemptive work through Jesus on Good Friday and Easter, linking it with the onset of a harvest of souls in response to the proclamation of the Messiah's cross. ("Messiah" is the Hebrew form of the Greek word "Christ" and is an especially appropriate title for the risen Jesus in the overwhelmingly Jewish setting of the early chapters of Acts.) The privilege of being the first to make that proclamation fell to Peter.

Pointed Message, Dramatic Response

The central effect of the Spirit's unusual presence involved the announcement of the gospel of Jesus the Messiah. An international assortment of Jewish pilgrims in Jerusalem for Pentecost—2:9–11 names over a dozen nations or ethnic groups, representing perhaps scores of languages—heard "the wonders of God" (2:11) proclaimed in their own native tongues. Not all onlookers were equally impressed, to be sure: Some quipped that they were observing nothing more than a disgraceful instance of early-morning public drunkenness (2:13)!

But Peter's message was stunningly sober. Drawing on the Old Testament prophet JOEL, he asserted that the end times of prophetic pronouncement were now at hand. It was time to call on the Lord, the God of Old Testament history and Scripture, with new fervor and intensity. For he was as close to them, and as fiercely firm in his expectations, as the person of Jesus had been in recent weeks.

Yet it was not primarily fervor that Peter called for: It was repentance (2:38). Peter's Jewish hearers, or at least their leaders, had conspired along with the Romans to put Jesus to death. The publicly attested facts that Jesus had been raised, and then ascended to heaven (2:32), demonstrated that God endorsed the one they had bitterly opposed. Because they had not heeded Jesus or his message when he himself preached it earlier, it was imperative they do so as his disciples preached it now. If they refused, the judgment Jesus had repeatedly an-

deniable public death (Lk 24:39). Jesus ascended to the place from whence he first came. And he would be back (1:11). Until then, his followers had work to do. Jesus himself through the Spirit saw to it that they got started.

The First Christian Pentecost (1:12–2:47)

Days of Preparation

The dramatic appearance of the Spirit that Jesus promised was some days in coming. The eleven waited obediently in continual prayer, joined by Jesus' mother, some other women, and his (formerly skeptical) brothers (1:13–14). This assembly, following Peter's suggestion, acted to appoint a replacement for the traitor Judas. The lot fell to MATTHIAS (1:26), about whom little else is known. The apostolic circle was again at full strength.

Pentecost (2:1) refers to the ancient Hebrew holiday instituted in Moses' time (Dt 16:16, there called the Feast of Weeks). It took place seven weeks after the Passover

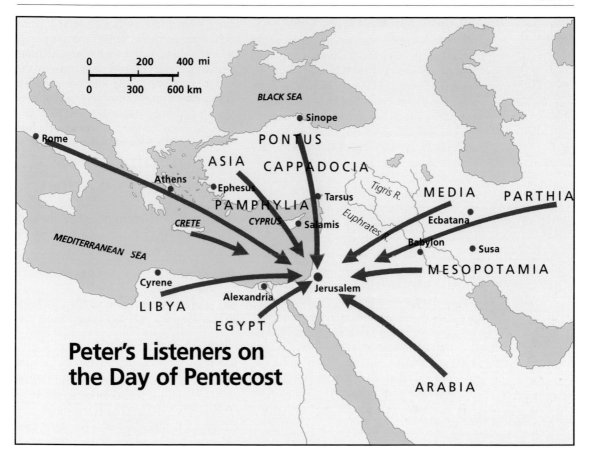

Peter's Listeners on the Day of Pentecost

nounced would befall them. If they accepted, they would receive the Holy Spirit and new life, now and forever. This would fulfill "the promise" (2:39), presumably the covenant promise made to Abraham (Gn 12:1–3), and assure their place among the people of God (2:39).

Acts gives only a summary of Peter's sermon (2:40). Peter's remarks were direct, sensitive, and persuasive, yet also threatening, all features reminiscent of messages preached by his master Jesus. His electrifying claims met a massive response: Over three thousand men (see 4:4; women and children were either not present or not counted) presented themselves for baptism.

Common Life

Acts 2:42–47 maps out the longer-term outcome of the Pentecost conversions. At least seven distinct results are mentioned. First, the apostles' teaching occupied center stage. This is understandable, because Jesus had commanded them to make disciples ("disciple" means pupil or learner), and because they, and in those earliest days

no others, were the spokesmen whom Jesus had authorized to relay the saving message of his death and resurrection.

A second outcome involved "fellowship," which may be taken as including both "breaking of bread" and "prayer." "Fellowship" apparently refers to what now marked all their lives and bound them intimately together: Jesus Christ and his Spirit, whom they had all received. Shared meals, which almost certainly included observance of the Lord's Supper, and corporate prayer indicated a common bond with one another and expressed devotion to the Lord. No wonder Acts next mentions two further outcomes: a sense of awe, in part due to wondrous works done by the apostles, and the sharing of physical goods and possessions. Such sharing may have been necessitated by social rejection and loss of employment by Jews who chose to accept Jesus as the promised Messiah (see Heb 10:32–34). Then as now in many locations around the world, becoming a serious follower of Jesus carried painful consequences.

A fifth outcome—meeting together in the temple courts—seems at first strange to mention. For many, if not most, this would have been normal practice prior to hearing Peter's message. But now they were not merely Jews but messianic Jews, descendants of Abraham who had bravely and gladly received the apostolic word that God's ancient promises to their divinely chosen progenitor had been fulfilled in Jesus the Messiah. Their presence in the temple was therefore significant as a witness that the God who had instituted temple worship had now delivered an additional and climactic word.

A sixth outcome was the heartfelt praise of God and favor with outsiders they enjoyed. Their home-to-home camaraderie, shared meals, and mutual gladness were apparently as distinctive at that time as they would be in modern Western society today.

A seventh outcome was growth. Luke takes pains to specify that "the Lord added to their number daily those who were being saved" (2:47). Here Acts tells not so much of human religious activity or social organization as of the amazing work of God's Spirit. He was marvelously transforming persons both in their inner beings and in the way they related to each other. The gospel's outworkings were dramatic at both personal and social levels.

Spreading the Message, Gathering Opposition (3:1–7:60)

Three themes dominate the remainder of Acts' opening chapters: the continuing work of the gospel through the joint working of miracle and message, life together in the community of believers, and conflict.

Miracles and Message

The same unusual signs of the divine presence that attended Jesus' ministry continued as the early days of church life stretched

The earliest Christians continued regular worship at the Jerusalem temple. But they also began to meet from home to home.

Do Miracles Happen?

New Testament scholar Rudolf Bultmann once said, "The world-view of the Scripture is mythological and is therefore unacceptable to modern man whose thinking has been shaped by science. Nobody reckons with direct intervention by transcendent powers" (*Jesus Christ and Mythology*, 36). Pretty strong stuff, but Bultmann is wrong on at least four counts. First, almost everybody believes in direct intervention by transcendent powers, especially God. The worldview of Scripture is quite acceptable to "modern man." All of the recent polls show this. Second, even the scientific community is beginning to come around. The older idea of a closed universe that explains everything simply will not do anymore. There are too many mysteries left unexplained and the more we learn about the correlation between prayer and health, to use just one example, the more we realize there's more to

life than just this earth. Third, it leaves God entirely out of the picture. If God can make a world, why can't he act in the world he has made? Most people believe it is more reasonable to think that he does than that he doesn't. And finally, the New Testament is full of miraculous events, from the virgin birth, to Jesus' healings and exorcisms and resurrection, to the apostles' continued miraculous minstry in the Book of Acts. We must either cut the heart out of the New Testament or dare to believe that God works. It is a challenge to our faith, but if God can raise Jesus from the dead, Peter can say to the crippled man, *"In the name of Jesus Christ of Nazareth, walk"* (Acts 3:6).

For extended discussion on the question of miracles, see R. D. Geivett and G. R. Habermas, eds., *In Defense of Miracles: A Comprehensive Case for God's Action in History* (Downers Grove: InterVarsity, 1996).

into weeks, months, and years. A beggar crippled since birth leaped to his feet with joy upon hearing Jesus' name (3:8). Even the disciples' enemies could not deny that a great work had occurred (4:16). And more signs of God's power lay ahead. Upon praying, the believers' meetinghouse was shaken (4:31). A married couple who conspired to deceive other believers dropped dead under circumstances too eerie to be coincidental (5:5, 10).

As the disciples' ranks swelled, signs and wonders continued. Apparently even the passing shadow of an apostle might be sufficient to bring about healing (5:15). As they preached their message, Jesus' original followers, who were the authoritative bearers of the message about him, were enabled to duplicate the work they had done when their Master first sent them out: healing the sick and delivering those tormented by demonic influence (5:16; see Lk 9:1–2).

When imprisoned, the apostles were delivered by an angel (5:19). Amazingly under the highly polarized circumstances, a number of Jewish priests declared their allegiance to the dead and risen Messiah

(6:7). Wonder-working power spread from the apostles to at least a few additional stalwart believers, among them Stephen (6:8). When put on trial Stephen not only managed to state his case with grace and elegance; he also was granted a heavenly vision (7:55). Still more notably, as stones battered his dying form, he nobly echoed the dying Messiah who had met a similar end (cf. Lk 23:34).

Truly, the power and very presence of Jesus were still at work.

Evidence of the gospel's power is also seen in the intensity and consistency with which it is preached. When Peter and John heal a lame beggar, they call the astonished crowd that gathers to repentance in view of Jesus' return and a coming fearful judgment (3:19–23). On trial before the religious authorities, Peter and John repeat their Jesus-centered message (4:12). Under arrest a second time, Peter and other apostles continue to insist that God's ancient promises to his people through Abraham have been fulfilled in Jesus' cross and ascension to heaven (5:29–31). Flogged for their refusal to hush up or tone down

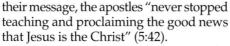

their message, the apostles "never stopped teaching and proclaiming the good news that Jesus is the Christ" (5:42).

Highly representative of the apostolic message is Stephen's lengthy sermon (7:2–53). It may well sum up key elements of apostolic instruction in the earliest church, tracing the work of God's saving grace from Abraham through his son Isaac and grandson Jacob to the Israelites in Egypt. Stephen points to the Israelites' stubborn defiance of Moses, God's chosen deliverer, as an example of his hearers' rejection of Jesus (7:51–53).

The same generous yet stern gospel seen at the church's beginning continues to go forth as the church expands. A major result of this message is a high level of growth and social cohesion among converts.

Christian Community

Growth is not an infallible sign of the gospel's progress, for religious movements may prosper quite apart from the gospel's light. Even religious movements that seriously distort the gospel (e.g., Christian Science, Mormonism) may enjoy notable levels of popular acceptance. But growth does sometimes attend faithful preaching and living of the Christian message, as it did in the years covered by this section of Acts (4:4; 5:14; 6:7).

In addition to growth, these years were marked by an enviable social cohesion. That is, people lived with an eye to the needs of others and with a common spirit of sacrifice and love that lifted up one's neighbor rather than centering on oneself. This high degree of common concern was rooted, however, in a high regard for Christ and his commands, not in bare humanitarian impulse. Luke states that there were "no needy persons among them" (4:34) and speaks of "the daily distribution of food" to needy widows (6:1). Prayer and preaching had a tangible, practical effect.

Conflict

No account of early church life should minimize the opposition that believers faced. Jesus had promised that persecution would come (Jn 15:20), and it did. In this portion of Acts leaders are repeatedly jailed and sometimes physically brutalized. Stephen is martyred.

The persecution was unjust but understandable. Christian preaching seemed to undermine widely accepted views of what mattered in religion and society. It appeared that Jerusalem and Jewish custom were under siege in the name of Jesus (6:14). The threat of harsh Roman response to prolonged social unrest (see Jn 11:48) was real, as the events of A.D. 70 later showed.

Acts 7 ends with Stephen's stoning in the same city where Jesus was crucified. Among his persecutors stood one named Saul (7:58). Premier enemy of the fledg-ling church, this Saul came to be one of the greatest advocates of Jesus Christ that the early church produced. The next chapters of Acts relate the drama of his conversion, as well as the continued spread of the gospel's transforming truth.

Focus 14: The Gospel to All Peoples: The African Example

Acts relates how the gospel spread to people from varying cultural settings, including Africa (people from Cyrene and Egypt were at Pentecost according to Acts 2:10). That complex process continues today. Africans in today's churches find themselves locked in a tension between three worlds, none of which they can ignore.

First there is the world of Christian teaching, customs, and practices. Then there is the world of African identity—a person's name, ancestry, tribal identity, location near or far from ancestral grounds and homeland, social situation (rich or poor, more educated or less educated, employed or unemployed, politically "free" or repressed), and family situation (single or married, first-born child). The third world that an African typically must cope with is the world of modern and postmodern culture—Western cultural influences (such as clothing, music, media, and consumerism); Islamic culture and language in much of Africa; global politics; education; medicine; science; technology; and the need for money to finance involvement in the emerging global economy.

Acts is reassuring because it confirms that early Christians faced similar challenges. There were questions about sound doctrine and faithful living. There were personal and social identity questions. Issues arose in connection with local and imperial governmental authorities. The similar situations faced by the first generations of believers assure us that God's word has counsel for our times, in Africa and elsewhere, just as it had for theirs.

As African Christians come to terms with this tension, they do so with at least three fundamental commitments: (1) commitment to Jesus Christ's lordship over the powers of this world (see Eph 6:10–13); (2) commitment to the Bible read with the help of God's Spirit and the aid of tested doctrinal formulations (creeds) as the final authority in questions of faith and practice; and (3) commitment to applying their biblical, Christ-centered faith to life in Africa within the context of the church.

—See *Issues in African Christian Theology,* ed. Samuel Ngewa, Mark Shaw, and Tite Tiénou (Nairobi/Kampala/Dar es Salaam: East African Educational Publishers, 1998), xi–xiv.

Key People

Joel
Matthias
Saul

Key Term

historical narrative

Study Questions

1. What three statements from Lk 1:1–4 apply to Acts as well and help to explain what Acts contains?

2. Briefly discuss Acts' historical and theological significance.

3. How can we determine which parts of Acts are descriptive and which are prescriptive?

4. What was the primary theme of Peter's sermon at Pentecost (Acts 2)? What is its relevance today?

5. What was the connection between the miracles of the apostles and the message they preached?

6. Describe the roles played by community and conflict in the early church.

Review Questions

1. Two factors that establish the common authorship of Acts and Luke are ancient _____ and similar _____ _____.

2. The Book of Acts makes extensive reference to the geography of the _____ region, mentioning over thirty countries and fifty towns and cities.

3. Combined with Luke's Gospel, the Book of Acts makes up over _____ percent of the New Testament.

4. Acts employs a wide-ranging _____.

5. Acts furnishes trustworthy _____ and not just reliable _____ information.

6. The person who announced the gospel of Jesus the Messiah at Pentecost was _____.

7. During the early days of the Christian church, the most striking evidence that God was at work was demonstrated by _____.

8. A result of the generous yet stern gospel at the church's beginning was _____ among converts.

9. Among those who persecuted Stephen was _____, a man who later became one of the greatest advocates of Christ.

Summary

1. The Book of Acts was written by Luke probably no later than the early A.D. 60s.

2. Acts is distinguished by its historical value and its theological insight.

3. In Acts Luke narrates the development, discussion, and dissension surrounding the spread of the early preaching of Christ.

4. There are two major divisions in Acts: (a) chapters 1–12 focus on the gospel's spread in and around Jerusalem, Judea, and Samaria; (b) chapters 13–28 focus on early witness to the ends of the earth.

5. Acts is a historical narrative that focuses on Jesus' followers rather than on Jesus' deeds and teachings.

6. Luke in Acts discusses Jesus' legacy in his leaving his own personal testimony, in his leaving standing orders, and in the recounting of Jesus' ascension.

7. At Pentecost the unusual presence of the Holy Spirit involved the announcement of the gospel of Jesus the Messiah.

8. Prominent features of early Christian life and impact in the wake of Pentecost included: (a) the centrality of the apostles' teaching, (b) the developing of fellowship, (c) a prevailing sense of awe, (d) sharing of material possessions, (e) meeting in the temple courts, (f) heartfelt praise of God, (g) the favor the apostles enjoyed with outsiders, and (h) the spiritual growth of believers.

9. Miracles continued through the work of the apostles.

10. The gospel's power is seen in the intensity and consistency with which it was preached.

11. Christians were persecuted in this period, and Stephen was the first known martyr.

Further Reading

See also reading suggestions at the end of chapters 15 and 16.

Bruce, F. F. *The Book of Acts.* Rev. ed. Grand Rapids: Eerdmans, 1988. Advanced but readable commentary.

Cadbury, H. J. *The Making of Luke–Acts.* New York: Macmillan, 1927. A classic study on Luke–Acts as a literary unity.

Gasque, Ward. T*he History of the Criticism of the Acts of the Apostles.* Rev. ed. Peabody, Mass.: Hendrickson, 1989. Fascinating survey of how different scholars have handled Acts in very different ways.

Green, Michael. *Thirty Years That Changed the World: The Book of Acts for Today.* Grand Rapids: Eerdmans, 2002. Thematic study of early church beliefs and practices.

Hemer, C. *The Book of Acts in the Setting of Hellenistic History.* Tübingen: Mohr, 1989. Technical investigation of the ties between early chapters of Acts and first-century sources and evidence outside the New Testament.

Johnson, Dennis E. *The Message of Acts in the History of Redemption.* Phillipsburg, N.J.: Presbyterian & Reformed, 1997. Treats some of Acts' major themes with learning, conviction, and imagination.

Marshall, I. Howard. *The Acts of the Apostles.* Grand Rapids: Eerdmans, 1980. Less technical but still thorough commentary.

Polhill, John B. "Interpreting the Book of Acts." In *Interpreting the New Testament,* ed. D. A. Black and D. S. Dockery. Nashville: Broadman & Holman, 2001, pp. 391–411. Surveys recent scholarship and comments on matters like genre, author, date, sources, and themes of Acts.

Sherwin-White, A. N. *Roman Society and Roman Law in the New Testament.* Grand Rapids: Baker, 1991. An ancient historian examines the New Testament in the light of first-century Roman culture.

Winter, Bruce, ed. *The Book of Acts in Its First Century Setting.* 6 vols. Carlisle/Grand Rapids: Paternoster/Eerdmans, 1993–97. Dozens of scholarly studies dealing with literary, historical, and cultural issues. Contributions affirm the general reliability of Acts as a historical source.

15 Acts 8–12
Salvation for Both Jew and Gentile

Outline

- **Outline of Acts 8–12**
- **Perspective of Acts 8–12**
- **Minor Figures: Ten More Who Believed**
  Philip (8:5–13, 26–40)
  The Ethiopian Eunuch (8:26–40)
  Ananias (9:10–19)
  Aeneas (9:33–35)
  Tabitha (9:36–42)
  Simon the Tanner (9:43; 10:6, 17, 32)
  Cornelius (10:1–11:18)
  Barnabas (11:22–30)
  Agabus (11:28)
  James, Brother of John (12:2)
- **Two Who Disbelieved**
  Simon the Sorcerer (8:9–25)
  Herod Agrippa I (12:1–23)
- **Major Figures**
  John (8:14–25)
  Peter (8:14–25; 9:32–43; 10:1–11:18; 12:3–18)
  Saul (8:1–3; 9:1–31; 11:25–30; 12:25)

Objectives

After reading this chapter, you should be able to

- Write a content outline of Acts 8–12
- List the ten individuals who responded to the gospel
- Explain the situations surrounding two individuals who did not respond to the gospel favorably
- Identify the contributions of three persons who were prominent in the rise and growth of the early church

Jews of Jesus' time shunned Samaria and Samaritans. But Jesus commanded his disciples to take the gospel there. Philip was among the first to obey.

Perspective of Acts 8–12

Acts 8–12 reflects a slight change of perspective. Earlier chapters focus more on the content and impact of the message preached. Acts 8–12 continues this focus but also takes interest in a number of individual persons. In order to dramatize early church response to Jesus' mandate ("you will be my witnesses in Jerusalem, and in all Judea and Samaria . . ."), it artfully portrays the gospel's impact on various individual lives. Usually the impact involves acceptance of Christ. In some cases it involves rebuke and even judgment for disobeying Christ. In all cases this section of Acts shows God's personal awareness of and interest in the lives of all persons, whether Jew (like Jesus and those around him) or Gentile (like the majority of people in both ancient and modern worlds).

Some of these persons are minor figures in the overall scope of the early church's formation. Others are more central. All are affected by the same gospel. Below we consider both of these groups—minor figures and major figures—in turn.

The gospel of Jesus' saving death and resurrection was preached first in JERUSALEM. Its earliest preachers and hearers were Jewish. But Jesus had called his followers to move out into greater JUDEA and SAMARIA with their message, too (Acts 1:8). Acts 8–12 relates high points of the gospel's surge beyond the streets and walls of Jerusalem.

Outline of Acts 8–12

I. **The Witness to Christ in Judea and Samaria** (8:1–12:25)
   A. Saul the Persecutor and Philip the Evangelist (8:1–40)
   B. The Conversion of Saul (9:1–31)
   C. Peter's Ministry in Judea (9:32–11:18)
   D. The Antioch Church: Barnabas's Ministry (11:19–30)
   E. Peter's Miraculous Deliverance (12:1–25)

Minor Figures: Ten More Who Believed

In all four Gospels and in Acts 1–7, twelve hand-picked followers of Jesus hold a prominent place. Their importance does not diminish in Acts 8–12, but the spotlight enlarges to include various individuals who responded to, and in some cases furthered, the message that Jesus had commanded be taken to all persons (Acts 1:8).

Philip (8:5–13, 26–40)

Philip was one of seven chosen to oversee food distribution in the Jerusalem church (6:5; not to be confused with Philip the apostle [1:13]). Because of the persecution of Christians that followed Stephen's stoning, Philip and others fled Jerusalem. But they did not leave the gospel behind. They

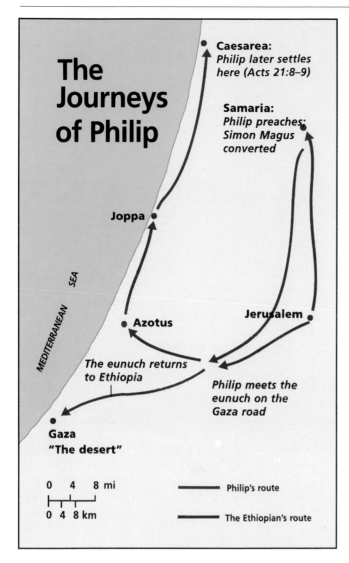

The Journeys of Philip

Caesarea:
Philip later settles here (Acts 21:8–9)

Samaria:
Philip preaches; Simon Magus converted

Joppa

MEDITERRANEAN SEA

Azotus

Jerusalem

The eunuch returns to Ethiopia

Philip meets the eunuch on the Gaza road

Gaza
"The desert"

```
0    4    8 mi
0  4  8 km
```

———— Philip's route

━━━━ The Ethiopian's route

spoke it to those they encountered as they went along.

Philip entered Samaria, a region shunned by most Jerusalem Jews (see Jn 4:9). He shared the messianic proclamation that the apostles, Stephen, and others had already spread in Jerusalem. The response was enthusiastic. Philip's preaching produced many of the same signs that had accompanied Jesus' ministry (8:7).

Philip is significant in Acts because he is among the first to take the gospel outside Jerusalem. Others probably preceded him (e.g., some of the converts mentioned in Acts 2, or the unknown founders of the group mentioned in 9:38), but records are sketchy. The gospel preached first to the Jews (Acts 1–7) is now proclaimed to the Samaritans by Philip. It is worth noting that persecution was the prod that first pushed the early church to obey Jesus' command (Acts 1:8). Among Philip's converts were a sorcerer named Simon (8:13) and a high official of the Ethiopian government.

The Ethiopian Eunuch (8:26–40)

Despite favorable response to the gospel in Samaria, Philip remained sensitive to divine leading when the time came to head elsewhere. At the prompting of an angel he left Samaria, which was north of Jerusalem, and headed for GAZA, which was to the southwest (8:26). Before long he encountered a distinguished traveler: the treasurer of the African kingdom of ETHIOPIA (not identical with modern Ethiopia, known in ancient times as ABYSSINIA). Ethiopia (referred to as CUSH in the Old Testament) was located in the area of present-day southern Egypt and northern SUDAN.[1] It had historic ties to Jerusalem and the Jewish faith.

The Ethiopian official (who may or may not have been physically emasculated; the term "eunuch" did not always imply castration) may have been visiting Jerusalem for religious reasons. Philip found him puzzling over a scroll containing Isaiah 53, which tells of an innocent victim dying willingly to atone for the sins of others. Philip seized the occasion to inform him how Jesus fulfilled Isaiah's prophecy. The Ethiopian requested baptism when they encountered water (8:36). Philip honored his request before he was again prompted to move on (8:39), laboring along the Mediterranean coast until he came to CAESAREA, where he apparently settled. He was known in the early church as Philip the evangelist (Acts 21:8), perhaps to distinguish him from the apostle of the same name.

The Ethiopian, who went on his way a changed man, may well have shared the message of Christ with his countrymen upon his return. The gospel continued to touch lives as it spread beyond Jerusalem, just as Jesus had foretold.

Ananias (9:10–19)

The same Saul whose persecution caused the gospel to spread across Judea and Samaria (8:1) took steps to arrest any followers of Jesus who might be in DAMAS-

Isaiah 53:1–10

This is the passage that the Ethiopian asked Philip to help him interpret. Isaiah (eighth century B.C.) speaks of a "servant of God" who suffers mistreatment for God's sake. Philip interpreted the passage as a prophecy about Jesus Christ.

Who has believed our message and to whom has the arm of the LORD been revealed? He grew up before him like a tender shoot, and like a root out of dry ground. He had no beauty or majesty to attract us to him, nothing in his appearance that we should desire him. He was despised and rejected by men, a man of sorrows, and familiar with suffering. Like one from whom men hide their faces he was despised, and we esteemed him not. Surely he took up our infirmities and carried our sorrows, yet we considered him stricken by God, smitten by him, and afflicted. But he was pierced for our transgressions, he was crushed for our iniquities; the punishment that brought us peace was upon him, and by his wounds we are healed. We all, like sheep, have gone astray, each of us has turned to his own way; and the LORD has laid on him the iniquity of us all. He was oppressed and afflicted, yet he did not open his mouth; he was led like a lamb to the slaughter, and as a sheep before her shearers is silent, so he did not open his mouth. By oppression and judgment he was taken away. And who can speak of his descendants? For he was cut off from the land of the living; for the transgression of my people he was stricken. He was assigned a grave with the wicked, and with the rich in his death, though he had done no violence, nor was any deceit in his mouth. Yet it was the LORD's will to crush him and cause him to suffer, and though the LORD makes his life a guilt offering, he will see his offspring and prolong his days, and the will of the LORD will prosper in his hand.

CUS (9:1–2). His confrontation with Jesus will be related below. When he arrived at Damascus, temporarily blind and refusing all food and drink, God sent Ananias to announce the restoration of his sight.

We are not told how Ananias came to embrace the gospel, nor whether he was a native of Damascus or perhaps had fled there from Jerusalem. He is significant in Acts not only for his role in Saul's conversion, but also for the evidence he furnishes for a significant Christian community in Damascus, over one hundred miles from Jerusalem, only a few years after Jesus' death. Acts' brief record of his conversation with God (9:10–16) points to the warmly personal nature of early Christian faith, the vital role that prayer (both speaking and listening) played, and the courage that obeying God required.

Aeneas (9:33–35)

Aeneas receives mention in connection with Peter's ministry. As the gospel spread outside Jerusalem, the apostolic church sent Peter and John out to check on the new developments (8:14). Peter continued to travel and speak outside Jerusalem. His travels took him to LYDDA, a thriving commercial center some thirty miles northwest of Jerusalem. There he visited "the saints" (9:32), Jews who were followers of Jesus Christ. Among their number was a man called Aeneas.

Aeneas had been paralyzed for eight years. Peter called on him to rise and pick up the mat on which he had lain helplessly for nearly a decade. This remarkable healing linked Peter's ministry with that of Jesus, in whose name Peter commanded the man to rise (Mk 2:11). The healing also drew additional numbers to faith in Christ. Aeneas's recovery became widely known in both Lydda and SHARON (9:35). Sharon was not a city, but the fertile coastal plain that linked Judea with Samaria and with the strategic port city of Caesarea to the north.

Tabitha (9:36–42)

Some ten miles beyond Lydda lay JOPPA on the Mediterranean coast, near modern-day TEL AVIV. Joppa served as the port city of Jerusalem. It is not known how the community of "disciples" (9:38) was founded there. When a beloved, saintly woman among them named Tabitha died, they sent word to Peter, who was still in Lydda where he had healed Aeneas.

Peter responded to their plea. He was clearly moved by their distress at Tabitha's death. Her name meant "gazelle" in Aramaic. (Her Greek name, "Dorcas," meant the same thing. Like many in this bi- or trilingual region, she had names in each of the current dominant languages.) She had been exemplary in care for the poor and other good works during her life.

Peter may have recalled a similar incident when Jesus brought a dead twelve-year-old girl back to life after putting everyone out of the room except her parents and Peter, James, and John (Mk 5:37–40). He fell to his knees in prayer, then called the dead woman's name. Her eyes opened and she sat up. The incident became widely known throughout the region, drawing many more to faith in the Lord that Peter preached.

Like Aeneas, Tabitha is a reminder of the spread of the gospel beyond the area directly touched by Jesus and his first disciples. She and Aeneas also point to God's active concern for needy individuals, especially those like widows and paralytics who tended to be overlooked by the broader society.

Simon the Tanner (9:43; 10:6, 17, 32)

Reference to this Simon (one of nine persons by that name in the New Testament) is brief but significant. Peter stayed at his home during the many days he was in Joppa (9:43). It was on the flat roof of Simon's house that Peter had a vision that changed the course of early church history (9:9–16). Simon the tanner is important in part because Peter received this vision at his home.

Simon's occupation points to another sense in which he is significant. He was a tanner, or leathermaker. His livelihood involved daily contact with dead animals. Jewish tradition based on the Old Testament (Lv 11:39–40) pronounced him ceremonially unclean. First-century groups like the Pharisees tended to look down on such persons. Peter's willingness to stay with Simon, whose home would be viewed by many as unclean due to his occupation, suggests that Peter was already being liberated from some of the prejudices that prevented the gospel from receiving the hearing it deserved. Jesus, of course, had done battle with many of these same prejudices. By staying under Simon's roof, Peter was following the lead of Jesus, who accepted those deemed unacceptable by religious authorities of the day (Mk 2:16).

Cornelius (10:1–11:18)

Peter's vision at the house of Simon the tanner prepared him for his historic visit with Cornelius, a Roman military commander. Cornelius was an unusual Roman **centurion**. He attempted to honor the God of the Jews in various ways (10:2). The typical Roman soldier worshiped the emperor and the patron deities of his military unit, called a legion.

God responded to Cornelius's devotion by sending a heavenly messenger. Cornelius was to send for Peter in Joppa. He did so, inviting a large number of relatives and friends to hear Peter's message (10:24).

Cornelius was a key figure in Peter's realization that Jewish customs forbidding

Widows, the sick, and the poor often had nowhere to go in the ancient world. Jesus taught God's care for them. Peter's ministry followed Jesus' lead.

Simon the tanner's occupation involved handling dead animals. Religious laws pronounced him unclean because of this. But Peter stayed under his roof anyway.

contact with Gentiles were inconsistent with following Jesus (10:28). When Cornelius and other non-Jews received the Holy Spirit in the same way that Peter and other Jews did, Peter understood that the people of God were not limited to those of Jewish ancestry and social custom (10:34–35, 44, 47).

The Cornelius incident became a test case in the early church, which was still largely Jewish. It raised the issue of the relation between Jewish religious practice and the necessary conditions for receiving forgiveness and new life through Jesus Christ. God used Cornelius to show Peter, and the early church, that Gentiles who repented and believed in Christ were acceptable to God. They did not need to adopt Jewish social customs first (11:17–18). As Jesus had taught, the gospel was for all persons, not just physical descendants of Abraham.

Barnabas (11:22–30)

The church at Jerusalem sent Barnabas north to ANTIOCH over three hundred miles away to check out reports that non-Jews were receiving "the good news about the Lord Jesus" (11:20, 22). Barnabas, whose name means "encourager," was well known from the days when he sold

Opposite:
Remains of the great Roman harbor at Caesarea, where Cornelius was stationed.

property to help meet pressing needs among destitute believers in Jerusalem (4:37).

Barnabas endorsed and encouraged the new believers at Antioch, the capital city of the large Roman province called SYRIA. He is thus a key figure in the spread of the gospel to this strategic political center where believers were first called Christians (11:26). He also had the wisdom to enlist Saul as a teacher in the Antiochene church (11:25). Earlier he had the insight and courage to associate with the dangerous Saul shortly after his conversion (9:27). Both Barnabas and Saul play central roles in the spread of the gospel in later chapters of Acts.

Agabus (11:28)

Agabus accurately predicted that a famine would occur during the reign of CLAUDIUS (A.D. 41–54). He is one of a number of persons called "prophets" in the early church. Elsewhere prophets are mentioned along with apostles, evangelists, and pastor-teachers as individuals uniquely called and gifted for the building up of the Christian community (Eph 4:11). Agabus's forecast spurred the believers in Antioch to take action on behalf of their needy brethren in Judea. Apparently Judean be-

Corruption in the Church

In Acts 8:20, Peter rebukes a huckster magician named Simon, a man who wanted to use holy things for personal gain.

In recent years North American churches have seen church leaders misuse their holy calling. On the Protestant side, an openly gay Episcopalian priest was elected to serve as bishop. It has come to light that some previous bishops were gay but did not admit it. And a United Methodist minister teaching at a United Church of Christ seminary in Chicago has published a study claiming that Jesus was involved in a same-sex relationship.

Among Roman Catholics, clergy have been guilty of sexually abusing their members. Many of the victims were teenagers and children. In 2003 a bishop in Phoenix who had admitted sheltering guilty priests left the scene of a hit-and-run accident in which the car he was driving fatally struck a pedestrian. Catholics have expressed outrage at the irresponsible behavior and attitudes of their leaders.

Problems exist in evangelical circles too. In his book *Can Fallen Pastors Be Restored? The Church's Response to Sexual Misconduct* (Chicago: Moody, 1995), John H. Armstrong documented the existence of shocking levels of immoral behavior by pastors and others in church leadership.

The Book of Acts is a reminder that although the church is called to holiness, its members may be guilty of unholy actions. Some, like Simon the Sorcerer or unnamed persons against whom Paul later warned (Acts 20:29), may actually be wolves among the sheep of God's flock. It is the responsibility of others in the church to call the rebellious to repentance rather than blandly tolerating behavior that Scripture clearly condemns.

Agabus is a reminder of God's provision for his people's needs. In its earliest years the church had no New Testament Scriptures. Prophets, many of whom seem to have been itinerant, furnished guidance and exhortation to augment instruction from the Old Testament, Christian teachers, and the apostles themselves. As decades passed, the office of prophet appears to have declined in importance, eventually disappearing altogether. Yet the testimony of its centrality to the spread and application of the gospel in Acts remains.

Agabus is also a reminder that God is ruler over history. He knows what the future holds. As he sees fit, he reveals aspects of his plans for both present and future times to those with ears to hear.

James, Brother of John (12:2)

James serves as a potent though grim reminder of the close link between Acts and the Gospels. James was the brother of the apostle John. Along with John and Peter, he was one of Jesus' original twelve followers and a member of Jesus' three-man inner circle. In Matthew 20:23 Jesus predicts that James will meet the same earthly end as he will: death by execution. Acts 12:2 records the fulfillment of that prophecy.

James thus became the first of the twelve to die for his allegiance to Jesus. He reminds us of the fierce opposition that many if not most early believers faced. Even the civil ruler HEROD AGRIPPA I (A.D. 37–44) joined in harrying Judean Jews who professed faith in the crucified Jesus. This increased Herod's esteem in the eyes of other Judeans (12:3). James paid the ultimate price for his loyalty to Jesus and the gospel.

Two Who Disbelieved

Most of the persons mentioned in Acts 8–12 respond favorably to the gospel or promote its spread. There are two accounts, however, of negative response to the message about Jesus Christ. The figures involved are a sorcerer and a king.

lievers were continuing to experience economic hardship as a result of heeding the gospel (Acts 2:45; 4:32).

simony

Simon the Sorcerer (8:9–25)

Philip the evangelist's preaching in Samaria, already mentioned above, attracted the attention of a local celebrity named Simon. He appeared to have magical powers, and he was not shy about boasting of them. He attracted a following of persons who felt that divine power must be at work in him. When Philip's preaching drew some of these persons to Christ rather than to Simon, Simon responded by making a public profession of faith and being baptized.

The nature of Simon's conversion, however, was called in question when Peter and John arrived from Jerusalem to survey the gospel's spread. Simon offered them money if they would share their apostolic powers with him (hence the word **simony**, the buying or selling of church office or privilege). Peter's reply was immediate and forthright: Simon's heart was still in bondage to the charlatan's greed from which he had pretended to repent. While Simon's response sounds noble (8:24), second-century reports suggest that he expressed momentary fear rather than lasting contrition. His name became synonymous with heresy. His brief story is a reminder that accepting the gospel means giving power over one's life to the Lord, not using the Lord to get power for one's own personal betterment.

Herod Agrippa I (12:1–23)

Herod, the persecutor of James (12:1–4), knew enough about the gospel to suppress it by force. Born about 10 B.C., he was brother of the woman (HERODIAS) who engineered John the Baptist's beheading. He would have had knowledge of Jesus' earthly ministry since its early days. When Claudius became Roman emperor in A.D. 41, he added Judea and Samaria to Herod's kingdom, which was previously limited to a much smaller area.

Herod ordered the execution of guards who stood watch as an angel released Peter from jail (see below and Acts 12:19). From Jerusalem he journeyed to the Mediterranean coast to negotiate with citizens of the cities of TYRE and SIDON. Delivering a public address, he basked in public adulation. He was even called a god (12:22). Despite the stir raised by the Christian movement in his lands, he was not moved to decline or rebuke such blasphemy. As a result, he was struck down, becoming a public example of the seriousness of defying God and opposing the gospel. He died a short time later.

Major Figures

Acts 8–12 mentions three persons who are prominent in the rise and growth of the early church: John, Peter, and Saul (Paul).

John (8:14–25)

While a number of persons named John appear in the New Testament, this John is the apostle, the son of Zebedee, the "beloved disciple" who wrote the Fourth Gospel. He also wrote three New Testament Epistles and the Book of Revelation. He is mentioned in Acts 1, 3, and 4, each time along with Peter. In Acts 8 he accompanies Peter to Samaria. He and Peter were sent by the Jerusalem church to Samaria to confirm the believers there.

John, along with Peter, prayed and laid hands on the new Samaritan converts. They "received the Holy Spirit" (Acts 8:17), which seems to indicate that they showed the same signs of divine visitation as John, Peter, and others had experienced earlier in Jerusalem. John thus became a witness and supporter of the spread of the gospel from Judea as well as lands beyond (8:25). While he is not mentioned by name in Acts after this (except as James's brother, 12:2), we can assume that he played a prominent role in the gospel's spread. Specifics of John's activity in Samaria and among the Jerusalem leadership (see Gal 2:9) are not preserved in detail, but indications from his writings and ancient church tradition are that his contribution and sacrifice for the cause of Jesus Christ were considerable.

Peter (8:14–25; 9:32–43; 10:1–11:18; 12:3–18)

In some respects Peter plays the leading role in Acts 8–12, much as he does in Acts 1–7. He joined John in confirming Philip's work in Samaria. Then he warned Simon the sorcerer to turn from his greed. In the course of spreading the gospel he healed Aeneas and Tabitha.

As we have already noted, Peter had a vision while staying with Simon the tan-

The Roman world pictured the gods in human form, like this sculpture of Serapis, who was widely worshiped. When Herod Agrippa I received acclaim as a god (Acts 12:22), he died shortly afterward.

ner. This vision underscored a truth that Jesus had taught: People are defiled by what proceeds from their hearts, not by what they eat (Mk 7:15–23). While diet is not irrelevant to spirituality, the role of "clean" and "unclean" foods as understood in much first-century Judaism was misguided. God's concern is with human hearts, not meal plans.

When messengers from Cornelius the Roman general came to escort Peter from Joppa to Caesarea, Peter followed. The distance was about thirty miles. Peter applied the lesson that the vision had taught: "God does not show favoritism" (10:34). The gospel was for Jew and Gentile alike on the same terms. As Peter preached, the Holy Spirit came upon the listeners. This astonished Peter's Jewish comrades (10:45). They could not understand how uncircumcised non-Jews could be acceptable in God's eyes, just like Jews, if they heeded the gospel. But Peter's vision (to say nothing of Jesus' teaching) had prepared him for this development. New converts did not need to adopt Jewish social customs (circumcision, dietary restrictions, observance of a Jewish religious calendar). He gave orders for them to be baptized in Jesus' name. Then he remained with them for a number of days to confirm them in their new faith (10:48).

Word of Peter's action met immediate criticism among Jewish believers in Judea.

They charged Peter with wrongdoing by fraternizing with Gentiles (11:3). Peter related his vision to them. He told of the angel who spoke to Cornelius. He also recalled pertinent words of Jesus and John the Baptist (11:16). Peter concluded that if God had granted his spirit to Gentiles, it would be foolhardy to oppose God. Perhaps Peter recalled Jesus' stern warning against obstructing the Holy Spirit's work (Mk 3:29). This appeared to satisfy the Judean believers, who praised God for calling both Jews and Gentiles to "repentance unto life" (11:18).

Peter won his case before his fellow Jewish believers, but this did not save him from Herod's schemes. For political reasons Herod had James the brother of John put to death and then had Peter arrested (12:3). This was during the Passover season, the same time of year that Jesus was arrested and crucified. Peter would likely have been next to die. But God intervened, and Peter walked out of prison unscathed (12:10). His fellow believers, in the midst of prayer for his deliverance, were astonished to see him free (12:16). Peter asked them to inform James (Jesus' half-brother who was a leader in the Jerusalem church) and other leaders of his good fortune (12:17). Peter is not mentioned again until Acts 15.

Peter is important in this segment of Acts because of his key role in furthering the gospel's spread beyond its original geographical boundaries. While in the longer sweep of time it would be Paul, not Peter, who became the "apostle to the Gentiles" (Gal 2:8), God worked through Peter to lay a foundation for Paul's work. As Peter himself put it, "God made a choice . . . that the Gentiles might hear from my lips the message of the gospel and believe" (Acts 15:7).

Saul (8:1–3; 9:1–31; 11:25–30; 12:25)

Acts 8–12 offers four glimpses of Saul (later in Acts called Paul). First, he presided over Stephen's stoning and helped instigate a vicious persecution against other Jews who accepted Jesus as the Messiah (8:1–3).

Second, while still engaged in work against Jesus' followers, Saul was confronted by the one he assumed was dead: Jesus. Acts 9:1–31 is one of three accounts,

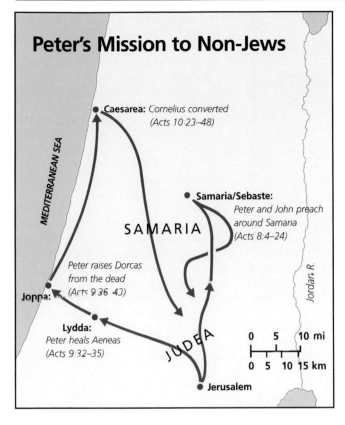

Peter's Mission to Non-Jews

MEDITERRANEAN SEA

Caesarea: *Cornelius converted (Acts 10:23–48)*

Samaria/Sebaste: *Peter and John preach around Samaria (Acts 8:4–24)*

SAMARIA

Peter raises Dorcas from the dead (Acts 9:36–43)

Joppa:

Lydda: *Peter heals Aeneas (Acts 9:32–35)*

JUDEA

Jordan R.

0   5   10 mi
0   5   10   15 km

Jerusalem

each slightly different, of this experience, which occurred on the road between Jerusalem and Damascus (see also Acts 22:4–16; 26:9–18). After three days of fasting, Saul received the spirit of Jesus, whose followers he had been persecuting (Acts 9:17–18). He aired his startling new convictions in the synagogues of Damascus, pressing his case with such vigor that a plot was hatched to kill him (9:23). He managed to escape to ARABIA for a time before returning to Damascus (Gal 1:17).

About three years after his conversion, he finally visited Jerusalem. With Barnabas's help he was received by at least some of the believers there, though many were naturally suspicious. Was his turn to Jesus Christ genuine (9:26)? Might he be pretending to follow Jesus as a way of gathering information to use against the Christians later? When Jews in Jerusalem tried to kill him, Saul withdrew with the help of other believers to Caesarea on the coast. He then sailed north to his place of birth, the city of TARSUS. Acts records that after this, the churches of Judea, Samaria, and GALILEE enjoyed a time of relative calm and growth.

Focus 15: One More Who Believed

Philip, Tabitha, Agabus, Cornelius—and the list of those who believed in Jesus Christ and whose names appear in the Book of Acts goes on. Since the first century, millions have heard the gospel and believed.

In the nineteenth century another man believed. He grew in the Lord and had a major impact on the Christian community reaching far beyond his native England.

As a youth he struggled with guilt; he was miserable under the burden of sin. Even though he tried to find relief, he was unable to rid himself of the crushing load. One snowy winter night he entered a small Methodist chapel in Essex, England, where the service was being conducted without a preacher. A poorly educated layman was making an appeal from the text, Is 45:22, *"Look unto me, and be ye saved, all the ends of the earth: for I am God, and there is none else."* The layman then turned to the young man and said, "Young man, you look so miserable; young man, look to Jesus, look and be saved."

Speaking later about this experience that young man said, "And I looked that night unto Jesus, and I lived." That bitter night, another believer's name was added to the roster begun in Acts. That young convert was Charles Haddon Spurgeon (1834–92), who went on to become one of the most gifted preachers in history. His work for the poor and orphans was also noteworthy. Not only did those who worshiped at the Metropolitan Tabernacle in London hear his sermons, but they were translated into many languages. They continue to be read and studied around the world.

Key People/Places

Abyssinia
Antioch (Syrian)
Arabia
Caesarea
Claudius
Cush
Damascus
Ethiopia
Galilee
Gaza
Herod Agrippa I
Herodias
Jerusalem
Joppa
Judea
Lydda
Samaria
Sharon
Sidon
Sudan
Syria
Tarsus
Tel Aviv
Tyre

Key Terms

centurion
simony

to Saul's gifts and efforts, "great numbers of people" were taught the gospel (11:26). When Agabus prophesied a famine, the Antioch believers decided to take up a collection for Jewish Christians in Judea. Saul, along with Barnabas, was selected to deliver a substantial cash gift (11:30). This would be Saul's second known post-conversion visit to Jerusalem. It is often referred to as the famine visit. The number and timing of Saul's visits to Jerusalem will become an issue when we examine Paul's letter to the Galatians in a later chapter.

Fourth, in Acts 12:25, Barnabas and Saul complete their mission. They returned to Antioch with someone named John Mark in tow. Many think that this was the Mark who wrote the second gospel.[2] In any case he, along with Saul and Barnabas, figures significantly in the next several chapters of Acts.

Third, in Acts 11:25–30, Saul is recruited by Barnabas for pastoral duties in the fledgling church at Antioch. Due in part

Summary

1. Acts 8–12 demonstrates that God takes note of each individual and is interested in them as persons.

2. Philip is significant because he is among the first to take the gospel outside Jerusalem (to Samaria).

3. Ananias was a significant figure because he was sent by God to restore Saul's vision.

4. Tabitha died in Joppa but Peter came and raised her from the dead.

5. Because of his contact with Cornelius, Peter learned that Jewish customs forbidding contact with Gentiles were inconsistent with following Christ.

6. Agabus was one of the prophets of the early church.

7. Simon the sorcerer and Herod Agrippa I did not respond appropriately to the message of Christ.

8. The three most prominent figures in the rise and growth of the early church as recounted in Acts 8–12 were John, Peter, and Paul.

Review Questions

1. The earliest preachers and hearers of the gospel were ethnically _____.

2. Among the first to take the gospel outside Jerusalem was _____.

3. Aeneas, who had been paralyzed for eight years, was healed by _____.

4. The woman who was raised from the dead by Peter was named _____, which means _____.

5. The person that God used to show Peter and the early church that Gentiles who repented were acceptable to God was _____.

6. The key figure in spreading the gospel to Antioch was _____.

7. The person who served as a reminder of God's provision for his people's needs was _____.

8. The first of the twelve disciples to die for his faith was _____.

9. The man who offered John and Peter money for sharing their apostolic powers with him was _____ .

10. The three men who were most prominent in the rise and growth of the early church were _____, _____, and _____.

Study Questions

1. What can we learn from the stress on individual persons in Acts 8–12?

2. Why did Philip and others first leave Jerusalem with the gospel message? See Acts 8:1, 4–5.

3. Name and briefly characterize five "minor characters." Name and describe one who disbelieved.

4. Why was Peter's visit to Cornelius controversial?

5. Why were many early Christians leery of Saul?

6. Name the three accounts of Saul's (Paul's) conversion (Acts 9:1–31; 22:4–16; 26:9–18). List three similarities and three differences between them.

Further Reading

On Acts 8–12 generally, see reading list at the end of chapters 14 and 16. See also:

Bornkamm, Günther. *Early Christian Experience.* London: SCM, 1969. A series of studies dealing with various aspects of early Christian life.

Carrington, Philip. *The Early Christian Church.* Vol. 1. Cambridge: Cambridge University Press, 1957. A standard work on the early church.

Chadwick, Henry. *The Early Church.* Rev. ed. London: Penguin, 1990. A brief but very helpful survey of the church's early years.

Daniel-Rops, H. *The Church of the Apostles and Martyrs.* London: Dent, 1960. An in-depth study of the early days of the church.

Duchesne, Louis. *Early History of the Christian Church.* 3 vols. London: Murray, 1925. An older but excellent treatment of the life and thought of the early church.

Frend, W. H. C. *Martyrdom and Persecution in the Early Church: A Study of a Conflict from the Maccabees to Donatus.* Grand Rapids: Baker, 1981 [1965]. The definitive work on the life and sufferings of the early believers.

———. *The Rise of Christianity.* Philadelphia: Fortress, 1984. Important work on the rise of the church.

Green, Michael. *Evangelism in the Early Church.* Grand Rapids: Eerdmans, 1991. The definitive study of how the church spread the gospel in its early years.

Gooding, David. *True to Faith.* London: Hodder & Stoughton, 1991. An excellent and easy-to-follow commentary on Acts from an evangelical perspective.

Johnson, Luke T. *Religious Experience: A Missing Dimension of New Testament Studies.* Minneapolis: Fortress, 1998. Shows how the incidents related in Acts 8–12 remain significant for an understanding of history and Christian belief, then and now.

Larkin, W. J. *Acts.* Downers Grove: InterVarsity, 1995. A fine commentary on Acts from an evangelical perspective for students and pastors.

Marshall, I. Howard, and David Peterson, eds. *Witness to the Gospel: The Theology of Acts.* Grand Rapids/Cambridge: Eerdmans, 1998. Two dozen essays covering various aspects of Acts's theological outlook and teaching.

Newman, Carey C. *"Acts."* In *A Complete Literary Guide to the Bible,* ed. Leland Ryken and Tremper Longman III. Grand Rapids: Zondervan, 1993. Stimulating tips on Acts' message and how Luke drives it home.

16 Acts 13–28
The Light of Christ to the Ends of the Earth

Outline

- **Outline of Acts 13–28**
- **First Missionary Journey (13:1–14:28)**
- **The Jerusalem Council (15:1–35)**
- **Second Missionary Journey (15:36–18:22)**
- **Third Missionary Journey (18:23–21:15)**
- **Arrest in Jerusalem and Imprisonment in Caesarea (21:15–26:32)**
- **Voyage to Rome (27:1–28:10)**
- **Ministry at Rome (28:11–31)**
- **Conclusion**

Objectives

After reading this chapter, you should be able to

- Illustrate how God showed that his love was not limited to one race or ethnic group
- Outline the content of Acts 13–28
- Trace the first missionary journey
- Identify the significance of the second missionary journey
- List the highlights of the third missionary journey
- Discuss events in Paul's life after his arrest in Jerusalem

The world community faces critical issues in the twenty-first century. One major problem, usually brought on by war and its first cousin famine, involves refugees. What is to be done with the millions of dislocated peoples? What aid should be offered? What immigration policies are best? Governments and international agencies debate these questions continually. People on all continents are fearful of too many strangers pouring into their country, threatening their living standard and way of life.

Wariness toward foreigners is not new. In fact it seems to be a basic human trait. But the Old Testament taught "love your neighbor as yourself" (Lv 19:18). It prescribed the same attitude toward "aliens" (Lv 19:34). Jesus likewise taught, "Do to others as you would have them do to you" (Lk 6:31). Jesus' followers were instructed to extend such kindness not only to each other but even to their enemies (Lk 6:35).

Acts 13–28 describes the continued spread of the gospel to new peoples and lands. God's love is not for any one race or ethnic subgroup alone but for all who will respond to the gospel call. Xenophobia—unfounded fear of strangers or foreigners—has no place in God's kingdom. The central figure in this portion of Acts is Paul, the former Pharisee, who was once zealous for Jewish ways and hostile toward any threat to Jewish religion and ethnic purity.

Acts 13–28 describes three separate missionary journeys, each of which carries the gospel to new regions. It summarizes a theological debate about what to do with aliens (non-Jews, or Gentiles) in the church. It also sketches Paul's imprisonment in two different locations, imprisonment caused largely because of his message that the Gentiles, too, are welcome in God's household by faith. Many zealous Jews opposed this message and toiled to silence Paul. Acts concludes with the story of how Paul's long-standing goal of preaching the gospel in the great city of ROME was finally fulfilled.

Outline of Acts 13–28

I. The Witness to Christ to the Ends of the Earth (13:1–28:31)
  A. Paul's First Missionary Journey (13:1–14:28)
  B. The Jerusalem Council (15:1–35)
  C. Paul's Second Missionary Journey (15:36–18:22)
  D. Paul's Third Missionary Journey (18:23–21:15)

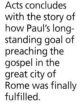

Acts concludes with the story of how Paul's long-standing goal of preaching the gospel in the great city of Rome was finally fulfilled.

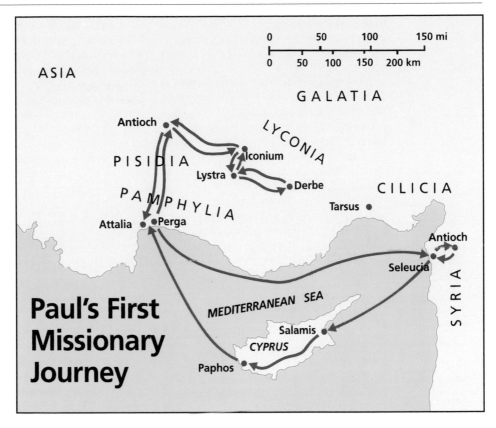

Paul's First Missionary Journey

E. Paul's Arrest in Jerusalem and
    Incarceration at Caesarea
    (21:15–26:32)
F. Paul's Voyage to Rome
    (27:1–28:10)
G. Paul's Ministry at Rome
    (28:11–31)

First Missionary Journey (13:1–14:28)

In Acts the postresurrection church of Jesus Christ gets its start in JERUSALEM (Acts 2). For about a decade (the A.D. 30s) Jerusalem retains its central importance. Of course its symbolic importance as Zion, the city of God, endures to this day. But in apostolic times a different city came to overshadow Jerusalem in some respects. That city was ANTIOCH, capital of the Roman province of SYRIA. Its population may have been around three hundred thousand.[1] It lay more than three hundred miles to the north of Jerusalem.

In the first century many Jews made their home in Antioch.[2] Some of them, along with many non-Jews, became the nucleus of a Christian church (or churches) there. This church was founded by people fleeing persecution in Jerusalem (Acts 11:19–21) shortly after Stephen's stoning (early in the A.D. 30s). Barnabas, and later Paul, assumed leadership of the Antioch congregation (Acts 11:22–26).

Antioch's importance is twofold. First, it modeled the ethnic diversity appropriate to the gospel that brings people of all backgrounds into the one family of God (see Eph 2:11–22). Second, it became the primary missionary church of earliest Christianity. All three of Paul's missionary journeys began at Antioch.

Today the notion that the religion of some people should be urged on others who already have their own religion is widely rejected. But it should be remembered that Jesus taught that he was the only way to the heavenly Father (Jn 14:6) and that to be his disciple meant taking the Good News of salvation through him to others (Mt 28:19–20).

The church at Antioch took this responsibility seriously. As they worshiped and fasted, the Holy Spirit impressed them to send Barnabas and Saul (Paul) out on a preaching and church-planting mission. So they did (Acts 13:1–3). The year was roughly A.D. 47.[3]

Their journey took them first to the island of CYPRUS (Acts 13:4–12). This was Barnabas's home turf (Acts 4:36). They met opposition from a charlatan named Bar-Jesus (Aramaic for "son of Joshua"). But they also witnessed the conversion of the Roman proconsul (governor) of the island, a man called SERGIUS PAULUS.

From Cyprus they sailed north to the mainland of ASIA MINOR, landing at PERGA in PAMPHYLIA. There John Mark, Barnabas's cousin (Col 4:10), returned to Jerusalem for unknown reasons. Paul and Barnabas soldiered on, traveling a circuit through the southern stretches of the Roman province of GALATIA. Wherever possible they visited towns that had Jewish synagogues. This afforded a foothold for their message, which they regarded as the fulfillment of Jewish belief and practice. The towns they visited included ANTIOCH (near PISIDIA, not Syria), ICONIUM, LYSTRA, and DERBE.

Their message centered on God's preparation for Christ's saving ministry through Old Testament times and on Jesus' death and resurrection (13:16–41). This message met both glad reception (13:48; 14:1, 21) and bitter rejection (13:50; 14:2, 19). Eventually Paul and Barnabas evidently felt they had traveled far enough. They retraced their steps, visiting each town they had preached in to encourage converts and to establish more permanent leadership (14:23). Finally they returned to Antioch in Syria with the glad tidings that in Galatia, as already in Syrian Antioch itself, God "had opened the door of faith to the Gentiles" (14:27).

We will consider the gospel message of Acts 13–14 more fully later in the chapter on Galatians. In the literary flow of Acts the first missionary journey is important because it sets the stage for the earliest—and quite heated—theological dispute that the apostolic church was forced to decide.

The Jerusalem Council (15:1–35)

Opposition to the gospel crops up repeatedly in Acts. The message about Jesus Christ that some Jews like Peter, Stephen, Barnabas, and later Paul preached antagonized other Jews, who rejected the claim that Jesus was the Jewish Messiah. At stake was the question of how a person is "saved"—forgiven of sins, enabled to further God's kingdom work on this earth, and privileged to enjoy heaven in the age to come. Jewish Christians insisted that salvation was a free gift of God's grace acquired through trusting in Jesus Christ. It was not gained by some mixture of faith and human merit. Non-Christian Jews disagreed. They did not accept Jesus' death on the cross as the sac-

The Orontes River, between Antioch and its port, Seleucia. Syrian Antioch was the Roman provincial capital of Syria and the base of Paul's missionary operations.

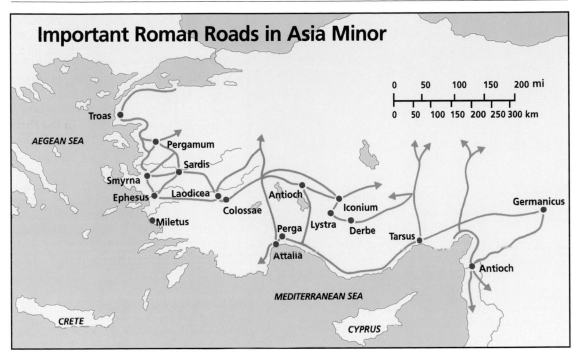

Important Roman Roads in Asia Minor

rifice for their sins. They insisted that to be acceptable to God it was necessary to follow Jewish beliefs and customs, especially (for males) the rite of circumcision.

Eventually a variation of this view surfaced within the church itself, still largely Jewish at the time (about A.D. 49). "Some men . . . from JUDEA," perhaps the same group who had criticized Peter earlier (11:2), came to Antioch to teach against the gospel that Paul and Barnabas had been spreading (15:1). They insisted that to receive salvation a person must believe in Christ but also follow the law of Moses as understood by most first-century Judaism. Years earlier Jesus had already registered protest against the Jews' understanding and misuse of the Mosaic law (see, e.g., Mt 23; Mk 7:9). He accused them of substituting human traditions for an authentic personal relationship with the Lord.

Paul and Barnabas, church leaders at Antioch, opposed the views of the visitors from Jerusalem. It is likely that Paul had written his Galatian Epistle at about this very time to address the same issues as they arose in the Galatian churches. To resolve the matter a meeting was called in Jerusalem. Those who disagreed with Paul and Barnabas spoke first. "The Gentiles must be circumcised and required to obey the law of Moses" (15:5), they claimed.

After consultation, Peter and others weighed in. Their verdict: "We believe it is through the grace of our Lord Jesus that we are saved, just as they are" (15:11). By "we" Peter meant "we Jews," and by "they" he referred to non-Jews. Barnabas and Paul obviously agreed (15:12), and so did James, Jesus' half-brother and a leader in the Jerusalem church (15:13–21).

A letter was then drafted for distribution to churches in Antioch, greater Syria, and CILICIA that had apparently been shaken by the dispute. (It was unnecessary to send it to the Galatian churches, because Paul had already instructed them on the matter through his own Epistle.) Acts 15:23–29 gives the text of this letter. It sets the theological record straight by discrediting the false teaching that salvation is through Christ plus works. It affirms the letter's couriers, Judas and Silas. Finally, it suggests four areas of Jewish concern that Gentile Christians should be considerate to observe. These are not a "short list" of rules to attain salvation but points of cultural or moral observance at which Jews and non-Jews held vastly different views. The letter urged Gentile believers to abstain from dietary and moral practices that would be unnecessarily repugnant to those in the church whose cultural heritage was Jewish. Salvation is by

241

An Epistle (Letter) in the Book of Acts

The Book of Acts is not a letter, but it contains the texts of at least two letters. One is the all-important decision taken by the apostles in their historic conference (Acts 15:23–29):

The apostles and elders, your brothers, To the Gentile believers in Antioch, Syria and Cilicia: Greetings. We have heard that some went out from us without our authorization and disturbed you, troubling your minds by what they said. So we all agreed to choose some men and send them to you with our dear friends Barnabas and Paul—men who have risked their lives for the name of our Lord Jesus Christ. Therefore we are sending Judas and Silas to confirm by word of mouth what we are writing. It seemed good to the Holy Spirit and to us not to burden you with anything beyond the following requirements: You are to abstain from food sacrificed to idols, from blood, from the meat of strangled animals and from sexual immorality. You will do well to avoid these things. Farewell.

grace alone through faith alone, but Gentile Christians must be willing to forgo their own freedoms in the interest of cultural sensitivity when this could be done without theological compromise. Paul himself practiced this policy and commended it to others (Rom 14; 1 Cor 8:9–13).

The modern church easily forgets the early church's Jewish origins. In many quarters it takes for granted that salvation is "by grace through faith." The Jerusalem Council is important as the record of how this key truth was debated and established. The church through the ages has not always been true to this insight. But by Scripture and the Holy Spirit's leading (15:15–18, 28) the authentic gospel was established with clarity at an early date in the church's growth. In every age the church does well to review the difficult but correct decision laid down at Jerusalem to make sure it has not somehow strayed from the insights that establish and preserve its spiritual vigor.

Second Missionary Journey (15:36–18:22)

Not long after the Jerusalem Council Paul proposed another mission thrust (15:36). The result was Paul's second missionary journey. This time he took Silas with him instead of Barnabas (15:40). They began by visiting nearby churches in Syria and Cilicia (15:41). Then they revisited churches founded on the first missionary journey (16:1–5). At Lystra they were joined by young Timothy, who became an increasingly valuable aide to Paul in years to come.

They eventually reached Troas on the coast of the Aegean Sea (16:8). A divinely given vision led them from there to the eastern edge of the European Continent, Macedonia in northern Greece. Judging from the "we" in 16:10, Luke joined Paul's party there at Troas. Paul's long, fruitful, and world-changing ministry in Europe was about to begin.

The second missionary journey lasted some three years and covered nearly three thousand miles, much of it on foot.[4] Paul, Silas, and Timothy took the gospel to towns or cities that included Philippi, Thessalonica, Berea, Athens, and Corinth. The message was received warmly by some and coolly by others. In several instances there was extreme hostility. More than once Paul faced physical intimidation and outright violence.

Yet despite such opposition the church-planting efforts bore fruit. Paul's letters to the Thessalonians, Philippians, and Corinthians are eloquent testimony to the profound effects that the gospel of Jesus Christ had wherever it was preached. We will look more closely at those cities and the churches Paul founded there when we consider Paul's letters in later chapters.

The second missionary journey drew to a close as Paul departed from Corinth, where he had ministered for a year and a half (18:11), and returned to Antioch in Syria. On the way he stopped at Ephesus

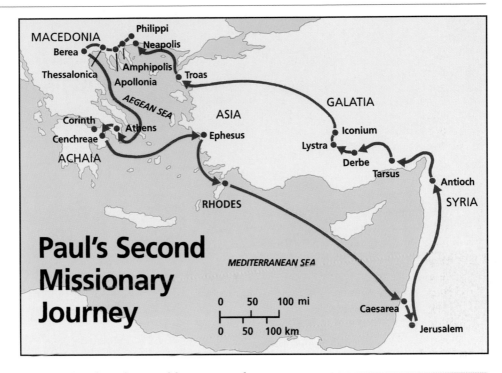

Paul's Second Missionary Journey

MACEDONIA
Philippi
Neapolis
Berea
Thessalonica
Amphipolis
Troas
Apollonia
AEGEAN SEA
ASIA
GALATIA
Corinth
Athens
Iconium
Cenchreae
Ephesus
Lystra
ACHAIA
Derbe
Tarsus
Antioch
RHODES
SYRIA
MEDITERRANEAN SEA
0 50 100 mi
0 50 100 km
Caesarea
Jerusalem

(18:19–21), where he would soon spend three fruitful years. Eventually Paul landed at CAESAREA near Judea, visited the Jerusalem church, and returned to Antioch. The second missionary journey was now history. But a third got underway almost immediately.

Ephesus was the center for worship of Artemis, goddess of fertility. Artisans who made their living from creating silver idols in her honor rioted when the gospel message that "man-made gods are no gods at all" (Acts 19:26) threatened their livelihood.

Third Missionary Journey (18:23–21:15)

After only a short time in Antioch Paul began a third swing through "Galatia and PHRYGIA, strengthening all the disciples" (18:23). This seems to indicate that he once again visited churches that he and Barnabas had planted on their first missionary journey. As Paul pressed westward he eventually came to Ephesus (19:1), one of the leading cities of the Roman Empire and capital of the Roman province of ASIA.

In Ephesus Paul began his longest known continuous ministry in one particular location. Beginning in a synagogue, as was his custom (19:8), Paul preached until opposition forced the disciples to relocate in a lecture hall. Over a span of three years (roughly A.D. 54–57) Paul witnessed miraculous cures (19:11–12), the effect of demonic oppression (19:13–16), and the conversion of many who were formerly involved in occult practices (19:17–20).

During those same years he also penned 1 and 2 Corinthians to deal with problems that had arisen in the Corinthian church,

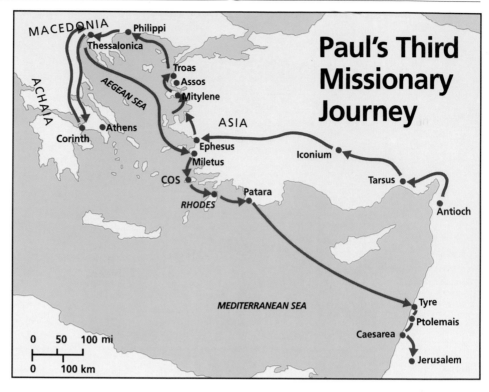

Paul's Third Missionary Journey

some 250 miles distance from Ephesus across the Aegean Sea. Another notable achievement was the so-called Jerusalem collection, an ingathering of money from the predominantly Gentile "Pauline" churches for the needy Christians in Judea, most of whom were Jewish. We will have more to say about this collection when we treat the Corinthian Epistles in detail.

The success of the gospel ministry in Ephesus eventually provoked a showdown. Christianity was damaging the local economy, especially the silver-smithing guilds, because idols were no longer selling at their former pace. Local residents also felt that their patron goddess, ARTEMIS, was being "robbed of her divine majesty" (19:27) by Christian proclamation and practice. A great riot resulted (19:23–41). Paul was in the process of leaving Ephesus anyway and had already set necessary preparations in motion (19:21–22).

The third missionary journey, just as productive as the first two, ended with Paul making a swing through both northern and southern Greece (Macedonia and ACHAIA). His movements seem to have taken him as far as ILLYRICUM, the general region of modern ALBANIA (Rom 15:19).

He wrote the historic Epistle to the Romans in early A.D. 57 during his three months in Achaia (Acts 20:2–3). On the way back to Jerusalem he addressed the Ephesian church leaders at MILETUS (20:17–38) before pressing on. At Caesarea the prophet Agabus warned Paul that if he returned to Jerusalem his Jewish enemies would arrest him and hand him over to Gentile officials (21:10–11). This prophecy proved truer, perhaps, than the prophet realized. Paul lived in chains for at least the next four years, the remainder of the time covered by the Book of Acts.

Arrest in Jerusalem and Imprisonment in Caesarea (21:15–26:32)

Paul was warmly received by James and the other elders of the Christian church in Jerusalem (21:17). They advised Paul of the danger he faced from adversaries and how he might best defuse local hard feelings (21:20–25). But despite Paul's best efforts

Roman Procurators of Palestine 44–66

	A.D.
Fadus	44–46
Tiberius Alexander	46–48
Cumanus	48–52
Felix (Acts 23:24–24:27)	52–60
Festus (Acts 24:27–25:27)	60–62
Albinus	62–64
Gessius Florus	64–66

procurator

the guile of his enemies prevailed. He was arrested on false charges in the midst of a riot that nearly cost him his life (21:27–36). His attempt to explain his views to the mob, held at bay by Roman soldiers, seemed successful until the word "Gentiles" escaped his lips (22:21). At that point the riot rekindled, and Paul was whisked away to be questioned by flogging.

Paul's Roman citizenship saved him from the sometimes fatal ordeal of scourging (22:25–29). On the following day the Roman commander brought Paul instead

before the Sanhedrin, or Jewish high court, a powerful legal and political body with whom Paul had once had close ties. Paul cleverly managed to divert attention from himself by luring the two main Jewish factions, the Pharisees and Sadducees, into a noisy squabble (22:30–23:11). Further legal inquiry was hindered by an assassination plot against Paul, who was subsequently moved sixty-five miles away by night to Caesarea on the coast (23:12–35). There, in protective custody, Paul awaited word of his immediate legal fate. He already had divine assurance regarding his longer-term destination, as the Lord had recently appeared to Paul by night and said, "Take courage! As you have testified about me in Jerusalem, so you must also testify in Rome" (23:11).

But between Caesarea and Rome lay some two years of prison life and legal maneuvering to stave off the powerful lobbying efforts of Jewish authorities seeking to extradite Paul back to Jerusalem for trial—or rather murder (25:3). The Roman **procurator** FELIX, who ruled in Judea A.D. 52–60, was first to hear his case (24:1–22). He handled Paul leniently, permitting him some freedom and the visits of friends (24:23). But he did not release him. Acts cites two reasons: Felix wanted a bribe,

When rioting broke out against Paul in Jerusalem, Roman soldiers restored order. They were garrisoned in the city center in the Antonia Fortress.

and he "wanted to grant a favor to the Jews" (24:26–27).

By A.D. 60 FESTUS had succeeded Felix as procurator of Judea. Paul's enemies in Jerusalem pressed anew for a resolution to Paul's case. They wanted him tried in Jerusalem, they claimed—but in fact their plan was to assassinate him (25:1–5). Paul appeared for yet another legal defense in the face of the Jews' numerous charges. When it appeared that Festus would give in to Jewish demands, Paul played his trump card: He appealed to CAESAR, which was the right of any Roman citizen who feared his civil rights were being violated (25:6–11). Festus really had no choice: "You have appealed to Caesar. To Caesar you will go!" (25:12).

Acts preserves one more lengthy transcript from Paul's two-year lock-up in Caesarea: his defense before Festus and HEROD AGRIPPA II (25:13–26:32). In this speech Paul again narrates his conversion experience (see 9:1–19; 22:4–16) and explains why he felt the Jews' charges were unfounded: "I am saying nothing beyond what the prophets and Moses said would happen— that the Christ would suffer and, as the first to rise from the dead, would proclaim light to his own people and to the Gentiles" (26:22–23).

Festus and Agrippa agreed that Paul was innocent of breaking civil or criminal law (26:30–32). But his appeal to Caesar had set wheels in motion that could not be stopped.

Voyage to Rome (27:1–28:10)

When Paul is sent to Rome for trial, the author of Acts once again becomes part of his narrative (note the "we" that begins in 27:1 and see 16:10–17; 20:5–15; 21:1–18). The colorful and dramatic story of how Paul and 275 other passengers almost lost their lives at sea is therefore not creative guesswork or legend: The author was actually part of the action he describes.

Focus 16: Overcoming Barriers to Mission

Now, no less than in Paul's day, Christians around the world are commanded to take part in spreading the gospel message. There is something for everyone to do. But many are no-shows in responding to the missions mandate. There are several reasons for this.

In the West, materialism, the fast pace of life, and the pursuit of career may tempt believers to shun their responsibility for world evangelization. Christians become syncretists—they combine elements of Christian faith with convictions of a world order bent on human priorities rather than divine ones. The gospel message they should be spreading is squelched.

The power of non-Christian culture to suppress Christian witness is a problem not only in the West. One study of Muslim converts to Christianity documents profound struggle to break loose from dominant cultural convictions. Among people professing faith in Christ 100 percent said they prayed to Jesus for forgiveness of sins and 97 percent that Jesus is the only Savior. But 96 percent say there are four sacred scriptures, not one; 66 percent say the Koran is the greatest of these; and 45 percent do not affirm the Trinity (P. Parshall, "Danger! New Directions in Contextualization," *Evangelical Missions Quarterly* 34 no. 4 [Oct. 1998]: 404–17)

A newsweekly article by David Van Biema raises an even more fundamental question: "Should Christians Convert Muslims?" (*Time*, June 30, 2003). Perhaps one-fifth of the world's population is Muslim at least in name. Many Muslims resent evangelistic efforts directed at them. Some voices in the West agree that it is imperialistic and arrogant to encourage persons of one religion to switch to a different one.

How can the gospel surge forth from those it touches in the face of so many opposing convictions? Paul tackled this question in numerous settings in the Book of Acts. Similar issues confront believers everywhere today.

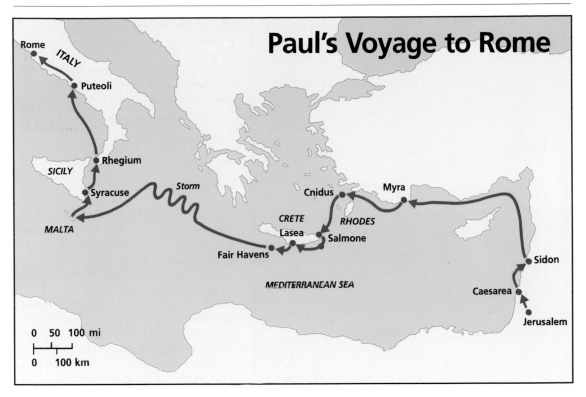

Paul's Voyage to Rome

The voyage is at once both a fascinating account of ancient seafaring and a tribute to God's providential protection. Through storm (27:13–26) and shipwreck (27:27–44) Paul and all the others were preserved from harm despite desperately adverse circumstances. Paul was even spared from death, which watchful natives of the island of MALTA were certain they would witness, when a deadly viper fastened onto his hand (28:1–7). Throughout the voyage Paul testified to God's good purposes, which, he was confident, would see them through all danger (27:22–25, 33–35).

Ministry at Rome (28:11–31)

Acts concludes with Paul safely in Rome awaiting trial for some two years (A.D. 60–62; see 28:30). Many scholars feel that this is a clue to the date when Acts was written: It ends when it does because at the time of writing all developments had been brought up to date.

Paul's imprisonment was not overly harsh. He was allowed his own (guarded) lodgings (28:16), and he was permitted visitors (28:17, 23, 30). Because God had planned and granted Paul this chance to preach in Rome, a chance he had long awaited (see Rom 1:13; 15:23), Paul made full use of it. "Boldly and without hindrance he preached the kingdom of God and taught about the Lord Jesus Christ" (28:31).

Four of Paul's letters, the so-called Prison Epistles (Ephesians, Philippians, Colossians, Philemon), were probably written at this time. (Some argue for Caesarea or even Ephesus as the site for Paul's authorship of one or more of these Epistles. But the prevailing consensus among those who see the letters as Pauline, and the understanding of most interpreters through the centuries, points to Rome.)

In one of Paul's prison letters he comments on the situation in Rome. "What has happened to me has really served to advance the gospel. As a result, it has become clear throughout the whole palace guard and to everyone else that I am in chains for Christ. Because of my chains, most of the brothers in the Lord have been encouraged to speak the word of God more courageously and fearlessly" (Phil 1:12–14). No doubt Paul would not have

247

Key People/Places

Achaia
Aegean Sea
Albania
Antioch (Pisidian)
Antioch (Syrian)
Artemis
Asia
Asia Minor
Athens
Berea
Caesar
Caesarea
Cilicia
Corinth
Cyprus
Derbe
Ephesus
Europe
Felix

Festus
Galatia
Greece
Herod Agrippa II
Iconium
Illyricum
Jerusalem
Judea
Lystra
Macedonia
Malta
Miletus
Pamphylia
Perga
Philippi
Phrygia
Pisidia
Rome
Samaria
Sergius Paulus
Syria
Thessalonica
Troas

Key Term

procurator

dreamed that his hopes of reaching Rome would come true through the inglorious means of false charges and chains. Yet—his Lord had gained glory by an illegal trial and a cross. Paul understood he was following in his master's steps.

Conclusion

The Gospels close with Jesus preparing his followers to make disciples "of all nations"—which could also be translated "of all Gentiles" (Mt 28:19–20). Acts begins with Jesus' assertion that the church would indeed fulfill their commission by the Holy Spirit's power, taking Christ's message not only to Judea and SAMARIA but also "to the ends of the earth" (1:8).

Acts concludes with the ringing testimony that the gospel did indeed establish a beachhead, and more, in the powerful imperial city of Rome. The word about Jesus Christ had not yet reached the "ends of the earth." But it was well on its way.

Review Questions

1. The central figure in Acts 13–28 is _____.

2. The city that replaced Jerusalem as the city of greatest importance in apostolic times was _____.

3. The first missionary journey was made by _____ and _____.

4. All three of Paul's missionary journeys began in the city of _____.

5. The issue of what salvation requires was debated at the _____.

6. Paul set out on a second missionary journey with _____ ; _____ joined him later at Lystra, and _____ joined them at Troas.

7. On Paul's return to Jerusalem after his third journey, he was arrested when he spoke the word _____.

8. It was necessary for his safety to move the imprisoned Paul to _____.

9. Paul appealed to _____ and was sent to _____ for trial.

10. While in Rome, Paul wrote letters to Philemon and to the _____, _____, and _____.

Summary

1. Acts 13–28 makes the point that God's love is for all who will respond to the gospel, not for any one race or ethnic group.

2. At least three missionary journeys were taken by Paul and each began in the city of Antioch in Syria.

3. The first missionary journey went from Syrian Antioch to Cyprus to Perga in Pamphylia to Galatia and back to Syrian Antioch.

4. Some Jews could not accept the fact that salvation was a free gift of God's grace; they insisted that to be acceptable to God it was necessary to establish one's righteousness through Jewish beliefs and customs.

5. The Jerusalem Council provides an important record of how an issue should be debated and settled; the result was that the authentic gospel was clearly established early in the growth of the church.

6. The principle that Gentile Christians should forgo their own freedom in the interest of cultural sensitivity when this could be done without theological compromise was suggested by James. Peter and Paul had already endorsed the same principle.

7. The second missionary journey opened a ministry in Europe.

8. At Ephesus on his third missionary journey, Paul began his longest continuous ministry in a single location.

9. Paul was imprisoned in Caesarea and his case was heard by Felix, Festus, and Herod Agrippa II. He appealed to Caesar and was sent to Rome.

10. Paul's imprisonment in Rome gave him the opportunity to spread the gospel there.

Study Questions

1. What is xenophobia? What do the Old Testament, Jesus, and Acts 13–28 have in common in the way they address this problem?

2. What role did Antioch play in the life of Paul and the early church?

3. What issue did the Jerusalem Council debate? How should we apply its decisions today?

4. What effect did the spread of the gospel have at Ephesus?

5. How did Paul, a prisoner, know that he would eventually reach Rome?

6. How did Paul's appeal to Caesar both save and trap him?

7. For what reason, in Paul's own view, was he "in chains"? What reasons might others give?

8. In what sense did Paul's arrival in Rome represent a fulfilling of what God told Ananias in Acts 9? How many years was it from Paul's conversion to his arrival in Rome?

Further Reading

See also reading lists at the end of chapters 14 and 15.

Brierley, Peter, and Heather Wraight. *Atlas of World Christianity: A Complete Visual Reference to Christianity Worldwise, Including Growth Trends into the New Millennium.* Nashville: Thomas Nelson, 1998. As the subtitle indicates, an invaluable guide for thinking about world issues and Christian mission in coming decades.

Dowley, Tim, ed. *Baker Atlas of Christian History.* Grand Rapids: Baker, 1997. Maps and commentary covering dozens of locales and eras beginning with ancient Mesopotamia and continuing right to the present. In graphic ways shows the spread of God's word before Acts and since.

House, Paul R. "Suffering and the Purpose of Acts." *Journal of the Evangelical Theological Society* 33 (1990): 317–30. Useful study that highlights the importance of suffering by God's servants in order for the gospel to go forth as it did in the era of the Book of Acts. Important implications for gospel ministry today.

Green, Joel B. "Acts of the Apostles." In *Dictionary of the Later New Testament and Its Developments,* ed. R. P. Martin and P. H. Davids. Downers Grove/Leicester: InterVarsity, 1997, pp. 7–24. Survey of discussion on Acts' genre, text, speeches, narrative unity, theology, and purpose. Extensive bibliography.

Netland, Harold. *Encountering Religious Pluralism: The Challenge to Christian Faith and Mission.* Downers Grove/Leicester: InterVarsity/Apollos, 2001. Excellent study of the challenge posed by today's global village to Christians who take seriously the missions mandate of Acts.

Pilch, John J., and Bruce J. Malina, eds. *Handbook of Biblical Social Values.* Peabody, Mass.: Hendrickson, 1998. Sections like "Hospitality" (pp. 115–18) shed light on concerns of Acts 13–28.

Part

3

Encountering Paul and His Epistles

17 All Things to All People
Life and Teachings of the Apostle Paul

Outline

- Brief Overview of the Life of Paul
- Missionary Journeys and Paul's Letters
- Which Letters Did Paul Write?
- Paul and Jesus
- Paul's Teaching about God
- Evil and the Human Dilemma
- Paul and the Law
- Children of Abraham, Children of God: Paul's View of the People of God
- Revelation and Scripture
- Messiah
- Redemption
- The Cross
- Resurrection
- The Church
- Ethics
- Last Things
- Conclusion

Objectives

After reading this chapter, you should be able to

- Write a brief sketch of the life of Paul
- Identify the major cities on Paul's missionary journeys
- List the books Paul wrote and give evidence for his authorship
- Demonstrate how God was the center of Paul's theology
- Discuss Paul's position on legalism
- Document how Paul viewed Jesus as the Messiah
- Summarize Paul's teaching on redemption, the cross, and the resurrection
- Illustrate how Paul related ethics to theology

In recent years scientists have expressed dismay over objections to the teaching of evolution in public schools. These objections come not only from parents on religious grounds but from academicians expressing intellectual concerns. A Rutgers University mathematician states that he thought all educated people were in general agreement about the validity of science and the truth of evolutionary theory. Yet other scholars question certain aspects of today's "science." They also question the integrity of a dominant Western university outlook that trivializes and ridicules Christian truth claims and beliefs.[1] Some scientists are distressed over the views expressed by others. Wars of words result.

Previous chapters on Acts reveal that wars of words are not new to modern times. They were part of the world of the New Testament as well. We have already seen that an energetic and brilliant Jewish leader named Paul was at the center of a great struggle surrounding the meaning of Jesus Christ for both Jews and Gentiles. Below we learn more about Paul's life. We will summarize his teachings on various themes. We will become more familiar with one of the most influential figures in church and world history. This will shed additional light on the Book of Acts that we have al-ready read. It will also prepare us for subsequent study of each of Paul's letters. Most of all, it will help us see more clearly the glory and the challenge that the Lord Jesus Christ presents through the gospel call.

Brief Overview of the Life of Paul

Paul's exact date of birth is unknown. It is reasonable to surmise that he was born within a decade of the time of Jesus' birth. He died, probably martyred in ROME, in the mid- to late A.D. 60s.

His birthplace was not the land Christ walked but the Hellenistic city of Tarsus, chief city of the Roman province of CILICIA. Tarsus, modern-day TERSOUS in southeastern TURKEY, has never been systematically excavated to first-century levels, so extensive archaeological data are lacking. Literary sources confirm that Paul's native city was a hotbed of Roman imperial activity and Hellenistic culture. Yet his writings show little significant influence of pagan authors. The one book dominating his thinking is the Old Testament. Paul "remains a Jew through and through."[2] He underscores this in calling attention to

Saul of Tarsus was converted at Damascus, spent three years in Arabia, briefly revisited Damascus, returned to Jerusalem, and finally took up residence in Tarsus.

his circumcision, Benjaminite lineage, Hebrew ancestry, and Pharisaic training (Phil 3:5).

Paul, in the New Testament known by his Hebrew name Saul until Acts 13:9 (see Acts 7:58; 8:1; 9:1, etc.), was apparently educated from boyhood in JERUSALEM, not Tarsus (Acts 22:3). It is not clear whether his family moved to Jerusalem while he was young or whether Paul was simply sent there for his education. He studied under the ranking rabbi of the era, GAMALIEL I. His use of the Old Testament bears testimony to his rabbinic training.[3] He was at least trilingual. His letters attest to excellent command of Greek, while

Important Dates and Events in Paul's Life

Date	Christian History	Roman History
14–37		Tiberius emperor
ca. 28–30	Public ministry of Jesus	
ca. 33	Paul converted	
ca. 35	Paul's first postconversion visit to Jerusalem	
35–46	Paul in Cilicia and Syria	
37–41		Gaius emperor
41–54		Claudius emperor
46	Paul's second visit to Jerusalem	
47–49	Paul and Barnabas in Cyprus and Galatia	
ca. 48–49	*Letter to the Galatians*	
49	Jerusalem Council	Jews expelled from Rome
49–50	Paul and Silas travel from Syrian Antioch through Asia Minor to Macedonia and Achaia	
50	*Letters to the Thessalonians*	
50–52	Paul in Corinth	
51–52		Gallio proconsul of Achaia
Summer 52	Paul's third visit to Jerusalem	
52–59		Felix procurator of Judea
52–55	Paul in Ephesus	
54–68	Nero emperor	
55–56	*Letters to the Corinthians*	
55–57	Paul in Macedonia, Illyricum, and Achaia	
early 57	*Letter to the Romans*	
May 57	Paul's fourth and last visit to Jerusalem	
57–59	Paul imprisoned in Caesarea	
59		Festus procurator of Judea
Sept. 59	Paul begins voyage to Rome	
Feb. 60	Paul arrives in Rome	
ca.60–62	Paul under house-arrest in Rome	
62		Albinus procurator of Judea
?60–62	*Prison Epistles*	
July 64		Fire of Rome
?65	Paul visits Spain	
?	*Pastoral Epistles*	
?67	Paul executed	

—From F. F. Bruce, *Paul: Apostle of the Heart Set Free* (Grand Rapids: Eerdmans, 1977), 475.

life and studies in PALESTINE presuppose knowledge of Hebrew and Aramaic. Facility in Latin cannot be ruled out. His writings show intimate knowledge of the Greek Old Testament, the Septuagint, though there is no reason to suppose that he was ignorant of the Hebrew original.

Some scholars (e.g., William Ramsey, Adolf Schlatter) insist that Paul had personal knowledge of Jesus during his earthly ministry. One goes so far as to assert that "it is very possible, indeed almost probable, that the young Saul even witnessed Jesus' death."[4] In any case, only a couple years after Jesus' crucifixion (ca. A.D. 30), Paul's hostile attitude toward the messianic movement spawned by John the Baptist and Jesus underwent radical change. As he traveled the 150 miles from Jerusalem to DAMASCUS armed with legal authority to hunt down Jewish Christians (Acts 9:1–2), bright light and a heavenly voice stopped him in his tracks. It was Jesus—to Paul's chagrin not a dead troublemaker but the risen Lord. Paul's conversion was never the focal point of his preaching—he preached Christ, not his personal experience (2 Cor 4:5)—but neither does it fail to influence him in later years (Acts 22:2–12; 26:2–18).[5]

We can only sketch the rough outlines of Paul's life from his conversion to his first missionary journey in the late A.D. 40s.

He spent various lengths of time in ARABIA, Damascus, and Jerusalem, eventually spending a lengthier stint far to the north in SYRIA and his native Cilicia (Gal 1:15–21). From there Barnabas enlisted his services for teaching duties in the church at SYRIAN ANTIOCH (Acts 11:25). Ironically, this multiracial church had been founded by Christians driven out of Palestine by persecutions instigated by Saul of Tarsus (Acts 11:19–21). It is from this period that our sources permit us to speak in greater detail of Paul's life and theology.

Missionary Journeys and Paul's Letters

Paul's writings arise from the crucible of missionary activity and the theological effort required to educate and sustain those who found Christ through his preaching. Galatians was probably written following Paul and Barnabas's tour of the Roman province of GALATIA (ca. A.D. 47–49). This is the so-called first missionary journey (Acts 13–14). A second foray, this time with Silas and Timothy, lasted most of three years (ca. A.D. 50–53) and resulted in churches founded in PHILIPPI, BEREA, THESSALONICA, and Corinth. The Thessalonian letters were written during this period.

Barnabas enlisted Paul's services for teaching duties in the church at Syrian Antioch.

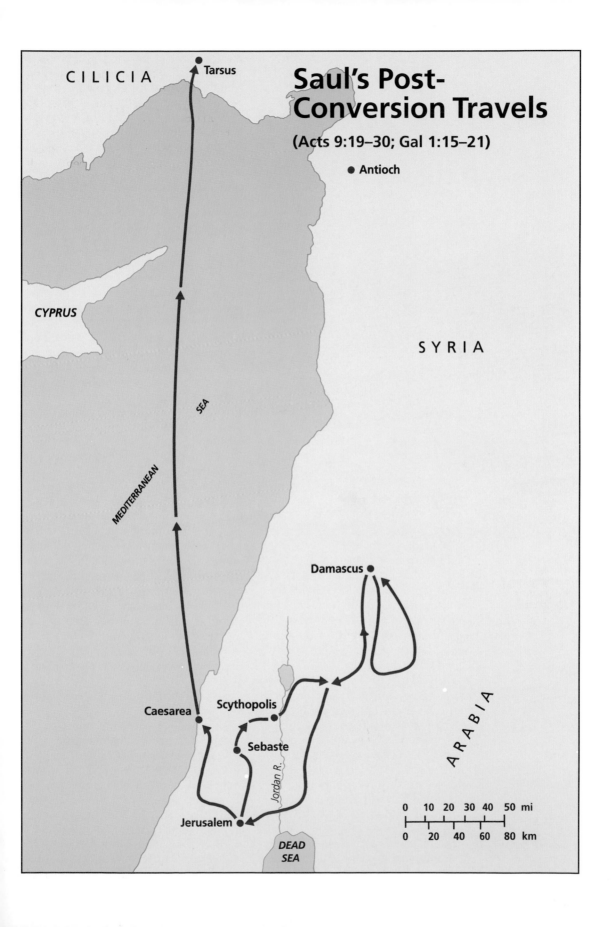

CILICIA

Tarsus

Saul's Post-Conversion Travels

(Acts 9:19–30; Gal 1:15–21)

Antioch

CYPRUS

SYRIA

MEDITERRANEAN SEA

Damascus

ARABIA

Caesarea

Scythopolis

Sebaste

Jordan R.

Jerusalem

DEAD
SEA

| 0 | 10 | 20 | 30 | 40 | 50 mi |
| 0 | 20 | 40 | 60 | 80 km |

west as SPAIN and then back into the Aegean area. One or more of the Pastoral Epistles may date from this period. Second Timothy concludes with Paul once more in chains. Reports of uncertain reliability place Paul's death at ca. A.D. 67 under the deranged oversight of Nero.

Which Letters Did Paul Write?

Below we will attempt to summarize Paul's views. But the exact shape of his theology depends on which writings are used to reconstruct his thought. Since the Enlightenment (eighteenth century) most scholars have agreed that Romans, 1 and 2 Corinthians, Galatians, Philippians, 1 Thessalonians, and Philemon are definitely from Paul's hand. Some have denied Paul's authorship of Ephesians, Colossians, and 2 Thessalonians. Others demur, and there is ample scholarly justification for drawing on them in outlining Paul's theology. Many deny that Paul wrote the so-called Pastoral Epistles (1 and 2 Timothy, Titus). Yet scholars like D. Guthrie, E. Ellis, and L. T. Johnson urge that Pauline authorship is entirely feasible—the documents do state that Paul wrote them, and even research not intent on proving that Paul wrote the Pastorals turns up evidence that he might have.[6] On purely scholarly grounds it is not irresponsible to draw from the entire thirteen-letter New Testament collection in summarizing Paul's theology. Christians convinced of divine authorship of the entire New Testament canon or sensitive to ecclesiastical authority have additional causes for accepting all thirteen Pauline letters as genuine.

An equally interesting and pressing question is whether data from Acts can be merged with material in Paul's letters. Some insist that "Acts must be excluded entirely as a source for the content of Paul's preaching."[7] This complex issue hinges on Acts' historicity. Those who see Acts as probably well-meaning, perhaps literarily skillful, but ultimately fanciful storytelling will naturally reject it as a source for reliable information about Paul and his

Paul's third missionary journey (Acts 18–21) lasted from about A.D. 53 to 57 and centered on a long stay in EPHESUS, from which he wrote 1 Corinthians. During a sweep through MACEDONIA he wrote 2 Corinthians. At the end of this time, awaiting departure for Jerusalem, he wrote Romans from Corinth (ca. A.D. 57).

His arrival in Jerusalem was followed quickly by arrest (on false charges of bringing a Gentile onto temple grounds reserved for Jews only) and a two-year imprisonment in CAESAREA MARITIMA. Thereafter he was shipped to Rome on appeal to the imperial court of NERO. There (see Acts 28) he apparently wrote his so-called Prison Letters: Ephesians, Philippians, Colossians, and Philemon. From this point reconstructions of Paul's movements are tentative. Assuming release from imprisonment Paul may have managed a fourth journey, perhaps as far

God's Glory in Paul's Theology

Rom 16:27	. . . **to** the only wise **God be glory** forever through Jesus Christ! Amen.
Gal 1:5	. . . **to whom be glory** for ever and ever. Amen.
Eph 3:21	. . . **to him be glory** in the church and in Christ Jesus throughout all generations, for ever and ever! Amen.
Phil 4:20	**To our God and Father be glory** for ever and ever. Amen.
1 Tm 1:17	Now **to** the King eternal, immortal, invisible, the only **God, be** honor and **glory** for ever and ever. Amen.
2 Tm 4:18	**To him be glory** for ever and ever. Amen.

Clearly there are differences between Jesus' proclamation of the kingdom of God and Paul's of the risen Jesus. But the differences are incidental to the overarching truth that God was manifesting himself definitively, in the threat of judgment and the offer of free pardon, in the ministry of Jesus Christ. Jesus announced, explained in advance, and finally carried out the atoning ministry God laid on him; Paul acknowledged Jesus' saving death and resurrection, became his follower, and spread the word of his glory across the Roman world.

Paul and Jesus are not identical in either their words or their work, but they are wonderfully complementary.[10] Paul's theology is Christ's own authorized extension of the gospel of salvation for Jew and Gentile alike (Acts 9:15).

Below we break down Paul's theology into a number of subsections in order to gain a better grasp of the power and importance of the gospel he proclaimed—a gospel that has changed the lives of millions right down to the present hour.

message. A sizable body of research, however, is more optimistic that Luke was as careful about his reports as he claimed to be (see Lk 1:1–4; see also chapter 14 above). Paul's own writings remain the primary source for his theology, but mounting evidence suggests that Acts is a reliable guide for the historical framework of Paul's life and travels.[8] It is also a dependable third-person (and sometimes first-person) account of the kinds of things Paul was wont to urge on his listeners in the various situations he faced.

Paul and Jesus

Since the Enlightenment the claim recurs that Jesus taught a simple ethical spirituality or called for political or social revolution; then Paul came along and transmuted the gentle or revolutionary Jesus into an idealized divine man. Classic creedal Christianity, in this view, was never Jesus' intention but purely the brainchild of Paul. It is in this vein that a recent writer calls Paul "the most misleading of the earliest Christian writers" and "very unripe" spiritually; in fact, "he didn't understand Jesus at all" and "wasn't even interested in Jesus, just in his own idea of the Christ."[9]

Paul's Teaching about God

The New Testament uses the word "God" over 1,300 times. Over 500 of these occurrences are in Paul's writings. At the center of Paul's theology is God. Several doxological statements (statements expressing praise of God) capture Paul's majestic vision. God's wisdom and knowledge stretch beyond human reach; he is infinitely wise and all-knowing; all things are "from him and through him and to him" (Rom 11:33–36). "To him be the glory forever" (Rom 16:27; Gal 1:5; Eph 3:21; Phil 4:20; 1 Tm 1:17; 2 Tm 4:18) might well be the best summary of Paul's theology yet suggested as in the title of a recent study: *Paul: Apostle of God's Glory in Christ.*[11]

"By the command of the eternal *God*" the gospel of Jesus Christ is made known "so that all nations might believe and obey him" (Rom 16:26). *God* comforts the afflicted and raises the dead (2 Cor 1:3, 9). *He* is faithful (2 Cor 1:18); his "solid foundation stands firm" (2 Tm 2:19). *He* causes believers to persevere in their faith, if indeed they do, granting them his own Spirit as a down payment of greater glory in the coming age (2 Cor 1:21–22). The "living *God* who made heaven and earth and sea and everything in them" (Acts 14:15) is, quite simply, "the King, eternal, immortal, invisible, the only *God*" (1 Tm 1:17). Or again, *he* is "the blessed and only Ruler, the King of kings and Lord of Lords, who alone is immortal and who lives in unapproachable light, whom no one has seen or can see" (1 Tm 6:15–16). No wonder Paul, like his Master before him, lays such great stress on hearing, obeying, and proclaiming the Lord *God*.

Against polytheism Paul insisted that God is one. Against Stoicism Paul preached a God who was personal and accessible rather than impersonal and inscrutable. Against most pagan religion Paul presented a God concerned with social morality and personal ethics; God is not a cipher for a spirit experienced through rites of worship, ascetic denial, or mystical sensuality. Paul's example and teaching affirm that God is to be feared, loved, served, and worshiped.

Evil and the Human Dilemma

God, all of whose ways are perfect and just (Rom 3:5–6), is solely sovereign over all. All reality will one day reflect his perfect justice and glory, even if the human eye cannot yet see or the human mind imagine this. Under God's ultimate sway there is evil, orchestrated by Satan (the name occurs ten times in Paul) or the devil (five times). Paul does not speculate on evil's origin. But his belief in a personal, powerful, malevolent being (and subservient underlings, human and angelic: 2 Cor 11:12–15; Eph 6:11–12) is an important feature of his outlook. It is also one that links him readily to Jesus, whose dramatic encounters with Satan form a major motif in the Gospels.

Evil is real and influential (Eph 2:2) but fleeting. In the end it will not triumph. "The God of peace will soon crush Satan under your feet" (Rom 16:20). But until that day, sinners (every single person: see Rom 3:23) languish in "the trap of the devil, who has taken them captive to do his will" (2 Tm 2:26). They need someone to save them. The reality of evil, nearly as basic to Paul's theology as the reality of God, sets up the need for the deliverance Paul preaches. This need is stated most clearly in his teaching about the law.

Paul and the Law

Paul believes that the Old Testament, as expressive of the God of all, is binding upon all. A central tenet of the Old Testament is the radical lostness of humankind. "There is no one righteous, not even one; there is no one who understands, no one who seeks God" (Rom 3:10–11, quoting Ps 14:1–3). The litany continues for many verses. Paul, like Jesus, takes the Old Testament as authoritative and avows that "all have sinned and fall short of the glory of God" (Rom 3:23). The law stops every self-justifying mouth and underscores humankind's universal bondage to a pattern of rebellion against God, leading to estrangement from God. The law also condemns legalism (the view that salvation is attained by the merit of one's good works) in the name of God. It points to the radical need of all for pardon and liberation lest they waste their lives and face eternal perdition for their willful error (2 Thes 1:8–10). It thereby points to Christ (Rom 3:21; Gal 3:24).

Both Romans and Galatians warn against the snare of self-salvation by law keeping alone. "We maintain that a man is justified by faith apart from observing the law" (Rom 3:28). The Galatian letter was occasioned by a move within a number of churches to establish circumcision and other traditional Jewish observances as necessary—and sufficient—for salvation. In response Paul speaks disparagingly of the "law," by which he often means his opponents' misrepresentation of the Old Testament in the light of then-current oral tradition. "A man is not justified by observing the law, but by faith in Jesus Christ" (Gal 2:16). Such criticism of legalism is not a Pauline innovation; it was already a prominent feature of the Old Testament (1 Sm 15:22; Pss 40:6–8; 51:16–17; Is 1:11–15; Mi 6:6–8) and appears repeatedly in Jesus' teaching (Mt 23; Mk 7:1–13; Lk 11:37–54).

Like his master, Jesus, Paul was an avid student of the Old Testament Scriptures. Paul knew the Hebrew Old Testament well, though he often quoted it in Greek translation.

Yet on other occasions, even in Romans and Galatians where faith's virtues are extolled, Paul speaks positively of the law (Rom 3:31; 7:12, 14; Gal 5:14; 6:2). His dozens of Old Testament quotations, many from the books of Moses, challenge the theory that Paul rejected out of hand the Mosaic law for Christians. The mixed nature of Paul's assessments of the law results from the contrasting situations he addresses. If opponents threaten to replace the gospel of free grace with a message of salvation by works, Paul responds that the law, understood in that way, leads only to death and destruction. But if Spirit-filled followers of Christ seek the historical background of their faith or moral and theological instruction, then the Old Testament corpus, including the legal portions, may have a beneficial function.

In recent decades Paul's view of the law has been the most disputed aspect of his theology.[12] Building on groundwork laid by W. Wrede and A. Schweitzer, E. P. Sanders[13] rejects justification by faith as the center of Paul's theology. Sanders and others have mounted a radical reinterpretation of Paul's various statements about the law, the human dilemma, and the nature of salvation in Christ as understood by Protestants and earlier figures such as Augustine. Studies such as P. Stuhlmacher's *Revisiting Paul's Doctrine of Justification*[14] respond to the challenge of what J. Dunn has called the "new perspective" on Paul. Justification by faith is not the sole concern of Paul's theology, but no concern is more vital. Newer research shows that Paul's own writings, properly understood, undermine key contentions of the "new perspective."[15]

Children of Abraham, Children of God: Paul's View of the People of God

Paul's preaching in Acts 13:17 and his numerous references to Abraham in Romans and Galatians (nine references in each Epistle; see also 2 Cor 11:22) confirm that Paul did not see himself as founder of a new religion.[16] The foundation of the gospel Paul preached was the covenant

God made with Abraham (see Gn 12:1–3; 15:1–21). As Paul writes, "The Scripture . . . announced the gospel in advance to Abraham. . . . So those who have faith are blessed along with Abraham, the man of faith" (Gal 3:8–9).

This is not to deny the importance of other dimensions of the Old Testament, the bounties of Israel that are the taproot of the church (Rom 11). These include "the very words of God" that God entrusted to Old Testament sages and seers (Rom 3:2). They also include "the adoption as sons . . . the divine glory, the covenants, the receiving of the law, the temple worship and the promises," as well as "the patriarchs [Abraham, Isaac, and Jacob] and . . . Christ" (Rom 9:4–5).

Nor is it to deny that Jesus Christ, as the fulfillment of God's prior promises, transcends all that went before. It is however to underscore that Paul's gospel was, in his view, in continuity with God's saving work over past millennia. Paul's references to *tekna theou* ("children of God"; Rom 8:16, 21; 9:8; Phil 2:15; cf. Eph 5:1, 8) or "children of promise" or "heirs" of salvation (Rom 8:17; 9:8; Gal 3:28, 31) hark back in every case to God's saving work in Old Testament times. In this sense Paul was not the originator of Christianity but merely its faithful witness and divinely guided interpreter (1 Cor 7:40)—granted, with the advantage of hindsight available after "the fullness of time had come" when "God sent his son . . . to redeem those who were under the law, so that we might receive adoption as children" (Gal 4:4–5 NRSV).

But the mention of hindsight raises the question of Paul's source of insight. How did he arrive at the startling and controversial body of lore and counsel found in his Epistles?

Revelation and Scripture

Paul saw himself claimed by the God of the ages, who had chosen him—of all people—even though he had persecuted Christ by persecuting the church (Acts 9:4; cf. 22:4; 26:11; 1 Cor 15:9; Gal 1:13, 23; Phil 3:6) to reveal secrets that were previously hidden (Eph 3:4–9). The heart of this *mysterion* (mystery in the sense of a God-revealed truth) was, first, the very word of salvation in Christ itself—on which more below. But additionally and significantly, at the center of the gospel of Christ was the good news that believing Gentiles are co-heirs with believing Israel of God's covenant favor. Peter had anticipated Paul in announcing this (Acts 10–11), just as Jesus foresaw that the gospel would open God's saving grace to the Gentiles in unprecedented ways (Mt 8:11–12; 28:19–20; Jn 12:20–24; Acts 1:8). But Paul bore the brunt of the responsibility of announcing the new wrinkle in the work God was bringing to pass. He was the primary founder of many assemblies of worship and mission that would take the word yet farther. God granted him special cognitive grace, an authoritative knowledge of what to teach, equal to his task (see Paul's references to "the grace given me" in Rom 12:3; 15:15; 1 Cor 3:10; Gal 2:9; Eph 3:7–8).

Yet it would be misleading to overemphasize the uniqueness of what was revealed to Paul. His views were seconded by other apostles (Gal 2:6–9). His teachings further and apply that which Jesus himself inaugurated and accomplished. Most of all, the revelation of which Paul speaks was corroborated by Scripture: His gospel and "the revelation of the mystery hidden for long ages past" are now "revealed and made known," not only by Paul's divinely given wisdom but "through the prophetic writings" of the Old Testament (Rom 16:25–26; cf. 1:2). Paul testified before Felix: "I believe everything that agrees with the Law and that is written in the Prophets" (Acts 24:14). Old Testament writings and the revelation Paul received—much of which became New Testament writings—combined to form an authoritative deposition, God's own sworn testimony as it were, grounding his saving work in centuries past and confirming it in the days of Jesus. Those same writings, combined with others of earliest New Testament times, were destined to serve as a primary source and standard for all Christian theology in the centuries since Paul's earthly course was run.

Jesus and Paul: Foundational Agreement

Jesus taught that "salvation is from the Jews" (Jn 4:22) and that the Old Testament "Scripture cannot be broken" (Jn 10:35). Paul likewise believed that Christian salvation flowed forth from what God had done in Old Testament times. Below are eight gifts of God to Israel that in various ways are also gifts to gospel believers (see Rom 9:4–5):

1. Adoption as sons
2. God's glorious presence
3. The covenants
4. The receiving of the law
5. Temple worship
6. The promises
7. The patriarchs (Abraham, Isaac, Jacob)
8. The Messiah

Messiah

Old Testament writings promised a God-sent savior figure who would establish an everlasting kingdom, bringing eternal honor to the Lord by exalting God's people and punishing his enemies.[17] "The case for the expectation of a divine Messiah is strong in the Old Testament."[18] By the first century messianic expectations were many and varied. Under the pressures of Roman rule in Palestine dozens of revolutionary figures arose.[19] It is hazardous to guess just what Saul the Pharisee believed about the Messiah. But first-century writings, es-pecially the New Testament, confirm that Jesus was rejected by the Jewish hierarchy as a messianic candidate. Clearly Saul shared this conviction.

It is therefore all the more striking that Paul later produced writings in which messianic honor is repeatedly ascribed to Jesus. By rough count of the Greek text, Paul uses the word "Christ" (a Greek word brought into common usage by Christians, translating the Hebrew word *mashiah*) close to four hundred times. He often uses the combination "Jesus Christ," other times writes "Christ Jesus," and most often uses the name "Christ" alone, as in the phrase "in Christ" (see below).

This frequency of use is probably best explained by analogy with Paul's even more frequent mention of God. God, not a concept or idea but the living divine person who creates and redeems, is the sole ordering factor over all of life. He is the basis and goal of all Paul does. But Paul was convinced that this same God had come to earth in human form, died for the forgiveness of human sin, and ascended to heaven to blaze a path for all who love him to follow. "Jesus" (over two hundred occurrences in Paul's letters) was the human locus of God's incarnate self-revelation. "Christ Jesus" and "Christ" are simply synonyms for the divine-human person in whom God brought his gracious saving will to pass.

A trio of texts encapsulates Paul's teaching on Christ's excellencies. First, Philippians 2:6–11 underscores Christ's essential oneness with God, yet his willingness to humble himself by taking on human form and enduring the shameful cross. God shares his very "name" (biblical shorthand for "personal identity" or "self") with him;

Paul's High View of Christ

In 1 Tm 3:16 Paul writes almost poetically about Christ's excellencies. Literary symmetry in Greek is evident in the sixfold rhyming -θη (*thē*) ending to the first word of each line. Note also the fivefold occurrence of ἐν (*en*).

ἐφανερώθη ἐν σαρκί,	revealed in human likeness
ἐδικαιώθη ἐν πνεύματι	vindicated by the Spirit
ὤφθη ἀγγέλοις,	witnessed by angels
ἐκηρύχθη ἐν ἔθνεσιν,	proclaimed among the nations
ἐπιστεύθη ἐν κόσμῳ,	believed on in the world
ἀνελήμφθη ἐν δόξῃ.	taken up in glory

soteriological

he is the king-designate before whom every knee will bow (Phil 2:9–10). Second, Colossians 1:15–20 (cf. Eph 1:20–23) expands on this **soteriological** vision to emphasize the cosmic dimensions of Christ Jesus' work. He was integral in creation and even now upholds the created order (Col 1:16–17). The fullness of the unseen God dwelt in him as he undertook his redemptive work (Col 1:19–20). Third, in compressed confessional form Paul summarizes his teaching about Jesus Christ in 1 Timothy 3:16, laying stress on his heavenly glory (see box at bottom of p. 263).

In theory Paul's high view of Jesus Christ (Paul knows no dichotomy between a "Christ of faith" and the "Jesus of history" in the modern sense, nor is "Christ" a spiritual being or symbol somehow discontinuous with Jesus of Nazareth) could be justified simply by virtue of his divine identity. Who would be so rash as to quibble with God (Rom 9:20)? Praise and honor befit whatever he deigns to do. But Paul's praise of Jesus Christ is not born of sheer necessity. It springs from the joyful awareness that God in Christ has regard for sinners in their lowly estate. He has expressed fierce, transforming love for his people through Christ's gracious work of redemption.

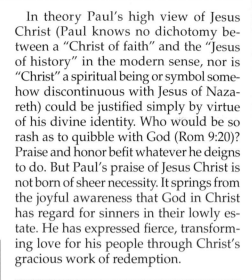

"High" Christology

Key Pauline passages reveal a lofty yet humane view of Jesus—he was fully human, though not merely human. A second-century document called the Epistle to Diognetus echoes Paul's sentiments:

He sent [Christ] unto them. Was he sent, think you, as any man might suppose, to . . . inspire fear and terror? Not so. But in gentleness [and] meekness has He sent Him, as a king might send his son who is a king. He sent Him, as sending God; He sent Him, as [a man] unto men; He sent Him, as Savior; as using persuasion, not force: for force is no attribute of God. He sent Him, as loving, not judging. . . . O the sweet exchange, O the inscrutable creation, O the unexpected benefits; that the iniquity of many should be concealed in One Righteous Man, and the righteousness of One should justify many that are iniquitous! Having then in the former time demonstrated the inability of our nature to obtain life, and having now revealed a Savior able to save even creatures which have no ability, He willed that for both reasons we should believe in His goodness and should regard Him as nurse, father, teacher, counselor, physician, mind, light, honor, glory, strength, and life.

—From J. B. Lightfoot, *The Apostolic Fathers* (London/New York: Macmillan, 1891), 507ff.

Redemption

Arguing from everyday experience Paul points out that only in a rare case would someone lay down his or her own life for the sake of another (Rom 5:7). But God has shown the depth of his love for the lost (see Lk 19:10) in that Christ died on their behalf while they were still in their woeful state (Rom 5:8). Through Christ there is "redemption" from sin. "Redemption" refers to the paying of a price for the release of prisoners from captivity and occupies a central place in Paul's understanding of Christ's ministry. It has rich Old Testament associations in the liberation of God's people from Egyptian bondage and other quandaries.

Jesus spoke of redemption in connection with events surrounding the return of the Son of Man (Lk 21:28). Paul uses the same word to describe the process by which sinners are justified (reckoned righteous in God's sight) through Jesus' death (Rom 3:24–25; cf. 1 Cor 1:30). But redemption is not only a past event. It is a future hope, as believers eagerly await the redemption of their bodies (Rom 8:23), their resurrection at the end of this age. Elsewhere Paul speaks of redemption most often in Ephesians, where he associates it with forgiveness of sins through Christ's death (1:7; cf. Col 1:14), the future heavenly inheritance of believers (1:14), and the coming day of vindication for Christ's followers.

Crucifixion by Altdorfer, 1518. Romans reserved crucifixion for heinous criminals and noncitizens. (Roman citizens were normally beheaded.) When Julius Caesar crucified a band of pirates, "he first mercifully cut their throats" (Suetonius). Jesus was shown no such mercy.

The logic of redemption requires that a price, or "ransom," be paid for prisoners' release. That price was the life of Jesus, "who gave himself a ransom for all" (1 Tm 2:6 NRSV). Christ died in place of sinners, bearing the punishment that should have been theirs. Theologians refer to this as the **substitutionary atonement.** In Paul's theology the cross is the means and central symbol of Christ's redeeming death.

The Cross

Paul can summarize the message he preaches as "the word of the cross" (1 Cor 1:18; cf. 1:23; 2:2). In itself the cross, re-

served by Roman overlords for the most despicable crimes and criminals, had no connotation but agony and shame. Jews in Jesus' day interpreted Deuteronomy 21:23 ("anyone who is hung on a tree is under God's curse") to apply to crucified persons, and this helps explain why Jewish leaders pressed for a Roman death sentence for Jesus. This would mean crucifixion, and crucifixion would be proof that Jesus was not God's messianic deliverer.

The strategy succeeded—but then backfired. Yes, Jesus was cursed by God. The Gospels imply this in recording Jesus' cry of dereliction, the prolonged midday darkness, and an earthquake at his death. But Paul points out that he became "a curse for us" so that "the blessing given to Abraham might come to the Gentiles through Christ Jesus" and so that "by faith we might receive the promise of the Spirit" (Gal 3:13–14). It is one of the grand ironies of history that the execrable cross should serve as the central symbol for history's most sublime religion.[20] Christianity's elevation of the cross is directly related to the fixation on it in Paul's writings.

Paul uses the noun "cross" ten times and the verb "crucify" eight times. His numerous references to Jesus' "death" and "blood" likewise cast a spotlight on the cross (Col 1:20). Yet it is not only a symbol for the means by which God in Christ atoned for sins. It is also the means by which believers walk in the footsteps of the one who calls them. As the cross is the source of strength in Christ's ministry, it is the source of strength for Paul (2 Cor 13:4; cf. Gal 6:14). For all believers the cross serves as inspiration and effective agent in mortifying "the sinful nature" with "its passions and desires" (Gal 5:24). A key link between Jesus and Paul is their shared emphasis on death to sin and self as requisite for life to righteousness and God. For both, the cross functions as Moses' bronze serpent (Jn 3:14; cf. Nm 21:8–9), a most unlikely symbol mediating eternal life to all who gaze on it with trust.

The cross, however, does not stand alone in Paul's theology. His gospel is not a grim summons to bottomless pain. The Pauline cross stands firmly planted in the rich soil of the resurrection.

Resurrection

The Christian message stands or falls with the truth or falsity of the claim that following his death for sin Jesus Christ rose bodily from the dead (1 Cor 15:14). Paul's preaching on the first missionary journey keyed on the resurrection (Acts 13:34, 37). Several years later at ATHENS Paul's stress was the same (Acts 17:31): God "has given proof . . . to all men" of coming judgment through Jesus Christ "by raising him from the dead" (cf. Rom 1:4). While it is generally true to say that Paul's witness in Acts is Christ-centered, it can also be said to be resurrection-centered. Scarcely a major message or testimony passes without mention of Christ's resurrection or the assurance of future resurrected blessedness that Christ's resurrection guarantees those who trust him (Acts 17:18, 32; 23:6; 24:15, 21; 26:23).

Paul refers to the resurrection over five dozen times in his letters. Only 2 Thessalonians, Titus, and Philemon lack such mention. Like "cross" and "crucify," "resurrection" and "raised" refer both to an event in Christ's life and a reality for believers. Cross and resurrection serve together to make the benefits of Christ's righteousness available: "He was delivered over to death for our sins and was raised to life for our justification" (Rom 4:25).

The resurrection is a key truth for daily Christian living. Jesus' resurrection from the dead means victory over sin (the ultimate cause of death, Rom 5:12), and believers are urged to appropriate this victory in their own lives: "offer yourselves to God, as those who have been brought from death to life" (Rom 6:13). The logic of growing in Christ-likeness, or **sanctification**, is based on Jesus' resurrection: "If the Spirit of him who raised Jesus from the dead is living in you, he who raised Christ from the dead will also give life to your mortal bodies" (Rom 8:11).

Paul's final extant letter urges Timothy to "remember Jesus Christ, raised from the dead" (2 Tm 2:9). This core Christian claim, still disputed yet defended today,[21] remains the fundamental hope of all true believers, for it defines the promise and power of the salvation that the gospel has granted them.

The Church

In Paul's theology it is not believers as autonomous, self-sufficient units to whom God directs his saving efforts. Yes, God views persons as individuals. But the horizon of his saving acts extends to the entirety of the "all peoples on earth" cited in God's promise to Abraham (Gn 12:3; cf. Eph 2:11–13). Christ died and rose to rescue a corporate body, the company of the redeemed, the elect, the people of God as a whole stretching from earliest Old Testament times to the present. In Paul's writings the term that denotes this entity is "church," a word that occurs some sixty times and is found in every Pauline Epistle except 2 Timothy and Titus. Perhaps most distinctive to his usage is the claim that Christ's very purpose was to have created "one new man out of the two" of Jew and Gentile, "thus making peace, and in this one body to reconcile both . . . to God through the cross" (Eph 2:15–16). For this reason the church is not a side issue or subpoint for Paul but a first-level corollary of his teaching about Christ.

The trademark Pauline phrase "in Christ (Jesus)" requires mention in connection with Paul's stress on the church. Paul uses this phrase (or "in the Lord") some 150 times. While its uses are varied, more than one-third relate to God's saving work through Christ (e.g., Rom 3:24) and one-third to the manner in which Christians should behave (Phil 4:4) or the redeemed state they enjoy (Rom 16:3).[22] Perhaps most fundamentally, "in Christ" (virtually absent from non-Pauline New Testament writings) bespeaks believers' unity and interdependence. It refers to their organic relatedness to the heavenly Father and to each other as his redeemed children because of what Christ has accomplished on their behalf.

The social reality denoted by "church" is often expressed using the metaphor of "body." Believers are to live humbly and to exercise their gifts for the sake of others in the body of Christ (Rom 12:3–5; cf. 1 Cor 12–14). Their organic connection to Christ, their being "members of Christ himself" (1 Cor 6:15), is the basis for many a Pauline imperative (e.g., that the

The garden tomb, Jerusalem. The resurrection, along with the cross, was the touchstone of early Christian preaching.

Corinthians defy their social norms and practice marital fidelity or celibacy rather than engage in casual or ritual sex; 1 Cor 6:12–20). The Ephesian Epistle is especially notable for its preponderance of references to "church" (nine times) and "body" (six times) in the sense of God's people in Christ. Under God's all-encompassing purpose the church is the direct recipient of Christ's fullness (Eph 1:22–23). Ephesians 4 stresses the unity of the triune God's work in Christ and the effects of this in the church, of which Christ is head (4:15; cf. 1:22; Col 1:18; 2:10, 19). Ephesians 5:22–33 spells out the glories of Christ's love for the church, and the church's high calling of attending to its Lord, in a didactic discussion of Christian marriage.

In the individualistic climate of the West it is difficult to overstate the importance of the corporate solidarity of God's people in Christ. Paul's frequent use of "church," "body" (along with other metaphors), and "in Christ" assures that careful readers will not impose modern or postmodern theories of selfhood and politics on Paul's radically Christ-centered affirmations.

Ethics

Paul's letters go beyond theological teaching and religious directives. Prin-
ciples and precepts regulating practical behavior, both individual and social, permeate his writings. It would be reductionist error to reduce Paul's ethic to a solitary basis; he seems to make use of a multiplex rationale (quite apart from the imponderables of divine guidance). Drawing on Old Testament precedent he charges believers with ethical imperatives based on the theological indicative of God's character, as when he calls on them to be imitators of God (Eph 5:1; cf. Lv 11:44: "I am the LORD your God; consecrate yourselves and be holy, because I am holy"). Their conduct should be regulated by God's presence in their midst (1 Cor 3:17) and his holy purpose in their election and calling (Eph 1:4, 4:1; cf. 2 Tm 1:9). Old Testament commands have a prominent place in Paul's ethic, but so does Christ's powerful example of humility and self-sacrifice (Phil 2:5–11). Put slightly differently, believers' lives should be regulated by what God has accomplished for them through Christ (1 Cor 5:7; Eph 5:8). Love is the crowning virtue (1 Cor 13:13), in Paul's ethic as in Jesus' (Mk 12:29–31). In the end, "the only thing that counts is faith expressing itself through love" (Gal 5:6; cf. 1 Tm 1:5).

Pauline ethics is a subject too vast to be treated as a subpoint of his theology, but it is important to note that Paul's doctrine is not rightly comprehended when it does not translate into transformation

267

Theology and Ethics in Paul

Paul stressed both universal qualities of true Christian character and the importance of good works. For Paul, "good works" do not earn salvation. They are defined by biblical teachings and commands.

Importance of Virtues
(1 Cor 13)
faith
hope
love

Importance of Good Works
(from Paul's letter to Titus; NIV translation modified)

2:7 In everything set them an example by doing **good works**.

2:14 who gave himself for us to . . . purify for himself a people . . . eager to do **good works**.

3:1 Remind . . . to be ready to do **good works** . . .

3:8 Stress these things, so that those who have trusted God may be careful to devote themselves to doing **good works** . . .

3:14 Our people must learn to devote themselves to doing **good works** . . .

eschatology

parousia

Abba

of behavior at both personal and corporate levels. Paul's theology is important, but it does not stand alone. The Epistle to Titus commends good works to God's people repeatedly (2:7, 14; 3:1, 8, 14) and condemns pseudo-Christians who confess God but live ethically indifferent lives (1:16; cf. Rom 12:1–2).[23]

Last Things

Paul's **eschatology** is an even more vast and complex subject than his ethics. The two areas are in fact related. Jesus' preaching of God's at-hand kingdom, vindicated by his resurrection from the dead, means that the end of the age has already dawned (Rom 13:12). As they live out their daily lives on earth, believers' "citizenship is in heaven," from which they "eagerly await a Savior . . . the Lord

Jesus Christ" (Phil 3:20; cf. Col 3:3). Paul's view of things to come has profound implications for the way life is to be lived now. As Schreiner states, "Being ready for the Lord's coming does not mean calculating the day when he will arrive; it means that believers are to live their everyday lives in a different fashion from unbelievers, with moral alertness and seriousness, because they know the Lord will return."[24]

Pauline eschatology, like all of Paul's teaching, grows out of his convictions about God generally and Jesus Christ in particular. Because Jesus was the Messiah, his victorious ministry signaled the arrival of the last stages of God's redemptive work prior to the consummation. This will include final judgment at the **parousia** (second coming; see Rom 2:1–11; 14:10–12; 1 Cor 3:12–15; Phil 2:16; 1 Thes 3:13; 2 Thes 1:5–10). Evildoers who have not obeyed the gospel will face God's wrath (Rom 1:18; Eph 5:6; Col 3:6). It is incumbent on believers, following in Paul's train, to proclaim the gospel to the nations (also to unrepentant Israel; Rom 9–11) as a faithful witness to the unfolding of God's eschatological aims.

Eschatological boon is already available in the present. Believers enjoy the Holy Spirit, a sure sign of the end of the age. He is "the firstfruits" of their coming redemption (Rom 8:23), the "guarantee" or "downpayment" of greater things to come (2 Cor 1:22; 5:5; Eph 1:14), a seal of the inheritance and adoption that enables them to call God "**Abba**" (Rom 8:15–17). For Christians who believe in a rapture (taking up) of Christians prior to Christ's return and his founding of a millennial reign on the earth, the Holy Spirit enables them to live in a state of readiness as they await those great events.

Conclusion

In the contemporary setting, Paul's dramatic emphasis on an imminent future order that calls for immediate, radical personal reorientation is readily written off as quaint mythology or apocalyptic excess. It even becomes the stuff of Hollywood parody. Such dismissal is

Key People/Places

Antioch (Syrian)
Arabia
Athens
Berea
Caesarea
Maritima
Cilicia
Corinth
Damascus
Ephesus
Galatia
Gamaliel I
Jerusalem
Macedonia
Nero
Palestine
Philippi
Rome
Spain
Syria
Tarsus
Tersous
Thessalonica
Turkey

Key Terms

Abba
eschatology
parousia
sanctification
soteriological
substitutionary
   atonement

perilous if Paul, like Jesus, possesses the authority that he claims. Endorsing wholeheartedly the Pauline vision with its cosmic implications means true life, life "in Christ," in this age and unspeakable enjoyment of God in the coming one (Rom 8:18; 1 Cor 2:9). Equally urgent is Paul's insistence that rejecting his gospel will in due course bring God's eternal displeasure. This is not to mention the tragedy of a life that squanders the opportunity to worship and share the resurrected Lord.

Focus 17: Not Even One

It's a familiar story. A public figure receives trust and honor. He is elected to high office, or his books sell millions.

Then the truth comes out: the person thought to be morally upright turns out to be guilty of gross wrongdoing. This is true of any number of recent political leaders, both in the U.S. and abroad. It is also true of a well-known historian (who shall here remain nameless). His book on intellectuals was a bestseller. It exposed the moral state of leading thinkers of modern times: Rousseau, Shelley, Marx, Ibsen, Tolstoy, Hemingway, Brecht, Sartre, Hellman, and others. The book performs the service of showing the hypocrisy and danger of certain dubious but now accepted convictions that these thinkers helped enshrine in the Western mind.

But the same author who blew the whistle on others seems to have committed a grave indiscretion himself. Another honored figure bites the dust. Public cynicism flourishes.

Moral lapse came as no surprise to Paul. While we rightly think of his message as pointing to Christ, it points with equal emphasis to humans—our moral weakness, our spiritual blindness, our social fragmentation. People are fallen, and there are no exceptions. Quoting a familiar Old Testament theme, Paul exclaims, "There is no one righteous, not even one" (Rom 3:10). He included himself in this grim assessment.

But then why was Paul's preaching so full of hope? Why did he not grow cynical? In Jesus Christ he met a man who had passed every moral test. His death absorbed the punishment due our human failing. His resurrection gives resources for living now on a new ethical plane (Rom 8:11).

Summary

1. Through his own writings and the Book of Acts, we are familiar with Paul, who was one of the most important figures in the apostolic church.

2. Paul was well educated and understood Judaism thoroughly, having studied under the leading rabbi, Gamaliel I.

3. Paul made at least three missionary journeys on behalf of the early church.

4. The primary sources for discovering Paul's theology are his own writings and Acts.

5. God is at the center of Paul's theology.

6. Paul believed that evil is real and influential but will be eternally curbed and punished by God.

7. Paul believed that the Old Testament has application for all persons, yet condemned legalism.

8. The foundation of the gospel Paul preached was the covenant God made with Abraham.

9. Paul held a high view of Christ not only because of his divine identity but because he is an expression of God's concern for sinners.

10. The cross is the means and central symbol of the redemption Christ won.

11. The resurrection is important because the Christian message depends on its truth.

12. Paul's treatment of the church places it at the heart of his Christology.

13. Paul taught that the gospel transforms believers' personal behavior and corporate identity.

14. Paul's theology is closely intertwined with his distinctive ethics and eschatology.

Study Questions

1. Describe two significant events from Paul's life in each of these four decades: the A.D. 30s, 40s, 50s, and 60s.

2. What is ironic about Paul serving as teacher and missionary of the church at Antioch?

3. How do Jesus' and Paul's messages differ? How are they alike?

4. Why did Paul speak of the law in both negative and positive terms?

5. Characterize the role played by Abraham in Paul's teaching.

6. Why did Paul stress "the grace given to me" in his writings?

7. Why did Jewish leaders press for Jesus' crucifixion? Why did Paul see redemption in Jesus' cruel death?

8. What does Paul mean by "in Christ" or "in Christ Jesus"?

9. How does Paul base ethics in theology?

10. Name three aspects of Paul's teaching about last things.

Review Questions

1. Paul was born in the Hellenistic city of
   _____.

2. Before his conversion Paul was called
   _____.

3. Paul's writings were all produced as a
   result of his _____ activity.

4. After his arrival in Jerusalem at the end
   of his third missionary journey, Paul
   was _____.

5. According to Enlightenment critics,
   Paul turned the gentle or revolutionary
   Jesus into an idealized _____ man.

6. In contrast to widespread _____
   belief, Paul insisted that God is one.

7. Paul and the law both condemn
   _____.

8. The foundation of the gospel Paul
   preached was the _____ covenant.

9. Paul was the primary founder of many
   assemblies of _____ and missions.

10. Paul's writings repeatedly ascribe
    messianic honor to _____.

11. The logic of redemption requires a
    _____ for the release of the prisoner.

12. The key truth for daily Christian living
    is the _____—but for Paul this truth
    stands in close proximity to the word
    of the _____.

Further Reading

Brown, Raymond. *An Introduction to the New Testament*. New York: Doubleday, 1997. Chs. 16 and 17 contain a concise update and assessment of Pauline studies.

Bruce, F. F. *Paul: Apostle of the Heart Set Free*. Grand Rapids: Eerdmans, 1977. Magisterial survey of Paul's life and the ties between his Epistles and Acts.

Doty, William G. "The Epistles." In *A Complete Literary Guide to the Bible*. Ed. Leland Ryken and Tremper Longman III. Grand Rapids: Zondervan, 1993, pp. 445–57. Reflections on ancient letters as a literary form and how to understand them.

Dunn, James. *The Theology of Paul the Apostle*. Grand Rapids: Eerdmans, 1997. Most comprehensive recent British synthesis of Pauline theology.

Hawthorne, Gerald, Ralph P. Martin, D. G. Reid, eds. *Dictionary of Paul and His Letters*. Downers Grove: InterVarsity, 1993. A standard reference work dealing with virtually every aspect of Paul's life and thought.

Kim, Seyoon. *Paul and the New Perspective: Second Thoughts on the Origin's of Paul's Gospel*. Grand Rapids: Eerdmans, 2001. A scholar noted for his work on the importance of Paul's conversion (see his *The Origin of Paul's Gospel*) restates his outlook in light of newer discussion.

Koperski, Veronica. *What Are They Saying about Paul and the Law?* New York/Mahwah, N.J.: Paulist, 2001. A fine summary of recent viewpoints on a critical issue for Pauline interpretation.

McGrath, Alister E. *The Mystery of the Cross*. Grand Rapids: Zondervan, 1988. Challenging but uplifting reflections on the importance of the cross for Christian thinking and living.

McRay, John. *Paul: His Life and Teaching*. Grand Rapids: Baker, 2003. A thoroughgoing investigation informed by the author's extensive travel and archaeological experience in areas where Paul was active. Focuses on history and backgrounds rather than theology.

Schreiner, Thomas R. *Interpreting the Pauline Epistles*. Grand Rapids: Baker, 1990. Valuable tips on how to get started understanding Paul's letters in a serious and responsible way.

———. *Paul, Apostle of God's Glory in Christ*. Downers Grove/Leicester: InterVarsity/Apollos, 2001. A fresh and wide-ranging summary of Paul's theology.

Wenham, David. *Paul and Jesus: The True Story*. Grand Rapids: Eerdmans, 2002. Demonstrates at a readable level the positive connections between Paul and Jesus.

18 Romans
Right with God

Objectives

After reading this chapter, you should be able to

- Characterize the impact of Romans on church history
- Present the purposes of Romans
- Outline the content of the Book of Romans
- Explain how Romans encouraged Christian believers to live their lives

Gospels—Acts—Epistles

The four Gospels tell the story of the Good News about Jesus Christ, and Acts tells how that Good News spread over the span of more than three decades. But if all we had were the Gospels and Acts, our grasp of earliest Christian **faith** and practice would be seriously limited. We can be grateful that nearly two dozen letters round out the picture. All the Epistles date from the first century, and many scholars argue that all of them come from the hand of writers whom Jesus Christ personally appointed to receive and teach the word of salvation. In this and following chapters we consider the Epistles one by one. But we will not discuss them in the chronological order in which they were written. We will rather follow the order that they appear in the New Testament. The single exception is Philemon, which we treat with

---

New Testament Epistles

The New Testament contains thirteen Pauline letters and eight others. From ancient times they seem to have been arranged in two groupings, Pauline and non-Pauline, and from longest to shortest within these groupings.

Pauline	Others
(13 total):	(8 total):
Romans	Hebrews
1 and 2 Corinthians	James
Galatians	1 and 2 Peter
Ephesians	1, 2, and 3 John
Philippians	Jude
Colossians	
1 and 2 Thessalonians	
1 and 2 Timothy	
Titus	
Philemon	

Paul's other so-called Prison Epistles. Although no one can say for sure why the early church arranged the Epistles like they did, it seems that they started from the longest Pauline letter (Romans) and then proceeded to the shortest (Philemon). They used the same procedure with the non-Pauline letters, beginning with Hebrews and ending with the little Book of Jude.[1]

Why Wade through Romans?

Paul's letter to the Romans has the reputation of being hard to understand and even boring. Many a congregation has groaned inwardly when their pastor announced a sermon series on Romans, and many a daily Bible reading schedule has come to grief in its pages!

Yet this Epistle, probably more than any other single book of the Bible, has influenced world history in dramatic ways. The great North African intellectual and church leader Augustine (354–430), for example, found new life in Romans after years of pagan philosophy and sometimes loose living. To slake the thirst of his soul, Augustine writes, he "most eagerly seized upon . . . the works of the apostle Paul."[2] And in the midst of wrestling with a tortured conscience and profound doubt about his life's direction, Augustine's "bondage of . . . desire for sex"[3] was broken when he read Romans 13:13–14:

> Let us behave decently, as in the daytime, not in orgies and drunkenness, not in sexual immorality and debauchery, not in dissension and jealousy. Rather, clothe yourselves with the Lord Jesus Christ, and do not think about how to gratify the desires of the sinful nature.

Writing about his conversion years later Augustine recalls, "I had no wish to read further; there was no need to. For . . . it was as though my heart was filled with a light of confidence and all the shadows of my doubt were swept away."[4] Augustine's writings exerted a profound influence on European civilization for a thousand years, and his ideas still command respect today.

Paul's Epistle to the Romans electrified Martin Luther's (1483–1546) life, too, as he pondered "night and day" how he, a sinner, could ever stand forgiven before God who is perfectly righteous and will one day judge all persons. Deeply troubled in conscience and aware from Scripture of the depth of his sin, he wrestled with the words of Romans 1:17, "The righteous will live by faith." That statement, itself a quote from Habakkuk in the Old Testament, convinced Luther that "through grace and sheer mercy God justifies us through faith."[5] Salvation is not by our good works or any other merit of ourselves, our church, or our religion: It is through Jesus Christ alone. The face of EUROPE was transformed by the Protestant Reformation that Luther helped launch. Romans was the springboard of the revolution he helped set in motion.

But it was not just the early church (Augustine) and the Reformation (Luther) that Romans stirred up. The spiritual revivals that swept ENGLAND in the 1700s were also kindled through the effect of Romans—on John Wesley. He attended a church meeting on May 24, 1738, and listened as the leader read from Luther's preface to his Romans commentary. He later recounted his experience that evening: "While he was describing the change which God works in the heart through faith in Christ, I felt my heart strangely warmed. I felt that I did trust in Christ, Christ alone for my salvation: And an assurance was given me, that he had taken away my sins, even mine, and saved me from the law of sin and death."[6]

Volumes could be filled with tales of the light that has filled human hearts through study of Romans. Luther testified that through reading it he felt himself "to be reborn and to have gone through open doors into paradise. The whole of Scripture took on a new meaning. . . . This passage of Paul became to me a gate of heaven."[7] It may be, then, that to call Romans boring would tell us more about ourselves than about it. An effort to rethink its message will be worthwhile—and could change our lives.

The City of Rome and Christianity

The greatest city of classical antiquity in the West, ROME was the capital of a vast

Paul's Epistle to the Romans opened Luther's heart to the gospel *(right)*.

Through Luther's writings on Romans John Wesley felt his heart "strangely warmed" *(far right)*.

275

empire. In Jesus' day perhaps one hundred million people inhabited Roman territory.[8] Rome's vast domain extended westward to modern GREAT BRITAIN, northward to modern GERMANY, eastward to modern IRAN, and southward hundreds of miles up the NILE in EGYPT. Few empires at any time in world history have rivaled its size, might, and splendor.

Christianity probably came to Rome first with Jews who heard Peter's preaching at Pentecost (Acts 2:10) and brought the gospel message back to the synagogues of the imperial capital. Ancient traditions that Peter ministered in Rome in the late A.D. 30s cannot be easily set aside. In any case, by about A.D. 49 the Christian presence among Jews in Rome was great enough to provoke riots in that community.[9]

The New Testament mentions Rome eight times. Twice Paul states he intends to go and preach there (Acts 19:21; 23:11). And two other times he mentions Rome when he dictates (see Rom 16:22) his Epistle that bears the great city's name (Rom 1:7, 15).

The Occasion and Purpose of Romans

There is general agreement that Paul wrote Romans during his three-month stay in GREECE (Acts 20:2–3). This was about A.D. 57, near the completion of his third missionary journey and on the eve of his departure for his last known visit to JERUSALEM. Comparison of Romans 16:23 with other passages (Acts 19:29; 20:4; 1 Cor 1:14) implies that Paul was in the vicinity of CORINTH as the letter took shape. This is confirmed by Paul's commendation of Phoebe as the person who carried it from Corinth to Rome: Her home church was in CENCHREAE, a small town eight miles from Corinth (Rom 16:1).

The purpose of Romans is one of the most disputed topics in modern New Testament scholarship.[10] Everyone agrees that Paul writes in part to rally support for the upcoming mission to SPAIN that he hopes to undertake (Rom 15:24). But the view held in the church for centuries that the main purpose of Romans is theological—to teach about salvation and

Romans in Early Church History	
Romans seems to have been known and used by such early church leaders as:	
	A.D.
Clement of Rome	95
Polycarp	ca. 110
Justin Martyr	ca. 140
Irenaeus	ca. 175
Clement of Alexandria	ca. 200
Tertullian	ca. 200
Origen	ca. 250
Eusebius	ca. 315

further Christ's kingdom in the world—is "not a serious option today" for many scholars.[11] New understanding is therefore sought in one of two theories: that Romans is primarily a letter about Paul's own concerns, or that it is "primarily occupied with the concerns of the Roman church."[12]

All three options may, however, be worth bearing in mind. First, no doubt Paul was concerned for the health of the church in Rome. The many greetings he conveys in chapter 16 indicate that he knew scores of believers there. It would be natural for him to tailor his remarks to his readers' situation. (The technical name for this is called **contextualization**.) Second, there can also be little doubt that Paul's personal hopes and aims inform his thinking—his passion to see his Jewish kinsmen accept their Messiah, for example (Rom 9:3; 10:1).

But third, although academic study of Scripture often discounts the theological message of the Bible, there is no law saying that we must submit to this particular—and certainly not universal—academic belief.

Therefore, in our discussion of Romans below we will be alert to any of these three emphases as they surface. We should observe in advance, however, that Christians through the centuries were probably on firm ground in reading Romans primarily with an eye for its life-changing truth about God, humankind, and redemption.

Outline

C. In Loving Acts of Service and Hospitality (12:9–13)
D. In Imitation of Jesus' Teaching (12:14–21)
E. In Rendering to Caesar What Is Caesar's (13:1–7)
F. In Loving One's Neighbor as Oneself (13:8–10)
G. In Living as in the Day, Not in Darkness (13:11–14)
H. In Pursuing Peace between Weak and Strong (14:1–15:13)

VI. **Conclusion** (15:14–16:27)
A. Paul's Missionary Purpose and Reason for Writing Boldly (15:14–22)
B. His Missionary Agenda for Jerusalem, Rome, and Spain (15:23–33)
C. Final Greetings, Warnings, and Doxology (16:1–27)

The Argument of Romans

We have already stated, and the outline above makes clear, that Paul had at least one obvious and direct intention in writing: to help the Romans get ready for Paul's visit, after which he hoped to journey westward to preach in Spain (Rom 15:23–33). This should be kept in mind even though the bulk of Romans is devoted to other matters.

Introduction (1:1–18)

The Epistle begins with the longest of all Paul's introductory statements, called a salutation (1:1–7). In it Paul identifies himself, customary in a Hellenistic letter of that time.[13] He also characterizes the message that had changed his life, speaking of its roots in the Old Testament, its basis in the resurrected Jesus Christ, and its expression through the apostolic ministry. To round out the salutation he names the recipients of the letter and bids them hello, though not with the secular "Greetings!" usually found in ancient Greek letters. Instead Paul pronounces a blessing "from God our Father and from the Lord Jesus Christ" (1:7).

Again following usual letter-writing custom of the day, Paul gives thanks for his readers. He expresses the desire to visit them soon (1:8–13). It is at this point that Paul anticipates the body of the letter. He speaks first of his eagerness to "preach the gospel also to you who are at Rome," then of the gospel itself. Like a composer laying down a concerto's theme, Paul praises the gospel as "the power of God for the salvation of everyone who believes: first for the Jew, then for the Gentile" (1:16).

Why such lofty claims for such a simple message? Because in the gospel "the righteousness of God" has been revealed. Debate has raged for centuries over what "the righteousness of God" means. One thing is certain: The meaning is sheer good news for all who embrace it. For the gospel message makes salvation available by faith (complete personal trust, not just mental agreement) to whoever desires to share the awe and joy of knowing the true and living God.

But why is the righteousness of God such an issue for Paul? Because of the wrath of God, which Paul takes up in the next section.

Diagnosis (1:19–3:20)

The gospel is good news. All of Paul's letters shine with an assurance and excitement that trusting God through Christ and serving him is a great thing—in fact, the greatest thing that people could ever experience. Why is Paul so stirred up about the faith he preaches?

For Paul, the good news is so good because the bad news is so bad. What is the bad news? All people are cut off from God and subject to eternal judgment because of their built-in tendency to ignore who he really is and to turn away from him. In Romans 1:18–23 Paul describes typical people of his day. They have an idea that there is a God because they see the beauty and grandeur of nature all around. But instead of seeking the true God who created nature, they worship nature itself.

The result of such religion is sad to read (1:24–32). Indifferent to the God who liberates people from their bondage to evil and vice, the pagans Paul describes fall into homosexual practices. Their minds become warped; their moral compass spins wildly. Murder, malice, deceit, and heartless cruelty prevail.

Homosexuality

In Rom 1:26–27 Paul underscores that homosexual relations, like all sexual intimacy outside monogamous marriage, are displeasing to God. Like other sins that he lists in Rom 1:28–31, it is an offense against God's law (Lv 18:22; 20:13). It is a twisting of the good gift of marital intimacy that God created for both procreation and enjoyment within heterosexual marriage (Gn 2:24; Prv 5:15–19; Mt 19:4–6; 1 Tm 4:3–5).

By the time Paul wrote Romans, he had observed gays becoming obedient to the Christian faith (see 1 Cor 6:9–11). Homosexuality, like premarital or extramarital sexual sin, is not unpardonable. The life-giving force that raised Christ from the dead can empower victims of both homosexual and heterosexual enslavements to break sin's chains and live pure lives that honor God (Rom 8:11).

The modern tendency to condone homosexuality is a denial of God's creation, his law, and his power through Christ's cross to loosen the grip of sin. Yes, some people do feel a strong attraction to the gay lifestyle, just as others feel trapped by illicit heterosexual desire. But is sin's stranglehold on the human will greater than God's liberating grace? The Bible's answer is a clear no. Even if the temptation to sexual sin involves fierce struggles, God's grace insists that we make an immediate and complete break with sinful deeds. God's Word is best even when it seems difficult.

It is wrong, of course, to single out gay offenders as worse sinners than others. Yet without softening the harsh verdict that Scripture delivers on both homosexual and heterosexual sin, divine forgiveness and the higher road of moral fidelity to a good and caring God need to be proclaimed in both true word and gracious deed.

Paul first reached Rome by foot along this Roman highway, the Appian Way, in about A.D. 62. He wrote his Epistle to Rome in about A.D. 57.

But the bad news is not just for idol worshipers, murderers, and sexual offenders. In 2:1–3:20 Paul widens the net of conviction. "Every mouth" is "silenced and the whole world held accountable to God" (3:19). Compared to a perfectly righteous God, the moral religious person is no better off than the immoral criminal. All alike, Jew and Gentile, are without hope, because all alike have sinned.

Romans is about the Good News of Jesus Christ. But we miss the glory of his goodness if we downplay the darkness of the human condition. The diagnosis is grim, and divine wrath is the inevitable result.

Is there any hope at all?

Prognosis I: Justified by Faith in Jesus Christ (3:21–8:17)

There is hope for sinners, Romans continues, because of Jesus Christ. He opens the way to receiving God's righteousness rather than wrath. All people in all times violate God's laws (3:23). But through Christ's death on the cross, God's just punishment for sin can be averted. Sinners can receive new life.

Paul uses several words that are important here. "Justified" (3:24) implies that God gives sinners a new status before him; where once they stood under a "guilty" sentence, God now counts them righteous on the basis of Christ's sacrifice. They receive "redemption" (3:24), which points to deliverance from sin's domination and liberation to the Lord's service. This is made possible by a "sacrifice of atone-

Questions and Answers in Romans

In Romans Paul asks a number of questions, then emphatically replies no. He employs a form of rhetoric called *diatribe*. Knowledge of this persuasive device can help to grasp Paul's message. Some samples:

Passage	Question	Reply
3:3	Does the fact that some do not believe the gospel mean that it might not be true?	NO!
3:5	Is God unjust in bringing wrath on those who break his law?	NO!
3:9	Are Jews morally superior to Gentiles in God's sight?	NO!
6:1	Should Christians sin more so they can be forgiven more?	NO!
6:15	Should Christians sin because they are not under law but grace?	NO!

ment," Jesus' death on the cross in which he bore the divine wrath that would otherwise have been ours (3:25).[14]

Another important word is "faith." If Christ is the basis and active agent in redemption, then what is the means? How can sinful people lay hold of the salvation Christ has won for them?

In Paul's day, as in ours, several answers to that question are possible. One possibility: "by good works." Before meeting Christ that was Paul's answer. Along with many others of his day and ours, he believed that by doing enough good things he could cancel out bad things. God would forgive Paul if he would earn God's favor by sufficiently honoring God's laws.

But in Romans Paul rejects that answer (3:27–31). Instead he sets forth a new, and at the same time ancient, way. Abraham knew that way (ch. 4). So did David (4:6–8). It is the way of faith. Faith means trust in God's promise to accept those who come to him, admitting their wrongdoing and clinging to the Lord as their only hope for deliverance. As Adam's sin brought calamity on the human race, God's gift of new life in Christ ushers in a new future for all who receive him by faith (5:12–21).

Paul's message is daring. It asserts that salvation is by grace through faith. Humans can do nothing to merit God's acceptance. They can only receive it as a gift, coming before God with the broken spirit evident in Martin Luther's deathbed remark: "We're all beggars, and that's the truth." But Paul's daring message could be misunderstood or distorted, and Paul next takes steps to prevent this.

Those who receive God's grace for their sins must not suppose that it would be good to keep sinning so there would be more grace (6:1–14). Grace means that Christ has entered our lives. This will diminish sin, not promote it. If we love him, we will keep his commandments (Jn 14:21). Next Paul speaks of sanctification (6:19, 22), a word that describes the Christian's increasing obedience to the Lord as faith grows. Grace does not mean that sin is now permissible because the penalty for disobeying God's commands has been lifted (6:15–7:6).

The opposite is the case. Before a person receives Christ, God's commands can have the effect of stirring up the desire to do wrong. Imagine a child playing outdoors who hears a parent call, "I've put fresh cookies in the cookie jar. Now don't touch them!" What temptation will that child probably struggle with? In the same way, our inner human sinfulness tempts us to misuse, ignore, or otherwise exploit God's good commands (7:11). Paul deals extensively with the struggle that Christians wage with sin (7:7–25). (Some think this passage describes those who are not yet Christians, however, and others think that Paul describes those who are in the process of facing their sins and coming to Christ.)

But one thing is clear: Receiving Christ by faith makes a new mode of living possible (8:1–17). Rather than being subject to the natural human spirit with its tendency to turn away from God and his commands, believers receive God's own Spirit (8:4). The divine Spirit's work overrides and transforms the sinful human nature's tendencies and deeds (8:13). The Spirit also gives believers assurance within themselves that they belong to the Lord, as surely as an adopted child belongs to the parents who have taken the child in (8:16).

Romans 8 teaches that salvation extends to the whole of creation—space, time, matter—as well as to the individual soul.

weight of the evil that wracks it. It eagerly awaits the liberation God has promised (8:19–22). Believers groan, too, as they live in the hope (assurance) of a future heavenly age that they can now only glimpse from afar (8:23–25). Even the Holy Spirit shares in the groaning as he hears the prayers of believers pouring out their needs and woes to God (8:26–27).

Yet victory for the Lord and those who seek him is assured, because nothing can thwart his purposes (8:28–39). The Lord will deliver his people, thereby bringing redemption to the whole created order currently marred by sin and suffering. The message of Romans, then, goes beyond personal salvation to include God's ability to bring about the good purposes he has established, not just in hearts but across the reaches of all created matter, space, and time.

The gospel's good news also means that God's word of salvation will prevail in another sense. That is, his promises to his people, Abraham's descendants, will not fail (9:1–6). In Paul's day the question could be raised: How can Jesus have been the Jewish Messiah when so many Jews do not think he was? If Paul is right, doesn't this imply that God's promise to save his people has failed?

Paul's answer: Abrahamic descent is not primarily a matter of ethnicity. To share Abraham's blessedness before God means rather to share Abraham's faith in God (9:8). Paul goes to considerable length to explain that God is true to his promises, that no human action (or inaction) can derail his good purposes, and that God will never reject the people whom he awakens to faith. Romans 9–11 is too rich and complex to discuss at length here, but its general drift is clear: The Lord has not abandoned his people and never will.

God's steadfastness in the face of human fickleness leads Paul to one of the loftiest ascriptions of praise to God ever penned (11:33–36). We have begun to grasp the gospel's good news when it moves us to the same depths of worship and love for God that it did Paul.

The same Spirit who gives assurance, however, also leads God's children into God's service. This will inevitably involve what Paul calls "sufferings" (8:17), and Paul deems these sufferings important enough to treat them at some length.

Prognosis II: Redeemed by Grace (8:18–11:36)

In the previous section we outlined Paul's "prognosis" in terms of the sinner's reception of forgiveness and new life in Christ. Christ's death and resurrection, received by faith, break sin's current stranglehold and eventual penalty. All possible condemnation is removed (8:1).

But the Good News means much more than individual salvation. Paul's further "prognosis" points to a broader redemptive impact by the gospel of grace Paul bears.

The gospel's good news involves believers in the struggle of cosmic battle—a battle that involves the whole created order, seen and unseen—with the Lord ensuring victory. Because of sin's presence in the world, the world is marked by bondage and decay. It groans under the

Prescription (12:1–15:13)

Paul spends the bulk of this lengthy Epistle (chs. 1–11) on issues that are theological more than practical. Why? Is he ad-

Ancient religions practiced animal sacrifice. The gospel calls for believers to offer their lives to God in worship, obedience, and outreach.

adiaphora

dressing a Jew–Gentile dispute in the Roman church? Is he primarily wrestling aloud, so to speak, with theological questions that weigh heavily upon him personally? Did he intend to set forth a sketch of his gospel for its own obvious value in itself? As we noted earlier, the "problem of Romans" concerning just why Paul wrote what he wrote remains unsolved.

But we need not wonder how Paul thought believers should live as a result of the gospel. Their daily lives should reflect the beliefs about Christ that they have embraced. They should present their very bodies wholly to the Lord's service, like an animal presented for sacrifice (12:1–2). Each person is called to place the capacities God gives him or her fully at God's disposal (12:3–8). Paul gives numerous pithy pointers for successful spiritual service, many of them echoes of Jesus' own teachings (12:9–21). He also calls for respect for government authorities, love for others, and understanding of "the present time," a time for devotion to Christ rather than indulgence of self (ch. 13).

Perhaps reflecting tensions among Jews and Gentiles at Rome, Paul deals with what theologians have called ***adiaphora***, or nonessential aspects of Christian practice (ch. 14). He insists that some matters of Christian conduct must be decided by each individual Christian before the Lord. Believers must not judge each other in

such matters but allow freedom for the Holy Spirit to guide as he wishes. Nor should they insist on exercising freedom if it will harm the cause of Christ in the eyes of others. Sometimes freedom means self-restraint for the sake of God's honor and the gospel's progress (14:15–21).

It is important to recall that Paul has in mind items of diet and religious custom here, not matters that Scripture gives clear teaching on. He would not, for example, say that stealing or sexual sin are matters for each Christian to decide about for himself or herself.

Paul concludes the body of Romans as he began it: by pointing to Jesus Christ. He is our example in putting others ahead of ourselves (15:1–7). His work on behalf of Jew and Gentile alike will progress to the lofty destination of which Old Testament Scripture prophesied (15:9–12). Hope, joy, and peace are the benefits that Paul wishes for God's people as a result (15:13).

Conclusion (15:14–16:27)

Romans' conclusion, like its introduction, is unusually long. Paul outlines his unique insight and mission in taking the Good News to the Gentiles (15:14–22) and calls for support of his proposed mission to Spain (15:23–29). He asks the Romans to struggle in prayer along with him (15:30–33). Finally, he passes on numer-

possible "by the command of the eternal God, so that all nations might believe and obey him." At the end of this lengthy Epistle Paul's wonder at God's mercy seems if anything more heartfelt than it did when he began.

Although Paul had not yet visited Rome when he wrote his Epistle to the church there, he greeted dozens of people. Personal ties were important in the early church.

ous greetings to various Roman believers (16:1–16), a warning against troublemakers (16:17–20), and greetings from several of Paul's co-workers who are with him as he writes (16:21–24).

The concluding doxology (16:25–27) ascribes praise to God by recounting the glories of God's saving purposes in Christ as "revealed and made known" in the Old Testament and now proclaimed through the gospel Paul preaches. All this is made

The Importance of Romans

At the beginning of the chapter we spoke of Romans' role in the conversion of a trio of historic figures: Augustine, Martin Luther, and John Wesley. They are by no means the only influential figures who helped change the course of civilization through what was imparted to them by this key Pauline writing.

A twentieth-century example of Romans' influence would be Swiss theologian Karl Barth (1886–1968). Barth's study of this Epistle resulted in a now-famous commentary (1919) that helped break the dominance of liberal theology in many circles in the modern West, at least for a time. Once again, behind theological revolution stood Paul's letter to the Romans.

Focus 18: Where Is Peace?

What does it mean to envision peace?

Some years ago at Du Sable High School, in a rundown section of South Chicago, a school courtyard was rebuilt to create a haven of peace for the larger community, made up of high-rise public housing buildings that look more like prisons. The $850,000 public oasis was to be named the Urban Ecology Sanctuary. It included water pools and a section to mourn the dead featuring a monument to the murdered children of the neighbor-

hood. The school was surrounded by gangs, guns, and ghosts of family and friends snatched away prematurely by acts of violence. Students who had been forced to face loss long before they reached ninth grade were yearning for peace. Their answer: a sanctuary.

In Israel the people are weary of conflicts, bombings, and terrorism. Their folk hero and prime minister of the mid-1990s was trying to find peace through negotiations with the Arabs. Then on November 4, 1995, Yitzhak

Rabin was assassinated. The people in the land of the Bible again cry out for peace, but there is no peace.

In Romans 5:1, Paul makes the message plain: *being justified by faith, we have peace with God through our Lord Jesus Christ.*

Neither peace talks nor man-made sanctuaries will bring lasting peace anywhere in the world. Whether in Chicago or Israel, real peace can be achieved only through the Prince of Peace.

Summary

1. All of the Epistles were written in the first century by men who knew Christ or his close associates personally.

2. Romans was the book that changed the course of the early church through Augustine, the medieval church through Luther, and the eighteenth-century church in England through Wesley.

3. Paul wrote Romans in A.D. 57–58 during a three-month stay in Greece.

4. One of the purposes of Paul's letter to the Romans was to prepare them for his visit prior to his projected journey to Spain.

5. Romans is about the Good News of Jesus Christ.

6. Sinful people receive the salvation made possible by Christ by grace through faith alone.

7. Sharing Abraham's faith in God does not require sharing his ethnicity.

8. Paul provides a clear prescription for Christian living in his Epistle, which addresses worship, the use of gifts, acts of service and hospitality, the role of government, loving one's neighbor, living in the day, and pursuing peace.

Over a century ago two English scholars summarized the Epistle's significance aptly:

> There are few books which it is more difficult to exhaust and few in regard to which there is more to be gained from renewed interpretation by different minds working under different conditions. If it is a historical fact that the spiritual revivals of Christendom have been usually associated with closer study of the Bible, this would be true in an eminent degree of the Epistle to the Romans.[15]

But centuries earlier John Calvin (1509–64) had heaped on Romans perhaps the greatest praise possible: "For when anyone understands this Epistle, he has a passage opened to him to the understanding of the whole Scripture."[16]

Calvin was surely correct. For all the valuable insights contained in Romans itself, it is most important for the entrance it provides into Scripture as a whole, and thereby into personal relationship with God in Christ.

Critical Issues

In addition to the purpose of Romans,[17] several other items have commanded scholarly attention. Foremost among these in recent years has been Paul's view of the law. This is a subset of another, equally important topic that has also provoked discussion: Paul's use of the Old Testament.[18] The question of Paul's view of the law is in part the result of profound questioning of the traditional Christian understanding of the gospel and human need for it. Questions are raised about Paul's relationship to Jesus, his understanding of Judaism, the nature of the message he preached, the function of the law in his theology, and even the very meaning of "law" in Paul's writings.[19]

There is virtually no question about whether Paul wrote the Epistle or what its destination was. The date of Romans and its place in the sequence of Paul's letters and early church history are questioned by some who are rethinking Pauline

Key Places

Cenchreae
Corinth
Egypt
England
Europe
Germany
Great Britain
Greece
Iran
Jerusalem
Nile
Rome
Spain

Key Terms

adiaphora
contextualization
faith

chronology,[20] but to date most scholars are content with a date in the A.D. 57–58 range. Social science theories and methods are being applied to issues of Pauline interpretation generally,[21] with obvious implications for understanding Romans. Oddly, however, in a recent social and cultural analysis of early Christian history, Romans receives almost no mention at all,[22] perhaps the result of social science indifference to the theological concerns that permeate the Epistle from start to finish.

Review Questions

1. Early Christians seemed to have arranged the Pauline letters roughly in the order of their _____.

2. An impetus for the Protestant _____ was the Book of Romans as interpreted by _____.

3. An early church leader who was influenced by Romans was _____.

4. Romans impressed Martin Luther because it taught justification by _____.

5. Paul wrote Romans during a three-month visit to _____.

6. The introductory statement in Romans is called a _____.

7. The darkness of the human condition is important to realize as we learn that Romans is about the _____ of Jesus.

8. When people accept Christ by faith, this makes possible a new _____.

9. When Paul teaches that believers must be free to conduct themselves as they feel is correct, he is not referring to matters of clear scriptural teaching but rather to items of _____ and _____.

10. According to _____, understanding Romans opens an understanding of the entire Scripture.

Study Questions

1. Why do some people find Romans boring? Why do you think others do not?

2. Name two ways that Christianity may have first come to the city of Rome.

3. Where did Paul hope to travel after visiting Rome? What did he intend to do there?

4. How is the greeting of Romans different from the usual greetings in letters of that day?

5. What does Paul say the gospel is, and what does it reveal?

Further Reading

Bockmuehl, Markus. *Jewish Law in Gentile Churches.* Edinburgh: T & T Clark, 2000. Reprinted Grand Rapids: Baker, 2003. Sheds fresh light on how New Testament figures like Paul utilized Jewish teaching in formulating early Christian ethics.

Davies, William D. *Paul and Rabbinic Judaism.* Philadelphia: Fortress, 1980. A seminal work on Paul as a rabbinic thinker.

Donfried, Karl P., ed. *The Romans Debate.* Rev. ed. Peabody, Mass.: Hendrickson, 1991. Anthology of scholarly essays dealing with the "problem" of why Paul wrote Romans.

Godsey, J. D. "The Interpretation of Romans in the History of the Christian Faith." *Interpretation* 34 (1980): 3–16. Surveys the profound impact Romans has had through the course of its history of interpretation.

Longenecker, Richard N. *Paul, Apostle of Liberty.* Grand Rapids: Baker, 1980. A scholarly but readable study of Paul's background, teaching, and practice.

Moo, Douglas J. *Encountering the Book of Romans.* Grand Rapids: Baker, 2002. A user-friendly survey of the entire epistle. Includes bibliography and discussion of contemporary relevance.

Ortlund, Raymond C. *A Passion for God: Prayers and Meditations on the Book of Romans.* Wheaton, Ill.: Crossway, 1994. A book that will bolster understanding of Paul's Roman Epistle—and worship of the Christ Paul preached.

Ridderbos, Herman. *Paul: An Outline of His Theology.* Grand Rapids: Eerdmans, 1975. One of the most thorough recent expositions of Pauline theology.

Schreiner, Thomas R. *Romans.* Grand Rapids: Baker, 1998. An erudite commentary that focuses on the message of Romans.

Seifrid, Mark. *Christ, Our Righteousness: Paul's Theology of Justification.* Downers Grove: InterVarsity, 2001. Thorough study of the Pauline doctrine of justification. Offers helpful correction to the "new perspective" on Paul and defends a Reformation understanding.

Stewart, James S. *A Man in Christ.* Grand Rapids: Baker, 1975. A devout yet scholarly study of Paul's religious thought.

Stuhlmacher, Peter. *Paul's Letter to the Romans.* Louisville: Westminster John Knox, 1994. A fine contemporary commentary on Romans, stressing the Jewish backgrounds, Jesus, and the church.

19 Corinthians and Galatians
Apostolic Counsel for Confused Churches

Objectives

**After reading this chapter,
you should be able to**

- Describe features of the city of Corinth
- Explain why Paul wrote to the Corinthians
- Outline the Book of 1 Corinthians
- Identify the issues Paul deals with in 1 Corinthians
- Outline the Book of 2 Corinthians
- Define the purpose of 2 Corinthians
- Discuss the significance of the Jerusalem collection
- Identify the purpose of Galatians
- Outline the Book of Galatians
- List the key elements of Paul's teaching in Galatians

First and Second Corinthians

The New Testament contains Pauline letters to various cities: EPHESUS, PHILIPPI, COLOSSAE, THESSALONICA, and others. But Paul's lengthiest surviving writings to any single locale consist of a pair of letters to the church in CORINTH.

The Corinthian church holds the dubious distinction of being the most confused congregation, or group of congregations, that Paul addressed. Despite Paul's eighteen-month church-planting labors there (Acts 18:11), the Corinthian believers seemed to have difficulty charting a consistent pattern of Christian belief and lifestyle. In 1 Corinthians Paul must rebuke them for tolerating an incestuous relationship in their midst (5:1). They even took pride in their tolerance of this mischief (5:2)! The overall thrust of 2 Corinthians is to defend the very gospel message itself from being twisted by what Paul calls "false apostles, deceitful workmen, masquerading as apostles of Christ" (11:13).

This suggests that the Corinthian letters are especially suited to give guidance to men and women in today's religiously troubled times. How troubled has religion become? In 1993 the Second Parliament of the World's Religions produced a nine-page summary document that failed to make any mention of God. Devotees of witchcraft were among the conference participants. Another example: In an Illinois prison an inmate filed suit in U.S. District Court because he was denied the right to worship in the prison chapel—naked. The inmate claimed that nude worship was required for members of "Technicians of the Sacred," a religion founded in 1983.

The problems at Corinth were not always so extreme, but sometimes they came close. Paul's counsel to the believers there is among the most fascinating and challenging of all his writings.

The City of Corinth

Corinth was the largest city in first-century GREECE, serving as capital of the Roman province of ACHAIA. It prospered due to its location on a narrow (about 3.5 miles wide) neck of land, or isthmus, between seas to the east and west. Most shipping heading to or from Rome passed through Corinth. Cargo was unloaded on one side

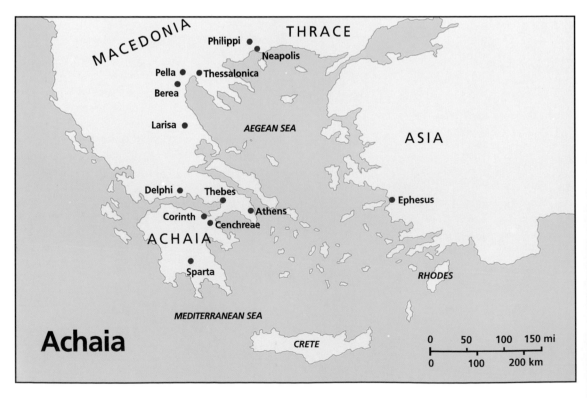

Achaia

In the middle of this great bay is Cenchreae, the harbor for ancient Corinth, where Paul took a boat for Ephesus.

bema

of the isthmus, transported across, and reloaded onto another boat on the other side. Small boats with intact cargo may have been skidded across on a path constructed for that purpose. Corinth was thus an important center of commercial and social interchange.

Corinth was famous not only for its bustling trade and wealth but also for its immorality.[1] Greco-Roman sexual practices, never lofty by biblical standards, descended to remarkable lows in the form of extensive and lucrative prostitution. This activity was sometimes part of pagan worship and may help explain the sexual excesses among the Corinthian believers: Paul mentions that prior to their conversion to Christ, some of the Corinthians had been "sexually immoral," "idolaters," "adulterers," "male prostitutes," and "homosexual offenders" (1 Cor 6:9, 11). Through Christ, however, there was liberation from such dehumanizing practices.

There was a sizable Jewish presence in Corinth, and it likely grew larger after the Roman emperor CLAUDIUS expelled Jews from ROME in A.D. 49 (Acts 18:2). It was in a Jewish synagogue that Paul began to preach Christ, teaming up with Jewish Christians from Rome named Aquila and Priscilla. They were tentmakers like Paul, who in his younger days like most Phar-

isees learned not only rabbinic theology but a practical trade.

Founding of Christianity in Corinth

Acts 18:1–18 tells in more detail how there came to be a Christian assembly in such a raucous city. Paul arrived in Corinth during his second missionary journey after preaching in Philippi, Thessalonica, BEREA, and ATHENS (see map on p. 243). When he had worn out his welcome at the synagogue, Paul and those who had believed moved next door to a private home. The synagogue ruler, however, was among the many who had embraced Paul's proclamation of Christ (Acts 18:7–8).

When the Roman official GALLIO assumed power in about A.D. 51,[2] hostile Jews brought Paul before him for prosecution. Gallio refused to try the case, then stood idly by as Paul's angry Jewish enemies took out their frustration on a Christian named SOSTHENES, whom they beat in full view of the judicial platform on which Gallio stood.

Archaeologists have uncovered this platform, or *bema*, which has been termed "one of the clearest links between Corinth's archaeology and Scripture."[3] Another link between Paul's time in

Letters between Paul and the Corinthians

The New Testament contains two letters from Paul to the Corinthians. But these are only two of a larger collection of writings that passed between the apostle and the church.

1. An initial letter from Paul to the Corinthians, now lost (1 Cor 5:9)
2. A letter from the Corinthians to Paul (1 Cor 7:1)
3. Paul's reply to their letter—our 1 Corinthians
4. A subsequent "painful letter" (2 Cor 2:3; 7:8) from Paul to the Corinthians
5. A third letter from Paul to the Corinthians— our 2 Corinthians

1 and 2 Corinthians in Early Church History

One or more of the Corinthian letters seem to have been known by such early church leaders as:

	A.D.
Clement of Rome	95
Polycarp	ca. 110
Justin Martyr	ca. 140
Irenaeus	ca. 175
Clement of Alexandria	ca. 200
Tertullian	ca. 200
Origen	ca. 250
Eusebius	ca. 315

Corinth and archaeological data is the ERASTUS inscription. This consists of a large limestone slab dating to Paul's time and bearing the message, "Erastus in return for his appointment as city treasurer laid [the pavement] at his own expense."[4] It is likely that this is the same Erastus whom Paul mentions in Romans 16:23 when, writing from the Corinth vicinity, he speaks of Erastus, "the city's director of public works."

Letters to and from Corinth

It is always challenging to interpret Paul's letters because they represent only one side of a two-sided communication process. We must infer from what Paul says to what we think the Corinthians were saying or doing. (This is sometimes called "mirror reading.") The Corinthian letters present a particular challenge since what we call 1 Corinthians may actually be Paul's second letter to them. In that case 1 Corinthians 5:9 could be translated "I wrote you in my letter" and may refer to an earlier letter, to which the Corinthians then replied in a letter to Paul (1 Cor 7:1). This would make 1 Corinthians the third component of a larger exchange. If, as some think, 2 Corinthians 2:3 and 7:8 refer to a "painful letter" that is not 1 Corinthians, then 2 Corinthians becomes the fifth letter between Paul and the church at Corinth.

The point is that 1 and 2 Corinthians are pieces in a larger and sometimes complex puzzle. Much of what they say is clear, but some is obscured by our ignorance of all that passed between Paul and his audience. We should not be surprised if there are statements or ideas in these letters whose full meaning we sometimes cannot quite penetrate.

First Corinthians

Author, Date, Place of Writing

Paul's authorship of 1 Corinthians (see 1 Cor 1:1) is virtually undisputed in both ancient and modern times. It may be among the letters mentioned by Peter in 2 Peter 3:16, and CLEMENT OF ROME speaks of it in about A.D. 95. Second-century figures like IGNATIUS, MARCION, and IRENAEUS were also familiar with 1 Corinthians. Paul wrote it during his two- or three-year ministry in Ephesus (Acts 19:10; 1 Cor 16:8, 19), or around A.D. 55. This was during his third missionary journey.

Why Paul Wrote

During his ministry in Ephesus Paul received word by way of three prominent members of the Corinthian congregation, Stephanas, Fortunatus, and Achaicus (1 Cor 16:17). Their urgent message: The Corinthian congregation was being torn apart by quarreling (1 Cor 1:11). Dissatis-

faction had arisen regarding Paul's authority (1 Cor 4:3). Paul anticipated having to make a visit to address the complaints (1 Cor 4:19). The distance from Ephesus to Corinth was over 250 miles by boat—not a casual junket. Apparently Paul could not make it immediately upon hearing of the problems. So he wrote (or dictated: 1 Cor 16:21 may mark the point at which Paul enters his own closing words, someone else having penned the rest as Paul spoke) a lengthy letter to quell the disturbance and give positive guidance in his absence. He sent Timothy to them to deliver the letter (1 Cor 4:17). The details that Paul took up are evident from the following outline.

Outline

I. Epistolary Introduction (1:1–9)

II. Paul's Response to Reports about the Community at Corinth (1:10–6:20)
- A. A Report of Factions within the Community (1:10–4:20)
- B. A Report of Immorality, Arrogance, and Improper Judgments (5:1–6:20)

III. Paul's Response to Questions from the Corinthians (7:1–16:4)
- A. Questions about Marriage, Divorce, and Celibacy (7:1–40)
- B. Questions about Food, Idolatry, and Freedom (8:1–11:1)
- C. Questions about Worship, Gifts, and Order (11:2–14:40)
- D. Questions about the Resurrection and Life in the Age to Come (15:1–58)
- E. Questions about the Collection and Paul's Plans (16:1–9)

IV. The Recommendation of Others (16:10–18)

V. Final Greetings and Formal Closing (16:19–24)

Message

Paul gives specific counsel about a number of issues, and these will be considered in the next section. But his specific directives are based on an overarching premise: the truth of the cross-centered gospel he preached. He communicates this basic message in the first four chapters, after which he turns to particular matters.

Paul commends the Corinthians for their initial reception of the gospel, and thanks God for the gospel's work among them (1:4–9). But they are now bitterly divided (1:10–12). Paul implies that this is the result of heeding human rather than divine wisdom (1:18–31). They have preferred the way of the "wise man," "the scholar," or "the philosopher" rather than the way of God in Christ (1:20). Paul calls them back to the gospel they first received. He calls them back to the real cause of their salvation, Jesus Christ (1:30)—not their own cleverness or strength or social standing (1:26). And he underscores the scandal of the gospel of Jesus Christ, which Jews rejected because they couldn't accept the doctrine of a crucified Messiah, and which Greeks rejected because the notion of an atoning death and bodily resurrection seemed absurd (1:23; cf. Acts 17:32). There is no way around this scandal. It cannot be bent into a less jagged shape and marketed in a more pleasing form. It would no longer be the gospel. It would no longer be the true message about Jesus Christ as established from the beginning by God in his wisdom and kindness.

The Corinthians had departed from Paul's instruction, apparently because ideas current in their own social setting appeared to make better sense. But in seeking to refine the gospel they were moving it onto different foundations. Paul responds, "No one can lay any foundation other than the one already laid, which is Jesus Christ" (3:11). They needed to become "foolish" once more, respecting God's truth instead of opting for worldly wisdom (3:18). They needed to reaffirm

that Jesus Christ, crucified and risen, was their hope and their Lord, and to stop promoting divisive alterations of the apostolic message.

Specific Issues

Paul's rather sharp opening statements eventually climax in a grave specific charge: The Corinthians are giving their blessing to open sexual immorality in the church (5:1). Paul calls on them to expel the offender (5:13) in the hope that he will repent. They should be tolerant of rank sinners who are outside the church and firm when dealing with each other "in house" rather than vice versa.

Next Paul treats a series of questions that the Corinthian messenger party (16:17) brought with it. These include questions about marriage, divorce, and celibacy (ch. 7); questions about diet, idolatry, and personal Christian freedom (chs. 8–10); questions about worship, spiritual gifts, and congregational order (chs. 11–14); and questions about resurrection and the age to come (ch. 15). Paul's answers are lengthy and sometimes difficult to understand

Spiritual Gifts Today?

"Eagerly desire spiritual gifts," Paul writes in 1 Corinthians 14:1. He lists a number of them in various passages (Rom 12; 1 Cor 12; Eph 4). How did people obtain these gifts? Are they still valid today?

The word "gift" in Greek is related to the word "grace." When people hear and respond to the gospel of God's "grace" in Christ, they receive a spiritual "gift." The gifts vary, but they are all meant to be used for the good of others (1 Cor 12:7) rather than for selfish purposes.

Controversy surrounds the use of a few of the gifts, such as tongues, prophecy, healing, and miraculous powers. Interpreters disagree on what these gifts consisted of and how they were exercised in the early church. Some claim that all of the apostolic-age gifts are still available today by faith. Others insist that God

granted them during the early decades of the church but subsequently allowed them to die out, just as some of Jesus' miracles (like walking on water) seem to have been limited to Jesus' own ministry. They were given to verify his message rather than to suggest that his followers ought to walk on water themselves.

Whatever view we take of the gifts, we should bear in mind that the virtues of faith, hope, and love are greater still (1 Cor 13:13). The center of Christian ministry is God's gospel, not our gifts. We should not deny our sovereign God the right to do wondrous deeds today as he sees fit. But we should avoid falling prey to the Corinthian syndrome of letting Christian self-expression stray from the sound doctrinal basis Paul insists on. The gospel's focus is on service to others and clear communication of gospel truth (1 Cor 14:19).

Corinth, looking southwest into the Peloponnese.

Paul's theology as reflected in the teaching he lays down on the various points mentioned in the previous section.

Because Paul's view of the law has dominated critical discussion in recent years, his references to the law in 1 (and 2) Corinthians have come in for renewed scrutiny. The so-called charismatic movement, a powerful force in world Christianity since the 1960s, has resulted in fresh attention to Paul's teachings on spiritual gifts and public worship (1 Cor 12–14). Passages like 1 Corinthians 11:2–16 and 14:33b–36 have attracted the attention of feminist interpreters, who have accused Paul of "inarticulate, incomprehensible, and inconsistent" assertions in 1 Corinthians 11,[5] and who suggest that Paul did not write 1 Corinthians 14:33b–36 at all.[6] These verses are instead alleged to be later additions to 1 Corinthians by an unknown editor. Both claims are vigorously challenged,[7] sometimes even by scholars who hold feminist views themselves.[8]

Second Corinthians

Setting and Purpose

If Paul wrote 1 Corinthians in about A.D. 55, slightly past the midpoint of his third missionary journey (A.D. 52–57; see map on p. 244), then 2 Corinthians can be dated perhaps a year later. The exchanges of letters between Paul and Corinth, and the visits there by Paul's aides and Paul himself, make an interesting but lengthy and complicated story. It is told well elsewhere.[9] For our purposes we need only note that 1 Corinthians, and Timothy's visit to Corinth to deliver it, did not bring about the good effects Paul hoped. The situation worsened.

It is likely that Paul himself paid a "painful visit" (2 Cor 2:1) to Corinth after Timothy's unsuccessful mission. But he, too, was apparently rebuffed. Rather than press matters to the breaking point he departed, following up his personal presence with a sternly worded letter delivered by Titus (2 Cor 2:3–9; 7:8–12). By this time the concluding months of his third missionary journey had taken Paul to MACEDONIA, far to the north of Ephesus, where he eagerly awaited word from Titus as to how the Corinthians would respond to his stern letter (2 Cor 7:5–7). The word was positive,

today. But their general drift is clear. Christ's example, and his ongoing instruction through Scripture, the apostles, and the Spirit, require that the Corinthians shape up. They need to trust and follow through on the direction God has given them instead of wandering off rebelliously in dangerous directions.

Prior to closing Paul reminds them of an ongoing collection they are supposed to be taking (16:1–4). This fund, the so-called Jerusalem collection, was an offering by (generally poor) Gentile churches for the Jewish Christians in Palestine, many of whom were suffering hardship because of professing Christ as Messiah (see 1 Thes 2:14; Heb 10:33–34). This collection becomes a central issue in 2 Corinthians 8–9.

Critical Issues

Scholars debate a number of issues related to 1 Corinthians. These include the identity of Paul's opponents and the nature of their views, the Epistle's literary unity, and

*theologia
gloriae*

theologia crucis

via dolorosa

and chapters 1–9 of 2 Corinthians reflect Paul's euphoria that the Corinthians seem to have begun mending their ways.

Paul's tone shifts, however, beginning in chapter 10. It has been suggested that the writing of 2 Corinthians took weeks, owing in part to Paul's travels, and that in the course of writing he learned of fresh difficulties at Corinth brought on by new and dangerous teachers. This would explain Paul's altered tone and urgent warnings, though other explanations are possible, and all explanations are hard pressed to answer the full range of questions that can be raised.[10]

In sum, Paul writes 2 Corinthians to praise the Corinthians for their progress, warn them of new threats, and prepare them for a third visit by Paul (13:1). At that time Paul will settle the issues raised by the false teachers, though he hopes to avoid being harsh (13:10). He and his associates will also take charge of the monies that have accumulated for the Christians in JUDEA, the so-called Jerusalem collection (chs. 8–9).

Outline

I. Epistolary Introduction (1:1–11)

II. Paul's Explanation of His Conduct in Recent Matters (1:12–2:13)
  A. The Basis for Paul's Behavior and an Appeal for Understanding (1:12–14)
  B. The Cause for Paul's Change of Plans (1:15–2:2)
  C. The Purpose of Paul's Last Letter (2:3–11)
  D. The Motive for Paul's Movement from Troas to Macedonia (2:12–13)

III. Paul's Reflection upon His Ministry (2:14–5:21)
  A. The Source and Character of Paul's Ministry (2:14–3:6a)
  B. The Message of Paul's Ministry (3:6b–4:6)
  C. The Cost of Paul's Ministry (4:7–5:10)
  D. The Perspective of Paul's Ministry (5:11–21)

IV. Paul's Appeal to the Corinthians (6:1–13:10)

  A. An Appeal for Complete Reconciliation (6:1–7:4)
  B. A New Basis for Appeal (7:5–16)
  C. An Appeal for Full Response to the Collection (8:1–9:15)
  D. An Appeal for Full Allegiance to Apostolic Authority (10:1–18)
  E. Support for the Appeal (11:1–12:13)
  F. The Conclusion of the Appeal (12:14–13:10)

V. Epistolary Conclusion (13:11–14)

Message

The flow of thought in 2 Corinthians is not always easy to follow. One scholar notes, "1 Corinthians has a clear line of argument from beginning to end. But 2 Corinthians often reads more like an anthology of Paul's advice on different subjects."[11] "Advice" may be too weak a word for the tone Paul adopts. But it is true that 2 Corinthians covers many subjects, making numerous dips and turns along the way.

Yet there is a consistent underlying theme: The way to glory is the way of the cross. Theologians sometimes speak of two very different understandings of the gospel—one that yields a *theologia gloriae* (theology of glory) and another that results in a *theologia crucis* (theology of the cross). Judging from Paul's letters, the Corinthians had adopted a *theologia gloriae*. This means that they viewed Christ primarily as a means of self-betterment, the way to success, the way to power and affirmation by peers. This is one reason there were factions at Corinth: Their underlying theology put themselves at the center of things rather than Christ. But not everyone can be at the center. Rivalries were the inevitable result.

Paul, however, lived and taught a different gospel. It was a means of self-betterment and success, to be sure, but its central symbol was a sign of suffering and death: the cross.[12] In service to Christ, the way to true glory—"glory" that elevates the Lord, not man—is often the *via dolorosa*, the way of suffering. A quick survey of the Epistle confirms this: Paul commends troubles and suffering that result from knowing Christ from the opening verses (1:3–7). He speaks of the constructive outcome of the perils he faced in Ephesus (1:8–10). He talks of the travail of the apostolic ministry, in which those who know life in Christ "are always being given over to death for Jesus' sake, so that his life may be revealed" in them (4:11). He cites his sufferings as evidence of the legitimacy of his ministry (6:4–10). He commends "godly sorrow" to the Corinthians as a painful but necessary stage in growing closer to the Lord (7:9–10). Paul's boast is his weakness (11:30), and his delight is in "insults, in hardships, in persecutions, in difficulties" (12:10). Why? "For when I am weak, then I am strong" (12:10).

Paul is not saying that suffering is good or that he enjoys it, but that declaring Christ as Lord means handing oneself over to responsibilities and sometimes griefs that could otherwise be avoided. Paul understood that following Jesus meant saying no to self (see Lk 9:23), that the way to find one's life was to lose it (Jn 12:25). Too many of the Corinthians, or their leaders, had other ideas. The overall message of 2 Corinthians challenges the self-serving nature of their outlook and exhorts them to examine themselves to see whether they are really in the true faith at all (2 Cor 13:5).

Apostolic Authority

Paul's stress on a *theologia crucis* is a matter of the *content* of his message. But 2 Corinthians, and to some extent 1 Corinthians too, deals with the equally fundamental question of the *authority* of his message. In other words, who speaks for God? As we will see below in considering Galatians, Paul regularly met challenges to his claim that the gospel he preached, in the form he and others of the apostolic circle preached it, was necessarily true. (Jesus, we may recall, met similar challenges; see Lk 20:2.) At Corinth this challenge reaches its high point: We know of no other church that so roundly set aside Paul's insight as inferior to its own. This is why Paul directly commends the message that he bore (1 Cor 2:1–16; 2 Cor 5:11–21) and the apostolic ministry generally (see 1 Cor 4:9–13; 2 Cor 2:14–3:12; 4:1–18; 10:1–11). In the end, however, Paul is not commending himself. He is rather ensuring the salvation of his hearers by refusing to tamper with the message that Jesus Christ passed on to his chosen envoys (2 Cor 12:19).

Today, when public figures and publications regularly discount, and sometimes ridicule, the truth claims of the Christian faith,[13] Christians need to recall that the

The Roman governor Gallio stood at this site to hear complaints about Paul's ministry.

core teachings of their faith have always been under fire.[14] In 2 Corinthians Paul provides a sobering reminder that sometimes even "the church" can lose its appetite for orthodoxy (true biblical teaching and practice). If this took place in the apostolic era, it is no wonder that novel interpretations of the gospel, and sometimes outright heresies, have been part of church history through the centuries, right down to the present hour.

The Jerusalem Collection

The financial assistance by Gentile churches for Jewish churches in Palestine (2 Cor 8–9) was one of the crown jewels of Paul's ministry. Jew–Gentile animosities were at least as active and deadly as racial or ethnic tensions anywhere in the world today. Pogroms (violent attempts to exterminate the Jewish population of a city or region) were not unknown. It would have been easy for Paul in Gentile areas to cater to negative Gentile assumptions about the Jews, especially when Jews so consistently snubbed or opposed the ministry of Paul and the Gentile churches.

Instead, Paul prayed and lobbied for churches from Macedonia to Achaia to ASIA to set aside money regularly for alleviation of the physical needs of Jewish Christians in PALESTINE—the hotbed of resistance to the Pauline churches. This amounted to a living object lesson illustrating several profound theological truths: the virtue of doing good to those who persecute you (Lk 6:27–28); the oneness of Jew and Gentile in Christ (Eph 2:11–22); the interdependence of Jew and Gentile in the forward progress of the kingdom Jesus announced (Rom 11:13–24).

Paul's conviction was that God could use such kindness to melt hardened Jewish hearts to receive Jesus as their Messiah (Rom 11:14). The strategy he adopted still has its applications in modern times.

Critical Issues

Scholarly debate surrounding 2 Corinthians is dominated by theories about its literary unity. Because Paul's tone and focus vary, some have suggested that the Epistle is a compilation of various segments of letters that Paul wrote. From here it is only a short move to the further suggestion of

a few that parts of 2 Corinthians are not from Paul at all but were inserted by later writers. Such theories are interesting, but all ancient copies of the Epistle contain it in its present form. There are no compelling reasons to deny that it is a unit, written by Paul in the form it has appeared in Bibles through the centuries.[15]

There is also debate centering on Paul's opponents in 2 Corinthians, the effect of social and rhetorical movements on the Corinthian congregation and its leaders, and the contribution of 2 Corinthians to our overall knowledge of Paul's life and theology. It cannot be said that the Epistle is at the center of current discussion, but its importance should not be underestimated: 2 Corinthians 10–13 has been called "the most intense, revealing, and emotional of all [Paul's] writings."[16]

Galatians

"Drivers Ignoring Red Lights," shouts a recent newspaper headline. In Boston, in Washington, in Philadelphia, basic traffic rules are flaunted. A Massachusetts traffic engineer calls it "total anarchy." Officials fear for public safety unless respect for law can be restored.

Law is important in many areas of life. For Christians it is even important in religion. This is because the Bible reveals a God who expresses his character and will in commandments. True, he also expresses them in other ways, like narrative and proverbs and poetry. Yet his laws—from the Ten Commandments to the commandments given by Jesus and his apostles—are central to knowing and honoring him.

But when does a high regard for God's law become an unhealthy fixation with rules? When does obedience to commandments threaten to substitute for personal relationship with the God who gives the commandments?

Paul's letter to the Galatians takes up these and other questions.

South Galatia or North Galatia?

On Paul's first missionary journey (see map on page 297), he and Barnabas led an evangelistic thrust from SYRIAN ANTIOCH

South Galatian
theory

North Galatian
theory

Galatians in Early Church History

Galatians appears to have been known and used by such early church leaders as:

	A.D.
Clement of Rome	95
Polycarp	ca. 110
Justin Martyr	ca. 140
Irenaeus	ca. 175
Clement of Alexandria	ca. 200
Tertullian	ca. 200
Origen	ca. 250
Eusebius	ca. 315

Many scholars conclude that Paul's Galatian Epistle is addressed to these congregations. They suggest that Paul wrote the letter to give guidance on issues that arose after he and Barnabas visited and established churches. These scholars note that GALATIA in the first century was the name for the Roman province in CENTRAL ASIA MINOR that extended south almost to the MEDITERRANEAN. As maps in the back of most modern Bibles show, Galatia included the towns of Pisidian Antioch, Iconium, Lystra, and Derbe. Scholars who think that Galatians is addressed to these southern Galatian towns spoken of in Acts 13–14 are said to hold the **South Galatian theory.**

to the island of CYPRUS (Acts 13:1–13), then northward to the mainland of what is now TURKEY. There they preached in a number of cities and villages: PERGA, PISIDIAN ANTIOCH, ICONIUM, LYSTRA, and DERBE (Acts 13:13–14:25).

Many scholars, however, take another view, suggesting that Paul wrote to a different set of towns in north-central Asia Minor. This is called the **North Galatian theory.** These two theories result in different dates and places of origin for the Epistle. They also result in different understandings of how Galatians relates to Acts.[17]

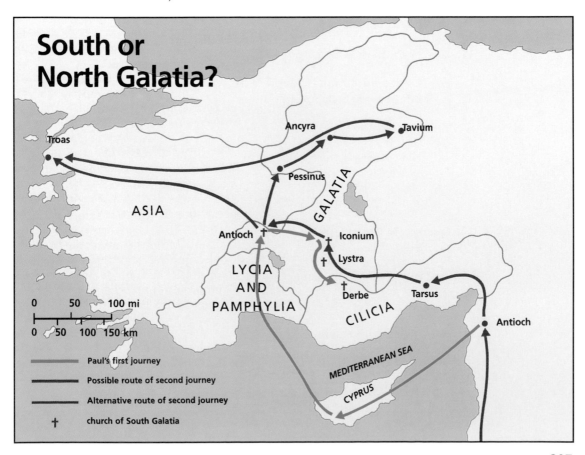

South or North Galatia?

Troas

Ancyra
Tavium

Pessinus

ASIA

GALATIA

Antioch †

Iconium
† Lystra
†

LYCIA
AND
PAMPHYLIA

† Derbe   Tarsus

CILICIA

Antioch

MEDITERRANEAN SEA

CYPRUS

0	50	100 mi

0	50	100	150 km

Paul's first journey
Possible route of second journey
Alternative route of second journey
† church of South Galatia

Technical discussion of this problem is available elsewhere.[18] Below we follow a "South Galatian" approach because we feel that it best accounts for all the literary, historical, geographical, and archaeological evidence.[19]

Outline

I. Introduction (1:1–10)
  A. Salutation (1:1–5)
  B. Occasion for Writing (1:6–9)
  C. Review of Accusations (1:10)

II. Paul and the Nature of His Apostleship (1:11–2:21)
  A. Preconversion Days (1:11–14)
  B. Conversion (1:15–17)
  C. First Meeting with Jerusalem Leadership (1:18–24)
  D. Second Meeting with Jerusalem Leadership (2:1–10)
  E. Correcting Cephas (2:11–21)

III. Treatise: The Efficacy of Grace over Law (3:1–4:7)
  A. The Argument from Experience (3:1–5)
  B. The Argument from Scripture (3:6–18)
  C. The Purpose of the Law (3:19–25)
  D. The Results of Faith (3:26–29)
  E. Maturing into Sonship (4:1–7)

IV. An Appeal to the Galatians (4:8–31)
  A. An Appeal to Maturity (4:8–11)
  B. An Appeal to Their Personal Relationship (4:12–20)
  C. An Allegorical Appeal (4:21–31)

V. Freedom in Christ (5:1–6:10)
  A. Thesis (5:1)
  B. Warnings and Reproof (5:2–12)
  C. Proof of One's Grounding (5:13–26)
  D. Practical Ethics (6:1–10)

VI. Conclusion with Personal Appeal (6:11–18)

Purpose

We stated earlier that controversy surrounds the exact date and destination of the Galatian Epistle. The purpose of the letter, however, is not in much doubt.

Paul writes to call a group of churches in Galatia (1:2) back to the gospel they have suddenly deserted (1:6). The new "gospel" they have embraced is really no gospel at all (1:7). The true gospel, the one Paul preached and they accepted, came through Jesus Christ by revelation directly to Paul (1:12). It is the same gospel preached by the other apostles (2:7–9). This means that altered versions of it must necessarily be unacceptable distortions. Not even angelic visions, or a different message from Paul himself, should entice the Galatians to exchange their earlier faith for a substantially revised one (1:8).

But Paul's purpose is not merely to rebuke and admonish. As the outline above indicates, he takes pains to give reasons for his warnings. He carefully describes the process by which he was granted the gift of apostleship, thus validating the truth of his message (1:11–21). He explains the relation between grace and law (3:1–4:7). He gives extended counsel on how the Christian life is to be lived (chs. 5–6).

Paul's purpose in writing, then, is both specific and broad. It is specific in its insistence that to accept altered views of the apostolic message about Jesus Christ is to nullify the whole Christian faith. It is broad in the range of arguments Paul musters and in the applications to faith and life he makes.

True and False Gospel

If Paul's purpose in writing is to oppose a false gospel, what is the true gospel? This is where Acts' account of Paul's preaching in Galatia becomes useful (Acts 13–14). Acts does not record all that Paul and Barnabas said on the first missionary journey, but it does record in some detail the main points of an entire Pauline sermon at Pisidian Antioch in the southwest corner of Galatia (Acts 13:16–41). We may take this sermon as illustrative of Paul's gospel message in Galatia generally.

Paul's basic claims are these: (1) The God of Israel, the true and living God, has from ancient times been at work saving a people from their sins so they may worship him and be a redemptive presence in the world. This saving work stretches back to

Remains of a Roman aqueduct at Pisidian Antioch, in Galatia.

Abraham and down through Moses, Samuel, and David (Acts 13:16–22). (2) David's descendant Jesus, announced by John the Baptist, is the Savior sent from God (Acts 13:23–25). (3) The message that salvation lies in Jesus has been entrusted to Jews like Paul as well as to non-Jews who will receive it. While many Jews rejected Jesus, even pressing for his execution, God raised him from the dead and caused him to appear alive to many witnesses (Acts 13:26–31). (4) Not only living witnesses but also the writings of Old Testament prophets attest to the good news that there is salvation in Jesus Christ whom God raised from the dead (Acts 13:32–37). (5) Therefore, all who hear the message about Jesus are urged to receive it and be joined to God's people. They are also sternly warned not to scoff at the gospel message, as far-fetched as it may sound to the ears of its detractors (like Paul before his conversion) and to those hearing it for the first time (Acts 13:38–42).

Virtually all of the points of Paul's sermon in Acts 13 are echoed in Galatians. For example, in summing up the gospel that the Galatians originally received Paul says, "Before your very eyes Jesus Christ was clearly portrayed as crucified" (3:1), a clear reference to his death for sins. In Galatians, as in Acts 13, Paul refers repeatedly to Abraham, mentioning him eight times in Galatians 3 alone.

We conclude, then, that the true gospel Paul preached centered on Jesus Christ's atoning death, foretold by Old Testament prophets. In light of the cross, all need to rely fully on Christ's self-sacrifice for salvation and new life, just as Abraham relied on God's promise in times of old (see, e.g., 3:6–14).

But what, then, was the false gospel? To answer this question we must consider the agitators against whom Paul directs many of his comments.

Misguided Leadership

After Paul and Barnabas preached in various Galatian towns and returned to their sending church in Syrian Antioch (Acts 14:26), the Galatian churches apparently gave in to pressure from "agitators" (Gal 5:12) whose understanding of salvation differed from what Paul preached. These shadowy figures, whom Paul did not need to name specifically since they were well known to his readers, are the key to understanding the false gospel that Paul opposes in his Galatian Epistle.

Once again information from Acts 13–14 comes into play. Paul's sermon at Antioch in PISIDIA (Acts 13:15–41) met a positive response from both Jews and "devout converts" alike (Acts 13:43). A "devout convert" was a non-Jew who accepted Jewish faith and practice, yet without becoming a proselyte (full convert), which for males involved circumcision. "Devout converts" therefore retained the legal status of Gen-

Judaizers

tile or pagan but were involved in Jewish worship. Acts refers to devout converts (literally "God-fearers" or "God worshipers") repeatedly (10:2, 22; 13:16, 26, 43, 50; 16:14; 17:4, 17; 18:7).

But there was also negative response to Paul's message. Jews who were not convinced by the gospel stirred up opposition to Paul and Barnabas in Pisidian Antioch (Acts 13:45, 50). This same opposition arose in Iconium (14:2), where Paul and Barnabas narrowly escaped a plot to silence them by stoning (14:5). They moved on to Lystra and Derbe and won many converts. But Jews from Antioch and Iconium dogged their steps and rallied a mob against them. Paul was stoned and left for dead (Acts 14:19). Many years later, near the end of his life, the memory of those tumultuous days was still fresh in Paul's mind (2 Tm 3:11).

Relief of a Roman lawyer. Paul contrasts grace and law in the Galatian Epistle.

As Paul writes his Epistle to the Gentile churches, it appears that the wrath of those who opposed Paul and Barnabas has been transferred to the new communities of faith that Paul and Barnabas founded and left behind (Acts 14:23). He writes that "some people are throwing you into confusion and are trying to pervert the gospel of Christ" (Gal 1:7). He rebukes the folly of those who follow this perverted gospel, calling them "bewitched" (3:1). The gospel of Jesus Christ had freed them from pagan gods as well as Jewish traditions that could not save them (4:8–11). But now they have fallen prey to treacherous leaders with a false message. "Those people are zealous to win you over," Paul writes, "but for no good" (4:17).

Specifically, it appears that the agitators were insisting that salvation required strict adherence to Jewish customs like circumcision (6:12). (Scholars sometimes call these agitators **Judaizers** because their message centered on combining aspects of the Christian message with Jewish practices to which they required even Gentiles to submit.) Paul is so distraught by this that he writes, "As for those agitators, I wish they would . . . emasculate themselves!" (5:12).

Why is Paul so upset?

Grace and Law

At the center of the Galatian Epistle is the truth that salvation is God's free gift. It is not earned by human merit. Christ has come to free people from the tyranny of moral or religious self-justification (5:1). Christ's death is what justifies people before God, not the effort they expend to live up to God's standards (3:11–13). Galatians has been called the Magna Carta of Christian liberty because of its stress on freedom from a performance-based approach to pleasing God.

Galatians was central to the Protestant Reformation with its reassertion of the sole sufficiency of divine grace to liberate the imprisoned human will.[20] To rely on rules, even the Old Testament law that Paul elsewhere praises (Rom 7:12), is to abandon the gospel's message of grace (Gal 5:4).

Paul is disturbed, then, because the Galatian churches seem on the verge of falling away from the faith Paul preached to them (5:4). At stake is not Paul's personal feelings and authority but the integrity of the Galatians' beliefs and ultimately the eternal destiny of their souls.

Paul's love for them is intense (4:19–20). Understandably, so is his concern for the soundness of the faith they profess. Paul, like his master Jesus, was concerned not merely *that* people have a religious experience. He was also concerned with *what* the substance of their beliefs was. This is why Paul in his letters, like Jesus in his daily ministry, spent so much time teaching. Contrary to some modern understandings of "faith," the content of *what* is believed matters. Erroneous beliefs can signal failure to grasp, or refusal to accept, who Jesus Christ really is and how profoundly the sinner is dependent on Christ's saving work. Paul sensed that the Galatian churches were sliding into a belief system in which the truth of Jesus Christ and the nature of the salvation he offers were being obscured. These were the very truths for which Christ had died and Paul had practically been killed! No wonder he writes with frankness and ardor.

Positive Ethic

Paul insists that salvation is by grace, not by human merit. Just as Abraham received God's promise through no merit of his own, so do believers who become Abraham's children, so to speak, when they receive the gospel by faith (3:6–9).

But it would be a mistake to conclude that obeying God is no longer important because salvation is through faith, not good works. Paul opposes works when viewed as the Galatian false teachers viewed them: as deeds that earn salvation. But he upholds works viewed as "faith expressing itself through love" (5:6). When a person believes the gospel, Christ enters that person's life and begins to change it (2:20). Christ's Spirit bears the fruit of attitudes and deeds like "love, joy, peace, patience, kindness,

Social Gospel?

"Do good to all people," Paul writes (Gal 6:10). Does this mean that Christians should be concerned mainly with preaching the gospel? Or should they also be working for social improvement?

Protestant teaching has traditionally tended to stress gospel preaching. In this view the world will improve only as more people are transformed by accepting Christ. At times this view has led to neglect of the poor, indifference to people's material needs, and silence in the realm of public policy where mass resources for relief are often allocated. (Stephen Carter's *The Culture of Disbelief* [New York: Basic, 1993] makes some of this silence in modern times understandable: The prevailing social welfare agenda intentionally rules out the Bible's prescriptions for addressing society's ills. Christians are then silent—because they have been silenced.)

In the nineteenth century the view that humankind could be perfected through change in society spread. An optimistic view of man and his upwardly evolving social state became popular. At times preaching the gospel of Christ's cross was replaced by social work activities and educational, economic, and political strategies. The "social gospel" movement was born and still flourishes today.

If apostolic writers like Paul are our guides, we dare not minimize the centrality of individual repentance and faith in Christ. But Paul also writes that Christians should *"do good to all people, especially to those who belong to the family of believers"* (Gal 6:10). This means helping people, all people, in practical ways, not just preaching to them.

Groups like the Salvation Army seek to combine gospel ministry and social relief so that the two flow together. Many churches are now following suit, and mission agencies around the world recognize that to get a hearing for the Christian message it is important to address physical needs.

antinomian

goodness, faithfulness, gentleness and self-control" (5:22–23). With a hint of irony Paul observes, "Against such things there is no law" (5:23).

The gospel of grace, then, does not mean an ethic (code of conduct) with no rules. True, the gospel abolishes rules seen as a means of self-justification. It removes the negative "thou shalt not" from center stage of pleasing God. Just avoiding the "acts of the sinful nature" (5:19–21) is not Christianity; it is mere moralism. In contrast, the gospel calls—and enables—people to be filled with Christ's Spirit. Only in this way can they find the resources not "to gratify the desires of the sinful nature" (5:16) but to move forward by the Holy Spirit's power in a life that honors the Lord.

Paul's ethic, then, is not anti-rule or anti-law (**antinomian**). It is positive in the sense that it bases Christian conduct on God's active working in the believer. God is pleased, and his kingdom furthered, through the positive measure of responsiveness to Christ's living presence through the gospel. The negative,

self-justifying approach of the Galatian false teachers, though no doubt sincere, was profoundly mistaken.

Critical Issues

Scholars continue to debate whether the South or North Galatian view (see above) does more justice to the full range of evidence. They also inquire into the identity of the false teachers whom Paul opposes. It has been suggested that Galatians (like other Pauline writings) should be understood with the help of categories drawn from Greco-Roman handbooks of rhetoric. While this has raised interesting possibilities in understanding Paul's strategy of persuasion, "rhetorical criticism" has been shown to run up against significant limits to its explanatory power when applied to Galatians and other Pauline letters.[21]

As already mentioned in a previous chapter, the work of E. P. Sanders has dominated academic study of Paul in the last quarter of the twentieth century.[22] His insistence that Judaism in Paul's day was far less legalistic (based on rules) than Paul assumed has met serious challenge,[23]

Focus 19: Persecution Today

Persecution of Christians did not end with Nero and the Coliseum in Rome. It has continued over the centuries, and it is very much with us today. From China to Saudi Arabia to Sudan, Christians are routinely subjected to harassment, physical abuse, and, yes—even death.

In Sudan more than 1.5 million people have died as a result of the "holy war" waged against the largely Christian south. Thousands of children of Christian parents have been taken and sold as slaves in Libya, Chad, and elsewhere—some as young as six!

In China the persecution of Christians has often been

supported by official policy. Many have been imprisoned, tortured, or sent to labor camps.

Across the Middle East, Christians are frequently suppressed in their expression of faith. Missionaries have been murdered. Congregations have been bombed and shot up by intruders whom police seem powerless to stop. Christians have also come under fire in India from Hindu interests and in various parts of Indonesia from Muslims.

As contemporary Christians we must be prepared for persecution and remember what Paul wrote of the

apostles in 2 Corinthians 4:8–9: *"We are troubled on every side, yet not distressed; we are perplexed, but not in despair; persecuted, but not forsaken; cast down, but not destroyed."*

On the modern situation, see Paul Marshall with Lela Gilbert, *Their Blood Cries Out: The Growing Worldwide Persecution of Christians* (Dallas: Word, 1997); James and Marti Hefley, *By Their Blood* (Grand Rapids: Baker, 2004); and Peter Hammond, *Faith under Fire in Sudan*, rev. ed. (Newlands, South Africa: Frontline Fellowship, 1998).

though his fresh reading of ancient Jewish sources is an important reminder of the complexity of the Judaisms—plural not singular—that flourished in the first century. Sanders has raised questions that clarify the faith of first-century Jews who declined to follow the lead of Jesus and later Paul. In this way Sanders's work contributes to better understanding of the writings of Paul himself.

Summary

1. The Corinthian church was full of dissent and confusion, and as a result the Corinthian letters provide helpful guidance for those in similar settings today.

2. Corinth, the largest city in Greece, was noted for its immorality.

3. Paul founded the church at Corinth on his second missionary journey.

4. The Corinthian church was being torn apart by quarreling; Paul first wrote to them about cross-centered truths before addressing specific issues.

5. In 1 Corinthians Paul addressed issues related to sexual misconduct, marriage, celibacy, idolatry, personal Christian freedom, worship, spiritual gifts, congregational order, the resurrection, and the age to come.

6. Paul wrote 2 Corinthians to praise the church at Corinth for their progress, to warn them of new threats, and to prepare them for his next visit.

7. The underlying theme of 2 Corinthians is that the way to glory is the way of the cross.

8. Galatians was written to the churches at Perga, Pisidian Antioch, Iconium, Lystra, and Derbe.

9. The purpose of Galatians was to call the churches back to the true gospel that Paul had preached and from which some of them had recently departed.

10. Paul carefully makes clear the true nature of the gospel, centered on Christ's atoning death foretold by the Old Testament prophets.

11. At the center of the Galatian Epistle is the truth that salvation is God's free gift.

12. Paul makes it clear to the Galatians that the gospel of grace rules out the use of mere rules or some code of conduct as a means of self-justification.

Key People/Places

Achaia	Greece
Antioch (Pisidian)	Iconium
Antioch (Syrian)	Ignatius
Asia	Irenaeus
Athens	Judea
Berea	Lystra
Central Asia Minor	Macedonia
Claudius	Marcion
Clement of Rome	Mediterranean Sea
Colossae	Palestine
Corinth	Perga
Cyprus	Philippi
Derbe	Pisidia
Ephesus	Rome
Erastus	Sosthenes
Galatia	Thessalonica
Gallio	Turkey

Key Terms

antinomian
bema
Judaizers
North Galatian theory
South Galatian theory
theologia crucis
theologia gloriae
via dolorosa

Review Questions

1. Considerable difficulty in maintaining a consistent Christian life-style was experienced by Christians in the city of _____.

2. The city of Corinth was famous for its trade and its _____.

3. Paul founded the Corinthian church on his _____ missionary journey.

4. Two archaeological finds that link Corinth with the Scriptures are the *bema* and the _____.

5. Paul wrote _____ because of quarreling among Christians.

6. First Corinthians is of great interest today because of the _____ movement.

7. Paul began 2 Corinthians by _____ the Corinthian believers.

8. Paul not only focused on self-betterment in 2 Corinthians but also on _____.

9. Gentile churches gave financial assistance to Jewish churches through the _____.

10. Galatians is addressed to churches Paul and _____ visited on the _____ missionary journey.

11. Many of the points that Paul makes in Galatians resembles points made in his sermon recorded in _____.

12. Those whose teaching combined parts of the Christian message with Jewish practices are called _____ by scholars.

Study Questions

1. In what ways do the Corinthian letters sound like they are addressed to a modern situation?

2. How has archaeology contributed to our understanding of Paul's Corinthian ministry?

3. What major issues does 1 Corinthians address?

4. What underlying theme unites 2 Corinthians? Do you think this theme is relevant for the modern church?

5. Distinguish between the true gospel and the false gospel as these relate to Galatians.

6. Who were the Judaizers? What was their role in the grace versus law controversy?

Further Reading

See also suggested readings at the end of chapter 17.

Carson, D. A., Douglas J. Moo, and Leon Morris. *An Introduction to the New Testament.* Grand Rapids: Zondervan, 1992, pp. 301–3. Listing of dozens of books and articles on technical aspects of Galatians.

Garland, David. *1 Corinthians.* Grand Rapids: Baker, 2003. A scholarly but readable treatment of the entire epistle in great detail. Strong on literary questions and social background.

Gill, David. "1 Corinthians." In *Zondervan Illustrated Bible Backgrounds Commentary*, vol. 3, ed. Clinton E. Arnold. Grand Rapids: Zondervan, 2002, pp. 100–193. Helpful comments, photos, and diagrams shedding light on ancient Corinth and giving background for understanding Paul's first letter to the church there.

Horton, Michael S. *The Law of Perfect Freedom.* Chicago: Moody, 1993. Gripping discussion of the relationship between law-keeping and freedom in Christ. Pertinent to both Galatians and the Corinthian letters.

Machen, J. Gresham. *Christianity and Liberalism.* Grand Rapids: Eerdmans, 1946 [1923]. Classic study of true and false versions of the gospel in the early twentieth century, shedding light on conflicts between Paul and his opponents.

Morris, Leon. *Galatians.* Downers Grove: InterVarsity, 1996. A commentary with many valuable insights. Suitable for the non-specialist.

Scott, James M. *2 Corinthians.* Peabody, Mass./ Carlisle: Hendrickson/Paternoster, 1998. Concise but insightful handling of a long and often complicated epistle. Pages 269–71 update bibliography on this letter.

Seifrid, Mark. "The 'New Perspective on Paul' and Its Problems." *Themelios* 25 (2000): 8–12. Helpful synopsis of issues that critics of the new perspective have continued to raise. Pertinent especially to Galatians.

Winter, Bruce. *After Paul Left Corinth: The Influence of Secular Ethics and Social Change.* Grand Rapids: Eerdmans, 2001. Draws on evidence from the Greco-Roman world to shed light on the problems Paul faced at Corinth and the counsel he prescribed.

Witherington, Ben, III. *Conflict and Community in Corinth.* Grand Rapids: Eerdmans, 1995. A commentary on the Corinthian letters making full use of socio-rhetorical insights.

20 Ephesians, Philippians, Colossians, and Philemon

Letters from Prison

Outline

Objectives

After reading this chapter, you should be able to

- Describe features of the towns of Ephesus, Philippi, and Colossae
- Outline the content of the Books of Ephesians, Philippians, Colossians, and Philemon
- State the purpose for each of these Epistles
- Evaluate critical issues that have been raised about each of the Epistles

The Prison Epistles in Early Church History

Three of Paul's four Prison Letters (Ephesians, Philippians, Colossians) were widely used by early church leaders. All of those listed below show knowledge of them. Only Eusebius cites or alludes to a fourth prison letter, the tiny letter to Philemon.

	A.D.
Polycarp	ca. 110
Justin Martyr	ca. 140
(fails to cite Philippians)	
Irenaeus	ca. 175
Clement of Alexandria	ca. 200
Tertullian	ca. 200
Origen	ca. 250
Eusebius	ca. 315

Adversity sometimes brings out the best in people. Over the past century the grim experience of arrest and detention gave rise to profound, prophetic reflections from individuals as varied as Dietrich Bonhoeffer in Germany, Alexander Solzhenitsyn in the Soviet Union, and Martin Luther King Jr. in the United States. All three generated powerful writings during periods of imprisonment.

The apostle Paul also endured incarceration. During his house arrest in ROME in the early A.D. 60s, he had the freedom to receive visitors and propagate the gospel (Acts 28:28–31). One of the ways he did this was through letter writing. It is believed that four of his extant Epistles arose during this time: namely, Ephesians, Colossians, Philippians, and Philemon.[1] Each names Paul as its author in the very opening lines, and each makes mention of its author being a prisoner or in chains (Eph 3:1; 4:1; 6:20; Phil 1:7, 14; Col 4:18; Phlm 1, 9, 10, 13).

The ideas of such writers as Bonhoeffer, Solzhenitsyn, and King receive more careful attention because their sacrifice lends urgency and credibility to their writings. This is all the more true of Paul. He had sought for years to be allowed to minister in Rome (Acts 19:21; Rom 1:13; 15:23). When he finally arrived there, he was in chains. The Prison Epistles (or Captivity Letters) are rich in courageous reflection. Their tone (see, e.g., Phil 4:11–13) also teaches by example the same selfless confidence in God that characterized Jesus' own life, marking Paul as a true disciple of his Master.

Ephesians

Introduction

"Demons, spirits, ancestors, and gods all exist as realities in the human mind, and possess the power to harm and harass the living." This quote from an anthropology textbook[2] is not only descriptive of today's world. It is true of the ancient world as well—though in both ancient and modern worlds, Satan is not merely a mental reality! Research into the cultural background of the ancient city of EPHESUS suggests that the occult—belief in and worship of unseen beings and powers other than the God of Old and New Testament tradition—may furnish important background for understanding Paul's reasons for writing this Epistle and for centering on the themes he chooses.[3] Given current worldwide interest in the occult,[4] Ephesians becomes a timely challenge to modern as well as ancient beliefs and practices.

The City of Ephesus

Details of Paul's lengthy ministry in Ephesus are found in Acts 19 (see also 20:16–38). A port city at the mouth of the CAYSTER RIVER on the AEGEAN SEA, Ephesus was the capital of the Roman province of ASIA (now extreme western TURKEY). Its population in the first century may have approached half a million. Among them were wealthy civic leaders of both sexes, called **asiarchs**, some of whom Paul counted as friends (Acts 19:31). The fame of Ephesus was not only political and commercial: it was the center for worship of the pagan goddess ARTEMIS (DIANA). It was also known as a center of occult (magic) practices.

The Artemision, Ephesus, site of the celebrated Temple of Artemis (Diana), considered to be one of the seven wonders of the ancient world.

A. Three Spiritual Blessings in Christ (1:3–14)
B. The Importance of Knowing about It All (1:15–23)
C. Redemption: Clearing the Ground (2:1–10)
D. Re-creation: Removing the Barriers (2:11–22)
E. Digression: Paul, Outsiders, and God's Glory (3:1–13)
F. Empowerment: Realizing the Future (3:14–19)
G. Doxology (3:20–21)

III. **Re-creating the Human Family: What God Is Doing** (4:1–6:20)
A. Creating Unity: The Body Forged (4:1–16)
B. Mind Control: The Inward Change (4:17–24)
C. Becoming Christian: The "Little" Things (4:25–5:5)
D. Light and Wisdom: Living Undeceived (5:6–21)
E. The Circle of Responsibility: Mutual Submission (5:22–6:9)
F. Making the Right Stand in the Right Strength (6:10–20)

IV. **Closing Remarks** (6:21–24)

The temple dedicated to Artemis was considered one of the seven wonders of the ancient world. Along with PERGAMUM and SMYRNA, other leading but lesser Asian cities, Ephesus was home to a temple for worship of the Roman emperor and his family.

If religious life was dominated by emperor worship, idolatry, and the black arts of occultism and spiritism, moral life was typical of a Greco-Roman city: Shortly after Paul's time, a large brothel stood at one of the major intersections. Excavations have uncovered an impressive amphitheater seating 24,000 people (see Acts 19:29). IRENAEUS, a second-century church leader, reports that the apostle John resided and ministered in Ephesus late in the first century.

Outline

I. Introduction (1:1–2)

II. **Re-creating the Human Family: What God Has Done** (1:3–3:21)

Purpose

The outline above stresses the implications of Ephesians for the family, both the human family generally and the nuclear family. The contents of the Epistle certainly lend themselves to such a reading. It may also be read as a treatise for and about the "family of God" known as the church. But while "church" or "family" may be examples of Ephesians' unifying themes, such headings fall short of providing the reason why the letter was written in the first place.

For centuries scholars have debated the most likely central purpose for this Epistle. No unanimity has been reached. Many conclude that the question must be left open, that no one specific purpose can be said to give the primary background for understanding what Paul writes. Yet the numerous occurrences of "power language" may furnish an important clue.[5]

Paul writes of God's "incomparably great power" and "the working of his

Ancient Magic Formula

Part of occult practice at Ephesus would have been the reciting of formulas or spells. Following is one recommended by a magician named Pibechis for driving away demons.

Take oil made from unripe olives, together with the plant mastigia and lotus pith, and boil it with marjoram (very colorless), saying, "Joel, Ossarthiomi, Emori, Theochipsoith, Sithemeoch, Sothe, Joe, Mimipsothiooph, Phersothi, Aeeioyo, Joe, Eochariphtha: come out of such an one (and the other usual formulae)."

Then make an amulet of a little sheet of tin containing these words: "Jaeo, Abraothioch, Phtha, Mesentiniao, Pheoch, Jaeo, Charsoc," and hang it round the sufferer: it's a thing that every demon will tremble at and fear.

—From Adolf Deissmann, *Light from the Ancient East*, trans. L. R. M. Strachan (London: Hodder & Stoughton, 1911), 255f. (translation and some spellings slightly altered).

against the central Pauline thesis of the supremacy of Christ. They expose their practitioners to moral error, spiritual deception, and possibly demonic affliction. It is possible that Paul wrote Ephesians to commend Christ as Lord to readers who had once (and perhaps in some ways still) bowed the knee to occult or imperial figures. Of course the Epistle's message holds importance for all who read it, not just those whose background is pagan worship at Ephesus. But known local religious background may furnish the most plausible clue available to shed light on the letter's distinctive emphasis.

Declarations and Exhortations

Ephesians consists of a series of statements about God, Christ, and salvation, followed by exhortations (or prayers) urging readers to reflect God's truth and will in their lives.

Chapter 1 opens with a lengthy ascription of praise to God for his blessings in Christ (1:3–23). Such lofty praise is warranted in view of the series of spiritual benefits Paul lists: election, love, predestination, redemption, forgiveness, inheritance. These are components in the overarching realities of God's grace and glory. Father, Son, and Holy Spirit are alike active in bestowing divine favor on unworthy sinners. Paul prays for these truths to enlighten his readers (1:18), giving them strength like that which raised Christ from the dead and elevated him to God's right hand (1:20). This would be an apt reflection of the sovereignty and excellence of Christ (1:21–23).

Chapter 2 turns from heavenly glory to human poverty. Paul calls his readers, and himself, "dead in . . . transgressions and sins" (2:1) prior to reception of the gospel message. Yet precisely in the midst of such need, God's mercy went to work (2:4; cf. Rom 5:8). Salvation came, not by good works but by God's unmerited favor, his grace (2:8–9). Good works are the outcome, not the meritorious cause, of God's forgiveness and gift of new life (2:10). Having declared their salvation in Christ, Paul exhorts them not to forget that they have been called to a new community. In this

mighty strength" (1:19). He pictures Christ in a position of power at God's right hand, "far above all rule and authority, power and dominion" (1:21). All things lie under the Son's jurisdiction, both in this age and in the age to come (1:21–22). That same power gives Paul his apostolic authority (3:7) to equip the church in its mission of making the gospel known to "rulers and authorities in the heavenly realms" (3:10). Christ is "head" of the church, its founder and reigning Lord (1:22; 4:15; 5:23; cf. Jn 13:13). Other examples of "power language" include 3:16, 20–21 and the famous "spiritual armor" passage of 6:10–17.

From Acts we know that sorcery and evil spirits were part of the religious climate for those both inside and outside the Ephesian church (19:13–19). This is corroborated by sources outside the New Testament. Worship of the Roman emperor and his family was also extensive.[6] All such beliefs and practices run

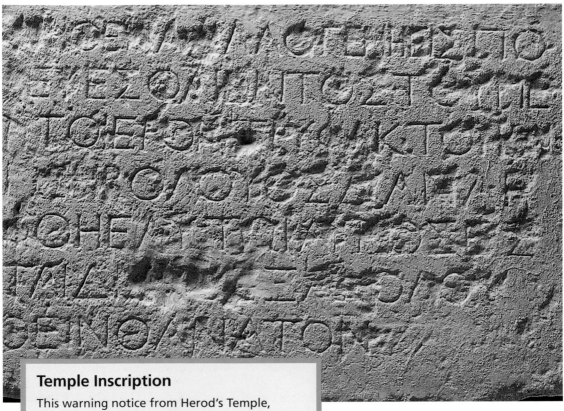

Temple Inscription

This warning notice from Herod's Temple, discovered in 1871, reads:

"No man of another nation to enter within the fence and enclosure round the temple. And whoever is caught will have himself to blame that his death ensues."

Non-Jews faced death on the spot if they passed from the Court of the Gentiles to the Court of the Women at the Jerusalem temple. However, the gospel destroyed the "middle wall of partition" between Jew and Gentile (Eph 2:14 KJV).

community old enmities are put to rest by Christ, who brings peace (2:14). Gentile Christians become "fellow citizens with God's people and members of God's household" (2:19) rather than estranged pagans outside the circle of the Lord's favor.

Chapter 3 consists largely of a prayer and benediction (3:14–21) but includes a description of the revelatory insight granted to Paul by God (3:2–13; cf. Rom 16:25–27). Both this description and the latter half of chapter 2 give Paul grounds for voicing a prayer that his readers will grow strong in the truth and love revealed in Christ.

Chapter 4 begins an extended exhortation to live worthily of the divine call (4:1). This section continues through chapter 5 and into chapter 6. Paul continues to alternate between declarations

of what God has done (4:7–11; 5:2, 23, 25–27, 29) and how the Ephesians ought to conduct their lives. Special mention is made of unity, ministry, and doctrinal stability in 4:1–16. In the latter half of chapter 4 Paul speaks of the need for breaking with pagan ways and living in conformity to Jesus Christ (4:17–21). Christ's presence can and should produce truth-telling rather than lies, self-control rather than loss of temper, charitable giving rather than stealing, and healing conversation rather than destructive babble and behavior (4:22–32).

Chapters 5 and 6 continue to stress personal transformation through the person and Spirit of Jesus Christ (5:1–21). The radical changes Christ brings should be especially evident in marriage, where Christ's relationship to the church furnishes the model for interaction between husband and wife (5:22–33). Relations between parent and child come under Christ's lordship, as well (6:1–4). So does interaction between slave and master (6:5–9).

Ephesians concludes on a strong note of the believer's need for divine protec-

Ephesians 6 uses the metaphor of military armor to describe preparation for Christian living.

Gnostic

tion and empowerment in the course of daily life (6:10–20). The image of God's armor is perhaps drawn from the Old Testament (see Is 11:5; 59:17). The Christian life is an ongoing struggle against evil powers that only the Lord can contain (6:12). Christ offers truth, righteousness, readiness, faith, salvation, Scripture, and prayer as defensive and offensive aids.

Paul concludes the Epistle with commendation of the letter's courier, Tychicus, and blessings of peace and grace on the reader (6:21–24).

Critical Issues

In the past two centuries some have questioned whether Paul wrote Ephesians. It clearly claims to come from the apostle's hand (1:1; 3:1). Kümmel admits that it "is extraordinarily well attested in the early church" as an authentic Pauline writing.[7] There is no unanimity regarding reasons for rejecting Pauline authorship, and numerous reputable scholars continue to affirm that Paul wrote it. In light of recent studies[8] we are justified in following their lead.

There is debate over the destination

of Ephesians. About five ancient copies lack the words "in Ephesus" in 1:1. It has been suggested that Paul originally intended the Epistle to be circulated to all the churches in ASIA MINOR. In this view "in Ephesus" got inserted into the copy that eventually became the master for almost all subsequent copies. It should be noted that even the ancient copies that leave "in Ephesus" out of 1:1 contain the words "To the Ephesians" in the title. Perhaps an early copyist left the words out because they were unnecessary given the title. Interpretation of the Epistle is not seriously affected regardless of whether it was originally addressed to the Ephesian church alone or to a larger circle of regional churches. Local conditions at Ephesus would have been at least somewhat similar in surrounding civic centers.

Other critical discussions involve the relation of Ephesians to Colossians (see below under Colossians), possible parallels between Ephesians and the writings found at QUMRAN, the possible presence of **Gnostic** ideas or motifs, and the nature of the Epistle's various doctrinal emphases. Regarding the last point, questions center around the doctrines of Christ, the church, and male–female roles in marriage. Such questions become most urgent for those whose view of biblical authority allows them to judge statements in Ephesians as unfit for the church to advocate today. But if Paul is not to be trusted by Christians on the topics about which he teaches, who is?

Philippians

Introduction

A classic rock tune by the Beatles, as defective in grammar and rhyme as in soundness of thought, contained the lyrics "Money don't buy everything it's true. But what it don't buy, I can't use." Paul did not, of course, hold this view of money. But money was essential to physical survival during his house-arrest in Rome (see Acts 28:16). Christians at PHILIPPI, a church he and Silas founded (see Acts 16:12–40 and the discussion in ch. 16 above), helped supply this need.

Via Egnatia

The Epistle to the Philippians acknowledges their generosity. It also urges them to resist false doctrine and, by reaffirming the primacy of Christ in their midst, to overcome dissension in their ranks.

The Town of Philippi

Details of how the Philippian church began are found in Acts 16:12–40. It was founded during Paul's second missionary journey (see map on p. 243), but the city had an illustrious history long before that. Named for PHILIP II OF MACEDON, father of ALEXANDER THE GREAT, it later gained importance as the site of a major Roman battle (42 B.C.). Soldiers from this and other battles settled there, and by Paul's time its heritage as a Roman colony, possessing civic and tax privileges, still endured. The town's importance stemmed in part from its location on the **Via Egnatia**, the major east–west commercial highway. Modern excavations have uncovered the likely site of Paul's arraignment before the local magistrates (Acts 16:19–21), an inscription to the father of CLAUDIUS (Roman emperor when Paul founded the Philippian church), and other inscriptions bearing such New Testament names as Rufus and Priscus. The site of Lydia's streamside conversion and the jail that housed Paul and Silas can also still be viewed.

Outline

I. **Introduction** (1:1–11)
   A. Salutation (1:1–2)
   B. Prologue: Thanksgiving and Prayer (1:3–11)

II. **Biographical Prologue: Paul's Present Circumstances in Serving the Gospel** (1:12–26)
   A. Advance of the Gospel in Rome (1:12–18a)
   B. Outlook Toward Death and Deliverance (1:18b–26)

III. **Exhortations to a Lifestyle Worthy of the Gospel** (1:27–2:30)
   A. To Unity and Steadfastness (1:27–30)
   B. To Christ-like Humility (2:1–11)
   C. To Obedience and Blamelessness (2:12–16)
   D. As Seen in Paul, Timothy, and Epaphroditus (2:17–30)

IV. **Warnings against False Teachings Contrary to the Gospel** (3:1–4:1)
   A. Stand Firm against Self-Righteous Legalists (3:1–16)

Roman ruins, including the agora at Philippi.

B. Stand Firm against Self-
Centered Libertines (3:17–4:1)

V. Further Exhortations to Application of Earlier Themes (4:2–9)
A. To Unity in the Cause of the Gospel (4:2–3)
B. To Joyful Peace in the Midst of Difficult Circumstances (4:4–7)
C. To Steadfastness in Thought and Practice (4:8–9)

VI. Personal Epilogue: Paul's Gratitude for Partnership in Spreading the Gospel (4:10–20)
A. For the Recent Gift (4:10–14)
B. For the Previous Gifts (4:15–20)

VII. Closing Salutation (4:21–23)
A. Greetings (4:21–22)
B. Benediction (4:23)

Purpose

Careful reading of Philippians suggests several reasons why Paul may have written it. He was about to send one of his personal aides, Epaphroditus, back to Philippi for health and other reasons (2:25–26). It would be natural to send a letter along with him to update the Philippian believers regarding Paul's circumstances. He was also planning to send Timothy their way (2:19). Perhaps even Paul himself would soon be released from jail and show up on their doorstep (2:24). A letter was called for to prepare them for these impending visits.

Further reflection on Paul's purpose in writing should bear in mind the history of his ties with the Philippian believers. He had enjoyed a fruitful relationship with them during the decade or so since he first brought Christ to them (the church was founded about A.D. 50; Paul writes in the early A.D. 60s). He probably visited them in about A.D. 55 and renewed old ties (see Acts 20:1–2). Over the years they had sent him financial support more than once (4:15; also 2 Cor 11:9). This helps explain why Paul writes with such depth of personal familiarity. It also accounts for his assumption that the recipients of his Epistle will have real interest in his circumstances and welfare.

Consideration of the evident friendship between apostle and church may point to the letter's most basic purpose: to voice Paul's pastoral concern for them in their present situation. Paul feels they need reassurance that the gospel they have trusted is continuing its conquering march, despite the apparent setback of Paul's lengthy imprisonments (nearly four years). This he gives in chapter 1. They also need encouragement to keep Christ before them in their life and Christian service together; this is what much of chapter 2 takes up. Whether for general or particular reasons, Paul feels he must warn them about religious leaders who might try to lead them astray. Chapter 3 profiles their toxic claims and practices and sets forth the truly Christian antidote to them. Finally, Paul seeks to promote the following: harmony among quarreling persons; Christian joy and peace; and a sense of satisfaction for the financial support they had made available to Paul over the years, especially most recently. These matters fill the bulk of chapter 4.

Paul's overarching pastoral concern, however, does not rule out zeal for addressing more specific matters. Two items much on his mind are the enemies the Philippians face and the Savior they serve.

Enemies of the Gospel

Philippians mentions three groups that are hindering the effective progress of the gospel message, whether by opposing it directly, tampering with its contents, or failing to apply it within the church.

One group is in Rome itself. They are apparently part of the Christian community there. Yet they envy Paul and see themselves in competition with him (1:15). While Paul is in chains (1:17) they hope to increase their own influence and following. Paul's response is kind, reserved, and wise. As long as they do not distort the message about Christ, Paul is content to be maligned. It is the gospel, not Paul's reputation or feelings, that matters (1:18). Why does Paul bring this up at all, since it does not directly affect the Philippians? First, Paul's triumph over such opposition gives the Philip-

Roman remains at Philippi.

pians reason to take heart (1:19, 25–26). Second, Paul may be aware of parallel opposition to the gospel at Philippi or elsewhere in MACEDONIA. If so, his example of restraint and aplomb will be valuable for them to see and learn from (3:17).

A second group of troublemakers is much less easy to make room for. In fact Paul does not make room for them at all. For they are not preaching the authentic gospel of Christ. Instead they advocate, it appears, a (false) gospel similar to the one Paul condemns in his letter to the Galatians. Paul calls them "mutilators" (3:2). His language suggests that they advocate a combination of trust in Christ and maintenance of the rituals (like circumcision) common to first-century Judaism. Paul objects that the true heirs of the Old Testament promises are those who acknowledge Jesus as the Christ, not those whose faith rests in religious rituals like circumcision (3:3). Such "enemies of the cross of Christ" (3:18) are to be resisted. Just as Jesus wept over JERUSALEM (Lk 19:41), Paul weeps as he laments their error (3:18). He is full of deep concern for them (see also Rom 9:3; 10:1). But their views will eventually land them in destruction (3:19). Paul warns the Philippians not to follow them there.

A third group of troublemakers consists of the Philippians themselves. While we lack detailed knowledge, two women appear to be at each other's throats (4:2). There is evidence that Paul envisioned selfishness and factiousness as widespread in the Philippian congregation (1:27; 2:2–4, 14). Paul speaks of joy (1:4, 25; 2:2, 29; 4:1) or rejoicing (1:18; 2:17, 18, 28; 3:1; 4:4, 10) over a dozen times. His positive stress may be an attempt to counter a negative situation. Here as often elsewhere in the New Testament (and in church history), God's people appear to be out of step with God's kingdom. Yet Paul does not lash out or despair. Instead, he points to Jesus Christ.

Christology

In the midst of admonishing the Philippians about their self-centeredness Paul reminds them of the example Christ set (2:5–11). This passage is of rare literary excellence and theological richness. Whole books have been devoted to exploring its origin, use in the early church, and message.[9] Paul's overall point is to rally the Philippians to more Christ-like living. How Jesus lived and died has a daily bearing on how they ought to be living out their lives in relation to each other (see Lk 9:23).

In the course of making this point Paul offers several significant statements about who Christ was and what he accomplished. He was not just a man—he was

315

God's Will

How can I know God's will for my life? This is one of the most important questions that a person can ask. Paul sketches an answer when he writes, *"Work out your salvation with fear and trembling, for it is God who works in you to will and to act according to his good purpose"* (Phil 2:12–13).

Christians walk by faith and not always by sight (2 Cor 5:7). Often we must make decisions without tangible confirmation that we are doing the right thing. Life contains a risk factor for everyone, followers of Christ included.

But Paul's guidance in Phil 2 sheds light on our way. *"Work out your salvation."* This does not mean work to earn salvation. It means throw yourself wholeheartedly into serving the Lord who has loved and saved you. The first step in knowing God's will for the future is to be diligent and faithful in the present. Jesus taught that being entrusted with great things starts with being faithful in little things (Lk 16:10–12).

"God . . . works in you to will and to act." Paul was confident that Christians who lived faithful lives unto God would develop inner will and outer responses in keeping with God's desires. God's will would come to be their will.

"According to his good purpose." God has a plan, a good plan, for all his children (Jer 29:11). He wants us to know and do his will. We should not expect detailed long-range maps and schedules to be dropped into our laps. But we can depend on the Lord to oversee our way so that it eventually leads to him. *"In all your ways acknowledge him, and he will make your paths straight"* (Prv 3:6).

divinity itself (2:6) who took on human form (2:7). Despite his regal heritage as eternal Son of the heavenly King, he gladly lowered himself to serve sinful humans by dying on the cross (2:8). Yet his humiliation, far from being a tragedy, was God's path to glory for him (2:9). God shared (and shares) his very name, *kurios* (Lord), with the one who so selflessly carried out his intentions (2:9–11).

These lofty affirmations about Jesus Christ are the heartbeat of all Paul has to say to the Philippians. Christ gave himself for others despite being infinitely superior to them by virtue of being equal to, inherently one with, the eternal God. How much more ought the Philippians be willing to swallow their pride, live more for others rather than for self, and allow God a free hand in their lives to bring about his good intentions (2:13)? This question, of course, is no less pertinent to those who claim to follow Christ in modern times.

Critical Issues

While the Pauline authorship of Philippians has rarely been questioned, it is sometimes suggested that the Epistle as we have it is a composite document. It is argued that 4:10–20 might have been a separate letter and that Paul's "finally" in 3:1 could have signaled the original closing lines of the Epistle; 3:2–4:9 would then be part of still a third Pauline composition. Against these suggestions are two weighty considerations: No ancient manuscripts reflect any such divisions, and the letter makes tolerably good sense in its canonical form. There are, then, no compelling reasons for doubting the Epistle's literary unity.[10]

Many twentieth-century scholars have asked if Paul in 2:5–11 might not be quoting an early Christian hymn or confession. This view first gained prominence in the 1920s. It is a plausible theory since the passage has powerful poetic qualities, but hard evidence for it is lacking.[11] As a conjecture, it can hardly serve as a basis for discounting the christological force of the verses because they are poetic in nature (much of the Old Testament is poetic, but this does not mean we can discount what it says when it adopts that literary form) or because they are non-Pauline (even if they are hymnic, Paul may have composed them, or endorsed their content by virtue of quoting them).

Colossians

Introduction

Theologian Carl F. H. Henry observes that "paganism is now more deeply entrenched than in the recent past, and it holds a firmer grip on Western society."[12] Debate rages today about how the church is being affected, and perhaps seduced, by popular culture, network television and reporting, and powerful institutions like government, university, and public school, all of which seem to be drifting away from Judeo-Christian moorings. The church is of necessity "in the world"; how can it keep from being swallowed up by forces hostile to it? How can followers of Jesus attain and maintain the status of "salt of the earth" and "light of the world" (Mt 5:13–14)?

Such questions are not unique to modern times. Long ago the apostle Paul realized the challenge society at large could pose to the integrity of Christian faith and practice among the congregations he helped found. In his Epistle to the Colossians he addressed the issue directly.

The Town of Colossae

The site of this ancient village has never been excavated so details about it are lacking. Its precise size is unclear, but it was not a large city. Located about one hundred miles east-southeast of Ephesus, it lay in the Lycus Valley in the district called Phrygia. Like the neighboring towns of Laodicea and Hier-

APOLIS, first-century Colossae was plagued by earthquakes. Its population consisted of local natives (Phrygians), Greeks, and Jews. It may have first heard the gospel during Paul's two-year ministry at Ephesus (Acts 19:10), although Phrygian Jews may have taken the gospel there immediately after Pentecost (Acts 2:10). New Testament figures who came from or lived in Colossae include Epaphras, Philemon, Apphia, Archippus, and Onesimus. Most of these persons are discussed further below.

Outline

I. **Salutation** (1:1–2)
 A. Sender (1:1)
 B. Addressee (1:2a)
 C. Greeting (1:2b)

II. **Thanksgiving and Prayer** (1:3–14)
 A. Thanksgiving for the Colossians' Love (1:3–8)
 B. Prayer for Knowledge and Godly Conduct (1:9–14)

III. **Body** (1:15–3:4)
 A. Christ's Work and the Reconciling of the Gentiles (1:15–23)

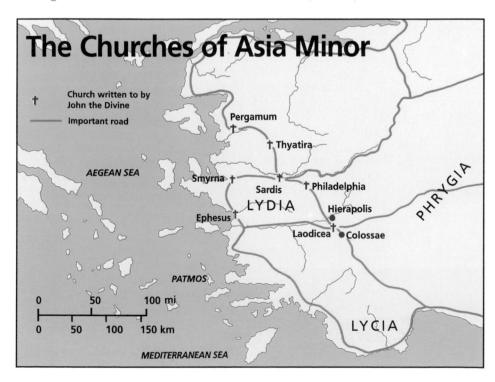

B. Paul's Ministry to the Gentiles
   (1:24–2:5)
C. Error and Antidote (2:6–19)
D. New Life in Christ (2:20–3:4)

IV. **Ethical Exhortations and
   Instructions** (3:5–4:6)
   A. Put to Death What Is Earthly
      (3:5–11)
   B. Put on Christian Virtues
      (3:12–17)
   C. Relations within Christian
      Households (3:18–4:1)
   D. Continue in Prayer (4:2–4)
   E. Conduct toward Outsiders
      (4:5–6)

V. **Closing** (4:7–18)
   A. Greeting (4:7–17)
   B. Benediction (4:18)

Setting and Purpose

During Paul's imprisonment he had occasion to address the Colossian Christians. He was not the founder of their church. That honor fell to Epaphras, who was a native of the area and had labored for its evangelization (1:7; 4:12). Paul gives a twofold reason for writing. One is to assure the Colossians (and the Laodicians, who are supposed to receive a copy of the letter, too [2:1; 4:16]) of his interest and care. He wants them to be fully receptive to Christ in their midst (2:2–3). The second reason involves false teaching and teachers who may be misleading some in the church. Their arguments sound impressive (2:4) but are based on "human tradition and the basic principles of this world rather than on Christ" (2:8). To a large extent the entire Epistle may be seen as an apostolic antidote to popular but erroneous opinions that threaten the purity of Christian doctrine and the integrity of Christian practice at Colossae.

Message

As the outline above indicates, Colossians is structured like a normal Hellenistic letter: salutation, thanksgiving and prayer, body, exhortation, closing. But its message is quite different from that of a normal letter. At its center is a

Deities Named in the New Testament	
Artemis (Diana)	Acts 19:24, 27, 28, 34, 35
Castor and Pollux	Acts 28:11
Hermes (Mercury)	Acts 14:12
"unknown gods"	Acts 17:23
Zeus (Jupiter)	Acts 14:12–13

series of profound assertions regarding Jesus Christ (1:15–20).

First, Christ "is the image of the invisible God" (1:15). No mortal has seen or can see God (see Jn 1:18), but God has revealed as much of himself as humanity can contain in the person of Jesus. In the same verse he is also called "the firstborn over all creation." "Firstborn" was a Hebraic-Jewish way of saying "specially honored." In the Old Testament the nation of Israel was called "firstborn" (Ex 4:22). So was David (Ps 89:27). In such contexts the reference is not to physical birth but to position of honor before God. Paul is saying that Christ has "pride of place" over all creation. And no wonder: All creation came about through and for him (1:16).

Second, "all things hold together" in Christ. It is impossible to exhaust the full meaning of such a statement. But it at least implies that Christ is the upholder and sustainer of the physical universe regarded as part of God's domain. Science can discover and manipulate matter, but the mysteries of matter's properties, essence, and origin relate ultimately to Christ. Human research can determine much about the "what" of the natural world, but the "why" is ultimately to be found only in God and the reign he establishes through his Son. His reconciling work (1:20) qualifies him to serve as the sustaining and redeeming lifeline between the spiritual, holy God and the physical, sinful world.

Implications of Christ's Supremacy

More could be said regarding Paul's presentation of Christ's uniqueness and preeminence, but it is clear that the

Paul and the Environment

Greenhouse effect . . . waste disposal . . . ozone depletion . . . population explosion . . . energy crisis . . . world hunger.

Environmental issues have moved to center stage in recent decades. Why should Christians be concerned? After all, isn't heaven their final home? Can't they afford to be indifferent to this fleeting world?

"All things were created by him and for him," Paul writes of Christ (Col 1:16). The created order belongs to God and to the Son of God. How God's people treat the created order is a reflection of their regard for God. Environmental issues matter.

This does not mean that God wants nature to be worshiped. Idolizing nature is a dangerous temptation to be guarded against (Rom 1:18–23). But God's people should be good stewards of the resources (air, water, land, sea) that God created. To squander God's good gifts is to fail to love God. It is also a failure to love our neighbor as ourselves. Good environmental stewardship is part of the twofold great commandment to love both the Lord and our fellow humans.

The New Testament gives a firm basis for environmentally responsible living. Jesus taught appreciation for the beauty of the world and God's rule over it (Mt 6:25–30). Paul spoke of a life-style of contentment (Phil 4:11–13; 1 Tm 6:6–12) that contrasts with the selfish grasping of a materialistic consumer society.

Paul's teaching about Christ the Creator adds new depth to the words of the hymn, *"This is my Father's world."* Christians' worship of God in Christ should express itself in consistent prayer concerning environmental issues, in non-materialistic spending patterns, in responsible political involvement, and in environmentally responsible habits like recycling and conservation of resources. It is sin to set our hearts on this passing world. But it is also sin to trash it.

---

basic message of Colossians is explicitly about Christ. He rescued the Colossians from darkness and delivered them into light (1:13). Their allegiance, therefore, belongs to Christ, not to persuasive peddlers of religious speculation. Because of who Christ is and what he has done, Paul goes on to exhort the Colossians to affirm and live out certain truths.

They are to identify and resist false teaching (2:8). Some notions may carry more intellectual appeal than Christ, but none is living, true, and powerful like he is, as Paul goes on to detail (2:9–15). With a series of admonitions Paul alludes to various misconceptions current at Colossae (2:16–23). Scholars have dubbed these views the "Colossian heresy." The exact nature of these false doctrines, and even whether there was a definite "heresy" at work at all, are disputed, but it is hard to deny that Paul speaks against some form of legalism (the view that saving merit is based on good works rather than God's free gift of grace) and asceticism (harsh treatment of the physical body as a means of earning divine favor and growing spiritually). Paul says that to take these paths is to lose "connection with the Head," who is Christ (2:19). Such religious exercises actually encourage the very excesses they claim to curb (2:23).

Paul goes on to enumerate what some of those excesses are and how Christ can serve to keep them in check and produce godly behavior instead. Vices like "sexual immorality, impurity, lust, evil desires and greed, which is idolatry" (3:5), as well as "anger, rage, malice, slander, and filthy language" (3:8) are put to flight as the "old self" is overcome by "the new self, which is being renewed in knowledge in the image of its Creator" (3:9–10). The result will be Christ-like virtues such as "compassion, kindness, humility, gentleness and patience" (3:12).

Christ's reign is not merely personal and internal but public in its manifestation. Paul calls for recognition of Christ's will in marriage, childrearing, and slave-master relations (3:18–4:1). He closes with an exhortation to pray and to deal wisely, graciously, and persuasively with nonbelievers (4:2–6). He also commends Tychicus, the bearer of the Epistle, and passes along news and greetings to and from various co-workers in the faith (4:7–17). Paul's personal signature, request for prayer, and blessing make up the Epistle's last words.

Critical Issues

The careful reader will note a number of similarities between Colossians and Ephesians. (In some ways this is comparable to similarities between Galatians and Romans.) Some have suggested that one is a non-Pauline expansion or summary of the other. It is more likely, however, that Paul wrote both within a fairly short span of time and used similar language in each. Fewer scholars doubt that Paul wrote Colossians than that he wrote Ephesians. There are no compelling reasons to question that the letter's author was Paul.

The nature of the so-called Colossian heresy has called forth much discussion. Barring discovery of further evidence, there seems little hope of arriving at conclusions acceptable to all scholars.[13] The opinion that the heresy was specifically Gnostic in nature seems unlikely; a growing body of opinion concludes that New Testament teaching owes little, if anything, to that body of religious speculation that arose in the second century.[14] Attempts to prove links between Colossian religion and first-century Jewish sects are more promising but are presently inconclusive. While Paul's language is reminiscent of legalistic and ascetic excesses

that were part of the first-century Jewish scene, it is also broad enough to apply to most serious religious systems whose center is not Christ.

The origin of 1:15–20, the section richest in reflection on the person and work of Christ, has been termed hymnic by many. This can perhaps not be ruled out, but the cautions voiced above regarding Philippians 2:5–11 apply here as well.

Philemon

Introduction

Street people . . . the homeless . . . runaways. We encounter them almost daily, whether in person or on the news. Do they represent a new, unheard-of problem? Hardly. People in similar

A view toward the acropolis mound of ancient Colossae *(green, middle distance),* with the modern town of Honaz in the distance. The inhabitants of Colossae moved to Honaz after the destruction of the ancient city.

straits were part of the first-century scene. Paul's letter to Philemon deals with a runaway slave named Onesimus, who apparently emerged from his hiding place in Rome's twisting alleys to begin a new life by embracing the gospel.

Outline

I. Greeting (1–3)

II. Commendation of Philemon (4–7)

III. Intercession for Onesimus (8–22)

IV. Salutations and Benediction (23–25)

Purpose

Philemon was a personal acquaintance of Paul and apparently a man of means. He lived in Colossae (see Col 4:9; Philemon's slave Onesimus is called a Colossian) in quarters large enough to host Christian meetings (v. 2). He also owned slaves, a common practice in the Roman world. One of them, Onesimus, is the main reason Paul writes.

For causes unknown to us Onesimus ran away from his duties under Philemon. This was a serious crime, which resulted in stern punishment if the offender was caught. Burning, branding, maiming, or even death was possible. As a runaway today might journey to a major population center like New York or London to avoid detection, Onesimus predictably fled to the largest city he

could reach: Rome. But he did not remain a fugitive. He apparently found where Paul was staying and visited him. The result may have been unexpected: Paul led him to a saving knowledge of Jesus Christ (v. 10).

Onesimus must have decided that the right thing to do under the awkward circumstances was to return to his master and straighten things out. Paul writes to Philemon, urging him to treat Onesimus with mercy. He is confident that Philemon will do just that and even more (v. 21). This may indicate that Paul expected Philemon to give Onesimus his freedom. Paul also asks Philemon to prepare for a visit from Paul when he is released from jail in answer to Philemon's prayers (v. 22).

Literary and Historical Questions

The letter gives its author's name—Paul—three times (vv. 1, 9, 19). Appar-

A Roman slave badge.

Focus 20: Christianity and Cultural Change

While some today suggest that all values and cultures are relative, Paul did not agree. Pagan values of his time allowed husbands to mistreat their wives, but in the Prison Epistles Paul teaches love and respect (Eph 5; Col 3). Pagan culture permitted misuse of slaves, but Paul calls for charity and equity (Col 4; Phlm). The gospel calls for modifying culturally accepted practices when these conflict with the love and justice God expects.

Western European conquistadores who conquered Mexico were in many ways cruel and destructive. But at least the civilization they represented, due in part to Christian influence, put an end to the human sacrifice and

cannibalism that reigned in Mesoamerican culture (see K. Windschuttle, *The Killing of History* [New York; The Free Press, 1996], 60–67).

Christianity in modern Sri Lanka has helped reduce the effect of the caste system, enhanced the position of women in society, and improved the level of morals and sexual ethics. "It introduced monogamy into a society where there was no clear institution of marriage" ("The Church in Sri Lanka," in *Church in Asia Today,* ed. Saphir Athyal [Singapore: Asia Lausanne Committee for World Evangelization, 1998], 436) and has contributed to peace in a war-torn land.

Christians too often support the cultural status quo. For example, in the early

centuries of the church, its leaders do not seem to have challenged the institution of slavary as aggressively as Paul's example, and Jesus' teaching, calls for. W. E. Raffety writes, "The church issued no edict sweeping away this custom . . . , but the gospel of Christ with its warm, pentetrating love-message mitigated the harshness of ancient times and melted cruelty into kindness." While this may be true at the individual level, it did not translate very quickly into societal transformation in the early centuries of the church.

Failure of Christians in the past may well make us wonder where we are lax in applying Christian teaching in our own settings.

ently Timothy was with him at this point in his imprisonment (v. 1; cf. Col 1:1). There is no evidence that Timothy co-authored the letter, though he might have written it down as Paul dictated. Like other Pauline correspondence this Epistle follows the conventions of an ancient Greek letter.[15] It must have been written at about the same time as Colossians (see Col 4:9). Assuming that Paul was in prison (see vv. 1, 9, 10, 13) in Rome, this suggests a date in the early A.D. 60s.

The situation reflected in the Epistle is true to the times. An ancient inscription discovered at Laodicea, a village very near Colossae, was dedicated by a slave to the master who freed him. The master's name: MARCUS SESTIUS PHILEMON.[16] We cannot be certain that this is the same Philemon as the one Paul addressed, but the identical names from the same locale do raise the possibility.

The first-century setting is directly reflected in a more particular way. Under

Summary

1. Ephesus was noted as a center of emperor worship, the occult, idolatry, and spiritism.

2. Ephesians consists of a series of statements about God, Christ, and salvation, followed by exhortations urging readers to reflect God's truth and will in their lives.

3. Critical issues raised concerning Ephesians have to do with the authorship and destination of the letter, the relation of Ephesians to Colossians, parallels with the Dead Sea Scrolls, the presence of Gnostic ideas, and the nature of various doctrinal emphases.

4. The church at Philippi was founded by Paul and Silas on the second missionary journey.

5. Paul wrote the letter to the Philippians to express his pastoral concern over their current situation, to let them know about his circumstances, and to prepare them for a visit from Timothy and possibly himself.

6. In Philippians Paul identifies three groups hindering the gospel message: a group in the Christian community in Rome, a group not preaching the authentic gospel, and the self-centered Philippians themselves.

7. Paul wrote to the church at Colossae to assure it of his interest and to warn them about false teachers who were misleading them.

8. The basic message of Colossians is the uniqueness and preeminence of Christ.

9. Paul spoke against legalism and asceticism in his Epistle to the Colossians.

10. Paul's letter to Philemon, a personal friend, dealt with a runaway slave named Onesimus.

11. Because a large percentage of the population in this era consisted of slaves, this was an important matter for Paul to bring to Philemon's attention.

12. In his treatment of Onesimus, Paul admonishes Philemon to go beyond the legal customs of the day and to consider standards of justice and love that are rooted in the character of God.

Roman law a slave might seek refuge at a religious altar, whether public or in a private home.[17] The person presiding over the altar would then act as a go-between on the slave's behalf. This may have been the legal provision under which Onesimus approached Paul, though certainty on the point is hardly possible.[18]

In any case the question of master-slave relations was a weighty one in a social setting where a substantial percentage of the population consisted of slaves. One writer suggests that this percentage ranged from half in Rome to three-quarters in ATHENS.[19] Another states that only one in five residents of Rome were slaves.[20] Yet Seneca (4 B.C.?–A.D. 65) states that the Roman senate defeated a proposed law requiring slaves to wear distinctive clothing; there was fear that they would thereby realize how numerous they were.[21] In tackling an aspect of the slavery question, Paul's letter to Philemon echoes the concerns being voiced by other influential thinkers in those very years. Paul's solution, which drew on the love of Christ, contrasts sharply with the purely political and legislative approach favored by the Roman senate.

Practical Lessons

This shortest canonical letter of Paul reveals a deeply personal and practical concern for a social outcast. In this it is reminiscent of Christ's own care for the lowly, not merely as a class but as individual persons. It also points to the high level of camaraderie and trust that existed among members of the Christian community. Paul writes with a respectful yet easy familiarity that one does not always find even among family members. He could address a thorny topic so frankly and cheerfully because he knew Philemon shared his own commitment to do the right thing in the Lord's eyes. A former Jewish rabbi, languishing in jail for being a gospel missionary, gets a careful hearing from a Gentile slave owner hundreds of miles away in a town he has never even visited. Such is the interpersonal and finally social cohesion that authentic response to the gospel can and should produce.

Paul's approach to the culture of his day merits careful reflection. While elsewhere he advocates compliance with civil authorities and legal custom (Rom 13:1–7), here he urges Philemon not to stop there. He must also consider standards of justice and love that are rooted in the character of God as revealed in Jesus Christ and in Old Testament Scripture. The Old Testament affirms the equality of all persons and makes provision for fair treatment, not only of God's own people but also of foreigners and slaves living alongside of them. Paul applies this viewpoint in a cultural setting whose values were quite different, with slaves having few to no civil rights.[22] In Paul's view Christ had died for slave and free, Gentile and Jew, female and male alike (Gal 3:28). God is not partial in his selfless love for persons. Christians must imitate God and his ways (Eph 5:1) rather than have their behavior determined by the way their surrounding culture functions (Rom 12:2). Paul's Epistle to Philemon, while recognizably part of its ancient setting, at the same time calls for transformation of that setting through response to Christ's high call to love for others. "What this letter does is to bring us into an atmosphere in which the institution [of slavery] could only wilt and die."[23]

Did Philemon heed Paul's advice? Would this little Epistle have survived if he had not?

Key People/Places

Key Terms	Key People/Places	
asiarchs	Aegean Sea	Irenaeus
Gnostic	Alexander the Great	Jerusalem
Via Egnatia	Artemis	Laodicea
	Asia	Lycus Valley
	Asia Minor	Macedonia
	Athens	Marcus Sestius
	Cayster River	Pergamum
	Claudius	Philemon
	Colossae	Philip II of Macedon
	Diana	Philippi
	Ephesus	Phrygia
	Hierapolis	Qumran
		Rome
		Smyrna
		Turkey

Review Questions

1. Ephesus was the center of pagan worship and was the site of the temple of _____.

2. A clue to the purpose for Paul's writing of Ephesians is found in a number of references to _____.

3. Ephesians concludes with an emphasis on believers' need for _____ and _____ in their daily lives.

4. The Philippian church was founded by Paul and _____.

5. Paul had a strong _____ with the believers in Philippi.

6. Paul admonished the Philippians about their _____.

7. The founder of the Colossian church was _____.

8. Like all of Paul's epistles, Colossians has the structure of a _____ letter.

9. The misconceptions at Colossae that Paul admonishes the Colossians about are called by some scholars _____.

10. Paul wrote a _____ letter to his friend Philemon.

11. The subject of the letter to Philemon was his runaway slave _____.

12. Paul's concern for Onesimus, a social outcast, was a reflection of the concern of _____.

Study Questions

1. Cite one way that modern society resembles the social world of ancient Ephesus.

2. Name some of the major themes of Ephesians.

3. What issues does Colossians deal with that are also pertinent issues today?

4. Paul says much about Christ in Colossians. Give three facts about Christ based on what Paul teaches.

5. Who are the "enemies" about whom Paul warns the Philippian believers?

6. How does Paul's presentation of Christ in Philippians compare to Colossians? Give two similarities and two differences.

7. Why is Philemon an important document, seen in its ancient social setting? What applications can be drawn for it in the modern setting?

Further Reading

See also works cited in notes to this chapter. On Paul generally, see chapter 17.

Arnold, Clint, ed. *Zondervan Illustrated Bible Backgrounds Commentary.* Vol. 3. Grand Rapids: Zondervan, 2002. Covers all four Pauline Prison Epistles. Discussion of selected passages, showing their relation to both biblical and extra-biblical writings. Many diagrams, photos, and illustrative sidebars.

Barth, Markus. *Ephesians: Introduction, Translation, and Commentary.* 2 vols. Garden City, N.Y.: Doubleday, 1974. Major scholarly treatment. Dated but still helpful.

Barth, Markus, and Helmut Blanke. *The Letter to Philemon.* Grand Rapids: Eerdmans, 2000. A work of over 500 pages on this brief Pauline epistle! Contains numerous thoughtful excurses on both historical and theological matters.

Bockmuehl, Markus. *The Epistle to the Philippians.* Peabody, Mass.: Hendrickson, 1998. Thorough but readable commentary that reflects recent scholarship.

Brown, Raymond. *An Introduction to the New Testament.* New York: Doubleday, 1997. Relevant chapters survey and assess recent Pauline scholarship on each of the Prison Epistles.

Calvin, John. *The Epistles of Paul the Apostle to the Galatians, Ephesians, Philippians, and Colossians.* Trans. T. H. L. Parker. Grand Rapids: Eerdmans, 1965. Classic exposition, rarely equaled in theological intensity and insight.

Lightfoot, J. B. *Saint Paul's Epistles to the Colossians and to Philemon.* 6th ed. London: Macmillan, 1882. Classic comments based on acute historical learning. Forms the basis for much subsequent discussion of issues like the Colossian heresy.

Moritz, Thorsten. *A Profound Mystery: The Use of the Old Testament in Ephesians.* Leiden: Brill, 1996. Shows how fundamental the Old Testament is to Pauline theology even in an epistle in which he does not quote from it extensively.

O'Brien, Peter. *Colossians, Philemon.* Waco: Word, 1982. Thorough exposition that combines historical rigor with theological insight. The author spent many years as a missionary teacher in India.

———. *Ephesians.* Grand Rapids: Eerdmans, 1999. Perhaps the best all-around commentary on this Epistle.

———. *The Epistle to the Philippians.* Grand Rapids: Eerdmans, 1991. Scholarly exposition that does not lose sight of Paul's doctrinal and worship concerns.

Stott, John R. W. *The Message of Ephesians.* Downers Grove: InterVarsity, 1979. A practical exposition ideal for students. Does a good job of suggesting real-life applications of what Paul writes.

Turcan, Robert. *The Cults of the Roman Empire.* Trans. Antonia Nevill. Oxford: Blackwell, 1997. Maps out the religious world of Paul's time and afterward. Deals with pagan deities and numerous religious movements and practices. Wrestles with the question of why these worship systems died out and Christian faith eventually won out. Useful bibliography for further reading and research (pp. 383–85).

21 Thessalonians, Timothy, and Titus

A Legacy of Faithfulness

Objectives

**After reading this chapter,
you should be able to**

- List reasons for the city of
  Thessalonica's importance
- Outline the content of 1 and 2
  Thessalonians
- Identify the purpose for the writing of
  1 and 2 Thessalonians
- Compare the reasons for the writing of
  the Pastoral Epistles
- Outline the content of 1 and 2 Timothy
- Outline the content of Titus
- Characterize the distinctive counsel of the
  Pastoral Epistles

First and Second Thessalonians

Threatened by a wide range of crises and uncertainties in today's world, many have sought refuge in a radical, self-absorbed individualism. Self-esteem has become a major theme of modern life in the West. Public education promotes it. Popular magazines praise it. "Feeling good about yourself" has come to be a fundamental priority for many. One study notes that "the self has become the main form of reality." But the same study questions the wisdom of this outlook.[1]

Christians in ancient times also faced threats to their sense of selfhood and indeed to their very existence. But in one notable case—that of believers in the Macedonian city of THESSALONICA—they did not flee into the illusory security of self-absorption and self-esteem. They opted rather for God-esteem, drawing their identity and self-understanding from what the Lord's work on their behalf told them about themselves rather than from what the abrasive surrounding society thought of them, or what it pressured them to think about themselves. Below we will see how God's

---

1 and 2 Thessalonians in Early Church History

First and Second Thessalonians appear to have been known and used by such early church leaders as:

	A.D.
Polycarp	ca. 110
Justin Martyr	ca. 140
Irenaeus	ca. 175
Clement of Alexandria	ca. 200
Tertullian	ca. 200
Origen	ca. 250
Eusebius	ca. 315

---

ministry to them through Christ gave them resources to live redemptive lives pleasing to God rather than timid or self-centered lives dominated by fear of the surrounding dominant culture or conformity to it.

Introduction

Paul's second missionary journey (see map, p. 243) took him and his companions from SYRIAN ANTIOCH (Acts 15:35), hundreds of miles westward across ASIA MINOR (Acts 15:41; 16:1, 6), and eventually to the Macedonian city of PHILIPPI (Acts 16:12). Following a brief, turbulent, but fruitful ministry there, Paul traveled through AMPHIPOLIS and APOLLONIA, where there were apparently no Jewish synagogues,[2] to Thessalonica, where the Jewish presence was substantial (Acts 17:1). Thessalonica was about one hundred miles from Philippi. It should be recalled that it was Paul's policy to take the gospel first to Jews in regions he sought to evangelize (Acts 16:13; 17:1, 10, 17; 18:4; 19:8; Rom 1:16).

Despite opposition Paul managed to found a church at Thessalonica. Later he would write two letters to the Christians there to encourage and instruct them. These letters are known as 1 and 2 Thessalonians.

The City of Thessalonica

Most of the ancient city's remains lie buried beneath modern THESSALONIKI, GREECE'S largest city except for ATHENS. Ancient sources establish that Thessalonica was no backwoods village. It lay on the Via Egnatia, the major east–west trade route. It was also a thriving seaport. The provincial governor made his residence there. Leading citizens enjoyed the fruits of economic prosperity, though as usual slaves and other lower classes did not necessarily benefit. Thessalonica boasted pagan temples as well as the Jewish synagogue where Paul and Silas ministered.

Origin of 1 and 2 Thessalonians

Acts makes it clear that the Thessalonian church was founded amid much opposition (Acts 17:1–9). The situation became so intense that Paul and Silas had to slip away under cover of darkness (Acts 17:10). They found refuge, and opportunity to minister, in BEREA (fifty miles from Thessalonica) for a short time (Acts 17:10). But

Paul's sermon in Athens may be seen today (in Greek) on a bronze tablet at the site where he is believed to have preached, on the Areopagus.

hostile parties in Thessalonica tracked them down and stirred up trouble in Berea, too. Apparently Paul was the main target of their ire, for Silas and Timothy found it possible to remain in Berea. But it was decided that Paul should travel some 250 miles south to Athens. There he awaited

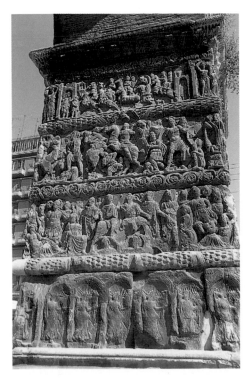

Arch of Galerius in modern Thessaloniki. Although not yet built when Paul was in Thessalonica, it depicts the ancient Roman presence there.

word from Silas and Timothy regarding the fate of the new believers in Thessalonica (Acts 17:15–34). Would they stand up under persecution, or would they cast off their new faith in Christ?

Paul tarried and preached for a brief time in Athens. But it was not until he traveled west to CORINTH (about fifty miles) that Silas and Timothy caught up with him (Acts 18:5). Upon hearing their news, Paul apparently wrote 1 Thessalonians and "mailed" it using Timothy as a courier. A few months later he followed up this first Epistle with a second.

First Thessalonians

Outline

  I. The Greeting (1:1)

  II. Personal Reminiscences (1:2–10)
    A. The Vitality of the Church (1:2–3)
    B. The Spiritual Roots of the Church (1:4–6)
    C. The Practical Expression of a Living Faith (1:7–10)

  III. The Nature of the Apostolic Ministry (2:1–12)
    A. Patience in Suffering (2:1–2)

B. Integrity of Motives (2:3–6)
C. Winsome in Manner (2:7–9)
D. Blameless in Behavior (2:10–12)

IV. **The Reception of the Gospel** (2:13–16)

V. **Paul's Concern for the Thessalonians** (2:17–3:13)
A. Frustrated Purposes (2:17–20)
B. Missionary Plans (3:1–5)
C. Joyful Praise (3:6–10)
D. Intercessory Prayer (3:11–13)

VI. **Exhortation to Christian Living** (4:1–12)
A. General Guidelines (4:1–2)
B. Morality (4:3–8)
C. Christian Love (4:9–12)

VII. **Problems Related to Christ's Coming** (4:13–5:11)
A. The State of the Dead (4:13–18)
B. The Times and the Seasons (5:1–11)

VIII. **The Internal Life of the Church** (5:12–24)
A. The Recognition of Leaders (5:12–13)
B. Interpersonal Relations (5:14–15)
C. The Life of Faith (5:16–18)
D. Life in the Assembled Community (5:19–22)
E. Paul's Second Prayer (5:23–24)

IX. **Closing Comments** (5:24–28)

Purpose and Message

In view of the historical setting sketched above, it seems likely that Paul wrote 1 Thessalonians primarily to encourage the new believers to persevere in their faith despite the opposition they faced. The outline in the preceding section breaks Paul's message down into small components. More generally we can recognize four ways Paul sought to lend his readers counsel and aid.

First, the Epistle confirms that hard times are part of God's plan for his people. The opposition they faced was not some strange thing (see 1 Pt 4:12) but was identical to what Paul and even the Lord Jesus himself had endured (1 Thes 1:6). Paul commends them for taking the apostolic word so deeply to heart that it brought the same adversity into their lives that it did earlier to the Judean churches (2:13–16). He has sent Timothy to them bearing the Epistle "so that no one would be unsettled by these trials" (3:3). In fact, part of Paul's basic instruction to new believers was that authentic faith in the gospel, lived out with the zeal it called for, would land them in hot water (3:4). Here Paul follows a strategy used earlier by Jesus himself. On the night he was betrayed Christ warned the eleven of the hard times that lay ahead so that when those times came they would be strengthened rather than demoralized (Jn 16:1–4). In 1 Thessalonians Paul takes a similar tack.

Second, Paul encourages the new believers by commending their faith and love, which he remembers in his prayers

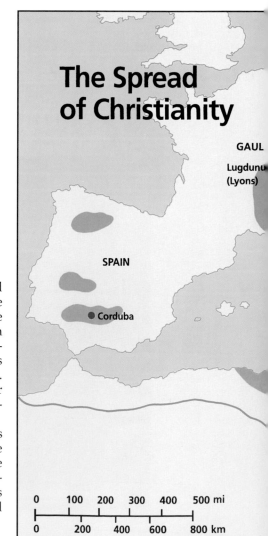

The Spread of Christianity

GAUL

Lugdunu (Lyons)

SPAIN

● Corduba

| 0 | 100 | 200 | 300 | 400 | 500 mi |
| 0 | 200 | 400 | 600 | 800 km |

continually (1:3). In ringing tones he extols their faith and the reputation for fidelity to the Lord that their faith has earned them throughout the young Christian world (1:8). He takes heart at what Timothy has told him about their faith and love (3:6). The tone of 1 Thessalonians makes clear that Paul was concerned for his readers' long-term survival in the faith, but the stance he adopts is one of confidence and commendation rather than doubt and criticism.

Third, he encourages by giving further instruction. While the level of their love for each other is exemplary, there is room and need for improvement (4:9–10). Areas of instruction on which Paul touches include the nature of the apostolic ministry (2:3–12), the authority of the proclamation and teaching he imparts (2:13; 4:2), the kind of sexual expression that is appro-

priate to Christ's followers (4:3–8), and the work habits that Christians should cultivate in order to express responsible love for each other (4:9–12). This is not all that Paul writes about, but it suffices to show that one way he achieves his purpose in writing is by giving further instruction. Like Jesus, when Paul saw God's people in need of shepherding, his impulse was to teach "them many things" (Mk 6:34–35).

Fourth, Paul encourages his readers by giving them insight into the last things. Theologians call this area of teaching eschatology, which means the study of what the Bible says will happen at the end of this age and beyond. One of 1 (and 2) Thessalonians' distinguishing features is a stress on eschatology (eighteen of forty-seven verses in 2 Thessalonians, or 38 percent of the letter, relate to eschatology). But Paul's goal is not to give comprehensive knowl-

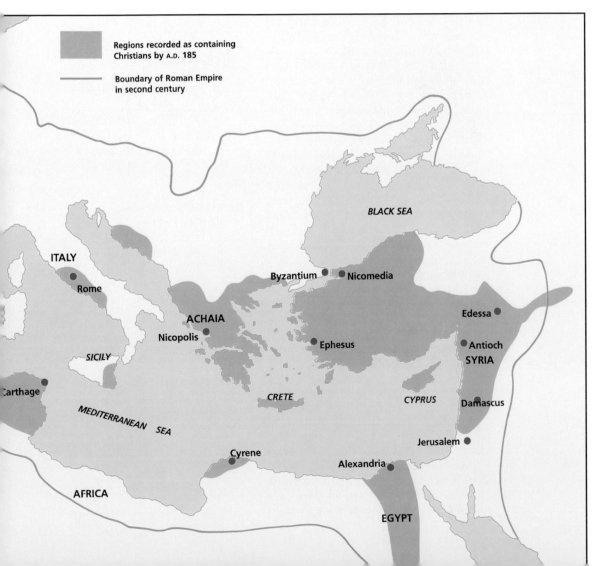

edge of the future. It is rather to give hope and encouragement in the present. His aim is edification, not speculation. But he achieves this aim by talking about things to come. These include the return of Jesus in judgment (1:10), rejoicing and reward at Christ's appearance (2:19; 3:13), the order of events when the Lord resurrects the righteous dead and raptures living Christians (4:13–18), and the danger of deception in the last days (5:1–11).

God-Focus at Thessalonica

The opening of this chapter spoke of the contrast between modern self-focus and the Thessalonians' God-focus. Given the hostility of both Jewish and pagan forces, it is remarkable that either the Thessalonian church or Paul's letters to them ever survived. Why did they? The central role that Paul ascribes to the Lord in their lives, as reflected by the frequency of mention of God, Christ, and related words in the Thessalonian correspondence, gives a partial answer to this question.

Note first that the word "God" appears some three dozen times in the Greek text of 1 Thessalonians. (Word counts in English translations may be slightly different.) "Jesus" appears about sixteen times. "Lord" appears about two dozen times. "Christ" appears about ten times. Looking ahead to 2 Thessalonians, a considerably shorter Epistle, "God" is found about eighteen times, "Jesus" thirteen times, "Lord" twenty-two times, and "Christ" ten times. First Thessalonians contains 89 verses and 2 Thessalonians 47 verses. This means that in 136 verses, there are nearly 150 references to God, Christ, or both. To this could be added over half a dozen references to the Holy Spirit.

Surveying 1 Thessalonians we note how Paul reassures his readers by reminding them that God chose them for salvation (1:4; see 2 Thes 2:13). God now takes center stage in their lives instead of idols (1:9). God gave Paul the strength and authority to preach his saving message to the Thessalonians (2:2–5). It is God who calls them "into his kingdom and glory" (2:12; see 2 Thes 1:11; 2:14). God is likewise the ultimate origin of the gospel they have accepted (2:13) and the one who presides over the church they have joined (2:14). God has a will for the lives of his people and will punish those who violate it (4:3–8).

In a word, Paul's language in 1 (as well as 2) Thessalonians bespeaks a personal and community awareness centered not on self but on God. This does not mean that self is unimportant. But it does serve as a reminder of where Christian self-esteem is most fruitfully sought: in recognition, worship, and service to the Lord. He can broaden human horizons and perspectives and lift them above the crushing limitations of self-fixations and oppressive circumstances. If there is any "secret" to the Thessalonians' success in bearing up under the conditions they faced, it may be due to the God-centeredness reflected in the exhortation from Paul that they received and adopted.

Second Thessalonians

Outline

    I. **The Greeting** (1:1–2)

   II. **The Judgment at Christ's Coming** (1:3–12)
      A. Trials Preceding Christ's Coming (1:3–5)
      B. Retribution at the Time of Christ's Coming (1:6–10)
      C. A Prayer for the Church in the Light of Christ's Coming (1:11–12)

  III. **Events Surrounding Christ's Coming** (2:1–12)
      A. The Call for Calmness (2:1–2)
      B. The Coming Apostasy (2:3–7)
      C. Antichrist Revealed (2:8–12)

  IV. **Right Attitudes Encouraged** (2:13–17)
      A. By Recalling the Foundations of Their Faith (2:13–14)
      B. By Exhortations to Stand Firm (2:15)
      C. By a Prayer for Spiritual Maturity (2:16–17)

   V. **Intercessory Prayer** (3:1–5)
      A. Requests for Prayer (3:1–2)
      B. Confidence in Prayer (3:3–4)
      C. A Wish-Prayer (3:5)

  VI. **Instruction in Faith and Life** (3:6–15)

Christ's Appearing and Eternal Consequences

Christians have high hopes about heaven. But what about hell?

As new Christians at Thessalonica suffer persecution, Paul assures them of a heavenly reward *"when the Lord Jesus is revealed"* (2 Thes 1:7). At that time their suffering will be more than compensated! Some think this speaks of a time when Christ will return and establish a physical earthly kingdom. Others think that *"when the Lord Jesus is revealed"* means after this world ends and all humans stand before God in judgment. Some will be placed on his right and some on his left to receive eternal reward or punishment (Mt 25:31–33).

The chronology of endtime events is debatable. But there is no debate about whether those who trust Christ will *"not perish but have eternal life"* (Jn 3:16). And by the same token those who reject Christ will suffer *"everlasting destruction"* (2 Thes 1:9). This view is not unique to Paul. Jesus spoke more about hell than about heaven. The whole Bible reflects the conviction that God's wrath is real and terrifying for those who spurn his grace.

Everlasting punishment is as assured as everlasting life. God promises both. He leaves it up to us to choose. The Thessalonians made the right choice, and Paul rejoiced. Paul's life and letters are a model for Christians today to take the message of God's grace in Christ to those who have not yet received it. Their eternal destiny, one way or the other, is at stake.

In modern times the view is popular that one day all will be saved (universalism). There is no hell. Others hold the theory of annihilation. After death the damned suffer intensely, but then they pass out of existence. Hell is not eternal but temporary. Such views may seem attractive, but so do many ideas based on human wisdom and not God's word (see Prv 14:12).

A. Attitude toward the Disorderly (3:6–10)
B. Correction of the Disorderly (3:11–13)
C. Discipline of the Disorderly (3:14–15)

VII. Final Greetings (3:16–18)
  A. The Prayer (3:16)
  B. The Authentication (3:17)
  C. The Benediction (3:18)

Purpose and Message

Much of what has already been said about 1 Thessalonians sheds light on 2 Thessalonians since the two letters were written only a few months apart. Paul continues to commend their faith and love (1:3) and their perseverance under trial (1:4). He continues to speak of Christ's return (1:5–10) and other eschatological matters (2:1–12). In these areas Paul's second letter to them is in some ways a shortened restatement of his first one.

Yet he does touch on other subjects. First, he takes particular pains to ensure that believers are not misled (2:1–3, 15; 3:2–4). Here Paul refers to people and writings circulating in or around the early church that somehow contradicted the true apostolic teaching. A major purpose of 2 Thessalonians is to counteract the influence of such forces.

Second, Paul gives instructions on how to handle wayward brethren (3:6–15). Not all the church's troubles come from hostile outsiders; sinful practices on the inside can also wreak havoc. Paul lays down guidelines for handling lazy busybodies. They are to be disciplined yet not treated as enemies (3:15).

Finally, a major purpose of 2 Thessalonians seems to be to assure believers of eventual victory, reward, and justice (1:4–10). Enemies of the gospel will receive their punishment in due time. Believers should rejoice that they are counted worthy to suffer indignity for Christ's sake. All who "do not obey the gospel of our Lord Jesus" (1:8) will bear the consequences, while Christ's followers will be granted a transforming vision of the Lord whom they have bravely served (1:10).

Critical Issues

The first words of both letters claim Paul as their author. (Silas and Timothy are named, too, and are part of Paul's traveling team on the second missionary jour-

The Pastoral Epistles in Early Church History

Paul's three extant pastoral letters appear to have been known and used by such early church leaders as:

	A.D.
Polycarp	ca. 110
	(1 Timothy only)
Irenaeus	ca. 175
Clement of Alexandria	ca. 200
	(not 2 Timothy)
Tertullian	ca. 200
Origen	ca. 250
Eusebius	ca. 315

All three letters are also listed in the Muratorian Canon, a list of writings accepted by Christian churches and dating to ca. A.D. 170.

Testament's portrayal of local conditions at Thessalonica was mistaken. Today, however, nearly three dozen ancient inscriptions confirm that the office of politarch existed in MACEDONIA in Paul's time.[4]

Second, the GALLIO inscription (four pieces of stone found last century in the Greek city of DELPHI) furnishes grounds for dating Paul's stay in Corinth, during which he wrote both Thessalonian letters. This inscription gives information that makes it possible to date Gallio's reign as proconsul (governor) over southern Greece (ACHAIA) to about A.D. 50–52. Because Paul appeared before Gallio at Corinth (Acts 18:12), and because he wrote 1 and 2 Thessalonians from that same city, we have reasonably secure dates for the composition of both Epistles.

First Timothy, Second Timothy, Titus

We now turn from the Thessalonian letters, which are among the earliest Pauline writings we possess, to three Epistles that most likely date from the very end of Paul's life: 1 Timothy, 2 Timothy, and Titus. These three are sometimes called the **Pastoral Epistles**. The term, coined in the eighteenth century, is fitting for two reasons. First, all three letters show pastoral concern for their recipients, Timothy and Titus. Second, all three deal with pastoral matters involving the care of souls and the orderly conduct of God's people in the church as well as in the world.

Fourth Missionary Journey and Authorship

All three Pastoral Epistles claim that Paul was their author. Yet it is not easy to fit the settings they describe into Paul's life as Acts presents it.[5] Following an ancient tradition that Paul was released from prison at ROME in about A.D. 62,[6] some scholars suggest that he then embarked on a fourth missionary tour. If so, he may have journeyed to SPAIN (Rom 15:24, 28; see also 1 Clem 5:7), then headed back east to CRETE (Ti 1:5), visiting former haunts like EPHESUS and Macedonia as well (1 Tm 1:3). Other travels could have taken him to MILETUS and Corinth (2 Tm 4:20), TROAS (2 Tm 4:13), and NICOPOLIS

ney, but there is no indication that they had active roles in formulating the letters' contents.) Virtually no scholars dispute the Pauline authorship of 1 Thessalonians. Questions have been raised about 2 Thessalonians because of its slightly different vocabulary, its allegedly more formal style, and its reference to "the lawless one" (2:8–9), a shadowy figure not specifically referred to elsewhere in Paul's writings. These questions are significant and interesting but do not seem weighty enough to call Paul's authorship into serious question.

Some have proposed that Paul wrote these two Epistles in the opposite order of their canonical appearance. Once again, while the arguments are interesting, they fall short of being persuasive.[3]

Critical investigation has uncovered two bodies of evidence that bolster our knowledge of the Thessalonian setting. The first relates to the title of the "city officials" who heard complaints against Paul's preaching (Acts 17:6). The Greek word for these officials is *politarch*. Because this term is not attested elsewhere in first-century writings, it used to be suggested that the New

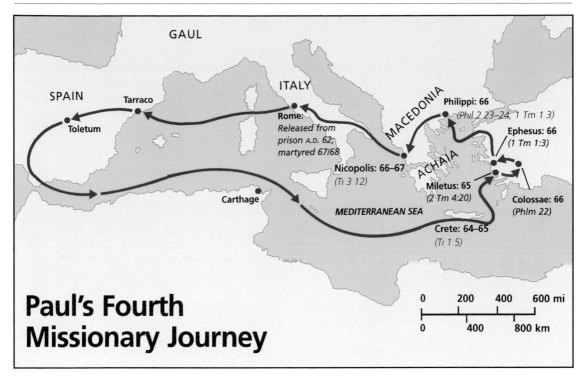

Paul's Fourth Missionary Journey

GAUL

SPAIN

Toletum

Tarraco

ITALY

Rome:
Released from
prison A.D. 62;
martyred 67/68

Carthage

Nicopolis: 66–67
(Ti 3 12)

MACEDONIA

Philippi: 66
(Phil 2 23–24, 1 Tm 1 3)

ACHAIA

Ephesus: 66
(1 Tm 1:3)

Miletus: 65
(2 Tm 4:20)

Colossae: 66
(Phlm 22)

MEDITERRANEAN SEA

Crete: 64–65
(Ti 1 5)

| 0 | 200 | 400 | 600 mi |
| 0 | 400 | 800 km | |

(Ti 3:12). During these travels he could have written 1 Timothy and Titus.[7] Paul's second imprisonment would then have been the occasion for writing 2 Timothy, in which Paul alludes to his chains (1:8; 2:9). Shortly after writing 2 Timothy Paul

Paul's Last Years

Ancient sources suggest that the Pastoral Epistles were written during the following period in Paul's life:

Under [Festus], Paul, after having pleaded his cause, was sent a prisoner to Rome. But Aristarchus was his fellow companion, whom he also somewhere in his epistles calls his fellow-prisoner; and here Luke, that wrote the Acts of the Apostles, after showing that Paul passed two whole years at Rome as a prisoner at large, and that he preached the gospel without restraint, brings his history to a close. After pleading his cause, he is said to have been sent again to the city [of Rome], where he finished his life with martyrdom.

—From Eusebius, *Church History* 2.22

apparently suffered death by beheading under persecutions instigated by the "degenerate madness"[8] of the Roman emperor NERO.

Despite the Epistles' clear claims that Paul wrote them, most scholars today view them as products of a later age. Someone else wrote in Paul's name, they urge, because they find various reasons for discounting the church's unanimous view over its first eighteen centuries that Paul was indeed the author.

The debate over Pauline authorship is too involved to be recounted here. An older essay still worth consulting argues that Pauline authorship has been too hastily dismissed; there are no compelling reasons for accepting modern alternative views.[9] Recently L. T. Johnson has argued convincingly for Paul's authorship of 1 and 2 Timothy. He exposes many fallacies in traditional critical scholarship on this topic.[10] No one has yet produced evidence that the ancient church accepted letters as apostolic that it knew to be written pseudonymously (under an assumed name, in this case Paul's).[11] In spite of the important questions that have been raised, we are justified in continuing to receive these Epistles as part of the Christian canon, penned by a chosen messen-

Opposite: The Arcadian Way, Ephesus.

ger of Jesus Christ himself, the apostle Paul.

First Timothy

Outline

I. **Salutation** (1:1–2)

II. **Warnings against False Teachers** (1:3–7)

III. **The Proper Use of the Law** (1:8–11)

IV. **God's Grace to Paul** (1:12–17)

V. **Paul's Charge to Timothy** (1:18–20)

VI. **Instructions Concerning Prayer** (2:1–8)

VII. **Instructions to Women** (2:9–15)
   A. Adornment (2:9–10)
   B. Teaching and Exercising Authority (2:11–15)

VIII. **Overseers and Deacons** (3:1–16)
   A. Overseers (3:1–7)
   B. Deacons (3:8–13)
   C. The Basis for Conduct in God's Household (3:14–16)

IX. **False Asceticism** (4:1–5)

X. **Ministerial Training** (4:6–16)

XI. **Christian Duties** (5:1–6:2)
   A. Exhortation (5:1–2)
   B. Widows (5:3–16)
   C. Instructions for Elders (5:17–25)
   D. Instructions for Slaves (6:1–2)

XII. **Final Indictment of False Teachers** (6:3–5)

XIII. **The Love of Money** (6:6–10)

XIV. **Final Exhortation** (6:11–16)

XV. **Instruction for the Rich** (6:17–19)

XVI. **Final Admonition** (6:20–21)

Occasion for Writing and Message

The Epistle opens with Paul urging Timothy to "stay there in Ephesus" (1:3) where Timothy was apparently serving as pastor. (On the city of Ephesus, see the previous chapter.) False teachers were threatening the stability and integrity of the Christian community (1:3–7). Paul gives instructions on proper interpretation of the law, by which he probably means the Old Testament (1:8–11). The false teachers were making improper use of it, suggesting that Paul's old Jewish adversaries were still seeking to discredit the preaching of salvation by grace (not lawkeeping) through faith in Jesus' atoning death and resurrection.

To encourage Timothy in the face of opposition Paul reminds him how he himself had once opposed the gospel (1:12–17). But God showed him mercy. There is therefore hope even in Timothy's difficult situation, and he should persevere (1:18–20). Paul reminds him of the sort of matters he ought to focus on: prayer and worship (ch. 2), high standards for those filling church offices (ch. 3), avoidance of heresy through maintenance of sound teaching (ch. 4), proper care for widows and elders (ch. 5), and godly respect by slaves for their masters (6:1–2). Paul concludes with final warnings regarding false teachers and teachings (6:3–5, 20–21) and final encouragement for Timothy, who should avoid love of money and pursue his calling with vigor despite the many distractions he faces.

Second Timothy

Outline

I. **Salutation** (1:1–2)

II. **Encouragement to Be Faithful** (1:3–18)
   A. Thanksgiving for Timothy (1:3–5)
   B. An Appeal for Boldness to Endure Suffering (1:6–14)
   C. Examples of Disloyalty and Loyalty (1:15–18)

III. **Be Strong and Suffer Hardship** (2:1–13)
   A. The Direct Appeal to Timothy (2:1–3)

Qualifications for Pastors

In the Pastoral Epistles, Paul sets forth demanding standards for those selected to fill the church's highest offices of service and leadership. Lists of qualifications are different but comparable:

1 Timothy 3:2–7	Titus 1:6–9
above reproach	blameless
husband of one wife	husband of one wife
temperate	children who believe and are not wild
self-controlled	not overbearing
respectable	not quick-tempered
hospitable	not given to drunkenness
able to teach	not violent
not given to drunkenness	not seeking dishonest gain
not violent but gentle	hospitable
not quarrelsome	promoter of what is good
not a lover of money	self-controlled
manages own family well	upright
not a recent convert	holy
good reputation with outsiders	disciplined
	firm advocate of the Christian message, to encourage believers and refute detractors

B. The Soldier, Athlete, and Farmer Images (2:4–7)
C. Remember Jesus Christ (2:8–10)
D. A Hymn of Endurance in the Face of Suffering (2:11–13)

IV. **What an Approved Workman Needs to Know and Do** (2:14–26)
A. Exhortation to Resist False Teachers (2:14–19)
B. The Analogy of Household Vessels (2:20–21)
C. Timothy's Responsibilities in the Midst of False Teaching (2:22–26)

V. **The Difficult Times of the Last Days** (3:1–9)

VI. **Another Appeal to Timothy to Continue in the Faith** (3:10–17)

VII. **The Charge to Preach the Word** (4:1–5)

VIII. **The Final Testimony of Paul** (4:6–8)

IX. **Personal Remarks and Instructions** (4:9–18)

X. **Final Greetings** (4:19–22)

Occasion for Writing and Message

Paul writes 2 Timothy from prison (1:8), probably in Rome where he awaits his final trial and execution (4:6–8, 16–18). His letter is designed to encourage Timothy and to urge him to come join Paul before winter sets in (4:21).

As the above outline indicates, much of 2 Timothy is devoted to reflections on suffering. Paul gives thanks for Timothy's sincere faith (1:3–5) and urges him to join Paul in "suffering for the gospel" (1:8). This is not a wish that Timothy would land in jail like Paul but an exhortation to be true to Christ, even when the price for such fidelity is high. In Paul's experience it usually was. Some have deserted Paul, presumably because of the danger involved in upholding their Christian confession in association with him. Yet Onesiphorus has not (1:15–18; 4:19). Timothy must likewise "endure hardship . . . like a good soldier of Jesus Christ" (2:3), like an athlete in training (2:5), or like a hardworking farmer (2:6). This is not a grim Stoic coping mechanism or asceticism; it is the example of the Lord Jesus himself (2:8–10) and the calling he extends to his servants (2:11–13).

Paul gives a healthy measure of pastoral counsel to guide Timothy and to pass on to the congregation in Ephesus. False teachers are to be resisted (2:14–19). Timothy must flee youthful lusts and quarrels, replacing them with Christian virtues that will facilitate effective pastoral leadership (2:22–26). But he should realize that the times are perilous, with religious deceivers poised to take advantage of the unwary (3:1–9). Timothy can overcome their threat through the apostolic example and teaching, through faith, and through attention to the Scriptures (3:10–17).

Paul closes with a dramatic charge to proclaim the Christian message faithfully, even when audiences would rather not hear it (4:1–5). He describes his own situation, passes on his greetings to a few of the Ephesian believers, relays greetings from his sole companion Luke, and gives Timothy instructions pertaining to the trip to Rome that Paul wants him to make (4:6–22). Timothy is to bring Mark and some of Paul's personal effects (4:11–13).

We simply do not know whether Timothy arrived in time for one last earthly reunion with his beloved mentor before the executioner's ax fell and Paul received the heavenly reward that he confidently awaited (4:8).

Titus

Outline

I. **Salutation** (1:1–4)

II. **Qualifications for Elders** (1:5–9)

III. **Silencing the False Teachers** (1:10–16)

IV. **Instructions for Various Groups** (2:1–10)
   A. Instructions for Older Men (2:1–2)
   B. Instructions for Older Women and Younger Women (2:3–5)
   C. Instructions for Young Men and Titus (2:6–8)

D. Instructions for Slaves (2:9–10)

V. **The Basis for the Instructions** (2:11–15)

VI. **Doing Good in Society** (3:1–8)
   A. Responsibilities as Citizens (3:1–2)
   B. The Basis for the Christian's Attitude (3:3–8)

VII. **Further Instructions about False Teachers** (3:9–11)

VIII. **Personal Instructions and Greetings** (3:12–15)

Occasion for Writing and Message
Titus is the shortest Pastoral Epistle. Its purpose is to give Titus, who is overseeing a number of other pastors on the island of Crete, practical direction until Paul's aides Artemas or Tychicus arrive (3:12). Then Paul wants Titus to come join him for the winter at Nicopolis, a port city lying some 140 miles northwest of Corinth.[12]

Paul had been in Crete with Titus earlier, leaving him behind to finish church organization and leadership training (1:5). He writes with reminders about the high standards required for elders or pastors (1:6–9). He also gives instructions on handling those who oppose the Christian message (1:10–16). They seem to be as numerous in Crete as they were most other places Paul ministered. Paul quotes a Cretan prophet to describe the wearisome sort of people that Titus found himself up against (1:12).

Paul is concerned that all age groups of both men and women relate to each other in ways that will show the love of Christ and the truth of the gospel. He gives explicit instructions for older men, older women, younger women, and younger men (2:1–6). He also gives counsel meant for Titus personally as well as for slaves (2:7–10). The goal in all this is, negatively stated, to keep the word of God from being maligned (2:5). Positively, Paul seeks to "make the teaching about God our Savior attractive" (2:10). It is only right to present Christian faith in its best possible light in view of all that the Lord has done on behalf of his people (2:11–15).

Paul closes by urging a submissive attitude toward "rulers and authorities" (3:1) and a considerate attitude toward nonbelievers generally. Why? Because "at one time we too were foolish, disobedient, deceived and enslaved by all kinds of passions and pleasures" (3:3). If Christians attain a more spiritual and moral level of life than others, it is not because of their own intrinsic goodness but God's grace. They should therefore be zealous, not complacent, in living up to the high calling they have received (3:4–8, 14).

The Wisdom of the Pastoral Epistles

Paul's last three known letters are rich in insight and instruction. They are often among Christians' favorite books of the Bible because they contain so much concise counsel. A few aspects of the wisdom Paul offers bear mention here.

The trust Paul placed in young Timothy is noteworthy. Apparently Timothy's youthfulness (1 Tm 4:12) tempted some to look down on him or take his leadership lightly. It is true that young and inexperienced people can cause difficulty for any institution, including the church. But it need not be so. In modern times the late evangelist and scholar J. Edwin Orr documented the great contribution of spiritual awakenings among college-age students to the life of the church internationally over the past two centuries.[13] Young people zealous for Christ, willing to repent of their sins and trust in him, and ready to follow him in costly service, have played a major role in the growth of God's kingdom. In this they have imitated faithful young Timothy. Paul's pastoral letters to his youthful partner are an enduring encouragement

Focus 21: Two Young Believers Stand Firm

Paul praises the Thessalonians for withstanding persecution and urges young Timothy to be ready to suffer if necessary. A century later, in Gaul (modern France), a young woman named Blandina and a fifteen-year-old youth named Ponticus lived out the brave spirit of Paul's exhortations. An ancient letter tells of their persecution:

. . . [O]n the last day of the gladiatorial sports, Blandina was again brought in with Ponticus. . . . They had been brought in every day to see the torture of the others. Efforts were made to force them to swear by the idols, and the mob was furious because they had remained steadfast and disregarded them. So there was neither pity for the youth nor respect for the sex of the woman. They exposed them to all the terrors and put them through every torture in turn, trying to make them swear, but not being able to do so. For Ponticus was encouraged by the Christian sister. Even the heathen saw that she was exhorting and strengthening him. After nobly enduring every torture he gave up his spirit. But the blessed Blandina, last of all, like a noble mother who had encouraged her children and sent them forth triumphant to the king, having herself endured all the tortures of the children, hastened to them, rejoicing and glad at her departure as though invited to a marriage feast rather than cast to the beasts. And after scourging, after the beasts, after the gridiron, she was at last put in a net and thrown to a bull. She was tossed about for a long time by the beast, having no more feeling for what happened to her through her hope and hold on what had been entrusted to her and her close fellowship with Christ. Thus she too was sacrificed. The heathen themselves confessed that never before had they seen a woman suffer so much and so long.

—From Eusebius, *Church History* 5.1.53–56

Women in the New Testament (1 Tm 2)

Recent trends in Western society have highlighted the role, and sometimes plight, of women in society. How does the New Testament view women? Is Paul's statement in 1 Timothy 2:11–12 demeaning?

Jesus ennobled women by speaking openly with them and teaching them, something that other Jewish teachers of his time frowned on. He upheld the Old Testament doctrine of male and female equality (Gn 1:27). Based on the Old Testament he condemned casual divorce practices in which men took advantage of wives (Mt 19:4–6). His healing touch was for sons and daughters of Abraham alike (Lk 13:16). A poor widow's tiny gift was greater than the hefty contributions of wealthy hypocrites (Lk 21:1–4). Women bravely joined courageous men in standing watch at Jesus' cross (Lk 23:27, 49). Women were the first to discover the empty tomb (Lk 24:2).

Paul followed Jesus in according women a much higher place than was common in many circles at that time. Husbands are to place their wives' welfare above their own (Eph 5:25). Paul commends many women co-workers in Christ (Rom 16:1, 3, 6, 7, 12; Phil 4:3). Women are heirs of salvation in Christ just as men are (Gal 3:28).

Discussion about the role of women in church and society today is sometimes heated. In dealing with a controversial text like 1 Timothy 2:11–12, the high esteem for women shown by the Lord Jesus and his apostolic followers, including Paul, should be borne in mind. There are different ways of understanding their practices and applying their teachings. But we should be slow to conclude that New Testament directives are outmoded simply because they are out of step with modern times. Sometimes it is modern times that need to get in step with Scripture.

for college-age believers not to underestimate the importance of faithfulness to Christ—not later but now.

In the Pastorals as in the Prison Epistles (see previous chapter) Paul sets forth a positive ethic. This means that serving the Lord is *not* primarily a matter of not doing bad things, though it is important not to disobey God. Rather the Christian call is to replace, and thereby to overcome, evil with good. As Paul tells Timothy, "Flee the evil desires of youth"—but Paul immediately goes on to state what Timothy should pursue: "righteousness, faith, love and peace" (2 Tm 2:22). Sometimes Christians become frustrated by their inability to overcome certain habits of thought or action. "I must quit thinking of this; I must quit doing that," they tell themselves. But the thought or deed only grows stronger. Paul's (the Lord's) solution is to channel drives, to focus and expend them productively for Christ, not simply try to eradicate them, which is often impossible. Careful study of the Pastorals reveals many examples of Paul outlining positive steps for Timothy to take, not merely negative advice on what Timothy must avoid.

Paul's letter to Titus contains a repeated stress on good works (2:7, 14; 3:1, 8, 14).[14] These references are a valuable reminder that Paul's stress on justification "by faith apart from observing the law" (Rom 3:28) should not be taken to mean that good works are unimportant or optional. Jesus taught that those who love him will keep his commandments (Jn 14:15). In the Pastorals, and especially in Titus, Paul underscores this truth.

The Christian understanding of the Bible finds one of its clearest expressions in 2 Timothy 3:16–17. "All Scripture is God-breathed," Paul writes. He refers specifically to the Old Testament, but the same holds true for the New, since it is Scripture too, including Paul's letters (2 Pt 3:15–16). Elsewhere Peter states the same truth using a different figure: "No prophecy of Scripture came about by the prophet's own interpretation. For prophecy never had its origin in the will of man, but men spoke from God as they were carried along by the Holy Spirit" (2 Pt 1:20–21). The point is that Christians are justified in holding a very high view of the reliability of the Bible, because it is not just a human book but of divine origin, and because it makes the claim to be "God-breathed" itself.

Critical Issues

We have already mentioned that scholars debate whether Paul wrote the Pastorals and if so at what stage of his life. There is also discussion regarding the church or-

Key People/Places

Ephesus
Gallio
Greece
Macedonia
Achaia
Miletus
Amphipolis
Nero
Antioch (Syrian)
Nicopolis
Apollonia
Philippi
Asia Minor
Rome
Athens
Spain
Berea
Thessalonica
Corinth
Thessaloniki
Crete
Troas
Delphi

Key Terms

Pastoral Epistles
politarch

ganization reflected in the Pastorals, the identity of the false teachers Paul mentions, and the relation of the theology found in the Pastorals to the theology found in the other Pauline letters.

Certain passages in 1 Timothy pose challenges to all who read them. How do Paul's positive remarks about the law in 1:8–11 square with less positive remarks elsewhere? How should the statement, "A woman should learn in quietness and full submission. I do not permit a woman to teach or to have authority over a man; she must be silent," be understood and honored in the church today (2:11–12)?[15] What does "women shall be saved through

Summary

1. In spite of opposition, Paul founded a church in Thessalonica on his second missionary journey.

2. Paul wrote 1 Thessalonians to encourage new believers by confirming that hard times are part of God's plan for his people, by commending their faith and love, by giving further instructions, and by providing insight into the last things.

3. In 1 Thessalonians Paul places the emphasis on God and not on self.

4. In 2 Thessalonians Paul continues the encouragement he began in 1 Thessalonians as well as emphasizing that believers must not be misled, providing instruction on handling wayward brothers, and assuring believers of eventual victory, reward, and justice.

5. First and Second Timothy and Titus are called Pastoral Epistles because they show pastoral concern for their recipients and deal with pastoral matters involving care of souls and orderly conduct in the church.

6. Paul wrote 1 Timothy to encourage Timothy to persevere with the church at Ephesus in spite of opposition.

7. In 1 Timothy Paul reminds Timothy to focus on prayer and worship, to hold high standards for filling church offices, to avoid heresy by maintaining sound teaching, to take proper care of widows, to have slaves show godly respect for their masters, to guard against false teachers, and to avoid love of money.

8. In 2 Timothy Paul focuses on the hardship to be endured by the servant of God.

9. The purpose of Paul's letter to Titus is to give him practical direction for his work on Crete until others can join him.

10. In Titus, special instructions were given for different groups, including older men, older and younger women, young men and Titus, and slaves.

childbearing" (2:15) mean? Should the modern church give the same priorities to care for widows that Timothy's church did (ch. 5)?

But the primary critical questions for the Pastorals as a whole surround their origin—from Paul or not?—and their setting—were they written during Paul's life, or perhaps decades later, thus addressing a very different social setting than could have existed in Paul's lifetime? Debate on these matters among scholars is lively, and the questions are not likely to find universally satisfactory answers any time soon.

Review Questions

1. Paul founded the Thessalonian church while on his _____ missionary journey.

2. Most of the remains of Thessalonica have not been excavated because they are buried beneath the city of _____.

3. The Thessalonian church experienced much _____.

4. Paul tried to encourage the Thessalonians by giving further _____ about such matters as demonstrating love for each other.

5. In 1 Thessalonians Paul's repeated use of the word _____ illustrates that his focus was on _____.

6. In 2 Thessalonians Paul seems to have written a _____ version of 1 Thessalonians.

7. The dating of Paul's stay in Corinth has been documented by the _____.

8. The Pastoral Epistles are _____, _____, and _____.

9. Paul's letters to Timothy and Titus all show _____ for them.

10. Timothy was serving as pastor in _____.

11. During the writing of 2 Timothy, Paul was in the city of _____.

12. Titus was overseeing a group of pastors on the island of _____.

Study Questions

1. How does the God-centeredness of 1 Thessalonians relate to the issue of self-esteem?

2. In what ways did suffering aid the Thessalonians in their Christian commitment?

3. Why are 1 and 2 Timothy and Titus called the Pastoral Epistles?

4. Describe Paul's positive ethic.

5. What are three features of the wisdom of the Pastoral Epistles?

Further Reading

See the works cited in the notes to this chapter. On Paul generally, see chapter 17.

Beale, G. K. *1–2 Thessalonians*. Downers Grove: InterVarsity, 2003. An accessible discussion of both letters.

Brown, Raymond. *An Introduction to the New Testament*. New York: Doubleday, 1997. Valuable chapters on each of the Pastoral Epistles. Extensive attention to critical discussion of whether Paul wrote certain New Testament books.

Carson, D. A. *The Inclusive Language Debate: A Plea for Realism*. Grand Rapids/Leicester: Baker/InterVarsity, 1998. Advanced but readable discussion of recent controversy over Bible translations.

———. "Pseudonymity and Pseudepigraphy." In *Dictionary of New Testament Background*, ed. Craig A. Evans and Stanley E. Porter. Downers Grove: InterVarsity, 2000, pp. 857–64. Important discussion relevant to the authorship of the Pastoral Epistles.

Castro, Ann F. "An Inconclusive Replay: Is There Conclusive Evidence for Women's Ordination?" *Touchstone* 15 (2002): 27–31. A Greek professor traces the results of her investigation of the "women's issue."

Donfried, Karl P. *Paul, Thessalonica, and Early Christianity*. Grand Rapids: Eerdmans, 2002. Updates and furthers scholarly discussion on the Thessalonian letters as they relate to Paul's doctrine, early church formation, the Dead Sea Scrolls, and other matters.

Doriani, Dan. *Women in Ministry*. Wheaton, Ill.: Crossway, 2003. Tackles all the difficult Pauline passages on the subject. Neither old-fashioned nor avant-garde in conclusions.

Fudge, Edward William, and Robert A. Peterson. *Two Views of Hell: A Biblical and Theological Dialogue*. Downers Grove: InterVarsity, 2000.

Debate between two interpreters who hold opposing views on what the Bible teaches. Fudge believes the unrepentant wicked will suffer for a limited time after death and then cease to exist. This is called the annihilation theory. Peterson argues the majority position of church history: the Bible teaches that after death the unrepentant wicked face unending conscious punishment.

Johnson, L. T. *The First and Second Letters to Timothy*. New York: Doubleday, 2001. A leading Roman Catholic scholar argues for Paul's authorship of the Pastoral Epistles. Comprehensive bibliography. Strong on Greco-Roman background.

Keener, Craig S. *Paul, Women, and Wives: Marriage and Women's Ministry in the Letters of Paul*. Peabody, Mass.: Hendrickson, 1992. Argues that passages like 1 Tm 2:9–15 are no longer binding on church practice.

Köstenberger, Andreas J., Thomas R. Schreiner, and H. Scott Baldwin, eds. *Women in the Church: A Fresh Analysis of 1 Timothy 2:9–15*. Grand Rapids: Baker, 1995. Comprehensive study of 1 Tm 2.

Mounce, William D. *Pastoral Epistles*. Nashville: Thomas Nelson, 2000. An exhaustive investigation (641 pages). Mounce argues for Pauline authorship. Focuses most of all on theological interpretation of each passage. Comprehensive bibliography.

Oden, Thomas C. *Ministry Through Word and Sacrament*. New York: Crossroad, 1989. A compilation of thoughts from church leaders through the centuries on the pastor's craft and calling. Topics include preaching, prayer, care for one's own soul, and many other aspects of pastoral leadership. Much of this wisdom is informed by Paul's Pastoral Epistles.

Weima, Jeffrey A. D., and Stanley E. Porter. *An Annotated Bibliography of First and Second Thessalonians*. Leiden: Brill, 1998. A valuable research tool containing hundreds of references to scholarship on the Thessalonian letters.

Part

4

Encountering the General Epistles and the Apocalypse

22 Hebrews and James
Maintaining Full Commitment to Christ

Objectives

After reading this chapter, you should be able to

- List the eight General Epistles
- Discuss the possible recipients of the Book of Hebrews
- Explain the purpose of the Book of Hebrews
- Outline the content of the Book of Hebrews
- Outline the content of the Book of James
- Illustrate how James reflects elements of both prophecy and wisdom writings from the Old Testament

General or Catholic Epistles

Hebrews	1, 2, 3 John
James	Jude
1, 2 Peter	

The General Epistles

In the five previous chapters we considered Paul's thirteen letters. We also summarized his thought and teaching. But Paul's letters are not the only ones contained in the New Testament. After Philemon, the shortest Pauline Epistle, we encounter Hebrews, which is nearly as long as any Pauline letter. Hebrews marks a new grouping within the New Testament writings: the General Epistles. They are eight in number. Like Paul's letters they come in the approximate order of their length, with the longest (Hebrews) first and the shortest (Jude) last. True, 2 and 3 John are each quite brief. But taken together with 1 John they form a body of writings that is longer than Jude.

They are called "general" because they appeal either to no specific audience (Hebrews, 2 Peter, 1 John, Jude) or to an audience whose exact identity is somewhat broad (James, 1 Peter) or vague (2, 3 John) to us. Sometimes these eight

Hebrews in Early Church History

Hebrews was widely used by early church leaders and in various writings, including:

	A.D.
Clement of Rome	ca. 95
Epistle of Barnabas	ca. 130
Irenaeus	ca. 175
Clement of Alexandria	ca. 200
Tertullian	ca. 200
Eusebius	ca. 315

Epistles are called the "catholic" Epistles. Here the word "catholic" simply means "universal, general" (from the Greek *kath' holon,* meaning "throughout"), and does not refer specifically to the Roman Catholic Church.

In this chapter we take up the first two of the General Epistles, Hebrews and James.

Hebrews: Sermonic Epistle

The Mystery of Hebrews' Authorship

It is not clear who wrote Hebrews. In contrast to Paul's thirteen canonical letters, Hebrews does not name its author. It is written in a Greek style that seems different from Paul's. It never uses the phrase "Christ Jesus," a title used elsewhere by Paul some ninety times. It lacks the Pauline greeting at the letter's beginning. Ancient church leaders were accordingly unsure of who wrote it. They made various suggestions, ranging from Paul (note the reference to Timothy in Heb 13:23), to a student of Paul, to Luke, to Barnabas. Martin Luther suggested that the author was Apollos. The fact is that we simply do not know for sure who the author was. The book's tone and content convinced the ancients that it deserved a place in the small collection of authoritative writings that eventually came to be known as the New Testament. Today most Bible-believing Christians around the world would endorse the soundness of their judgment.

Date, Recipients, Purpose, and Genre

Because CLEMENT OF ROME cites Hebrews in his Epistle to the Corinthians (A.D. 95), Hebrews must have been written well before that time. Timothy was still alive as the author wrote (13:23), and the impression is given that the recipients of Hebrews had heard the gospel from eyewitnesses of Jesus' ministry (2:3). It is possible that the temple in Jerusalem is still standing as the author writes; otherwise he would surely have used its destruction in A.D. 70 to clinch his argument that Christ's sacrifice supersedes the temple's bloody offer-

It is likely that the temple in Jerusalem is still standing as the author writes the Epistle to the Hebrews.

ings (10:2). No one can say with certainty when Hebrews was written, but any time between the A.D. 40s and 60s fits the known facts.

Several lines of evidence indicate that Hebrews was written to a Jewish Christian audience. The first readers were former adherents of Judaism who accepted Jesus as the promised Messiah and became his followers. This claim is supported, first, by the book's title "Hebrews" or "To the Hebrews." The evidence that it ever circulated under a different name is limited. Such ancient testimony should not be set aside lightly. Second, the author assumes a level of knowledge of Old Testament sacrificial practices and Jewish teaching that hardly befits a Gentile Christian audience. Third, the core of Hebrews' argument is that Jesus Christ has perfected, and in that sense rendered obsolete, the levitical institutions of the Old Testament (see 7:11; 8:7; 10:1–2) for the people of God in the days following the Messiah's advent. The writer's exhortation for his readers to make a decisive break with the Jewish "camp" (13:13) implies that they had once made their religious home there.

If Hebrews was written to Jewish Christians, do we know why the author wrote it? It seems that he wrote to warn his readers not to turn back to Judaism and to encourage them to stay true to faith in Jesus Christ. Hebrews 10:32–39 offers a window into the situation. After initial courageous reception of the gospel in the face of bitter persecution (10:32–34), they must not throw away the high level of confidence they had attained (10:35). To stand firm is salvation; to shrink back would mean defeat and destruction (10:39). While the writer's arguments are numerous, varied, and sometimes complex, his central purpose is fairly elementary: Trust in the Lord and stand your ground! In this sense Hebrews sounds a theme that is common throughout much of Scripture (see, e.g., Jos 1:6; Ps 27:14; 1 Cor 15:58; Eph 6:10).

Technically speaking Hebrews lacks the most common feature of an ancient letter: the formal greeting at the very beginning. On the other hand, the conclusion indicates that the writer has a particular audience and setting in mind (13:22–25). Yet the writer calls his work a "word of exhortation" (13:22). This same term is used to describe a sermon in Acts 13:15. "Sermonic Epistle" is perhaps a helpful way to think of the letter overall since it combines aspects of both forms of literary expression.

Outline

I. The Superiority of the Christian Faith (1:1–10:18)
  A. Jesus Christ Superior to the Prophets (1:1–4)

Mosaic code

B. Jesus Christ Superior to Angels (1:5–2:18)
C. Jesus Christ Superior to Moses (3:1–4:13)
D. Jesus Christ Superior to Aaron (4:14–10:18)

II. **Exhortations to Persevere in Christian Faith** (10:19–12:29)
A. The Danger of Apostasy (10:19–31)
B. Encouragements to Press On (10:32–39)
C. Faith Defined and Exemplified (11:1–40)
D. Jesus, the Superior Example of Faith (12:1–4)
E. The Meaning and Merit of Discipline (12:5–13)
F. Warning Not to Turn Away from God (12:14–29)

III. **Concluding Exhortations** (13:1–19)

IV. **Benediction and Greetings** (13:20–25)

Focal Points

The above outline indicates that Hebrews has two main aims. One is to remind the readers of the incomparable greatness of Jesus Christ (1:1–10:18). Old Testament

---

Old Testament Examples for New Testament Faith

Hebrews 11 cites over a dozen Old Testament figures as examples for Christians to follow:

Abel	Gideon
Enoch	Barak
Noah	Samson
Abraham	Jephthah
Isaac	David
Jacob	Samuel
Joseph	The prophets
Moses	Numerous
People of Israel	unnamed men
Rahab	and women

---

prophets, angels, Moses, and Aaron serve grand purposes in God's redemptive plan. But none of these can compare with God the Son, who "is the radiance of God's glory and the exact representation of his being, sustaining all things by his powerful word" (1:3). Like other New Testament writings, then, Hebrews calls on believers to look to Jesus Christ. He can furnish insight into their dilemma and grace to help them find their way forward (4:16).

The second focal point follows from the first: The readers need to reaffirm their courageous Christian faith of former days (10:19–12:29). Because God is faithful to his promises, believers can have confidence even in their current troubled times (10:23).

Down with the Old Testament?

We will examine the message of Hebrews more fully in the next section, but first we must examine a common misconception. It is sometimes held that Hebrews amounts to an attack on Old Testament religion. In this view the faith of Old Testament believers was qualitatively inferior to what Christians enjoy. The Old Testament is significant chiefly as a tribute to a religious system that saw its day and is now rightly the object of pity if not scorn.

Against this view we note, first, that Hebrews 11 draws its examples of faith from Old Testament characters or times, whether before, during, or after the institution of the **Mosaic code**. Second, Hebrews refers to the Old Testament extensively as the foundation for its own teachings and warnings; it would be a basic logical error to base arguments on writings thought to be mistaken or no longer in force. Third, the "fault" that the writer diagnoses in God's people in the days before Christ's first coming involves their misuse of God's covenant love, not the Old Testament or the covenants God established there (Heb 8:8: "But God found fault with the people"; cf. Jer 31:32: "they broke my covenant"). Fourth, there is a basic continuity assumed between the nature of God and his dealings with his people in Old Testament times, on the one hand, and in New Testament times, on the other (see, e.g., 10:26–31). Hebrews' obvious criticisms of certain attitudes and practices of Old Testament characters do not constitute a dismissal of Old Testament faith.

Hebrews attacks a false conception of faith in God that too often prevailed in Old Testament times, not the Old Testament or its message in itself. In this false conception, God could be appeased by dutiful observance of religious rituals. The law, the priesthood, the sacrifices—in the Old Testament these were intended to instruct God's people in their need for redemption and to lift their gaze to their Lord and to a deliverer whom he would one day send. Tragically, many set their hope in their ritual observance—and thus ultimately in themselves—not in God's promise to save. The result was a sterile and rebellious stance toward God, one that prophets from Samuel (1 Sm 15:22) to Malachi (Mal 1:10) were sent from God to address. In fact, even parts of Moses' sermons in Deuteronomy (see, e.g., Dt 9:4–6) may be seen as warnings against the human tendency to twist God's provision of salvation by free grace into a message of justification by idolatrous good works. By the first century we find Jesus, Paul, and others blowing the whistle on such misunderstanding of what knowing the Lord entails.

It is just this false understanding of the Old Testament that the writer of Hebrews criticizes. He exposes misuse of Old Testament institutions in order to allow the brilliance of Christ's ministry, as foreshadowed in the Old Testament, to shine in its fullness. Obviously the days of animal sacrifice and high priestly ritual are things of the past now that what they symbolized has taken place. But, far from setting the Old Testament aside, the writer calls his readers to ponder its abiding message in the fuller light of God's dramatic self-disclosure in Christ.

Exhortation

The major practical concern of Hebrews is that Christians not be intimidated by the difficult circumstances they face. They should rather stand firm in their devotion to Christ. We may trace this concern in four passages. In each case the writer issues a warning, a reason for taking the warning seriously, and encouragement to heed the warning with faithfulness rather than fear.

In 2:1–4 the writer calls on his readers to pay more attention to the saving word they have heard lest they "drift away." Why would drifting away be so dangerous? Because of the dire consequences. The writer rightly reasons that if God's people in Old Testament times did not get off lightly when they defied God, then God's people who enjoy the added privilege of hearing about Christ will face even stiffer penalties (2:2–3). In other words, against a common modern view that Old Testament religion involved strict laws and harsh punishment, while the New Testament speaks only of love and forgiveness, Hebrews insists on the opposite. New Testament believers face a sterner judgment since they have received a more unmistakable revelation in Jesus Christ and all that accompanied his first coming (2:4). But there is also encouragement: Christ himself stands ready to give assistance. He has personal knowledge of the woes people face, and he can thus give aid to them in their time of trial (2:18).

In 3:12–14 and 4:1–2 the exhortation continues. Here the writer stresses the need to persevere, to follow through on the confession of Christ that brought his readers into the church in the first place. Believers have a secure "share in Christ if we hold firmly till the end the confidence we had at first" (3:14). The reason for this warning seems to involve the deceitfulness of both sin and the human heart (3:12–13). It is possible to be active in the community of believers without personal knowledge of the Lord and devotion to the Lord's interests. It is possible to profess belief but to live in rebellion. The writer refers to Old Testament examples of this and warns Christians not to fall into the same trap. But he also encourages, again pointing to Jesus Christ: He can "sympathize with our weaknesses." He is our high priest before God and enables us to approach God, despite our failings, "with confidence." We can thus "receive mercy and find grace to help us in our time of need" (4:15–16).

The next exhortation appears in 5:11–6:8. Here the warning is that once Christians turn their backs on Christ, it is difficult if not impossible for them to muster the will to return to him. Some interpret this passage to mean that true Christians can lose their salvation. To use

apostasy

a more technical term, they can "commit **apostasy**," or fall away from the faith. But others argue that those who finally reject Christ never really knew him to begin with. Whichever way we interpret these verses, its point is unmistakable. It is no small matter to go back on a commitment we have made to the Lord. Yet even in the midst of such grave warnings the writer repeats a message of hope (6:9–12). The writer is convinced that his readers can resist the temptation to give in to the pressure they face. Through God's faithfulness to them and through imitating faithful role models (6:12) they can face the future with peace and courage rather than fear.

A final exhortation comes in 10:26–31, perhaps the most harrowing warning of Hebrews if not of the whole Bible. "If we deliberately keep on sinning after we have received the knowledge of the truth, no sacrifice for sins is left, but only a fearful expectation of judgment and of raging fire that will consume the enemies of God" (10:26–27). Or again: "It is a dreadful thing to fall into the hands of the living God" (10:31). Yet once more the writer ends on a note of confidence and encouragement. He declares that his readers will not slink back into old bad habits but will rather rise to the high call of faithfulness (10:39).

From the 1940s into the 1980s students at a North American Christian college were privileged to sit under the instruction of Merrill C. Tenney. His love for the Bible, knowledge of ancient history and languages, high academic standards, and affection for students aided thousands along the sometimes rocky road of Christian faith. A student once asked Dr. Tenney to autograph a book he had written. Reluctantly, for he was a modest man, Dr. Tenney did so. Later the student was amazed to see that under his signature this great man of faith and learning had writ-

The Wrath of God

"It is a dreadful thing to fall into the hands of the living God" (Heb 10:31). Is belief in a wrathful God still appropriate in modern times?

Many say no. For generations some thinkers have sought to remake Christianity, bringing it in line with modern conceptions of religion and humankind not based on the Bible. In this view, the Bible's teachings are exchanged for a different outlook. One scholar has described the new version of Christianity in this way: "A God without wrath brought men without sin into a kingdom without judgment through the ministrations of a Christ without a cross" (H. Richard Niebuhr). The most common term for this new outlook was "liberalism."

The writer of Hebrews, however, like Jesus himself, knew the God who had sent the Great Flood, destroyed Sodom and Gomorrah, and (in 587 B.C.) overthrew even the city of Jerusalem when its people turned away from their God and refused to repent.

The Old Testament teaches that God's fiery wrath is but the other side of his zealous love. It took passionate devotion to sinners, and burning contempt for sin, for Jesus to endure the cross. Why should it seem wrong that those who reject his offer of free pardon will suffer the promised consequences?

Even if some modern persons refuse to take seriously the prospect of a coming day of judgment, God's people are on firm ground in affirming it. Not that they are eager to take revenge: that is God's business alone. But they trust God's word. They eagerly await God's justice, trusting in his mercy through Christ's cross to save them from the wrath to come. And they devote their lives to spreading the gospel, so that whoever is willing to avoid destruction and choose life, abundant life, has opportunity to repent and be saved.

ten a single Bible reference: Hebrews 10:38. It reads: "But my righteous one will live by faith. And if he shrinks back, I will not be pleased with him."

Was Tenney living under a shadow of fear? Did he fail to realize that God is love and that Christians have no need to be afraid of God's judgment? On the contrary, he knew the fuller truth. Knowing the Lord does not mean lapsing into a sloppy self-confidence that encourages laxness and excuses disobedience. It rather means exercising diligent faith out of a fierce desire to please rather than dishonor Christ. Tenney, confident yet not complacent, had taken to heart the exhortation that the writer of Hebrews issues.

Critical Issues

Much ink has been spilled in discussing the identity, circumstances, and setting of both the writer and readers of Hebrews. Evangelical scholars are at the forefront of discussion here, and excellent resources are available for deeper study of these questions and possible solutions.[1] Other areas of ongoing scrutiny include the view of Christ that Hebrews presents, the significance of Melchizedek and other Jewish elements of the letter especially in light of ongoing Dead Sea Scroll discoveries, the role of the Old Testament in Hebrews, and such themes as faith, the Epistle's view of history, and "rest" (see Heb 4).[2]

James: Epistle of Straw?

The next General Epistle after Hebrews is James. Only five chapters in length, it is rich in content. At times the church may be guilty of neglecting it, perhaps because it places so much stress on good works, and this seems to contradict Paul's emphasis on faith. As long ago as 1522 Martin Luther called it *"eyn rechte stroern Epistel"* ("a rather strawy letter") in comparison to Romans, Galatians, Ephesians, and 1 Peter. Yet even Luther did not exclude it from the New Testament, and he quoted it often and approvingly. Rather than suspicion, James deserves the honor of careful study and response.

There is, to be sure, an apparent contradiction between James 2:24 ("a person is justified by what he does and not by faith alone") and Romans 3:28 ("a man is justified by faith apart from observing the law"). The disagreement dissolves, however, when each passage is seen in its own context. In Romans Paul addresses the error that says that salvation is earned by human merit. No, Paul responds, salvation is God's free act of grace, which we receive by faith, not by acts of merit. James addresses a different error. This is the error that equates faith with mere assent to certain doctrinal truths like the existence of

James's Times and Death

Our knowledge of James and his times is not limited to Christian sources. The Jewish historian Josephus preserves the following important information, which substantially but not totally agrees with information from other sources:

Upon Festus' death [A.D. 62], Caesar [Nero] sent Albinus to Judea as procurator. But before he arrived, King Agrippa [II] had appointed Ananus to the priesthood, who was the son of the elder Ananus ["Annas" in the New Testament Gospels]. This elder Ananus, after he himself had been high priest, had five sons, all of whom achieved that office, which was unparalleled. The younger Ananus, however, was rash and followed the Sadducees, who are heartless when they sit in judgment. Ananus thought that with Festus dead and Albinus still on the way [from Rome], he would have his opportunity. Convening the judges of the Sanhedrin, he brought before them a man named James, the brother of Jesus who was called the Christ, and certain others. He accused them of having transgressed the law, and condemned them to be stoned to death.

—From Paul L. Maier, trans. and ed., *Josephus: The Essential Writings* (Grand Rapids: Kregel, 1988), 275.

God. This is a "faith" that even demons possess (Jas 2:19) and is not genuine trust in Christ at all. Genuine trust involves not merely the mind but the whole person. Paul and James agree that authentic trust in Christ results in good works (Eph 2:10; 1 Thes 1:3).

A number of other good suggestions have been put forward for explaining the similarities and differences between Paul and James. But at the basic level of who Jesus Christ is and what the gospel calls for, James's message, while distinctive, is not essentially different from that contained in other Epistles.

Author, Date, Recipients, and Purpose

The Epistle gives its author as "James, a servant of God and of the Lord Jesus Christ" (1:1). This is most likely James the

(half-) brother of Jesus (Mt 13:55; Mk 6:3). At first a skeptic (Mk 3:21), later he became a leading pastor of the JERUSALEM church (see Acts 15; Gal 2). It is moving to think of the change of heart he must have undergone in moving from hostility toward Jesus (Jn 7:3–5) to acknowledging him as Messiah. According to an ancient report James's steadfast faith cost him his life: He refused to deny Jesus as Lord when Jewish authorities demanded that he publicly do so in about A.D. 62. This report is well worth reading for the light in sheds on early church life—and death.[3]

If James died in the early 60s, his Epistle must have been written no later than that time. Because James writes to "the twelve tribes scattered among the nations" (1:1), his letter must date from an era long enough after Christ's resurrection for the gospel to have spread to various locations. The Epistle must have been written, therefore, sometime between the late A.D. 30s and the early A.D. 60s.

The "twelve tribes scattered" of 1:1 may be a clue to James's intended audience. "Scattered" is a translation of the Greek words *en tē diaspora,* which could also be translated "in the diaspora." In earlier chapters we learned that the "diaspora" refers to the Jewish community outside its original homeland in PALESTINE. James may well have in mind Jewish Christian readers in various far-flung communities where the gospel had gained a foothold. Several additional features make a Jewish audience plausible: the natural, almost casual reference to Old Testament law (1:25; 2:8–13); the use of the word "synagogue" to describe their place of meeting (2:2); the numerous Jewish and Old Testament metaphors throughout the Epistle.[4] Moreover, as we will see below, James's tone combines elements of both prophecy and wisdom literature as these appear in the Old Testament. A reason for this may be that he knows his readers are accustomed to such modes of discourse.

Outline

   I. Address and Greeting (1:1)

  II. Trials and Temptation (1:2–18)
     A. Overcoming Trials (1:2–13)
     B. The Source of Temptation (1:13–18)

III. Putting the Word into Practice
(1:19–2:26)
- A. Anger and the Tongue (1:19–20)
- B. "Be Doers of the Word" (1:21–27)
- C. The Sin of Favoritism (2:1–13)
- D. True Christian Faith Seen in Its Works (2:14–26)

IV. Worldliness in the Church
(3:1–4:12)
- A. The Taming of the Tongue (3:1–12)
- B. Peaceable Relations among Christians (3:13–4:3)
- C. A Call for Repentance (4:4–10)
- D. Arrogance and the Critical Tongue (4:11–12)

V. Looking at Life from a Christian Perspective (4:13–5:11)
- A. Recognizing Who We Are before God (4:13–17)
- B. The Dangers of Wealth (5:1–6)
- C. Waiting on the Lord (5:7–11)

VI. Concluding Exhortations
(5:12–20)
- A. Oaths (5:12)
- B. Prayer (5:13–18)
- C. Being Our Brother's Keeper (5:19–20)

James's Prophetic Wisdom

We noted earlier that James's tone echoes two forms of Old Testament literature: prophecy and the wisdom writings. James is prophetic in his passion for faithfulness to the Lord and in his repeated blunt denunciations of faithless behavior. Like the prophet Jeremiah, who wept over the people he preached to, James shows tenderness of heart as he repeatedly addresses his readers as "brothers" or "my dear brothers" (1:2, 16, 19; 2:1, 5; 3:1, 10, 12; 4:11; 5:7, 9, 10, 12; in Greek the word translated "brothers" can include both men and women). Like Nathan, who denounced David to his face (2 Sm 12), James pulls no punches as he urges obedience on his readers. Some of the most pungent charges in the New Testament come from James: "Do you want to be shown, you senseless person, that faith apart from works is barren?" (2:20 NRSV). "You adulterous people, don't you know that friendship with the world is hatred toward God?" (4:4). "Wash your hands, you sinners, and purify your hearts, you double-minded. Grieve, mourn, and wail" (4:8–9). The zeal and style of the Old Testament prophets, and for that matter the New Testament prophet Jesus, are alive and well

There are similarities in Jesus' and James's teachings. They also shared unpleasant experiences on the heights of Jerusalem's buildings. Jesus was tempted by Satan (Mt 4:5). And decades later James was thrown to the ground from the battlement of the temple for refusing to denounce the belief in Jesus as the Messiah. Still alive despite the fall, he was then clubbed to death, according to an ancient report.

355

Poverty and Wealth

"Now listen, you rich people, weep and wail because of the misery that is coming upon you" (Jas 5:1). The Epistle of James is sensitive to the problem of the rich oppressing the poor.

Because wealth can be a snare, James speaks of the *"low position"* of the rich (1:10). Riches quickly fade (1:11). The church should take pains not to favor the wealthy (2:1–4). Wealth needs to be at the disposal of the needy (2:15–16) rather than hoarded for oneself.

Does this mean that all wealthy people are condemned by God? Does being righteous in God's eyes require living in poverty? No. James is making generalizations: The rich too often trust in their wealth instead of in the Lord. They take advantage of the downtrodden. The poor, stripped of material comfort, may seek spiritual comfort. But some who are poor remain godless in their poverty, while some who are wealthy seek the Lord.

James's warnings about the misuse of wealth fit well with warnings elsewhere in Scripture. Paul counsels those who have material plenty *"to do good, to be rich in good deeds, and to be generous and willing to share"* (1 Tm 6:18). Or, in Jesus' words, be *"rich toward God"* (Lk 12:21) in a life that pleases him in every respect.

The materialism and consumerism of the affluent around the world too often infect the church. James has much to say to Westerners of all economic levels as they strive to use their material resources to further God's kingdom rather than to indulge themselves or take advantage of others.

in James. In his Epistle's 108 verses there are more than 50 direct commands!

But James also reflects the Old Testament wisdom tradition. This is true, first, with respect to content (1:5). Wisdom lies not in purely intellectual cleverness but in the moral astuteness given by God to those who seek him. James is practical in nature and sees the goal of Christian life reached in putting God's Word into practice. And James reflects the Old Testament wisdom tradition, second, with respect to style. In some ways his letter reflects the distinctive structure of the Book of Proverbs. It touches on a theme, goes on to others, and returns to the first. While it would be unjust to call the letter disorganized, its coherence lies in its consistent call to fidelity to the Lord rather than in clear and logical literary progression.

To observe that James resembles prophetic and wisdom writings likely indicates that he knew the Old Testament well and naturally imitated it in his own written expression. But it may also reflect the influence of Jesus on his life.

James and Jesus

James's stress on the close link between practice and belief, between ethics and theology, stems in part from Old Testament influence. But it should be observed that James echoes Jesus' teaching, especially in the Sermon on the Mount, at a number of points. In 1:22, 25 James stresses the need to put God's word into practice, not just agree with it in theory. Jesus sounds a similar note in Matthew 7:26 when he refers to a foolish person who "hears these words of mine and does not put them into practice." In 3:12 James asks, "Can a fig tree bear olives, or a grapevine bear figs?" In Matthew 7:16 Jesus asks, "Do people pick grapes from thornbushes, or figs from thistles?" In 4:13 James rebukes those who presume on God by banking on the unknown future. They should rather be humbly serving the Lord in the daily present. In Matthew 6:34 Jesus says, "Do not worry about tomorrow, for tomorrow will worry about itself. Each day has enough trouble of its own."

This is not to suggest that James made use of Matthew or any other written Gospel. It is to observe that James was likely influenced by religious and social factors similar to those that influenced Jesus. After all, they apparently grew up in the same family. In addition, there is no reason to suppose that James remained ignorant of the kind of things his older brother taught in the three years of his public ministry. After Jesus' death, and after James along with many others recognized his messiahship and divinity, James became part of a chorus of early

Focus 22: Faith and Works

Swiss church leader and scholar Adolf Schlatter (1852–1938) composed the following devotional thoughts and prayer on a famous verse from James's Epistle:

What good is it, dear brothers and sisters, if someone says he has faith, but doesn't have works? Can even faith render him blesséd (Jas 2:14)?

That I say I have faith cannot possibly free me from sin, guilt, and punishment. How could something I say be my deliverance? Not that I say I have faith, but that I exercise faith that saves me, situates me in God's peace, brings me God's grace, and is my righteousness before God.

If I have faith, I also express that I have him. Faith causes us to confess faith, and where such confession is absent, so is faith. If I cannot even speak about faith, how shall I actually live it out? For that reason confession holds the same promise as our faith. For confession is faith's first fruit. Faith gives me words with which to respond to God, so that his message issues in thanksgiving and his promise calls forth my plea.

I cannot remain mute before God if I believe. Through faith we pray, James said. And faith also gives me the words to say in dealing with other persons. I believe, therefore I speak, wrote Paul. But does this describe God's grace entirely? If faith gave me merely words, then it would be of use, after all, to say I have faith. But that is a sinister thought. Is that all I am, a thinker and talker? God has given me life, and that means he has planted a will in me that can act—that must act, with unalterable necessity.

That goes for my dealings with God and likewise for my relations with other people. Service to God is action. Our fellowship with each other likewise arises through that which we do for each other. Now if I have no works, do nothing, if I do not even do what God wants from me, that is not salvation but sin and death. It is impossible for me to do nothing; if I don't do God's will, then my work arises from my own ambition and is therefore godless and harmful to others.

In that case I need James's warning urgently. For it is sweet to gaze on nothing except God's work and to let everything sink into that quiet stillness that I have because I suppose I am hidden in God.

Work always seems difficult when set alongside faith. Work is a battle. It arises through overcoming self. It brings me in dangerous proximity to the world. But the slothful and selfish tendency of my heart must not deceive me. There can be no doubt whatsoever that I must act. I should thank God that I can act as one who trusts, so that my work is not guilt and disaster but accomplishes God's will.

What you, gracious God, do for us and to us needs no help or supplementation. My works are not the ground of your grace. It has its ground in you and is as perfect as you are. Therefore we trust you and do not trust ourselves and our works. However, you give your grace to me in my situation and my occupation; you have bestowed on me the privilege of labor. I would be throwing your grace away if I did not do it. O give me, Father, the warm, strong, joyous love that obeys you.

Amen.

—From Adolf Schlatter, *Andachten* (Dresden-Klotzsche: Oskar Günther, n.d. [1927]), 277. Translated by Robert Yarbrough.

voices who passed along what they had received from their exposure to Christ.

Critical Issues

With the rise of social science methods in New Testament study,[5] the social setting of each New Testament book has come under scrutiny. This is especially true for James, whose emphasis on economic justice and other social inequalities is undeniable. It needs to be pointed out, however, that the political assumptions of the average modern interpreter have roots different from James's profound theological convictions. Modern scholars sometimes believe in humankind's innate goodness, in economic determinism, in the ultimate good of the state rather than God's kingdom, and in the power of human reason rather than divine revelation.

James operates in a different sphere. His thought is moored in the Old Testament and centered on the gospel of and about Jesus. James's zeal has God as its focus and the purity of the church as its aim. He is not laying out a utopian vision for reform of society at large. This does not mean that his scathing critique of societal ills of his time can be set aside as unimportant. On the contrary, it is central to his message. But it is issued in and to the church. To encounter James is, as a professing Christian, to be brought face to face with God, with "the Judge" who "is standing at the door!" (5:9). James is consistent with other New Testament writers in pointing to Christ as the means of salvation, and the people of God as his primary redemptive agents in the world. When the church humbly accepts James's message as a verdict on itself, and when God's people submit to God and relate to one another with the selflessness and compassion that James calls for, the purpose of James's letter has been achieved. For God's people are then poised to serve as the salt and light that Jesus called them to be (Mt 5:13–16).

Summary

1. There are eight books classified as General Epistles, and both Hebrews and James belong to this group.

2. The authorship of Hebrews is uncertain.

3. Hebrews was likely written for a Jewish audience.

4. Hebrews emphasizes the superiority of the Christian faith and teaches that Jesus is superior to the prophets, angels, Moses, and Aaron.

5. Hebrews can be viewed as a book of exhortations because it repeatedly exhorts its readers courageously to reaffirm their Christian faith.

6. The major practical concern of Hebrews is that Christians not be intimidated by the difficult circumstances they face.

7. James may have intended his letter for the Jewish Christians scattered in a variety of communities—he refers to them as the "twelve tribes scattered."

8. James's approach is similar to the prophecy and wisdom writings from the Old Testament.

9. James emphasizes the importance of practicing the Christian faith, not merely "believing" it.

Key Terms

apostasy
Mosaic code

Key Person/ Places

Clement of Rome
Jerusalem
Palestine

Review Questions

1. The General Epistles appear in the New Testament in an order that is based on their _____.

2. Possible authors of Hebrews are a student of Paul, Luke, Barnabas, _____, or _____.

3. Hebrews was probably written between A.D. _____ and A.D. _____.

4. The feature common to ancient letters missing in Hebrews is the _____.

5. Overall, Hebrews can be viewed as a _____ Epistle.

6. Hebrews reminds readers of the greatness of _____, who is superior to the prophets, angels, _____, and _____.

7. Hebrews points out that it is possible to be active in the _____ without _____ of the Lord.

8. James's teaching at points resembles what _____ taught in the ___ ___.

9. The "twelve tribes scattered" refers to _____.

10. James's language in some ways echoes the Old Testament literary forms of wisdom writings and _____.

Study Questions

1. What is the central theme of Hebrews?

2. Why can Hebrews be called a sermonic Epistle? What elements in Hebrews would be unusual for an Epistle?

3. In what sense is Hebrews critical of Old Testament religion? Is this an attack on the Old Testament itself?

4. How does Hebrews use warnings and encouragement to appeal for perseverance?

5. Does James's view of faith and works ultimately contradict Paul's teachings on this subject? Why or why not?

6. What seems to be the major point of James's Epistle?

Further Reading

Charles, J. Daryl. "Interpreting the General Epistles." In *Interpreting the New Testament,* ed. D. A. Black and D. S. Dockery. Nashville: Broadman & Holman, 2001, pp. 433–56. A stinging indictment of how scholarship has ignored or misconstrued the General Epistles. And not only scholarship: the church has neglected them too. Calls for recovery of what has too often been lost.

Gooding, D. W. *Unshakeable Kingdom: The Letter to the Hebrews for Today.* Leicester: InterVarsity, 1989. Excellent study of the message of the epistle.

Guthrie, George H. *Hebrews.* Grand Rapids: Zondervan, 1988. Seeks to determine original meaning of each section then bridges from the writer's day to present times and seeks to make application. Both scholarly and practical.

———. "Hebrews." In *Zondervan Illustrated Bible Backgrounds Commentary,* vol. 4, ed. Clinton E. Arnold. Grand Rapids: Zondervan, 2002, pp. 1–85. Commentary on selected verses and themes. Relates Hebrews and its message to the Greco-Roman as well as Jewish context of the early church.

Hagner, Donald A. *Encountering the Book of Hebrews.* Grand Rapids: Baker, 2002. Designed for undergraduate student use. Survey of each chapter of the letter. Gives attention to detail without getting bogged down. Helpful bibliographic aids; numerous sidebars, and other features to encourage understanding.

Hughes, R. Kent. *Hebrews: An Anchor for the Soul.* 2 vols. Wheaton, Ill.: Crossway, 1993. Sermons combining careful attention to Hebrews with discerning application to modern life.

Johnson, Luke Timothy. *The Letter of James.* New York: Doubleday, 1995. Among the most insightful and readable studies of James yet to appear.

Koester, Craig R. *Hebrews.* New York: Doubleday, 2001. Technical and scholarly but readable. Comprehensive survey of the history of interpretation of Hebrews. Rich theological exposition with attention to sociological and rhetorical aspects.

Martin, Ralph P., and Peter H. Davids, eds. *Dictionary of the Later New Testament and Its Developments.* Downers Grove/Leicester: InterVarsity, 1997. Helpful and concise articles on the General Epistles and related topics.

Moo, Douglas J. *The Letter of James.* Grand Rapids: Eerdmans, 2000. Informed by recent scholarship but written at a non-technical level. Shows how James and Paul are not in conflict but are dealing with the same topics (faith, righteousness) from different vantage points.

Stulac, George. *James.* Downers Grove/Leicester: InterVarsity, 1993. Stimulating and understandable treatment.

Trotter, A. H., Jr. *Interpreting the Epistle to the Hebrews.* Grand Rapids: Baker, 1997. Easy-to-follow examination of different ways to study the epistle. Focuses on how to read Hebrews more than on what Hebrews actually says.

23 Peter, John, and Jude
A Call to Faith, Hope, and Love

Objectives

**After reading this chapter,
you should be able to**

- Discuss the authorship of 1 and 2 Peter
- Outline the content of the Books
  of 1 and 2 Peter
- Identify the emphases of 1 Peter
- Compare the life of the pilgrim
  with the life of the world
- Identify the emphases of 2 Peter
- Provide evidence that John the apostle
  wrote 1, 2, and 3 John
- Outline the content of the Books
  of 1, 2, and 3 John
- State the purposes for the writing
  of 1, 2, and 3 John
- Outline the content of the Book of Jude
- Discuss the purpose of Jude

Imagine a carpenter showing up for work with his toolbox, but not knowing what the tools are used for or how to use them. Some carpenter!

Imagine a Christian who claims to believe in the New Testament with its twenty-seven different "books," but doesn't know what those books contain or how they might apply to the job of everyday living.

At least six of the last seven New Testament writings are not very familiar to most people. Yet they are just as important "tools" for understanding the Bible's message as some of the longer, better-known writings. Below we examine the brief but important Epistles of Peter, John, and Jude. We can learn much from each of them. At the very least we can make sure that we know what "tools" God has furnished us for the daily labor of understanding, worship, and service for his kingdom.

The Letters of Peter

Two of the letters in this group claim to be written by the apostle Simon Peter (1 Pt 1:1; 2 Pt 1:1, 16, 18). He is one of the best known figures in the early church, mentioned over 150 times in the New Testament. He grew up in BETHSAIDA along the coast of the SEA OF GALILEE, where he and his brother Andrew were fishermen (Jn 1:44). He was introduced to Jesus by Andrew and given a new name (Jn 1:40–42)—his original name was Simon; Jesus renamed him *Petros*, or "Rock." Later, when living in CAPERNAUM, he was called to the ministry by Jesus himself (Mk 1:16–18) and appointed as one of the original twelve apostles (Mk 3:13–16). He was part of an inner circle that surrounded Jesus and seemed to be the spokesman for the twelve. He was a man of great strength and courage but given to exaggerated self-confidence, in the end denying that he even knew Christ when taunted by a servant-girl during Jesus' last hours (Mk 14:66–72). Peter's faith was strengthened by appearances of the risen Christ (Lk 24:34; 1 Cor 15:5), by the empty tomb (Jn 20:6–7), and by the ascension of Jesus (Acts 1:7–9, 12–13). He became the Rock that Jesus said he would be.

At Pentecost, Peter preached the first Christian sermon, and three thousand people were saved that day (Acts 2:14–41). He quickly became a leader in the JERUSALEM church, worked miracles in Jesus' name (Acts 3:11–16), boldly defended the faith (Acts 4:8–12), experienced persecution and suffering (Acts 5:17–18, 33, 41; 12:1–5), and, although primarily an apostle to the Jews, helped open the church to the Gentiles (Acts 10:1–48; 15:6–11). He traveled as a missionary, probably going to ASIA MINOR (1 Pt 1:1) and "Babylon" (1 Pt 5:13). We are not told in the Scriptures about Peter's death, but tradition puts it in Rome by crucifixion at about the same time that Paul died (see Eusebius, *Ecclesiastical History* 2.25.5–8).

First Peter

"Peter, an apostle of Jesus Christ," claims to have written this letter (1:1). That claim was never disputed until recent times. All of the early evidence supports the view that Peter, was, in fact, the author. The arguments used currently to deny this fact are hardly compelling. For example, it is said that severe persecution is the background for this letter and that this could only refer to persecution under DOMITIAN near the end of the century or under TRAJAN even later. But the persecution under NERO could certainly have been the persecution Peter had in mind as he was facing death in Rome. Another argument is that Peter, an unlearned fisherman, could hardly have written such excellent Greek. But history is replete with unlikely geniuses, like John Bunyan, the uneducated "tinker of Bedford" who wrote *Pilgrim's Progress*. Who is to say that Peter did not know Greek very well? Besides, Peter himself says "with the help of Silas, whom I regard as a faithful brother, I have written to you briefly" (5:12). Professional scribes such as Silas would have no trouble at all writing eloquent Greek. It is also said that the theology of 1 Peter looks too dependent on Paul's thought. But why should this not be the case, even if it were an entirely accurate statement? Peter and Paul were not preaching two different gospels, and modern attempts to portray them as at mortal odds with one another are far from convincing. In the absence of any convincing alternative and given the unanimous positive early testimony, it is reasonable to affirm that Peter wrote this letter.

It claims to have been written from "Babylon" (5:13), but it is unlikely that the ruins of the Old Testament city is where the letter originated. Rather, Babylon should be taken as a code-word symbolizing ROME. It is commonly used in this way in both Christian and Jewish writings of the time.[1] This accords well with other testimony that places both Peter and Paul in Rome during Nero's persecutions. If true this places the date of 1 Peter sometime before A.D. 64–66. The letter was written to believers of northern Asia Minor south of the BLACK SEA in the provinces of PONTUS, GALATIA, CAPPADOCIA, ASIA, and BITHYNIA (1:1). All of these are in present-day TURKEY.

There has been some discussion of late as to the precise literary nature of the letter, with some suggesting that it is a baptismal liturgy or a baptismal sermon. However, it is in the ordinary style of a letter of that day, so there is no compelling reason to see it as anything other than a letter of encouragement to beleaguered believers. The following outline reflects this understanding of the letter.

Outline

I. Suffering as a Christian (1:1–2:10)
  A. The Hidden Inheritance, the Hidden Lord (1:1–9)
  B. Preparation for Action (1:10–2:3)
  C. The Hidden Spiritual House (2:4–10)

II. At Home, But Not in This World (2:11–3:12)
  A. The Christian's Inner Self (2:11–12)
  B. A Life of Submission (2:13–3:7)
  C. The Christian's Corporate Self (3:8–12)

III. Suffering—The Road to Glory (3:13–4:19)
  A. Suffering for Doing Good (3:13–22)
  B. Living for God (4:1–11)
  C. Sharing the Sufferings of Christ (4:12–19)

IV. Final Exhortations and Greetings (5:1–14)

The Comfort and Encouragement of Christ

Peter's heart was full as he wrote this letter, and a sense of urgency pervades it. "The end of all things is near," he says (4:7). This was true whether God brought history to a close at the second coming of Christ or whether persecution ended mortal lives. Peter was facing imminent death and so were many of those to whom he was writing. Consequently one of the major things he is trying to do is to com-

Simon Peter grew up in Bethsaida, along the coast of the Sea of Galilee, where he and his brother Andrew were fishermen.

The Deaths of Peter and Paul

Examine your records. There you will find that Nero was the first that persecuted this doctrine, particularly then when after subduing all the east, he exercised his cruelty against all at Rome. We glory in having such a man the leader in our punishment. For whoever knows him can understand that nothing was condemned by Nero unless it was something of great excellence. Thus publicly announcing himself as the first among God's chief enemies, he was led on to the slaughter of the apostles. It is, therefore, recorded that Paul was beheaded in Rome itself, and that Peter likewise was crucified under Nero.

—Tertullian (ca. A.D. 155–222)

The Roman emperor Nero.

fort and encourage his friends in the face of the savage treatment they could expect because they were believers in Christ. They were not to be surprised at the intensity of the suffering they were experiencing, as though something strange was happening to them; rather they were to rejoice (1:6; 4:13). These are striking words, but Peter reminds them that Christ also suffered and that they were participating in the very sufferings of Christ (4:13). And because it was God's will that Christ had suffered, being prophesied by Scripture (1:11), they also were to suffer according to the will of God (3:17; 4:19). This might sound strange to those who have never had to go through intense trials for Christ's sake, and some in our own day have even taught that suffering is never God's will. Church history and broader Christian experience teach us otherwise. Paul wrote, "Everyone who wants to live a godly life in Christ Jesus will be persecuted" (2 Tm 3:12), so it should not surprise Christ's followers if the world heaps abuse on them (4:4) or insults them (4:14) because they refuse to swear allegiance to it. We must remember that Christians are "aliens and strangers in the world" (1:1; 2:11), that is, foreigners and exiles, whose eternal home is elsewhere. This "world is not my home,

I'm just a' passin' through," as the old spiritual says. If this were really our attitude we would not be mourning what we might lose, but rejoicing in the glory that is to come.[2]

The Glory of Salvation

The glory that is to come, or salvation, is another of Peter's major themes. Because life is short, like the grass of the field that quickly wilts in the summer heat (1:24), we ought to keep our eyes on what cannot fade away rather than on earth's fleeting and unfulfilled promises. The Christian believer can look forward to an unfading, eternal inheritance in heaven (1:3–6). This includes the salvation of their souls, and for this reason they should be filled with profound and persistent joy (1:8–9).

The Believer as Pilgrim

Peter also has some practical things to say about living the Christian life in a fallen and hostile world. In some instances he sets this in explicit contrast to the ways of the world; in others, the comparison is so obvious as to need no elaboration. He develops these themes in no special order; they apparently appear in his letter as they occurred to him. All of them, however, are closely related to the pilgrim idea—we are strangers here, on our way to our true home.[3] We should live here as members of the world to which we ultimately belong, not as though enslaved by this one. In the box below is a brief outline of what Peter says.

In some instances Peter has specific instructions for specific people: husbands and wives (3:1–7), elders in the church (5:1–4), and young people (5:5). In all of this Peter realizes that in our own strength it would be impossible to live this way. It is only the grace of God himself and the power of Christ within that can make believers strong, firm, and steadfast (5:10).

Following Christ

The final thing that Peter wishes to emphasize is that as Christians our supreme goal should be to follow Christ. He is our Savior and example. As his disciples we follow in his steps (2:21)—even if it means following him into the vale of suffering. "Since Christ suffered in his body, arm yourselves also with the same attitude, because he who has suffered in his body is done with sin" (4:1). Peter said he had witnessed the sufferings of Christ that had led to his subsequent glory (5:1). If we arm ourselves with Christ's attitude, the power and glory of Christ will rest on us.

Second Peter

The author of this letter identifies himself as "Simon Peter, a servant and apostle of Jesus Christ" (1:1) and as the writer of an earlier letter that we know as 1 Peter (3:1). He further defines himself as an eyewitness of the transfiguration and a close associate of the apostle Paul (3:15). He says he is awaiting death in the manner predicted by Christ after his resurrection (1:13–15; see Jn 21:18–19). This is as clear a statement of authorship as we have in the New Testament. Yet, strangely enough, this very fact is being used today to say that someone pretending to be Peter wrote the letter.[4] However, it is hard to imagine that someone could write a letter that emphasizes the importance of truth so much (see 1:12; 2:12) and warning against teachers who "will exploit you with stories they have made up" (2:3), while being at the same time a prevaricator and someone who is making up stories about who he is. It is further argued that the tone of the letter seems to be later than Peter's day (some even put it into the second century), with the mention of false prophets, destructive heresies, and greedy, immoral leaders. It also speaks of Paul's letters as being Scripture (3:16), and this could only have hap-

The Life of the Pilgrim

Be obedient to God (1:14, 22)
Be holy (1:15)
Live as servants (2:16; 4:11)
Be prayerful (3:7; 4:7)
Live openly, transparently (2:16; 3:16)
Do what is good (2:15; 3:16–17)
Be gentle and respectful (3:15)
Love one another deeply (1:22; 4:8)
Exercise self-control (1:13; 4:7; 5:8)
Live humbly (5:6)
Reject evil (2:11)
Accept human rule (2:13, 17)
Control sinful desires (2:1, 11)
Do God's will (4:2)
Share with others (4:9)
Use our gifts for others (4:10–11)

The Life of the World

Rebellion against God
Unholiness
Live selfishly
Reject God
Live deceitfully
Do what is wrong
Live harshly and insolently
Hate one another
Live excessively, wildly
Be proud and arrogant
Embrace evil
Reject human rule
Give desires free rein
Reject God's will
Hoard one's possessions
Refuse to share

pened later. But neither of these arguments is conclusive. There were serious problems very early in the church, and Paul himself felt he was writing under the inspiration of the Holy Spirit, making what he said authoritative and the Word of God (see 1 Cor 7:17; 14:37; 1 Thes 2:13; 2 Thes 3:14). Why couldn't Peter have recognized that? It seems best, all things being considered, to take the letter's statements at face value and accept Peter as the author of this letter. This would place it sometime before A.D. 68 (the latest date suggested for Peter's martyrdom). The place of writing was perhaps Rome, although this is not certain.

Outline

I. Salutation (1:1–2)

II. Concern for Sanctification (1:3–11)

III. Confidence in the Scripture (1:12–21)

IV. Caution toward False Teachers (2:1–22)
    A. Their Threat and Judgment (2:1–3)
    B. God's Judgment in the Past (2:4–10)
    C. Their Character (2:10–16)
    D. Their Empty Teaching (2:17–22)

V. Constancy in Light of the Last Days (3:1–16)

VI. Conclusion (3:17–18)

Purpose and Teaching

As can be seen from the outline there are basically four areas of concern covered by this short letter: sanctification, Scripture, warnings against false teachers, and the end of the age. Let's look at these in a little more detail.

First, Peter begins and ends his letter by encouraging growth in the Christian walk. He assures his readers that God has given everything needed for life (1:3). He then lists virtues that will promote growth—faith, goodness, knowledge, self-control, perseverance, godliness, brotherly kindness, and love (1:5–8). Knowing this, believers are to go forward, not backward, in their Christian lives (3:18).

Second, Peter wants to assure his readers that what God promised through the prophets, spoke through his word, and taught through his apostles is true. Some were beginning to doubt if God really meant what he said (3:4). Peter assures them prophecy is not a human invention, but "men spoke from God as they were carried along by the Holy Spirit" (1:21). If we twist the Scriptures, we do it to our own destruction (3:16).

Third, in a lengthy section that is similar to the Book of Jude, Peter warns of the false teachers and doctrines that will arise some day (2:1–22). These people will be false, destructive, shameful, greedy, arrogant, blasphemous, boastful, and sinful. Worst of all, they will turn their backs on God's sacred commandments (2:21). But God knows how to rescue his people from this. They are called to turn to him in renewed faith (2:9).

Finally, Peter wants to clarify the nature of the end of the age. He begins by explaining why the coming of Christ has not yet occurred. We must remember that time is different for God than for us—a thousand years is only as one day with God, so the delay hasn't been all that long from God's point of view (3:3–8). But more than that, it is a sign of God's patience—he is in no hurry to destroy the earth; rather, he does not want anyone to perish, but for all to come to repentance (3:9). Peter then explains what the event will be like: It will be the fiery destruction of the existing cosmic order (3:10–12). But this is not the end of God's dealings with the universe he created. He will replace this sinful world order with "a new heaven and a new earth, the home of righteousness" (3:13), which will endure throughout all of eternity. He concludes his survey of this topic with the admonition to prepare for it by living blameless and spotless lives, at peace with God (3:14).

The Epistles of John

There are three letters in the New Testament that have from the earliest days of the church been associated with the apostle John, who also wrote the Gospel that

1 Clement

Didache

bears his name. The first of the three, which is the longest, does not have the usual characteristics of an ancient letter—it looks more like a small treatise or tract. The other two are constructed as letters and are very short. In fact 2 John is the shortest book in the New Testament.

Author

There is uniform early testimony that John the apostle wrote these three letters. The existence of 1 John is reflected in **1 Clement,** the **Didache**, PAPIAS, and POLY-CARP (i.e., by the first quarter of the second century). IRENAEUS and CLEMENT OF ALEXANDRIA during the later second century specifically speak of the letters as coming from John. No new evidence has been discovered, either archaeologically or otherwise, to call this into question. Where skepticism exists as to Johannine authority, other elements become the dominant factor: "Almost inevitably, the most fundamental reasons advanced today for rejecting Johannine authorship of these letters turn not on the hard evidence . . . but on reconstructions of the development of the Johannine 'circle' or 'community' or 'school.' This reconstruction exercises such controlling power in contemporary discussions that the possibility of apostolic

authorship is prematurely ruled out of court."[5] That John the apostle wrote these letters remains the most likely possibility.

Let's review who John was. He grew up in Galilee, probably in Bethsaida, where his father Zebedee was a wealthy fisherman. His mother's name was Salome; she later accompanied Jesus on some of his travels, along with her two sons John and James. John early became a disciple of John the Baptist but after Jesus' baptism followed him. After the arrest of John the Baptist, John was called by Jesus to leave his fishing nets to become a permanent part of Jesus' group (Mk 1:16–20) and was later made one of the twelve apostles (Mk 3:13–19). He formed part of an "inner circle" of apostles and was personally present with Jesus at the raising of Jairus's daughter (Lk 8:51), on the MOUNT OF TRANSFIGURATION (Lk 9:28), and in the garden of GETHSEMANE (Mk 14:33).

Because he knew the high priest John was able to be present at the trial of Jesus (Jn 18:15–16) and at Jesus' crucifixion, where he accepted responsibility for Mary, Jesus' mother (Jn 19:26–27). He was one of the first to see the empty tomb (Jn 20:1–8) and to witness the risen Christ, first in the locked room (Jn 20:19–28) and later by the Sea of Galilee (Jn 21:1–24). After

John ministered in Ephesus from around A.D. 68 to around A.D. 98.

Jesus' ascension, John stayed in Palestine for some time—how long we are not sure—but he was still there in the mid-A.D. 40s when Paul visited Jerusalem along with Barnabas (Gal 2:6–10). He left for EPHESUS sometime after that, perhaps around A.D. 68 when the Christians fled before the fall of Jerusalem.[6] He ministered there until his death, which could have been as late as A.D. 98,[7] although this is not certain. At one point he was on the island of PATMOS, where he received the visions that are recorded in the Book of Revelation (Rv 1:9). Early in his life John was of vigorous and almost fiery temperament (Jesus called him and his brother James "Sons of Thunder"; Mk 3:17), but as the reality of Christ deepened in his heart over the years he became the great apostle of love, as his writings show.

We are not certain when these letters were written, but somewhere closer to the end of John's life, rather than toward the beginning, would seem to be required by the content.

First John

Outline

I. **The Incarnation Makes Fellowship Possible** (1:1–4)
   A. John Expresses the Substance of His Proclamation (1:1–2)
   B. John Expresses His Purposes for Writing (1:3–4)

II. **Fellowship with God Is Based on Truth and Love** (1:5–5:17)
   A. The Apostolic Message Declares the Partners in Fellowship (1:5–2:2)
   B. Fellowship Bears Certain Distinctives (2:3–27)
   C. Fellowship Demands Certain Prerequisites (2:28–4:6)
   D. Love Leads to Fellowship (4:7–5:5)
   E. Faith Enhances Fellowship (5:6–17)

III. **Fellowship Comprises Three Certainties** (5:18–21)

Purpose and Teaching

It is characteristic of John to say why he wrote something, and that is particularly

true of 1 John, where he mentions the fact of his writing to them thirteen times.

In the first instance (1:4) he says he is writing so that their joy may be full in the knowledge that Jesus is the Son of God who has appeared in the flesh. This opens up for us fellowship with the Father, and in fact, God himself dwells in us if we confess that Jesus is the Son of God (4:15).

In the second instance he says he is writing so that they will not sin (2:1). This is an important part of 1 John, occupying almost all of the third chapter. The true child of God cannot live a life of continuous, willful sinning, because he or she is born of God (5:1) and hence is a new creation. However, if we do sin, as sometimes we will, we must confess that sin and be cleansed by the blood of Christ to restore our fellowship with God (1:9–2:2).

In a third instance (2:7–8) John emphasizes that he is both writing and not writing a new commandment to them—to love one another. It is not new, because it is present throughout the Old Testament and the teachings of Jesus. But it is new, in that we have now actually seen the embodiment of that love in Christ. Because Christ dwells in us, the love of God dwells in us and we may (indeed, must) love those around us (4:7–12). Twice John says "God is love" (4:8, 16), and because he first loved us, we are to love one another. We are not to love the world (2:15–17), because the world is false and passing away; it is the arena of antichrist, who is already at work (2:18–19). We are to test every spirit to see if it is from God (4:1–6). If it acknowledges that Jesus Christ is come in the flesh it is of God (4:2). If not, it is to be rejected as the spirit of falsehood. So, John says, as a fourth point, he is writing to warn about those who would lead the believers astray (2:26–27).

Finally, John says he is writing to assure his readers of their victory in Christ and of the certainty of their salvation (5:13). The believers have triumphed over all evil because "the one that is in you is greater than the one that is in the world" (4:4). The world cannot defeat us because "everyone born of God has overcome the world" (5:4) and, as the old hymn says, "Faith is the victory that overcomes the world." We

At one point John was on the island of Patmos, where he received the visions that are recorded in the Book of Revelation.

know this when we believe in the name of the Son of God; hence we may know that we have eternal life (5:13). In this assurance we are to live our lives unafraid in the world.

Second John

Outline

I. The Elder Greets the Elect Lady and Her Children (1–3)

II. Abiding in the Truth Is the Basis for Walking in Love (4–11)
   A. Commendation: Walking in the Truth Keeps the Command from the Father (4)
   B. Exhortation: Walking in Love Keeps the Command from the Son (5–6)
   C. Warning: Confessing and Keeping the Truth about Christ Determine the Circle of Fellowship in Love (7–11)

III. The Truth Is the Basis of Christian Fellowship (12–13)

Purpose and Teaching
John addresses this short letter to "the chosen lady" (and her children), whom some take to be a woman who allowed a church to meet in her house and others take to be a personification of a particular church. In either case the message is the same. Sec-

ond John emphasizes the same things that are found in 1 John. John underscores the necessity of walking in love, repeating the statement that this is no new command but one Christians have had from the beginning (5–6). He warns about those who deny either the humanity or the deity of Christ. There are already many such deceivers at large in the world (7–8). John's readers are to reject those who reject the teaching of Christ as it is found in the true church. John concludes by saying he has run out of paper (papyrus) but will elaborate on these themes during a coming visit, face to face (12).

Third John

Outline

I. The Elder Addresses Gaius in Love (1)

II. Love Must Prevail in the Circle of the Truth (2–12)
   A. Commendation of Gaius: He Walks in the Truth and Love (2–8)
   B. Condemnation of Diotrephes: He Rejects Authority and Lacks Love (9–10)
   C. Recommendation of Demetrius: He Does Good (11–12)

III. Peace Should Prevail among Friends (13–14)

Purpose and Teaching

Unlike 2 John this letter states explicitly who its recipient is. It is Gaius, a convert of John. Gaius is commended for being faithful to and walking in the truth (3–4). He is also commended for showing hospitality to traveling Christian evangelists or missionaries (8). All is not well, however. Diotrephes is not willing to help other Christian workers. He prefers to gossip, rejects John's advice, and expels from the church those who seek to help those laboring to further the true gospel (9–10). He does this, apparently, because he cannot stand any competition and wants to be first. Demetrius, on the other hand, is well spoken of by everyone—the embodiment of good and not a troublemaker like Diotrephes. John closes his short letter to Gaius as he closed 2 John, by saying he has much to communicate but prefers to do it face to face rather than on paper (13–14). His concluding greeting emphasizes the friendship that existed among the early believers—a rare commodity in that or any age.

Jude

There are three men named Jude (or Judas) in the New Testament, other than the infamous Judas Iscariot, who are closely associated with the church in Jerusalem: Jude, the son of James, who was one of Jesus' original apostles (Lk 6:16); Judas, also called Barsabbas, who went with Paul, Barnabas, and Silas to ANTIOCH after the Council at Jerusalem (Acts 15:22); and Jude, listed along with James, Joseph, and Simon as a brother of Jesus (Mt 13:55; Mk 6:3). It is this last-named Jude who identifies himself as the author of the Epistle bearing his name (1). In humility he calls himself only a *servant* of Jesus Christ and a brother of James. Little is known about Jude except that he, along with his other brothers, did not believe in Jesus during his earthly ministry (Mt 12:46–50; Jn 7:1–5). But he was apparently convinced as a result of the resurrection, as his brother James was (1 Cor 15:7). He was in the upper room along with the

Focus 23: Martin Luther (1483–1546) on 1 John

This is an outstanding epistle. It can buoy up afflicted hearts.

Furthermore, it has John's style and manner of expression, so beautifully and gently does it picture Christ to us. It came to be written because at that time heretics and sluggish Christians had rushed in, which invariably happens when the Word has been revived. Then the devil harries us constantly and seeks in every way to cast us down, in order that we may give up preaching and good works. In John's time there were the Corinthians, who denied the divinity of Christ; and there were sluggish Christians, who thought that they had heard God's Word enough and that it was not necessary to forsake the world and to do good to their neighbors. Here the apostle attacks both evils and urges us to

guard the Word and to love one another. Thus we shall never learn so much and be so perfect that need for the Word of God will not remain. For the devil never rests. Thus exhortation and the use of God's Word are needed everywhere. It is a living and powerful Word. But we snore and are lazy. It is the Word of life. But we are in death every day. And because we are never without sins and the danger of death, we should never cease to ruminate on the Word. And this epistle is in the nature of an exhortation. In short, in this epistle the apostle wants to teach faith in opposition to the heretics, and true love in opposition to those who are wicked.

—From *Luther's Works,* vol. 30, *The Catholic Epistles,* ed. Jaroslav Pelikan (Saint Louis: Concordia, 1967), 219.

Key People/Places

Antioch
Asia
Asia Minor
Bethsaida
Bithynia
Black Sea
Capernaum
Cappadocia
Clement of Alexandria
Domitian
Ephesus
Eusebius
Galatia
Galilee
Gethsemane
Irenaeus
Jerusalem
Mount of Transfiguration
Nero
Palestine
Papias
Patmos
Polycarp
Pontus
Rome
Trajan
Turkey

Key Terms

the Didache
1 Clement

when they told him that Christ's kingdom was coming at the end of the age and was no threat to current Roman rule (*Ecclesiastical History* 3.19.1–20.6).

Jude's authorship of this letter is rejected by many modern scholars for the same reasons that 2 Peter is assigned to a later time. But for Jude, just as for 2 Peter, no compelling reason exists for rejecting the straightforward testimony of the book itself. It is not possible to speak with certainty about the place or time of writing, since sufficient evidence is lacking. Placing it somewhere in PALESTINE where it is thought Jude ministered in the A.D. 60s to the 80s would not be far wrong.

Outline
  I. **Salutation** (1–2)
  II. **Reason for Writing** (3–4)
  III. **God's Judgment in the Past** (5–7)
  IV. **Warning against False Teachers** (8–16)
  V. **A Call to Persevere** (17–23)
  VI. **Doxology** (24–25)

eleven apostles, Mary Jesus' mother, and his other brothers awaiting the promise of the Holy Spirit after the ascension of Jesus (Acts 1:12–14). According to EUSEBIUS, Jude's grandsons were leaders in the church and were once interrogated by the emperor Domitian (A.D. 81–96) but were released

Summary

1. The letters of Peter were written by the apostle Peter, one of the best known figures in the New Testament.

2. The theme of 1 Peter is salvation in the midst of suffering.

3. In 1 Peter, the ways of the Christian and the ways of the world are contrasted.

4. Second Peter focuses on sanctification, Scripture, warnings against false teachers, and the end of the age.

5. While there is considerable discussion about the authorship of 1, 2, and 3 John, there are good reasons to affirm that John the apostle was the author.

6. In 1 John the Christians were exhorted to love one another.

7. Second John was written to "the chosen lady" and her children and emphasizes the same matters as 1 John.

8. Third John was written to Gaius, whom John commends for being faithful and walking in the truth.

9. Jude was written to urge the Christians to contend for the faith.

10. Jude lists the sins of evildoers, whom he urges Christians to resist.

Purpose and Teaching

Jude begins the letter by telling his readers specifically why he wrote to them: "I felt I had to write and urge you to contend for the faith that was once for all entrusted to the saints" (3). The believers were to go on the offensive (but not be offensive!) for what they believed against those who denied that Jesus Christ is the sovereign Lord (4). The deity of Christ is, of course, a crucial issue. If one denies that, the very essence of Christianity is gone. Jude recognizes, however, that rejection of Christ rarely stands alone. It usually includes the rejection of Christian morality as well. Consequently, he spends the better part of his letter warning his readers against the godless evildoers of his day (4–16). This section of his letter is very similar to 2 Peter 2:4–17, and it is difficult to tell if Jude is reflecting 2 Peter, if Peter is reflecting Jude, or if both are voicing shared traditional material. However, the theological point remains the same in either case: evildoers are to be resisted at all costs because they will destroy the church. The catalog of their sins ranges from slander and greed to sexual immorality and perversion. They are without any concern at all for the church and seek only what is to their own obscene advantage. But Jude's readers had been told that this would happen. They are to resist such people and their enticements with all the strength that God provides. They are to build one another up, pray in the Holy Spirit, dwell in God's love, show mercy to those who are weak, and do all within their power to save the lost (20–23).

Review Questions

1. The "Babylon" of 1 Pt 5:13 is probably the city of _____.

2. The persecution referred to in 1 Peter was probably at the hands of _____ or possibly earlier.

3. The believer is presented in 1 Peter as a _____.

4. Peter exhorts his readers by reminding them that he had been an eyewitness of the _____ of _____.

5. Second Peter was probably written in the city of _____.

6. In 2 Pt 1:5–8, Peter lists the following virtues that will promote growth: faith, goodness, knowledge, self-control, perseverance, _____, _____, and _____.

7. First Clement, the Didache, and Papias in the first century and Irenaeus in the second all speak of the existence of the Book of _____.

8. The shortest book in the New Testament is _____.

9. Second John asserts that the basis for walking in love is abiding in the _____.

10. Third John was written to one of John's converts named _____.

11. Jude became a believer after he was convinced of the truth of Christ following the _____.

12. According to Jude, a crucial issue in contending for the faith is the _____.

General Epistle Summary

Since page 347 we have been looking at the General Epistles: Hebrews, James, 1 and 2 Peter, 1, 2, and 3 John, and Jude. It is now time to summarize their message.

Despite their diversity, all these letters share a focus on Jesus Christ. Most of their authors identify themselves as *messengers* (apostles) *of* Jesus Christ. Two of them bear the stamp of privileged administration of the gospel *about* Christ (2 Jn 9; 3 Jn 9). Two of them are clearly extended applications of God's will as revealed *in* and *by* Christ (Heb 1:1–2; 13:20; Jude 1, 4, 24–25). Christ is the core of the content of all these documents—no doubt because he was the core of the beliefs and lives of those who wrote the epistles as well as those who received them.

But their focus on Christ is not purely doctrinal. It is intensely practical. They are a compendium of insight into the following truths that have the ability to renew our daily lives:

- Hebrews: Christ and he alone is God's supreme revelation to all peoples on earth. No different or truer gospel message will ever arise. It is urgent for Christians to embrace and proclaim the new life they have received, locally and around the globe.

- James, 2 Peter, Jude, and Johannine Epistles: New challenges arise to authentic Christian practice all of the time. The gospel lifts believers above do-nothing complacency (James), moral laxity (2 Peter, Jude), and religion that is sloppy in doctrine, ethics, or devotion of the heart (John's letters).

- 1 Peter: The Gospel calls believers to be ready to make painful sacrifices in the course of carrying out their callings. This will not always mean overt persecution, but it could. Wise and dedicated followers of Christ will be fortified with 1 Peter's counsel when it does. A touching yet tough fidelity to the Lord will result, as it has already in centers of ongoing persecution like the Middle East, Indonesia, North Korea, China, India, and many other locations.[8]

Study Questions

1 Peter

1. Who was Peter? Briefly outline his life.

2. What comfort does Peter offer to his suffering friends?

3. How is the pilgrim-believer to live?

4. What is the supreme goal of the believer?

2 Peter

1. What has God given us for our Christian life?

2. What does Peter say about the end of the age?

1 John

1. Who was John? Briefly outline his life.

2. What is the "New Commandment" and what does John say about it?

3. John urges believers to forsake sin. What basis does he give for this command in 1 Jn 3:8?

2 John

1. How would you summarize the teaching of this small letter?

3 John

1. What are the major points of 3 John?

Jude

1. Who was Jude? Briefly outline his life.

2. How would you summarize the teaching of Jude?

Further Reading

Bauckham, Richard. *2 Peter and Jude*. Waco: Word, 1983. Probably the best commentary on these two letters. Argues that 2 Peter is pseudepigraphical.

———. *Jude and the Relatives of Jesus in the Early Church*. Edinburgh: T & T Clark, 1990. A careful and creative study of overlooked but important figures.

Brown, R. E. *The Epistles of John*. Garden City, N.Y.: Doubleday, 1982. An advanced commentary by an eminent Roman Catholic scholar.

Bruce, F. F. *The Epistles of John*. Grand Rapids: Eerdmans, 1988. An excellent verse-by-verse exposition of these letters.

Burge, Gary. *The Letters of John*. Grand Rapids: Zondervan, 1996. Highly readable and practical in orientation.

Clowney, Edmund P. *The Message of 1 Peter*. Downers Grove: InterVarsity, 1988. An excellent treatment of 1 Peter's message for today.

Elliott, John H. *1 Peter*. New York: Doubleday: 2000. A massive (956 pp.) study. Denies Peter's authorship of the letter yet contains much of value. Usually understandable to the nonspecialist. Valuable bibliography.

Guthrie, Donald. "The Development of the Idea of Canonical Pseudepigrapha in New Testament Criticism." In *The Authorship and Integrity of the New Testament*. London: SPCK, 1965, pp. 14–39. A somewhat technical essay on the subject of using someone else's name when writing in antiquity.

Kruse, Colin. *The Letters of John*. Grand Rapids/Leicester: Eerdmans/Apollos, 2000. A thorough but concise treatment interacting with a good range of contemporary scholarship.

Lieu, Judith. *The Theology of the Johannine Epistles*. Cambridge: Cambridge University Press, 1991. Thorough discussion of issues and options in understanding the epistles' message as a whole.

Martin, Ralph P., and Peter H. Davids, eds. *Dictionary of the Later New Testament and Its Developments*. Downers Grove/Leicester: InterVarsity, 1997. Helpful and concise articles on the General Epistles and related topics.

Moo, Douglas J. *Second Peter and Jude*. Grand Rapids: Zondervan, 1996. A usable commentary on these letters by an eminent evangelical scholar.

Stott, John R. W. *The Letters of John*. Grand Rapids: Eerdmans, 1988. Pays close attention to both literary and theological features.

24 Revelation
God Is in Control!

Objectives

**After reading this chapter,
you should be able to**

- Identify the author of Revelation and support this identification with specific facts
- Outline the content of the Book of Revelation
- Compare the four theories used to interpret Revelation
- List the four major theological ideas developed in Revelation
- Illustrate how God is working between the supernatural world and the world of recorded time
- Enumerate the various names given to God in Revelation

For many people today, the Book of Revelation is a closed book—literally. They never read it. They are either afraid of it or think they cannot possibly understand it. This is unfortunate because from the early days of the church this book was turned to in times of persecution as a source of strength and encouragement. Of all the books in the Bible, it has the most panoramic sweep of history and of God's ultimate control over it. Things might be rough, but God knows what he is doing and is leading us to the New Jerusalem, where he will wipe away all tears and we will dwell with him forever.

Still, the book is hard to understand. That should not stop us from trying to understand it, however. There are many things that are hard to understand at first, but the meaning becomes clear after some effort. T. S. Eliot's *Four Quartets* and some of Gerard Manley Hopkins's poems are like that. The Book of Revelation falls in the same category.

A few basic guidelines are helpful to start with. First, the book consists of a long and complicated series of visions—over sixty of them. They blend into one another, overlap at times, go back and start over, pick out and expand details, give overviews of colossal events, and much more. They need to be read for what they are: visionary accounts of reality that were given by God to portray profound spiritual and theological truths. We also need to remember that the images John used were familiar to the people of his day, even if they aren't to us. Most of them are taken from the Old Testament—there are about 350 allusions or references to it—and the rest come from other books that were current in that day. We need to think ourselves back into their situation in order to make sense of what John is saying.

Second, the style that John used was also familiar to his readers. It was called apocalyptic, and John's readers were able to digest much of what he was saying because they were used to reading that sort of literature. As a literary style, apocalyptic was highly symbolic. The likes of Revelation's beasts, dragons, and even dissolving universes were pictorial representations of deep historical and theological realities. They were familiar to John's readers, coming as they did from

well-known books in the Old Testament, such as Exodus, Psalms, Ezekiel, Daniel, Isaiah, and Zechariah.

Finally, we have to remember that basic Christian theology is woven throughout the book. That gives it an inner coherence and unity that ties it together. Try not to get completely enthralled by the symbols; look for the theological truth being presented.

Author and Date

The author calls himself John (1:1) and says he was on the island of PATMOS as a result of being a "companion in the suffering and kingdom and patient endurance" that are common to those who are in Jesus (1:9). Patmos is a small island off the coast of ASIA MINOR in the AEGEAN SEA. It was a barren, rocky place. John was exiled there, no doubt to die. There is very strong early testimony (JUSTIN MARTYR, IRENAEUS, TERTULLIAN, ORIGEN, HIPPOLYTUS) that this John was John the apostle, who also wrote the Gospel and three letters. There is some ancient dissent to this, but it was usually for dogmatic reasons. DIONYSIUS OF ALEXANDRIA, for example, later followed by Eusebius, disliked the book's teaching on the millennium (a view he did not share), so he argued against its apostolic origin.

Much of contemporary scholarship also rejects the apostolic origin of Revelation. But this negative position rests on internal grounds, claiming that the theology of the book and the Greek used are so different from the Gospel's that the same person could not have written both. Since most of these modern scholars do not accept the Johannine authorship of the Gospel, it is hard to see the force of their argument, but even granting the differences, they are not as great as some contemporary scholars make them out to be. Those far closer to the situation historically, and who spoke Greek as their native language, had no problem with acknowledging John the apostle as the author of both the Gospel and the Book of Revelation.[1]

The date usually assigned to Revelation is during the persecutions of the emperor DOMITIAN (A.D. 81–96), Irenaeus saying "towards the end of Domitian's reign"

St. John's
Monastery,
Patmos,
Greece.

(*Against Heresies* 5.30.3). But some today are suggesting an earlier date, most likely in Nero's reign (ca. A.D. 68).[2] Of the two, the later date seems to have the most going for it, primarily because Revelation seems to imply that Nero was already dead. This would, of course, put its origin later than Nero, but during a time of persecution, and Domitian's reign suits that.

John's Mysticism

Isaiah, then, prophesies these things. But let us see if John uttered things similar to his. For this man, being in the island of Patmos, saw a revelation of awe-inspiring mysteries, which he relates unreservedly and teaches [to] others. Tell me, O blessed John, Apostle and pupil of the Lord, what have you seen, and what have you heard about Babylon:—awake and speak, for she also banished you. "And there came one of the seven angels, who had the seven vials."

—Hippolytus (ca. A.D. 170–236)

Outline

D. Christ as Triumphant Lamb (5:6–10)

E. Universal Adoration of God (5:11–14)

IV. Opening of the Seals on Destiny's Scroll (6:1–17)
A. First Seal Opened (6:1–2)
B. Second Seal Opened (6:3–4)
C. Third Seal Opened (6:5–6)
D. Fourth Seal Opened (6:7–8)
E. Fifth Seal Opened (6:9–11)
F. Sixth Seal Opened (6:12–17)

V. Interlude before the Seventh Seal (7:1–17)
A. Sealing of the 144,000 of Israel (7:1–8)
B. Vision of the Redeemed Multitude of the Earth (7:9–11)
C. Explanation of the Multitude (7:12–17)

VI. The Seventh Seal and the Seven Trumpets (8:1–9:21)
A. Opening the Seventh Seal and the Vision of the Censer (8:1–5)
B. Blowing of the First Four Trumpets (8:6–13)
C. Blowing of the Fifth Trumpet (9:1–12)
D. Blowing of the Sixth Trumpet (9:13–21)

VII. Interlude and the Seventh Trumpet (10:1–11:19)
A. Vision of the Mighty Angel and the Scroll (10:1–11)
B. Vision of the Two Witnesses (11:1–14)
C. Blowing of the Seventh Trumpet (11:15–19)

VIII. The Cosmic Conflict of Good and Evil (12:1–13:1a)
A. The Woman Clothed with the Sun (12:1–6)
B. War in Heaven (12:7–12)
C. Spiritual Warfare on Earth (12:13–13:1a)

IX. The Beasts, the Believers, and the Judgment of Earth (13:1b–14:20)
A. The Beast from the Sea (13:1b–10)
B. The Beast from the Earth (13:11–18)

C. The Lamb and the 144,000 (14:1–5)
D. The Announcements of the Three Flying Angels (14:6–13)
E. The Reaping of the Earth in Judgment (14:14–20)

X. The Seven Last Bowls of the Wrath of God (15:1–16:21)
A. The Song of Moses and the Lamb (15:1–4)
B. The Seven Angels with the Seven Last Plagues (15:5–8)
C. Pouring out of the Seven Bowls of the Wrath of God (16:1–21)

XI. The Fall of Rome Predicted (17:1–18:24)
A. Destruction of the Woman on the Beast (17:1–18)
B. Fall of Babylon the Great (18:1–24)

XII. The Return of Christ in Glory (19:1–21)
A. The Multitude of Heaven Rejoices (19:1–10)
B. Destruction of Evil by the Rider on the White Horse (19:11–21)

XIII. The Millennial Reign of Christ (20:1–15)
A. The Thousand-Year Reign (20:1–6)
B. Satan's Doom (20:7–10)
C. The Judgment at the Great White Throne (20:11–15)

XIV. The Eternal New Order (21:1–22:6)
A. The New Heaven and the New Earth (21:1–8)
B. The New Jerusalem, the Wife of the Lamb (21:9–27)
C. The River and the Tree of Life (22:1–6)

XV. The Promise of Jesus' Return (22:7–21)

As can be seen from the outline, the content of Revelation is complex and somewhat confusing. However, it does break out into three basic sections: the introduction and letters (chs. 1–3), the unfolding of history up to the return of Christ

antichrist

great white throne

(chs. 4–19), and the millennial reign of Christ and eternal new order (chs. 20–22).

The middle section begins with a magnificent vision of God triumphant on his throne (chs. 4–5), followed by three sets of seven visions (seals, trumpets, bowls) interspersed with various interludes, backtrackings, and overlappings. A large number of commentators see these three series of visions running parallel to each other, with each ending in a vision of the second coming (the seals ending in 6:12–17; the trumpets ending in 11:15–18; the bowls ending in 16:17–21).

Theories of Interpretation

There have been numerous theories of how to interpret Revelation throughout the history of the church.[3] Donald Guthrie lists nine basic theories, but for our purposes, four stand out as most significant: the historic premillennial view, the amillennial view, the dispensational premillennial view, and the postmillennial view.[4]

The historic premillennial view, dating back to Papias, Irenaeus, Justin Martyr, and Hippolytus, holds that the book relates to the life of the church. The various persecutions are to be experienced by the believers up to the time of the end, when they will be delivered from the power of **antichrist** by the return of Christ (described in ch. 19). There will be a resurrection of believers at the time of Christ's coming, followed by a millennium, a lengthy period during which Christ reigns on this earth. Then comes a final judgment of unbelievers at the "**great white throne**" (depicted in 20:11–15). After that, a new heaven and a new earth are instituted, and the eternal day dawns.[5]

The amillennial view also dates back to the early days of the church, being vigorously defended by Origen and Augustine. It was held by Luther and Calvin, and has probably been the majority view throughout church history. It rejects the idea of a literal thousand-year reign of Christ after his return at the end of the age (hence its name, a-millennialism, i.e., no millennium). It sees the millennium as being fulfilled in a spiritual fashion in the ministry of the church during this present age. The Book of Revelation is understood to be a description of the historical course of the persecuted church that will end with Christ's second coming, at which time there will be a general resurrection of everyone, the saved and lost alike. The last judgment takes place and a new heaven and a new earth are inaugurated as the home of the believers. The lost are cast into the lake of fire.[6]

The dispensational premillennial view is of relatively recent origin and is a bit more complicated than the former two views. In this view, typically, the first three chapters of Revelation deal with the church (or church age), after which the saints are raptured (removed) from the earth. This is usually placed at 4:1, 2—"come up here" is taken to refer to the rapture. The middle section of the book (chs. 4–19) deals with Israel on earth during a seven-year period of great tribulation that does not affect the church, because it is in heaven with Christ. At the battle of ARMAGEDDON in chapter 19, Christ brings with him the raptured Christians and establishes a Jewish millennium in fulfillment of the Old Testament prophecies. The Christian saints rule with Christ during this thousand-year period. At the end of this time, Satan is released from his confinement for a final rebellion and at the great white throne, he, his angels, and all the lost are cast into the lake of fire. A new heaven and a new earth are created and we enter into our eternal state. This view is sometimes called the pretribulation rapture theory because the church is removed from the earth *before* the great tribulation, or the any-moment rapture theory because it postulates that the rapture of the saints may take place at any moment and without warning.[7] There are variations to this view, postulating a mid-tribulation or even a post-tribulation rapture of the church.

Postmillennialism is a view that dates back to the eighteenth century and postulates that through the preaching of the gospel the world will gradually be won to Christ. In this way the idea of the millennium is fulfilled. The age of the church *is* the millennium, where righteousness and justice reign and good prevails throughout the earth. The great commission is fulfilled and the knowledge of the Lord covers the earth like the waters cover the sea.

After the world has thus been made worthy of Christ, he returns in glory to the world he has saved—hence the name "postmillennialism," Christ returns *after* the millennium. This view is similar to amillennialism in that a general resurrection, general judgment, and inauguration of the eternal state accompany Christ's second coming. The Book of Revelation is interpreted in a preterist fashion, that is, understood as referring to events of John's day, not as prophetic of the future.[8]

Devout Christians have held all of these views (and several more), and it is tragic when the return of Christ becomes a point of controversy. The important thing is that *Jesus* is coming back, not when or exactly how he will accomplish it. Martin Luther said we ought to live as though Christ was crucified yesterday, risen today, and coming tomorrow. If we follow that wise counsel, we will be ready when Christ does return.

The Teachings of Revelation

Although there are some strong differences of opinion about the end-time drama depicted in Revelation, there is virtual unanimity about its essential theological teachings. Revelation is a profound theological document. Many ideas are developed in it. Let us look at four of the most important.[9]

God

The central fact of the book is that God exists, has created the universe, is guiding the course of its history, has overcome evil, and will bring everything to a triumphant conclusion in his own good time. Numerous Old Testament images are woven together to give a rich depiction of God. The commanding vision of chapters 4 and 5 shows God on his throne, ruling over the universe, with all the heavenly hosts and the redeemed of earth bowing down before him. It is significant that as the book begins to unfold the course of future history, "every creature in heaven and on earth and under the earth and on the sea, and all that is in them" join in the concluding doxology to God who created all things and to the Lamb (4:11; 5:13). This is to prepare the reader for what is to come. The descriptions that follow hardly look like a creation that is praising God, but we would be totally wrong to see it that way. In reality, all of creation, in its own way, is praising God, even those beings (supernatural and human) that are fighting against the will of God. This is reminiscent of a profound Old Testament theme: God does his will in heaven and earth, and no one can hinder him.

God is introduced in trinitarian fashion in 1:4–5, first as the one "who is and who was and who is to come," second as the "seven spirits before his throne" (symbolically representing the Holy Spirit's sevenfold ministry as seen in Is 11:2–3), and third as "Jesus Christ, who is the faithful witness, the firstborn from the dead, and the ruler of the kings of the earth." Emphasis on the Spirit and his ministry is somewhat limited in Revelation (2:7; 3:1; 4:2; 5; 14:13; 17:3; 21:10; 22:17), with the heaviest emphasis being laid on the divine glory of the Son.

One of the keys to understanding the book is to grasp the idea of God's relation to the world. There are two realities in which we live: the supernatural order, where God is all in all, and the world of recorded time, where God is working out his earthly purposes. The book is constantly shifting back and forth between these two dimensions, challenging us to see the hand of God at work in the world around us, even though that world is hostile to God. God is the supreme reality, and this world is subordinate to him and passing away. It is moving toward its appointed end, regardless of how things look now.

The Son of God

No book in the New Testament speaks in such exalted fashion of Jesus Christ, the Son of God. From the overpowering vision of 1:12–18 to the return of Jesus as King of kings and Lord of lords (19:16), he is seen as nothing less than the Divine Being himself (1:18; 3:7; 22:13). The doxologies of the book are directed to both, and the Father and the Son have the same divine qualities (4:11; 5:12–13; 7:12). God calls himself "the Alpha and the Omega, the beginning and the end" (1:8; 21:5–6) and Jesus refers to himself in the same way (22:12–13).

John's favorite expression (twenty-eight times) to describe Jesus is "the Lamb," recalling from his Gospel the redemptive work of God in Christ (Jn 1:29). Jesus is supremely the Savior of the world. The Lamb receives worship from the saints (5:8) and glory and honor for ever and ever (5:13); he brings the salvation of God (7:9–10); the saints conquer through the blood of the Lamb, and the Lamb is the glory of God in the eternal city of heaven (21:23). This Lamb is the Lion of the Tribe of Judah who has come to crush the nations and rule with a rod of iron (5:5; 19:15).

The People of God

The redeemed people of God play a prominent role in the Book of Revelation. As individual churches, they have their strengths and weaknesses (see chs. 2–3 for the seven churches), but as the redeemed of God, over against Satan and the world, they are those who are "victorious over the beast and his image and over the number of his name" (15:2), even if it costs them their lives.

The believers are variously described in Revelation as servants of God (7:3); a kingdom (1:6; 5:10); priests (1:6; 5:10; 20:6); saints (18:20); the blameless (14:5); the called and chosen (17:14); the wife of the Lamb (19:7; 21:9); and those who are redeemed as a firstfruit to God and the Lamb and who follow the Lamb wherever he goes (14:4). The believers' task is to hold fast to the testimony of Jesus and to the word of God (6:9; 11:7; 12:11, 17; 19:10; 20:4). They do this by watching (16:15), keeping God's commands (3:8, 10; 12:17; 14:12), keeping themselves pure (14:4), and doing the work that God has assigned to them (2:2, 13, 19; 3:1, 8; 14:13). This is all summarized as "the patient endurance and faithfulness of the saints" (13:10).

Eschatology

Theologians speak of personal eschatology (what happens at the end of our lives) and cosmic eschatology (what happens at the end of the world). Both are to be found in abundance in Revelation. Elements of things to come include the certainty of life after death (6:9–11); the comfort of the believer in the presence of God and Christ (7:9–17); the resurrection and reward of the saints (20:4–6) and their glorious eternal state (21:6–8); the second coming of Christ (6:12–17; 19:11–21); the assignment of all to their eternal place (20:1–15); the creation of

Is Everybody Going to Heaven?

Universalism is the view that ultimately everything and everyone will be saved, even Satan, his angels, and demons. This view is becoming more popular in our own day through the spreading notion of the essential divinity of every human being, no matter how deliberately they reject God or the gospel. We are all part of Ultimate Being and Being is divine, so that makes us partly god ourselves. Because we are essentially divine, we cannot ultimately be lost. In the end, all things will be brought back together in a cosmic harmony as a redeemed humanity.

This view has enormous popular appeal because it tells us that no matter what we are or do we will ultimately make it to "heaven." Unfortunately, it is not the view of Jesus or the Bible. The Bible tells us not that we are in essence saved, but that we are, in fact, lost. We are not partly divine, but rather, alienated from God by our sinful condition. Our sinfulness and lostness have put us in a state of condemnation, destined for hell, not heaven. It is only the grace of God expressed in the death and resurrection of Jesus, the only human being ever to possess deity, that saves us from our lostness and qualifies us for heaven.

The New Testament is clear on the fact that it is only those who accept Jesus as their Savior, the one who died for them, who will enter heaven. Heaven is the free gift of God to those who will repent of their sins and open their hearts to the Son of God, who loved us and gave himself for us. People are lost not because God does not offer them salvation, but because some refuse to accept the gracious offer that is made to them.

Focus 24: The New Heaven and the New Earth

In Rv 21:1 we read that the apostle John, in his vision on Patmos, *"saw a new heaven and a new earth, for the first heaven and the first earth had passed away."* His description of this new universe is rich in symbolism, speaking of the streets of the New Jerusalem as being *"of pure gold, like transparent glass"* (21:21) and of the *"river of the water of life, as clear as crystal"* (22:1). It is a marvelous picture of what awaits the believer when Christ returns for his church and brings history to a dramatic close.

The Christian apologist and scholar C. S. Lewis wrote a famous series of children's books, The Chronicles of Narnia. But as any adult who has ever read them knows, they are not just stories for children. Rather, they relate the story of God's creation and redemption of the earth and humankind, symbolized in the books by the country

of Narnia and its inhabitants. In the following passage from the final book in the series, *The Last Battle*, Lewis draws this picture of the new heaven and the new earth at the end of recorded time:

It is hard to explain how this sunlit land was different from the old Narnia, as it would be to tell you how the fruits of that country taste. Perhaps you will get some idea of it, if you think like this. You may have been in a room in which there was a window that looked out on a lovely bay of the sea or a green valley that wound away among mountains. And in the wall of that room opposite to the window there may have been a looking glass. And as you turned away from the window you suddenly caught sight of that sea or that valley, all over again, in the looking glass. And the sea in the mirror, or the valley in the mirror, were in one sense just the same as the real

ones: yet at the same time they were somehow different— deeper, more wonderful, more like places in a story: in a story you have never heard but very much want to know. The difference between the old Narnia and the new Narnia was like that. The new one was a deeper country: every rock and flower and blade of grass looked as if it meant more. I can't describe it any better than that: if you ever get there, you will know what I mean.

It was the Unicorn who summed up what everyone was feeling. He stamped his right fore-hoof on the ground and neighed and then cried:

"I have come home at last! This is my real country! I belong here. This is the land I have been looking for all my life, though I never knew it till now. The reason why we loved the old Narnia is that it sometimes looked a little like this. Bree- hee-hee! Come further up, come further in!"

Key People/Places

Aegean Sea
Armageddon
Asia Minor
Dionysius of Alexandria
Domitian
Hippolytus
Irenaeus
Justin Martyr
Nero
Origen
Patmos
Tertullian

Key Terms

antichrist
great white throne

a new heaven and a new earth (21:1–17); and the promise that we will see God personally face to face, and reign with him forevermore (22:1–6). The book ends with the prayer of every sincere Christian heart: "Amen, Come Lord Jesus" (22:20).

It is with good reason that the New Testament ends with the Book of Revelation. In it a philosophy of history is developed that shows God as supreme over all the universe and in particular over the course of human events. It also shows in a marvelous, symbolic way the two elements of Christ's messianic ministry—that of suffering servant (the Lamb) and that of ruling sovereign (the lion). The Old Testament had spoken of the coming Messiah in both these ways. Jesus was rejected by his own people at his first coming because they wanted him to be their king so they could rule the world with him. They did not realize that the cross must precede the crown and that only after sinners accept their role of servant will glory follow. Jesus showed this to be true and commanded followers to take up their cross and live for him (Mk 8:34). Revelation shows us that our life here will be one of service and great trial. But just as Jesus triumphed, so too his faithful followers of all times and places will triumph with him.

Summary

1. The Book of Revelation was most likely written by John the apostle.

2. Four prominent theories of interpretation of Revelation are historic premillennialism, amillennialism, dispensational premillennialism, and postmillennialism.

3. The central themes of Revelation are that God exists and is guiding the course of history, that he has overcome evil, and that he will bring everything to a triumphant conclusion in his time.

4. One key to understanding Revelation is to grasp God's relation to the world.

5. The major theological teaching of Revelation focuses on God, the Son of God, the people of God, and eschatology.

6. Symbolism is used throughout the Book of Revelation; Christ's messianic ministry is one example, the Lamb representing the Suffering Servant and the Lion representing the ruling Sovereign.

Review Questions

1. The Book of Revelation is difficult to study because of the number of _____; there are over _____ of them.

2. An apocalyptic literary style is highly _____.

3. The author of Revelation calls himself _____.

4. Revelation refers to letters written to seven Asian _____.

5. The three sets of seven visions are _____, _____, and _____.

6. The position that rejects the idea of a literal thousand-year reign of Christ on earth is called _____.

7. The dispensational premillennial theory holds that at the end of the millennium, Satan and all his angels will be judged at the _____.

8. In Revelation God is introduced in Trinitarian fashion, but heaviest emphasis is laid on the _____ of the _____.

9. John's favorite name for Jesus is the _____.

10. The Book of Revelation provides much material for study of the division of theology known as _____.

Study Questions

1. What are some possible reasons that Revelation is sometimes avoided?

2. Give one distinguishing feature of each of the four major theories of interpretation of Revelation.

3. What does Revelation teach about God?

4. What does Revelation teach about the Son of God?

5. What does the subject of eschatology have to say to us today as we live our daily lives?

6. Look up the references to Jesus as Lion and Lamb. Describe in detail what each image signifies.

Further Reading

Bauckham, Richard. *The Theology of the Book of Revelation.* Cambridge: Cambridge University Press, 1993. A methodical examination of central themes.

Beale, G. K. *The Book of Revelation.* Grand Rapids: Eerdmans, 1999. A massive study stressing Old Testament and Jewish backgrounds and historical setting.

Clouse, Robert G., ed. *The Meaning of the Millennium: Four Views.* Downers Grove: InterVarsity, 1977. Airs views regarding an important teaching in Revelation. Somewhat technical for beginners.

Guthrie, Donald. *The Relevance of John's Apocalypse.* Grand Rapids: Eerdmans, 1987. Four essays on how the teaching of Revelation relates to today.

Hemer, Colin J. *The Letters to the Seven Churches of Asia in Their Local Setting.* Grand Rapids: Eerdmans, 2001. A scholarly study of the seven churches, but still easy enough to read and very enlightening.

Himmelfarb, Martha. *Ascent to Heaven in Jewish and Christian Apocalypses.* New York/Oxford: Oxford University Press, 1993. A study of apocalyptic literature outside the New Testament.

Ladd, George E. *A Commentary on the Revelation of John.* Grand Rapids: Eerdmans, 1972. An easy-to-follow commentary from the historic pre-millennial point of view.

Martin, Ralph P., and Peter H. Davids, ed. *Dictionary of the Later New Testament and Its Developments.* Downers Grove/Leicester: InterVarsity, 1997. Helpful and concise articles on Revelation and related topcis.

Metzger, Bruce M. *Breaking the Code: Understanding the Book of Revelation.* Nashville: Abingdon, 1996. An easy-to-follow look at Revelation.

Mounce, Robert H. *Revelation.* Rev. ed. Grand Rapids: Eerdmans, 1997. A comprehensive commentary from a historic premillennial point of view.

Osborne, Grant. *Revelation.* Grand Rapids: Baker, 2002. A thorough treatment interacting extensively with recent scholarship. Historic premillennial outlook.

Wainwright, A. W. *Mysterious Apocalypse: Interpreting the Book of Revelation.* Nashville: Abingdon, 1966. A look at the history of interpretation, cultural context, themes, and content of Revelation.

Walvoord, John F. *The Revelation of Jesus Christ.* Chicago: Moody, 1976. A standard commentary from a leading exponent of dispensational premillennialism.

Epilogue
Matters to Ponder

Outline

- **The New Testament Story: Over But Not Ended**
- **The Legacy of the Apostolic Age**
  Old Testament Roots
  Balanced Vision
  Empowering Example
  Basis for Reflection and Action
- **Unfinished Business**
  Contextualization
  Church and Culture
  Gospel and Society
  Keeping Faith Fresh
  Great Awakening?

Objectives

After reading this chapter, you should be able to

- List the church's inheritance from the New Testament writings
- Give illustrations of the continuity between Old and New Testaments
- Give examples of how the New Testament provides a balanced vision
- Explain how the New Testament gives us a standard for engaging contemporary culture
- Identify questions that are not answered directly in the New Testament

The New Testament Story: Over But Not Ended

Any good story has a beginning, main body, and ending. The New Testament begins with God's eternal plan to create and redeem as related in the Old Testament. The main body of the New Testament is the story of Jesus Christ. The New Testament ends, ominously yet gloriously, with the Book of Revelation.

But the New Testament story does not end in the first century. Think of Abraham Lincoln and the courageous leadership he gave to a fledgling nation at a crucial time. Society is still striving to implement the principles of justice and equality for which he was willing to lead a nation into its deadliest war. Or think of a more modern statesman like Winston Churchill as he rallied Great Britain early in the dark days of World War II. Both men are long gone, but their legacies continue.

In the same way, the lives of Jesus Christ and his followers continue on into the future long after their deaths. What have later generations inherited from the rich deposit of truth and insight preserved in the New Testament's sacred pages? Perhaps we should put a finer point on the question: What are some of the lessons that we ourselves should take to heart from our survey of New Testament times and writings?

The Legacy of the Apostolic Age

Old Testament Roots

One lesson is the importance of the Old Testament. This is not because the New Testament is always a direct continuation of Old Testament times and traditions. By the first century Jewish life in the Roman world contrasted sharply with the way things were under Moses, or David, or Ezra many centuries before. Neither New Testament faith nor New Testament history can be adequately understood as a simple straight-line projection forward from the Old Testament.

Nevertheless, there is profound continuity. New Testament writers make it plain that the God of Jesus Christ is identical to the God of Abraham, Isaac, and Jacob. God's righteousness is unchanged from Old Testament to New. His rule extends unbroken from Eden to the eschaton. Human nature is regarded as fallen and in need of radical transformation in both great divisions of the Bible.

Use of the New Testament that casts aside or misconstrues the Old Testament runs the risk of becoming an abstract philosophy of religion or mere moral drama. The good news of Jesus Christ is neither of these. New Testament writers built on the foundation of God's prior acts and words as the Old Testament attests to them. That foundation remains secure for all ages of the church who wish to stay true to the message of Jesus and his first followers.

Balanced Vision

To some degree we all live our lives according to an overarching vision. If that vision is distorted—if we think that the main thing in life is making money, for example, or pursuing sexual pleasure—our lives will be off center as a result. The New Testament's vision is balanced. It focuses on contrasting truths in such a way that each is preserved without any receiving unhealthy emphasis.

Take the twin truths of this age and the age to come, the world and heaven, history and eternity. Here theologians speak of "immanence" (that which has to do with purely temporal and material existence) and "transcendence" (that which has to do with the unseen spiritual world). For the New Testament both exist. Both are part of God's universe. Both have importance in their own right. Yet neither is stressed to the exclusion or minimizing of the other. Just because we long for heaven, that does not justify ignoring the tasks God gives us on earth. Christians of all people should seek to make the world a place of less misery and more true happiness. On the other hand, just because we see the dire needs of the great nations, cities, and sprawling suburbs of our time, that does not mean that we can forget about life's spiritual dimension. Problems of poverty, hunger, health care, or a sense of life's

Billy Graham addresses an estimated crowd of 1,100,000 in Yoido Plaza, Seoul, Korea, 1973, in what is believed to be the largest religious meeting in the world.

meaningless are never issues of money, food, medicine, and education alone. A better world requires better people, and only the gospel can cleanse and change the deceitful human heart. The New Testament keeps both the tangible world and the intangible world before our eyes and demands that we live in daily recognition of both.

The New Testament's vision is also broad enough to incorporate what some see as the apparent opposites of religious faith, on the one hand, and the historical events that are the basis for faith, on the other. It stresses facts like Jesus' virgin birth, his miracles, and his resurrection. Yet these facts are not presented as the message by themselves alone. Rather, they are viewed in such a way as to encourage trust in the God who stands behind the facts as their ultimate cause and interpreter. Faith and fact are intertwined. They cannot be abstracted from each other without canceling out the real import of both. In the modern setting, where history is widely disregarded as a fit means of conveying truth, the New Testament calls us back to a vision of openness to seeing the very hand of God in certain persons, incidents, and words that various biblical sources have preserved.

Empowering Example

Moving stories can inspire us to aspire to noble acts. The New Testament is far more than a moving story. But through the story it tells it beckons the reader to a higher plane of existence than he or she might otherwise settle for.

It abounds, for example, in displays of measured zeal, courageous dedication, and sacrificial commitment. Moreover, much of this is in the face of persecution. Whether Jesus enduring the indignities of his trial with rock-solid trust in God, or Paul braving the rigors of shipwreck with remarkable hope, we are confronted with loyalty to truth and to God himself that urges us to more spiritually robust lives.

The holy bravery of the New Testament is exemplary in other ways. It is not the harsh zeal of hateful fanaticism but the active devotion of love. Jesus, Paul, and others expose themselves to ridicule without lapsing into bitterness in return. Jesus on the cross prays for his tormentors (Lk 23:34). Stephen does the same as he is cruelly stoned to death (Acts 7:60). Paul expresses anguish over his countrymen who thwart his mission and everywhere dog his steps (Rom 9:2–3; 10:1). This is more than simply nonviolent resistance, a political strategy advocated by Thoreau, Gandhi, and Martin Luther King. It is that greatest and most difficult of graces: placing full trust in the heavenly Father when present circumstances seem to require drastic measures for the sake of self-preservation. There are times, of course, to defend oneself (Acts 25:11). But to follow Jesus means to stand ready to lose our lives in order to gain true life. The reader of the New Testament is seldom far from a passage pointing to this sobering but liberating truth.

Another point at which the New Testament stands as a shining example is the missionary zeal and effectiveness it documents. In a few short decades the gospel of Jesus Christ went forth in all directions and into dozens of different ethnic and language groups.[1] Christians believed in the kingdom of God! Their lives had been changed by the gospel of Jesus Christ! They knew that same Word could give light and life to others! So they went forth with joyful determination, not to oppress others with a burdensome ideology but to free them from sin's shackles by the truth of Christ's coming.

Today Christian missions in the West is undermined by flat or falling levels of missions giving and doubt among some whether people without Christ are really lost. Influential religious leaders question whether Jesus and other biblical writers really speak of a place of conscious eternal torment called hell.[2] Some suggest that there are other names for the God who saves than Jesus Christ, and other religions that may "work" if people believe in them sincerely. Of course God is free to save whom he chooses. But the New Testament remains a monument to a generation or more of men and women who knew Jesus—and who at great cost committed their lives to making him known in every place still ignorant of his cross and resurrection. Their example can brace us who face similar challenges today in the midst of churches often more concerned with self-betterment, preservation of tradition, or style of worship than with the meat-and-potatoes fare of going to the lost, whether poor or rich, with the gospel that can change lives and bring blessing and hope.

A final area where the New Testament

is an example for today lies in how it sees truth and life as a unity. To live upright lives, the New Testament insists, we must (1) know truth and (2) do the right thing. To know without doing is hypocrisy. To do without knowing is blindness. The New Testament places us firmly before both of these priorities. In more technical terms it keeps life's ethical dimension (doing the right thing) tied firmly to the shared certainties of the New Testament's writings (doctrine). It does not set forth a body of teaching to be learned and affirmed—and nothing more. Nor does it call to moral activism, good works, social improvement, by themselves.

It can be tempting to reduce the Christian faith to intellectualism. Doctrine becomes everything. "Truth" (of a sort) takes center stage. The actual doing of truth becomes secondary. What is important is to *be* right, not to *do* right. "Faith" means correct belief. Clearly this falls short of the "faith" to which New Testament writers call with its explicit goal of active love for God and others. Biblical faith bears the fruit of good works; it is not content just to refine good ideas.

Yet another temptation is no less dangerous. It is the tendency to scoff at truth, to minimize the importance of sound understanding. Here the stress is on practical action, on "getting out and getting it done." Study, thought, critical analysis, learning are unimportant; what matters are concrete acts of compassion and concern. Yet mindless activism comes no closer to capturing the essence of gospel obedience than barren intellectualism.

The New Testament's example is one of both solid teaching, firm and increasing grasp of biblical doctrines and their meaning, and obedient response, selfless and progressive attention to human needs and their solution. Truth and life, theology and practice, are not torn apart. They were perfectly joined in Jesus' own life, as the New Testament records. By his Spirit the same happy combining of gospel *teaching* and gospel *doing* has been a recurring feature of the lives of his loyal followers through all the centuries since.

Basis for Reflection and Action

The last legacy of the New Testament era to be mentioned here is the New Testament as a standard for thinking about and engaging the world. As the twenty-first century dawns, much of the world finds itself awash in skepticism about the possibility of certainty—not just about God but about anything at all. "There is no such thing," a handbook of modern thought asserts, as "a way of reaching the truth about natural phenomena." In fact, "everything we 'know' is . . . a temporary acquisition based on information at present available and a useful basis for speculation and analysis, but by no means absolute truth."[3] In this view, with sure knowledge of physical matter denied, it is easy to imagine how hopeless the quest for truth about God becomes. No wonder religious relativism—the logically baffling doctrine that there is no true religion, yet all religions are true—flourishes.

The New Testament (in combination with the Old) furnishes a way to sort truth from error. This does not mean that all truth about everything is contained in the Bible. But it does mean that sound and substantial answers to fundamental questions are found on its pages—such questions as Who are we? Where did we come from? Why are we here? Where are we headed? Is there a God? What is he like? How can I know him? What does he expect of me? A brief glance at the religion/philosophy section of a modern bookstore reveals a bewildering array of answers (or rejection of answers) to such questions. How can we cut through the confusion?

The New Testament answers with twenty-seven writings that join in pointing to Jesus Christ. As witnesses to God's climactic word to humanity (Heb 1:1–2), these writings give a foundation for finding one's way in the world in terms of both understanding and doing. True, it is a foundation only; each generation must renew and refine the superstructure erected on the New Testament basis by previous generations of loyal Christians. It should also be underscored that the discovering, nurturing, and passing along of sure knowledge is a daunting enterprise; to say that there is truth, and that the New Testament aids in grasping it, is not to say that truth is always simple to comprehend and easy to apply. But the fact remains that Scripture does provide some sure

knowledge at numerous key junctures (for example, what happens after we die?). It is humbling but heartening to be reminded of the Christian mission of making known to the world the truth of God in Christ as revealed in the New Testament. The New Testament furnishes a home base and constant companion for this mission.

Unfinished Business

This book is a survey of the New Testament, not a manual for Christian living today. But there are a number of key issues the New Testament raises but hardly settles. In the nature of the case many questions had to be left to later generations—among them our own.

Contextualization

First, there was the problem of how the gospel should be extended beyond the Greek-, Aramaic- (or Hebrew-), and Latin-speaking regions where it first went forth. This is the issue of contextualizing the gospel for successive new cultural settings. From the outset, the gospel had to be stated in new languages and expressed in different forms without distorting the message in the process. This task continues to the present day as the gospel penetrates new frontiers and as older, once Christian societies have to be called back to the meaning of a gospel that they have ceased to understand, much less trust.

Church and Culture

A second and related unfinished task involves working out the connection between the gospel and the government, the larger society outside the church, and the ruling thought forms of each successive era. How should the church and its message relate to culture? The New Testament offers models but no one single strategy. Answers to this question are sufficiently challenging to engage the best minds and resources of any generation of Christians willing to try to find them. (Augustine's *City of God* is a classic example from the fifth century.) There is the need for reconfigured systems of theology, keeping pace with (and setting the pace for!) human society's constant growth and flux. There is likewise need for reworking practical responses to the unique challenges to gospel influence that each era and locality presents. In all of this the New Testament offers normative guidance, but Christians are left to figure out a great deal for themselves with the light available to them from both biblical and extrabiblical quarters.

Gospel and Society

Third, the social dimensions of the gospel remain to be worked out more fully. To become a Christian necessarily involves personal decision and change. The result is transformation of personal life to some extent. But individual Christians can never be content just to be better off themselves. The cross of Christ has application to the whole world (1 Jn 2:2). The New Testament raises issues involving all of society, not just personal religion and church life. What it says requires attention to racism and the environment and materialism and education and the social plight of orphans and the poor, not simply the state of our own hearts.

Keeping Faith Fresh

Fourth, the New Testament calls for wrestling with the question of how to handle success when God grants it. When the gospel is preached and accepted on a large scale, it has historically received wide acceptance and made a dramatic impact. Then, what was at first an electrifying message becomes a familiar religious system. How can the freshness of selfless and costly trust in the living God be kept alive and passed on to the next generation? Particularly after decades or centuries of gospel influence in a society, how can the domestication of God be avoided? How can the fire of divine judgment and deliverance be kept burning, consuming any who approach with the idea of using God for personal, national, or other purely human ends? Through its history the church, just like Israel in the Old Testament, has tended to fall short of fidelity to the truth and love that gave it birth. How can it nurture and live out the seminal message of redemption in Christ instead of smothering that message with some kind of churchianity?

Great Awakening?

This brings up a final issue, the issue of renewal (or revival, a term that must be defined carefully). The New Testament is first of all a book given by God to God's people for God's people. Both Old and New Testament make it painfully clear that God's people are often their own worst enemies, worse by far than the "world" outside the church, when it comes to faithful appropriation of the gospel message. Many observers see Christianity in a crisis situation at the present hour.

It is not so much the threat of opposition and persecution, as in Muslim countries like Sudan or totalitarian strongholds like China there is vicious suppression of Christian witness. The church has always flourished where suffering has in effect purified Christians' lives and proclamation. We can be sure that the blood of the martyrs will continue to be the seed of tomorrow's church.

The survival of Christianity is rather most questionable in areas where Christian belief was once widespread but is now compromised by materialism and the crass (though widely accepted) pursuit of pleasure and self-fulfillment. This describes the situation in much of what has been traditionally called the West. The church is not openly opposed; it has simply become impotent, absorbed and largely neutralized by the pagan world around it. Sometimes this involves compromise of Christian doctrines, so-called liberalism. But churches with "conservative" beliefs are beset by the same illness—and they are self-righteous to boot, thankful that they are not like others, whose sin they judge as worse than their own. Yes, there is much to be thankful for in many quarters. But overall the decay of societies (as seen in growing violence, falling education standards, high rates of illegitimate births and divorce, normalization of gay marriages, etc.) is mirrored by decline in true Christian belief and obedience in the Western world (conditions are currently more encouraging in Third World areas where the gospel seems to be mushrooming in its good effects). Religion or spirituality may

Focus 25: What Does Revival Do?

Restores Faith in the Word of God
Restores Definiteness to the Meaning of "Christian"
Advances the Gospel with Amazing Swiftness
Always Has Moral Impact upon Communities
Changes Understanding of the Christian Ministry
Will Change the Public Worship of the Churches

—From Iain H. Murray, *Pentecost—Today? The Biblical Basis for Understanding Revival* (Edinburgh/Carlisle, Pa.: Banner of Truth, 1998), 170–93.

be healthy in some sectors of the West, but in most places costly following of Christ along the lines of the New Testament precedent is not.

The New Testament offers hope. If the message of Jesus Christ could revolutionize the desperately sick world of classical antiquity, challenging paganism and calling key segments of a decadent Judaism back to its own truths and messianic destiny, we can be assured that widespread renewal of church and society today is by no means out of the question.[4] But Jesus left his disciples with a chilling question: "When the Son of Man comes, will he find faith on the earth?" (Lk 18:8). It is a point to ponder upon reaching the end of a survey of the New Testament and as a new millennium continues to unfold.

Summary

1. The Old Testament provided the foundation for the New Testament, and there is a profound continuity between the testaments.

2. The vision of the New Testament is always a balanced (though not a domesticated!) one. It upholds contrasting truths in a manner that will prevent any of them from receiving one-sided emphasis.

3. The New Testament provides examples of holy bravery, zeal, dedication, and commitment.

4. The New Testament provides us with examples of missionary fervor and effectiveness.

5. Truth and life, theology and practice are unified in the New Testament.

6. The Bible provides guidelines that will assist us in sorting out truth from error.

7. The New Testament by itself does not settle every detail of how new generations and cultures must receive and apply the gospel.

8. The New Testament does not always provide complete instructions for how we should respond to issues related to the relationship between the church and culture, details of the social dimensions of the gospel, or suggestions on how to keep faith fresh.

9. The church today must reevaluate how well it is following Christ as he is presented in the New Testament.

Review Questions

1. The New Testament is not a direct _____ of Old Testament times and traditions.

2. God's righteousness is _____ from Old Testament to New.

3. Every human being lives his or her life by a _____.

4. That which pertains solely to material existence is called _____.

5. We should be motivated to live better Christian lives when we read New Testament examples of loyalty to truth and to _____.

6. The zealous bravery of many New Testament figures is due not to harsh _____ but to devoted _____.

7. The New Testament teaches that to live upright lives, Christians must both know _____ and do _____.

8. The New Testament example rejects both barren _____ and mindless _____.

9. The problem of how the gospel should be presented to new cultures is called _____.

10. The church has always survived and grown during times of _____.

Study Questions

1. In what ways does the New Testament reflect continuity with the Old Testament?

2. How does the New Testament keep both the tangible and intangible worlds before our eyes?

3. What are some New Testament examples of holy bravery?

4. What are some questions concerning how we are to engage the world that are not answered in the New Testament?

5. What are some questions that are not fully answered in the New Testament but to which contemporary Christians must formulate responses?

6. How is modern Christianity in the West most compromised?

Glossary

Abba The intimate Aramaic word for father used exclusively by Jesus (Mk 14:36) and the early Christians for God (Rom 8:15; Gal 4:6). It is not found in ancient Jewish writings.

Abraham's Bosom A term used in Luke 16:19–31 to denote that portion of Hades where believers who died in Old Testament times find their rest in company with the patriarch Abraham.

A.D. Description of time deriving from the Latin *anno domini,* "in the year of our Lord," using the birth of Christ as the point of reference. Some prefer to use C.E. (Common Era) as its equivalent. See B.C.

Adiaphora "Things indifferent," that is, morally neutral with respect especially to the public religious sphere. How an individual chooses to treat these "things indifferent" is a matter of conscience, since they are neither forbidden nor commanded by Scripture.

Allegory A literary device wherein the details of a story are given symbolic meaning. Philo of Alexandria interpreted much of the Old Testament this way. Jesus (Mt 13:1–9, 18–23; 24–30, 36–43) and Paul (Gal 4:21–31) sometimes make use of allegory-like methods.

Amen A Greek (and Hebrew) word meaning "true" or "truthfully," put at the end of prayers. Jesus characteristically began his statements "*Amen* I say to you . . ." to emphasize his supreme authority. Whatever he said would be true.

Am ha-aretz Hebrew term meaning "people of the land" and referring to the common, uneducated masses, who were looked down upon by the upper levels of society. They are probably referred to in John 7:49. The Greek equivalent is *hoi polloi.*

Antichrist The ultimate enemy of Christ who appears prior to Christ's second coming, only to be defeated. Until his appearance there are many "antichrists" in the world for believers to contend with (1 Jn 4:1–3; 2 Jn 7).

Antinomianism The view that believers in Christ are freed from all moral obligations whatsoever. Paul (1 Cor 5:1–5) and John (1 Jn 3:7–10) both had to contend with this.

Apocalyptic Term describing both a theological movement and its literature. It postulates the increase of evil in the world, the near end of the age, and the decisive intervention of God to inaugurate the age to come. Both Jewish and Christian apocalyptic literature exists, and its characteristic motifs are to be found in the New Testament (Mt 24–25; Rv).

Apocrypha Specifically, a collection of fourteen Jewish books written mainly between 200 B.C. and A.D. 100 not found in the Hebrew Old Testament, but included in the Roman Catholic Bible. These books are sometimes called the deutero-canonical books of the Old Testament. More generally, the term means "inauthentic" or "false" and refers to a large body of writings, both Old and New Testament, such as the Psalms of Solomon (OT) and the Gospel of Thomas (NT). See also Apocalyptic; Pseudepigrapha.

Apostasy The ultimate rejection of one's former religious belief or practice. The Book of Hebrews warns against this sin.

Apostle Term meaning "a messenger" or "one who is sent," applied to the twelve leaders appointed by Jesus (Mk 3:13–19). Qualifications for apostleship included seeing the risen Lord (Acts 1:13–14). Paul could claim apostleship for this reason (1 Cor 9:1). They are sometimes called simply "the Twelve" (Jn 20:24; 1 Cor 15:5).

Aramaic A Semitic language related to Hebrew commonly spoken in Palestine during Jesus' day and used by him in ordinary discourse. It dates back to ancient Syria (biblical Aram). Part of the Old Testament is written in Aramaic.

Areopagus Term designating a hill NW of the acropolis in Athens or the council or court that met there. Paul made his case for Christianity here (Acts 17:16–34).

Armageddon A Hebrew word meaning Mount Megiddo, used in Revelation 16:16 to designate the place where the last great battle of the ages will take place. Historically, the broad plain before Megiddo had been a place of decisive battles (e.g. Jgs 4–6; 1 Sm 31).

Ascension Term used to describe the return of Jesus to heaven forty days after his resurrection (Lk 24:50–53; Acts 1:9).

Asiarchs Roman administrative officials chosen annually by a league of cities in the province of Asia. Asiarchs were among the wealthiest and most aristocratic citizens. One of their duties was oversight of local patriotic cultic activities on behalf of Rome and the emperor. Acts 19:31 describes some of them as friends of Paul.

Atonement To make amends for sin. Israel's "Day of Atonement" included blood sacrifices to restore fellowship between God and the sinful nation. Jesus' death fulfilled that ceremony by making atonement through the cross (Gal 3:13).

Baptism The Christian ceremony whereby a person is publicly received into the church by application of or immersion in water (Acts 2:38–41). A type of baptism was practiced by John the Baptist and other Jews before the church adopted it.

B.C. Abbreviation meaning "Before Christ." Some prefer B.C.E., "Before the Common Era." See also A.D.

Beatitudes The nine blessings pronounced by Jesus upon those who live in the kingdom of God and embody the principles he called for. They introduce the Sermon on the Mount (Mt 5:3–12).

Bema Judgment seat or tribunal of a Roman official. The term denoted an elevated platform from which political orations or judicial decisions were delivered.

Bible Term derived from the Greek *biblion* (book) designating the 66 books (39 OT, 27 NT) that constitute the Christian Scriptures as the church's ultimate rule of faith and life. Roman Catholics add 14 Apocryphal books to the Old Testament. See Apocrypha; Canon.

Bishop A leader in the early church, sometimes called an "overseer" or "elder." Qualifications for office are listed in 1 Timothy 3:1–10 and Titus 1:5–9.

Calvary See Golgotha.

Canon Term meaning standard or basis for judgment. In theology it refers to the Scriptures received by the church as authoritative for its life and thought. See Bible.

Canonical Criticism One of a number of interpretive approaches concerned with the nature, function, and authority of canon. It takes as its starting point the nature of Scripture as revealed by historical criticism and then asks how the biblical text functions in the communities of faith that have preserved and treasured it.

Catholic Letters Those seven letters (James; 1 and 2 Peter; 1, 2, 3 John; and Jude) that are not addressed to specific churches, but to Christians generally. Hence they are called "general" or "catholic" (universal) letters. Some include Hebrews in this grouping.

C.E. See A.D.

Centurion Commander of a hundred men (a "century") in a Roman legion. He was typically a prestigious member of a small military governing class; a high-ranking centurion held a position comparable to that of a knight. The centurion's duties were: (1) to drill his subordinates; (2) to inspect them (arms, clothing, etc.); and (3) to command them in both the camp and the field. The Gospel writers present centurions in a favorable light (see Mt 8:5; Mk 15:39; Lk 23:47).

Cephas Aramaic name meaning "Rock," the Greek form of which is "Peter," given to Simon, one of Jesus' twelve apostles (Jn 1:42; 1 Cor 1:12; Gal 1:18).

Charisma Greek word meaning "gift graciously bestowed." Specifically, it refers to those "gifts of the Spirit" mentioned several times by Paul and others, given by God to the church for its outreach, upbuilding, and growth (Rom 12:3–8; 1 Cor 12; Eph 4:7–13; 1 Pt 4:10).

Christ See Messiah.

Christology Study of the person and work of Christ Jesus, covering all aspects of his divine and human natures, both before, during, and after his incarnation, death, and resurrection.

Church Translation of the Greek word *ekklesia* (assembly), referring to the congregation of believers in Christ, whether as a whole (the universal church) or in particular (e.g., the church in Ephesus, Rv 2:1 or the church in Corinth, 1 Cor 1:1). Paul calls the church the "Body of Christ," those who are organically united to him (1 Cor 12:27–28; Eph 5:29–31).

Community Construction Recent trend in New Testament historiography in which social science methods and models are used to describe the dynamics of community formation in early Christianity.

Concursus The complementary interworking of God and human writers in the composition of the Bible.

Contextualization Presentation of the gospel in various languages and cultural settings without distorting its message.

Corban Term used to declare something dedicated to God (Lv 1:2; Nm 7:13). In Mark 7:11–13 Jesus castigates the Jews for the practice of pronouncing something corban and thus unavailable for the lawful support of aging parents.

Covenant An agreement established by God with his people, binding the two together. There are several covenants mentioned in the Old Testament and in the New Testament. Jesus establishes a New Covenant based upon the promise of God (Gen 12:1–3; Jer 31:31–34) and sealed with his sacrificial blood (Mk 14:22–25; 1 Cor 11:23–26).

Cynic(ism) A Greek philosophy founded by Antisthenes, a friend of Socrates in the fifth century B.C. It taught that virtue lay in living intelligently and independently of anything external to the person, such as human customs or institutions. Wandering Cynic philosophers still existed in New Testament times.

Deacon Transliteration of a Greek word meaning "servant." In the early church, a deacon was an officer dedicated to service, qualifications for which are listed in 1 Timothy 3:8–13.

Dead Sea Scrolls Group of Jewish documents written between 250 B.C. and A.D. 68 found in caves near the Dead Sea in the late 1940s. Fragments from over 800 volumes are represented, ranging from Old Testament and possibly New Testament texts to current blessings, hymns, and prayers. See also Qumran.

Deconstructionism Postmodern position that maintains that any attempt to take an objective approach to the facts of experience will lead to the paradoxical conclusion that such an approach is impossible. Language does not refer to objects as referents; rather, words refer only to other words, or to the difference between words. In theology, then, the aim is to "deconstruct" the traditional objects of thought and traditional methods of the discipline.

Dedication, Feast of An eight-day Jewish festival, beginning on the

25th of Kislev (November/December), commemorating the rededication of the temple by Judas Maccabeus in 164 B.C. and the relighting of the temple candles (1 Mc 4:52–59). It was also called the Feast of Lights and today is known as Hanukkah. Jesus attended this Feast (Jn 10:22–39).

Demythologizing Reinterpretation of biblical images so as to provide self-understanding acceptable to the modern scientific mind. This technical term, coined by Hans Jonas, appeared in the biblical hermeneutics of Rudolf Bultmann. Bultmann's thesis was that contemporary humanity, which claims to hold a scientific worldview, cannot accept the mythological worldview of the Bible (myth, for Bultmann, was the use of thisworldly language symbols or images to conceptualize the otherworldly). Bultmann's concern was to reinterpret the mythological language of the Bible in anthropological (human-oriented) or existential (personal) categories.

Diadochi Military successors to Alexander the Great who fought among themselves as they carved up his empire following his death. Antigonus Cyclops seized Asia Minor; Ptolemy took Egypt and North Africa; Seleucus Nicator took the territory stretching from Mesopotamia eastward to India; others took more insignificant portions.

Diaspora, Dispersion Terms designating those Jews who were living outside of Palestine, scattered or dispersed among the Gentiles.

Didache An anonymous Christian manual dealing with doctrine, ethics, and church practice. It has been dated variously from A.D. 85–135.

Disciple From the Latin *discipulus* (Greek, *mathetes*) meaning "learner, pupil," a term used over 250 times in the New Testament to refer broadly to those who follow Christ and learn from him (Mt 14:26; Acts 6:1). It is sometimes used narrowly to refer to the twelve apostles (Mt 10:1–2; 11:1). See also Apostle.

Discourse Analysis Investigation of a text's form and function, in all its parts and levels, to arrive at a better understanding of both the parts and whole of the text. An important assumption of this method is that the meaning of an extended text (or discourse) is found above the sentence level.

Docetism Early Christian heresy, related to Gnosticism, asserting that Christ only appeared to be human and never really suffered, died, or rose again as a human being. It is based on the premise that matter is evil, so a divine being could not have taken on flesh in a real incarnation.

Doxology A formal expression of praise, offering glory and honor to God. In the New Testament doxologies are offered to the Son as well as to the Father (Rom 11:33–36; Jude 24–25; Rv 5:12–13).

Ekklesia See Church.

Elder See Bishop.

Epicureanism Materialistic philosophy of the Greek thinker Epicurus (342–270 B.C.). He taught that pleasure or happiness was the supreme end of life, everything was made of material atoms, and nothing survived death. Paul encountered Epicureans at Athens (Acts 17:16–18).

Eschatology That division of theology dealing with last things (Greek *eschatos*, last), both the end of human life and of the world, including death, the afterlife, the end of the age, the second coming, the resurrection of the dead, the last judgment, and the eternal state.

Essenes A sect of Judaism at the time of Jesus that emphasized apocalyptic, asceticism, and strict obedience to the law. The Qumran community by the Dead Sea was probably Essene. See Apocalyptic; Dead Sea Scrolls; Qumran.

Ethnarch A subordinate ruler. The term's precise meaning varied throughout the Greco-Roman era during which it was used.

Eucharist See Lord's Supper.

Exegesis The process of drawing the author's original meaning and intent from a text, by considering all relevant data related to it, such as language, circumstances of writing, style, purpose, etc. After this has been determined, one may then proceed to contemporary relevance and application.

Existentialism Term that denotes a variety of philosophies and attitudes toward life that flourished in Germany from the time of World War I and in France during and immediately after World War II. Its influence was also felt in Great Britain, North America, and Western culture generally. It is largely associated with major philosophers such as Karl Jaspers and Martin Heidegger, but some of its leading proponents have been writers (e.g., Albert Camus, Jean-Paul Sartre). Existentialism's concern is above all with the problems of human life in the modern world.

Expiation The act of "making right" or fully atoning for sin. In the New Testament the death of Jesus is the atoning sacrifice that establishes peace between sinful humans and God (Rom 3:25; Heb 2:17; 9:11–14). See also Propitiation.

Fall, The Mankind's loss of original righteousness by deliberate disobedience to God's express command, resulting in physical and spiritual death, alienation from God, and universal human sinfulness (Gn 3; Rom 5:12–21; 1 Cor 15:22).

1 Clement Letter written in the late first or early second century from Rome addressed to the church in Corinth and intended to address disputes over leadership.

Form Criticism A method of literary analysis (especially of the Gospels) that classifies the written material by form and attempts to work back through the various "life-situations" in an assumed earlier oral period to the original form of a saying of Jesus. This method was supposed to help sort between what is primary and secondary in a text and aid the process of exegesis. See Exegesis; *Sitz im Leben.*

Formgeschichte See Form Criticism.

Gehenna Hebrew word meaning "Valley of the sons of Hinnom," a place south of Jerusalem where in Old Testament times pagan sacrifices had been offered (2 Chr 28:1–3). In New Testament times the area had become a garbage dump where fires smoldered continually. The term was used by Jesus as a synonym for eternal judgment (Mt 10:28; Mk 9:47–48) and is usually translated "Hell."

Gemara The second major part of the Jewish Talmud, consisting primarily of extensive commentary on the Mishnah. See Mishnah; Talmud.

General Letters See Catholic Letters.

Genre Type of literature or literary "species." In biblical studies the term designates literary forms, such as Gospel, Epistle, apocalypse, and historical narrative.

Gentile In Jewish thought, one who is racially a non-Jew and who, theologically speaking, is not in covenant relationship with God. Typically, Gentiles were considered "unclean" by the Jews of Jesus' day.

Gethsemane An olive grove and garden on the Mount of Olives east of Jerusalem where Jesus customarily took his disciples. On the night before his crucifixion he prayed there in agony and was arrested (Lk 22:39–53; Jn 18:1–11).

Glossolalia See Tongues, Speaking in.

Gnostic See Gnosticism.

Gnosticism An esoteric blend of Christian, Jewish, and Greek ideas that was vigorously opposed as heresy by the church during the second and third centuries after Christ. It taught salvation through special knowledge (*gnosis*), a complicated series of divine emanations from a hidden "One," and (in a few versions) a divine deliverer who showed the secret path back to the divine Ground of Being.

Golgotha Aramaic word meaning "skull," designating the place outside Jerusalem where Jesus was crucified (Jn 19:17). The term "Calvary" as designating this place is derived from the Latin word for skull, *calvaria.*

Gospel Greek word meaning "good news" that described the message preached by the early Christians concerning the life, death, and resurrection of Jesus Christ (1 Cor 15:1–8). It is also used to designate any of the first four books in the New Testament.

Great White Throne God's final judgment of humanity at the end of the millennium (Rv 20:11–15). Premillennial theory maintains that at the end of Christ's thousand-year earthly reign, Satan and his followers will be judged at this throne.

Hades The place of the dead, equivalent to the Old Testament Sheol (Acts 2:27, 31). The Septuagint translated "Sheol" as "Hades." In some instances, it came close to meaning "Hell" (Mt 16:18; Lk 16:3). See also Gehenna.

Haggadah Hebrew term designating the nonlegal material of rabbinic literature found in the Talmud. Its teachings were not held to be as authoritative as the Halakah. See also Halakah; Midrash; Mishnah; Talmud.

Halakah Hebrew term designating the legal portions of the Talmud that deal with conduct or one's way of life. It was held to be binding by the Rabbis. See also Haggadah; Midrash; Mishnah; Talmud.

Hanukkah See Dedication, Feast of.

Hasidim Hebrew term used to designate those pious Jews who would not abandon their faith, even if it meant their death, during the persecutions of Antiochus IV, Epiphanes, in the second century B.C. (1 Mc 2:42).

Hasmonean The family name of those Jews (the Maccabees) and their descendants who instigated the revolt against the Syrians in 167 B.C. (1 Mc 14:25–45; Josephus, *Antiq.* 20.8.11). See also Maccabee(s).

Hell See Gehenna.

Hellenists A term designating Jews who often lived outside of Palestine, who spoke the Greek language, and who to a greater or lesser degree adopted Greek ways (Acts 6:1; 9:29).

Hellenization, Hellenistic The process that began following Alexander the Great's conquest (4th century B.C.) whereby non-Greek peoples were brought, sometimes by force, into conformity with Greek ideas and way of life, including the use of the Greek language. The process was so pervasive that this period of time is called "the Hellenistic (Greek-like) Age." The New Testament is written in Hellenistic Greek.

Heresy A false teaching; one that does not conform to the official standards of the religious community. Christianity was called a heresy ("sect," NIV, Acts 24:14) by some of the Jewish leaders. Paul warns Timothy (1 Tm 1:3–7) and Titus (Ti 3:10) against the false teaching of heretics.

Hermeneutics Term derived from a Greek word meaning "to interpret." It designates the science and art of interpreting a text. It includes exegesis and concerns both what the text meant originally and what it means today. See also Exegesis.

Herodians Jewish party of Jesus' day that sought to keep Herod's dynasty in power. Their theological views were similar to the Sadducees', but they lined up with the Pharisees in trying to discredit Jesus with the question of paying taxes to Caesar (Mt 22:16; Mk 12:13). Some actually wished to kill him after a miracle in Galilee (Mk 3:6).

Historical Criticism Discipline that deals with the historical setting of a document; the time and place it was written; its sources (if any); the events, dates, persons, and places mentioned or implied in the text; and other historical matters. It sometimes implies a philosophical stance that is hostile to biblical claims about God's dealings in human affairs.

Historical Narrative A sequential recounting of events, particularly focused on their nature and interconnection.

Immanuel Hebrew name meaning "God (is) with us" found in Isaiah 7:14. The ultimate fulfillment of this prophetic word was found in Jesus Christ, born of a virgin, who through the incarnation was and is truly God present with his people (Mt 1:22, 23).

Incarnation Latin word meaning "having become flesh." Theologically, it is the doctrine that the second person of the eternal Trinity became a human being by taking on human flesh in being born of the Virgin Mary (Jn 1:14; Phil 2:6–8; 1 Tm 3:16). See Immanuel.

Inspiration The truth that the Bible has as its origin God himself. Behind each human author of Scripture is divine initiative and activity that gives that author's words a reference beyond himself. A classic New Testament text for this doctrine is 2 Timothy 3:16–17.

Internal Criticism Method of textual and literary criticism that examines a text on the basis of elements internal to it (e.g., level of Christology, word order of Jesus' sayings, etc.).

Intertestamental General term denoting the period of time from the completion of the Old Testament to the writing of the New Testament.

Jamnia Town some twenty-five miles west of Jerusalem that became a site of traditional Jewish learning after ca. A.D. 90, when the Romans allowed a religious academy to flourish there. Under Johanan ben Zakkai's leadership, the foundations for what was to become modern Judaism were developed.

Jerusalem Council Meeting between delegates from the church in Antioch (Paul, Barnabas, and others) and delegates from the church in Jerusalem (Acts 15:1–35). It was convened to settle the issue of whether Gentile converts could be saved apart from Mosaic rites like circum-

cision. The Council probably took place between Paul's first and second missionary journeys.

Jesus Seminar Group of radical contemporary scholars who have worked for almost a decade to answer the questions: What did Jesus really say? What did Jesus really do?

Judaism General term denoting the religious system upheld by the Jews; their theological, ethical, and social beliefs and practices based upon their authoritative writings, which currently includes the Old Testament and above all the Talmud. Judaism began during the captivity in Babylon/Persia (586–539 B.C.). There were many divergent forms of Judaism during New Testament times. See also Jamnia.

Judaizer(s) Radical Jewish Christians who opposed Paul by arguing that a person must be circumcised according to the law of Moses to be saved, making works a part of salvation. The council at Jerusalem (ca. A.D. 50) settled in favor of Paul on the questions the Judaizers raised (Acts 15:1–21).

Justification The act whereby God declares a person righteous and in a right relationship with himself. It is based upon the perfect life, atoning death, and resurrection of Jesus Christ and appropriated by faith, apart from any works or merit on our part (Rom 3:21–26; 4:1–8; Eph 2:8, 9).

Kerygma Greek word meaning "proclamation" used in New Testament theology to designate the message of the early church concerning the life, death, and resurrection of Jesus Christ as preached to those who had yet to receive Christ.

Kingdom of God The sovereign reign or rule of God; it was the essence of Jesus' teaching. It was inaugurated by Jesus' first coming and will be consummated at his second coming. It refers to the full sweep of God's redemptive activity.

Koine Greek word meaning "common." Koine Greek was the

everyday language spoken in Jesus' day. It developed from earlier classical Greek and spread throughout the Mediterranean world following Alexander's conquests. The New Testament is written in Koine (or Hellenistic) Greek.

Koran Sacred text of Islam, believed by adherents to contain Allah's (God's) revelation to Muhammad.

Last Supper See Lord's Supper.

Law Term with several meanings in the New Testament. It can refer to the legal and moral teachings of the Old Testament (Jn 7:19) or to the first five books of the Old Testament, the Pentateuch (Mt 7:12). It can denote a general principle or standard at work within persons (Rom 7:23, 25; Jas 2:12) or Jewish rules generally (Acts 25:8).

Lectionaries Books containing brief selections (or pericopes) of New Testament Scriptures (except the Book of Revelation) for use in worship services or private devotions organized in accordance with the church year.

Levite(s) Temple officials who worked along with the priests instructing the people and offering sacrifices. They arose early in Israel's history and were still in existence in Jesus' day (Lk 10:30–35; Jn 1:19).

Lights, Feast of See Dedication, Feast of.

Literary Criticism The study of biblical books as literature, analyzing their forms, structure, figures of speech, and general literary characteristics. It is closely connected with historical analysis, although today it is exercised independently of historical analysis and using the techniques of literary study in general.

Logos See Word.

Lord's Supper The final Passover meal that Jesus held with his disciples on the night he was betrayed. He established a ceremonial meal consisting of bread (commemorating his body) and wine (commemorating his blood) confirming the New Covenant prophesied by Jeremiah (Jer 31:31–34; Mt 26:27–28). It became the central ceremony of fellowship of the Christian church (1 Cor 11:17–32). It is also called "communion" and "the Eucharist."

LXX See Septuagint.

Maccabee(s) Nickname meaning "the Hammer" that was applied to Judas, son of Mattathias, who led his brothers and others in a successful war against their Syrian oppressors ca. 167 B.C. Their family, called the Hasmonean dynasty, ruled in Judah until the Roman occupation of Palestine in 63 B.C. See also Hasmonean.

Magi Non-Jewish religious astrologers who, from their observations of the heavenly bodies and probably the Old Testament, inferred the birth of a great Jewish king. They came to Bethlehem to do homage to Jesus (Mt 2:1–12).

Mammon Aramaic word transliterated into Greek in the New Testament meaning "wealth" or "money" (Mt 6:24; Lk 16:13). Wealth is not considered evil in the New Testament, but it is condemned when it replaces God or leads away from him.

Manuscript A handwritten copy of the whole Bible or a part of it.

Marcan Hypothesis Hypothesis that Mark was the first written Gospel and a primary source for both Matthew and Luke.

Masoretic Text The name given to the standardized Hebrew text of the Old Testament that was established in the seventh to ninth centuries A.D. The Masoretes were a group of Jewish scholars who transcribed the text of the Hebrew Old Testament and added vowel points to the consonants. The Masoretic Text itself goes back into antiquity, as evidenced by the Dead Sea Scrolls. It is abbreviated MT.

Messiah Hebrew word meaning "Anointed One." In the Old Testament it referred to one who was specially designated by God to perform a particular task. The prophets announced the coming of a Messiah who would restore the kingdom to Israel (Ps 110; Dn 9:25–26). Jesus Christ fulfilled those prophesies, bringing in the kingdom of God (Mt 16:13–20; Acts 17:3). "Christ" is the Greek word for Messiah and quickly became a proper name for Jesus (see, for example, Gal 3:14, 16, 17, 22, 24, 26).

Mezuzah Doorpost of a city gate, sanctuary, or private home. In Judaism, the term eventually denoted the container affixed to a doorpost in which scriptural passages were placed.

Midrash Commentary on the Hebrew text of the Old Testament by the rabbis. Such commentary began as early as 50 B.C. Midrash falls into two major categories: Halakic, dealing with legal matters, and Haggadic, moral homilies on the text. See also Haggadah; Halakah.

Millennium Latin term meaning a thousand-year period of time. The term derives from Revelation 20:1–8 where Christ rules and reigns for a thousand years after Satan is bound and the saints are resurrected. Amillenarians and postmillenarians interpret this passage as symbolic of the church and its ministry, whereas premillenarians see this as future and subsequent to the second coming of Christ.

Minuscule Term used by textual critics to define a large group of Greek biblical manuscripts, dating from the ninth to early sixteenth centuries A.D. They were written in a running script of smaller letters. The term "minuscule" (Latin, *minusculus*) means "somewhat small." See also Textual Criticism; Uncial.

Mishnah A collection of Jewish legal teachings dating from the second century B.C. to the second century A.D., when they were codified by Rabbi Judah ha-Nasi (the Patriarch). They are Pharisaic in tone, designed to draw out the full meaning of the law (Torah). Together with the Gemara (commentary upon it) it constitutes the Talmud. See also Gemara; Talmud; Tosefta.

Monotheism The belief that there is only one God.

Mosaic Code The laws given by God to Moses at Mount Sinai.

Mystery Term used to describe some non-Christian religions whose rites and doctrines were secret. Used in the New Testament by Jesus and Paul to speak of spiritual truths no longer secret but revealed. Jesus speaks of the mystery of the kingdom that is made known to the disciples (Mt 13:11; Mk 4:11; Lk 8:10), and Paul explains the mystery of Christ (Eph 3:3, 4), of the Gospel (Eph 6:19), of God's will (Eph 1:9), and of godliness (1 Tm 3:16). It is, in essence, the saving will of God now made known to the world through the gospel.

Mystery Religions Popular religions of the Hellenistic era, some of which go back to earlier times, that promised a better life after death, practiced secret initiation rites, and pursued a closer relation to the gods. They were frequently violent and orgiastic. The most prominent were the Eleusinian and the Dionysian mysteries.

Narrative Criticism An approach to the New Testament that tries to incorporate modern insights on the study of ancient and modern literature, giving full weight to the Bible as a literary production. Focus is on literary techniques, plot, structure, ordering of events, dramatic tension, intended impact on the reader, and other elements. There is less emphasis on the specific theological ideas present, grammar and lexicographical matter, and historical reference.

Neo-Kantianism A philosophical movement of the late nineteenth century. It was built on Immanuel Kant's epistemology and was a reaction against Hegelianism and materialism.

Nicene Creed A short statement of Christian belief drafted in A.D. 325 by the Council of Nicea. The creed emphasized the proper relationship between the Father and the Son as well as the humanity of Jesus.

Nisan The first month of the year in the Hebrew calendar; it corresponds to March/April. Jesus died on the fourteenth of Nisan.

North Galatian Theory View that Paul wrote Galatians to churches founded on his second missionary journey in north-central Asia Minor.

Oral Tradition Traditions of a group that are passed from person to person or from generation to generation in oral form before they are written down. In the New Testament period the time when oral tradition was passed on by word of mouth was very short. Eyewitnesses were still alive during the process (see Lk 1:1–4).

Papyrus A paper made from reeds and used in ancient times. The earliest New Testament manuscripts were written on papyrus.

Parable Story used by ancient teachers, prophets, and frequently by Jesus to convey a profound spiritual truth. It usually had points of contact with everyday life and sometimes contained elements of hyperbole or surprise to arrest one's attention. Parables frequently required some significant decision on the hearer's part. Their fundamental point in Jesus' ministry was to change lives, not just to entertain or provide information.

Paraclete Transliteration of a Greek word meaning "One called to someone's aid," translated variously "Comforter," "Counselor," "Advocate." It is used most frequently of the Holy Spirit (Jn 14:16, 26; 15:26; 16:13), but also of Jesus in 1 John 2:1.

Paradise Term used in New Testament times to describe heaven, the place of the blessed dead. Jesus said to the dying thief, "You will be with me in Paradise today" (Lk 23:43); Paul speaks of having been caught up into Paradise during his lifetime (2 Cor 12:3–4), and Revelation 2:7 paints a beautiful picture of Paradise as the place where the tree of life grows, never to be taken away again.

Paranesis, Paranetic Designates those portions of the New Testament letters containing moral instruction, such as James 4:7–12.

Parousia See Second Coming.

Passion Term derived from a Latin word meaning "to suffer." It is most frequently used to designate the sufferings of Jesus, especially those related to his atoning death on the cross (see Acts 1:3).

Passover, Feast of Annual Jewish festival held on Nisan 14 (March/April of the Jewish calendar) that begins the seven-day Festival of Unleavened Bread. The original Passover meal included roast lamb, unleavened bread, and bitter herbs (Ex 12:14–30; 13:3–10) and commemorated the night before the exodus from Egypt when the angel of death "passed over" the children of Israel because of the blood of the sacrificial lamb smeared over the door posts (Ex 12:12, 13). Jesus celebrated a last Passover with his disciples. Paul calls Jesus "our Passover Lamb" who was sacrificed for us (1 Cor 5:7–8).

Pastoral Letters 1 and 2 Timothy and Titus. These letters were written by Paul to the leaders (pastors) of two groups of churches—Timothy in Ephesus and Titus in Crete.

Pax Romana Latin phrase meaning "the Roman Peace." This period of peace, which lasted three hundred years, began with the consolidation of the Roman Empire in the first century B.C. The *pax romana* contributed to the rapid spread of Christianity throughout the Mediterranean world.

Pentecost, Feast of Jewish Feast of First Fruits (Nm 28:26), also known as the Feast of Weeks (Ex 34:22; Dt 16:10). It was held on the fiftieth day after Passover—counting seven times seven weeks, then the next day. It was on Pentecost that the Spirit was poured out upon the early believers in Jerusalem, beginning a new work of God in the church (Acts 1:8; 2:1–41).

Pericope In form criticism, a literary unit of tradition, such as parable, healing story, or miracle story. According to form critics these units of tradition circulated independently before being gathered together to become our Gospels. See also Form Criticism.

Pharisee(s) During New Testament times one of the dominant groups of Jewish thought. The Pharisees accepted both Scripture and tradition as authoritative; affirmed the traditional theological doctrines of God's providence, angels, resurrection, and the afterlife; held to a strict observance of Jewish legal rules (their name meant "separated"); and opposed Jesus and early Christianity, for, among other reasons, the Christians' apparent disregard of key Jewish rules. Although small in number (estimated at 6,000) their influence was widespread and in many ways typified Jewish thinking at that time.

Phenomenology A philosophical movement that studies human consciousness and the objects of human consciousness.

Phylactery Small leather container that held copies of four Old Testament Scriptures (Ex 13:1–10, 11–16; Dt 6:4–9; 11:13–21). It was worn by Jewish men on the left arm or forehead during prayer. Jewish tradition interpreted Exodus 13:9, 16 and Deuteronomy 6:8; 11:18 as requiring this. Jesus criticized improper use of phylacteries (Mt 23:5).

Politarch A Greek term referring to the ruler of a city. Luke uses the word in Acts 17:6, 8 to speak of the city officials in Thessalonica.

Polytheistic Syncretism Combining the beliefs of different religions. This combination results in a new religion that includes the worship of many gods. See also Religious Syncretism.

Praeparatio Evangelium Term used by many Church Fathers and contemporary theologians; it means "preparation for the gospel" and is used to convey the idea that all prior history was a prelude leading up to the coming of Christ.

Presbyter New Testament term that refers to a church official or elder. See also Bishop.

Priest Person authorized to offer ritual sacrifices and make intercession before God in a specially designated place of worship. In Jesus' day such sacrifices were offered in the temple in Jerusalem. Jesus predicted the destruction of the long-standing sacrificial system (Mt 24:1, 2). Early Christianity taught that all believers are a "royal priesthood" (1 Pt 2:9), that their bodies are a temple of the Holy Spirit (1 Cor 6:19), and that the whole of life is "a fragrant offering, a sacrifice acceptable and pleasing to God" (Phil 4:18). Everyone, not just a priestly class, should make supplications, prayer, and intercessions (1 Tm 2:1).

Proconsul Governor appointed by the Roman senate to administer a province for a period of one year. These senatorial provinces were considered secure enough to need no standing army. Two proconsuls are mentioned in the Book of Acts: Sergius Paulus of Cyprus (Acts 13:7–12) and Gallio of Achaia (Acts 18:12–17).

Procurator Roman official appointed by the emperor to oversee his affairs, especially financial, in one of the provinces. In the case of Judea the procurator also acted as governor and military administrator. Three procurators are mentioned by name in the New Testament: Pontius Pilate (A.D. 26–36; Jn 18:19); Antonius Felix (A.D. 52–59; Acts 23:24–25:14); Porcius Festus (A.D. 59–62; Acts 24:27–26:32).

Prophet One called to proclaim the will of God. The prophet's task was to denounce sin, call to repentance, remind the people of God's deeds in the past, preach warnings of judgment to come, predict future events, and offer mercy to those who responded in faith. There were New Testament as well as Old Testament prophets, and both men and women prophesied.

Prophets, The The second division of the Hebrew Bible. It contains longer works like Isaiah along with very short ones like Joel and Obadiah.

Propitiation An offering that turns aside the wrath of God. In the New Testament, God himself turns aside his wrath through the offering of himself in the death of the Son of God, the second person of the eternal Trinity (1 Jn 2:2). See also Expiation.

Proverb A short and compact saying that expresses a well-known truth or idea. In the Scriptures proverbs usually relate theological truth to practical living, but abstract doctrinal ideas can sometimes be found.

Pseudepigrapha Often fanciful religious books written between 200 B.C. and A.D. 200 falsely ascribed to well-known figures of the past, such as Elijah, Moses, or Enoch. Such books sometimes have points of contact with the Old or New Testament but were never accepted as part of the Bible.

Ptolemaic Dynasty The family that descended from Alexander the Great's general, Ptolemy I. It ruled Egypt from about 323 to 30 B.C., when the Romans gained control over that part of the world.

Publican Individual drawn from the Jewish population who collected taxes for Rome. They were known for dishonesty and despised as traitors. Jesus chose Matthew, a publican or tax collector, to be one of his apostles (Mt 9:9–13).

Q From the German, *Quelle,* "source." Designates a hypothetical document that contained primarily sayings of Jesus. According to one theory, Matthew and Luke used it when they composed their Gospels. The bulk of its content is assumed to be the approximately 230 verses common to Matthew and Luke that are not found in Mark.

Qumran Archaeological site near Jericho at the northwest corner of the Dead Sea where an Essene sect lived in strict communitarian fashion. The Dead Sea Scrolls were found in the caves near the community and were probably part of their library, hidden just before the Romans destroyed the community buildings in A.D. 68. See also Dead Sea Scrolls; Essenes.

Rabbi Title of respect meaning "Teacher" or "Master," given in Jesus' day to those who excelled in the law of Moses and were qualified to teach it. Jesus was referred to as "Rabbi" by his followers (Mt 26:25; Mk 11:21; Jn 3:2). Jesus at one point told his followers not to seek such titles of honor (Mt 23:7, 8).

Reader–Response Theory Theory of interpretation that asserts that the meaning of a text does not lie in the author's intended message but in the thoughts and feelings of readers as they encounter the text.

Redaction Criticism Method of critical study of the Gospels. It seeks to isolate the earlier units of tradition from the editorial (redactional) elements in order to place them all in their proper life-setting (*Sitz im Leben*). In this way a history of the tradition can be reconstructed, in theory. The editor is referred to as the redactor. See also Form Criticism; *Sitz im Leben*.

Redemption Term meaning "to purchase" or "to buy back." Theologically it is the doctrine that God saves, liberates, and delivers his people (Is 49:26; 60:16). In the New Testament the foundation of God's redeeming activity is the death and resurrection of Jesus Christ (Rom 3:24, 25; 1 Pt 1:18–21).

Religious Syncretism Combining the beliefs of different religions. This practice was common in Hellenistic times because of the popular idea that all deities and religions ultimately amounted to the same thing. See also Polytheistic Syncretism.

Resurrection To be brought to life again after death. Central to New Testament theology is the resurrection of Jesus from the dead and the promise that believers will be resurrected at the end of the age to newness of life (1 Cor 15:1–57). The resurrected body will not be subject to decay, but will be a spiritual body

(1 Cor 15:42–44, 49). Unbelievers will be raised to condemnation (Jn 5:28, 29).

Revelation To make known, lay bare, uncover. In general, we have knowledge of God only because he chooses to make himself known, that is, reveals himself. Sometimes God reveals specific things he wants us to know (Gal 1:12; 2:2; Eph 3:3). Because the Scripture is the Word of God in its entirety, it is the revelation of God, as is Jesus Christ, who supremely makes God known. "Revelation" also refers to the last book of the New Testament, because John began it "The revelation of Jesus Christ, which God gave him . . ." (Rv 1:1).

Rhetorical Criticism A method developed to understand better a biblical author's intended meaning. It involves analyzing the text according to the methods of speech, argumentation, and persuasion that were in use at the time of the author.

Righteousness That quality of God (and derivatively of human beings) that consists of moral uprightness, totally just actions, and proper relationships. God is absolute moral perfection in all that he is, does, and establishes between himself and the created order. Human beings are righteous through faith in Jesus Christ and the renewing power of the Holy Spirit.

Sabbath The seventh day (Saturday) of the Jewish week, set apart by God for rest and as a sign of the covenant made with Israel (Ex 20:8–11; Dt 5:12–15). Jesus said the Sabbath was made for the benefit of the human race (Mk 2:23–28). The Book of Hebrews sees in the Sabbath a foreshadowing of our rest in heaven (Heb 4:9–11). Christians worship on the first day of the week (Sunday) in honor of Jesus' resurrection from the dead.

Sacrament A visible sign expressive of an invisible, spiritual grace that is bestowed by God through Jesus Christ. Most Protestant Christians accept baptism and the Lord's Supper as sacraments; Roman Catholicism and Eastern Orthodoxy add five more. See also Baptism; Lord's Supper.

Sacrifice An offering of value made to God in recognition of his glory and of our dependence upon him. In the Old Testament an elaborate system of animal sacrifices was established. This was fulfilled by the death of Jesus, who offered himself as the final sacrifice, once for all (Heb 9:11–14; 10:10). Believers are to offer themselves as living sacrifices to be used by God in his service (Rom 12:1, 2).

Sadducee(s) A group of Jews in Jesus' day comprised primarily of the priestly aristocracy, who relied only upon the first five books of the Bible (the Pentateuch). They rejected the idea of angels, life after death, providence, and the resurrection. They were willing to cooperate with the Romans to preserve the nation.

Saint(s) Word derived from the Latin *sanctus* meaning "holy." In the New Testament Christians are called to be saints (holy) because they serve a holy God, should live holy lives, and are filled with the Holy Spirit (Rom 1:7). Because of this believers are sometimes called simply "saints" (Col 1:4; 1 Tm 5:10).

Salvation The action of God, who alone is Savior, whereby human beings are delivered from the power and consequences of sin, death, and the devil through the atoning work of Jesus Christ. We may experience the benefits of salvation in the present by faith in Christ; ultimate salvation is the believer's future hope.

Samaritan(s) Resident of a region roughly equivalent to Israel in the Old Testament, lying west of the Jordan River between Galilee to the north and Judea to the south. The Samaritans separated from the other Jews around 400 B.C. and had their own Bible (Torah), temple on Mount Gerizim, sacrifices, and worship. They were bitterly resented by the Jews as apostates. Most Jews would have nothing to do with them (Jn 4:9).

Sanctification That continuous action of God whereby the believer is progressively being made holy. Justification is an act; sanctification, which follows upon that, is a process.

Sanhedrin The supreme judicial council of Judaism. It began around the fourth century B.C. and in Jesus' day consisted of seventy-one members, divided into three categories: the high priests, the elders, and the scribes. The council arbitrated matters of Jewish law, and its decision was final. Jesus (Mt 26:59), Stephen (Acts 6:12–15), Peter and John (Acts 4:5–21), and Paul (Acts 22:30–23:10) were all tried, in one way or another, by the Sanhedrin.

Scribe(s) Men originally skilled in copying texts who, after the exile and into Jesus' day, were scholars skilled in teaching, copying, and interpreting Jewish law for the people. They were closely associated with the Pharisees in opposition to Jesus' teaching.

Scripture See Bible.

Second Coming The visible return of Jesus Christ to earth at the end of the age as Lord of all (Acts 1:11; Rv 11:15; 19:11–16). Jesus prophesied his second coming (Mt 24:29–31), as does the rest of the New Testament (1 Thes 4:13–18; 2 Pt 3:3–13). It is also called the parousia, from a Greek word meaning "presence" or "coming." Some Christians distinguish between a coming of Christ for believers and a subsequent coming again with his believers to earth.

2 Maccabees History of the Maccabean revolt written from a different perspective than 1 Maccabees. Whereas 1 Maccabees is concerned with praising Judas, Jonathan, and Simon for their role in the liberation of the Jews from Seleucid oppression, 2 Maccabees focuses on the insult to the temple and its cult, blaming the Jewish Hellenizers.

Second Temple Judaism Term used to describe the society and culture of the Jews after they returned from exile in Babylon and built the second temple. This era ended with the temple's destruction in A.D. 70.

Seleucid Dynasty The dynasty founded by Alexander the Great's general Seleucus after Alexander's death in 323 B.C. It ruled Syria from approximately 312 B.C. until Roman times. The Seleucids' capital city was Antioch. They controlled Palestine in the second century B.C. until driven out by the Maccabees after the defeat of Antiochus IV.

Septuagint The Greek translation of the Hebrew Old Testament. It arose between approximately 250 B.C. and A.D. 50. It was used by diaspora Jews who no longer spoke Hebrew as their native language. It is sometimes called "The Seventy" (hence LXX) because according to tradition 70 (or 72) scholars translated it in 72 days. See also Apocrypha; Diaspora, Dispersion; Jamnia.

Shema The supreme Jewish confession of belief as found in Deuteronomy 6:4–9; 11:13–21; Numbers 15:37–41, expressing Judaism's monotheistic faith. It was recited at home and in the synagogue in Jesus' day. Jesus referred to it when formulating the two great commandments (Mk 12:28–31). "Shema" is the first word of Deuteronomy 6:4 in Hebrew, "Hear . . ."

Sheol See Hades.

Simony The buying or selling of church office or privilege. The term comes from Acts 8:9–25, where Simon offered Peter and John money if they would share their apostolic powers with him.

Sin Any thought, act, word, or state of being that is contrary to the law or will of God. Sin thus breaks one's fellowship or communion with God. According to the New Testament all human beings are sinners (Rom 3:23), but they may be forgiven through faith in Jesus Christ whose death and resurrection secured remission of sin (Rom 5:12–21).

Sitz im Leben German term meaning "setting in life," used by form critics to define the hypothetical situations out of which the units of Gospel tradition grew. A unit of tradition may pass through several "life settings" (*Sitze im Leben*) before it reaches its final form. See also Form Criticism.

Sociological Criticism Method of interpretation that uses modern social science theories and insights to examine the social setting in which the biblical text was written.

Son of God In the New Testament, a messianic title used of Jesus (Ps 2:7; Jn 1:49), but also used in a deeper sense of Jesus' unique relation to God the Father (Mt 11:25–27; Jn 1:14–18; 1 Cor 1:9). Believers are also called sons (children) of God, by virtue of having been adopted into God's family through faith in Jesus Christ (Jn 1:12; Gal 4:4–7).

Son of Man Jesus' favorite self-designation, drawn from Daniel 7:13, 14. The term was not a common messianic title in Jesus' day; hence he could fill it with his own understanding of the Messiah's task, which he defined as bringing in the kingdom of God, dying and rising again, and returning in glory at the end of the age (Mt 16:13–28; 26:62–64; Mk 10:32–34; 13:24–27).

Soteriology Theological term meaning "teaching about salvation." In Christian theology it relates to human sinfulness, those qualities of God that define how sinful humans relate to him, the atoning death of Christ, faith, forgiveness, justification, and sanctification.

Source Criticism Method of critical study of the Gospels. It seeks to reconstruct the sources the Gospel writers may have used to write their accounts.

South Galatian Theory View that Paul wrote the letter of Galatians to churches in southern Asia Minor prior to the Jerusalem Council. This would include churches in cities Paul and Barnabas visited on their first missionary journey: Perga, Pisidian Antioch, Iconium, Lystra, and Derbe.

Stoicism A Greek philosophy of pantheistic materialism popular in Paul's day. It understood "God" to be an immanent principle of reason within the universe that ordered all things according to rational principles. The goal of life is to find happiness by mastering oneself, one's passions and emotions, and living independently of circumstances. Paul encountered Stoic philosophers in Athens (Acts 17:18).

Structuralism An approach to biblical studies contending that underlying all expression and narrative is a structure in our minds, a "deep structure," which determines courses that our thoughts and expressions take. Understanding that deep structure allows the reader to understand the "real" meaning of any narrative or story.

Substitutionary Atonement Refers to Christ's dying in place of sinners and bearing the punishment that should have been theirs.

Synagogue Local places of worship and teaching in Judaism. Synagogues developed during the intertestamental period, beginning after the destruction of the temple in 587 B.C., as places where Jews could study the law, meet together, worship God, and administer justice according to the law. When the temple was rebuilt during Herod's reign, synagogues continued to exist as many people could not travel to the Jerusalem temple to worship. There were numerous synagogues throughout the Roman Empire, with many in Palestine itself. Early Christian worship paralleled the synagogue service in many respects.

Synoptic Gospels Term applied to Matthew, Mark, and Luke because they contain similar material and look at Jesus' life from roughly the same perspective, emphasizing the Galilean ministry of Jesus. The Gospel of John relates primarily to Jesus' Jerusalem ministry.

Synoptic Problem, The Denotes the challenge posed by the fact that the Gospels of Matthew, Mark, and Luke are very similar to one another, yet also show numerous differences.

Tabernacles, Feast of One of the three major festivals of the Jewish year (Lv 23:33–43). It commemorated the completion of the agricultural year and in New Testament times lasted eight days, beginning Tishri (Sept./Oct.) 15. During the festival people lived in small tabernacles (Booths), recalling the time in the wilderness. Jesus attended at least one Feast of Tabernacles (Jn 7:1–39).

Talmud Collection of Jewish traditions that forms the basis of Judaism's life and thought. It developed over several centuries and was codified in two collections, the Palestinian and the Babylonian, in the late fourth and fifth centuries A.D. The Babylonian is by far the longer and more complete. Both versions consist of two main parts: (1) the Mishnah, interpretations of the Torah, and (2) the Gemara, commentaries on the Mishnah, as well as other tractates, or chapters.

Tannaim Rabbis of the first and second centuries who taught the Mishnah. Their work culminated with the compilation of Mishnaic teachings in the late second century by Rabbi Judah the Patriarch (died A.D. 217).

Targum Free translation of the Hebrew Old Testament into Aramaic at the time when Hebrew was no longer fully understood by all Jews. Aramaic, a language related to Hebrew, had become the common language of the Middle East. Targums arose during the intertestamental period. Many are still extant.

Tephillin A small leather box containing Scripture. It was to be worn by Jewish men when they prayed.

Textual Criticism The study of the ancient texts and versions of the Bible to determine what the original writer or scribe is most likely to have penned. Currently there are over 5,000 portions of the New Testament in Greek, and thousands more in other ancient languages. Together they contribute to our understanding of the process underlying the copying and transmitting of the original text.

Theologia Crucis "Theology of the cross"; a way of understanding the gospel that focuses on the weakness, suffering, and death involved in

enduring, and conquering through, faith in Christ and sharing in his cross.

Theologia Gloriae "Theology of glory"; a way of understanding the gospel that views Christ primarily as a means of self-betterment, the way to success, the way to power, affirmation by peers, and acceptance by God.

Tithe The contribution of a tenth of one's income, in money or in possessions, to the Lord for use in supporting the nation's religious activities (Lv 27:30–33; Dt 14:22–29; Neh 10:37, 38). Jesus spoke against distorting the emphasis of tithes (Mt 23:23), and Paul speaks of giving as one is able (2 Cor 8:3), according to the decision of one's own heart (2 Cor 9:7).

Tongues, Speaking in A spiritual gift bestowed by the Holy Spirit (1 Cor 12:10, 30) that enables one to speak intelligibly in other languages (Acts 2:1–12) or in unknown or "angelic" tongues (1 Cor 13:1). Paul is sharply critical of the improper use of tongues (1 Cor 14:6–25) and urges believers to have orderly worship services (1 Cor 14:26–33).

Torah Hebrew word meaning "guidance," "law," or "teaching," most commonly used to refer to the first five books of the Bible, the Pentateuch. "Torah" is also used broadly to mean all of God's teachings combined to form a way of life.

Tosefta A collection of Jewish legal writings that parallel the Mishnah. This material was written roughly the same time as the Mishnah, but it was not deemed as authoritative, so it was excluded from the Mishnaic canon. The word "Tosefta" means "supplement." See also Mishnah.

Tradition Religious teachings that run parallel to the canonical Scriptures, in some instances considered equally authoritative with those canonical Scriptures. The Pharisees in Jesus' day honored their traditions along with the Old Testament Scriptures; the Sadducees did not. In our own day Roman Catholics base their doctrine upon

Scripture and tradition, while Protestants seek to base their doctrine on *sola scriptura*, Scripture alone.

Transfiguration The transformation of Jesus on a high mountain in Palestine (probably Mount Hermon) during which his essential deity was glimpsed by Peter, James, and John. Moses and Elijah were also there, conversing with Jesus. God the Father closed the revelatory scene with the words, "This is my Son, whom I love; with him I am well pleased. Listen to him!" (Mt 17:1–13).

Trinity The doctrine that God is both one and three—the one and only God exists eternally as Father, Son and Holy Spirit. The revelation of this mystery unfolds through the Old Testament and is most clearly seen in Jesus Christ, the Son of God (Mt 3:16, 17; 28:19; 1 Cor 12:4–6; 2 Cor 13:14; 1 Pt 1:2). The Father is God (1 Cor 8:6), the Son is God (Jn 1:18), and the Spirit is God (Eph 4:4, 5). The Trinity is central to the Christian faith, and upon it virtually every major doctrine is logically dependent.

Twelve, The See Apostle.

Typology Method of biblical interpretation that sees in Old Testament persons, actions, events, or rituals prophetic foreshadowings of Jesus Christ, as well as other New Testament truths. For example, Jesus saw in the bronze serpent a picture of his own coming death (Jn 3:14); Paul saw in the water from the rock a type of Christ (1 Cor 10:1–4), and Hebrews saw Jesus as a new Melchizedek (Heb 6:19, 20).

Uncial Term used by text critics to define a large group of Greek biblical manuscripts written in large, carefully formed letters something like our capital letters. Uncial manuscripts date from the third to about the ninth centuries A.D. See also Minuscule; Textual Criticism.

Via Dolorosa "Way (or path) of suffering." Literally, the path Jesus walked through Jerusalem on his way to

Golgotha. Figuratively, it is a reminder that in Christian service, true glory—glory for God, not man—comes in part through suffering.

Via Egnatia A major east–west commercial highway of the Roman world. The city of Philippi, which Paul visited, derived much of its importance from its location on this highway.

Virgin Birth This doctrine is perhaps better stated as the virginal conception of Jesus. It holds that Mary conceived of Jesus by a miraculous act of God, independent of any human involvement (Mt 1:18–25; Lk 1:26–35).

Vulgate Term derived from the Latin *vulgatus*, meaning "common" or "popular." It refers to the Latin translation of the Bible made by Jerome near the end of the fourth century A.D. which became the authorized Roman Catholic version.

Weeks, Feast of See Pentecost, Feast of.

Word In John 1:1–14 and Revelation 19:13 Jesus is referred to as the Word (Greek *logos*). Hence, Christians often speak of Jesus as the Logos or the Word of God. Just as human words express the innermost depths of our hearts and minds, so Jesus is the perfect expression of what God is really like. The Scriptures are also referred to as the Word of God because they too infallibly make known the mind and heart of God.

Writings, The The third division of the Hebrew Bible. It contains some historical books, Psalms, Proverbs, and other poetic books.

Yahweh Modern rendering of the divine name of God as revealed in the Old Testament (Gn 4:26; Ex 6:2–4). The Hebrew form is YHWH (KJV sometimes translates it "Jehovah"). Because it contains four letters it is also called the Tetragrammaton. It is derived from the Hebrew verb "to be" and hence means "He (who) is" or "He who causes to be," emphasizing God as the creator and sustainer of the universe.

Zealot(s) A Jewish party of extreme nationalism in Jesus' day that advocated armed rebellion to usher in the kingdom of God. Their actions precipitated the Jewish War of A.D. 66–70 that culminated in the destruction of Jerusalem by Titus, the Roman general and future emperor. One of Jesus' disciples, Simon, was a former Zealot (Mk 3:18; Acts 1:13).

Answers to Review Questions

Chapter 1: Why Study the New Testament

1. Torah, Prophets, Writings
2. Torah
3. testament
4. apocryphal/deuterocanonical
5. cultural literacy
6. Gospels, Acts, letters, prophecy
7. Josephus
8. canon
9. concursus
10. papyrus

Chapter 2: The Middle East in the Days of Jesus

1. five
2. Galilee
3. Alexander the Great
4. Herod Antipas
5. Titus
6. way of life
7. synagogue
8. Pharisees
9. Essenes
10. Old Testament

Chapter 3: The Gospel and the Four Gospels

1. heart, whole
2. kerygma
3. eighty
4. orderly
5. memoirs
6. biography
7. Roman Empire
8. three

Chapter 4: The Gospel of Matthew

1. Irenaeus, Origen, Eusebius
2. John Wenham
3. Syria, Antioch of Syria, Palestine
4. life, words
5. prophecy
6. David, Abraham
7. supreme authority
8. Caesarea Philippi

Chapter 5: The Gospel of Mark

1. sixteen
2. 325
3. narrative
4. Peter
5. Gentiles
6. Son of God
7. supernatural
8. confession
9. religious leaders
10. death, resurrection

Chapter 6: The Gospel of Luke

1. Theophilus
2. Marcion
3. Acts
4. historical facts
5. history
6. Mary his mother
7. Simeon, Anna

Chapter 7: The Gospel of John

1. three
2. Ephesus
3. Old Testament
4. Trinity
5. Israel, all humanity
6. humanity
7. faith

Chapter 8: Man from Galilee

1. Josephus, Suetonius, Tacitus, Talmud
2. 30
3. Nazareth
4. twelve
5. Bethany beyond the Jordan
6. demons
7. praise, persecution
8. Caesarea Philippi
9. Jerusalem
10. Jewish leaders

Chapter 9: Lord, Teach Us

1. teacher, preacher
2. Old Testament
3. communicators
4. parable
5. God
6. repent
7. providence
8. equal
9. Isaiah
10. Son of Man

Chapter 10: Modern Approaches to the New Testament

1. modern approaches
2. reasoned, responsible
3. skepticism
4. hermeneutics
5. revelation
6. authority
7. prayer
8. missiological
9. exegesis
10. lifelong

Chapter 11: The Modern Study of the Gospels

1. Augustine
2. J. J. Griesbach
3. Marcan Hypothesis
4. Synoptic Problem
5. form
6. communities
7. compilers, writers
8. reader–response
9. Q

Chapter 12: The Modern Search for Jesus

1. Europe
2. about
3. supernatural
4. Bultmann
5. demythologizing
6. Third Quest
7. 82
8. multiple source attestation

Chapter 13: The World and Identity of the Earliest Church

1. Roman Empire
2. Antioch
3. Nero, Domitian
4. Greek
5. Hellenization
6. occult
7. philosophy
8. fate
9. Pentecost
10. divinity, oneness

Chapter 14: Acts 1–7

1. tradition, literary features
2. Mediterranean
3. 25
4. vocabulary
5. teaching, historical
6. Peter
7. miracles
8. social cohesion or growth
9. Saul

Chapter 15: Acts 8–12

1. Jewish
2. Philip

3. Peter
4. Tabitha, gazelle
5. Cornelius
6. Barnabas
7. Agabus
8. James (brother of John)
9. Simon the sorcerer
10. John, Peter, Paul

Chapter 16: Acts 13–28

1. Paul
2. Antioch
3. Paul, Barnabas
4. Antioch
5. Jerusalem Council
6. Silas, Timothy, Luke
7. "Gentiles"
8. Caesarea
9. Caesar, Rome
10. Ephesians, Philippians, Colossians

Chapter 17: All Things to All People

1. Tarsus
2. Saul
3. missionary
4. arrested
5. divine
6. polytheistic
7. legalism
8. Abrahamic
9. worship
10. Jesus
11. ransom
12. resurrection, cross

Chapter 18: Romans

1. length
2. Reformation, Luther
3. Augustine
4. faith
5. Greece
6. salutation
7. Good News
8. way of life
9. diet, custom
10. John Calvin

Chapter 19: Corinthians and Galatians

1. Corinth
2. immorality
3. second
4. Erastus inscription
5. First Corinthians
6. charismatic
7. praising
8. suffering
9. Jerusalem collection
10. Barnabas, first
11. Acts 13
12. Judaizers

Chapter 20: Ephesians, Philippians, Colossians, and Philemon

1. Artemis or Diana
2. power
3. divine protection, empowerment
4. Silas
5. friendship
6. self-centeredness
7. Epaphras
8. Hellenistic
9. the Colossian heresy
10. personal
11. Onesimus
12. Christ

Chapter 21: Thessalonians, Timothy, and Titus

1. second
2. Thessaloniki
3. opposition
4. instruction
5. God, God
6. shorter
7. Gallio inscription
8. 1 Timothy, 2 Timothy, Titus
9. pastoral concern
10. Ephesus
11. Rome
12. Crete

Chapter 22: Hebrews and James

1. length
2. Paul, Apollos

3. 40, 60
4. formal greeting
5. sermonic
6. Jesus Christ, Moses, Aaron
7. community of believers, personal knowledge
8. Jesus, Sermon on the Mount
9. Jewish Christians
10. prophecy

Chapter 23: Peter, John, and Jude

1. Rome
2. Nero
3. pilgrim
4. transfiguration, Jesus
5. Rome
6. godliness, brotherly kindness, love
7. 1 John
8. 2 John
9. truth
10. Gaius
11. resurrection
12. deity of Christ

Chapter 24: Revelation

1. visions, sixty
2. symbolic
3. John
4. churches
5. seals, trumpets, bowls
6. amillennialism
7. great white throne
8. divine glory, Son
9. Lamb
10. eschatology

Epilogue

1. continuation
2. unchanged
3. vision
4. immanence
5. God
6. zeal, love
7. truth, the right thing
8. intellectualism, activism
9. contextualization
10. persecution

Notes

Chapter 1: Why Study the New Testament?

1. W. H. C. Frend, *The Rise of Christianity* (Philadelphia: Fortress, 1984), 457–60.

2. On the Bible and the Qur'an, see Ergun Mehmet Caner and Emir Fethi Caner, *Unveiling Islam* (Grand Rapids: Kregel, 2002), 231–34; Jacques Jomier, *The Bible and the Qur'an*, trans. Edward P. Arbez (San Francisco: Ignatius, 2002).

3. Over fifty translations or revisions of the New Testament appeared in the latter half of the twentieth century—to speak only of the English-language situation. See Bruce M. Metzger, "To the Reader," in *The New Revised Standard Version* (New York/Oxford: Oxford University Press, 1989), xii.

4. But for information along these lines, see, e.g., Peter R. Ackroyd et al., eds., *The Cambridge History of the Bible*, 3 vols. (Cambridge/New York: Cambridge University Press, 1963–70).

5. For a recent survey, see Larry R. Helyer, *Exploring Jewish Literature of the Second Temple Period* (Downers Grove: InterVarsity, 2002); David A. deSilva, *Introducing the Apocrypha* (Grand Rapids: Baker, 2002).

6. Allan Bloom, *The Closing of the American Mind* (New York: Simon & Schuster, 1987), 60.

7. Ibid.

8. Jaroslav Pelikan, *Jesus through the Centuries: His Place in the History of Culture* (New York: Harper & Row, 1987 [1985]), 1.

9. For similar bravery on the part of Blandina, a young Christian woman at Lyons in France in the second century, see Frend, *The Rise of Christianity*, 184.

10. *The New Testament: Its Background, Growth, and Content*, 2nd ed. (Nashville: Abingdon, 1983), 276.

11. For elaboration of this viewpoint, see Herman N. Ridderbos, *Redemptive History and the New Testament Scriptures*, trans. H. De Jongste, rev. Richard B. Gaffin Jr. (Phillipsburg, N.J.: Presbyterian & Reformed, 1988).

12. *Biblical Hermeneutics*, trans. Robert W. Yarbrough (Wheaton, Ill.: Crossway, 1994), 130–31.

13. For extensive discussion of the doctrine of inspiration, see René Pache, *The Inspiration and Authority of Scripture*, trans. Helen I. Needham (Salem, Wis.: Sheffield, 1992 [1969]).

14. See Peter Balla, "Evidence for an Early Christian Canon (Second and Third Century)," in *The Canon Debate*, ed. L. M. McDonald and James A. Sanders (Peabody, Mass.: Hendrickson, 2002), 372–85.

15. William Wrede, "The Task and Methods of 'New Testament Theology,'" in *The Nature of New Testament Theology*, ed. and trans. Robert Morgan (London: SCM, 1973), 71.

16. Robert M. Grant, *Heresy and Criticism: The Search for Authenticity in Early Christian Literature* (Louisville: Westminster John Knox, 1993), 32. "Trent" refers to the Council of Trent, a Roman Catholic conference convened in the 1540s to counteract the rise of Protestantism. See also Raymond F. Collins, *The Birth of the New Testament: The Origin and Development of the First Christian Generation* (New York: Crossroad, 1993), 293n93: "To speak of an official proclamation of a New Testament canon for the universal church, one would have to look . . . to the fourth session of the Council of Trent (February 4, 1546 . . .)."

17. Bruce M. Metzger, *The New Testament* (Nashville: Abingdon, 1983), 276.

18. Bruce M. Metzger, *The Text of the New Testament: Its Transmission, Corruption, and Restoration*, 3rd ed. (New York/Oxford: Oxford University Press, 1992), 35.

19. Dewitt Matthews, *Capers of the Clergy: The Human Side of Ministry* (Grand Rapids: Baker, 1976), 34–35.

Chapter 2: The Middle East in the Days of Jesus

1. There are twenty-one Epistles proper (thirteen from Paul, eight from others). Luke, Acts, and Revelation are not actually epistles but are epistle-like in the way they address their recipients.

2. For discussion and maps, see Yohanan Aharoni and Michael Avi-Yonah, *The Carta Biblical Atlas*, 3rd ed. (New York: Macmillan, 1993); Thomas V. Briscoe, *The Holman Bible Atlas* (Nashville: Broadman & Holman, 1998); Barry Beitzel, *The Moody Atlas of Bible Lands* (Chicago: Moody, 1985).

3. Some prefer to speak of seven regions, adding the plain of Esdraelon in the north and the Negev in the south.

4. For a full discussion, see Seán Freyne, "Galilee (Hellenistic/Roman)," in *Anchor Bible Dictionary*, ed. David Noel Freedman, 6 vols. (New York: Doubleday, 1992), 2:895–9.

5. William M. Thomson, *The Land and The Book*, 3 vols. (New York: Harper & Bros., 1882), 2:110.

6. Josephus gives a summary of their views in *Antiquities* 18.1.3. For a summary of scholarship on the Pharisees see S. Westerholm, "Pharisees," in *Dictionary of Jesus and the Gospels*, ed. J. B. Green, S. McKnight, and I. H. Marshall (Downers Grove: InterVarsity, 1992), 609–14. See also John P. Meier, *A Marginal Jew*, vol. 3, *Companions and Competitors* (New York: Doubleday, 2001), 311–40, though Meier is too skeptical of the Gospels' witness to interaction between Jesus and the Pharisees.

7. Josephus summarizes their views in *Antiquities* 18.1.4. For recent assessment, see Meier, *A Marginal Jew*, 3:389–487.

8. Josephus gives a summary of the Essenes in *Antiquities* 18.1.5. See also Allen H. Jones, *Essenes: The Elect of Israel and the Priests of Artemis* (Lanham, Md.: University Press of America, 1985); Meier, *A Marginal Jew*, 3:488–532, 569–94.

9. For a full study of this group, see Martin Hengel, *The Zealots: Investigations into the Jewish Freedom Movement in the Period from Herod I until 70 A.D.*, trans. David Smith (Edinburgh: T & T Clark, 1989);

Meier, *A Marginal Jew,* 3:565–68 and 257n20.

10. For discussion and extensive bibliography, see Larry Kreitzer, "Apocalyptic, Apocalypticism," in *Dictionary of the Later New Testament and Its Developments,* ed. R. P. Martin and P. H. Davids (Downers Grove: InterVarsity, 1997), 55–68; also John J. Collins, *The Apocalyptic Imagination,* 2nd ed. (Grand Rapids: Eerdmans, 1998).

11. Important recent discussion is examined by David J. Bryan, "The Herodians: A Case of Disputed Identity. A Review Article," *Tyndale Bulletin* 53, no. 2 (2002): 223–38.

12. Stanley E. Porter, "Did Jesus Ever Teach in Greek?" *Tyndale Bulletin* 44, no. 2 (1993): 199–235. For additional bibliography, see Daniel B. Wallace, *Greek Grammar Beyond the Basics* (Grand Rapids: Zondervan, 1996), 13.

13. G. Gordon Stott, "Am Ha'arez," in *A Dictionary of Christ and the Gospels,* ed. James Hastings, John Selbie, and John Lambert, 2 vols. (Edinburgh: T & T Clark, 1906), 1:52.

14. Alan D. Crown, ed., *The Samaritans* (Tübingen: J. C. B. Mohr [Paul Siebeck], 1989). For additional studies, see Meier, *A Marginal Jew,* 3:594–95.

15. For fuller discussion of this, see R. T. France, *Jesus and the Old Testament: His Application of Old Testament Passages to Himself and His Mission* (Downers Grove/London: InterVarsity/Tyndale, 1971); John W. Wenham, *Christ and the Bible,* 3rd ed. (Grand Rapids: Baker, 1994); R. V. G. Tasker, *The Old Testament in the New Testament* (Grand Rapids: Eerdmans, 1963); E. Earle Ellis, *The Old Testament in Early Christianity: Canon and Interpretation in the Light of Modern Research* (Grand Rapids: Baker, 1992).

16. A recent introduction to the subject is David deSilva, *Introducing the Apocrypha: Message, Context, and Significance* (Grand Rapids: Baker, 2002).

17. For discussion and the texts themselves, see G. W. E. Nickelsburg, *Jewish Literature between the Bible and the Mishnah* (Philadelphia: Fortress, 1981); James H. Charlesworth, *The Old Testament Pseudepigrapha and the New Testament* (Cambridge: Cambridge University Press, 1998); James H. Charlesworth, ed., *The Old Testament Pseudepigrapha,* 2 vols. (Garden City, N.Y.: Doubleday, 1983–85); Michael E. Stone, ed., *Jewish Writings of the Second Temple Period: Apocrypha, Pseudepigrapha, Qumran, Sectarian Writings, Philo, Josephus* (Assen, Netherlands/Philadelphia: Van Gorcum/Fortress, 1984).

18. For the texts, see Florentino García Martínez, *The Dead Sea Scrolls Translated,* 2nd ed. (Grand Rapids: Eerdmans, 1996). For introduction and reference, respectively, see James C. VanderKam, *The Dead Sea Scrolls Today* (Grand Rapids: Eerdmans, 1994); Lawrence H. Shiffman and James C. VanderKam, eds., *Encyclopedia of the Dead Sea Scrolls,* 2 vols. (Oxford: Oxford University Press, 2000).

19. See Hermann Strack and Günther Stemberger, *Introduction to the Talmud and Midrash,* trans. and ed. Markus Bockmuehl, 2nd ed. (Philadelphia: Fortress, 1996); Abraham Cohen, *Everyman's Talmud* (New York: Dutton, 1949); C. G. Montefiore and H. Loewe, *A Rabbinic Anthology* (New York: Schocken, 1974 [1938]); Jacob Neusner, *Introduction to Rabbinic Literature* (New York: Doubleday, 1994).

20. Herbert Danby, *The Mishnah* (London: Oxford University Press, 1933); David W. Halivini, *Midrash, Mishnah, and Gemara: The Jewish Predilection for Justified Law* (Cambridge, Mass.: Harvard University Press, 1986).

21. See Jacob Neusner, *Rabbinic Literature and the New Testament: What We Cannot Show, We Do Not Know* (Valley Forge, Pa.: Trinity Press International, 1994).

22. For information on the targums, see Bruce Chilton, "Targums," in *Dictionary of Jesus and the Gospels,* ed. J. B. Green, S. McKnight, I. H. Marshall, 800–804. For the texts in translation, see Kevin Cathcart, Michael Maher, and Martin McNamara, eds., *The Aramaic Bible: The Targums,* 19 vols. (Collegeville, Minn.: Liturgical Press, 1987–).

23. See Jacob Neusner, *What Is Midrash?* (Philadelphia: Fortress, 1987); Gary G. Porton, *Understanding Rabbinic Midrash: Texts and Commentary* (Hoboken, N.J.: Ktav 1985); R. Travers Herford, *Christianity in Talmud and Midrash* (Hoboken, N.J.: Ktav, 1975 [1903]).

24. Samuel Sandmel, *Philo of Alexandria: An Introduction* (New York: Oxford University Press, 1979); Harry A. Wolfson, *Philo,* 2 vols. (Cambridge, Mass.: Harvard University Press, 1947); Ronald Williamson, *Jews in the Hellenistic World: Philo* (Cambridge/New York: Cambridge University Press, 1989); C. D. Yonge, trans., *The Works of Philo,* rev. ed. (Peabody, Mass.: Hendrickson, 1993).

25. Tessa Rajak, *Josephus: The Historian and His Society* (Philadelphia: Fortress, 1984); Shayne J. D. Cohen, *Josephus in Galilee and Rome: His Vita and Development as a Historian* (Leiden: E. J. Brill, 1979); F. J. Foakes-Jackson, *Josephus and the Jews: The Religion and History of the Jews as Explained by Flavius Josephus* (Grand Rapids: Baker, 1977 [1930]); William Whiston, trans., *The Works of Josephus* (Peabody, Mass.: Hendrickson, 1987 [1893]).

Chapter 3: *The Gospel and the Four Gospels*

1. On the importance of facts for saving faith, see Gordon R. Lewis, "Is Propositional Revelation Essential to Evangelical Spiritual Formation?" *Journal of the Evangelical Theological Society* 46, no. 2 (June 2003): 269–98.

2. On this, see Charles H. Talbert, *What Is a Gospel? The Genre of the Canonical Gospels* (Macon, Ga.: Mercer University Press, 1985 [1977]).

3. R. T. France, *Matthew: Evangelist and Teacher* (Grand Rapids: Zondervan, 1989), 123–27. See also Paul Barnett, *Jesus and the Logic of History* (Grand Rapids: Eerdmans, 1997), 159–61, on how the Gospels both belong to and transcend the "biography" genre.

4. David E. Aune, *The New Testament in Its Literary Environment* (Philadelphia: Westminster, 1987), 17–76.

5. Arriving at a very similar conclusion is Udo Schnelle, *The History and Theology of the New Testament Writings,* trans. M. Eugene Boring (Minneapolis: Fortress, 1998), 160–61.

Chapter 4: *The Gospel of Matthew*

1. *Studies in the Gospel of Mark,* trans. John Bowden (London: SCM, 1985), 64–84.

2. For a modern defense of Matthean authorship, see R. T. France, *Matthew: Evangelist and Teacher* (Grand Rapids: Zondervan, 1989), 50–122; D. A. Carson, Douglas J. Moo, and Leon Morris, *An Introduction to the New Testament* (Grand Rapids: Zondervan, 1992), 66–74.

3. Paul S. Minear, *Matthew, the Teacher's Gospel* (London: Darton, Longman and Todd, 1984), 23–24.

4. *Redating Matthew, Mark, and Luke* (London: Hodder & Stoughton, 1991).

5. *Redating the New Testament* (Philadelphia: Westminster, 1976).

6. Wenham, *Redating Matthew, Mark, and Luke*, 243.

7. For this and other options, see Udo Schnelle, *The History and Theology of the New Testament Writings*, trans. M. Eugene Boring (Minneapolis: Fortress, 1998), 223.

Chapter 5: *The Gospel of Mark*

1. Kirsopp Lake, *Eusebius: Ecclesiastical History*, 2 vols. (London: Heinemann, 1953), 1:297.

2. See on this whole question Martin Hengel, *Studies in the Gospel of Mark* (London: SCM, 1985). For the negative view, see D. E. Nineham, *St. Mark* (Philadelphia: Westminster, 1977 [1963]).

3. Richard Bauckham, "The Eyewitnesses and the Gospel Traditions," *Journal for the Study of the Historical Jesus* 1, no. 1 (2003) 28–60.

4. So Adolf von Harnack, *The Date of the Acts and the Synoptic Gospels*, trans. J. R. Wilkinson (New York/London: Putnam/Williams & Norgate, 1911), 126.

5. Willoughby C. Allen, *The Gospel According to St. Mark* (London: Rivingtons, 1915), 5–8.

6. John A. T. Robinson, *Redating the New Testament* (Philadelphia: Westminster, 1976), 116.

7. John W. Wenham, *Redating Matthew, Mark, and Luke* (London: Hodder & Stoughton, 1991), 238.

8. Benjamin W. Bacon, *The Gospel of Mark: Its Composition and Date* (New Haven, Conn.: Yale University Press, 1925), 73.

9. S. G. F. Brandon, *The Fall of Jerusalem and the Christian Church: A Study of the Effects of the Jewish Overthrow of AD 70* (London: SPCK, 1957), 185ff.

10. Royce G. Gruenler, "Mark," in *Baker Commentary on the Bible*, ed. Walter A. Elwell (Grand Rapids: Baker, 1989), 765.

11. William Wrede, *The Messianic Secret*, trans. J. C. G. Greig (Greenwood, S.C.: Attic Press, 1971). Against this view see Ralph P. Martin, *Mark: Evangelist and Theologian* (Grand Rapids: Zondervan, 1973), 91ff.; and James D. G. Dunn, "The Messianic Secret in Mark," *Tyndale Bulletin* 21 (1970): 92–117.

Chapter 6: *The Gospel of Luke*

1. For detailed discussion, see Donald Guthrie, *New Testament Introduction*, 4th ed. (Leicester/Downers Grove: Apollos/InterVarsity, 1990), 113–31.

2. See "Early Church (The)," in *Handbook of Biblical Criticism*, ed. Richard N. Soulen and R. Kendall Soulen, 3rd ed. (Louisville: Westminster John Knox, 2001), 51.

3. Thomas R. Schreiner, "Luke," in *Baker Commentary on the Bible*, ed. Walter A. Elwell (Grand Rapids: Baker, 1989), 804–5.

4. For a summary of Luke's theology, see Michael Wilcock, *The Savior of the World: The Message of Luke's Gospel* (Downers Grove: InterVarsity, 1979); Leon Morris, *New Testament Theology* (Grand Rapids: Zondervan, 1986), 144–221.

5. For detailed discussion, see Ben Witherington III, *Women in the Earliest Churches* (Cambridge: Cambridge University Press, 1988), 128–57.

Chapter 7: *The Gospel of John*

1. Plutarch, *The Lives of the Noble Grecians and Romans*, trans. John Dryden, rev. Arthur H. Clough (New York: The Modern Library, 1932), 293. See also his comments on the life of Alexander, 801.

2. Robert M. Grant puts it this way: "After the end of the second century no Christian author doubted that the gospel was written by an apostle." *A Historical Introduction to the New Testament* (London: Collins, 1963), 148.

3. D. Moody Smith, "Johannine Studies," in *The New Testament and Its Modern Interpreters*, ed. Eldon J. Epp and George W. MacRae (Philadelphia/Atlanta: Fortress/Scholars, 1989), 273.

4. Irenaeus, *Against Heresies* 3.1.1. See also 3.16.5; 3.22.2; 5.1.8.2 for similar statements.

5. Irenaeus, *Against Heresies* 3.3.4.

6. Eusebius, *Ecclesiastical History* V, 20, 5–6.

7. Brooke F. Westcott, *An Introduction to the Study of the Gospels* (London/Cambridge: Macmillan, 1860), 240.

8. Robert Kysar, "Community and Gospel: Vectors in Fourth Gospel Criticism," in *Interpreting the Gospels*, ed. James L. Mays (Philadelphia: Fortress, 1981), 277.

9. *The Writings of the New Testament* (Minneapolis: Fortress, 1999), 525.

10. Grant, *A Historical Introduction to the New Testament*, 159.

11. Werner G. Kümmel, *Introduction to the New Testament* (Nashville: Abingdon, 1972), 246.

12. See, for example, John A. T. Robinson, *Redating the New Testament* (Philadelphia: Westminster, 1976), 254–311. See also the earlier dates reported in the literature by Udo Schnelle, *The History and Theology of the New Testament Writings*, trans. M. Eugene Boring (Minneapolis: Fortress, 1998), 477n120.

13. For further study on the themes of the Gospel, see D. A. Carson, *The Gospel According to John* (Leicester/Grand Rapids: InterVarsity/Eerdmans, 1991), and the sources quoted there.

Chapter 8: *Man from Galilee*

1. See F. F. Bruce, *Jesus and Christian Origins outside the New Testament* (Grand Rapids: Eerdmans, 1974); James H. Charlesworth, *Jesus within Judaism: New Light from Exciting Archaeological Discoveries* (New York: Doubleday, 1988); R. Travers Herford, *Christianity in Talmud and Midrash* (Hoboken, N.J.: Ktav, 1975 [1903]); Gary R. Habermas, *Ancient Evidence for the Life of Jesus* (Nashville: Thomas Nelson, 1984).

2. For the modern development of the treatment of the Gospels and the scholarly search for Jesus, see chs. 11 and 12 below.

3. There have been numerous books written on the life of Jesus at the basic level; the following are suggested: John W. Shepard, *The*

Christ of the Gospels: An Exegetical Study, 3rd ed. (Grand Rapids: Eerdmans, 1946); Ferdinand Prat, *Jesus Christ: His Life, His Teaching and His Work,* trans. John J. Heenan, 2 vols. (Milwaukee: Bruce, 1950); F. F. Bruce, *Jesus: Lord and Savior* (Downers Grove: InterVarsity, 1986); Donald Guthrie, *A Shorter Life of Christ* (Grand Rapids: Zondervan, 1970); James S. Stewart, *The Life and Teaching of Jesus Christ* (Nashville: Abingdon, 1978).

4. If you wonder how Jesus could be born "B.C." it is because a Christian chronographer named Dionysius Exiguus in the early sixth century A.D. incorrectly calculated the time of Jesus' birth in the Roman calendar.

5. For full discussion, see Jack Finegan, *Handbook of Biblical Chronology: Principles of Time Reckoning in the Ancient World and Problems of Chronology in the Bible,* rev. ed. (Peabody, Mass.: Hendrickson, 1998), 279–369; Harold Hoehner, *Chronological Aspects of the Life of Christ* (Grand Rapids: Zondervan, 1977).

6. On the magi, see Edwin M. Yamauchi, *Persia and the Bible* (Grand Rapids: Baker, 1990), 467–91.

7. On John the Baptist, see Ben Witherington III, "John the Baptist," in *Dictionary of Jesus and the Gospels,* ed. Joel B. Green, Scot McKnight, and I. Howard Marshall (Leicester/Downers Grove: InterVarsity, 1992), 383–91. For detailed critical discussion, see John P. Meier, *A Marginal Jew,* vol. 2: *Mentor, Message, and Miracles* (New York: Doubleday, 1994), 1–233.

8. An excellent source of detailed listings of miracles and other events in Jesus' ministry can be found in William Graham Scroggie, *A Guide to the Gospels* (Grand Rapids: Kregel, 1995 [1948]).

9. This aspect of Jesus' ministry is emphasized in a life of Jesus by A. B. Bruce, *The Training of the Twelve* (New Canaan, Conn.: Keats, 1979 [1871]).

10. For a good summary of the trial of Jesus, see Bruce Corley, "The Trial of Jesus," in *Dictionary of Jesus and the Gospels,* ed. Joel B. Green, Scot McKnight, and I. Howard Marshall (Leicester/Downers Grove: InterVarsity, 1992), 841–54; Stephen S. Smalley, "Jesus Christ, Arrest and

Trial of," in *International Standard Bible Encyclopedia,* ed. Geoffrey W. Bromiley, 4 vols. (Grand Rapids: Eerdmans, 1979–88), 2:1049–55. For a longer discussion, see David R. Catchpole, *The Trial of Jesus: A Study in the Gospels and Jewish Historiography from 1770 to the Present Day* (Leiden: E. J. Brill, 1971).

11. It is sometimes alleged that the accounts of Jesus' resurrection are hopelessly confused. A reasonable resolution of difficulties can be found in John W. Wenham's *Easter Enigma: Are the Resurrection Accounts in Conflict?,* 2nd ed. (Grand Rapids: Baker, 1992). See also Michael Green, *The Empty Cross of Jesus* (Downers Grove: InterVarsity, 1984).

Chapter 9: *Lord, Teach Us*

1. For general introduction, see Robert H. Stein, *The Method and Message of Jesus' Teachings* (Philadelphia: Westminster, 1978); Roy B. Zuck, *Teaching as Jesus Taught* (Grand Rapids: Baker, 1995); Herman H. Horne, *Jesus the Master Teacher* (New York: Association Press, 1920); Joel B. Green and Max Turner, eds., *Jesus of Nazareth: Lord and Christ* (Grand Rapids/Carlisle, England: Eerdmans/Paternoster, 1994); Claude C. Jones, *The Teaching Methods of the Master* (St. Louis: Bethany, 1957); Robert H. Stein, *A Basic Guide to Interpreting the Bible: Playing by the Rules* (Grand Rapids: Baker, 1994); Joachim Jeremias, *New Testament Theology: The Proclamation of Jesus* (London: SCM, 1971), 8–29.

2. There is ongoing interest in the difficult sayings of Jesus. See, in particular, Robert H. Stein, *Interpreting Puzzling Texts in the New Testament* (Grand Rapids: Baker, 1996); F. F. Bruce, *The Hard Sayings of Jesus* (Downers Grove: InterVarsity, 1983); William Neil and Stephen H. Travis, *More Difficult Sayings of Jesus* (Grand Rapids: Eerdmans, 1979); William Neil, *What Jesus Really Meant* (London: Mowbrays, 1975).

3. On the parables, see Craig L. Blomberg, *Interpreting the Parables* (Downers Grove: InterVarsity, 1990); David Wenham, *The Parables of Jesus* (Downers Grove: InterVarsity, 1989); Arland J. Hultgren, *The Parables of Jesus: A Commentary* (Grand Rapids: Eerdmans, 2002); David B. Gowler, *What Are They Saying about the*

Parables? (New York: Paulist, 2000); Richard N. Longenecker, ed., *The Challenge of Jesus' Parables* (Grand Rapids: Eerdmans, 2000).

4. There are many books on Jesus' teachings available. In addition to the works listed in the further reading section at the end of this chapter, see Craig Blomberg, *Jesus and the Gospels* (Nashville: Broadman & Holman, 1997); Thomas Walker, *The Teaching of Jesus* (London: George Allen and Unwin, 1923); Donald Guthrie, *New Testament Theology* (Downers Grove: InterVarsity, 1981); Leonhard Goppelt, *Theology of the New Testament,* trans. John E. Alsup, ed. Jürgen Roloff, 2 vols. (Grand Rapids: Eerdmans, 1981–82); Leon Morris, *New Testament Theology* (Grand Rapids: Zondervan, 1986), 91–286.

5. See G. R. Beasley-Murray, *Jesus and the Kingdom of God* (Grand Rapids: Eerdmans, 1986); Bruce Chilton and J. I. H. McDonald, *Jesus and the Ethics of the Kingdom* (Grand Rapids: Eerdmans, 1987); John Gray, *The Biblical Doctrine of the Reign of God* (Edinburgh: T & T Clark, 1979); John Bright, *The Kingdom of God: The Biblical Concept and Its Meaning for the Church* (Nashville: Abingdon, 1953); Werner G. Kümmel, *Promise and Fulfillment: The Eschatological Message of Jesus,* 2nd ed. (London: SCM, 1961).

6. See B. B. Warfield, *The Lord of Glory: A Study of the Designations of Our Lord in the New Testament with Especial Reference to His Deity* (Grand Rapids: Zondervan, n.d.), 1–173; Oscar Cullmann, *The Christology of the New Testament,* trans. Shirley C. Guthrie and Charles A. M. Hall, rev. ed. (Philadelphia: Westminster, 1963); Murray J. Harris, *Jesus as God: The New Testament Use of* Theos *in Reference to Jesus* (Grand Rapids: Baker, 1992); Murray J. Harris, *3 Crucial Questions about Jesus* (Grand Rapids: Baker, 1994), 65–103; Vincent Taylor, *The Person of Christ in New Testament Teaching* (London/New York: Macmillan/St. Martin's, 1958); D. M. Baillie, *God Was in Christ: An Essay on Incarnation and Atonement* (London: Faber & Faber, 1948), 106–56; Robert L. Reymond, *Jesus, Divine Messiah: The New Testament Witness* (Phillipsburg, N.J.: Presbyterian & Reformed, 1990).

7. See George B. Stevens, *The Theology of the New Testament* (New York: Scribner, 1907), 187–98; Thomas W. Manson, *The Teaching of Jesus* (Cambridge: Cambridge University Press, 1963), 116–70, 285–312.

8. See T. F. Glasson, *The Second Advent: The Origin of the New Testament Doctrine*, 2nd ed. (London: Epworth, 1947); Bruce Milne, *The Message of Heaven and Hell* (Downers Grove: InterVarsity, 2003); Leon Morris, *The Biblical Doctrine of Judgment* (Grand Rapids: Eerdmans, 1960); relevant articles in Joel B. Green, Scot McKnight, and I. Howard Marshall, eds., *Dictionary of Jesus and the Gospels* (Leicester/Downers Grove: InterVarsity, 1992).

Chapter 10: *Modern Approaches to the New Testament*

1. Martin Albertz, *Die Botschaft des Neuen Testaments*, vol. II/2 (Zollikon-Zürich: Evangelischer Verlag, 1957), 14. The fallen young pastor and Ilse Friedrichsdorff are honored in the opening pages of vol. II/1.

2. Helmut Koester, *Introduction to the New Testament*, 2 vols. (Philadelphia/Berlin and New York: Fortress/Walter de Gruyter, 1982), xviii, warns students against expecting "largely secure results." See also the statement by Russell Pregeant, *Engaging the New Testament: An Interdisciplinary Approach* (Minneapolis: Fortress, 1995), 36. This introduction to the New Testament brings the student to the text, finally, on p. 174. Prior to this the student is inundated with theory, methods, and hypotheses.

3. On the danger of simplistic appeal to "the surface of the text," see Grant R. Osborne, *The Hermeneutical Spiral: A Comprehensive Introduction to Biblical Interpretation* (Downers Grove: InterVarsity, 1991), 9.

4. For a defense of this approach, see Gerald Bray, "Scripture and Confession: Doctrine as Hermeneutic," in *A Pathway into the Holy Scripture*, ed. Philip E. Satterthwaite and David F. Wright (Grand Rapids: Eerdmans, 1994), 221–35.

5. *The New Testament and Criticism* (Grand Rapids: Eerdmans, 1967), 37.

6. "Historical Criticism," in I. Howard Marshall, ed., *New Testament Interpretation: Essays on Principles and Methods* (Grand Rapids: Eerdmans, 1977), 127–32.

7. This summary of Enlightenment historical criticism draws from Francis Watson, "Enlightenment," in *A Dictionary of Biblical Interpretation*, ed. R. J. Coggins and J. L. Houlden (London/Valley Forge, Pa.: SCM/Trinity Press International, 1990), 191–94.

8. Ibid., 194.

9. See Richard N. Soulen and R. Kendall Soulen, *Handbook of Biblical Criticism*, 3rd ed. (Louisville: Westminster John Knox, 2001), 79.

10. See, e.g., relevant entries in Donald McKim, ed., *Historical Handbook of Major Biblical Interpreters* (Downers Grove: InterVarsity, 1998); John H. Hayes, ed., *Dictionary of Biblical Interpretation*, 2 vols. (Nashville: Abingdon, 1999).

11. Robert W. Funk and Roy W. Hoover, eds., *The Five Gospels: The Search for the Authentic Words of Jesus* (New York: Macmillan, 1993). The same views in more radical dress are found in Robert W. Funk, *Honest to Jesus: Jesus for a New Millennium* (San Francisco: Harper San Francisco, 1996). More recently see S. Patterson, J. M. Robinson, and H. Bethge, *The Fifth Gospel* (Philadelphia: Trinity Press International, 1999).

12. James L. Price, *The New Testament: Its History and Theology* (New York/London: Macmillan/Collier Macmillan, 1987), 4.

13. Philip Jenkins, *Hidden Gospels* (Oxford: Oxford University Press, 2001), 8.

14. "Historical Criticism," in Marshall, *New Testament Interpretation*, 133.

15. For a moderate (and witty) investigation of faulty historical critical procedure, see David R. Hall, *The Seven Pillories of Wisdom* (Macon, Ga.: Mercer University Press, 1990).

16. "Less than ideal" is an understatement. Many think that it has much to do with the dramatic turn of Western nations away from the Christian faith in recent generations. It has been suggested that historical criticism helped pave the way for the Third Reich in Germany (see William R. Farmer, *The Gospel of Jesus: The Pastoral Relevance of the Synoptic Problem* [Louisville: Westminster John Knox, 1994], 8). It has discouraged millions from taking the gospel of Jesus Christ as seriously as they might otherwise have done. It poses provocative, even brilliant questions—but is less effective at replacing what it tears down.

17. *The Scope and Authority of the Bible* (London: SCM, 1980), 8–9.

18. Eta Linnemann, *Historical Criticism of the Bible*, trans. Robert Yarbrough (Grand Rapids: Kregel, 1990); idem, *Biblical Criticism on Trial*, trans. Robert Yarbrough (Grand Rapids: Kregel, 2001).

19. Donald A. Hagner, "The New Testament, History, and the Historical-Critical Method," in *New Testament Criticism and Interpretation*, ed. David Alan Black and David S. Dockery (Grand Rapids: Zondervan, 1991), 88.

20. Joseph Cardinal Ratzinger, "Biblical Interpretation in Crisis: On the Question of the Foundations and Approaches of Exegesis Today," in *Biblical Interpretation in Crisis: The Ratzinger Conference on Bible and Church*, ed. Richard John Neuhaus (Grand Rapids: Eerdmans, 1989), 1.

21. David S. Dockery, "New Testament Interpretation: A Historical Survey," in *Interpreting the New Testament*, ed. David Alan Black and David S. Dockery (Nashville: Broadman & Holman, 2001), 37.

22. Gerhard Maier, *Biblical Hermeneutics*, trans. Robert W. Yarbrough (Wheaton, Ill.: Crossway, 1994), 256–60.

23. Erich Heller, "The Hazard of Modern Poetry," in idem, *The Disinherited Mind: Essays in Modern German Literature and Thought*, 4th ed. (London: Bowes & Bowes, 1975), 261–300.

24. Ibid., 273.

25. Osborne, *Hermeneutical Spiral*, 5.

26. Dan Doriani, *Putting the Truth to Work* (Phillipsburg, N.J.: Presbyterian & Reformed, 2001), 59–80.

27. Maier, *Biblical Hermeneutics*, ch. 6.

28. For valuable discussion, see Craig L. Blomberg, "The Diversity of Literary Genres in the New Testament, in *Interpreting the New Testament*, ed. David Alan Black and David S. Dockery (Nashville: Broadman & Holman, 2001), 272–95.

29. *Knowing Scripture* (Downers Grove: InterVarsity, 1977), 63–99. Equally valuable, and more detailed, is Daniel Doriani, *Getting the Message* (Phillipsburg, N.J.: Presbyterian & Reformed, 1996).

30. Chapters are devoted to each of these approaches in *Interpreting the New Testament,* ed. David Alan Black and David S. Dockery (Nashville: Broadman & Holman, 2001).

31. See Jenkins, *Hidden Gospels;* also Thomas C. Oden, *The Rebirth of Orthodoxy* (San Francisco: Harper San Franciso, 2003), 99–100.

32. Maier, *Biblical Hermeneutics,* 402–9; Doriani, *Putting the Truth to Work.*

33. Osborne, *Hermeneutical Spiral,* 6, 12.

34. Ibid., 6.

35. Robert Morgan with John Barton, *Biblical Interpretation* (New York/Oxford: Oxford University Press, 1988), 196.

Chapter 11: *The Modern Study of the Gospels*

1. *Latin and Greek: A History of the Influence of the Classics on English Life from 1600 to 1918* (Hamden, Conn.: Archon, 1964), xiv.

2. Klaus Scholder, *The Birth of Modern Critical Theology: Origins and Problems of Biblical Criticism in the Seventeenth Century,* trans. John Bowden (London/Philadelphia: SCM/Trinity Press International, 1990).

3. Standard works that deal with this subject include: William Baird, *History of New Testament Research,* 2 vols. (Minneapolis: Fortress, 1992–2003); Stephen Neill and Tom Wright, *The Interpretation of the New Testament 1861–1986* (New York/Oxford: Oxford University Press, 1988); Werner G. Kümmel, *Introduction to the New Testament* (Nashville: Abingdon, 1972).

4. Frederick C. Grant, *The Gospels: Their Origin and Growth* (New York: Harper & Bros., 1957), 51.

5. For an overview, see Edgar V. McKnight, *What Is Form Criticism?* (Philadelphia: Fortress, 1969).

6. Vincent Taylor, *The Formation of the Gospel Tradition* (London: Macmillan, 1933), 51.

7. Martin Hengel, *Acts and the History of Earliest Christianity,* trans.

John Bowden (Philadelphia: Fortress, 1980), 25.

8. For an overview, see Norman Perrin, *What Is Redaction Criticism?* (Philadelphia: Fortress, 1969); Joachim Rohde, *Rediscovering the Teaching of the Evangelists,* trans. Dorothea M. Barton (London: SCM, 1968).

9. Günther Bornkamm, *Tradition and Interpretation in Matthew,* trans. Perry Scott (Philadelphia: Westminster, 1963), written with two of his students, Gerhard Barth and Heinz J. Held.

10. Willi Marxsen, *Mark the Evangelist: Studies on the Redaction History of the Gospel* (Nashville: Abingdon, 1969), 21.

11. Perrin, *What Is Redaction Criticism?* 33–34.

12. Robert H. Stein, *Gospels and Tradition: Studies in Redaction Criticism of the Synoptic Gospels* (Grand Rapids: Baker, 1991), 15.

13. Such as Helmut Koester. "How can we know when written documents are the source for such quotations and allusions? Redaction Criticism is the answer. . . . However, this task has become much more difficult than it appeared to me forty years ago" (*Journal of Biblical Literature* 113, no. 2 [1994]: 297).

14. Daniel Patte, *Structural Exegesis for New Testament Critics* (Minneapolis: Fortress, 1989).

15. Edgar V. McKnight and Elizabeth Struthers Malbon, eds., *The New Literary Criticism and the New Testament* (Valley Forge, Penn.: Trinity Press International, 1994).

16. Consult Robert Alter, *The Art of Biblical Narrative* (New York: Basic, 1981); Mark Allan Powell, *What Is Narrative Criticism?* (Minneapolis: Fortress, 1990). A good general survey is found in Christopher M. Tuckett, *Reading the New Testament: Methods of Interpretation* (Philadelphia: Fortress, 1987).

17. See Robert C. Holub, *Reception Theory: A Critical Introduction* (New York: Routledge, Chapman and Hall, 1984); Jane P. Tompkins, ed., *Reader-Response Criticism: From Formalism to Post-Structuralism* (Baltimore: Johns Hopkins University Press, 1980).

18. See George A. Kennedy, *New Testament Interpretation through*

Rhetorical Criticism (Chapel Hill: University of North Carolina Press, 1984).

19. See David M. May, ed., *Social Scientific Criticism of the New Testament: A Bibliography* (Macon, Ga.: Mercer University Press, 1991); Bengt Holmberg, *Sociology and the New Testament: An Appraisal* (Minneapolis: Fortress, 1990); David G. Horrell, ed., *Social-Scientific Approaches to New Testament Interpretation* (Edinburgh: T & T Clark, 1999).

20. M. P. Parvis, "New Testament Criticism in the World-Wars Period," in *The Study of the Bible Today and Tomorrow,* ed. Harold R. Willoughby (Chicago: University of Chicago Press, 1947), 63.

21. Typical is James H. Charlesworth, ed., *Jesus' Jewishness: Exploring the Place of Jesus in Early Judaism* (New York: Crossroad, 1991).

22. Brad Young, *Jesus the Jewish Theologian* (Peabody, Mass.: Hendrickson, 1995).

23. To take only two examples, both of which extend their insights to the whole of the early church, see Oskar Skarsaune, *In the Shadow of the Temple* (Downers Grove: InterVarsity, 2002); Markus Bockmuehl, *Jewish Law in Gentile Churches* (Edinburgh: T & T Clark, 2000; reprinted Grand Rapids: Baker, 2003).

24. William R. Farmer, *The Synoptic Problem* (Macon, Ga.: Mercer University Press, 1964).

25. Hans-Herbert Stoldt, *History and Criticism of the Marcan Hypothesis,* trans. and ed. Donald L. Niewyk (Macon, Ga./Edinburgh: Mercer University Press/T & T Clark, 1980).

26. William R. Farmer, *Jesus and the Gospel: Tradition, Scripture, and Canon* (Philadelphia: Fortress, 1982); *The Gospel of Jesus: The Pastoral Relevance of the Synoptic Problem* (Louisville: Westminster John Knox, 1994).

27. John W. Wenham, *Redating Matthew, Mark, and Luke* (London: Hodder & Stoughton, 1991); Bo Reicke, *The Roots of the Synoptic Gospels* (Philadelphia: Fortress, 1986); David Alan Black, *Why Four Gospels? The Historical Origins of the Gospels* (Grand Rapids: Kregel, 2001). See also Mark Goodacre, *The Synoptic Problem: A Way through the*

Maze (Philadelphia: Trinity Press International, 2004).

28. A. M. Farrer, "On Dispensing with Q," in *Studies in the Gospels*, ed. D. E. Nineham (Oxford: Blackwell, 1955), 55–88.

29. A good survey is Graham N. Stanton, "Q," in *Dictionary of Jesus and the Gospels*, ed. Joel B. Green, Scot McKnight, and I. Howard Marshall (Leicester/Downers Grove: InterVarsity, 1992), 664–50. For a different perspective, see Eta Linnemann, *Biblical Criticism on Trial*, trans. Robert Yarbrough (Grand Rapids: Kregel, 2001), 18–39. See also David R. Catchpole, *Studies in Q* (Edinburgh: T & T Clark, 1992); Darrell Bock, "Questions about Q," in *Rethinking the Synoptic Problem*, ed. David Alan Black and David R. Beck (Grand Rapids: Baker, 2001), 41–64.

30. See A. K. M. Adam, *What Is Postmodern Criticism?* (Minneapolis: Fortress, 1995).

31. *Why Four Gospels?*, 7–8.

Chapter 12: *The Modern Search for Jesus*

1. Markus Bockmuehl, *This Jesus: Martyr, Lord, Messiah* (Edinburgh: T & T Clark, 1994), ix.

2. Among many surveys of this topic, see Chester C. McCown, *The Search for the Real Jesus: A Century of Historical Study* (New York: Scribner, 1940); Charles C. Anderson, *Critical Quests of Jesus* (Grand Rapids: Eerdmans, 1969); Gustaf Aulén, *Jesus in Contemporary Historical Research* (Philadelphia: Fortress, 1976); Mark Allan Powell, *Jesus as a Figure in History: How Modern Historians View the Man from Galilee* (Louisville: Westminster John Knox, 1998).

3. For the full story, see Colin Brown, *Jesus in Modern European Thought, 1778–1860* (Grand Rapids: Baker, 1988).

4. In Hans Werner Bartsch, ed., *Kerygma and Myth*, 2 vols., 2nd ed. (London: SPCK, 1962), 1–44.

5. Marcus J. Borg, *Jesus: A New Vision* (San Francisco: Harper & Row, 1987).

6. Burton L. Mack, *A Myth of Innocence: The Gospel of Mark and Christian Origins* (Philadelphia: Fortress, 1988).

7. S. G. F. Brandon, *Jesus and the Zealots: A Study of the Political Factor in Primitive Christianity* (New York: Scribner, 1967).

8. Morton Smith, *Jesus the Magician* (New York: Harper & Row, 1978).

9. A. N. Wilson, *Jesus: A Life* (New York/London: W. W. Norton, 1992).

10. John Dominic Crossan, *The Historical Jesus: The Life of a Mediterranean Jewish Peasant* (San Francisco: Harper, 1991).

11. Milan Machovec, *A Marxist Looks at Jesus* (London: Darton, Longman and Todd, 1976).

12. Barbara E. Thiering, *Jesus the Man: A New Interpretation from the Dead Sea Scrolls* (London/New York: Doubleday, 1992).

13. See Donald Guthrie, *Jesus the Messiah: An Illustrated Life of Christ* (Grand Rapids: Zondervan, 1972); Everett Harrison, *A Short Life of Christ* (Grand Rapids: Eerdmans, 1968); B. F. Meyer, *The Aims of Jesus* (London: SCM, 1979); Bockmuehl, *This Jesus*.

14. *The New Testament and Its Modern Interpreters*, ed. Eldon J. Epp and George W. MacRae (Philadelphia/Atlanta: Fortress/Scholars, 1989), 520–24.

15. Ibid., 524.

16. Marcus J. Borg, "Jesus, Teaching of," in *Anchor Bible Dictionary*, ed. David Noel Freedman, 6 vols. (New York: Doubleday, 1992), 3:804–812.

17. John Riches, "Jesus, Words of," in *Anchor Bible Dictionary*, ed. David Noel Freedman (New York: Doubleday, 1992), 3:802–804.

18. Robert W. Funk and Roy W. Hoover, eds., *The Five Gospels: The Search for the Authentic Words of Jesus* (New York: Macmillan, 1993).

19. For surveys of how these criteria are used, see D. G. A. Calvert, "An Examination of the Criteria for Distinguishing the Authentic Words of Jesus," *New Testament Studies* 18 (1971): 209–18; Robert H. Stein, "The Criteria for Authenticity," in *Gospel Perspectives: Studies of History and Tradition in the Four Gospels*, ed. R. T. France and David Wenham (Sheffield: JSOT, 1980–86), 1:225–63; M. D. Hooker, "Christology and Methodology," *New Testament Studies* 17 (1970): 480–87.

20. This was true from the very outset, beginning with such works as August Neander, *The Life of Jesus Christ*, trans. John M'Clintock and Charles E. Blumenthal, 3rd ed. (New York: Harper & Bros., 1849). It continues to be true today with such writers as Graham N. Stanton, *The Gospels and Jesus* (Oxford/New York: Oxford University Press, 1989); N. T. Wright, *Who Was Jesus?* (Grand Rapids: Eerdmans, 1992); Bockmuehl, *This Jesus*; Richard A. Burridge, *Four Gospels, One Jesus?* (Grand Rapids: Eerdmans, 1994); Darrell Bock, *Jesus according to Scripture* (Grand Rapids/Leicester: Baker/Apollos, 2002).

21. Rudolf Bultmann, "Is Exegesis without Presuppositions Possible?" in *Existence and Faith: Shorter Writings of Rudolf Bultmann*, ed. Schubert M. Ogden (New York: Meridian, 1960), 289–96.

22. As quoted in John A. T. Robinson, *Redating the New Testament* (Philadelphia: Westminster, 1976), 360.

23. See Peter Stuhlmacher, *Jesus of Nazareth, Christ of Faith*, trans. Siegfried S. Schatzmann (Peabody, Mass.: Hendrickson, 1988), 1–38; I. Howard Marshall, *The Origins of New Testament Christology*, 2nd ed. (Downers Grove: InterVarsity, 1990); C. F. D. Moule, *The Origin of Christology* (Cambridge/New York: Cambridge University Press, 1977).

Chapter 13: *The World and Identity of the Earliest Church*

1. The shape and tone of Julius Caesar's world is preserved in his own gripping account: *The Battle for Gaul*, trans. Anne and Peter Wiseman (Boston: David R. Godine, 1980). See also the biographical study by Plutarch in his *Fall of the Roman Republic*, trans. Rex Warner (Baltimore: Penguin Books, 1958), 217–76.

2. For studies on the interface between Rome, early Christianity, and first-century Judaism, see Karl P. Donfried and Peter Richardson, *Judaism and Christianity in First-Century Rome* (Grand Rapids: Eerdmans, 1998).

3. New York: Penguin, 1989.

4. Wheaton, Ill.: Tyndale, 1976.

5. See, e.g., Frederick Copleston, *A History of Philosophy*, vol. 1, pt. 2: *Greece and Rome* (Garden City, N.Y.: Image, 1962); James S. Jeffers, *The*

Greco-Roman World of the New Testament Era (Downers Grove: InterVarsity, 1999).

Chapter 14: Acts 1–7

1. See John W. Wenham, *Redating Matthew, Mark, and Luke* (London: Hodder & Stoughton, 1991), 186, 230–37.

2. See I. Howard Marshall, *Luke: Historian and Theologian* (Grand Rapids: Zondervan, 1989).

3. The best recent reflection on this issue is probably Daniel M. Doriani, *Putting the Truth to Work* (Phillipsburg, N.J.: Presbyterian & Reformed, 2001), ch. 8 ("Issues in Applying Narrative Texts").

Chapter 15: Acts 8–12

1. Now dominated by Islam, this was the vicinity of a vibrant and powerful church that arose around the fourth or fifth century. See Paul Bowers, "Nubian Christianity: The Neglected Heritage," *East Africa Journal of Theology* 4, no. 1 (1985): 3–23.

2. Robert H. Gundry, *Mark: A Commentary on His Apology for the Cross* (Grand Rapids: Eerdmans, 1993), 1034–35.

Chapter 16: Acts 13–28

1. John McRay, *Archaeology and the New Testament* (Grand Rapids: Baker, 1991), 227.

2. For a sketch of their settlement there, see Barry J. Beitzel, *The Moody Atlas of Bible Lands* (Chicago: Moody, 1985), 178.

3. F. F. Bruce, *Paul: Apostle of the Heart Set Free* (Grand Rapids: Eerdmans, 1977), 475.

4. According to calculations in Andrew E. Hill, *Baker's Handbook of Bible Lists* (Grand Rapids: Baker, 1981), 235.

Chapter 17: All Things to All People

1. See Phillip E. Johnson, *Defeating Darwinism by Opening Minds* (Downers Grove: InterVarsity, 1997); George M. Marsden, *The Outrageous Idea of Christian Scholarship* (New York/Oxford: Oxford University Press, 1997).

2. Martin Hengel, *The Pre-Christian Paul*, trans. John Bowden (London/Valley Forge, Pa.: SCM/Trinity Press International, 1991), 3.

3. D. Brewer, *Techniques and Assumptions in Jewish Exegesis before*

70 CE (Tübingen: J. C. B. Mohr [Paul Siebeck], 1992); John B. Polhill, *Paul and His Letters* (Nashville: Broadman & Holman, 1999), 30–32.

4. Hengel, *The Pre-Christian Paul*, 63.

5. See S. Kim, *The Origins of Paul's Gospel*, 2nd ed. (Tübingen: J. C. B. Mohr [Paul Siebeck], 1984); idem, *Paul and the New Perspective* (Grand Rapids: Eerdmans, 2001).

6. See the spirited and erudite defense of Paul's authorship of 1–2 Timothy in Luke Timothy Johnson, *The First and Second Letters to Timothy* (New York: Doubleday, 2001), 55–99.

7. V. Furnish, "Pauline Studies," in *The New Testament and Its Modern Interpreters*, ed. Eldon J. Epp and George W. MacRae (Philadelphia/Atlanta: Fortress/Scholars, 1989), 331. For a recent discussion arriving at a largely negative assessment of Acts' reliability, see David H. Akenson, *Saint Paul* (Oxford/New York: Oxford University Press, 2000), 134–43. John G. Gager speaks of Acts as a "harmonious tale" (*Reinventing Paul* [Oxford/New York: Oxford University Press, 2000], 69).

8. David Wenham, *Paul and Jesus: The True Story* (Grand Rapids: Eerdmans, 2002).

9. Stephen Mitchell, *The Gospel according to Jesus: A New Translation and Guide to His Essential Teachings for Believers and Unbelievers* (New York: Harper Collins, 1991), 41.

10. I. Howard Marshall, "Jesus, Paul and John," in idem, *Jesus the Saviour* (Downers Grove: InterVarsity, 1990), 35–56; Wenham, *Paul and Jesus*.

11. By Thomas Schreiner (Downers Grove/Leicester: InterVarsity/Apollos, 2001).

12. For a survey of discussion, see V. Koperski, *What Are They Saying about Paul and the Law?* (New York/Mahwah, N.J.: Paulist, 2001).

13. *Paul and Palestinian Judaism* (Philadelphia: Fortress, 1977); *Paul, the Law, and the Jewish People* (Philadelphia: Fortress, 1983).

14. Downers Grove: InterVarsity, 2001.

15. See Donald A. Hagner, "Paul and Judaism: Testing the New Perspective," in Peter Stuhlmacher,

Revisiting Paul's Doctrine of Justification: A Challenge to the New Perspective (Downers Grove: InterVarsity, 2001); D. A. Carson, P. T. O'Brien, and Mark Seifrid, eds., *Justification and Variegated Nomism*, 2 vols. (Tübingen/Grand Rapids: J. C. B. Mohr [Paul Siebeck]/Baker, 2001–4).

16. Stephen in Acts 7:1–8 (cf. Peter in Acts 3:25) likewise traces the gospel message back to God's promise to Abraham; is Paul Luke's source for what Stephen said on that occasion? Did Stephen have a hand in instructing Paul?

17. See Philip E. Satterthwaite, Richard S. Hess, and Gordon J. Wenham, eds., *The Lord's Anointed: Interpretation of Old Testament Messianic Texts* (Carlisle, England/Grand Rapids: Paternoster/Baker, 1995).

18. J. Alec Motyer, *The Prophecy of Isaiah* (Downers Grove: InterVarsity, 1993), 85.

19. It is not clear however that these figures understood themselves as "messiahs." Raymond Brown (*An Introduction to the New Testament* [New York: Doubleday, 1997], 820n6) claims that "there is no evidence that any Jew claimed or was said to be the Messiah before Jesus of Nazareth. . . ." Jesus' claim may well have been unique at the time.

20. See Alister E. McGrath, *The Mystery of the Cross* (Grand Rapids: Zondervan, 1988).

21. See Gary R. Habermas and Anthony G. N. Flew, *Did Jesus Rise from the Dead?*, ed. Terry L. Miethe (San Francisco: Harper & Row, 1987); Thomas C. Oden, "Did Jesus Christ Really Rise from the Dead?" in *This We Believe*, ed. J. Akers, J. Armstrong, and J. Woodbridge (Grand Rapids: Zondervan, 2000), 100–119.

22. M. Seifrid, "In Christ," in *Dictionary of Paul and His Letters*, ed. Gerald F. Hawthorne and Ralph P. Martin (Leicester/Downers Grove: InterVarsity, 1993), 436.

23. For an approach to Christian ethics that well captures Paul's teaching, see David C. Jones, *Biblical Christian Ethics* (Grand Rapids: Baker, 1994).

24. Schreiner, *Paul, Apostle of God's Glory in Christ*, 463.

Chapter 18: *Romans*

1. For details on the order of Paul's letters in ancient manuscripts, see John McRay, *Paul: His Life and Teaching* (Grand Rapids: Baker, 2003), 273–81.

2. *The Confessions of St. Augustine,* bk. 7, ch. 21.

3. Ibid., bk. 7, ch. 6.

4. Ibid., bk. 7, ch. 12.

5. Roland H. Bainton, *Here I Stand: A Life of Martin Luther* (Nashville: Abingdon, 1950), 49.

6. *The Works of John Wesley,* 14 vols., 3rd ed. (Grand Rapids: Baker, 1991 [1872]), 1:103.

7. Bainton, *Here I Stand,* 49–50.

8. Michael Grant, *History of Rome* (New York: Scribner, 1978), 247.

9. See Acts 18:2, generally regarded as referring to the expulsion of Jews from Rome by the emperor Claudius (A.D. 41–54) because of "disturbances at the instigation of Chrestus" (Jews or others who were preaching Christ). See Suetonius, *The Twelve Caesars,* trans. Robert Graves (New York: Penguin, 1989), 202.

10. See Karl P. Donfried, ed., *The Romans Debate,* rev. ed. (Peabody, Mass.: Hendrickson, 1991).

11. Ibid., xliv.

12. Ibid.

13. On Paul as a letter writer, see M. Luther Stirewalt Jr., *Paul, the Letter Writer* (Grand Rapids: Eerdmans, 2003).

14. See Leon Morris, *The Apostolic Preaching of the Cross* (Grand Rapids: Eerdmans, 1955), 125–85.

15. William Sanday and Arthur C. Headlam, *A Critical and Exegetical Commentary on the Epistle to the Romans,* 5th ed. (Edinburgh: T & T Clark, 1902), i.

16. John Calvin, *Commentaries on the Epistle of Paul the Apostle to the Romans,* trans. and ed. John Owen (Grand Rapids: Baker, 1981 [1849]), xxiv.

17. See Donfried, *The Romans Debate.*

18. The literature is enormous. For orientation, see V. Koperski, *What Are They Saying about Paul and the Law?* (New York/Mahwah, N.J.: Paulist, 2001); Andrew Das, *Paul, the Law, and the Covenant* (Peabody, Mass.: Hendrickson, 2001).

19. For bibliography in these and all areas of Pauline study, see Mark Seifrid and Randall Tan, *The Pauline Writings,* IBR Bibliographies 9 (Grand Rapids: Baker, 2002).

20. For discussion, see John B. Polhill, *Paul and His Letters* (Nashville: Broadman & Holman, 1999), 76–80.

21. For literature, see Luke T. Johnson, *The Writings of the New Testament,* rev. ed. (Minneapolis: Fortress, 1999), 275–76.

22. Howard Clark Kee, "The Context, Birth, and Early Growth of Christianity," in idem et al., *Christianity: A Social and Cultural History* (New York: Macmillan, 1991), 13–74. Romans is covered in one scant paragraph (pp. 58–59). For other focal points of scholarly inquiry into Romans, and other Pauline writings, see Thomas R. Schreiner, "Interpreting the Pauline Epistles," in *Interpreting the New Testament,* ed. D. A. Black and D. S. Dockery (Nashville: Broadman & Holman, 2001), 412–32.

Chapter 19: *Corinthians and Galatians*

1. John McRay, *Paul: His Life and Teaching* (Grand Rapids: Baker, 2003), 166.

2. See J. Murphy-O'Connor, "Paul and Gallio," *Journal of Biblical Literature* 112, no. 2 (1993): 315–17.

3. John McRay, *Archaeology and the New Testament* (Grand Rapids: Baker, 1991), 335.

4. Ibid., 331f.

5. J. E. Bassler, "1 Corinthians," in *The Women's Bible Commentary,* ed. Carol A. Newsom and Sharon H. Ringe, (London/Louisville: SPCK/Westminster John Knox, 1992), 327.

6. Ibid., 328.

7. For a very different analysis of 1 Corinthians 11, see Peter Cotterell and Max Turner, *Linguistics and Biblical Interpretation* (Downers Grove: InterVarsity, 1989), 316–28. On 1 Cor 14:33b–36, see D. A. Carson, "'Silent in the Churches': On the Role of Women in I Cor. 14:33b–36," in *Recovering Biblical Manhood and Womanhood: A Response to Evangelical Feminism,* ed. Wayne A. Grudem and John Piper (Westchester, Ill.: Crossway, 1990), 140–153, 487–90.

8. Craig S. Keener, *Paul, Women, and Wives: Marriage and Women's Ministry in the Letters of Paul* (Peabody, Mass.: Hendrickson, 1992), rejects the theory that 1 Cor 14:33b–36 is a later insertion.

9. See, e.g., F. F. Bruce, *Paul: Apostle of the Heart Set Free* (Grand Rapids: Eerdmans, 1977), 318; D. A. Carson, Douglas J. Moo, and Leon Morris, *An Introduction to the New Testament* (Grand Rapids: Zondervan, 1992), 264–83.

10. See Carson, Moo, and Morris, *An Introduction to the New Testament,* 267–72.

11. John W. Drane, *Introducing the New Testament* (San Francisco: Harper & Row, 1986), 322.

12 For further discussion on this central and profound point, see D. A. Carson, *The Cross and Christian Ministry: An Exposition of Passages from 1 Corinthians* (Grand Rapids/Leicester: Baker/InterVarsity, 1993).

13. See, e.g., Stephen L. Carter, *The Culture of Disbelief: How American Law and Politics Trivialize Religious Devotion* (New York: Basic, 1993); Robert W. Funk, *Honest to Jesus: Jesus for a New Millennium* (San Francisco: Harper San Francisco, 1996). For the scandalously sloppy and sensationalist manner in which even "scholarly" study of Christian beginnings sometimes proceeds, see Philip Jenkins, *Hidden Gospels: How the Search for Jesus Lost Its Way* (Oxford/New York: Oxford University Press, 2001).

14. Many "modern" objections to the gospel are already mentioned in the Bible itself. For a full-scale rhetorical and philosophical attack on Christianity dating from the second century, see Celsus, *On the True Doctrine: A Discourse Against the Christians,* trans. R. Joseph Hoffmann (New York/Oxford: Oxford University Press, 1987).

15. On so-called interpolation theories relating to 2 Corinthians and other Pauline writings, valuable counsel is found in Frederick W. Wisse, "Textual Limits to Redactional Theory in the Pauline Corpus," in *Gospel Origins and Christian Beginnings: In Honor of James M. Robinson,* ed. James E. Goehring et al. (Sonoma, Calif.: Polebridge, 1990), 167–78.

16. Carson, Moo, and Morris, *An Introduction to the New Testament,* 282.

17. On this relation, see the help-

ful summary in E. Earle Ellis, *Paul and His Recent Interpreters* (Grand Rapids: Eerdmans, 1961), 16–17.

18. Defending the South Galatians view is F. F. Bruce, *The Epistle to the Galatians* (Grand Rapids: Eerdmans, 1982), 3–18. Rejecting it and arguing for the North Galatians theory is Werner G. Kümmel, *Introduction to the New Testament*, trans. Howard Clark Kee, rev. ed. (Nashville: Abingdon, 1975), 296–304. Luke Timothy Johnson, *The Writings of the New Testament*, rev. ed. (Minneapolis: Fortress, 1999), 327, claims that the dispute makes little difference to our understanding of Galatians, but this minimizes the light that Acts 13–14 sheds on Galatians if the South Galatian theory proves correct.

19. Archaeological data are presented in McRay, *Archaeology and the New Testament*, 235–41.

20. See, e.g., Martin Luther, *The Bondage of the Will*, trans. Henry Cole (Grand Rapids: Baker, 1979), which needs to be read after consulting Erasmus's *Discourse on the Free Will*, trans. and ed. Ernst F. Winter (New York: Frederick Ungar, 1966). See also the important essays in *Still Sovereign*, ed. Thomas R. Schreiner and Bruce A. Ware (Grand Rapids: Baker, 2000).

21. See Thomas Schreiner, "Interpreting the Pauline Epistles," in *Interpreting the New Testament*, ed. D. A. Black and D. S. Dockery (Nashville: Broadman & Holman, 2001), 422–23.

22. Most important here is Sanders's *Paul and Palestinian Judaism: A Comparison of Patterns of Religion* (Philadelphia: Fortress, 1977). A concise depiction of Sanders's understanding of Paul is found in his *Paul* (Oxford: Oxford University Press, 1991).

23. Most notably from D. A. Carson, P. T. O'Brien, and Mark Seifrid, eds., *Justification and Variegated Nomism*, 2 vols. (Tübingen/Grand Rapids: J. C. B. Mohr [Paul Siebeck]/Baker, 2001–4).

Chapter 20: *Ephesians, Philippians, Colossians, and Philemon*

1. Some have suggested that one or more of Paul's Prison Epistles date from Paul's two-year detention in Caesarea Maritima (Acts 24:27) or even an imprisonment in Ephesus (2 Cor 1:8–10). These are possibilities that have yet to win widespread agreement.

2. Arthur C. Lehmann and James E. Myers, *Magic, Witchcraft, and Religion: An Anthropological Study of the Supernatural*, 2nd ed. (Mountain View, Calif.: Mayfield, 1989), 254.

3. Clinton E. Arnold, *Power and Magic: The Concept of Power in Ephesians* (Grand Rapids: Baker, 1997); idem, "Ephesians," in *Zondervan Illustrated Bible Backgrounds Commentary*, ed. Clinton E. Arnold (Grand Rapids: Zondervan, 2002), 3:300–41.

4. Lehmann and Myers, *Magic, Witchcraft, and Religion*, offers numerous examples, both Western and non-Western.

5. See Arnold, *Power and Magic*, especially ch. 3.

6. John McRay, *Archaeology and the New Testament* (Grand Rapids: Baker, 1991), 256f.

7. Werner G. Kümmel, *Introduction to the New Testament*, rev. ed., trans. Howard Clark Kee (Nashville: Abingdon, 1975), 357.

8. See, e.g., Aart van Roon, *The Authenticity of Ephesians* (Leiden: E. J. Brill, 1975). See also Arnold, *Power and Magic*, 171; Eta Linnemann, *Biblical Criticism on Trial*, trans. Robert Yarbrough (Grand Rapids: Kregel, 2001), chs. 3–5.

9. See, e.g., Ralph P. Martin, *A Hymn of Christ: Philippians 2:5–11 in Recent Interpretation and in the Setting of Early Christian Worship* (Downers Grove: InterVarsity, 1997).

10. For an advanced study of this subject, see Jeffrey T. Reed, "Philippians 3:1 and the Epistolary Hesitation Formulas: The Integrity of Philippians, Again," *Journal of Biblical Literature* 115, no. 1 (1996): 63–90.

11. See Frank Thielman, "Philippians," in *Zondervan Illustrated Bible Backgrounds Commentary*, ed. Clinton E. Arnold (Grand Rapids: Zondervan, 2002), 3:355.

12. *Twilight of a Great Civilization: The Drift Toward Neo-Paganism* (Westchester, Ill.: Crossway, 1988), 23.

13. But see Clinton E. Arnold, *The Colossian Syncretism: The Interface between Christianity and Folk Belief at Colossae* (Grand Rapids: Baker, 1996), for a convincing new proposal.

14. See Craig A. Evans, *Noncanonical Writings and New Testament Interpretation* (Peabody, Mass.: Hendrickson, 1992), 166f.

15. See the comparison between Paul's letter to Philemon and a non–New Testament letter in McRay, *Archaeology and the New Testament*, 365.

16. Ibid., 247.

17. See F. F. Bruce, *Paul: Apostle of the Heart Set Free* (Grand Rapids: Eerdmans, 1977), 400.

18. William Baird, "Philemon, the Letter of Paul to," in *Harper's Bible Dictionary* (San Francisco: Harper & Row, 1985), 784–85.

19. Xavier Léon-Dufour, *Dictionary of the New Testament*, trans. T. Pendergast (New York: Harper & Row, 1983), 40.

20. Everett Ferguson, *Backgrounds of Early Christianity* (Grand Rapids: Eerdmans, 1987), 46.

21. Seneca, *De Clementia*, 1.24.1; see *Seneca: Moral Essays*, vol. 1, trans. John W. Basore (London/New York: Heinemann/Putnam, 1927), 421.

22. Assuming that Paul addresses slavery and the laws governing it in a Roman and Hellenistic framework, not a specifically Hebrew or Jewish one; see Francis Lyall, *Slaves, Citizens, Sons: Legal Metaphors in the Epistles* (Grand Rapids: Zondervan, 1984), 238.

23. Bruce, *Paul*, 401.

Chapter 21: *Thessalonians, Timothy and Titus*

1. R. N. Bellah et al., *Habits of the Heart: Individualism and Commitment in American Life* (San Francisco: Harper & Row, 1985), 143.

2. Cf. John McRay, *Archaeology and the New Testament* (Grand Rapids: Baker, 1991), 289.

3. See D. A. Carson, Douglas J. Moo, and Leon Morris, *An Introduction to the New Testament* (Grand Rapids: Zondervan, 1992), 350–51.

4. McRay, *Archaeology and the New Testament*, 295.

5. John A. T. Robinson makes the attempt in *Redating the New Testament* (Philadelphia: Westminster, 1976), 67–85.

6. Eusebius, *Ecclesiastical History* 2.22.

7. Perhaps from Nicopolis; see McRay, *Archaeology and the New Testament*, 338.

8. Eusebius, *Ecclesiastical History* 2.25.

9. E. Earle Ellis, "The Authorship of the Pastorals: A Resume and Assessment of Recent Trends," in idem, *Paul and His Recent Interpreters* (Grand Rapids: Eerdmans, 1961), 49–57.

10. *The First and Second Letters to Timothy* (New York: Doubleday, 2001), 55–97.

11. See Terry L. Wilder, "Pseudo-nymity and the New Testament," in *Interpreting the New Testament,* ed. D. A. Black and D. S. Dockery (Nashville: Broadman & Holman, 2001), 296–335.

12. On Nicopolis, see McRay, *Archaeology and the New Testament,* 338–40.

13. J. Edwin Orr, *Campus Aflame: A History of Evangelical Awakenings in Collegiate Communities,* rev. ed. (Wheaton, Ill.: International Awakening Press, 1994).

14. The NIV translates "what is good" or "whatever is good." The translation "good works" may be more apt.

15. A full-length study of the question is *Women in the Church: A Fresh Analysis of 1 Timothy 2:9–15,* ed. Andreas J. Köstenberger, Thomas R. Schreiner, and H. Scott Baldwin (Grand Rapids: Baker, 1995).

Chapter 22: *Hebrews and James*

1. See commentaries and other studies listed in Donald A. Hagner, *Encountering the Book of Hebrews* (Grand Rapids: Baker, 2002), 197–200.

2. For a fuller survey, see D. A. Carson, Douglas J. Moo, and Leon Morris, *An Introduction to the New Testament* (Grand Rapids: Zondervan, 1992), 405.

3. Eusebius, *Ecclesiastical History* 2.23.

4. See Carson, Moo, and Morris, *An Introduction to the New Testament,* 415.

5. See, e.g., John H. Elliott, *What Is Social-Scientific Criticism?* (Minneapolis: Fortress, 1993); M. Robert Mulholland Jr., "Sociological Criticism," in *Interpreting the New Testament,* ed. D. A. Black and D. S. Dockery (Nashville: Broadman & Holman, 2001), 170–186.

Chapter 23: *Peter, John, and Jude*

1. See *Sib. Orac.* 5:139; 143; 2 Baruch 10:1, 2; 67:7; 4 Esdras 3:1–2; Rev. 14:8; 17:5; 18:2, 10, 21.

2. Excellent treatments of these themes can be found in Herbert B. Workman, *Persecution in the Early Church* (Oxford: Oxford University Press, 1980 [1906]); and W. H. C. Frend, *Martyrdom and Persecution in the Early Church: A Study of a Conflict from the Maccabees to Donatus* (Grand Rapids: Baker, 1981 [1965]). For a brutally graphic firsthand account of persecution in the early church, see Eusebius's account of the martyrs in Gaul (France), *Ecclesiastical History* 5.1. For a contemporary Christian analysis and reflection on suffering, see Isaiah Majok Dau, *Suffering and God: A Theological Reflection on the War in Sudan* (Nairobi: Paulines Publications, 2002).

3. Contemporary sociological analysis takes the word "pilgrim" in a more literal sense, meaning "resident-alien," rather than as a spiritual description of those whose home is heaven. Peter's addressees were displaced persons. See John H. Elliott, *A Home for the Homeless: A Sociological Exegesis of First Peter, Its Situation and Strategy* (Philadelphia: Fortress, 1981), 24–37.

4. See, e.g., Werner G. Kümmel, *Introduction to the New Testament* (Nashville: Abingdon, 1972), 302; or Robert M. Grant, *A Historical Introduction to the New Testament* (London: Collins, 1963), 228–331. For a discussion of the question of pseudonymity, see D. A. Carson, Douglas J. Moo, and Leon Morris, *An Introduction to the New Testament* (Grand Rapids: Zondervan, 1992), 367–71; E. M. B. Green, *2 Peter Reconsidered* (London: Tyndale, 1961); Ralph P. Martin, *New Testament Foundations: A Guide for Students,* 2 vols. (Grand Rapids: Eerdmans, 1975–78), 2:281–87, 2:383–88.

5. Carson, Moo, and Morris, *An Introduction to the New Testament,* 450.

6. Eusebius mentions this in his *Ecclesiastical History* 3.5.3.

7. Irenaeus says "He [John] remained among them [the disciples] up to the times of Trajan (A.D. 98–117)." *Against Heresies* 2.22.5.

8. On persecution in these and other countries, a starting point is the entry "Persecution of Christians" in the index of Philip Jenkins, *The Next Christendom: The Coming of Global Christianity* (Oxford/New York: Oxford University Press, 2002), 276.

Chapter 24: *Revelation*

1. For a good discussion of this, see Donald Guthrie, *New Testament Introduction* (Chicago: InterVarsity, 1964), 929–85; D. A. Carson, Douglas J. Moo, and Leon Morris, *An Introduction to the New Testament* (Grand Rapids: Zondervan, 1992), 465–86; I. T. Beckwith, *The Apocalypse of John* (Grand Rapids: Baker, 1967), 343–93.

2. See, e.g., Carson, Moo, and Morris, *An Introduction to the New Testament;* John A. T. Robinson, *Redating the New Testament* (Philadelphia: Westminster, 1976), 221–53.

3. See Ned B. Stonehouse, *The Apocalypse in the Ancient Church* (printed dissertation, 1929); J. Paulien, "Recent Developments in the Book of Revelation," *Andrews University Seminary Studies* 26 (1988): 159–70. R. H. Charles, *Studies in the Apocalypse* (Edinburgh/New York: T & T Clark/Scribner, 1913), 1–78, details the history of the interpretation of the book.

4. For a discussion of these views, see Robert G. Clouse, ed., *The Meaning of the Millennium: Four Views* (Downers Grove: InterVarsity, 1977); Guthrie, *New Testament Introduction,* 970–77.

5. See Robert H. Mounce, *The Book of Revelation* (Grand Rapids: Eerdmans, 1977); George E. Ladd, *A Commentary on the Revelation of John* (Grand Rapids: Eerdmans, 1972); and Leon Morris, *The Revelation of St. John: An Introduction and Commentary* (Leicester/Grand Rapids: InterVarsity/Eerdmans, 1987) for commentaries that represent this point of view.

6. Michael Wilcock, *I Saw Heaven Opened: The Message of Revelation* (Downers Grove: InterVarsity, 1975); and William Hendriksen, *More Than Conquerors: An Interpretation of the Book of Revelation* (Grand Rapids: Baker, 1940) represent this point of view. A slightly different form of

this view can be found in William Milligan, *The Book of Revelation,* 8th ed. (London: Hodder & Stoughton, 1903).

7. There are varieties of dispensationalism today. *The Scofield Reference Bible;* John F. Walvoord, *The Revelation of Jesus Christ* (Chicago: Moody, 1966); and Dwight Pentecost, *Things to Come: A Study in Biblical Eschatology* (Grand Rapids: Zondervan, 1958) represent this point of view. For the newer "progressive dispensationalism," see Craig S. Blaising and Darrell L. Bock, *Progressive Dispensationalism* (Grand Rapids, Baker, 1993); Robert L. Saucy, *The Case for Progressive Dispensationalism: The Interface between Dispensational and Non-Dispensational Theology* (Grand Rapids: Zondervan, 1993).

8. See Loraine Boettner, *The Millennium* (Philadelphia: Presbyterian & Reformed, 1957); J. Marcellus Kik, *An Eschatology of Victory* (Phillipsburg, N.J.: Presbyterian & Reformed, 1974).

9. For fuller discussion, see Henry Barclay Swete, *The Apocalypse of St. John,* 2nd ed. (London/New York: Macmillan, 1922), clix–clxxiii; Leon Morris, *New Testament Theology* (Grand Rapids: Zondervan, 1986), 292–97.

Epilogue

1. For a fascinating sociological study of factors behind Christianity's survival and spread to become the dominant religion of the Roman world, see Rodney Stark, *The Rise of Christianity* (San Francisco: Harper Collins, 1997). For a comprehensive historical account, see Eckhard Schnabel, *Early Christian Mission,* 2 vols. (Downers Grove: InterVarsity, 2004).

2. For a response to current alternate views of the Bible's teaching, see Chris Morgan and Robert Peterson eds., *Hell Under Fire* (Grand Rapids: Zondervan, 2004).

3. Kenneth McLeish, "Scientific Method," in *Key Ideas in Human Thought,* ed. Kenneth McLeish (Rocklin, California: Prima, 1995 [1993]), 662–63.

4. For a projection of what world Christianity may look like in coming decades, see Philip Jenkins, *The Next Christendom: The Coming of Global Christianity* (Oxford/New York: Oxford University Press, 2002).

Scripture Index

Name Index

Subject Index

Note: Italic page numbers refer to illustration captions